The Reception of Greek Lyric Poetry in the Ancient World: Transmission, Canonization and Paratext

Mnemosyne Supplements

MONOGRAPHS ON GREEK AND
LATIN LANGUAGE AND LITERATURE

Executive Editor

C. Pieper (*Leiden University*)

Editorial Board

A. Chaniotis (*Institute for Advanced Study, Princeton*)
K.M. Coleman (*Harvard University*)
C.C. de Jonge (*Leiden University*)
T. Reinhardt (*Oxford University*)

VOLUME 430

The titles published in this series are listed at *brill.com/mns*

The Reception of Greek Lyric Poetry in the Ancient World: Transmission, Canonization and Paratext

Studies in Archaic and Classical Greek Song, Vol. 5

Edited by

Bruno Currie
Ian Rutherford

BRILL

LEIDEN | BOSTON

Library of Congress Cataloging-in-Publication Data

Names: Currie, Bruno, editor. | Rutherford, Ian, 1959- editor.
Title: The reception of Greek lyric poetry in the ancient world : transmission, canonization and paratext / edited by Bruno Currie, Ian Rutherford.
Other titles: Mnemosyne, bibliotheca classica Batava. Supplementum ; 430.
Description: Leiden ; Boston : Brill, 2019. | Series: Mnemosyne supplements, 0169-8958 ; volume 430 | Most of the chapters in this volume were originally presented at a conference organized by Oxford University and Reading University under the auspices of the Network of Archaic Greek Song at the University of Reading in 2013. | Includes bibliographical references and index.
Identifiers: LCCN 2019039749 (print) | LCCN 2019039750 (ebook) | ISBN 9789004414518 (hardback) | ISBN 9789004414525 (ebook)
Subjects: LCSH: Greek poetry–History and criticism–Congresses. | Greek poetry–Influence–Congresses. | Classical literature–History and criticism–Congresses. | LCGFT: Conference papers and proceedings.
Classification: LCC PA3092 .R43 2019 (print) | LCC PA3092 (ebook) | DDC 881/.0109–dc23
LC record available at https://lccn.loc.gov/2019039749
LC ebook record available at https://lccn.loc.gov/2019039750

Typeface for the Latin, Greek, and Cyrillic scripts: "Brill". See and download: brill.com/brill-typeface.

ISSN 0169-8958
ISBN 978-90-04-41451-8 (hardback)
ISBN 978-90-04-41452-5 (e-book)

Copyright 2020 by Koninklijke Brill NV, Leiden, The Netherlands.
Koninklijke Brill NV incorporates the imprints Brill, Brill Hes & De Graaf, Brill Nijhoff, Brill Rodopi, Brill Sense, Hotei Publishing, mentis Verlag, Verlag Ferdinand Schöningh and Wilhelm Fink Verlag.
All rights reserved. No part of this publication may be reproduced, translated, stored in a retrieval system, or transmitted in any form or by any means, electronic, mechanical, photocopying, recording or otherwise, without prior written permission from the publisher.
Authorization to photocopy items for internal or personal use is granted by Koninklijke Brill NV provided that the appropriate fees are paid directly to The Copyright Clearance Center, 222 Rosewood Drive, Suite 910, Danvers, MA 01923, USA. Fees are subject to change.

This book is printed on acid-free paper and produced in a sustainable manner.

Printed by Printforce, the Netherlands

Contents

Preface IX
Note on Abbreviations, Texts, and Translations X
Notes on Contributors XI

1 The Reception of Greek Lyric Poetry in the Ancient World: Transmission, Canonization, and Paratext 1
   Bruno Currie and Ian Rutherford

PART 1
Transmission

2 New Philology and the Classics: Accounting for Variation in the Textual Transmission of Greek Lyric and Elegiac Poetry 39
   André Lardinois

3 Tyrtaeus the Lawgiver? Plutarch and Diodorus Siculus on Tyrtaeus fr. 4 72
   Eveline van Hilten-Rutten

PART 2
Canons

4 On the Shaping of the Lyric Canon in Athens 95
   Gregory Nagy

5 Melic Poets and Melic Forms in the Comedies of Aristophanes: Poetic Genres and the Creation of a Canon 112
   Claude Calame

6 Structuring the Genre: The Fifth- and Fourth-Century Authors on Elegy and Elegiac Poets 129
   Krystyna Bartol

PART 3
Lyric in the Peripatetics

7   The Peripatetics and the Transmission of Lyric   151
    Theodora A. Hadjimichael

8   The Self-Revealing Poet: Lyric Poetry and Cultural History in the Peripatetic School   182
    Elsa Bouchard

PART 4
Early Reception

9   Lyric Reception and Sophistic Literarity in Timotheus' *Persae*   205
    David Fearn

10 "Total Reception": Stesichorus as Revenant in Plato's *Phaedrus* (with a New Stesichorean Fragment?)   239
    Andrea Capra

11 Indirect Tradition on Sappho's *kertomia*   257
    Maria Kazanskaya

PART 5
Reception in Roman poetry

12 Alcaeus' *stasiotica*: Catullan and Horatian Readings   279
    Ewen Bowie

13 Pindar, Paratexts, and Poetry: Architectural Metaphors in Pindar and Roman Poets (Virgil, Horace, Propertius, Ovid, and Statius)   295
    Gregor Bitto

PART 6
Second Sophistic Contexts

14 Sympotic Sappho? The Recontextualization of Sappho's Verses in Athenaeus   321
Stefano Caciagli

15 A Sophisticated *hetaira* at Table: Athenaeus' Sappho   342
Renate Schlesier

16 Solon and the Democratic Biographical Tradition   373
Jessica Romney

17 Strategies of Quoting Solon's Poetry in Plutarch's *Life of Solon*   395
Jacqueline Klooster

18 Playing with Terpander & Co.: Lyric, Music, and Politics in Aelius Aristides' *To the Rhodians: Concerning Concord*   417
Francesca Modini

PART 7
Scholarship

19 Historiography and Ancient Pindaric Scholarship   441
Tom Phillips

20 Poem-Titles in Simonides, Pindar, and Bacchylides   461
Enrico Emanuele Prodi

21 *Ita dictum accipe*: Pomponius Porphyrio on Early Greek Lyric Poetry in Horace   516
Johannes Breuer

22 Pindar and His Commentator Eustathius of Thessalonica   533
Arlette Neumann-Hartmann

Index of Passages   553
Index of Subjects   568

Preface

This is the fifth volume in a series within Brill's Mnemosyne Supplements that presents the proceedings of the Network for the Study of Archaic and Classical Greek Song (http://www.ru.nl/greeksong/). Previous volumes in the series are *The Look of Lyric: Greek Song and the Visual* (2016), eds. Vanessa Cazzato and André Lardinois; *The Newest Sappho (P. Sapph. Obbink and P. GC inv. 105, Frs. 1–4)* (2016), eds. Anton Bierl and André Lardinois; and *Authorship and Greek Song Authority, Authenticity, and Performance* (2017), ed. Egbert Bakker. A further volume on genres of Greek lyric poetry, edited by Leslie Kurke, is also forthcoming. The Network was founded in 2007 as a means of facilitating interaction among scholars interested in the study of archaic and classical lyric, elegiac, and iambic poetry. Most of the chapters included in this volume were originally presented at the conference organized by Oxford University and Reading University under the auspices of the Network of Archaic Greek Song at the University of Reading in the Summer of 2013. The volume was edited by Bruno Currie, with input from Ian Rutherford in the early stages. The chapters underwent a double process of peer reviewing by core members of the Network of Archaic Greek Song and by an anonymous reviewer acting on behalf of the publisher (Brill). The contributors had the opportunity to read each other's papers and comment on them before the manuscript went to press. The editors are especially grateful to André Lardinois for plentiful assistance of various kinds throughout the whole process. The indices were compiled by Emily Barradell, Aniek van den Eersten, Myrthe Spitzen, André Lardinois, and Ian Rutherford.

BGFC
ICR

Note on Abbreviations, Texts, and Translations

Names of ancient authors and titles of texts are abbreviated in accordance with the list in *The Oxford Classical Dictionary*, fourth edition (2012) xxvi–liii. Unless otherwise specified, Greek and Latin authors are quoted from the Oxford Classical Texts, but the early Greek lyric poets—with the exception of those listed below—are cited from D.A. Campbell, *Greek Lyric*, volumes I–V (Cambridge MA and London, 1982–1993); the early Greek iambic and elegiac poets from M.L. West, *Iambi et elegi Graeci* (Oxford, second edition, 1989–1992); Sappho and Alcaeus are quoted from the edition of E.-M. Voigt, *Sappho et Alcaeus: Fragmenta* (Amsterdam, 1971); Pindar is quoted according to the text editions of B. Snell and H. Maehler, *Pindarus: Pars I: Epinicia* (Leipzig, 1987) or H. Maehler, *Pindarus: Pars II: Fragmenta; Indices* (Leipzig, 1989). Translations are by the contributors themselves, unless noted otherwise. Other standard abbreviations used are below.

BNJ *Brill's New Jacoby*, ed. I. Worthington, http://referenceworks.brillonline.com/browse/brill-s-new-jacoby

DK H. Diels and W. Kranz, eds. *Die Fragmente der Vorsokratiker*. Volumes I–III. 6th edn., 1951. Berlin.

FGrH *Die Fragmente der griechischen Historiker*, ed. by F. Jacoby. Volumes I–. 1923–. Leiden.

PCG *Poetae Comici Graeci*, ed. by R. Kassel and C. Austin. Volumes I–VIII. 1983–2001. Berlin and New York.

PLF *Poetarum Lesbiorum Fragmenta*, ed. by E. Lobel and D. Page. 1955. Oxford.

PMG *Poetae melici Graeci*, ed. by D.L. Page. 1962. Oxford.

TGrF *Tragicorum Graecorum fragmenta*, ed. by B. Snell, S. Radt, and R. Kannicht. Volumes I–V. 1971–2004. Göttingen.

Notes on Contributors

Krystyna Bartol
is Full Professor of Classics at Adam Mickiewicz University, Poznań, and President of the Scientific Committee on Ancient Culture of the Polish Academy of Sciences. She has published extensively on Greek lyric poetry as well as on Greek Imperial prose. She recently co-authored with Jerzy Danielewicz the first ever Polish translation of Athenaeus (2010) and a commented Polish translation of a selection of Greek comic fragments (2011).

Gregor Bitto
was Assistant Professor (*wissenschaftlicher Assistent*) to the Chair of Classical Philology at the Catholic University of Eichstätt-Ingolstadt until 2017 and is currently working as a teacher for Latin and Greek. He is working on the reception of Alexandrian philology in Roman poetry and has published a monograph on this topic (*Lyrik als Philologie. Zur Rezeption hellenistischer Pindarkommentierung in den Oden des Horaz* [2012]) and together with Anna Ginestí Rosell an edited volume entitled *Philologie auf zweiter Stufe. Literarische Rezeptionen und Inszenierungen hellenistischer Gelehrsamkeit* (2019). His second monograph offers an interpretation of Statius' *Achilleid* as an epic designed to be perceived as the work of an ageing poet (*Vergimus in senium. Statius' Achilleis als Alterswerk* [2016]).

Elsa Bouchard
is Associate Professor at the Université de Montréal. She is the author of *Du Lycée au Musée. Théorie poétique et critique littéraire à l'époque hellénistique* (2016).

Ewen Bowie
is Emeritus Fellow of Corpus Christi College, Oxford University and has written numerous articles on Greek lyric poetry and later Greek literature. He is the author of a commentary on Longus, *Daphnis and Chloe* (2019), editor of a collection entitled *Herodotus: Narrator, Scientist, Historian* (2018), and co-editor of collections of papers on Philostratus (2009) and *Archaic and Classical Choral Song* (2011).

Johannes Breuer
is *akademischer Oberrat* of classics at the University of Mainz (Germany). His fields of research comprise, amongst others, Augustan poetry (*Der Mythos in*

den Oden des Horaz. Praetexte, Formen, Funktionen [2008]) and the transformation of pagan education in early Christian literature.

Stefano Caciagli
currently teaches at an Italian school and at Bologna University, where he was formerly a research fellow. He has published a number of articles on Sappho, Alcaeus, Alcman, and Aristophanes, as well as a book about the contextualisation of Aeolic poetry (*Poeti e società. Comunicazione poetica e formazioni sociali nella Lesbo del VII/VI secolo a.C.* [2011]). Recently he has been editor of *Eros e genere in Grecia arcaica* (2017) and has published *L'eteria arcaica e classica* (2018).

Claude Calame
is Director of Studies Emeritus at the École des Hautes Études en Sciences Sociales in Paris (Centre AnHiMA: Anthropologie et Histoire des Mondes Antiques). In English he has published, among other books, *Masks of Authority: Fiction and Pragmatics in Ancient Greek Poetics* (2005), *Poetic and Performative Memory in Ancient Greece* (2009), and *Greek Mythology: Poetics, Pragmatics and Fiction* (2009).

Andrea Capra
is Reader in Greek Literature at Durham University. He has published widely on Plato, Aristophanes, the Greek novel, and lyric poetry.

Bruno Currie
is an associate professor at Oxford University. He is the author of *Pindar and the Cult of Heroes* (2005) and *Homer's Allusive Art* (2016).

David Fearn
is Associate Professor at Warwick University. He is the author of *Bacchylides: Politics, Performance, Poetic Tradition* (2007) and *Pindar's Eyes: Visual and Material Culture in Epinician Poetry* (2017).

Theodora A. Hadjimichael
is WIRL Marie Skłodowska-Curie COFUND Fellow at the University of Warwick, working on a project on Plato and Greek lyric poetry. She has published *The Emergence of the Lyric Canon* (2019) and articles on the poetics of Bacchylides and on his reception in antiquity, and co-edited *Paths of Song: The Lyric Dimension of Greek Tragedy* (*Trends in Classics* Supplementary Volume 58, 2018).

Maria Kazanskaya
is Assistant Professor of Classics at Saint-Petersburg State University. She is currently working on a book on speech and narrative in Herodotus.

Jacqueline Klooster
is Assistant Professor of Greek Language and Literature at the Rijksuniversiteit Groningen. She is the author of *Poetry as Window and Mirror, Positioning the Poet in Hellenistic Poetry* (2011).

André Lardinois
is Professor of Greek Language and Literature at Radboud University, Nijmegen (the Netherlands), and the Academic Director of OIKOS, the national Dutch research school in Classical Studies. He has published extensively on Sappho and other Greek poetry. He is co-author of *Tragic Ambiguity: Philosophy and Sophocles' Antigone* (1987) and *Sappho: A New Translation of the Complete Works* (2014), and co-editor of *Making Silence Speak: Women's Voices in Greek Literature and Society* (2001), *Solon of Athens: New Historical and Philological Approaches* (2006), and *The Look of Lyric: Greek Song and the Visual* (2016).

Francesca Modini
is a PhD student at King's College London. Her research project focusses on the reception of ancient lyric in imperial Greek rhetoric.

Gregory Nagy
is Francis Jones Professor of Classical Greek Literature at Harvard University and Director of the Centre for Hellenic Studies, Washington, DC. His many books include *Pindar's Homer: The Lyric Possession of an Epic Past* (1990).

Arlette Neumann-Hartmann
is a research fellow in the Classics Department of the University of Fribourg and Editor for Classical Studies at Schwabe publishing house. She has published on epinician poetry, especially on Pindar and Bacchylides.

Tom Phillips
is a Leverhulme Postdoctoral Research Associate in the Faculty of Classics, Oxford University. He is the author of *Pindar's Library: Performance Poetry and Material Texts* (2015).

Enrico Emanuele Prodi
is a stipendiary lecturer at Balliol College, Oxford. His main research interests are archaic Greek lyric, papyrology, the history of the book in antiquity, and

ancient scholarship on Greek and Roman poetry. He is working on a commentary of the fragments of Pindar's *Prosodia* and a monograph on ancient scholarship on archaic *iambos*.

Jessica Romney

is a visiting assistant professor of classical studies at Dickinson College. Her PhD thesis at Bristol University examined the expression and manipulation of group identity in Archaic elegy, iambus, and lyric, and she has published on ethnic and political identities in early lyric poetry. Her book, *Lyric Poetry and Social Identity in Archaic Greece*, is under contract with the University of Michigan Press.

Ian Rutherford

is Professor of Greek at Reading University. He is the author of *Canons of Style in the Antonine Age* (1998), *Pindar's Paeans* (2001), and *State Pilgrims and Sacred Observers in Ancient Greece* (2013).

Renate Schlesier

is Professor Emerita of the Study of Religion at Freie Universität Berlin. She has published extensively on tragedy as well as on Dionysos, including the conference volume *A Different God? Dionysos and Ancient Polytheism* (2011) and, especially in recent years, on Sappho and the symposium as arguably the main poetic and pragmatic space of her compositions.

Eveline van Hilten-Rutten

is a graduate student at the Radboud University Nijmegen, Netherlands.

CHAPTER 1

The Reception of Greek Lyric Poetry in the Ancient World: Transmission, Canonization, and Paratext

Bruno Currie and Ian Rutherford

1   Introduction

To approach a fuller understanding of any work of ancient Greek literature we need to pay attention to reception, not only its immediate reception by contemporary and near-contemporary audiences (insofar as there is any direct evidence for that), but also its longer-term reception in later Greek and Roman culture. There are two main parts to this inquiry. One is transmission: the process by which literary works were passed on to later generations and made available to listeners and readers. The other is the broader impact on Greco-Roman intellectual culture: the ways in which the texts are used by writers, critics, or visual artists. Their views are bound to be shaped to some extent by the tastes of the particular historical period in which they lived, but they may also draw on established interpretative traditions, which in some cases go back to the period when the works were first composed. These two issues of tradition and broader impact are closely linked, both because a citation or allusion may provide at least indirect evidence for transmission, and because the attitudes of later writers and intellectuals can help to explain why it was believed to be necessary to transmit the texts in the first place.

For the study of Greek song—melic, iambic, and elegiac poetry—of the seventh to fifth centuries BCE, understanding ancient reception is particularly important. In this case the process of transmission had an exceptionally transformative effect, seeing the conversion of musical performances into written texts lacking any form of musical (or choreographical) notation. With the creation of a literary "canon", the Greek lyric tradition underwent what Jan Assmann has called "excarnation": a process of becoming disembedded from its original context.[1] The creation of a canon in this context entails not only the creation of canonical *poets* (an exclusive list of specially favoured authors), but also of canonical *texts* (texts fixed in their precise wording and maybe even in

---

[1] Assmann (2006) 65–70; he credits Aleida Assmann with the invention of the term.

their colometry); both aspects are relevant to this volume.[2] A second reason for the importance of reception to early Greek song specifically is that comparatively few texts from these genres survive complete, and much of what comes down to us takes the form of short excerpts ("fragments") scattered in the texts of other writers. Many of these are presumably faithful citations (direct or indirect) of some version of a text that was in circulation, but others could be distorted or even invented. Thus it is crucial to be aware of the agendas of the embedding authors. Finally, the surviving texts of lyric poetry, even the nearly complete, are often not entirely comprehensible in themselves; many of them require that we grasp topical allusions or know something about the circumstances of performance, and some, such as Pindar's *Epinicia*, contain language that is, at least *prima facie*, obscure. For all these reasons, lyric poetry in antiquity was bound up with commentary and we for our part are more than usually dependent on the opinions of ancient writers and scholars who, whatever their limitations and idiosyncrasies, at least had access to much more primary material than we do.[3]

The aim of the chapters collected in the present volume is to examine aspects of the reception and transmission of ancient Greek song in the ancient world. It had its origins in an international conference, 'The Reception of Greek Lyric Poetry 600 BCE–400 CE: Transmission, Canonization, and Paratext' held at the University of Reading in September 2013, under the auspices of the Network for the Study of Archaic and Classical Greek Song. Neither the volume nor this introduction claims to give comprehensive coverage of the subject, and although all of the chapters here are self-contained, it may be helpful to attempt a sort of overview of the subject they address in their different ways.

A useful way of approaching the ancient reception of Greek lyric chronologically is to break it down into a number of stages, none of them entirely clear, but some clearer than others. Probably the best understood is the Hellenistic period, when scholars in Alexandria are believed to have produced editions of the texts (Stage 4 below). Before that, we find traces of Peripatetic interest in the fourth century BCE (Stage 3) and signs of an early canon forming in Athens (Stage 2). The hardest to make out is the period before the fifth century (Stage 1), with which our chronological survey, necessarily very partial and selective, begins.

---

2 On the interconnection of these two aspects of "canonization", see Lardinois' contribution to this volume, p. 49.
3 Hutchinson (2007) 36.

1.1 Stage 1: The Seventh and Sixth Centuries BCE

Most of the melic, elegiac and iambic poets who later became canonical date from the seventh and sixth centuries BCE, and they practised their art in different parts of Greece: Sparta, Ionia, and the West. How did their songs come through to the fifth century BCE? While a complete answer to this question is beyond our grasp, we can sketch out three aspects that may have played a role.

The first could be described as selection and Panhellenization. Although there must have been hundreds of singers in Greece in the seventh and sixth centuries BCE, only a small number achieved the status of classics. Many of them must have been forgotten quickly or were remembered for a single composition, such as the one-hit-wonder Tynnichus (Plato, *Ion* 534d). The successful ones must have owed much of their success to their ability to reach beyond their local communities, and to secure recognition at the Panhellenic level. In some cases Panhellenic recognition may have come after the poet's death, but in others it may have been achieved in his lifetime through travelling and performing at festivals or by constructing poems in such a way as to appeal to a general audience.[4] The poet's Panhellenic ambition is sometimes made explicit in the poetic texts (e.g. Pindar, *Olympian* 1.115b–116).

The second aspect is the role played by oral and written transmission. Some see transmission as largely oral right down to the fifth century BCE, and possibly later, with writing playing only a supporting role. Gregory Nagy,[5] for example, has seen the transmission of the poems in terms of generations of singers who, by performing the songs associated with a given poet, take on his or her persona. Thus what is passed down is not the song but the performance tradition and the associated persona, with writing playing at most a secondary role. Others see even the earliest melic poems as being written down from the start, a position that need not presuppose the existence of a significant reading public, as the main purpose of written texts may have been to ensure the continued performance of lyric compositions in a form faithful to the original.[6] This debate replicates one concerning early Greek epic, and equally eludes consensus.[7] Intermediate positions are also possible, such that writing was introduced in, say, the mid-sixth century BCE, an early sign of this potentially being Theognis' "Seal" elegy, if that implies a literal seal on a written document (which

---

4 For poets travelling and performing at festivals, see Hunter and Rutherford (2009). For poems as constructed so as to appeal to a wider audience, see Carey (2011) 442–445, but see also Currie (2017) 202–208.
5 Nagy (1990) 36–82.
6 Stehle (1997) 262–318, on Sappho.
7 Nagy (1990) 38–82, (1996) 29–63; Fowler (2004).

is uncertain).[8] Possibly there was a correlation between the increasing Panhellenization of song and the need for writing to stabilize the text when performed beyond the local communities. But even that is unclear; frequent performance even within local communities could give rise to a desire to standardize the text that was to be performed (as with Lycurgus' establishment of "official" texts of the three great tragedians in fourth-century BCE Athens).

The third aspect is control of the tradition. Was it simply left to itself or did some parties have a special role in shaping it? One interested party might be the lyric poets themselves, who could have helped to shape the emerging tradition. We know at least that poets cite their predecessors: Solon cites Mimnermus, Simonides cites Stesichorus, and Pindar refers to Archilochus and to the (to us) uncanonical Sacadas of Argos and Xenocritus of Locri. In other words, the question of how poets themselves viewed the lyric tradition arises already for the archaic and early classical periods, as well as for the later fifth century.[9] This all pertains to the creation of a "canon" of elite poets. The other aspect of the control of the tradition is the creation of "canonical", or authorised, fixed, texts. It is natural to think of the poets themselves as taking an interest in the textual preservation of their own work (consider Theognis' "Seal" again). While there is no sign of any central archive, the home cities of poets might also patriotically have played a part by preserving the texts of their poets.[10] Another factor shaping the early textual tradition could have been the tastes of the participants in the institution of the symposium. Vases depict Anacreon and Sappho at the symposium.[11] Already at a relatively early date, lyric anthologies may have been made to cater to sympotic reperformance.[12] Performance of Stesichorus at the symposium may be implied by the proverb, 'the three of Stesichorus'.[13]

Whether oral or written or possibly an interactive combination of the two, the nature of early transmission is likely to have resulted in a high degree of instability in the texts transmitted. (The classic illustration of this is the variation found between the text of a song of Alcaeus as preserved for us on papyrus from a Hellenistic book-edition of the poet, fr. 249.6–9, and as transmitted as an Attic drinking-song or *skolion*, 891 *PMG*.[14]) From the point of view of the

---

8   Cerri (1991); Bakker (2017).
9   This question is addressed in the contributions to this volume of Calame, pp. 114–119 (focussing on Aristophanes' citatory practice with the melic poets), and Fearn, pp. 210–220 (considering Timotheus' relationship with Simonides, Pindar, and Bacchylides).
10 See Lardinois' contribution to this volume, pp. 43–44.
11 Yatromanolakis (1997). Compare Nagy's contribution to this volume, p. 103.
12 See the contributions to this volume of Bartol, pp. 139–140, and Caciagli, p. 327.
13 See Capra's contribution to this volume, p. 251.
14 See Lardinois' contribution to this volume, pp. 60–62.

modern editor the question arises whether it is possible or desirable to seek to establish a single reading.[15] The nature of the early transmission would also have provided scope for pseudepigraphy of various sorts. In Athens in the later fifth century when the canon was coming into being there could well have been a tendency to ascribe a wide variety of cult songs emanating from Sparta to Alcman, for example.

1.2   Stage 2: Fifth-Century Athens

The next phase was Athens in the later fifth century BCE, which was, as far as we can tell, the principal centre of Greek musical culture at this time. None of the melic poets who later became canonical was an Athenian, though Simonides and Anacreon[16] were resident there under the tyrant Hipparchus,[17] and Pindar and Bacchylides composed dithyrambs for the Athenian Dionysia. Lyric poetry is a major intertext for tragedy.[18] Comedy, too, shows an awareness of most of the poets and genres who later came to make up the melic canon.[19] Aristophanes reveals a notable leaning to the older, deceased, lyric poets in preference to contemporary practitioners of the New Music.[20] Several comedies about or featuring Sappho were produced from the fifth century into the fourth century BCE.[21] Herodotus, active in the third quarter of the fifth century and plainly envisaging an Athenian readership, though not exclusively, refers to events in the lives of three melic poets, Alcaeus, Sappho,[22] and Simonides, as well as the non-melic "lyric" poets Archilochus and Solon. The dialogues of Plato, set in the Athens of the later fifth century, feature frequent quotations and discussions of melic poets such as Simonides, Pindar, and Stesichorus.[23]

Plato's dialogues, which look back to the late fifth century, confirm the impression that Athenian intellectuals were familiar with a wide range of Greek song and engaged keenly in debates about its merits. Stesichorus' *Palinode*

---

15   This question is a preoccupation of the contributions to this volume of Lardinois and van Hilten-Rutten.
16   For Anacreon, see now Bing (2014).
17   See Nagy's contribution to this volume, p. 101.
18   Swift (2011). For the reception of choral lyric in drama, an important guide is Herington (1985); in tragedy, Bagordo (2003); in comedy, Kugelmeier (1996). Excellent overviews are Hutchinson (2001) 427–439 and Stehle (2004).
19   See Calame's contribution to this volume.
20   See Hadjimichael's contribution to this volume, p. 165.
21   For Sappho on the stage, see Parker (1993) 309–310n2; Yatromanolakis (2007) 70–71; Olson (2007) 303–304; Schlesier's contribution to this volume, pp. 353, 365–366.
22   See Kazanskaya's contribution to this volume.
23   See Capra's contribution to this volume. Plato also cites the non-canonical lyric poets Tynnichus of Chalcis (*Ion* 534d = 707 *PMG*) and Cydias (*Charm.* 155d = 714 *PMG*).

plays a central role in the *Phaedrus*,[24] and the protracted discussion of the Scopas ode of Simonides in the *Protagoras* furnishes the first recorded case of textual exegesis.[25] Simonides also plays a major part in Xenophon's *Hiero* where he is imagined as engaging in dialogue with the Sicilian tyrant. The existence of a treatise *On Theognis* ascribed to Xenophon may be a sign of the popularity of Theognis among Athenians with oligarchic sympathies in this period.[26]

It is unclear to what extent there was a reading public for poetry at this time.[27] By contrast, various mechanisms are conceivable by which songs could be experienced in performance. It has been suggested that there was a permanent institutional venue in the Panathenaia festival.[28] Another venue would have been the symposium. Sympotic anthologies are thought to be have been created in the sixth and fifth centuries BCE.[29] Transmission in such anthologies would constitute a way in which texts of the archaic lyric poets (e.g. Alcaeus and Sappho) might reach later authors (such as Athenaeus) independently of Alexandrian editorial activity.

Lyric was still a living tradition at this time, but there is a sense of a "canon" emerging, the latest of the soon-to-be canonical melic poets (Simonides, Bacchylides, Pindar) having died around the middle of the fifth century.[30]

Around this time we hear of literary critical works, mainly focussing on Homer, for instance, by Theagenes of Rhegium. No treatises about lyric poetry are known from this period, though lyric poetry may have been discussed in the context of *mousike* by early musical writers such as Lasos of Hermione and Damon. Theoretical statements about lyric poetry were also made in passing by poets.[31] Our principal resource, though not a straightforward one, for reconstructing Athenian attitudes are the comedians, who suggest that by their time some, at least, of the lyric poets were seen as conservative,[32] presumably in contrast to the musical tastes of the later fifth century, which leaned towards

---

24 See Capra's contribution to this volume.
25 Most (1994).
26 Stobaeus, *Florilegium* 88.14. See Lane Fox (2000). For the use of the Theognidean corpus at Athens in this period, see Colesanti (2011) 329–330; Bartol's contribution to this volume, pp. 139, 142.
27 Compare Wright (2012) 146–147.
28 See Nagy's contribution to this volume.
29 See n. 12 above.
30 For the formation of the canon in Athens in this period, see Nicolai (2014) 35–37, (2006).
31 For poets' statements, see Rossi (1971) 75–76; Ford (1995) 10–13. Critias' use of the terms *elegeion* and *iambeion* is discussed in Bartol's contribution to this volume, pp. 136–137.
32 Cf. Ar. *Clouds* 1357–1358 on Simonides; Eupolis fr. 148 and 395 *PCG*.

the New Music and *avant-garde* figures such as Melanippides of Melos and Timotheus of Miletus.[33] The old order was changing.

The fifth-century sophists are likely to have played a part in the development of literary critical discourse, even if they may not, for the most part, have produced literary critical treatises.[34] (We may note, however, Theagenes and Protagoras' pronouncements on Homer, and 'Protagoras'' on Simonides in Plato's *Protagoras*.) It is unclear to what extent sophistic ideas are reflected in Old Comedy.[35] It is possible that the sophistic distinction between the instructional and recreational aspects of literary influenced the fifth-century transmission of elegy in an anthologised form.[36]

1.3 Stage 3: The Fourth Century BCE

The first known texts of melic poets are from the fourth century: the papyrus of Timotheus' *Persai* from Abusir in Egypt (possibly produced within the lifetime of Timotheus himself) and epigraphic texts such as the *Paean to Dionysus* by Philodamus of Scarpheia from Delphi.[37] It is striking that the two earliest preserved texts are of non-canonical poets, and both can be seen as innovative literary experiments. It is not until the beginning of the third century BCE that we encounter the earliest preserved text of any canonical lyric poet: the "Cologne papyrus" of Sappho.[38]

There is no evidence of Aristotle and the Peripatetic philosophers producing texts of the poets.[39] Aristotle had little to say about lyric in his *Poetics*,[40] though he makes extensive use of Solon's poetry as a historical source in his *Constitution of Athens*.[41] Chamaeleon and other Peripatetics, however, show an interest at least in the biographies of lyric poets.

1.4 Stage 4: The Hellenistic Period

Scholars in Hellenistic Alexandria are believed to have produced standard editions of the poets, together with commentaries. Most work was done by Aris-

---

33 On Timotheus, see Fearn's contribution to this volume.
34 For Gorgias as an important influence on Timotheus' *Persae*, see Fearn's contribution to this volume, pp. 226–234.
35 See Dover (1993) 31–32; Wright (2012) 106–107.
36 See Bartol's contribution to this volume, pp. 140–141.
37 For Timotheus, see van Minnen (1997).
38 See Gronewald and Daniel (2004) 1.
39 See Hadjimichael's contribution to this volume, pp. 174–175; Hadjimichael (2019).
40 See the contributions to this volume of Hadjimichael, pp. 177–178 and Bouchard, pp. 184–189.
41 See Stehle (2006), and Bouchard's contribution to this volume, p. 189.

tophanes of Byzantium (late third century BCE) and Aristarchus (early second century BCE), but Zenodotus and Callimachus (early third century BCE) had anticipated them to some extent: Zenodotus corrected the text of Pindar, and Callimachus had views on the genres of lyric poems.[42] All of them were probably using texts of the poets that had been collected for the use of the Library of Alexandria, perhaps drawing these from archives in local communities such as Sparta for Alcman and South Italy or Sicily for Stesichorus.[43]

The following are some of the key aspects of Hellenistic editorial practice.

(i) Genre: in the cases of many of the poets, poems were henceforth grouped by category, arranged in a scroll comprising poems judged to belong to the same genre (paean, dithyramb, and so on). This practice, which in some cases knowingly involved messy compromises for practical convenience (e.g. Pindar, *Nemeans* 9–11), may have created the impression that genres were more clear-cut than they were.[44] The idea that lyric poems fell into distinct genres was not new (it is clearly formulated in Plato's *Laws*, for example, and implied in Pindar, fr. 128c); but in the preceding centuries, instead of a rigid system of genres, we should probably think of fluid conventions and a degree of evolution, as in the case of elegy.[45]

(ii) Music: Hellenistic scholars followed fourth-century practice (as seen in the Timotheus papyrus) in not attempting to annotate the music of any song of the classical lyric poets.[46] It is not clear whether they assumed general knowledge of the music, or whether they just thought it unimportant. They did, however, arrange the texts in metrical cola: Aristophanes of Byzantium is usually said to have established the practice,[47] although an early Hellenistic papyrus of Sappho that has the text arranged in cola predates Aristophanes, and the Lille Papyrus of Stesichorus may be earlier as well.[48] It is unknown whether the Hellenistic colometry reflects

---

42   Pfeiffer (1968) 117–118; for Pindar in general, Dickey (2007) 38–40. For Callimachus and genre, a vivid illustration is P.Oxy. 2368; cf. also schol. Pind. *Pyth.* 2 inscr.
43   Alcman: Carey (2011); Stesichorus: Cassio (1997).
44   Harvey (1955); Rossi (1971) discusses written and unwritten laws of genres in general; see also Calame (1974).
45   On elegy, see Bartol's contribution to this volume. For *iambos*, see Rotstein (2010). The apparent evolution of dithyramb from Dionysiac hymn to narrative song, for which see Käppel (2000), is another famous case.
46   Musical notation itself goes back at least as far as the fourth century BCE, since Aristoxenus of Tarentum was moved to express disapproval of it: *Harm.* 2.39–41, but its applications were limited. Compare Hagel (2010) 1, 3.
47   Pfeiffer (1968) 187; Montana (2015) 120–121.
48   Nünlist (2015) 735; contrast West (1978) 3–4.

the musical practice of the original poets. A century ago, Wilamowitz was sure that there was no connection, but today many scholars are prepared to believe that there was at least an element of continuity.[49] In any case the experience of Hellenistic and Roman readers who knew the songs as music-free, colometrized columns of text was clearly radically different from that of audiences who heard them performed centuries before. The experience of reading the poems in the standard book editions may also be contrasted with that gleaned from some Hellenistic and Roman texts of non-canonical songs preserved on papyrus or stone that did not arrange the text in (the same) metrical cola, and did sometimes include musical notation.[50]

(iii) The "canon": there is reason to believe that Hellenistic scholars also produced an official list of nine melic poets judged to belong to the first class.[51] They may have produced a shorter list of preferred iambic poets as well.[52] For the melic poets, none later than Bacchylides was included, entailing the omission of Timotheus and Melanippides (the greatest of the dithyrambic poets, according to Xenophon, *Memorabilia* 1.4.3). We may contrast the Alexandrian list of epic poets, which accommodated one poet (Antimachus of Colophon) who lived around 400 BCE (Quintilian 10.1.53–54). The preference for the great poets of the period 700–450 BCE implied in this section seems to reflect the judgements implied in Aristophanes' comedies two centuries earlier (see above, under Stage 2).

In subsequent centuries the lyric poets are, for the most part, those nine, though there are exceptions, such as Timotheus, who continues to be regarded as a classic for some time (he was reperformed in Arcadia according to Polybius, 20.8–9),[53] although there are no signs of Hellenistic editions of his works. Another problematic case is Corinna of Tanagra, now generally believed to have lived in the fifth century BCE, whose songs may have been preserved in a local Boeotian archive, if they did not make it to Alexandria.[54] We may note also

---

49   Wilamowitz (1921) 83. See, differently, Montana (2015) 62, 121n278.
50   D'Alessio (2017) 242 (colometry) and 249–250 (musical notation).
51   Pfeiffer (1968) 207; Nicolai (1992) 251–265 and 275–296. Wilamowitz was mistaken to think nine represented all that survived: D'Alessio (2017) 233.
52   For the canon of iambographers see Rotstein (2010) 28n11, (2016). For a canon of archaic and classical elegiac poets there is less to go on, perhaps because they were superseded by the Hellenistic ones (Quintilian 10.1.59). See Kroehnert (1897) 30.
53   On Polybius' citation of Timotheus, see Prauscello (2009).
54   See Larson (2002); a Hellenistic date for Corinna had previously been argued by West (1970). For Corinna as the "tenth", see Nagy's contribution to this volume, p. 110. See also D'Alessio (2017) 232–233.

Thaletas of Gortyn, an obscure early poet, whose songs were apparently performed by ambassadors from Mylasa visiting Crete in the second century BCE; assuming these were genuine poems and not fakes, the question arises how these got to Mylasa: were they perhaps preserved in Gortyn?[55] This reminds us that the Alexandrians did not necessarily—at this stage—have a monopoly on the lyric tradition.

We know something, then, about Hellenistic scholarship; but we need to remember how much we do not know. For one thing, we cannot be certain that there were not alternative editions of some poets in circulation.[56] And we have very little information about how Hellenistic scholars dealt with elegiac and iambic poetry. It is striking that the only book of classical song that comes down to us in manuscript tradition apart from Pindar, Theognis' elegies, is a compilation from several early collections of poems, some likely to be by Theognis, some obviously not, and it is unclear what role, if any, Alexandrian scholars played in its creation.[57] Another mode of transmission was the poetic anthology, attested from about 300 BCE.[58] Equally, some poetry may have been transmitted in a way that bypassed the Hellenistic editors; for example, the famous Hymn to Asclepius from Erythrae, which survives in three copies, two from the fourth century BCE and one from Roman Egypt. It should be remembered too that in some cases even the Hellenistic scholars were uncertain of the authorship of particular poems.[59]

In the Hellenistic period we find lyric, elegiac, and iambic poets referenced and imitated by poets of the time, such as Callimachus, who himself wrote lyric poems and iambics.[60] Anacreon's simple symposiastic verse lent itself particularly well to imitation and so-called "Anacreontea" seem to have been composed from the Hellenistic period right through to the Byzantine period.[61]

---

55   Chaniotis (1988).
56   Compare Lardinois' contribution to this volume, pp. 55–57 (after E. Bowie), on two editions of Theognis from the fourth century BCE.
57   See the contributions to this volume of Bartol, p. 139, and Caciagli, p. 326, as well as West (1974) 40–59; Bowie (1997).
58   Pordomingo Pardo (2013), e.g. the songs of Elephantine, Pordomingo Pardo no. 21 = 917 *PMG*.
59   We find them uncertain about the hymn to Athene cited by Aristophanes (735 *PMG*: Lamprocles? Stesichorus? Phrynichus?). Compare the judgment of Eratosthenes, discussed by Pfeiffer (1968) 162. Similar uncertainty is shown in P.Oxy. 2737.i.22–26 = *SLG* 2, which discusses the genre of a line cited by Aristophanes: was it by Terpander, Ion, or Alcman?
60   See now Acosta-Hughes (2010).
61   West (1984) p. vxii; Rosenmeyer (1992).

Meanwhile, some of the great poets were the subject of veneration, most prominently Archilochus on Paros, a cult of whom was founded by one Mnesiepes in the third century BCE.[62] One of Callimachus' *Aitia* is devoted to the ruined tomb of Simonides of Ceos in Acragas.[63] Stesichorus had a celebrated octagonal tomb at Catania in Sicily, and Ibycus probably had one at Rhegium.[64] In this respect the treatment of canonical lyric poets resembled that of the preeminent epic and tragic poets.

1.5   Stage 5: The Roman Period

In the Empire, the centre of Greek literary culture is probably Rome,[65] but the best evidence for the reception of Greek lyric continues to be papyri from Egypt, which confirm what we would otherwise have suspected: that Greek lyric poetry continued to be read and taught in schools in the early imperial period. Papyri of all nine of the canonical melic poets have survived, along with some of Corinna. For the iambic and elegiac poets we have papyri for Archilochus, Hipponax, and Tyrtaeus. Commentaries are also known to have been written,[66] and it became the practice to include excerpts from these in the manuscripts of poems in the form of scholia.[67] A good example of how commentators may have shaped expectations of readers is provided by a fragment of a commentary on Alcman, P.Oxy. 2390, which argues that Alcman's poem contains a cosmic genealogy, something that may not have been in the poem at all.[68]

Greek song continues to be adapted, imitated, and cited in literature. Catullus translates Sappho, and Horace presents himself as introducing Greek song (Archilochus in the *Epodes*, Sappho and Alcaeus in the *Odes*) into Rome.[69] Patricia Rosenmeyer has pointed to Sapphic resonances in the poems of Julia Balbilla, a travelling companion of the emperor Hadrian, inscribed on one of

---

62   See Gerber (1999) Archilochus T3.17–25; Clay (2004).
63   Callimachus fr. 64 Pfeiffer; see Barchiesi (2009) 327–328; Rawles (2018).
64   Stesichorus: see Barbantani (2010) 29–39; Ibycus: Barbantani (2010) 19–22, referring to *AP* 7.714.
65   For the shift to Rome, see Irigoin (1994) 73.
66   Commentaries on Pindar and Bacchylides were written by Didymus of Alexandria (late first century CE); see Montanari (2015) 173–174; Braswell (2013); Theon worked on Alcman, Pindar and Stesichorus (Montanari [2015] 178); a section of his commentary on the *Pythians* survives on papyrus (P.Oxy. 2536: Theon). Tryphon of Alexandria wrote on the dialects of the lyric poets (Montanari [2015] 182).
67   Dickey (2015) 504.
68   See Most (1987).
69   See Paschalis (2002), Feeney (1993).

the colossi of Memnon in Roman Egypt.[70] One tendency we observe is for the idea of any particular poet to become simplified, a stereotyping process akin to that which cognitive theorists call "chunking". Thus Pindar is torrential and overpowering, like a river in full flood (Horace, *Odes* 4.2.5–8), while Anacreon is reduced to being a poet of the symposium and love, even though his poetry may have been broader than that.[71]

Lyric poets were popular with the prose writers of the Second Sophistic, partly, perhaps, for the stylistic embellishment that excerpts of poetry were seen to provide (see Hermogenes, *On Ideas* 331, 334 Radt). Plutarch often cites them for moral content, and Athenaeus not infrequently for what they say about the ancient symposium. The treatise *De musica* ascribed to Plutarch includes accounts of the development of Greek music, much of it culled from Peripatetic writers, with many references to Greek lyric poetry. The rhetor Heraclitus, author of the *Homeric Problems*, applies allegorical interpretation to Alcaeus and Anacreon.[72] Pindar becomes something of a religious source book in this period, being cited by, for instance, Pausanias in his guide to Greece and Aelius Aristides in his prose Hymn to Zeus (43.40). In the third century CE, Menander Rhetor recommends several of the lyric poems as models for different types of hymn.[73] One of the biggest surprises in recent years is the discovery that 'Ibycus of Rhegium' was probably a character in a Greek novel.[74]

1.6 *Stage 6: Late Antiquity and Byzantium*

Continued interest in lyric in the fourth century CE is shown by the Orations of Himerius, one of which seems to summarize a paean by Alcaeus (*Or.* 48), while another excerpts Sappho's *epithalamia* (9). The Emperor Julian uses iambus as a model.[75] Nonnus makes striking use of the idea, at least, of Pindaric victory odes in his *Dionysiaca*.[76]

---

70 Rosenmeyer (2008).
71 See Bernsdorff (2014). For "chunking" see Rotstein (2010) 11.
72 *Alleg.* 4, citing Alcaeus 208.1–9 Campbell and 6.13 Campbell and Anacreon *PMG* 417. For the ship of state in Alcaeus, see Bowie's contribution to this volume, pp. 286–293.
73 At *Treatise* 1, 333 (Russell and Wilson [1981] 7–9) he recommends Sappho, Anacreon, and Alcman for cletic hymns, Bacchylides for apopemptic hymns, and Simonides' hymn to Tomorrow is an example of a fictitious hymn. Sappho is a source for narratives about divine marriages (2, 402; Russell and Wilson [1981] 141); Menander's *Sminthiakos Logos* cites the example of Pindar (2, 437; Russell and Wilson [1981] 207).
74 This is known to us through a Persian translation: see D'Alfonso (2000); Hägg and Utas (2003) 230–231.
75 Hawkins (2014).
76 Hardie (2005).

Despite this, it seems likely that after the third or fourth centuries CE there was a decline in the range of texts in circulation, and that the melic poets gradually ceased to be read—with some exceptions. Sappho remained in circulation for a while (one codex of Sappho, P.Berl. 9722, is dated to the sixth or seventh centuries CE), but not into the later Byzantine period.[77] Pindar's *Epinicia* survived, saved by contemporary interest in competitions, most likely;[78] a commentary on Pindar was written as late as the twelfth century CE by Eustathius of Thessalonica.[79] Theognis also survived into the Byzantine period, and it is possible that a book of Hipponax was still available in this period as well.[80] The loss of the texts is to some extent compensated for by anthologies, such as that of Stobaeus (fourth to fifth centuries CE), who includes excerpts from most of the lyric poets, but particularly Theognis: paradoxically, Theognis' popularity as a source for *gnomai* in anthologies may have been a factor that sustained interest in his works and led to their survival.[81]

2   The Individual Chapters of This Volume

The foregoing must suffice as a chronological sketch within which to situate the chapters of this volume. The chapters themselves have been grouped into seven subsections ('1' to '7') highlighting distinct aspects of the process, whether thematic (transmission, canonization, reception, scholarship) or temporal (the classical period of the fifth to fourth centuries BCE; the Peripatetic movement of the fourth century BCE; the Roman period; and the Second Sophistic movement of the second century CE). It will be obvious that these divisions are for convenience only. Often more than one period is involved (Stages 1 and 5 are relevant in the contributions of van Hilten-Rutten and Caciagli), and very often more than one thematic aspect of the process of transmission is in play. As the following summaries will make clear, the chapters in many cases offer different and even contradictory perspectives on the same material; this plurality was welcomed.

---

77 See Pontani (2001).
78 Rutherford (2012) 100–104.
79 See Neumann-Hartmann's contribution to this volume; Pontani (2015) 386–387. For even later Byzantine work, see Pontani (2015) 417, 423–425; for Tzetzes' study of Pindaric metre, see Dickey (2015) 490.
80 See Masson 1962: 42–51; Degani (1984) 80–83.
81 See Campbell (1984).

2.1   Part 1: Transmission

André Lardinois, in 'New Philology and the Classics: Accounting for Variation in the Textual Transmission of Greek Lyric Poetry', advocates for ancient Greek lyric a methodology (the New Philology) developed by scholars of medieval European literatures. The traditional aim of the modern editor of reconstructing the "original" text of a Greek lyric poem comes under scrutiny here: what if our textual witnesses take us back to a time when there was no "canonical" version of the text (compare above on Stage 1)? Do we hope to be able to intuit the author's original text, or do we content ourselves with presenting all alternatives as equally valid? Even when we are confident that one version is "authentic", does that mean that "less authentic" versions that were current in antiquity should be disregarded? Lardinois surveys a number of texts that illustrate the challenges, from Solon, Theognis, Tyrtaeus, Alcaeus, and Sappho. At the heart of Lardinois' chapter is the interplay between notions of canonization (in the sense of the creation of fixed texts), and of reception (in the sense of ancient reworkings of that text). Lardinois makes the case that ancient reworkings should be an object of study as much as the canonical text itself. We are required to ask ourselves whose text we are interested in: the author's own, some later "authorised" version, or all versions that speak to the changing significance of the author and his or her text throughout antiquity? Depending on our perspective, each may have a particular claim on our attention. Also central to this discussion (as to many others in the volume) is the question of the relative value of the indirect tradition compared to the direct tradition.

The method of the New Philology is explored in detail through a single test case by Eveline van Hilten-Rutten in 'Tyrtaeus the Lawgiver: Plutarch and Diodorus Siculus on Tyrtaeus fr. 4'. Tyrtaeus' poem about the origins of the Spartan constitution as it appears in modern editions is a conflation of different versions transmitted by two historians, who cite it for different reasons. Van Hilten-Rutten questions whether Plutarch and Diodorus are best treated as two testimonia to a single original whose reconstruction should be scholarship's goal. The point here is not that there is no original and that we should resign all hope of recovering it (though the difficulty of that task is not underestimated). It is rather that our task should also be to strive to appreciate the palimpsestic quality of these texts as preserved in the indirect tradition, the layers of interpretation they have accrued in antiquity. Van Hilten-Rutten investigates the specific interpretations given to the Tyrtaean passage by Plutarch in his *Life of Lycurgus* and by Diodorus in an excerpt from the lost seventh book of his *World History*. Plutarch, she argues, seeks corroboration in Tyrtaeus' text of his own account of how a 'rider' was added to the Lycurgan 'Great *Rhetra*' by the two Spartan kings Polydorus and Theopompus, on the authority of the Delphic oracle; van Hilten-Rutten shows how Plutarch presses various indeterminacies in Tyrtaeus' language into the service of his interpretation. In the case of Diodorus, we have an excerptor excerpting Diodorus quoting Tyrtaeus, and the ten elegiac verses quoted are in fact introduced as being not of Tyrtaeus, but of an oracle (a rather extreme form, therefore, of the "excarnation"[82] of the work of a lyric poet). The Diodoran excerptor appears to have been interested in the elegiac verses as a memorable expression of the need for obedience to authority. Diodorus' own reasons for including the quotation of Tyrtaean in his *History* are less apparent; van Hilten-Rutten suggests that he may have been interested in citing poetic testimony to buttress his historical account of the laws and oracles of Lycurgus or for their moralizing content.

2.2 Part 2: Canons

Whereas the first two chapters addressed the question of fixed texts, the following are additionally concerned with the creation of a canon in the sense of a fixed list of supreme poets and/or poetic genres. Gregory Nagy's chapter, 'On the Shaping of the Lyric Canon in Athens', treats the establishment of both a fixed group of nine "canonical" lyric poets and of fixed "canonical" texts of those poets. He is interested, moreover, in the shift from performance to text, and in the role of fifth-century Athens as a crucial mediating stage in the lyric tradition before the Alexandrians.[83] Nagy diverges from U. von Wilamowitz-Moellendorff's classic discussion of the Greek lyric textual tradition in conceiving of the "lyric canon" as a phenomenon of the performative tradition before it became one of the textual tradition.[84] The canonization of the 'lyric nine', Nagy argues, was due to the Panathenaic performance repertoire: this fed into and informed Alexandrian tradition, which, however, abandoned the performative aspect. The parallelism between epic and lyric is key: the Homeric epics and the "lyric nine" were both performed at the Panathenaea: Nagy points to inscriptional and literary evidence for competitions at the Panathenaea of rhapsodes performing Homeric epic and of kitharodes and aulodes performing lyric. The institution of rhapsodic contests at the Panathenaea saw the two "Homeric" epics, the *Iliad* and the *Odyssey*, being made "canonical", in the sense of both being accorded a specially privileged status vis-à-vis other early epic poems and of becoming textually fixed via the so-called "Pisistratean recension". A parallel development for lyric is envisaged, whereby texts of the "lyric nine" were generated primarily from performance at the Panathenaea. The Alexandrians

---

82 See above, p. 1.
83 This is also a concern of the contributions to this volume of Calame and Bartol.
84 Wilamowitz (1900).

will have inherited this Athenian legacy, though not merely passively: we may think of them also as proactively expanding what came down to them, their collecting activities thus counterbalancing a probable narrowing of the Panathenaic performance repertoire of the lyric poets that set in around the first half of the fourth century BCE. Thus Nagy posits continuity between Athens of the fourth to third centuries BCE and third-century BCE Alexandria in scholarly and textual activity on the canonical representatives of all the three main poetic genres: Homer (for epic), Aeschylus, Sophocles, and Euripides (for tragedy), and the "Nine" (for lyric). That continuity in the scholarly-critical tradition is accompanied by discontinuity, however, in the performance tradition, which Nagy regards as ceasing with classical Athens.[85]

Claude Calame, in 'Melic Poets and Melic Forms in the Comedies of Aristophanes: Poetic Genres and the Creation of a Canon', looks at the evidence from Old Comedy for the reception of lyric poetry in late fifth-century BCE Athens. He finds that the notion of the nine canonical lyric poets of Alexandrian scholarship has no very clear adumbration in extant Aristophanic comedy or Old Comedy more generally. Five of the nine are mentioned by Aristophanes, and three others by Eupolis (with only Bacchylides going unmentioned), but non-canonical, especially dithyrambic, poets are also named (such as Lasus of Hermione, Cinesias, and Philoxenus). There is, moreover, no very clear articulation of the lyric "genres" that are fundamental to later Alexandrian scholarship. Rather, as Calame shows, several genres were clearly distinguished in the fifth century (and others might easily have been); but certain others (such as the *skolion* and the 'Harmodius song') eluded distinctive labelling, while others again (such as iambus and elegy)[86] were intrinsically not such as to submit to easy categorization. The Aristophanic evidence also offers other insights into the reception of lyric in Athens of the later fifth century. First, the symposium emerges as the key venue for the reperformance of melic poetry (most explicitly, in the scene involving Strepsiades' request for Simonides' Krios-ode from Pheidippides in *Clouds*). Second, we may see evidence of the phenomenon referred to in this introduction as "chunking", the tendency to reduce the significance of the lyric poets to just one or two salient aspects; thus Ibycus, Anacreon, and Alcaeus are associated in comedy with the singing of (homo-)erotic praise at symposia (for instance, in the Agathon scene of the *Thesmophoriazusae*). Third, a crucial component of comedy's (and likewise tragedy's) reception of lyric poetry consists not in what Calame calls 'simple

---

85 On the question of the (dis)continuity of the performance tradition, see also D'Alessio (2017).
86 See Bartol's contribution to this volume on elegy.

"allusions" to traditional melic forms', but in the novel creation of melic compositions for fictional ritual occasions that arise from the comic (or tragic) plot (for instance, the *hymenaia* at the end of *Birds* and *Peace*, or the paeanic songs found in *Thesmophoriazusae* and several other comedies). In all this, Calame stresses the importance of the fifth-century BCE Athenian song and dance culture (which itself represents a departure from the various epichoric song and dance cultures in which the traditional melic compositions came about in the first place) that fostered a flexibility and suppleness quite unlike the rigid systematization necessitated by the Alexandrian editorial project.

Krystyna Bartol, in 'Structuring the Genre: the Fifth- and Fourth-Century Authors on Elegy and Elegiac Poets', deals with the reception not of specific poems or poets but of a genre—elegy—in the classical period. Like Calame, she emphasizes that the fifth and fourth centuries represented a crucial transitional moment in the transmission of lyric, but differs somewhat from Calame in finding both performance and texts vital to the ways in which the conceptualization of elegy as a distinct genre evolved during this period. First, she considers the distinction of elegy from *melos*. While elegiac poetry was always distinguished from melic poetry, the basis of the distinction appears to have shifted. In the earlier period, both were conceived of as being sung and performed, though to a different musical accompaniment; later, the distinction turned into one between a sung genre (melic) and a recited one (elegiac). Second, Bartol examines the evolving understanding of the term *elegos*: originally a term relating to performance (apparently a particular melodic pattern suiting the metrical form), it came to be conceived, apparently from the later fifth century onwards, in terms of content (the lament). Third, Bartol considers the connotations of the term *elegeion*: towards the end of the fifth century, it seems to conjure up, in addition to its metrical scheme, a particular type of content: both praise poetry (thus we find *elegeion* as praise poetry being opposed to *iambos*, blame poetry) and paraenetic poetry. Fourth, Bartol reflects on the assumptions that underlie the creation of elegiac collections from an early date (at least the late fifth century BCE, and perhaps as early as the late sixth century BCE). The poems in these collections all relate to a sympotic context (as indeed do other, non-elegiac, anthologies);[87] but crucially, further to the metre and the sympotic ambience, they evidence paideutic, didactic, or gnomic content of a kind relevant to aristocratic education. Bartol points out that such early elegiac anthologies presuppose the sophistic distinction between collections

---

87   Compare Caciagli's contribution to this volume, p. 327.

made for pleasure and those made for edification.[88] In these elegiac collections we may again see the operation of "chunking": long narrative elegies are excluded, and only the shorter, sympotic, paraenetic, and paideutic poems are seen as elegy's canonical representatives by classical authors. Bartol's emphasis on the importance of written anthologies in the fifth century for the development of the classical conception of the elegiac genre can be contrasted with Calame's emphasis on performative factors for the fifth-century conceptions of genre.

2.3 *Part 3: Lyric in the Peripatetics*

Scholarship on the Greek lyric poets is especially associated with the Alexandrian critics of the Hellenistic period, but the lyric poets were already a concern of the Peripatetic philosophers of the fourth century BCE. In 'The Peripatetics and the Transmission of Lyric', Theodora Hadjimichael documents the "Peripatetic project" in relation to the lyric poets, focussing on such figures as Heraclides Ponticus, Dicaearchus, Chamaeleon, Praxiphanes, and Aristoxenus. The school produced treatises both on individual lyric poets and treatises of a more general nature. Characteristic features of this "project" as a whole are its complementarity (reduplication of the work of other members of the school was apparently avoided) and its aesthetic conservatism. Hadjimichael's discussion raises important questions about the transmission and canonization of lyric, touching on many of the issues that were central to the discussions of Nagy and Calame. First, take canonization: the lower chronological cut-off point for "canonical" lyric poets applied by the Peripatetics is the second half of the fifth century BCE (thus excluding New Music—apart from Aristoxenus on Telestes). Hadjimichael sees this as an example of the Peripatetics' pursuit of a conservative "classicized" agenda, influenced by Platonic (and Old Comic) views, which favoured the traditional and spurned the innovative. Next, transmission: Hadjimichael, focussing on the Peripatetics, finds Athens relatively unimportant to the transmission of lyric, inferring that the Peripatetics, though resident in Athens, relied on lyric texts obtained from elsewhere. This perspective contrasts with that of Nagy who, focussing on the Panathenaea, accords Athens a central position in the transmission of lyric to Alexandria. According to Hadjimichael, moreover, the Peripatetics did not themselves 'organise, classify, or edit the text of lyric', although editions were a prerequisite of their scholarly work. Members of the "Lyric Nine" whom the Peripatos ignored include

---

88   For the impact of sophists on fifth-century BCE lyric poets themselves, compare Fearn's contribution to this volume, pp. 226–234, on Gorgias and Timotheus.

Ibycus and Bacchylides; these may have lacked editions, or at least the Peripatetics would appear not to have possessed them. Alternatively, it is possible, Hadjimichael suggests, that Ibycus and Bacchylides were not seen as "classical", next to, respectively, Anacreon and Pindar. (We may here compare and contrast Calame's discussion, from the evidence of Old Comedy, of which poets were considered canonical in the fifth century.) A further question arises concerning the influence of the Peripatetics on the subsequent critical tradition. Hadjimichael sees the Peripatetics as initiating the properly "literary study" of lyric poetry, rather than merely philosophical or historical uses of it, as seen, for instance, in Plato or Herodotus. This development would then eventually pave the way for the great commentaries of Aristarchus and Didymus and, ultimately, of Eustathius.[89]

Elsa Bouchard's appraisal of the Peripatetics in 'The Self-revealing Poet: Lyric Poetry and Cultural History in the Peripatetic School' turns in a different direction to Hadjimichael's. In her view, the Peripatetics were not interested in the lyric poets (as they were in Homer) from a genuinely literary critical perspective. Instead, they attached to them a 'historical value', and used them on the one hand to create an account of the origins and the successive innovations in the art of *mousike* (illustrations are given from Chamaeleon and Clearchus) and on the other to exemplify the moral character and cultural practices of the early Greeks. For Bouchard, this 'antiquarian interest' can account for the Peripatetic disinterest in the New Music: the relatively late date of these poets meant that they could not serve as witnesses to the earlier period. (We may compare and contrast the 'classicized agenda' attributed to the Peripatetics by Hadjimichael, seeing the aesthetic conservatism of the school, following Plato and Old Comedy, as responsible for the exclusion of the New Music from the Peripatetic "canon".) Compared with Hadjimichael, Bouchard also downplays the influence of the Peripatetics on the Alexandrians, regarding the more distinctively literary and formalistic approaches to lyric poetry of the latter as lacking anticipations in the former (whereas Hadjimichael saw the Peripatetics as paving the way to the properly literary study of lyric). Bouchard bolsters her case with two further arguments. First, the Peripatetic attitude towards lyric poetry is related to that of Aristotle, who was disinterested in lyric poetry as poetry because it was non-mimetic (the lyric poets, unlike Homer or the tragedians, spoke in their own persona). And second, Chamaeleon's trademark biographically oriented criticism (the so-called "Chamaeleon's method", which

---

89   On Aristarchus and Didymus, see Phillips' contribution to this volume, pp. 441–450. On Eustathius, see Neumann-Hartmann's contribution to this volume.

takes the poet's text to give a window on the poet's life and vice-versa) is applied exclusively or at least pre-eminently to the lyric poets, rather than to the early hexameter poets or the tragedians.

2.4 Part 4: Early Reception

The New Music that was excluded from the treatises of the Peripatetics is the subject of David Fearn's chapter, 'Lyric Reception and Sophistic Literarity in Timotheus' *Persae*', where canonicity and reception also play central roles. Fearn illustrates how 'Platonic reactionism' is not just a feature of the reception of Timotheus by the Peripatetics (compare Hadjimichael's paper), and by the ancients more generally, but also of modern scholars and editors, such as Bacchylides' great Victorian editor, Richard Jebb; in both antiquity and modernity the canonical Bacchylides, though himself often denigrated in comparison to Pindar, enjoyed a respectability and admiration denied to the non-canonical Timotheus. However, the divergent treatment of the two poets in terms of ancient literary criticism and transmission history is only one part of the picture. A contrasting picture is implied by "literary history"; that is, by the poetic reception of the former by the latter. Through a study of Timotheus' intertextual, structural, and stylistic debts, Fearn reveals Timotheus as a self-styled continuator of the lyric, and especially dithyrambic, traditions found in Pindar and Bacchylides; the continuities are no less important than the discontinuities between the "canonical" and "non-canonical" poets. Fearn goes on to explore Timotheus' debts to the sophist Gorgias, as indicative of the complexity and self-consciousness of Timotheus and the range of his influences. Fearn's argument also shows how, as early as Timotheus, lyric poets may be responsive to the scholarly and critical tradition of which Gorgias in the *Helen* is an early representative. Much later, we see Horace and other Latin poets responding to Alexandrian scholarship on the Greek lyric poets.[90] This shows that the scholarly philosophical "paratext" can turn into something more like "intertext" even in the context of late fifth-century lyric.

Reception and canonization are likewise fundamental to Andrea Capra's '"Total Reception": Stesichorus as Revenant in Plato's *Phaedrus*'. Capra reveals that Plato's reception of Stesichorus in the *Phaedrus* is more pervasive than previously recognized; Stesichorean pastiche already bookends Socrates' first speech (237a7–9, 241d1) prior to his explicit quotation from Stesichorus' '*Palinode*' (243a6–9). Capra is interested above all in the contrast that Socrates draws between Stesichorus and Homer (243a4), which Capra interprets as a multifa-

---

90 See the contributions to this volume of Bowie and Bitto.

ceted programmatic opposition that gets developed at the end of the dialogue in particular (277e5–b2). In the terms of this opposition, Homer is associated, via the rhapsodes, with fixed texts (whether written or performed, verse or prose—as with the speech of Lysias with which the dialogue begins), with the ignorance of true causes, and with (metaphorical) blindness. Stesichorus, on the other hand, is associated with musical performance, flexibility, dialectical discourse, knowledge of true causes, (metaphorical) sightedness. Accordingly, on Capra's interpretation, the 'fixed impersonal discourse' of (the rhapsodes') Homer is unfavourably compared to the 'flexible personal speech' of the lyric poet Stesichorus. (Here we may note the contrasting valorization of the opposition of a 'mimetic' Homer versus 'non-mimetic' lyric poets that was found by Bouchard in the Aristotelian and Peripatetic school.) In this introduction we have discussed the transformation of lyric from a musical performance (in the archaic and classical periods) into a fixed written text lacking musical notation (in the Hellenistic period);[91] Socrates, according to Capra, in the later fifth century is interested in the difference between lyric poetry as a musical performance and Homeric poetry as a fixed text memorized and recited by rhapsodes. Capra, like Nagy, is also interested in the performance of Stesichorean lyric at the Panathenaea alongside rhapsodic performance of Homeric epic. But Capra's argument emphasizes the opposition between a "musical" Stesichorus and a non-musical (fixed-text-dependent) rhapsodes' Homer, while Nagy's argument stresses a parallelism between Homer and the lyric poets in that both become "canonical" (in both senses in which we are interested) as a consequence of the Panathenaea. According to Capra, Plato also has Socrates in the *Phaedrus* make play with the idea of "canonization" in the sense of a selection of poets worthy of cultivation for posterity. Rather as Socrates in the *Republic* indulges the fantasy of a radically unorthodox "canonization" (Homer and the tragedians being excluded from his model republic), here too he implies a "canon" of value in which Stesichorus surpasses Homer and he himself surpasses Stesichorus. Capra also stresses the interconnectedness of Stesichorus' text (that of the '*Palinode*') and paratext (in the form of the biographical tradition of Stesichorus). We are dealing with a case of reception on all fronts—what Capra calls 'total reception':[92] namely, verbatim quotation, pastiche, metrical allusion, and allusion even (Capra suggests) to the way Stesichorus' poems would have been acted out in performance.

---

91   Above, pp. 8–9.
92   Compare Calame's contribution to this volume, p. 123, on Aristophanic comedy's 'full-scale dramatization of lyric poetry, enacted both musically and ritually in the orchestra.'

With Maria Kazanskaya's chapter, 'Indirect Tradition on Sappho's *kertomia*', we move from the biographical tradition of Stesichorus' blinding in Plato (Capra, above) to the biographical tradition of Sappho apparently taking her brother Charaxus to task for his love affair with a courtesan from Naucratis. Kazanskaya is concerned with divergences on three points in the indirect tradition (comprising statements from Herodotus, Posidippus, Athenaeus, and Ovid): first, the name of the courtesan (whether Doriche or Rhodopis); second, the tone of the poem (whether hostile or friendly); and third, the butt of the censure (whether the brother or the courtesan). There are some methodological similarities here with van Hilten-Rutten's chapter, in that Kazanskaya pays close attention to the indirect tradition and is concerned with the question of how elements of an original archaic lyric poem may be reconstructed from the indirect tradition. However, here the poet's *ipsissma uerba* are not at stake, but rather the coarser-grained issue of the outline of the poem's content. Moreover, whereas van Hilten-Rutten's New Philological approach was premised on the impossibility or undesirability of establishing a unitary original text, the object here is to read the various authors of the indirect tradition in such a way as to reconcile the differences and so to establish the likely contours of Sappho's lost poem. Thus Kazanskaya feels able to infer that in Sappho's poem the sister's tone was admonitory towards Charaxus, but more outright hostile towards the courtesan; that the butt of Sappho's more biting censure was the courtesan, not Charaxus; and that the name of the courtesan was Doricha, not Rhodopis.

2.5   Part 5: Reception in Roman Poetry

In 'Alcaeus' *stasiotica*: Catullan and Horatian Readings', Ewen Bowie looks at how two Roman poets engage with Greek lyric poetry, specifically Alcaeus. The first case is Catullus' poem 11, the renunciation of Lesbia, which scholars assume is intended to recall Sappho; without disputing that, Bowie argues that the poem is rather a 'brilliant collage' that evokes both Alcaeus and Sappho. The argument has interesting implications for (once again) the way that "chunking" applies to the Greek lyric poets: we tend to think of Sappho as being "chunked" in Rome as a personal, amatory, feminine voice, well suited to Catullus' countercultural neoteric poetic programme; and to think of the Augustan lyric poet Horace as pointedly preferring the ostensibly more politically engaged and masculine persona of Alcaeus. However, Bowie's reading of Catullus 11 prompts a nuancing of this account. Not only do the Alcaic and Sapphic elements jostle with one another in Horace's construction of his lyric persona, they do so already in Catullus. The second poem Bowie considers is Horace *Odes* 1.14, in which the image of a ship in sea during a storm serves as a political allegory. According to a standard position in modern Horatian and

Alcaean scholarship, Horace's allegory is derived from a corresponding allegory in poems of Alcaeus, detected already by Heraclitus in his *Homeric Problems*. Bowie indicates, however, that a non-allegorical interpretation of Alcaeus is also viable, and goes on to point out that Horace in two further odes (1.32 and 2.13) uses the shipwreck image non-figuratively. Granted that Horace as *poeta doctus* was familiar with the commentary tradition on the Greek lyric poets as well as with the poets themselves,[93] Bowie argues that in *Odes* 1.14 and 1.32 Horace reflects alternative approaches in Hellenistic scholarship to Alcaeus' storm-tossed ship: allegorical and non-allegorical respectively. Thus consideration of Horace's reception of Alcaeus invites a reappraisal of Hellenistic scholarship on Alcaeus, which in its turn has implications for our interpretation of Alcaeus' own poetry. This particular case study therefore provides a fine illustration of how our interpretation of the text of an archaic melic poet (Alcaeus) can be dependent both on our reconstruction of the ancient scholarly paratext (the Hellenistic commentary tradition) and on our gauging of the poet's reception by other poets in the lyric tradition (here, Horace).

Similar issues, in connection with Pindar rather than Alcaeus, are the concern of Gregor Bitto's 'Pindar, Paratexts, and Poetry: Architectural Metaphors in Pindar and Roman Poets'. Bitto traces successive receptions of Pindar's architectural metaphor, 'a treasure-house of songs' (*Pythian* 6.7) through Horace, Propertius, Ovid, and Statius. Bitto shows that, alongside the elaborate window-referencing and contrast imitation at work in this series of poetic receptions, when these Roman *poetae docti* hark back to the Pindaric original they are engaging not just with the text of Pindar itself, but also and just as vitally with its paratext, the Hellenistic scholarly tradition that had grown up around the Pindaric text. Thus some of the changes rung on the extended Pindaric image are seen by Bitto as having been prompted by Hellenistic scholarly judgements (which have left traces in our Pindar scholia) on the aesthetic merits and demerits of the passage. But the Hellenistic literary critical aesthetic is used very creatively by the Latin poets: Horace's reworking of Pindar gestures assentingly to it, whereas Statius' reworking pointedly flouts it. Bitto also invokes the commentary tradition to argue that Virgil in his famous architectural metaphor (the poem as a temple) in the proem of the third *Georgic* is engaging substantively with Pindar (or rather, with the assemblage that is Pindar plus his ancient commentators), and not merely with Callimachus' Pindarizing epinician, the *Victoria Berenices*.

---

93   See also Bitto's contribution to this volume, p. 300.

2.6 Part 6: Second Sophistic Contexts

Stefano Caciagli's contribution, 'Sympotic Sappho? The Recontextualization of Sappho's Verses in Athenaeus', examines the use of the indirect tradition of Sappho's poetry to determine the original circumstances of the performance of Sappho's poems and the nature of her relationship to her 'companions' (*hetairai*). The idea that Sappho was a schoolmistress has been generally rejected as being a fabrication of the scholia, with many scholars today, Caciagli included, being more open to seeing her female addressees as a group of comrades (*hetairai*) on the analogy of Alcaeus' symposiastic *hetairoi*. But the construction of this "sympotic Sappho" has tended to rely on a privileging of the poetess's *ipsissima uerba* over the testimonia, a procedure that Caciagli now identifies as problematic: neither our implicit trust in the former nor our instinctive distrust of the latter are fully justified. Caciagli's discussion once again revolves around the relationship of text and paratext, although here the manner of the transmission of the poetry complicates even that distinction. On the one hand, as Caciagli points out, Sappho's poems may have been transmitted from archaic and classical times in anthologies for use at symposia. On the other, an embedding text such as Athenaeus' *Learned Banqueters* quotes excerpts of Sappho in the context of a narrative setting that is explicitly sympotic. Thus the *ipssima uerba* of Sappho that come to us through these routes are likely to come with a sympotic veneer that may owe nothing to the original circumstances of Sapphic performance (a kind of double form of "excarnation", therefore). So, Caciagli argues, with Sappho fr. 94, Athenaeus' manner of quoting creates a sympotic impression that may not have been present, either at all or to the same degree, in the original.[94] And in Sappho fr. 2, Caciagli detects reworking of the Sapphic original either by Athenaeus or his putative source—perhaps a sympotic anthology. The discussion leaves our confidence shaken in reconstructions of a "sympotic Sappho" (that is, a Sappho with a female *hetairia* analogous to Alcaeus' male *hetairia*) on the basis of the—assumed—*ipsissima uerba* as given by Athenaeus: these are liable to the suspicion of having been reworked precisely so as to accentuate the sympotic aspects. Although Caciagli still cautiously favours the idea of Sappho's having had such a female *hetairia*, he here counsels caution in the use of the fragments quoted by Athenaeus in order to reach such a position.

Renate Schlesier, in 'A Sophisticated *hetaira* at Table: Athenaeus' Sappho', shares with Caciagli interests in Athenaeus' presentation of Sappho, Sappho's relationship with the symposium, and the interpretation of Sappho's status as

---

[94] For the point, see Schlesier's contribution to this volume, p. 367, citing Jacob (2013).

hetaira; however, her discussion moves in different directions. On Caciagli's reconstruction of Athenaeus' Sappho, *hetaira* means 'fellow-member of a (female) aristocratic faction', analogously to Alcaeus' use of *hetairos* of his male companions, and the symposia envisaged are female equivalents of the male symposium seen in Alcaeus' poetry. On Schlesier's reconstruction of Athenaeus' Sappho, *hetaira* means 'courtesan' and the symposia are male drinking-parties to which the only women admitted as active participants were courtesans. After surveying the many references to and quotations of Sappho in Athenaeus, Schlesier identifies the symposium as a 'thematic frame' for Athenaeus' quotations of Sappho. From book 9 on, and especially in book 13, Sappho is associated with eroticism. Most Sapphic quotations come in book 13, where the discussion centres on courtesans (*hetairai*). Athenaeus' learned banqueters see Sappho, Schlesier argues, as participating in male symposia as a courtesan, and she is viewed as being as much at home in the context of the (male) symposium as male lyric poets, such as Anacreon. Further, Athenaeus' learned banqueters treat Sappho as a courtesan by freely admitting her into the literary and cultural space of their own symposium, in which she becomes a virtual participant. Schlesier argues further that the attributes and utterances of Sappho that receive prominence in the *Learned Banqueters* are consistent with a courtesan, and points out that Athenaeus' representation of Sappho as a courtesan is consistent with other strands of Sappho's reception in antiquity. This leaves open the question of how this view of Sappho's status relates to the seventh-century BCE reality, and how it should inform our interpretation of Sappho's poetry—questions that Schlesier has pursued more explicitly elsewhere.[95]

In 'Solon and the Democratic Biographical Tradition' Jessica Romney is interested in the way the ancient reception of Solon, in the form of the biographical tradition that starts in the fifth and fourth centuries BCE and culminates in Plutarch's *Life of Solon* in the first to second centuries CE, has conditioned the interpretation of his poetry as transmitted in the indirect tradition. Romney thus takes a similar approach to Plutarch's presentation of Solon as does Caciagli to Athenaeus' presentation of Sappho. Like Caciagli, Romney is interested in how the 'narrative frames' provided by source-authors dictate our understanding of the fragments. Her approach also invites contrast with the New Philological approach undertaken by Lardinois and van Hilten-Rutten; while they insist on the validity of the source-authors' readings (both their textual readings and their interpretative readings) of the lyric poets as an object of study in its own right, Romney's aim with the source-authors on Solon is to 'destabilize this tra-

---

95 See, e.g. Schlesier (2013) 217.

dition, contextualizing the fragments in the setting of archaic politics as seen in the Greek *poleis* as a whole'. Whereas the biographical tradition persistently presents Solon as an isolated, moderate, and mediating figure, standing above the factionalism of contemporary Athenian politics, Romney argues that Solon is much more likely to have been implicated in the *stasis* of his city-state and to have been the leader of a *hetaireia*, analogously with near-contemporary figures such as Alcaeus. Thus in fr. 11, rather than berating 'the Athenians' on allowing Pisistratus' tyranny, as the indirect tradition (Diodorus, Diogenes Laertius, and Plutarch) would have it, Solon is more likely, Romney argues, to be addressing his *hetairoi* (the members of his *hetaireia*). The pronouns used by Solon (τούτους, 'these men', fr. 11.3) and 'you (pl.)' (fr. 11, *passim*) will then have been accommodated by these source-authors to their own reading where they are referred to, respectively, Pisistratus and 'the Athenians' at large, rather than to a rival *hetaireia* and Solon's own *hetaireia*.[96] Similar points may be made about the reference of the pronominal adjective in Solon fr. 4.1 ἡμετέρη … πόλις, and about the contrasting of ἡμεῖς 'we' with αὐτοῖς (as read by Plutarch: v.l. τούτοις) in fr. 15.1–2; similar oppositions, Romney points out, are found in Alcaeus. Romney thus shares with Caciagli the insight that the *ipsissima uerba* of the poet are affected by the way that the poet is presented in the indirect tradition.

The Solonian biographical tradition and the indirect tradition of Solon's poetry in Plutarch are again the subject of Jacqueline Klooster's paper, 'Strategies of Quoting Solon's Poetry in Plutarch's *Life of Solon*'. Whereas Romney concentrates on how the vision of Solon's role in democratic Athenian politics has shaped Plutarch's reception of Solon, Klooster focusses on how Plutarch's moralistic approach both to the study of poetry and to the writing of the lives of exemplary men has conditioned his reception of Solon. Plutarch's moralizing attitude to poetry is set out in his tract *How to Study Poetry*, where he accords poetry a definite value as a propaedeutic to the study of philosophy, but also recognizes that there are many potentially pernicious features of poetry, and recommends various hermeneutic strategies for neutralizing these. Klooster points out that Plutarch employs several of these strategies in his treatment of Solon's poetry, not merely in the *Solon*, but also in the *Amatorius* and *Conuiuium*. One key strategy is that of offsetting an immoral passage with another more edifying passage from the same author. This is found in *Solon* 3.1, where Plutarch alludes to (but, significantly, does not quote from) poems of Solon that bespeak an extravagant and hedonistic lifestyle, but then offsets these

---

96 Compare van Hilten-Rutten's contribution to this volume, pp. 78–79, on Plutarch's reinterpretation of the unexpressed subject of the participle ἀκούσαντες in Tyrt. 4.1.

with a Solonian quotation in which the first-person speaker (taken to be Solon) professes poverty and virtue. Similarly in Plutarch's *Amatorius*, a fragment of unabashedly pederastic content (fr. 25) is offset with a fragment (fr. 26) that is interpreted (tendentiously) by Plutarch as expressing the older Solon's commitment to marriage and philosophy. That fragment, moreover, can only be given the desired meaning by implementing another of the strategies outlined in *How to Study Poetry*: the expedient of interpreting the gods' names metonymically rather than literally: when Solon's first-person speaker professes a devotion to Aphrodite, Dionysus, and the Muses, this is to be interpreted not as a devotion to wine, women, and song, but as a commitment to congenial social interactions ('Aphrodite' and 'Dionysus') and a cultured education (the 'Muses'). Thus Plutarch's reception of Solon may be influenced not only by the democratic–political colouring inherited by Plutarch (according to Romney's discussion), but also by the sanitizing attitude to poetry held by Plutarch and expounded in his *How to Study Poetry*. This sanitizing attitude affects not merely the way Plutarch interprets Solon's poetry, but also his reasons for quoting it or, indeed, for not doing so (a form of censorship): the existence of a body of erotic poetry by Solon is alluded to, but scarcely ever quoted from.

No writer of this period had a more intense engagement with Greek lyric than Aelius Aristides, who composed paeans in praise of Asclepius, but in his Hymn to Sarapis claimed that his prose hymns were superior to hymns by the classic poets. In 'Playing with Terpander & Co.: Lyric, Music, and Politics in Aelius Aristides' *To the Rhodians on Concord*', Francesca Modini examines a neglected aspect of his use of Greek lyric, namely his presentation of himself as a poet from outside sent to reconcile a community on the model of Terpander.

2.7   *Part 7: Scholarship*

Our main source for ancient scholarship on lyric poems are scholia in manuscipts and papyri, which draw on, among other things, the great Hellenistic commentaries of the likes of Aristarchus and Didymus; the scholia on Pindar's *Epinicia* are the subject of the chapter by Tom Phillips, 'Historiography and Ancient Pindaric Scholarship'. Bowie and Bitto considered implications of the fact that the Roman 'learned poets' read the Greek lyric poets—specifically, Alcaeus and Pindar—in conjunction with the Hellenistic commentary tradition. In a similar vein, Phillips explores what it could have meant for Hellenistic readers of Pindar's *Epinicia* of the second to first centuries BCE to encounter Pindar's text via the commentaries. Phillips focusses in particular on how notes that sought to provide historical context for Pindar's poems or that cited historiographical texts may have affected the reading experience of Pindar's Hellenistic readers. Two kinds of case are distinguished: those where commentators advanced a historicizing reading for a specific exegetical purpose, and those where commentators proffered incidental background historical information without any such purpose. Examples of the first category are scholia on *Olympian* 3 and *Nemean* 1, deriving from Aristarchus and Chaeris respectively, where historical contextualization is used to solve problems of seeming irrelevance in the odes. Thus the Dioscuri are invoked (rather than Heracles) at the beginning of *Olympian* 3 because they enjoyed an important cult in Acragas. In *Nemean* 1, the 'Heracliscus' myth and Tiresias' prophecy of Heracles' exploits are narrated because the historical circumstances of the laudandus Chromius' life offered certain parallels to that of Heracles. Phillips emphasizes how such notes, rather than closing down the interpretative possibilities, could serve to stimulate critical reflection on the reader's part. The adjective φιλοξείνοις applied to the Dioscuri in *Olympian* 3.1 prompts reflection on the possible relationship between an Acragantine Theoxenia festival in honour of the Dioscuri and the circumstances of the ode, while the reader of *Nemean* 1 is required to consider which elements in Heracles' career correspond to elements in Chromius' and which do not. Examples of scholia that furnish historical information without any explicit interpretative end in view are found in the notes on *Olympian* 13.23 (where Pindar refers to Corinth's military excellence in very general terms) and *Nemean* 3.13 (where Pindar refers to Myrmidons as ancient inhabitants of Aegina). In the former instance, the commentator cites a very specific story concerning Corinth's role in the Persian wars taken from the fourth-century BCE historian Theopompus and also attested in a fifth-century epigram of Simonides; Phillips speculates that the aim is to make Pindar more accessible by connecting him with a major Panhellenic event, and suggests that the citation of Simonides is an attempt to encourage the reader to approach Pindar through fifth-century rather than Hellenistic interpretative horizons. In the latter instance, the commentator supplements Pindar's own sober and elliptical reference to the Myrmidons in Aegina's early myth-history by quoting an unabashedly mythical narrative in 'Hesiod's' *Catalogue of Women*, where Zeus turned all the ants of the island into men and women, followed by a resolutely rationalizing account given by a local historian, Theogenes. Phillips suggest that one effect of the note is to prompt reflections on the relationship, on the one hand, between the archaic epic poet Hesiod and the classical lyric poet Pindar, and, on the other, between the rationalizing-euhemerizing historian Theogenes and the mythological poet Pindar (who in the same ode goes on to give a miraculous account of Achilles' early life). But, once again, the reader's own responses to Pindar's text are not trammelled by what he encounters in the commentary tradition: 'The extant scholium does not formulate how text and metatexts should be related, opening up a space for individual readers' interpretative decisions'.

Perhaps the single most significant paratextual device used in the transmission of Greek lyric is the title; in 'Poem-titles in Simonides, Pindar, and Bacchylides', Enrico Prodi presents an in-depth study of the attested poem-titles of these poets. In general, poem-titles can be regarded as a feature of the "canonical" Alexandrian editions of Simonides, Pindar, and Bacchylides, and so this investigation pertains to what we have called "Stage 4" of the transmission of Greek lyric. At this stage in the transmission, the poems were read as texts rather than experienced in performance, and so the title offered a form of rapid contextualization of the work for the reader, indicating, for example, which was the athletic victory that occasioned this epinician, which was the community who commissioned and performed this paean and at what religious venue, and so on, compensating for what would have been self-evident to an audience assisting at the first performance: 'by inscribing originally non-written, non-textual elements in written form they seal the textualization that these compositions had undergone.' However, the poem-titles of dithyrambs, such as Bacchylides' poems 15 (*Antenoridae*) and 17 (*Eïtheoi*), may actually go back to the fifth-century poets themselves, and would thus relate to "Stage 1". Poem-titles play a key role in the reception of lyric: they not only provide evidence for how poems were viewed in (Hellenistic) antiquity, but also exercise a decisive and long-lasting influence on the way the poems come to be viewed in their subsequent reception, once the title has become an inalienable part of the text's tradition, from antiquity to the present. Titles of whole books of lyric poetry (*Epinicians*, *Paeans*, etc.) have a key role in the conceptualization of the miscellaneous sub-genres of Greek lyric. Individual poem-titles interact crucially with book-titles by 'simultaneously individualiz[ing] each poem through the specific indications that they offer, and contribut[ing] to characterizing the genre through the elements that they consistently put forward for that purpose'.[97] Poem-titles may not only conform to and confirm the characteristics of the genre declared in the book-title; they may also offer complications, such as the hybridizing title that declares Pindar *Paean* D7 Rutherford 'a prosodiac paean', or even negations of them: thus an *oschophorikon* (Pindar fr. 6c, from the book of '*Isthmians*') is evidently not properly an Isthmian ode nor an epinician. The other major issue in Prodi's chapter is whether poem-titles have merely exegetical value (in the event that they represent just a scholarly inference

---

97   Prodi, this volume, p. 487.

from the text) or whether they may have independent evidentiary value (in the event that they preserve independently known information). Prodi considers the likelihood of whether the poem-titles of Pindar's epinicians are informed by the Olympic and Pythian victor lists compiled by Hippias and Callisthenes respectively, and whether the dithyrambs can be seen as taking their titles from Athenian victor lists (*didaskaliai*)—if these lists both named dithyrambic poets and recorded their poem-titles.

The reception, and transmission, of Greek lyric poetry in the Roman imperial period, specifically the third century CE, is the subject of Johannes Breuer's '*Ita dictum accipe*: Pomponius Porphyrio on Early Greek Lyric Poetry in Horace'. Breuer points out that the treatment of the Greek lyric poets by the third-century Horatian commentator Porphyrio is superficial. He will typically identify the poets referred to antonomastically by Horace; thus *Lesboum ... barbiton* (Horace, *Odes* 1.1) is explained as a reference to Sappho and Alcaeus, as is 'common knowledge' (*manifestum*). In general, he references the poets' biographical traditions rather than their actual poems. Thus, commenting on *Odes* 1.14 and 1.32, Porphyrio points to Alcaeus' opposition to Mytilenean tyrants, but does not reference any Alcaean poem about shipwreck or the allegorical interpretation of the Alcaean storm-tossed ship.[98] In commenting on *Odes* 2.13, Porphyrio concentrates on providing "biographical" information about Sappho and Alcaeus. Thus Sappho as *querentem / ... puellis de popularibus* is explained with reference to the biographical tradition about her love for Phaon. Alcaeus as *plenius sonantem* is explained with reference to the image of Alcaeus as embroiled in wars, in seafaring, and in bouts of exile at the hands of tyrants (an image developed by Horace himself in *Odes* 1.32), these being the 'fuller strain' of Alcaeus' song. In commenting on Horace *Epistles* 1.19, Porphyrio cites the biographical tradition of Sappho's love for women and the story concerning Archilochus, Lycambes, and Neobule. In explaining Alcaeus' 'threatening' Muses of *Odes* 4.9.7, Porphyrio instances Alcaeus' role in the expulsion of tyrants (alluded to by Horace at *Odes* 2.13.31). Porphyrio does indicate some of Horace's poetic debts to the lyric poets when these are not explicitly named by Horace (Alcaeus in *Odes* 1.10, Pindar in 1.12, Bacchylides in 1.15, Anacreon in 1.27); however, we are aware of many more obvious Greek lyric intertexts for Horace than Porphyrio acknowledges. Porphyrio's awareness of Greek lyric thus appears to be both attenuated and, often, mediated by the biographical tradition. Breuer introduces a telling control: Porphyrio is both interested and

---

98   On the allegorical interpretation of the Alcaean storm-tossed ship, see Bowie's contribution to this volume, pp. 287–293.

able to quote many Latin intertexts for Horace, and able also to put them to more constructive use, as linguistic, motival, or thematic parallels for Horace: the implication is that he would have done the same with the Greek lyric poets, had he been able to do so. A plausible argument from silence thus indicates that Prophyrio, and perhaps his peers in the third century CE, were barely conversant with early Greek lyric.

The ancient tradition of Pindaric scholarship, whose Hellenistic phase was examined by Phillips, lasted until the Byzantine period, and the last known commentary is by Eustathius of Thessalonica (twelfth century), which like its Hellenistic predecessors, is lost, apart from its introduction. Arlette Neumann-Hartmann, in 'Pindar and his Commentator Eustathius of Thessalonica', illuminates this commentary as far as possible, drawing not only, as other scholars have done, on its extant introduction, but also from the many (approximately 220) scattered references to Pindar in Eustathius' other surviving commentaries on poetic works—Homer's *Iliad* and *Odyssey*, and Dionysius Periegetes' *Description of the Known World*—which were evidently written after his work on Pindar (they refer to it eight times). It emerges that Eustathius' knowledge of Pindar seems to have been largely confined to the *Epinicia* (though, unlike us, he knew the complete book of *Isthmians*), and his knowledge of poems from other genres may have been owed to the indirect tradition, perhaps as this had already been incorporated into the Pindaric commentary tradition. Unlike the ancient Pindar scholia, Eustathius' commentary covered only a selection of Pindar's epinicians, ranging over all four books of the *Epinicia*. Poems certainly included were *Olympian* 10, *Pythians* 1, 2, 4, 12, *Nemean* 2, and *Isthmian* 5. The commentary was heavily dependent on the ancient Pindar scholia, but also included significant new material and insights. Thus it is possible to say that Eustathius had an interest in Pindar's Doric dialect (one note dealt with the use of ἐν with the accusative), Pindar's diction (for instance, his fondness for the verb μίγνυμι, in non-literal senses), and Pindar's mythology (the Sphinx/Medusa, Heracles, and the Moliones, Zeus Ammon, the name Typhaon, the Centaur, and Nephele). Perhaps unsurprisingly, the commentaries on Homer reveal that Eustathius also must have taken a keen interest in epithets in Pindar (such as ἐρισφάραγος and the uniquely Pindaric εὐρυφαρέτρας of Apollo). While much of course remains in the dark, Neumann-Hartmann thus manages to shed meaningful light on the Pindaric commentary tradition at the end of antiquity.

References

Agócs, P., Carey, C., and Rawles, R., eds. 2012. *Receiving the Komos: Ancient and Modern Receptions of the Victory Ode*. London.
Acosta-Hughes, B. 2010. *Arion's Lyre: Archaic Lyric into Hellenistic Poetry*. Princeton.
Assmann, J. 2006. *Religion and Cultural Memory: Ten Studies*. Stanford.
Bagordo, A. 2003. *Reminiszenzen früher Lyrik bei den attischen Tragikern: Beiträge zur Anspielungstechnik und poetischen Tradition. Zetemata 118*. Munich.
Bakker, E. 2017. Trust and Fame: The Seal of Theognis. In *Authorship and Greek Song Authority, Authenticity, and Performance. Studies in Archaic and Classical Greek Song 3*, ed. E. Bakker, 99–121. Leiden.
Barbantani, S. 1993. I poeti lirici del canone alessandrino nell'epigrammistica. *Aevum(ant)* 6: 5–97.
Barbantani, S. 2009. Lyric in the Hellenistic Period and Beyond. In Budelmann 2009: 297–318.
Barbantani, S. 2010. *Three Burials (Ibycus, Stesichorus, Simonides): Facts and Fiction about Lyric Poets in Magna Graecia in the Epigrams of the 'Greek Anthology'*. Alexandria.
Barchiesi, A. 2009. Lyric in Rome. In Budelmann 2009: 319–335.
Baumbach, M. and Dümmler, N. 2014. *Imitate Anacreon!: Mimesis, Poiesis and the Poetic Inspiration in the Carmina Anacreontea*. Berlin.
Bernsdorff, H. 2014. Anacreon's Palinode. In Baumbach and Dümmler 2014: 11–24.
Bing, P. 2014. Anacreontea avant la lettre: Euripides, *Cyclops* 495–518. In Baumbach and Dümmler 2014: 25–46.
Bitto, G. 2012. *Lyrik als Philologie. Zur Rezeption hellenistischer Pindarkommentierung in den Oden des Horaz*. Rahden.
Bowie, E.L. 1989. Greek Sophists and Greek Poetry in the Second Sophistic. *ANRW* II 33.1: 209–258.
Bowie, E.L. 1997. The Theognidea: A Step towards a Collection of Fragments? In *Collecting Fragments. Fragmente sammeln*, ed. G.W. Most, 53–66. Göttingen.
Bowie, E.L. 2008. Aristides and Early Greek Lyric, Elegiac and Iambic Poetry. In *Aelius Aristides between Greece, Roma, and the Gods*, ed. W.V. Harris and B. Holmes, 9–29. Leiden.
Braswell, B.K. 2013. *Didymos of Alexandria: Commentary on Pindar*. Basle.
Budelmann, F. 2009. *The Cambridge Companion to Greek Lyric*. Cambridge.
Calame, C. 1974. Réflexions sur les genres littéraires en Grèce antique. *QUCC* 17: 113–128.
Campbell, D. 1984. Stobaeus and Early Greek Lyric Poetry. In *Greek Poetry and Philosophy: Studies in Honor of Leonard Woodbury*, ed. D.E. Gerber, 51–57. Chico.
Cannatà Fera, M. 1992. *Il Pindaro di Plutarco*. Messina.

Carey, C. 2011. Alcman: From Laconia to Alexandria. In *Archaic and Classical Choral Song: Performance, Politics and Dissemination. Trends in Classics—supplementary volumes, 10*, ed. L. Athanassaki and E. Bowie, 437–460. Berlin.

Cassio, A.C. 1997. Futuri dorici, dialetto di Siracusa e testo antico dei lirici greci. *AION-(filol)* 19: 187–214.

Cerri, G. 1991. Il significato di sphregis in Teognide e la salvaguardia dell'autenticità testuale nel mondo antico. *QS* 17/33: 21–40.

Chaniotis, A. 1988. Als die Diplomaten noch tanzten und sangen. Zu zwei Dekreten kretischer Städte in Mylasa. *ZPE* 71: 157.

Clay, D. 2004. *Archilochos heros: The Cult of Poets in the Greek Polis*. Washington, DC.

Colesanti, G. 2011. *Questioni Teognidee. La genesi simposiale di un corpus di elegie*. Rome.

Currie, B.G.F. 2017. Festival, Symposium, and Epinician (Re)performance: The Case of *Nemean* 4 and Others. In Hunter and Uhlig 2017: 187–208.

D'Alessio, G.B. 2017. Performance, Transmission, and the Loss of Hellenistic Lyric Poetry. In Hunter and Uhlig 2017: 232–261.

D'Alfonso, F. 2000. Anassimene e Ibico alla corte di Policrate (Metiochos et Parthenope; 'Unsurî, Vâmiq u 'Adhrâ). *Helikon* 35–38 (1995–1998): 55–76.

Degani, E. 1984. *Studi su Ipponatte*. Bari.

Degani, H. 1991. *Hipponax: Testimonia et Fragmenta*. 2nd edn. Stuttgart.

Dickey, E. 2007. *Ancient Greek Scholarship*. Oxford.

Dickey, E. 2015. The Sources of our Knowledge of Ancient Scholarship. In Montanari, Matthaios, and Rengakos 2015: 1.459–514.

Dover, K.J. 1993. *Aristophanes* Frogs. Oxford.

Feeney, D. 1993. Horace and the Greek lyric poets. In *Horace 2000: A Celebration: Essays for the Bimillennium*, ed. N. Rudd, 41–63. London.

Ford, A. 1995. *The Origins of Criticism. Literary Culture and Poetic Theory in Classical Greece*. Princeton.

Fowler, R.L. 2004. The Homeric Question. In *The Cambridge Companion to Homer*, ed. R.L. Fowler, 220–232. Cambridge.

Gerber, D.E. 1999. *Greek Iambic Poetry*. Cambridge, MA.

Gronewald, M. and Daniel, R.W. 2004. Ein neuer Sappho-Papyrus. *ZPE* 146: 1–8.

Hadjimichael, T.A. 2019. *The Emergence of the Lyric Canon*. Oxford.

Hagel, S. 2010. *Ancient Greek Music: A New Technical History*. Cambridge.

Hägg, T. and Utas, B. 2003. *The Virgin and her Lover: Fragments of an Ancient Greek Novel and a Persian Epic Poem = Brill Studies in Middle Eastern Literatures, Supplements to the Journal of Arabic Literature, vol. XXX*. Leiden.

Hardie, P. 2005. Nonnus' Typhon: The Musical Giant. In *Roman and Greek Imperial Epic*, ed. M. Paschalis, 117–130. Herakleion.

Harvey, A.E. 1955. The Classification of Greek Lyric Poetry. *CQ* 5: 157–175.

Hawkins, T. 2014. *Iambic Poetics in the Roman Empire*. Cambridge.

Herington, J. 1985. *Poetry into Drama: Early Tragedy and the Greek Poetic Tradition*. Berkeley.

Hunter, R.L. and Rutherford, I.C., eds. 2009. *Wandering Poets in Ancient Greek Culture: Travel, Locality and Pan-Hellenism*. Cambridge.

Hunter, R.L. and Uhlig, A., eds. 2017. *Imagining Reperformance in Ancient Culture: Studies in the Traditions of Drama and Lyric*. Cambridge.

Hutchinson, G.O. 2001. *Greek Lyric Poetry: A Commentary on Selected Larger Pieces*. Oxford.

Hutchinson, G.O. 2007. Horace and Archaic Greek Poetry. In *The Cambridge Companion to Horace*, ed. S.J. Harrison, 36–49. Cambridge.

Irigoin, J. 1994. Les éditions de textes. In *La philologie grecque à l'époque hellénistique et Romaine*, ed. F. Montanari, 39–82. Geneva.

Irmscher, J. 1981. Pindar in Byzanz. In *Aischylos und Pindar. Studien zu Werk und Nachwirkung. Schriften zur Geschichte und Kultur der Antike* 19, ed. E.G. Schmidt, 296–302. Berlin.

Jacob, C. 2013. *The Web of Athenaeus*. Cambridge, MA.

Käppel, L. 2000. Bakchylides und das System der chorlyrischen Gattungen im 5.Jh. v. Chr. In *Bakchylides 100 Jahre nach seiner Wiederentdeckung. Zetemata* 106, ed. A. Bagordo and B. Zimmermann, 11–27. Munich.

Kroehnert, O. 1897. *Canones ne poetarum scriptorum artificum per antiquitatem fuerunt?* Königsberg/Kaliningrad.

Kugelmeier, C. 1996. *Reflexe früher und zeitgenössischer Lyrik in der alten attischen Komödie. Beiträge zur Altertumskunde* 80. Stuttgart.

Lane Fox, R. 2000. Theognis: An Alternative to Democracy. In *Alternatives to Athens*, ed. R. Brock and S. Hodkinson, 35–51. Oxford.

Larson, J. 2002. Corinna and the Daughters of Asopus. *SyllClass* 13: 47–62.

Massimilla, G. 2012. Callimachus and Early Greek Elegy. In *Hellenistic Studies at a Crossroads: Exploring Texts, Contexts and Metatexts*, ed. R.L. Hunter, A. Rengakos, and E. Sistakou, 3–12. Berlin.

Masson, O. 1962. *Les fragments du poète Hipponax. Études et Commentaires* 43. Paris.

Matthaios, S. 2015. Greek Scholarship in the Imperial Era and Late Antiquity. In Montanari, Matthaios, and Rengakos 2015: 184–296.

Montana, F. 2015. Hellenistic Scholarship. In Montanari, Matthaios, and Rengakos 2015: 60–183.

Montanari, F., Matthaios, S., and Rengakos, A., eds. 2015. *Brill's Companion to Ancient Greek Scholarship*. Leiden.

Most, G.W. 1987. Alcman's Cosmogonic Fragment (Fr. 5 Page, 81 Calame). *CQ* 37: 1–19.

Most, G.W. 1994. Simonides' Ode to Scopas in Contexts. In *Modern Critical Theory and Classical Literature*, ed. I. de Jong and J.P. Sullivan, 127–152. Leiden.

Nagy, G. 1990. *Greek Mythology and Poetics*. Ithaca.

Nagy, G. 1996. *Homeric Questions*. Austin.
Nicolai, R. 1992. *La storiografia nell'educazione antica*. Pisa.
Nicolai, R. 2006. Alle origini dei canoni letterari: da Omero al Museo di Alessandri, *Scienze umanistiche* 2: 43–62.
Nicolai, R. 2014. The Canon and its Boundaries. In *Submerged Literature in Ancient Greek Culture: An Introduction*, ed. G. Colesanti and M. Giordano, 33–45. Berlin.
Nünlist, R. 2015. Poetics and Literary Criticism. In Montanari, Matthaios, and Rengakos 2015: 706–755.
Olson, S.D. 2007. *Broken Laughter: Select Fragments of Greek Comedy*. Oxford.
Parker, H.N. 1993. Sappho Schoolmistress. *TAPhA* 123: 309–351.
Paschalis, M., ed. 2002. *Horace and Greek Lyric Poetry*. Rethymnon.
Pfeiffer, R. 1968. *History of Classical Scholarship from the Beginnings to the End of the Hellenistic Age*. Oxford.
Phillips, T. 2015. *Pindar's Library: Performance, Poetry, and Material Texts*. Oxford.
Pontani, F. 2001. Le cadaver adoré: Sappho à Byzance. *Byzantion* 71: 233–250.
Pontani, F. 2015. Scholarship in the Byzantine Empire (529–1453). In Montanari, Matthaios, and Rengakos 2015: 297–455.
Pordomingo Pardo, F. 2013. *Antologías de época helenística en papiro*. Florence.
Prauscello, L. 2009. Wandering Poetry, 'Travelling' Music: Timotheus' Muse and Some Case-Studies of Shifting Cultural Identities. In Hunter and Rutherford 2009: 168–194.
Rawles, R. 2018. Simonides on Tombs, and the 'Tomb of Simonides'. In *Tombs of the Ancient Poets: Between Literary Reception and Material Culture*, ed. N. Goldschmidt and B. Graziosi, 51–68. Oxford.
Rosenmeyer, P.A. 1992. *The Poetics of Imitation: Anacreon and the Anacreontic Tradition*. Cambridge.
Rosenmeyer, P.A. 2008. Greek Verse Inscriptions in Roman Egypt: Julia Balbilla's Sapphic Voice. *ClAnt* 27: 334–358.
Rossi, L.E. 1971. Generi letterari e le loro leggi scritte e non scritte nelle letterature classiche. *BICS* 18: 69–94.
Rotstein, A. 2007. Critias' Invective Against Archilochus. *CPh* 102: 139–154.
Rotstein, A. 2010. *The Idea of Iambos*. Oxford.
Rotstein, A. 2016. The Ancient Literary History of Iambos. In *Iambus and Elegy: New Approaches*, ed. L. Swift and C. Carey, 101–121. Oxford.
Russell, D.A. and Wilson, N.G., ed. 1981. *Menander Rhetor*. Oxford.
Rutherford, I.C. 2012. On the Impossibility of Centaurs: The Reception of Pindar in the Roman Empire. In Agócs, Carey, and Rawles 2012: 93–104.
Schlesier, R. 2013. Atthis, Gyrinno, and other *hetairai*: Female Personal Names in Sappho's Poetry. *Philologus* 157: 199–222.
Stehle, E. 1997. *Performance and Gender in Ancient Greece: Nondramatic Poetry in its Setting*. Princeton.

Stehle, E. 2004. *Choral Prayer in Greek Tragedy: Euphemia or Aischrologia? In Music and the Muses: The Culture of Mousike in the Classical Athenian City*, ed. P. Murray and P. Wilson. 121–155. Oxford.

Stehle, E. 2006. Solon's Self-reflexive Political Persona and its Audience. In *Solon of Athens: New Historical and Philological Approaches*, ed. J.H. Blok and A.P.M.H. Lardinois, 79–113. Leiden.

Swift, L. 2010. *The Hidden Chorus: Echoes of Genre in Tragic Lyric*. Oxford.

Van Minnen, P. 1997. The Performance and Readership of the Persai of Timotheus. *APF* 34: 246–255.

Vassilaki, E. 2005. Réminiscences de Pindare dans l'"Hymne à Sarapis" d' Aelius Aristide (Or. XLV). *Euphrosyne* 33: 325–339.

West, M.L. 1970. Corinna. *CQ* 20: 277–287.

West, M.L. 1974. *Studies in Greek Elegy and Iambus*. Berlin.

West, M.L. 1978. Stesichorus at Lille. ZPE 29: 1–4.

West, M.L. (1984), *Carmina Anacreontea* (Leipzig).

Whitmarsh, T. 2004. The Cretan Lyre Paradox: Mesomedes, Hadrian and the Poetics of Patronage. In *Paideia: The World of the Second Sophistic*, ed. B. Borg, 377–402. Berlin.

Wilamowitz-Moellendorff. U. von. 1921. *Griechische Verskunst*. Berlin.

Wilamowitz-Moellendorff. U. von 1900. *Textgeschichte der griechischen Lyriker*. Berlin.

Wright, M.E. 2012. *The Comedian as Critic: Greek Old Comedy and Poetics*. London.

Yatromanolakis, D. 2007. *Sappho in the Making: The Early Reception*. Cambridge, MA.

PART 1

Transmission

∴

CHAPTER 2

New Philology and the Classics: Accounting for Variation in the Textual Transmission of Greek Lyric and Elegiac Poetry

André Lardinois

1   Introduction*

In 2007, Julia Gaisser pointed out that the practice of philology has acquired a bad name in certain quarters, including in classical studies.[1] There is a widespread feeling among classicists that the most important philological work, the production of reliable editions of texts, has been done and that the consideration of textual variants is less important than the understanding of a text in its historical and social context. Significantly, the members of the American Philological Association voted in 2015 to change the name of their organization into the Society for Classical Studies.

Among medievalists the word "philology" does not have the same negative connotation. Here a renewed interest in the editing and close study of texts has emerged under the name of "new philology". This movement can be traced to a special issue of the journal *Speculum* that appeared in 1990, although earlier examples of New Philological practices and ideas can be found.[2] In the *Speculum* issue, six American medievalists use the term "new philology" to plead for a new kind of textual criticism that pays close attention to the social context of medieval literature, but also to modern linguistics and, most importantly, to the different versions in which texts appear.[3] I believe these insights are useful

---

* This chapter has been a long time in the making and I could thank many colleagues and audiences with whom I discussed this subject, but I would like to single out Ewen Bowie, Vanessa Cazzato, Bruno Currie, Ian Rutherford, and the anonymous reviewer, who read and commented on earlier drafts of this paper. I know they do not agree with all I say in this chapter, so they should not be held responsible for its failings.
1 Gaisser (2007). Compare already Tarrant (1995) 122–126.
2 Nichols (1990). The authors of the *Speculum* volume refer explicitly to Cerquiglini (1989). See also the work of Zumthor (1972, 1983) and Pearsall (1985), cited by Tarrant (2016) 33.
3 Some proponents of New Philology later preferred using the term "Material Philology", because of the significance of the physical appearance of manuscripts and new text variations: see Nichols (1997) and Westra (2014). Detractors have called the movement "Necro-Philology", because of its harsh criticism of older philologists: Busby (1993b) 29.

for the study of some ancient texts as well. In this chapter I will first lay out the principles of New Philology, especially its concern with different versions in which poetic texts are preserved. Next I will argue that significant variations in the transmission of Greek poetry did occur in antiquity, and finally I will focus on a few examples of such variations in the textual transmission of Greek lyric and elegiac poetry, which require, in my opinion, different editions than those we have today.

In Europe, the practice of New Philology gained momentum when the esteemed German medievalist Karl Stackmann endorsed it in an article published in 1994.[4] As Stackmann observes, the authors who wrote the 1990 *Speculum* issue seem to have integrated the most pertinent findings of poststructuralism into the practice of philology. For instance, New Philologists acknowledge that a text has multiple meanings, as do poststructuralists, but they tie these different meanings to concrete variations in the transmission of the texts themselves. Around the same time as Stackmann wrote his article, Richard Tarrant predicted that poststructuralism and philology might merge in classical studies,[5] but it never happened, in part because most classical scholars who engage in literary theory are not interested in text editing and vice versa, but also because the debate in Classics about variant readings has focussed primarily on the opposition between orality and literacy, especially in Homeric studies.[6]

Within classical studies, Bruno Gentili anticipated some of the principles of New Philology in his 1984 essay 'L'arte della filologia', in which he argues for taking into account changes resulting from reperformances when assessing the variations found in the texts of Greek lyric poetry.[7] In general it must be said that orality and folklore studies have long drawn attention to variations occurring in the performances of poetry.[8] New Philology is different, however, from folklore or oral studies in that it is a study of *texts* and therefore of *literate* products. Oral reperformances of early Greek poetry undoubtedly influenced its textual transmission, as we will see, and New Philology is therefore particu-

---

4   Stackman (1994). Compare Greetham (1993).
5   Tarrant (1995) 125.
6   E.g. the debate between Nagy and West on the constitution and proper editing of Homer's epics: Nagy (2000, 2003); M.L. West (2001b, 2004). For a summary and reasonable assessment of this debate, see Graziosi (2010) and Graziosi and Haubold (2019).
7   Gentili (1984). Nagy (1996) 10; Boedeker (2009) 74; Klooster (2014); and Kreij (2015) have pointed to the possible relevance of New Philology for the editing of ancient Greek poetry as well. Gellrich (1995) uses the term in a different sense, focussing on the application of modern literary theory to classical texts, which was indeed part of the agenda of the authors in the *Speculum* volume as well.
8   E.g. Parry (1971) 336 and Lord (1960) 100–101, quoted by Bird (2010) 29.

larly well-suited to study the literature of cultures in which oral performances of texts coexist with written versions, such as classical antiquity or medieval Europe, but the aim of New Philology is to explain the textual record, not the oral reperformances that may lie behind it. "Oral variations" of classical literature are theoretical constructs, just as "fixed texts" are. Oral variants only become visible to us after they have been written down, while texts that are truly fixed do not exist before the printing press.[9] All that classicists have are the variations in their written sources, and ancient commentators, copyists and authors who quote fragments of Greek poetry can be just as much responsible for these variations as reperformers.[10] New Philologists are interested in recording all significant changes that are made to a text in the course of its transmission.

The authors of the *Speculum* volume propose various ways in which the study of medieval literature can be improved, but the most important principle they advocate is that all variants of a text ought to be examined and appreciated in their own right and not only as possible witnesses to the original text.[11] As an example of such an approach I cite the analysis that the medievalist Thomas Bein has made of six strophes of the German lyric poet Walther von der Vogelweide, as represented in table 2.1.[12]

In the left hand column are the opening lines of six strophes that are all composed in a similar metre. The capital letters B, C, E, and F represent four different sets of manuscripts of Walther von der Vogelweide, each with their own arrangement of these strophes. They date from the beginning (B and C) to the middle of the fourteenth century (E) and the second half of the fifteenth century (F). The numbers in the columns correspond to the place of the strophes in the manuscripts: for example, the strophe starting with 'Ich wil nu teilen' ('I wish to share') is the 62nd strophe in group B, the 150th or 156th in group C, etc. In the column on the right is the arrangement of the strophes by Christoph Cormeau, a modern editor of Walther von der Vogelweide's songs, who has divided the six strophes over two songs: Song 36 and 36a.[13]

---

9 Even printed texts are only relatively fixed, because they can be found to differ from the autograph or undergo significant changes in new editions. See Schoor (2015).
10 For example, the variation in the transmission of Anacreon fr. 422 (Θρηκίην σίοντα χαίτην versus ὀρίκην σίοντα χαίτην), which Gentili (1988) 227–228 cites as an example of oral variation, is just as likely the result of a scribal error.
11 See especially the introduction to Nichols (1990). For a more recent articulation of the principles of New Philology, see Cerquiglini (2007).
12 Bein (2010).
13 Cormeau (1996) 128–132.

TABLE 2.1   Analysis by Bein of six strophes of Walther von der Vogelweide

	Manuscripts				
Strophes	B	C	E	F	Edition
Ich wil nu teilen	62 strophes of other songs	150 [156] strophes of other songs	174 directly connected to 175 E	29 directly connected to 30 F	36 I
Mir ist liep	87	219 [226]	–	–	36a I
Nu bitent	88	220 [227]	–	33	36 II
Sit mir din	–	–	175	31	36a II
Man mac wol	–	–	176	30	36a III
Ich han vil	–	–	177	32	36a IV

Bein's analysis shows that the six strophes appear in widely different places in the manuscripts and that, furthermore, in manuscripts B and C only the strophes starting with 'Mir ist liep' ('It pleases me') and 'Nu bitent' ('Now wait') are grouped together, and the next three strophes are not attested. In manuscripts E and F, by contrast, these three strophes are grouped together but in different arrangements, while other strophes are not included. Cormeau, in his edition, does not represent the different arrangements found in the manuscripts, but makes his own arrangement, which, however, does not appear in any of the medieval manuscripts: it is Cormeau's own abstraction of the manuscript tradition and his idea of what the original composition may have looked like. The New Philologist Bein, instead, pleads for an edition of this poet that informs the reader about the different arrangements in the manuscripts and acknowledges that there are at least three different ways in which the order of the strophes of this song, probably also in performance, diverged in the Middle Ages.[14]

The different manuscripts of Walther von der Vogelweide show a variation in the wording of the different strophes as well. As an example, I cite the first line of strophe 33 in manuscript F (number 88 in B, 220 and 227 in C). It reads: 'Nun schweÿget und lasset wieder kumen' (Now be quiet, and let [me] come again) instead of 'Nun bitent, lant mich widerkommen' (Now wait, let me come again). The change of 'Nun bitent' to 'Nun schweÿget' can hardly be the result of scribal

---

14   Bein in the meantime has produced such an edition: Bein (2013).

error. Instead it reflects a different performance tradition of this song, just as the rest of the line is "updated" to represent more contemporary German. The version with '*Nun bitent*' looks older and may go back to the poet himself, but both versions are "authentic" in the sense that they both represent a way in which the songs of Walther von der Vogelweide were remembered and performed in the Middle Ages.

The example of the variations in the songs of Walther von der Vogelweide is significant for another reason, namely for the limited influence of writing on the transmission of these kinds of poetry. As the manuscripts attest, the songs of this German poet were written down repeatedly from the beginning of the thirteenth century onwards, but new variations nevertheless continued to appear. This is possible, first of all, because most people who performed these songs did not learn them from books but from other singers who recited them from memory, leading inevitably to small changes in their wording of the song. Second, when scribes made new collections of Walther von der Vogelweide's songs, resulting in manuscripts B, C, E, and F, they did not copy earlier editions (or at least they did not only do that), but consulted their own memories or those of other contemporary singers who were particularly adept at performing these songs. They also updated the songs in terms of language, dialect, and orthography.[15]

I will not argue that Greek lyric poetry underwent exactly the same type of transmission from archaic Greek times down to the Hellenistic period as the songs of Walther von der Vogelweide—no historical periods are the same and the level of "panhellenism" may have been greater in archaic and classical Greece than in medieval Germany—but the history of the transmission of von der Vogelweide's songs may nevertheless be of value as *comparandum*, because we know so little about the transmission of Greek lyric poetry before the Hellenistic period. What we do know is that Athenians in the classical period enjoyed improvising on the songs of the archaic Greek poets,[16] and that they learned them, for the most part, as young children or at symposia by having the songs sung to them.[17] When they recited them, they did so from memory, and if they wanted a text of, for example, Sappho's poems, they probably did not sail to Lesbos to copy the master edition in Sappho's house (if such an edition even

---

15 Bein (2013) 20.
16 Collins (2004) esp. chs. 6–9. Compare Gentili (1988) 228 and Ford (1997) 91–99. For later examples, see Plutarch, *Quomodo adolescens* 33c–d, with Klooster's contribution to this volume.
17 Wilamowitz-Moellendorff (1900) 12; Prauscello (2006) 45–47.

existed),[18] but they would more likely ask a local expert, who was particularly good at performing Sappho's songs. Such experts may well have possessed written copies of (some of) Sappho's poems, which they used in turn when copying the songs, but they would not have hesitated to make changes or additions of their own.[19]

It is further worth noting that not all texts of the early Greek poets in antiquity were complete editions, such as the Alexandrian scholars later produced, but that different kinds of compositions were made, often grouping songs from different poets together for specific occasions, such as performances at symposia.[20] In such a context it is even more likely that changes were made to the songs to make them fit each other, as the Cologne papyrus fragments of Sappho seem to show (see below). In most cases such changes were probably made to the texts of the songs before their performance (recomposing and/or rearranging verses on paper for later recitation), as is probably the case with the more substantial actors' interpolations in dramatic texts (see below), but in other cases particularly striking or felicitous improvisations may have been recorded on paper after the reperformance of the songs. The latter could explain some of the variations we find in similar verses in the *Theognidea* (see below). Most improvisations in oral reperformances, however, will not have left a trace in the written record.

I consider this the most important distinction between a (partly) oral and a predominantly literate culture: the degree to which one accepts that texts are not fixed. Because no purely literate culture exists without any oral performance or memorization of rhymes and songs, cultures reveal a sliding scale in

---

18   It has been argued that the archaic Greek poets must have made more or less complete editions of their own poetry for so much to have survived into the Hellenistic period (e.g. Pöhlmann [2003] 13–15), but this argument does not take account of the fact that many of these poems may have been assigned to them later. This process already started in the classical period, when there are clear signs of the ascription of poems of anonymous or lesser-known composers to Homer, Hesiod, Simonides, Theognis and Solon: see Lardinois (2006) 15–17. Compare Boter (2008) 66 for the ascription of spurious works to famous prose authors, such as Plato, and D'Alessio (2015) on the possible inclusion of narrative poems by other authors in the Hellenistic edition of Stesichorus' poetry. Furthermore, if there had existed more or less complete editions made by the archaic Greek poets themselves, the Hellenistic scholars would not have had to produce new editions of this poetry with obviously new arrangements.
19   On changes being made in orally performed literature even after the appearance of written texts, see Thomas (1992) 44–51, and Vet (1996). The little we know about the dissemination of written texts in the fifth and fourth centuries BCE is discussed by Hadjimichael (2019) 171–211.
20   For examples of such editions, see Yatromanolakis (2008) 249.

which they accept the fluidity of texts. Modern Europeans accept, for example, that children's songs or nursery rhymes are subject to improvisation,[21] but expect their literary texts to contain the exact words of their authors. Classical Athenians insisted that certain religious formulae, laws, and prayers be remembered verbatim, but tolerated variations in their texts of Homer and the Greek lyric and elegiac poets, just as medieval Germans did in the songs of Walther von der Vogelweide.

In the Hellenistic period attitudes seem to have changed, when through a process of canonization, described below, and as the result of a growing literate culture, the demand for fixed texts increased. The Alexandrian scholars produced standard editions of most archaic Greek poets, although we do not know how widely accepted these editions were or who had access to them. Anthologies with selections from the works of different poets, such as the *Stephanos* of Meleager, continued to be made and the fact that different scholars produced new editions of the same texts, such as Homer's epics or Sappho's songs, shows that variant texts in practice continued to exist. Religious poetry, recorded in stone, admitted variations and was adapted to local circumstances down to the second century CE,[22] and morally offensive passages in older literature were deliberately altered or expunged.[23] Even the practice of quoting from memory rather than looking up the exact wording, shows that a certain fluidity of these texts continued to be tolerated. It is the aim of the New Philologist to register this fluidity in all its forms.

2   Criticism of New Philology

In the thirty years of its existence, the premises of New Philology have also been met with criticism, some of it justified, some less so. First, it has been pointed out that the practice of "New" Philology is not so novel as it claims to be and that multiform editions, recording variants of a text, had been produced in Medieval Studies before 1990.[24] Within classical studies one can point to the practice of bracketing, rather than deleting, suspected passages. This allows the reader

---

21   For an example of recorded improvisation in English nursery rhymes, see Lardinois (2006) 22.
22   Alonge (2011); Faraone (2011).
23   Zetzel (1993) 107–112. Compare Klooster's contribution to this volume, on Plutarch's advice to young readers to change the wording of poetic quotations if they find them morally offensive in *Quomodo adolescens* 33d–34a.
24   Schnell (1997) esp. 65–80.

to see the proposed original text as well as the state of the text in the medieval manuscripts. This practice goes back to the earliest philologists, the Hellenistic scholars, who placed an *obelos* or horizontal stroke next to a verse of Homer they suspected of being an interpolation, while leaving the verse in place.

It can be argued, however, that these editions are still aimed at reconstructing the original text. Little attention is paid, in editions or commentaries, to when or why these interpolations were made. The same is true of the critical apparatus: its position at the bottom of the page shows that the variants recorded there are literally deemed "inferior". New Philology is not interested in the hypothetical reconstruction of the original text, but in the recording of the development of a text from its first beginnings right through to its later appearances. As Tara Andrews phrases it:

> At its core, the difference between old and new philology can be seen as a subtle but crucial shift in purpose. The older practice of philology, whose methods are taken from traditional philology, emphasizes the "ideal" text whose authority supersedes that of any surviving witnesses; the specific ideal text might be the author's original, the recoverable archetype, or even the emended and conjectured version of a sole surviving witness. Conversely, the emphasis of New Philology is on the "real" text as it has been preserved, received, annotated, and used. The distinction between "ideal" and "real" is a simple shift that nevertheless prescribes radically different working methods.[25]

Second, it has been claimed that New Philologists deny the importance of the author in shaping the text and its meaning.[26] This assumption is partly due to the rhetoric in which some of the early champions of the new movement couched the debate, in which they equated author and scribe or introduced the copyist as a second author. The author is a complicated concept, not only in the Middle Ages but in Antiquity as well, and New Philologists are right to point out that the ancients thought differently about authorship than we do.[27] Their downplaying of the importance of the initial author again shows their interest in the development of a text, including creative rewritings, of which we will see several examples in the transmission of Greek lyric poetry. This is not to deny, of course, that someone at some point did produce the first version

---

25 Andrews (2013) 64. Compare Tarrant (2016) 24 on editions that focus on *Überleiferungsgeschichte*.
26 Busby (1993b) 38; Schnell (1997) 84.
27 See the collection of essays in Marmodoro and Hill (2013) and Bakker (2017).

of these poems, which reperformers or creative writers worked from. In that sense a New Philological edition is not incompatible with a traditional one, in which an attempt is made to reconstruct the original text as closely as possible. It should rather be seen as an *addition* to such an edition: it charts the vicissitudes of texts throughout their history, including their ascription to particular authors, and therefore helps rather than hinders the reconstruction of the oldest version. As Patrick Finglass remarks with respect to the reconstruction of the texts of Greek tragedy:

> Investigating the mutual relationship of reperformance and the transmission of texts should not force us to choose between either attempting to get as close as possible to the author's text, or appreciating the social and cultural circumstances which led to the adaptation of these texts in the decades that followed. They are both legitimate forms of historical inquiry, and a genuine analysis of the problems that they represent will lead to an enriched understanding of both.[28]

Third, it has been pointed out that the principles of New Philology are more applicable to certain genres and periods than to others. For example, while one can find significant variations in the songs of Walther von der Vogelweide, the textual transmission of the medieval courtly romances appears to be far more stable.[29] Texts that are orally reperformed are more likely to develop significant variations than texts that are primarily intended to be read.[30] The principles of New Philology are therefore more suitable for the Homeric epics or early Greek lyric poetry than to, for example, the histories of Herodotus or Thucydides, although some texts that were primarily read in antiquity also contain significant variations, especially technical treatises and popular romances.[31]

One should also distinguish between historical periods in which divergences are more likely to occur and other periods in which the transmission of the text is more stable. For example, the variations in the medieval manuscripts of the great classical texts are relatively minor and consist for the most part of unintended copying mistakes. One can and should therefore continue to apply to

---

28 Finglass (2015) 274–275. Compare Graziosi (2010) on the the importance of connecting reception to the editing of texts.
29 Busby (1993c) 91; Wolf (2002) 180.
30 Birge Vitz (1993) 76; Wolf (2002) 189.
31 See Reynolds and Wilson (1991) 234–237 and Zetzel (1993) 110–111 for examples from antiquity.

these manuscripts the principles of Lachmann and other traditional philologists who try to reconstruct the earliest possible variant of these texts.[32]

It is important to realize, however, that the so-called archetypes of the medieval manuscripts of our classical texts do not go back much further than late antiquity and that more variations of these texts did exist in antiquity itself in all likelihood. Richard Tarrant, in assessing the reliability of Latin text editions in antiquity, points out that most Latin readers corrected and emended copies of the texts that they possessed themselves.[33] They in turn would lend these texts to friends who wanted to have their own copy made.[34] In this way, alterations passed from one copy to the next. The situation in the Greek-speaking world was not very different, at least not in the Hellenistic and Roman period. Wilamowitz, however, rightly remarks that it took poetic texts of the archaic Greek period a much longer time to reach the relative degree of stability than the works of Callimachus, Horace, or Vergil enjoyed the moment they produced their books.[35] Especially in this earlier period, a close interaction between written versions and oral reperformances of poetic texts must have taken place and very different copies of the songs of the archaic Greek poets may have circulated.

A good example is the text of the three great tragedians. We know that their plays were regularly reperformed in the fourth century BCE and that actors and producers added or changed whole passages.[36] These changes became so pervasive that the Athenian statesman Lycurgus ordered new copies of the texts of the tragedians to be made at the end of the fourth century BCE. These copies were preserved in the state archives and actors henceforth were told to perform the plays in accordance with these texts.[37] This episode is interesting for two

---

32 For the principles behind this type of philology, including the need to study the history of the transmission of the texts, see Boter (2008) with earlier bibliography. Sometimes, deliberate changes were made in the medieval manuscripts of the classical authors, for example to purge texts of offensive passages or to bring them in line with Christian doctrine (Boter [2008] 67; M.L. West [1973] 18). Such variations are of course relevant for the reception of these authors in the Middle Ages.
33 Tarrant (1995) 99–103. Compare Zetzel (1993) 107 and Phillips (2016) 59: 'the nature of text production in the ancient world is such that we must allow for a good deal of variety in the constitution of individual texts'.
34 Reynolds and Wilson (1991) 23.
35 Wilamowitz-Moellendorff (1900) 3–4. Compare the four stages in the transmission of Greek literature distinguished by Pfeiffer (1968) 25–27; see also Ford (2003).
36 Page (1934); Hamilton (1974), Finglass (2015).
37 See Scodel (2007), who points out that the measure must have been largely symbolic. It would have been very difficult to reinforce and could only pertain to performances in Attica.

reasons. In the first place, it demonstrates that fourth-century actors and producers had no qualms about making significant changes in dramatic texts they were meant to perform.[38] These changes would find their way into other written copies of these plays, when they lent their copies to friends or colleagues who wanted to have their own copy made. The Lycurgus episode, however, also shows that at some point the wish for a stable text did emerge. It is no accident that Lycurgus' measure concerned the plays of Aeschylus, Sophocles, and Euripides. Contemporary sources, including speeches of Lycurgus himself, identify the tragedies of these three poets as the cultural heritage of the city of Athens.[39] Their plays had, in other words, become canonical. Once a text acquires a canonical status, there is a tendency to stabilize its transmission.[40]

Finally, New Philologists are sometimes accused of failing to distinguish between significant and insignificant variations in a text: a copying mistake is something different from a deliberate change and even among deliberate changes one can often distinguish between older and newer ones.[41] This is a fair point of criticism and it stresses again that it makes little sense to make a New Philological edition of an author like Thucydides, whose text is mainly transmitted through medieval manuscripts and whose transmission was probably fairly stable in antiquity already. In fact, I would argue that for the vast majority of ancient texts it makes no sense. But in some cases, like early Greek lyric poetry, which went through a long period of unstable transmission and for whose transmission we depend to a large degree on citations by later authors, it does pay off. Such an edition ideally should be accompanied by a commentary that tries to explain the likely origin and significance of the variations.

The reason one decides to make such an edition is because one expects there to be significant variations. It is nevertheless necessary that one record and assess *all* variations in such an edition, including variations that look like copying mistakes. The reason is that it is not always so easy to distinguish between a copying mistake and a deliberate change. Something that looks like a copying mistake, such as εἰπέμεναι versus εἰπεῖν μοι in the transmission of Solon fr. 22a, may in fact be part of a deliberate variation (see below). Second, copying mistakes may be significant for the way in which texts were later (mis)read and interpreted. Finally, it should be noted that poetic citations that are preserved in medieval manuscripts of later Greek authors, such as Athenaeus or Plutarch,

---

38 Finglass (2015) 270.
39 Hanink (2014) esp. 25–59.
40 Canonical texts, however, generate their own kind of variations in the form of translations, adaptations and reprints.
41 Westra (1993) 58; Wolf (2002) 179.

have their own manuscript traditions that should be taken into account and reported.[42] In this case, however, we can be fairly certain that the variations found in the medieval manuscripts of these authors ultimately go back to one original version, the text written by Plutarch or Athenaeus. For the Greek lyric poets this is far less certain.

Martin West lists over twenty ways in which Greek and Latin texts could have undergone changes in the course of their transmission.[43] Most of these pertain to copying mistakes, but they also include:

(1) Citations from memory (in the case of quotations transmitted in the manuscripts of later authors).
(2) Deliberate changes made to the text by the author himself, by later authors who quote the text, or by copyists. These include changes made for the reperformance of a text, such as actors' interpolations in dramatic texts.[44] They also include changes made to the text that may not have been thought of as real changes, such as changes in the orthography or in the dialect of the cited text.[45] Finally, the author himself may have produced more than one version of the text.[46]

To these ways of changing texts can be added:

(3) Different editions with different arrangements of the same poetry made in antiquity, (e.g. the Cologne papyrus versus the Oxyrhynchus papyrus of Sappho fr. 58; see below) or later (e.g. *Anthologia Palatina* versus *Anthologia Planudea*).[47]

If a great number of such significant variations are found in the transmission of a particular text, it warrants the production of a New Philological edition that displays these variations and explains their provenance.

---

42 See the contributions to this volume of Schlesier, Caciagli, Klooster, and Romney.
43 M.L. West (1973) 15–29. Significantly, he refers to these as ways in which a text may 'suffer' change (15).
44 On actors' interpolations, see note 36 above. The variations found in the so-called wild-papyri of Homer can perhaps be explained in this way as well: see S. West (1967); Haslam (1997); and Bird (2010). On significant variations in the texts of Hesiod and the Homeric hymns, see Rossi (1997) and Ferrari (2007).
45 A good example is Pausanias (5.24.3), who cites in Attic an inscription he saw in Laconia. The stone, which has been found, records the inscription in Doric and in the old-style Laconian alphabet, however (see Meiggs and Lewis [1988] 47). Pausanias may have changed the dialect and orthography of the inscription to facilitate his readers. I owe this reference to David Sider.
46 For an example, see Reynolds and Wilson (1991) 24.
47 Another example is an epigram of Palladas, which is found with different arrangements in the *Anthologia Palatina* 9.127 and in papyrus P.CtYBR inv. 4000: see Wilkinson (2012) 167. I owe this reference to the anonymous reviewer.

In the rest of this chapter I will focus on some of the significant variations in the texts of Greek lyric and elegiac poetry that are preserved from antiquity.[48] By putting together a number of examples I hope to show that the Greek lyric poets deserve a New Philological edition in which these variations are taken account of.

3   Variants in the Transmission of Greek Elegiac Poetry

I will start with two examples I have already discussed in my 2006 article on the transmission of Solon's poetry.[49] They concern the opening lines of fragment 5 and fragment 22a. I have reproduced these two fragments of Solon, as preserved in the manuscripts of different ancient Greek authors, below. Variations between the two different versions are indicated in bold:

(1) Solon fr. 5.1–2 (Aristotle and Plutarch)

(a) Solon apud Arist., *Ath. Pol.* 12.1.

> δήμωι μὲν γὰρ ἔδωκα τόσον **γέρας** ὅσσον **ἀπαρκεῖ**,
> τιμῆς οὔτ' ἀφελὼν οὔτ' ἐπορεξάμενος·

> For I have given the people as much **privilege** as **is sufficient**,
> neither taking away from their honour nor adding to it (or: reaching out to it).[50]

(b) Solon apud Plut. *Sol.* 18.5.

> δήμωι μὲν γὰρ ἔδωκα τόσον **κράτος** ὅσσον **ἐπαρκεῖ**,
> τιμῆς οὔτ' ἀφελὼν οὔτ' ἐπορεξάμενος·

> For I have given the people as much **power** as **suffices**,
> neither taking away from their honour nor adding to it.

---

48   I cite the Greek lyric poets from the editions of Campbell (1982–1993) and the elegiac poets from Gerber (1999), unless noted otherwise.
49   Lardinois (2006).
50   For the possible meanings of ἐπορεξάμενος, see Irwin (2005) 230n71. The papyrus' text of Aristotle's *Ath. Pol.* in fact reads ἀπορεξάμενος, which is a clear example of a scribal error, because it yields no meaning.

(2) Solon fr. 22a (Proclus and Aristotle)

(a) Solon apud Proclus *in Tim.* 20e (i.81.27 Diehl)

> εἰπέμεναι Κριτίηι ξανθότριχι πατρὸς ἀκούειν·
> οὐ γὰρ ἁμαρτινόῳ πείσεται ἡγεμόνι.

> **Tell thou yellow-haired Kritiês** to listen to his father
> for he will be heeding a guide of unerring judgement.

(b) Solon apud Arist. *Rhet.* 1.1375b34 Kassel

> εἰπεῖν μοι Κριτίαι πυρρότριχι πατρὸς ἀκούειν·
> οὐ γὰρ ἁμαρτινόῳ πείσεται ἡγεμόνι.

> **Please tell red-haired Kritias** to listen to his father
> for he will be heeding a guide of unerring judgement.

The differences between the two versions are usually explained by modern editors as being the result of scribal error or lapses in memory of the authors who cite them. They are treated, in other words, as corruptions, and editors try to reconstruct one original text out of them.

A good example is Martin West, who has edited the standard edition of the Greek iambic and elegiac poets.[51] He has reconstructed these two fragments of Solon as follows:

(1) Solon fr. 5.1–2

> δήμωι μὲν γὰρ ἔδωκα τόσον γέρας ὅσσον ἐπαρκεῖν,
> τιμῆς οὔτ' ἀφελὼν οὔτ' ἐπορεξάμενος·

> For I have given the people as much privilege as to suffice,
> neither taking away from their honour nor adding to it.

(2) Solon fr. 22a

> εἰπεῖν μοι Κριτίηι ξανθότριχι πατρὸς ἀκούειν·
> οὐ γὰρ ἁμαρτινόῳ πείσεται ἡγεμόνι.

---

51 M.L. West (1992).

> Tell yellow-haired Kritiês to listen to his father for me
> for he will be heeding a guide of unerring judgement.

West draws freely on the different variants in order to create a new text. He combines in line 1 of fragment 5 the word γέρας found in Aristotle with ἐπαρκεῖ found in Plutarch, which he then emends to ἐπαρκεῖν. In fragment 22a, he opts for the construction εἰπεῖν μοι of Aristotle with the more archaic sounding Κριτίηι ξανθότριχι of Proclus. Other variants are relegated to the critical apparatus. What is worse, by embedding the newly reconstructed fragments in textual quotations of Aristotle and Proclus, respectively, he makes it seem as if his version is the one they quoted and originally wrote. It is questionable, however, if his version of these poems ever existed in antiquity, just as Cormeau's reconstructions of the songs of Walther von der Vogelweide are only to be found in his edition but never as such in the Middle Ages.

To be fair, other editors do the same and what West, of course, tries to do is to reconstruct the version he believes Solon originally wrote. The problem is, however, that he treats the two versions in which the fragments are transmitted as if they are manuscript variants, but the changes between these texts were deliberately made, either by Plutarch or Aristotle themselves or by their sources. Proclus' version of fragment 22a—with its epic infinitive in -μεναι, the Ionic form of Critias' name, and its Homeric sounding epithet ξανθότριχι[52]— represents a more archaic form of the couplet than the version preserved in Aristotle's *Rhetoric*, which has adapted the language to more regular, contemporary usage.[53] Proclus, it seems, somehow had access to a more archaic-looking version of Solon's poetry, while the manuscripts of Aristotle's *Rhetoric* preserved the way the philosopher recited the lines in fourth-century Athens. In that case it is better to choose one of the two versions, as Bruno Gentili and Carlo Prato do in their edition of Solon's fragments, for example.[54] Classical scholars are, however, best served in my opinion by being presented with

---

52 Cf. Hom. *Od.* 13.399 and 431: ξανθὰς … τρίχας. πυρρός was a more common term to denote the colour of hair in fourth-century Athens: see LSJ s.v. πυρρός. An infinitive on -μεναι is also attested in Solon fr. 13.39.

53 Compare Wilamowitz-Moellendorff (1900) 54: 'die Perpatetiker lasen wenigstens einige Gedichte stark modernisiert'. Wilamowiz is generally sceptical of how much of the original dialect forms of the archaic Greek poets was preserved, even in the editions of the Alexandrian scholars.

54 Gentili and Prato (1988) 115. They choose the version of Proclus and only change Κριτίηι to Κριτίαι. Similarly Noussia-Fantuzzi (2010) 106.

both versions in which this fragment has been preserved, especially in this case where it is unclear which of the two versions is closest to what Solon may have composed. Proclus' version looks older, but it may also have been deliberately archaized. It is impossible to know for certain if this is the case or not.

In fragment 5, the content of the quoted lines differs significantly as well, because it makes quite a difference to have Solon say that he gave 'privilege' or 'power' to the people. I have argued elsewhere that I suspect different political agendas behind these two versions of Solon's fragment.[55] We know that Solon's poems were sung in Athenian symposia in the fifth and fourth centuries BCE, and it is easy to imagine an Athenian democrat performing version 1b, which says that Solon gave *kratos* to the *demos*; he would claim, in so doing, that Solon had established the Athenian *dêmo-kratia*. Plutarch may have found this version in one of the fourth-century BCE Atthidographers he used or it could have found its way into a Hellenistic edition or anthology of Solon's poetry.[56] It fits his own interpretation of Solon as a politician who gave in too much to the demands of the populace.[57]

A conservative Athenian, on the other hand, will have preferred to recite version 1a, which states that Solon merely gave a privilege to the people, but not power. Even if this conservative version is older and more "original" than the other one, the democratic version is interesting as an example of the way in which the poems of Solon were adapted and read in later times. In this case I would therefore also argue for an edition that prints both versions of the fragment with an explanation of how the differences had most likely come about. One may, of course, try to identify among these two versions an older and a younger one, but in order to do so one must first recognize the different traditions behind them.

Maria Noussia-Fantuzzi has questioned my analysis of these two fragments (and of Solon fr. 11) as examples of oral variations, because, she argues, the authentic versions of these fragments can clearly be distinguished from the later, derivative ones and the changes may be the result of writers, such as Plutarch, who deliberately changed the text.[58] I accept that in my 2006 article I may have overemphasized the oral background of the variations we find in the fragments of Solon. I agree that some of them may be the result of deliberate changes made by later writers to the text, although I cannot believe that this holds true, for example, for Solon fr. 22a. If Proclus preserved the authen-

---

55 Lardinois (2006) 28.
56 On the sources of Plutarch's *Life of Solon*, see Mühl (1942) and Blois (2006).
57 Compare Blois (2006).
58 Noussia-Fantuzzi (2010) 45–55.

tic version of this fragment, as Noussia-Fantuzzi believes, it is hard to see why Aristotle would have de-archaized this fragment. Instead, his quotation of these lines in contemporary Attic probably reflects the way in which Solon's poetry was performed in his day.[59]

The fact that a study of the transmitted variants of Greek lyric fragments may result in the identification of older, more "authentic" versions of the poetry as well as younger ones does not make the distinction between these variants less interesting for a New Philologist, because, as I have argued above, New Philologists are not only interested in the original version of a text but also in its subsequent developments. Even if the word *kratos* in Plutarch's version of fr. 5 is a later, democratic adaptation or a deliberate change made by Plutarch himself, it speaks to the perception of Solon and the reuse of his poetry in later times and is therefore worth recording. Such examples, furthermore, may serve as a cautionary reminder of how difficult it is to identify the "authentic" versions of Solon's fragments. In this case we happen to have another attestation of the fragment to show us that Plutarch's version is probably a later variant, but in most cases we only have one quotation and do not know whether it is authentic or not: before the discovery of Aristotle's *Athenaiôn Politeia* no one doubted the "authenticity" of Plutarch's reading of *kratos*.[60] A traditional edition, which only offers one (reconstructed) version of the poems, therefore offers the reader a false sense of security: it obscures the fact that what is preserved is only one of many possible versions produced in antiquity.

Another example of variation in the same corpus of elegiac poetry is found in the so-called *Theognidea*, a collection of elegiac verses ascribed to the Megarian poet Theognis. The doublets found in the manuscripts at the beginning and end of this collection have long been the source of heated debate.[61] Ewen Bowie has made a convincing case that these doublets go back to two different editions of Theognis, dating to the fourth century BCE.[62] These two editions in turn probably reflect different ways in which this poetry was performed at that time.[63] As one example, among many, I have reproduced below lines 39–

---

59 See note 53 above.
60 As no one today seems to doubt the word *kartos* in Tyrtaeus fr. 4.9. In light of my discussion of Solon fr. 5 and the late recording of our version of Tyrtaeus' poetry (see below), I believe that it is possible that the term represents a later adaptation of the text, perhaps in the context of democratic Athens.
61 For an overview of this debate, see Selle (2008) 196–205.
62 Bowie (1997) and (2012).
63 Compare Collins (2004) 111–134 and Selle (2008) 226–227. Collins compares the Theognidean doublets to the alternative endings of the so-called Attic skolia, which he connects with the sympotic game of 'capping' or improvising on known verses.

42, which appear in a different version at lines 1081–1082a near the end of the collection. The differences between the two versions are again in bold.

Version A (39–42)

> Κύρνε, κύει πόλις ἥδε, δέδοικα δὲ μὴ τέκηι ἄνδρα
>   **εὐθυντῆρα κακῆς ὕβριος ἡμετέρης.**
> ἀστοὶ μὲν γὰρ ἔθ' οἵδε σαόφρονες, ἡγεμόνες δέ
>   τετράφαται πολλὴν εἰς κακότητα πεσεῖν.

> Cyrnus, this city is pregnant and I fear she will give birth to a man
>   **who will set right our wicked insolence.**
> These townsmen are still of sound mind, but their leaders
>   have changed and fallen into the depths of depravity.

Version B (1081–1082b)

> Κύρνε, κύει πόλις ἥδε, δέδοικα δὲ μὴ τέκηι ἄνδρα
>   **ὑβριστήν, χαλεπῆς ἡγεμόνα στάσιος·**
> ἀστοὶ μὲν γὰρ ἔθ' οἵδε σαόφρονες, ἡγεμόνες δέ
>   τετράφαται πολλὴν εἰς κακότητα πεσεῖν.

> Cyrnus, this city is pregnant and I fear she will give birth to a man
>   **who commits wanton outrage, a leader of grievous strife.**
> These townsmen are still of sound mind, but their leaders
>   have changed and fallen into the depths of depravity.

Nagy has argued that these two versions reflect different political ideologies, much like the two versions of Solon's fragment 5 I discussed above.[64] He recognizes in version A the hand of an oligarch, who expects the arrival of a strong man who will heal the city. Version B would represent the more democratic ideology of a speaker who accuses the tyrant of being the cause of civil strife himself. Whatever the exact meaning one wishes to attach to the two different versions, the difference between them is deliberate and not the result of scribal error or faulty memorization. The two versions should therefore both be recognized as "authentic", even if one of the two was originally composed by Theognis and the other one was not. In this case it is in fact not easy to

---

64   Nagy (1983) and (1985).

decide which of the two versions is more original. As Derek Collins remarks about this doublet: 'It is not quite possible to say whether one of the distichs above presupposes and elaborates the other; instead, we can say that both reflect mutually-felt impulses for variation within a tradition, accomplished by the means of the innovative use of known material'.[65]

The same is true, in my opinion, of versions of the poetry of Solon, Tyrtaeus, and Mimnermus that are found in the *Theognidea* and differ significantly from the elegies preserved under the names of these authors.[66] The differences between these versions are so great that they cannot be explained as scribal errors. They either result from deliberate changes made to these verses by Theognis himself or the compiler of the *Theognidea*, or they reflect different performance traditions of these poems in classical Athens.[67] Of course, many different considerations may underlie these changes, not only political ones.

Another example of the deliberate manipulation of early Greek elegy are the opening lines of fragment 4 of the Spartan poet Tyrtaeus. This fragment is preserved in two different versions: in Plutarch's *Life of Lycurgus* 6.10 and in Diodorus Siculus' *Bibliotheca Historica* 7.12.6. It describes in elegiac couplets the Spartan constitution, which was supposedly given to the early kings of Sparta through a Delphic oracle. The two authors disagree as to which kings the oracle was delivered, however, and they cite as a result different opening lines. According to Plutarch, the early Spartan kings Polydoros and Theopompos received the oracle, and he quotes the relevant lines as follows:

Φοίβου ἀκούσαντες Πυθωνόθεν οἴκαδ' ἔνεικαν
μαντείας τε θεοῦ καὶ τελέεντ' ἔπεα·
ἄρχειν μὲν βουλῆς θεοτιμήτους βασιλῆας,
οἷσι μέλει Σπάρτας ἱμερόεσσα πόλις,
5   πρεσβύτας τε γέροντας· ἔπειτα δὲ δημότας ἄνδρας
εὐθείαις ῥήτραις ἀνταπαμειβομένους

Having listened to Phoebus, they brought home from Delphi
   prophecies of the god and words that will come true.

---

65   Collins (2004) 120.
66   E.g. Theognis 585–590 / Solon fr. 13.56–70, Theognis 1003–1006 / Tyrt. Fr. 12.13–16, Theognis 1020–1022 / Mimnermus fr. 5.1–3. For a complete list of the twelve passages that overlap with the poetry of Solon, Tyrtaeus, and Mimnermus, see Selle (2008) 212–213n350.
67   Deliberate changes: Blaise (2006) and Noussia-Fantuzzi (2010) 55–65. Different performance tradions: Nagy (1985); Collins (2004) 111–134; Irwin (2006) 51–63; and Selle (2008) 212–226.

> Counsel is to begin with (or to be led by?) the divinely honoured kings
>   in whose care is Sparta's lovely city,
> and with the ancient elders. Then the men of the people
>   responding in turn with straight utterances.

Diodorus quotes the poem as the recording of an oracle delivered to the legendary lawgiver Lycurgus, and opens it with a different couplet:

> (ὧ)δε γὰρ ἀργυρότοξος ἄναξ ἑκάεργος Ἀπόλλων
>   χρυσοκόμης ἔχρη πίονος ἐξ ἀδύτου·
> ἄρχειν μὲν βουλῆς, κτλ.

> For thus Apollo of the silver bow, the shooter from afar
>   with his golden hair, prophesied from his rich shrine:
> Counsel is to begin, etc.

Diodorus' opening lines are compatible with a single addressee, like Lycurgus, unlike those in Plutarch's version, which assumes a plural number who listened to (ἀκούσαντες) and brought home (ἔνεικαν) the oracle.[68] The two different versions seem to be the result of a difference of opinion about the person or persons to whom the oracle was delivered. Given the fact that the whole Spartan constitution was gradually assigned to Lycurgus, Plutarch may well have preserved the older version of the two, but that does not make Diodorus' version less interesting. It demonstrates the "Lycurgisation" of early Spartan history, which apparently extended to some of the poetry that was passed on. As in the case of Solon's fragment 5, this poetry was "updated" to fit the new history of the Spartan constitution.[69]

There are more fragments of Tyrtaeus that show signs of historical adjustments. Chris Faraone, adducing the structure of the elegy and the language of the four lines, has argued that lines 31–34 of fragment 12 represent a fifth-century insertion into an older, archaic composition. They refer to slain Spartan warriors as acquiring immortality below the earth, an idea more reminiscent

---

68 For a full discussion of the text, transmission, and significance of these two versions, see Nafissi (2010) 93–102 and van Hilten-Rutten's contribution to this volume.

69 These deliberate manipulations of the poetry of Solon and Tyrtaeus are a good example of what Dutch classicists have identified as "anchoring innovation". In this case the justification of a new political order by ascribing it to older, authoritative figures such as Solon or Lycurgus. For a programmatic article, explaining the concept, see Sluiter (2017).

of fifth-century grave inscriptions than of archaic Greek elegy.[70] If Faraone is right, it is significant that Stobaeus, who has preserved the poem for us, quotes it with these four lines, because it would show that his text of the poem went back to a post-classical recording of Tyrtaeus' poetry and not to an original Spartan copy, if such a text ever existed.[71] Tyrtaeus' elegies may have circulated orally in ancient Sparta before they were written down and even if they were written down in Sparta as early as the seventh century BCE, new editions with updated versions were probably made in Athens or Sparta in later times. This does not mean that lines 31–34 should be deleted from the poem or buried in a critical apparatus: they should be marked as a possibly fifth-century update of the archaic poem and appreciated as such.

Bruno Gentili has argued that the predominantly Ionic forms we find in the preserved quotations of Tyrtaeus are the result of an Athenian redaction of his poetry, because he believes that his elegies originally must have been composed in Doric.[72] As another example of such a change of dialect in the course of the transmission of elegiac poetry, Gentili cites the funeral inscription for the Corinthian war dead at Salamis, attributed to Simonides (Ep. 11 Page). This epigram is preserved in Doric on the original stone but in the Ionic-Attic dialect in the manuscripts of Plutarch and Favorinus.[73] It is quite possible that these famous lines, despite the fact that they were literally fixed in writing on a stone, were recomposed in the Ionic-Attic dialect when reperformed at symposia across ancient Greece or when they were copied into one of several anthologies of Simonides' epigrams.[74]

The reverse is, however, possible as well. The earliest citations of the infamous elegiac couplet the Spartan general Pausanias had inscribed for himself on a tripod at Delphi after the battle of Plataea are in Ionic (Thuc. 1.132, Ps-Dem. 59.97), as were other inscriptions the Spartans put up outside Laconia after this war. It reads as follows:

---

70   Faraone (2006) and (2008) 108–109.
71   See note 18 above.
72   Gentili (1988) 230. Traces of Doric forms can still be found in Tyrtaeus' elegies, for example ἀλοιησεῦμεν in fr. 1.55 and the accusative plural ending of the first declension on short—ας throughout the fragments. It is worth noting that the manuscripts of Plutarch preserve Σπάρτας with a Doric ending in fr. 4.5, while those of Diodorus render it in Ionic. On possible changes made to the dialect in which the poetry of Ibycus is preserved, see Ucciardello (2005).
73   Plut. *De malign. Herodot.* 870e; Favorinus (Ps. Dio Prus.) *Or.* 37.18. For a discussion of the constitution of this epigram, see Page (1981) 202–204 and Petrovic (2007) 144–157.
74   Reperformance: Nagy (1990) 53; on different early editions of Simonides' epigrams: Petrovic (2007) 90–109 and Sider (2007).

Ἑλλήνων ἀρχηγὸς ἐπεὶ στρατὸν ὤλεσε Μήδων
Παυσανίας Φοίβῳ μνῆμ' ἀνέθηκε τόδε.

Pausanias, leader of the Greeks, after he destroyed the army of the Medes,
dedicated this monument to Phoebus.
   THUC. 1.132

The same epigram is quoted, however, in the Doric dialect in a version preserved in the *Anthologia Palatina* (6.197), going back to a Hellenistic collection of Simonidean epigrams. In this version the third-person description of Pausanias' success is furthermore changed into a first-person statement:

Ἑλλάνων ἀρχαγὸς ἐπεὶ στρατὸν ὤλεσα Μήδων
Παυσανίας Φοίβῳ μνᾶμ' ἀνέθηκα τόδε.

I, Pausanias, leader of the Greeks, after I destroyed the army of the Medes,
dedicated this monument to Phoebus.

It looks like the epigram was changed deliberately in the course of its transmission to make it sound more personal (i.e. Doric) and more hybristic.[75] A New Philological edition of Simonides' epigrams would print both versions.

4 Variants in the Transmission of Greek Lyric Poetry

One would perhaps expect fewer changes in Greek melic poetry than in elegy, because of the greater complexities of the metres, which place greater constraints on variation in performance, but some significant variations can be found here as well. An example from the transmission of Alcaeus' songs are four lines that are preserved as part of a poem on a papyrus but also quoted as an Athenian *skolion* by Athenaeus:[76]

⟨καλὸν μὲν⟩ ἐκ γῆς χρὴ κατίδην πλόον
εἴ τις δύναιτο καὶ παλάμην ἔχοι,

---

75 Petrovic (2007) 270–271. There are more examples of significant variations in the transmission of the epigrams attributed to Simonides. See Higbie (2010).
76 Alcaeus fr. 249.6–9 = Attic skolion 891, preserved in Athenaeus' *Deipnosophistai* 15.695a.

ἐπεὶ δέ κ' ἐν ποντῶι γένηται
τῶι παρεόντι τρέχειν ἀνάγκη

One should look out from land for a (fair?) voyage
if one can and has the skill,
but if one is on the high seas
it is necessary to run in the conditions that exist.

Of the papyrus fragment (P.Oxy. 2298 fr. 1) not a lot is preserved but enough to show that the poem consisted of more than four lines, that it contained other readings (προΐδην instead of κατίδην), and that it was, like other papyrus fragments of Alcaeus, transmitted in the Lesbian dialect:

2 [   ]..ον χ[ό]ρον αἰ..[
   [   ]. νᾶα φ[ερ]έσδυγον
   [   ]ην γὰρ ο[ὐ]κ ἄρηον
5 [   ]ω κατέχην ἀήταις

   [ἐ]κ γᾶς χρῆ προΐδην πλό[ον
   [   ]ι καὶ π[αλ]άμαν ἔ[χ]ηι,
   [π]όν[τωι γ]ένηται
   [ἀνά]γκα.

10 [μ]αχάνα
   [ἄν]εμος φέρ[
   [   ]εν
   [   ].ι[

The Attic skolion cites only four lines of this poem and is predominantly recorded in the Attic or Ionic dialect.[77] This shows that Greek lyric poems could easily be excerpted, as we also know from the *Theognidea*, and that dialects

---

77 Manuscripts C and E of Athenaeus read Attic κατιδεῖν ('to look upon') in line 1 of the skolion, but manuscript A records the Aeolic infinitive κατίδην, thus adding an Aeolic flavour, reminiscent of Alcaeus, to the song. Following the principle of the *lectio difficilior* it is more likely that Athenaeus wrote the version with the Aeolic form in his original treatise, which later was changed by scribes into Attic, than the other way around. For other examples of readers and copyists changing non-Attic dialect forms into Attic, see Reynolds and Wilson (1991) 47–48.

could be changed.[78] Such examples show that we must be wary of restoring the "original" dialect in quotations of early Greek poetry found in our sources.[79]

An example both of grammatical and dialect variation are the two different endings of Sappho's fragment 2 recorded in Athenaeus and on a third century BCE potsherd, called the Florence ostrakon. These two sources present two different ways in which this poem of Sappho was preserved in antiquity. I have reproduced below the two versions with their significant differences:

2) Ostracon Flor.

> ἔνθα δὴ σὺ.... ἔλοισα Κύπρι
> χρυσίαισιν ἐν κυλίκεσσιν ἄ(β)ρως
> ⟨ὀ⟩μ(με)μείχμενον θαλίαισι νέκταρ
> ⟨οἰ⟩νοχόαισον

> Where you, having taken up (wreaths?), Cypris,
> pour nectar gracefully
> in golden cups
> mingled with the festivities.

2) Athenaeus 11.463e

> ..... ἐλθέ, Κύπρι,
> χρυσίαισιν ἐν κυλίκεσσιν ἁβρῶς
> συμμεμιγμένον θαλίαισι νέκταρ
> οἰνοχοοῦσα

> ..... Come, Cypris,
> pouring nectar gracefully
> in golden cups
> mingled with the festivities.

---

[78] On the excerpting of Greek lyric poems, thus creating in effect new variants, in the Hellenistic period, see Hose (2008).

[79] Olson (2006–2012), for example, in his Loeb edition of Athenaeus' *Deipnosophistai* changes Attic forms in Athenaeus' quotations of Sappho and Alcaeus back to Aeolic and, even more problematically, adopts the reconstructions of modern editors such as Eva-Maria Voigt in his text. Note his editorial statement on p. xvii of the introduction to the first volume: 'Where Athenaeus is our only author for a fragmentary text, I have given it as it appears in the best modern editions and thus not infrequently in a substantially emended form.' This makes it for future readers almost impossible to know what Athenaeus actually wrote and in which versions he knew the poems. Compare Kreij (2015) 31.

The potsherd contains many writing mistakes and its text is therefore not easy to reconstruct, but it seems to preserve a version of the song that ends on the imperative 'pour nectar' (οἰνοχόαισον) with what appear to be several Aeolic dialect forms: at least ἔλοισα and probably ⟨ὀ⟩μ⟨με⟩μείχμενον and ⟨οἰ⟩νοχόαισον.[80] Athenaeus, on the other hand, records a version of the song that contains several Attic forms and begins with the imperative 'come' (ἐλθέ). A New Philological edition of Sappho would record both variants as versions in which this song of Sappho was rendered in antiquity. In this case a deliberate change of the syntax and dialect by Athenaeus to make the quotation fit his text is a distinct possibility,[81] but it is also possible that Athenaeus and the Florence ostrakon preserve two different ways in which this song of Sappho was remembered in antiquity.[82]

This brings me to my final example: the Tithonos poem of Sappho. In 2004, the papyrologists Michael Gronewald and Robert Daniel published a new papyrus fragment of Sappho, which supplements an older fragment known as fragment 58 from the Oxyrhynchus papyri in significant ways.[83] The biggest question surrounding this newly restored poem of Sappho is the way it ends: more specifically whether or not it originally continued with the four lines that follow in the Oxyrhynchus papyrus. These four lines were assumed by Edgar Lobel and by all subsequent editors to belong to the poem, until the new papyrus fragment was found. They read as follows:

]ιμέναν νομίσδει
]αις ὀπάσδοι
ἔγω δὲ φίλημμ' ἀβροσύναν, ...] τοῦτο καί μοι
τὸ λά[μπρον ἔρος τὠελίω καὶ τὸ κά]λον λέ[λ]ογχε.

---

80 Ferrari (2010) 152, following Malnati (1993) proposes a different reconstruction of the text on the potsherd. I do not find this reconstruction convincing however, because it has to emend the participle ἔλοισα to ἐ⟨θέ⟩λοισα, for no good reason, and deviates too much from Atheneaus' version, quoted below.
81 See Kreij (2015) 24. Note that Athenaeus continues his quotation with the words 'for these my friends and yours' (τούτοισι τοῖς ἑταίροις ἐμοῖς γε καὶ σοῖς), which do not fit the language or metre of the song. On deliberate changes Athenaeus could make to the texts of prose authors that he cites, see Olson (2018).
82 Nicosia (1976) 93–107. We cannot exclude the possibility that the dialect in which the quotation was originally cited, was (further?) changed into Attic in the course of the transmission of Athenaeus' text: see note 77 above.
83 Gronewald and Daniel (2004a, 2004b). See also Gronewald and Daniel (2007) and Hammerstaedt (2009).

.....   ] ... (he / she) thinks
.....   ] ... might give
but I love delicacy ... this and love (of the sun) has obtained
for me the brightness and beauty of the sun.[84]

I have argued elsewhere why I believe that these four lines did at some point belong to the poem.[85] They provide the poem with a consolatory ending, reminiscent of other songs of Sappho. The version without these four lines, however, lends itself better for performances at a symposium, as Deborah Boedeker has argued.[86]

Whatever one's view is on the ending of this poem, the Cologne papyrus provides us with clear evidence that there existed different editions of Sappho's poetry in antiquity, because the Tithonos poem is preceded by a different composition on this papyrus from the one on the Oxyrhynchus papyrus. The Cologne papyrus dates from the beginning of the third century BCE and therefore predates the Alexandrian editions of Sappho's poetry, on which the Oxyrhynchus papyrus is based and of which there were also more than one.[87] It is not unlikely that these different editions of Sappho preserved different versions of her poetry. The preceding compositions, both on the Cologne papyrus and on the Oxyrhynchus papyrus, are written in the same metre as the Tithonos poem, raising the possibility that strophes from different compositions attributed to Sappho were differently combined with one another,[88] as was the case, as we have seen, with the strophes in the medieval collections of the lyric poems of Walther von der Vogelweide. A New Philological edition of her poetry would point out these possibilities in the transmission of Sappho's songs in antiquity.

---

84   Campbell (1990) 100–101. The last two lines are supplemented on the basis of a citation in Athenaeus 687b. One should construct τὠελίω both with ἔρος and with τὸ λάμπρον καὶ τὸ κάλον: 'love of the sun has obtained for me the brightness and beauty of the sun'. Love of the sun stands for love of life here: see Lardinois (2009) 44.

85   Lardinois (2009). Compare the contributions of Edmunds, Boedeker, and Nagy to Greene and Skinner (2009).

86   Boedeker (2009) 79. On the "excerpting" of Greek lyric poetry in antiquity, see note 78 above.

87   See Yatromanolakis (1999); Liberman (2007); and Acosta-Hughes (2010) 92–104. The newest Sappho fragments have greatly improved our understanding of the arrangement of poems in at least one of the Hellenistic editions of Sappho: see Obbink (2016).

88   On the possibility that different compositions of Sappho were combined with one another in the reperformances of her songs, see Boedeker (2009); Lidov (2009) 100; and Pittoto and Raschieri (2017).

5 Conclusion

Having argued for the benefits of the editing practice of New Philology to the editing of the Greek lyric and elegiac poets, I have discussed some divergences that can be found in the textual transmission of this poetry. These variations, I have argued, cannot be attributed to scribal error or the failure of memory of the authors who quote them, but result from deliberate changes made to this poetry in antiquity. I am convinced that a renewed study of the full transmission of the Greek lyric poets on papyrus, in quotations and in the limited number of medieval manuscripts, would yield many more examples. Such finds require new editions, which would adopt the principles of New Philology and print the fragments of these poets with all their variations. It is obvious that the computer is the best instrument to produce such a multiform edition.[89] In short, there remains a lot of (new) philological work to be done in Classics, especially in the field of Greek lyric poetry.

References

Acosta-Hughes, B. 2010. *Arion's Lyre: Archaic Lyric into Hellenistic Poetry*. Princeton.

Alonge, M. 2011. Greek Hymns from Performance to Stone. In *Sacred Words: Orality, Literacy and Religion*, ed. A.P.M.H. Lardinois, J.H. Blok, and M.G.M. van der Poel, 217–234. Leiden.

Andrews, T.L. 2013. The Third Way: Philology and Critical Edition in the Digital Age. *Variants* 10: 61–76.

Bakker, E., ed. 2017. *Authorship and Greek Song: Questions of Authority, Authenticity, and Performance*. Studies in Archaic and Classical Greek Song 3. Leiden.

Bein, T. 2010. "schlechte handschriften", "critische ausgaben", "äusgezeichnete copisten": Über die Bedeutung der Materialität für Edition und Interpretation am Beispiel von Ton 36/36a Walthers von der Vogelweide. In *Materialität in der Editionswissenschaft*, ed. M. Schubert, 267–274. Berlin.

---

89 Compare Andrews (2013); Dalen-Oskam (2015); and Tarrant (2016) 145–156. A good example is the LaParola online text edition of the Greek New Testament, showing on demand all the different manuscript readings: http://www.laparola.net/greco/index.php (last accessed: 5.7.2019). Scholars connected to the Center of Hellenic Studies have been working for some time on an online multitext edition of the Homeric epics, parts of which are available: http://www.homermultitext.org (last accessed: 5.7.2019). Ideally, such multiform editions are accompanied by a commentary, explaining the likely source and meaning of the variations, as provided, for example, by Dué and Ebbott (2010).

Bein, T. 2013. *Walther von der Vogelweide: Leich, Lieder, Sangsprüche: Aufgrund der 14., von Christoph Cormeau bearbeiteten Ausgabe, neu herausgegeben*. 15th edn. Berlin.

Bird, G.D. 2010. *Multitextuality in the Homeric Iliad: The Witness of the Ptolemaic Papyri*. Cambridge, MA.

Birge Vitz, E. 1993. On the Role of a Renewed Philology in the Study of a Manuscript- and an Oral-Culture. In Busby 1993a, 71–78.

Blaise, F. 2006. Poetics and Politics: Tradition Re-Worked in Solon's 'Eunomia' (Poem 4). In Blok and Lardinois 2006, 114–133.

Blois, L. de. 2006. Plutarch's Solon: A Tissue of Commonplaces or a Historical Account? In Blok and Lardinois 2006, 429–440.

Blok, J.H. and Lardinois, A.P.M.H., eds. 2006. *Solon of Athens: New Historical and Philological Approaches*. Leiden.

Boedeker, D. 2009. No Way Out? Aging in the New (and Old) Sappho. In Greene and Skinner 2009, 71–83.

Boter, G.J. 2008. Herkules oder Sisyphos? 23 Jahrhunderte Griechishe Philologie. In *Die Herkulesarbeiten der Philologie*, ed. S. Berto and B. Plachta, 63–96. Berlin.

Bowie, E.L. 1997. The Theognidea: A Step Towards a Collection of Fragments? In *Collecting Fragments—Fragmente sammeln*, ed. G. Most, 53–66. Göttingen.

Bowie, E.L. 2012. An Early Chapter in the History of the *Theognidea*. In *Approaches to Archaic Greek Poetry*, ed. X. Riu and J. Pòrtulas, 121–148. Messina.

Busby, K., ed. 1993a. *Towards a Synthesis? Essays on the New Philology*. Amsterdam.

Busby, K. 1993b. *Variance* and the Politics of Textual Criticism. In Busby 1993a, 29–45.

Busby, K. 1993c. Doin' Philology While the –isms Strut. In Busby 1993a, 85–95.

Campbell, D.A. 1982–1993. *Greek Lyric*. 5 vols. Loeb Classical Library. Cambridge, MA.

Campbell, D.A. 1990. *Greek Lyric I*, 2nd corr. edn. Cambridge, MA.

Cerquiglini, B. 1989. *Éloge de la variante: Histoire critique de la philologie*. Paris. Translated as *In Praise of the Variant: A Critical History of Philology*, trans. B. Wing. Baltimore 1999.

Cerquiglini, B. 2007. Une nouvelle philologie? http://magyar-irodalom.elte.hu/colloquia/000601/cerq.htm.

Collins, D. 2004. *Master of the Game: Competition and Performance in Greek Poetry*. Cambridge, MA.

Cormeau, C., ed. 1996. *Walther von der Vogelweide: Leich, Lieder, Sangsprüche*. 14th edn. Berlin.

Dalen-Oskam, K. van. 2015. In Praise of the Variant Analysis Tool: A Computational Approach to Medieval Literature. In Lardinois et al. 2015: 35–54.

D'Alessio, G. 2015. Review of M. Davies and P.J. Finglass, eds. *Stesichorus. The Poems*. Cambridge Classical Texts and Commentaries 54. *BMCR* 2015.10.40.

Dué, C. and Ebbott, M. 2010. *Iliad 10 and the Poetics of Ambush: A Multitext Edition with Essays and Commentary*. Washington, DC.

Faraone, C.A. 2006. Stanzaic Structure and Responsion in the Elegiac Poetry of Tyrtaeus. *Mnemosyne* 59: 19–52.

Faraone, C.A. 2008. *The Stanzaic Architecture of Early Greek Elegy*. Oxford.

Faraone, C.A. 2011. An Athenian Tradition of Dactylic Paeans to Apollo and Asclepius: Choral Degeneration or a Flexible System of Non-Strophic Dactyls? *Mnemosyne* 64: 206–231.

Ferrari, F. 2007. Orality and Textual Criticism. In *Politics of Orality*, ed. C. Cooper, 53–86. Leiden.

Ferrari, F. 2010. *Sappho's Gift: The Poet and Her Community*, translated by B. Acosta-Hughes and L. Prauscello. Michigan.

Finglass, P.J. 2015. Reperformances and the Transmission of Texts. *Trends in Classics* 7.2: 259–276.

Ford, A. 1997. The Inland Ship: Problems in the Performance and Reception of Early Greek Epic. In *Written Voices, Spoken Signs: Tradition, Performance, and the Epic Text*, ed. E. Bakker and A. Kahane, 83–109. Cambridge, MA.

Ford, A. 2003. From Letters to Literature: Reading the 'Song Culture' of Classical Greece. In *Written Texts and the Rise of the Literate Culture in Ancient Greece*, ed. H. Yunis, 15–37. Cambridge.

Gaisser, J.H. 2007. Some Thoughts on Philology. *TAPhA* 137: 477–481.

Gellrich, M. 1995. Interpreting Greek Tragedy: History, Theory and the New Philology. In *History, Tragedy, Theory: Dialogues on Athenian Drama*, ed. B. Goff, 38–58. Austin.

Gentili, B. 1984. L'arte della filologia. In *Poesia e pubblico nella Grecia antica*, 297–312. Rome. Translated in Gentili 1988: 223–233 and 307–309.

Gentili, B. 1988. *Poetry and Its Public in Ancient Greece: From Homer to the Fifth Century*. Baltimore.

Gentili, B. and Prato, C. 1988. *Poetarum elegiacorum testimonia et fragmenta. Pars I*. 2nd rev. edn. Leipzig.

Gerber, D.E. 1999. *Greek Elegiac Poetry*. Loeb Classical Library. Cambridge, MA.

Graziosi, B. 2010. Homer: From Reception to Composition. *Letras Clássicas* 14: 21–33.

Graziosi, B. and Haubold, J. 2019. Review of M.L. West, *Homerus. Odyssea* (Berlin 2017). *BMCR* 2019.01.05 (http://www.bmcreview.org/2019/01/20190105.html).

Greene, E. and Skinner, M.B., eds. 2009. *The New Sappho on Old Age*. Cambridge, MA.

Greetham, D.C. 1993. Editorial and Critical Theory: From Modernism to Postmodernism. In *Palimpsest: Editorial Theory in the Humanities*, ed. G. Bornstein and R.G. Williams, 9–28. Ann Arbor.

Gronewald, M. and Daniel, R.W. 2004a. Ein neuer Sappho-Papyrus. *ZPE* 147: 1–8.

Gronewald, M. and Daniel, R.W. 2004b. Nachtrag zum neuen Sappho-Papyrus. *ZPE* 149: 1–4.

Gronewald, M. and Daniel, R.W. 2007. 429. Sappho (Inv. 2351 + 21376r). *Kölner Papyri* 11: 1–11.

Hadjimichael, T.A. 2019. *The Emergence of the Lyric Canon*. Oxford.

Hamilton, R. 1974. Objective Evidence for Actors' Interpolations in Greek Tragedy. *GRBS* 15: 449–477.

Hammerstaedt, J. 2009. The Cologne Sappho: Its Discovery and Textual Constitution. In Greene and Skinner 2009: 17–40.

Hanink, J. 2014. *Lycurgan Athens and the Making of Classical Tragedy*. Cambridge.

Haslam, M. 1997. Homeric papyri and the Transmission of the Text. In *A New Companion to Homer*, ed. I. Morris and B. Powell, 54–100. Leiden.

Higbie, C. 2010. Epigrams on the Persian Wars: monuments, memory and politics. In *Archaic and Classical Greek Epigram*, eds. M. Baumbach, A. Petrovic and I. Petrovic, 183–201. Cambridge.

Hose, M. 2008. Der Leser schneide dem Lied Länge ab. *Hermes* 136: 293–307.

Irwin, E. 2005. *Solon and Early Greek Poetry: The Politics of Exhortation*. Cambridge.

Irwin, E. 2006. The Transgressive Elegy of Solon. In Blok and Lardinois 2006: 36–78.

Klooster, J. 2014. New Philology and Ancient Editors. In *The Making of the Humanities*, vol. 3, ed. R. Bod, T. Weststeijn, and J. Maat, 251–263. Amsterdam.

Kreij, M. de. 2015. Transmission and Textual Variants: Divergent Fragments of Sappho's Songs Examined. In Lardinois et al. 2015: 17–34.

Lardinois, A.P.M.H. 2006. Have we Solon's Verses? In Blok and Lardinois 2006: 15–35.

Lardinois, A.P.M.H. 2009. The New Sappho Poem (P. Koln 21351 and 21376): Key to the Old Fragments. In Greene and Skinner 2009: 41–57.

Lardinois, A.P.M.H., Levie, S., Hoeken, H., and Lüthy, C., eds. 2015. *Texts, Transmissions, Receptions*. Leiden.

Liberman, G. 2007. L'édition alexandrine de Sappho. In *Atti del convegno internazionale di studi 'I papyri di Saffo e di Alceo': Firenze 8–9 giugno 2006*, ed. G. Bastianini and A. Casanova, 41–65. Milan.

Lidov, J. 2009. Acceptance or Assertion? Sappho's New Poem in its Books. In Greene and Skinner 2009: 84–102.

Lord, A.B. 1960. *The Singer of Tales*. Cambridge.

Malnati, A. 1993. Reivisione dell'ostrakon fiorentino di Saffo. *APapyrol* 5: 21–22.

Marmodoro, A. and Hill, J. (eds.) 2013. *The Author's Voice in Classical and Late Antiquity*. Oxford.

Meiggs, R. and Lewis, D. 1988. *A Selection of Greek Historical Inscriptions to the End of the Fifth Century BC*. Revised edn. Oxford.

Mühl, P. von der. 1942. Antiker Historismus in Plutarchs Biographie des Solon. *Kleio* 35: 89–102.

Nafissi, M. 2010. The Great *Rhetra* (Plut. *Lyc*. 6): A Restrospective and Intentional Construct? In *Intentional History: Spinning Time in Ancient Greece*, ed. L. Foxhall, H.-J. Gehrke, and N. Luraghi, 89–119. Stuttgart.

Nagy, G. 1983. Poet and Tyrant: *Theognidea* 39–52, 1081–1082b. *CA* 2: 82–91.

Nagy, G. 1985. Theognis and Megara: A Poet's Vision of His City. In *Theognis of Megara: Poetry and Polis*, ed. T.J. Figueira and G. Nagy, 22–81. Baltimore.

Nagy, G. 1990. *Pindar's Homer: The Lyric Possession of an Epic Past*. Baltimore.

Nagy, G. 1996. *Poetry as Performance: Homer and beyond*. Cambridge.

Nagy, G. 2000. Review of West, *Homeri Ilias, Pars I*, BMCR 2000.09.12, reprinted in Nagy 2004: 40–74.

Nagy, G. 2003. Review of West 2001a, *Gnomon* 75: 481–501, reprinted with changes in Nagy 2004: 75–109.

Nagy, G. 2004. *Homer's Text and Language*. Urbana.

Nichols, S.G., ed. 1990. *The New Philology*, Special issue of *Speculum* 65: 1–108.

Nichols, S.G. 1997. Why Material Philology? Some Thoughts, *Zeitschrift für deutsche Philologie* 116: 10–30.

Nicosia, S. 1976. *Tradizione testuale diretta e indiretta dei poeti di Lesbo*. Rome.

Noussia-Fantuzzi, M. 2010. *Solon the Athenian, the Poetic Fragments*. Leiden.

Obbink, D. 2016. Ten Poems of Sappho: Provenance, Authenticity, and Text of the New Sappho Papyri. In *The Newest Sappho: P. Sapph. Obbink and P.GC inv. 105, frs. 1–4*, ed. A. Bierl and A. Lardinois, 34–54. Leiden

Olson, S.D. 2006–2012. *Athenaeus. The Learned Banqueters*. 8 vols. Loeb Classical Library. Cambridge, MA.

Olson, S.D. 2018. Athenaeus "Fragments" of Non-Fragmentary Prose Authors and their Implications. *AJP* 139: 424–450.

Page, D.L. 1934. *Actors' Interpolations in Greek Tragedy: Studied with Special Reference to Euripides'* Iphigeneia in Aulis. Oxford.

Page, D.L. 1981. *Further Greek Epigrams*. Cambridge.

Parry, M. 1971. *The Making of Homeric Verse: The Collected Writings of Milman Parry*, ed. A. Parry. Oxford.

Pearsall, D.A. 1985. Editing Medieval Texts: Some Developments and Some Problems. In *Textual Criticism and Literary Interpretation*, ed. J. McGann, 92–106. Chicago.

Petrovic, A. 2007. *Kommentar zu den Simonideischen Versinschriften*. Leiden.

Pfeiffer, R. 1968. *History of Classical Scholarship: From the Beginnings to the End of the Hellenistic Age*. Oxford.

Phillips, T. 2016. *Pindar's Library: Performance Poetry and Material Texts*. Oxford.

Pitotto, E. and A.A. Raschieri. 2017. Which Sappho? The Case Study of the Cologne Papyrus. In Bakker 2017: 265–286.

Pöhlmann, E. 2003. *Einführung in die Überlieferungsgeschichte und in die Textkritik der antiken Literatur*. Vol. 1: *Altertum*. 2nd edn. (1st edn. 1994). Darmstadt.

Prauscello, L. 2006. *Singing Alexandria: Music between Practice and Textual Transmission*. Leiden.

Reynolds, L.D. and Wilson, N.G. 1991. *Scribes and Scholars: A Guide to the Transmission of Greek and Latin Literature*. 3rd edn. Oxford.

Rossi, E.L. 1997. Esiodo, Le opere e i giorni: un nuovo tentativo di analisi. In *Posthomerica I*, ed. F. Montanari and S. Pittaluga, 7–22. Genova.

Schnell, R. 1997. Was ist neu an der 'New Philology'? In *Alte und neue Philologie*, ed. M.-D. Gleßgen and F. Lebsanft, 61–95. Tübingen.

Schoor, R. van de. 2015. Mutatis Mutandis: The Same Call for Peace, but Differently Framed Each Time. In Lardinois et al. 2015: 55–70.

Scodel, R. 2007. Lycurgus and the State Text of Tragedy. In *Politics of Orality*, ed. C. Cooper, 129–154. Leiden.

Selle, H. 2008. *Theognis und die Theognidea*. Berlin.

Sider, D. 2007. Sylloge Simonidea. In *Brill's Companion to Hellenistic Epigram*, ed. P. Bing and J.S. Steffen, 113–130. Leiden.

Sluiter, I. 2017. Anchoring Innovation: A Classic Research Agenda. *European Review* 25(1): 1–19.

Stackmann, K. 1994. Neue Philologie? In *Modernes Mittelalter: Neue Bilder einer populären Epoche*, ed. J. Heinzle, 398–427. Frankfurt am Main.

Tarrant, R.J. 1995. Classical Latin Literature. In *Scholarly Editing: A Guide to Research*, ed. D.C. Greetham, 95–148. New York.

Tarrant, R.J. 2016. *Texts, Editors and Readers: Methods and Problems in Latin Textual Criticism*. Cambridge.

Thomas, R. 1992. *Literacy and Orality in Ancient Greece*. Cambridge.

Ucciardello, G. 2005. Sulla tradizione del testo di Ibico. In *Lirica e teatro in Grecia*, ed. S. Grandoli, 21–88. Naples.

Vet, T. de. 1996. The Joint Role of Orality and Literacy in the Composition, Transmission and Performance of the Homeric Texts: A Comparative View. *TAPhA* 126: 43–76.

West, M.L. 1973. *Textual Criticism and Editorial Technique*. Stuttgart.

West, M.L. 1992. *Iambi et elegi Graeci*. Vol. 2. Second revised edition. Oxford.

West, M.L. 2001a. *Studies in the Text and Transmission of the Iliad*. Munich.

West, M.L. 2001b. West on Nagy and Nardelli on West, *BMCR* 2001.09.06.

West, M.L. 2004. West on Rengakos (*BMCR* 2002.11.15) and Nagy (*Gnomon* 75, 2003, 481–501) on West. *BMCR* 2004.04.17.

West, M.L. 2005. The New Sappho. *ZPE* 151: 1–9.

West, S. 1967. *The Ptolemaic Papyri of Homer*. Cologne.

Westra, H.J. 1993. New Philology and the Editing of Medieval Latin Texts. In Busby 1993a: 49–58.

Westra, H.J. 2014. What's in a Name: Old, New and Material Philology, Textual Scholarship and Ideology. In *Neo-Latin Philology: Old Tradition, New Approaches*, ed. M. van der Poel, 13–24. Leuven.

Wilamowitz-Moellendorff, U. von. 1900. *Textgeschichte der griechischen Lyriker*. Berlin.

Wilkinson, K.W. 2012. *New Epigrams of Palladas: A Fragementary Papyrus Codex (P. CtY BR inv. 4000)*. Durham, NC.

Wolf, J. 2002. New Philology / Textkritik: Ältere deutsche Literatur. In *Germanistik als Kulturwissenschaft: Eine Einführung in neue Theoriekonzepte*, ed. C. Benthein and H.R. Velten, 175–195. Reinbeck bei Hamburg.

Yatromanolakis, D. 1999. Alexandrian Sappho Revisited. *HSCPh* 99: 179–195.

Yatromanolakis, D. 2008. P. Colon. inv. 21351 + 21376 and P. Oxy. 1787 fr. 1: Music, Cultural Politics, and Hellenistic Anthologies. *Hellenika* 58: 237–255.

Zetzel, J.E.G. 1993. Religion, Rhetoric, and Editorial Technique: Reconstructing the Classics. In *Palimpsest: Editorial Theory in the Humanities*, ed. G. Bornstein and R.G. Willimas, 99–120. Ann Arbor.

Zumthor, P. 1972. *Essai de poétique mediévale*. Paris.

Zumthor, P. 1983. *Introduction à la poésie orale*. Paris.

CHAPTER 3

Tyrtaeus the Lawgiver? Plutarch and Diodorus Siculus on Tyrtaeus fr. 4

Eveline van Hilten-Rutten

1   Introduction*

In the opening lines of the *Life of Lycurgus*, Plutarch famously argues that everything about the Spartan lawgiver is a mystery: 'there is nothing in the life of this man which is not disputed'.[1] He could have said the same of another character in the early history of Sparta: Tyrtaeus. We know the poet's name, but even simple details, such as where he came from (Sparta or Athens?) or where his poetry was performed (were his elegiacs to be sung before battle, at symposia, or at festivals?), remain a matter of dispute. Even the authenticity of some of the poems transmitted under his name was debated in the nineteenth and early twentieth centuries. This so-called Tyrtaean Question may have been laid to rest over recent decades, but that does not mean that scholars now view all of Tyrtaeus' poems as being originally by his hand.[2] The fragment on which most debate has centred is the vexed fragment 4 West (1b and °14 Gentili-Prato), with which this chapter is largely concerned.

The poem of Tyrtaeus, now seen as part of the poem *Eunomia*, is found in two sources: six lines of it are quoted by Plutarch in the *Life of Lycurgus*, and ten lines were quoted by Diodorus Siculus in the *World History*, but survive only as a fragment in a book with excerpts. The quotations differ not only in length, but also come with different opening lines and several variations within the four lines that overlap. Scholars have proposed a variety of solutions to this problem. First, editors have tried to combine both versions into one poem. In Martin West's *Iambi et Elegi Graeci*, the two fragments are combined to form one poem of ten lines: West combines the first six lines of Plutarch with the

---

* I would like to thank the audience at the Reading Conference, the anonymous reviewers and the editors for their helpful comments and suggestions. André Lardinois and Vanessa Cazzato, with whom I co-presented the oral version of this chapter, also improved its written version in both thought and wording. Any remaining mistakes are my own.
1   Plut. *Lyc.* 1.1.
2   On the Tyrtaean Question, see Prato (1968) 8*–20*.

last four of Diodorus, but adopts two readings of Diodorus into the lines of Plutarch, together with several emendations.[3] This is similar to the solution proposed by Theodor Bergk in his edition of 1882, save that he chose to print Diodorus' opening lines, together with another apophthegm, as a separate Tyrtaean fragment (3 Bergk), dubbed *'nihil ad Tyrtaeum'* by West.[4] Second, editors have presented one of the two versions as derivative. Bruno Gentili and Carlo Prato did not wish to combine the two versions and edited the fragment of Plutarch as Tyrtaeus fragment 1b, and the fragment of Diodorus, which they considered a forgery, as fragment °14. Nevertheless, they have admitted one reading of Diodorus into the fragment of Plutarch, and four of Plutarch in Diodorus.[5] An earlier editor, Ernst Diehl, also printed the versions separately, as 3a and 3b. He printed Plutarch's version (3b) in a smaller type, which suggests that he considered Diodorus' version (3a) as the Tyrtaean original. He also corrected the ungrammatical words in Diodorus with the help of the text of Plutarch.[6] Third, historians who have interpreted the text, also have tried to construct their own edition of the two versions. Van Wees, for instance, believes that all the lines are genuine and prints lines 1–2 of Plutarch's version followed by lines 1–10 of Diodorus', again with corrections from Plutarch, and thus bases his discussion on an amalgam of both versions.[7] Meier has the same solution, but athetizes the last two lines of Diodorus' quotation.[8] Based on these reconstructions, some thought it possible to make a further reconstruction. The verses of Tyrtaeus mention an oracle, and Bergk has argued that the text of the original oracle can be reconstructed by deleting the pentameters from Tyrtaeus' poem.[9]

The above enumeration of the attempted reconstructions shows how contemporary scholars usually look at texts: there is one original and all subsequent versions derive from it. When we only have later versions (as we usually

---

3   West (1989–1992) ii.171–172; West (1974) 184–186. Σπάρτης instead of Σπάρτας (line 4) and πρεσβυγενέας (in Diodorus: -εῖς) for πρεσβύτας (line 5).
4   Bergk (1882) 9; West (1989–1992) ii.170. Bergk and West give slightly different readings of lines 8 and 9 of fragment 4.
5   Gentili and Prato (1988–2002) 21–22 (fr. 1b), 38–39 (fr. °14); also in Prato (1968) 24 (fr. 1b), 44 (fr. °14). Σπάρτης instead of Σπάρτας (line 4) in fr. 1b; βουλῆς for βουλῇ (line 3), ἱμερόεσσα for ἱχερόεσσα (line 4), τὲ for δὲ (line 5) and εὐθείαις ῥήτραις for εὐθείην ῥήτρας (line 6) in fr. °14.
6   Diehl (1922) 7–8, with reference to Wilamowitz-Moellendorff (1900) 109. He emends the same words as Gentili and Prato in fr. 1b and fr. °14.
7   Van Wees (1999) 6–9.
8   Meier (1998) 243–253; see also the subsequent debate between Meier (2002), Van Wees (2002), and Link (2003).
9   Bergk (1882) 10–11; cf. Tigerstedt (1965) 357n393.

do), we do all we can to reconstruct one original poem, maybe even its original source. These are valuable contributions to the field, and we can use these reconstructed texts as a basis to gain insights in the oeuvre of a single author, or to make connections with other authors and events in history. Moreover, no editor would claim that he or she has found *the* original text; such editors would merely claim that they had done the best that they could, and would leave it to new editors to come up with new versions of the text. I will argue here, however, that when we (temporarily) let go of the reconstructive mode, we may lose our original text, but we gain insights into the way in which texts were transmitted and interpreted in antiquity. For when we look at the texts as source material, as New Philology and reception studies encourage us to do, and transcend the debate on authenticity of the fragments, the versions' differences become an interesting case of reception in antiquity.[10]

The focus in this chapter will be on the interpretations that Plutarch and Diodorus give of Tyrtaeus' poem. In the following two sections, I will discuss first Tyrtaeus' fragment as transmitted by Plutarch and then the fragment of Diodorus Siculus. I will read each version of Tyrtaeus' poem without referring to the other, and reconstruct the respective interpretations that Plutarch and Diodorus Siculus gave of the lines. In the case of Diodorus Siculus, the poem's context survives incomplete, and it will be necessary to take the historiographer's own transmission into detailed account. It will be argued that both historians quote the fragment of Tyrtaeus as evidence connected to Lycurgus' politics, but come up with different interpretations. These differences are possible because both versions of the poem are vague about its recipients. My analysis sheds light, moreover, on how Tyrtaeus' poems were not seen as poems, but as sources for historical events in the otherwise scarcely documented early history of Sparta.

2   Plutarch and the Great Rhetra

One version of Tyrtaeus' poem is preserved in Plutarch's *Life of Lycurgus*, embedded in an intricate discussion on Sparta's first law: the Great Rhetra. This is one of the most hotly debated problems of archaic Sparta. My aim here is not to summarize all arguments for and against the Rhetra's authenticity,

---

10   This chapter bases itself on the theory of New Philology, combined with ideas from reception studies as represented foremost by Martindale (1993). For the background to New Philology, including criticism of its ideas, see Lardinois' contribution to this volume, pp. 39–50.

integrity, and influence on Spartan politics; these overviews can be found elsewhere.[11] Instead, I will focus on the way in which Plutarch embeds and interprets Tyrtaeus' poem. I use the text of Tyrtaeus as given by Plutarch, without additions from Diodorus' text.

According to Plutarch, Lycurgus' most important innovation was the institution of a *gerousia*, or council of elders, in the political constitution.[12] Through the establishment of the *gerousia*, which contained twenty-eight elderly Spartan men and the two kings, Sparta received its exemplary mixed government, which supposedly increased its stability over time.[13] Plutarch explains that Lycurgus received an oracle about this measure, and proceeds to quote a prose document that he calls *rhetra*. Plutarch first glosses and explains the Great Rhetra and explicitly takes some of his arguments from Aristotle.[14] He then discusses a later addition to the Great Rhetra (often called "the Rider" by modern scholars) made by two kings, Polydorus and Theopompus, and supports his reasoning with a quotation of Tyrtaeus.[15]

τοῦ δὲ πλήθους ἀθροισθέντος, εἰπεῖν μὲν οὐδενὶ γνώμην τῶν ἄλλων ἐφεῖτο, τὴν δ' ὑπὸ τῶν γερόντων καὶ τῶν βασιλέων προτεθεῖσαν ἐπικρῖναι κύριος ἦν ὁ δῆμος. ὕστερον μέντοι τῶν πολλῶν ἀφαιρέσει καὶ προσθέσει τὰς γνώμας διαστρεφόντων καὶ παραβιαζομένων, Πολύδωρος καὶ Θεόπομπος οἱ βασιλεῖς τάδε τῇ ῥήτρᾳ παρενέγραψαν· "Αἰ δὲ σκολιὰν ὁ δᾶμος ἔροιτο,[16] τοὺς πρεσβυγενέας καὶ ἀρχαγέτας ἀποστατῆρας ἦμεν," τοῦτ' ἔστι μὴ κυροῦν, ἀλλ' ὅλως ἀφίστασθαι καὶ διαλύειν τὸν δῆμον, ὡς ἐκτρέποντα καὶ μεταποιοῦντα τὴν γνώμην παρὰ τὸ βέλ-

---

11   The bibliography on the subject is vast, and this chapter's references are restricted to several recent contributions in which the focus is on Tyrtaeus' poem rather than Spartan history. Recent overviews on the widely differing opinions on the Great Rhetra, with full bibliography, are provided by, e.g. Meier (1998) 186–207; Cartledge (2001) 29–36; Nafissi (2010) 93n20.
12   Plut. *Lyc.* 5.10.
13   Already argued by Pl. *Leg.* 691d–692c, 712d–e; Arist. *Pol.* 1265b33–a1.
14   Plut. *Lyc.* 6.1–6. On Plutarch's general working method and source material, see Pelling (2002), esp. 91–115 and 143–170; and Klooster's contribution to this volume. Even though it is likely that much of the argument derives from Aristotle's lost *Lacedaemonian Constitution*, I take Plutarch as the main writer of this text, and do not follow Nafissi (2010) in his use of the combination Plutarch/Aristotle.
15   Plut. *Lyc.* 6.6–10. The text, including Tyrtaeus' poem, is taken from the edition of Ziegler (1973); all translations are my own.
16   αἴροιτο Reiske (preferred by Ziegler])| ἕλοιτο Sintenis | ἔροιτο MSS. The manuscript reading is now generally accepted; see further Ogden (1994) 88–89. The preferred translation has been 'to say (something crooked)', but most scholars now accept Ogden's thesis that it is an optative of ἔρομαι and means 'to ask for'.

τιστον. ἔπεισαν δὲ καὶ αὐτοὶ τὴν πόλιν ὡς τοῦ θεοῦ ταῦτα προστάσσοντος, ὥς που Τυρταῖος ἐπιμέμνηται διὰ τούτων·
Φοίβου ἀκούσαντες Πυθωνόθεν **οἴκαδ᾽ ἔνεικαν**[17]
μαντείας τε θεοῦ καὶ τελέεντ᾽ ἔπεα·
ἄρχειν μὲν **βουλῆς**[18] θεοτιμήτους βασιλῆας,
οἷσι μέλει Σπάρτας ἱμερόεσσα πόλις,
5   πρεσβύτας τε γέροντας, ἔπειτα δὲ δημότας ἄνδρας
εὐθείαις ῥήτραις ἀνταπαμειβομένους.

When the multitude was assembled, he [Lycurgus] allowed no one of the others to state a proposal (*gnômê*), but the people (*dêmos*) had the authority to decide on the proposal which was brought forward by the elders (*gerontes*) and the kings (*basileis*). Later however, when the multitudes by subtraction and addition distorted and violated the proposals (*gnômai*), kings Polydorus and Theopompus wrote the following as addition to the rhetra: 'but when the people ask for something crooked [literally: 'a crooked one', sc. *rhêtra*], the elders and kings are to be setters-aside'. This means that no ratification takes place, but they quit immediately and dissolve the people's assembly, because it turned and changed the proposal into something against the best interest. And they themselves actually persuaded the city on the grounds that the god ordered this, as Tyrtaeus surely makes mention of in these verses:

Having listened to Phoebus, they brought home (?) from Delphi
   prophecies of the god and accomplishing words:
Counsel is to begin with the divinely honoured kings,
   who have the lovely city of Sparta in their care,
5   and with the ancient elders; then the men of the people,
   responding in turn with straight *rhetras*.

Plutarch describes the way in which the assembly, the twenty-eight elders, and the two kings made decisions: the elders and kings together formed a *gnômê*, a decision or proposal, and then the people gave their final word.[19] In this pro-

---

17 οἴκαδ᾽ ἔνεικαν: Amyot | οἱ τάδε νικᾶν MSS.
18 τιμῆς in manuscript Z. This seems to be a transposition due to the following word θεοτιμήτους and is therefore identified as a scribal error; but an interesting one nevertheless, as it would lead to quite a different meaning of this passage for the reader of this manuscript.
19 The sentence in the Great Rhetra of which this is the explanation, is corrupt, and several reconstructions of it have been proposed: see Manfredini and Piccirilli (1980) 239–240. To what degree the explanation reflects the actual sentence remains unclear. The wide-

cess, the people are subordinate to the *gerousia*: the people can vote, but they cannot alter the proposal according to their own wishes or submit a new proposal. Plutarch then argues that the Spartan assembly had started to think that it could not only say yay or nay to the proposals, but also change the proposals to suit its needs.[20] But the people do not have this right of amendment.[21] The solution to this distortion of the Spartan order is that the meeting is cancelled by the aristocratic leaders: the *gerousia* denies the right to the people to ratify the *gnômai* (μὴ κυροῦν).[22] The stress, therefore, in Plutarch's interpretation of the Great Rhetra and the Rider, is on the subordinate position of the *dêmos* to the *gerousia*. Both before and after the addition to the Great Rhetra, the *dêmos* is not allowed to speak for itself: it can only ratify what the kings and council of elders have said. Plutarch thus interprets the Great Rhetra in Sparta with the help of concepts from later democratic governments: a clear sign that we should not take his explanation at face value.[23]

The additional clause to the Great Rhetra, then, is actually a re-statement of it, one could say a clarification of the *dêmos*' subordinate position. It is this sentiment that we should look for in the quotation of Tyrtaeus. For Tyrtaeus, in

---

ranging meaning of γνώμη, which in contexts of politics most often means 'insights of a collegial body gained by voting' is discussed by Gerhard Thür in *NP* s.v. *gnômê* [2]. As this text talks about the way in which the insight is gained, I translate with 'proposal', although 'decision' or 'motion' is also possible. Compare also Talbert's Penguin translation of this passage, and Van Wees (1999) 10 and (2002) 96.

20   The combination ἀφαίρεσις καὶ πρόσθεσις is found one more time in Plut. *Lyc*. 13.2: there it refers to contracts and other minor matters, which are not bound by writing to be unchanged forever, but are subject to 'addition and subtraction', i.e. can be changed according to the situation.

21   Aristotle, in comparing the Cretan, Spartan, and Carthaginian constitution, says that the Carthaginian people have the right 'to speak against the proposals (τοῖς εἰσφερομένοις ἀντειπεῖν), which the other constitutions do not permit.' (Arist. *Pol*. 1273a9–13). Wade-Gery (1943–1944) 71–72, wished to transpose this sentence in Aristotle, but this is rightly countered by Van Wees (1999) 34n62.

22   I take 'kings and elders' as implied accusative subject of ἀφίστασθαι καὶ διαλύειν, but when they are also taken as the subject of μὴ κυροῦν the translation runs something like 'the kings do not agree with the *demos*', whereas κυρόω is more likely here to signify ratification by the assembly, see e.g. Thuc. 8.69 for the terminology. I translate it, therefore, as impersonal ('no ratification takes place'), as I believe it glosses the εἰ-clause rather than the main clause of the rider. For other solutions, see Wade-Gery (1943) 68–69; Ogden (1994) 90–91.

23   On Plutarch's interpretation, see especially the comments on the text of the Great Rhetra in Nafissi (2010) 95–96. *Contra*, Wade-Gery (1943) 63, who argues the *dêmos* could have powers of amendment in the Great Rhetra and that the Rider merely limited rather than forbade these.

Plutarch's words 'surely makes mention of this in the following verses'.[24] This is all Plutarch says explicitly about these lines of Tyrtaeus, but it is clear that they are supposed to prove that the kings themselves supported their Rider with an oracle. Let us therefore compare the Rider and its interpretation to the text of Tyrtaeus given by Plutarch. In the story about the origin of the Rider, an oracle is mentioned, and this interpretation is clearly supported in Tyrtaeus' poem by the words μαντείας τε θεοῦ (line 2), which came from Apollo via the Pythia (Φοί-βου ... Πυθωνόθεν). But what the oracle says in lines 3–6, and to whom it was said, may be subject to discussion.

First of all, Plutarch interprets the Tyrtaean text as stating that two kings went to Delphi and brought back an oracle. Here, he makes an interpretive leap: although the plural ἀκούσαντες proves beyond doubt that more than one person listened to the oracle, there is no mention of kings in the first two lines, let alone of the two kings Plutarch has mentioned in his explanation of the Rider.[25] Some commentators assume that Polydorus and Theopompus must have been mentioned by Tyrtaeus in a verse that was not cited.[26] This is not impossible, since Theopompus is mentioned in Tyrtaeus fragment 5 as well. Andrewes argues that Tyrtaeus must have referred to the Heraclidae, the kings' ultimate ancestors, mentioned in Tyrtaeus' *Eunomia* in fragment 2.[27] Since then a new papyrus fragment has been discovered, however, which has expanded our knowledge of fragment 2. It offers another possible subject of the first line of Plutarch's version of fragment 4: the oracular messengers of the Spartans. These messengers, who were also messmates of the kings of Sparta, are called the Pythii by our historical sources, and are explicitly said to be memorizers of Pythian oracles.[28] This would make them a natural subject to present the words of an oracle. They are possibly mentioned in the poem *Eunomia*, as the

---

24　Van Wees (1999) 12 and Nafissi (2010) 100 think that Plutarch expresses doubt about this interpretation because of his use of the particle που, which they translate as 'perhaps'. But Koier (2013) has established that που in classical prose usually signifies 'a positive argumentative orientation, and the suggestion that the addressee has access to the information provided by means of reasoning or knowledge of the world' (296), and gives 'you know, surely' as common translation. See also her discussion on the difficulty of deciding whether που has a locative or modal meaning in the introduction to quotations at 209–210.

25　The last two words of line 1 had to be reconstructed from the manuscript tradition, which gives οἱ τάδε νικᾶν. Amyot's correction, already introduced in the sixteenth century, has been generally accepted and makes sense, but I will not use it here to reconstruct Plutarch's interpretation.

26　Nafissi (2010) 103, with further references.

27　Andrewes (1938) 99–100, followed by Van Wees (1999) 12–13.

28　Hdt. 6.57.2–4; Xen. *Lac.* 15.5. Herodotus calls them θεοπρόποι.

papyrus fragment shows traces of θεοπροπ[(diviner) in line 2, together with the word μαντείασα[in line 4.[29] Nothing is further known about the context of this fragment or of Plutarch's version of fragment 4. The actual referent of the plural subject of line 1 in Plutarch's version is therefore unknown and we cannot be certain that two kings were mentioned earlier in the poem.

It seems that Plutarch's interpretation of the plural verbs is connected to a second improvement to the political system of Sparta: the institution of the ephors, who were representatives of the Spartan *dêmos*. In *Life of Lycurgus* 7, Plutarch tells the story about the institution of the ephorate by King Theopompus, who tried to save Lycurgus' policy by diminishing the power of the elite. He clearly sees the *ephores* as the added democratic element in the Spartan constitution that gives the *dêmos* the power it asked for, but did not receive within the Great Rhetra and the Rider.[30] In his account of the ephorate, Plutarch does not mention Polydorus at all, and neither do his sources.[31] Theopompus was probably one of the few Spartan kings who could be securely dated to the archaic period, and Meier has argued that the institution of the ephorate was ascribed to Theopompus on the basis of his role in the Messenian Wars.[32] The link between Theopompus and the king of the other house, Polydorus, is based on king lists, and our only other source that mentions these two kings together is Pausanias: he, however, comments on a battle in the Messenian Wars, not on politics.[33] Plutarch, or his source material, seems to make an interpretive leap here, identifying Theopompus and Polydorus as the subject of the plural in lines 1–2, possibly based on a connection with another political decision taken at the same time.

The second interpretive leap that Plutarch makes is interpreting the saying of the oracle as evidence for an addition to the Great Rhetra. For what does the oracle in Tyrtaeus' poem say? The kings (βασιλῆας) have the right to counsel first (ἄρχειν μὲν βουλῆς), together with the ancient elders (γέροντας), then it is the people's turn (δημότας ἄνδρας), who respond with 'straight' utterances (εὐθεί-

---

29   Tyrt.W2 = P.Oxy. 2824, ed. Turner (1971). Turner himself already suggested that the word θεοπροπ[referred to the Spartan Pythioi.
30   Later on, in *Lyc.* 29, Plutarch claims that although the ephorate was seen as a measure of democratization, it was in fact reinforcing the aristocracy.
31   Plutarch explicitly draws upon Pl.*Leg.*691e–692a (Plato's name is given and words quoted) and Arist.*Pol.*1313a19–33 (paraphrased but not identified unless by φασιν 'some say'), who also ascribe the ephorate to Theopompus. The most important source who argues that not Theopompus but Lycurgus instituted the ephorate, is Herodotus (1.65). For more on the ephorate, see Luther (2004).
32   Meier (1998) 93; Link (2000) 70–75.
33   Paus. 3.3.1; 3.7.5; 4.7.7.

αις ῥήτραις).³⁴ Although, on first appearance, this merely looks like an order of sequence, Plutarch reads it as an order of merit: the kings begin and are therefore the most powerful and important, together with the *gerousia*, and the *dêmos* comes only after these two. Moreover, the response of the people must be 'straight'. Plutarch clearly sets the σκολιάν of the Rider against the εὐθείαις ῥήτραις of Tyrtaeus, and interprets the latter as voicing the same idea as the Rider.³⁵ The link between Tyrtaeus' 'straight' and the Rider's 'crooked' is clear and seems proof for Plutarch's argument. But on closer inspection it is evidence only for the first part of the Rider. For its second part ('the kings and elders are to be setters-aside') Plutarch cannot point to any line or word in Tyrtaeus. There is no mention of ἀφίστασθαι καὶ διαλύειν in the text of the poem. It may be deduced from the poem if we elaborate Plutarch's interpretation: the *gerousia* is more powerful and can, therefore, dissolve the meeting. But the measure is not fully proven.³⁶ The kings could have simply 'overruled' the *dêmos* and ignored its voice, instead of dissolving it.

Plutarch seems to draw upon the notion that an oracle needs explanation. That explanation may not tie in directly with the uttered words, but must be deduced: like all oracles, this one too is riddling. So when Plutarch describes a situation in which 'the kings *persuade* the people that Apollo ordered an addition' to the Great Rhetra, the addition itself does not necessarily have to be in the oracle: the idea of the oracle, however, must fit with the solution given. Moreover, as we have seen, the Rider is not portrayed as a reversal of the status quo: it is a re-statement of the law of Lycurgus, putting the *dêmos*, which deemed itself too powerful, in its place. The oracle of Tyrtaeus' poem can confirm the law of Lycurgus (which was after all an oracle itself) and contain evidence for the addition by the two kings at the same time.

3   Diodorus Siculus: Traces of *World History*

The second version of Tyrtaeus fragment 4 can be found in book 7 of Diodorus of Sicily's *World History*. Of Diodorus Siculus' *Bibliothêkê*, or *World History*, only books 1 to 5 and 11 to 20 survive completely. Indirect transmission secured

---

34   Van Wees (1999) 9–10 translates with 'to straight *rhetrai*'; for refutation of this possibility, see Nafissi (2010) 97n38.

35   Van Wees (1999) 10–11. On the widely debated addition σκολιόν to line 8 of Tyrt. fr. 4, based on this interpretation, see the clear refutation by van Wees loc. cit.; van Wees (2002) 97; Nafissi (2010) 100.

36   Compare Wade-Gery (1944) 1: 'The burden has to be borne by the one word εὐθείαις.'

some fragments of Diodorus' other books, including book 7.[37] The most important source for Diodorus' fragments is the *Excerpta Constantiniana*, an extensive collection of excerpts made in the 9th century at the Byzantine court. It contains quotations from the works of several Greek historians, sorted into thematic volumes. Of the fifty-three thematic volumes attested, only four are still extant. Tyrtaeus' fragment survives in the book *Sententiae*, which is preserved in only one manuscript copy.[38] This manuscript was taken apart in the fourteenth century and used as a palimpsest; as a result, the first quire of every author is missing, and the order of the remainder had to be reconstructed. The fact that it is a palimpsest also makes it difficult to read, and nineteenth-century scholars who subjected the parchment to chemicals have not improved its condition.[39]

This story reveals an important factor in the survival of lyric texts, namely "chance". It also demonstrates that the lines are an excerpt, a quotation of a quotation. Much of the reasoning of Diodorus Siculus on this fragment is lost. It is not so much a question of which part of the preserved text is from Diodorus; comparisons with extant parts of Diodorus' work show that the excerptors copied out his text quite precisely, only supplying necessary information on the speaker or situation at the beginning of some excerpts.[40] The difficulty lies in placing the fragments from different sources in the right order, providing them with a suitable context, and filling in the gaps between the excerpts.[41] A New Philological approach advocates that one considers a text in its *current context*, in whatever condition it may be. Because its current context is an excerpt collection, I will focus on the position of the fragment within this collection, and only reconstruct Diodorus' interpretation where I believe it is possible.[42]

Tyrtaeus' fragment is classified in the category *Sententiae*. This is, admittedly, rather vague, and an examination of the whole book shows that the excerptors

---

37   Detailed discussion of all sources can be found in the general introduction to the Budé edition (Chamoux et al. [1993] cxxiii–clii) and in the Budé edition of book 6–10 (Cohen-Skalli [2012] xxv–lxiv). The book numbers of Diodorus Siculus are reconstructed on the basis of cross-references in the *Bibliothêkê*.
38   Vat.Gr.73; described in Mercati and Franchi de' Cavalieri (1923) 67–78.
39   For a history of this manuscript and its discovery, see Boissevain (1906) v–xxiii.
40   For a detailed description of the working method, see Cohen-Skalli (2012) xxxi–xxxvi. For the sake of clarity, I will refer to both Boissevain's edition of the *Excerpta*, and to Cohen-Skalli's edition of Diodorus Siculus. The latter contains some changes to the numbering of the fragments in the editions of Vogel (1888–1906) and Oldfather (1939).
41   See again Cohen-Skalli (2012) xiv, lxi–lxxiv.
42   Diodorus has been analysed and viewed mainly as a sourcebook for lost works of historiographers. Diodorus, however, did have a voice of his own, especially in moral notions, as has recently been demonstrated by Sacks (1990, 1994) and Sulimani (2011). In this chapter

classified quite diverse entries under this heading. Their common denominator is the focus on kings or famous people, often in political situations and wars. The excerptors mainly included oracles received by such persons or wise sayings they uttered in the *Sententiae*, but poets, such as Alcaeus, Solon, and Callimachus get quoted or mentioned too, as is the philosopher Pythagoras.[43] Tyrtaeus' poem is found within a series of entries devoted to the Spartan lawgiver Lycurgus.

The *Excerpta de Sententiis* of Diodorus open with four entries devoted to the Spartan lawgiver Lycurgus. Perhaps there were more: at least two preceding quires are missing, and the first entry starts mid-sentence. Our extant text opens with the oracle on Lycurgus' divine status, which Herodotus quotes too: here, however, it is preserved in a different form with two added verses, in which the Pythia promises to give Lycurgus his 'Eunomia'.[44] The second oracle to Lycurgus speaks about two paths that can be taken in life, followed by an explanation of its meaning.[45] Two more oracles round off the section on Lycurgus; both follow here.[46] As they are transmitted in a very bad state with multiple writing mistakes and impossible constructions, I have chosen to reproduce the edition by Boissevain: corrections are printed in bold type, with the manuscript reading in the notes.

v. Ὅτι ὁ αὐτὸς Λυκοῦργος ἤνεγκε χρησμὸν ἐκ Δελφῶν περὶ τῆς φιλαργυρίας τὸν ἐν παροιμίας μέρει μνημονευόμενον,
    ἁ φιλοχρηματία Σπάρταν ἕλοι, ἄλλο δὲ οὐδέν.

vi. [Ἡ Πυθία ἔχρησε τῷ Λυκούργῳ περὶ τῶν πολιτικῶν οὕτως][47]
    ὧδε[48] γὰρ ἀργυρότοξος ἄναξ ἑκάεργος Ἀπόλλων

I try to distinguish between excerptor and Diodorus, and I will not pay attention to Diodorus' source material, but most scholars have assumed that Diodorus based himself on Ephorus for this part of his *Bibliothêkê*.

43 *Exc. Sent.* 48 = Diod. 9.20 (Alcaeus); *Exc. Sent.* 36–37, 53–57 = Diod. 9.4–5, 31–32, 37–39 (Solon), *Exc. Sent.*77 = Diod. 10.11 (Callimachus); *Exc. Sent.* 75–87 = Diod. 10.9–16, 18–19, 21–24 (Pythagoras).

44 *Exc. Sent.* 1 = Diod. 7.10B. Hdt 1.65. Diodorus' form is presumably also preserved in Eus. *Praep. Evang.* 5.27.8 but with the last line missing. See Parke and Wormell (1956) 14 (no. 29), 89 (no. 216); Fontenrose (1978) 115–116.

45 *Exc. Sent.*2 = Diod. 7.11. Parke and Wormell (1956) 90 (no. 218), also preserved in Eus. *Praep. Evang.* 5.28.7.

46 One more excerpt on the oracles is preserved in another tome, *De virtutibus et vitiis* 28. It is now commonly printed in Diodorus' editions as the introductory formula to the first oracle (Diod. 7.10A). See also Cohen-Skalli (2012) 65n94.

47 Line is added in the margin of the manuscript.

48 ὧδε Hermann | δε/δὴ MS.

χρυσοκόμης ἔχρη πίονος ἐξ ἀδύτου,
ἄρχειν μὲν βουλῇ θεοτιμήτους βασιλῆας,
οἷσι μέλει Σπάρτης ἱμερόεσσα⁴⁹ πόλις,
5 πρεσβυγενεῖς τε⁵⁰ γέροντας, ἔπειτα δὲ δημότας ἄνδρας,
εὐθείαις ῥήτραις⁵¹ ἀνταπαμειβομένους
μυθεῖσθαί τε τὰ καλὰ καὶ ἔρδειν πάντα δίκαια,
†μηδέτι ἐπιβουλεύειν⁵² τῇδε πόλει†
δήμου τε πλήθει νίκην καὶ κάρτος ἕπεσθαι·
10 Φοῖβος γὰρ περὶ τῶν ὧδ' ἀνέφηνε πόλει.

v. And the same Lycurgus brought an oracle from Delphi concerning love
   of money and its memory is preserved in the form of a proverb:
   Love of money will destroy Sparta, and nothing else.
vi. [The Pythia gave the following oracle to Lycurgus on political matters].
   For thus spoke Apollo of the silver bow and golden hair
   The lord who works from afar, from his rich shrine:
   Counsel is to begin with the divinely honoured kings
   who have the lovely city of Sparta in their care
5 and with the ancient elderly men. Then the men of the people
   responding in turn with straight enactments
   must say what is noble and do all that is just
   and do not plot against this city (?)
   and victory and power attend the multitude of the people.
10 For thus Phoebus declared to the city in these matters.

In this version, the quotation of Tyrtaeus has become an oracle of the Pythia, given to Lycurgus. Tyrtaeus' name is not mentioned and the text has been seen as non-Tyrtaean by the editors Gentili and Prato and other exegetes of these lines, most notably Wade-Gery and Nafissi.⁵³ The introductory note 'the Pythia gave the following oracle to Lycurgus' is a marginal note: it was written next to the lines of the poem, instead of above them.⁵⁴ Although we cannot be sure,

---

49 ἰχερόεσσα MS. Corr. from Plutarch.
50 δὲ MS. Corr. from Plutarch.
51 εὐθείην ῥήτρας MS. Corr. from Plutarch.
52 μηδέ τι ἐπιβουλεύειν MS. Corr. by Bach to μηδέ τι βουλεύειν τῇδε πόλει ⟨σκολιόν⟩, but see n. 35 above.
53 Prato (1968) 63–70; Wade-Gery (1944) 3–4; Nafissi (2010) 99.
54 Boissevain ad loc. In the manuscript the note occupies the margin of lines 23–27: verse lines are written as normal prose: the poem occupies four lines in the manuscript and starts on a new line.

the marginal note does not seem to contain Diodorus' *ipsissima verba*, when we compare it to the introductory notes of the other oracles in the *Excerpta de Sententiis*. First, the introduction is much shorter than that of most other oracles, not specifying more than the receiver and the subject. Second, the syntax of the sentence is different from that of introductions to other oracles. This is the only case in which the Pythia is placed as subject at the beginning of the sentence.[55] Third, the marginal note refers to the whole section (οὕτως), but in fact only applies to lines 3–9 of the poem. Phoebus Apollo does figure in other oracular texts from the *Excerpta*, but the verbs are then always in present or future tense, and contain such phrases as 'Phoebus Apollo sends you', or 'Apollo will lead you'.[56] Here, by contrast, both opening and closing verbs of the poem are put in the past tense, which makes clear that they are introductory words to the oracle and not part of the oracle itself. Fourth, the metre excludes the poem from being a Pythian oracle: all other oracles given in the Diodorean excerpts are either in hexameters or paraphrased in prose.[57] Diodorus was a skilled historiographer and we should not doubt his ability to respect the differences between hexameters and elegiacs. Diodorus was not unfamiliar with elegiacs, nor with Tyrtaeus: he quotes several elegiacs of Solon and preserves an anecdote about Tyrtaeus' Athenian origin.[58] Fifth, the *Excerpta* do preserve the introduction to the previous 'oracle' to Lycurgus, on greed. This oracle, however, is not said to be an oracle but a reflection of the original oracle, preserved in a proverb (τὸν ἐν παροιμίας μέρει μνημονευόμενον). We could posit a similar construction for the introduction of this poem. In my view, then, we should not take the introductory line as a reflection of Diodorus' interpretation of Tyrtaeus' poem.

Diodorus' interpretation is completely missing, and therefore I would like to compare Tyrtaeus' poem to the other Lycurgan oracles in the *Excerpta* to see whether we can distinguish Diodorus' and the excerptor's interests. As one may expect from the *Sententiae*'s themes set out above, all Lycurgan oracles and explanations focus on the good ruler and the right order, which will eventually lead to divine favour. For instance, in the first oracle, the stress is on the fact that because of Lycurgus' divine favour, he received all his laws directly from

---

55 The more usual order is *the receiver—question/problem—and she said—oracle*. Closest in formulation (but with the question put before the Pythia) is *Exc. Sent.* 38 = Diod. 9.6.
56 *Exc. Sent.* 15, 19, 32 = Diod. 8.15, 8.22, 8.40.
57 The oracle-poem as preserved in the manuscripts has several metrical corruptions and writing mistakes, but these are probably later than Diodorus Siculus. Other unmetrical or incomplete oracles e.g. *Exc. Sent.* 19, 24, 42 = Diod. 8.22, 8.29, 9.10.
58 Solon: Diod. 9.1–8, 12, 28, 31–32, 38; Tyrtaeus: *Exc. Sent.* 30–31 = Diod. 8.38–39.

Delphi. After the 'oracle' of Tyrtaeus, one more piece of moralizing instruction is quoted: 'that those who do not observe piety (εὐσέβεια) toward the gods do not observe justice (δίκαια) towards men'.[59] This point is adduced more often in Diodorus' work and cannot be linked with certainty to the Lycurgan passages.[60] But if we explain 'being εὐσεβής' as obeying Lycurgus' oracles, it is a clear indication that justice and good order will only prevail as long as Lycurgus' oracles are followed. This thought is strengthened by an excerpt from *De virtutibus et vitiis*, another tome of the *Excerpta Constantiniana*. In this passage, Diodorus reflects on the decline of Sparta, brought about by 'relaxing the strains of the laws'.[61] If we compare these thoughts, the excerptor seems to focus clearly on obedience and authority. The Tyrtaean lines fit this theme well, especially lines 7 to 9 ('the people ... must say what is noble and do all that is just ... [then] victory and power will attend the multitude'), and the stress on obeying the kings rather than acting for oneself, were probably the main attraction for the excerptor.

But is the attraction of the excerptor a good indication for Diodorus' own reasoning on the passage of Tyrtaeus? Diodorus was probably also interested in the constitution of Sparta itself, and Lycurgus' famous measures that pervaded all levels of Spartan society. Many interpreters have assumed that he cited and explained the oracle in Tyrtaeus' poem as evidence for Lycurgus' political measures. These scholars have also noted that the first two lines in this version, which are radically different from those preserved in Plutarch, fit the notion that the oracle was given to one person rather than two.[62] The rest of the poem, which mentions all political parties in Sparta (the kings, *gerousia*, and the people), could stand for the oracle through which Lycurgus gave power to the people. From the context as preserved, however, it is hard to tell how Diodorus exactly used or interpreted the poem.

From comparative evidence of the books that have been transmitted completely, it appears that Diodorus was interested both in history and moral edification through law texts, and that he quoted from poetry as evidence for the nature of these laws. This can be seen, for example, in his account of the lawgiver Charondas in book 12.[63] The lawgiver Charondas is part of the history of Sicily, where the Thurians and the Sybarites established a new city, Thurium.

---

59 *Exc. Sent.* 5 = Diod. 7.14.
60 E.g. *Exc. Sent.* 17–18 = Diod. 8.19–20. Cohen-Skalli (2012) 68n120.
61 *Exc. Virt. et Vit.* 29 = Diod. 7.15.
62 Andrewes (1938) 99; Nafissi (2010) 101.
63 This section on Sicily may have been based on different source material than the section on Sparta. Sulimani (2011) 138–146 has shown that the structural comments in Charondas' account are very similar to those used in other books of the *Bibliothêkê* and this suggests some reworking and selection by Diodorus himself.

After relating the military and societal struggles that came with this foundation (12.10–11), Diodorus writes that the lawgiver Charondas 'selected the most powerful laws' from the other cities, but also invented some of his own, and that it is 'not incongruous to commemorate these in order to improve our readers'.[64] In the following enumeration of the laws of Charondas (12.12–13), Diodorus selects some laws that are unique to Charondas' law code, and then provides evidence 'from poets who have borne witness (μεμαρτυρήκασι) to both of the aforementioned'.[65] He proceeds to quote a couple of dramatic passages, one from Euripides and two from New Comedy.[66] Of these dramatic passages, however, only fr. 148 *PCG* actually pertains to the laws by Charondas: it explicitly mentions his name at the beginning and paraphrases the law that forbids second marriages. The other two passages merely express gnomic sentiments that are *similar to* the laws of Charondas, but do not prove that Charondas instituted those laws.[67]

In my view, it is possible that Diodorus used the poetic fragment of Tyrtaeus in a similar way. Diodorus, in that case, presented information on Lycurgus' laws and oracles in prose, and then adduced the Tyrtaean poem as supporting evidence to show that the poets reflected the measures of Lycurgus, or to show simply that the deeds of Lycurgus were commemorated in poetry. The poets' function as μάρτυς is well known in historiographical treatises, and the poet's words then do not have to be interpreted in detail: the fact that a poet mentions similar aspects can be enough to establish a link.[68]

The moral aspect, which appears to be the main interest of the excerptor, can also be seen in the explanations by Diodorus: the laws of Charondas are men-

---

64 οὗτος δὲ ἐπισκεψάμενος τὰς ἁπάντων νομοθεσίας ἐξελέξατο τὰ κράτιστα καὶ κατέταξεν εἰς τοὺς νόμους· πολλὰ δὲ καὶ ἴδια ἐπινοησάμενος ἐξεῦρε, περὶ ὧν οὐκ ἀνοίκειόν ἐστιν ἐπιμνησθῆναι πρὸς διόρθωσιν τῶν ἀναγινωσκόντων (Diod. 12.11.4). See Sulimani (2011) 133–134 for the importance of readers and other "reader-comments" in Diodorus.

65 ἀμφότερα δὲ τὰ προειρημένα πολλοὶ τῶν ποιητῶν δι' ἐμμέτρου ποιήματος μεμαρτυρήκασι (Diod. 12.14.1).

66 Diodorus quotes only one poem with a name: the comic writer Philemon (fr. 51 *PCG*). The other passages are Eur.fr.812.7–9 *TrGF* (some quote it as Menander fr. 414), and anon.fr. 148 *PCG*.

67 In the case of the Philemon fragment (fr. 51 *PCG*), the comic fragment refers to seafaring rather than marriage: Diodorus himself replaces 'πέπλευκε' with 'γεγάμηκε' in his explanation. The fragment comes from the play *Nothos* (homecoming), and may simply warn for the sea rather than talk about remarriage.

68 Arist. *Rh.* 1375b25–33 is the *locus classicus* for using a poet as witness. A good indication of the use of poetry for all kinds of evidence is Strabo's *Geography*, on which see the work of Kim (2007, 2010) with bibliography. For a recent study organised by author, see Koning (2010) on Hesiod.

tioned 'for the benefit of the readers', and one of the other Lycurgan oracles preserved in Diodorus has been called 'an elegant piece of moralizing'.[69] It seems, then, that the excerptor had a close interest in morality, and chose the best sample of moralistic oracles and laws for his book on *Sententiae*. The excerptor indeed started to copy both chapters with the laws of Charondas completely, right after Diodorus' comment on the educational benefits for his readers, but did not preserve the account on the war that preceded these measures.[70] When reconstructing the meaning that Diodorus gave to the lines of Tyrtaeus, it is necessary to take into account that much of the historiographical background is lost. I have argued that Diodorus perhaps quoted the poetry as an appendix to an exposition on Lycurgus' measures, much in the same way as the laws of Charondas are reflected in some poetic quotations. The poetry of Tyrtaeus (if he named the poet at all), should then reflect basic outlines of Lycurgus' policies, and since it quotes an oracle, and includes both kings, *gerousia* and *dêmos*, it would have suited any interpretation of the political measures by Lycurgus. On the basis of the current evidence, it is impossible to know how exactly the poem and Lycurgus' measures are related in Diodorus' account.

4 A Comparison

The differences between Diodorus Siculus and Plutarch are great, especially in the version of the poem of Tyrtaeus that they quote. In past scholarly literature, most scholars have focussed on the differences in the length of the poem, and in the opening lines: was it Lycurgus or two of his successors who received the oracle? But if we compare the aim and method of interpretation that Plutarch and Diodorus seem to follow, it becomes noticeable that they use the poems for the same purpose. Both use poetry to clarify measures taken in the politics of Sparta, and both connect the poetry to the life of Lycurgus. Moreover, both interpretations stress that the people should be obedient to their superiors.

Although Plutarch attributes the oracle to two kings who lived long after Lycurgus, his quotation is still aimed at explaining the Spartan political system that Lycurgus instated, but later kings altered. As we have seen, the addition

---

69 *Exc. Sent.* 2 = Diod. 7.11. Parke and Wormell (1956) 87. See, for further inquiry on Diodorus' moralism Sacks (1990) 23–55.

70 *Exc. Sent.* 150–152 = Diod. 12.12–13.2. The manuscript of the *Excerpta* breaks off in the middle of paragraph 13.2 (one quire is missing which contained the rest of books 13 and 14), so we cannot establish whether the excerptor also preserved the poetic examples following the prose text of the laws.

to the Great Rhetra was merely a re-statement of Lycurgus' law rather than a reform of it, and Plutarch does quote the poem in the *Life of Lycurgus*, not in a general account on Spartan history. It seems he had to make sense of conflicting accounts in which, according to some, Lycurgus was responsible for the whole Spartan political system and, according to others, later rulers still made modifications and alterations. His solution is to present these alterations as *similar to* the aims of Lycurgus rather than completely different from them.[71] The poem of Tyrtaeus is evidence for an oracle given to two kings, on the basis of which they could reinstate Lycurgus' original policy. In the case of Diodorus, it is difficult to assess how exactly he used the poem. As I have argued, it is unlikely that Diodorus interpreted the oracle preserved in Tyrtaeus as *the exact* oracle given to Lycurgus. It is more probable that he used it as supportive evidence, a μάρτυς for a prose description of Lycurgus' actual measures. In the context of the *Excerpta de Sententiis*, the oracle becomes an example of good government, in which the people obey the kings, and the result is freedom and peace for the city.

Both Plutarch and Diodorus used their own version of the poem. It is likely that neither of them read a full edition of Tyrtaeus' *Eunomia*, but rather read the poem in other historical sources, and made assumptions on the basis of the text before them. They also made interpretive leaps on matters left unclear by the poet, for instance by providing a referent to an unexpressed subject. This can most clearly be seen in Plutarch's argument: he connects the plural verbs in the poem to the names of two kings, but for this assumption no other evidence from antiquity survives. The interpretation of Diodorus connected the poem probably to Lycurgus' own measure, and according to many, this chimes well with the absence of the plural verb.[72] But I believe it is too easy to think that Plutarch could have used only his version of Tyrtaeus' poem and not Diodorus' version, or vice versa. Plutarch's interpretation would have worked just as well with the poem of Diodorus, which also stresses the subordination of the *dêmos* to the kings, the linchpin of Plutarch's argument. And Diodorus could have used Plutarch's version, and simply give a different explanation to the plural subject of the first two lines, or pay no attention to the plural at all. In the case of Charondas' laws, the poems are also rather loosely connected to the laws of Charondas himself, and Diodorus does little to justify his claim that the poets refer to Charondas' laws. Precisely because the short quotations remain vague about basic points (who? where? when?), they can suit several interpretations.

---

71   See also Van Wees (1999) 20–21.
72   e.g. Andrewes (1938) 99; Nafissi (2010) 101.

From Andrewes onwards, scholars have tried to reconstruct the source material of Diodorus and Plutarch, focusing on the question of who was the first to link the oracle in Tyrtaeus to Lycurgus. Most have pointed to a pamphlet by the Spartan king Pausanias as its ultimate source. He was expelled from Sparta and supposedly wrote a pamphlet about Lycurgus, which contained some of the oracles on his laws.[73] All we know for sure is that Ephorus knew about the pamphlet and used its oracles in his account on Spartan history.[74] Since Diodorus probably used Ephorus as his main source, Nafissi assumes that the pamphlet also contained the version of Tyrtaeus' poem as preserved in Diodorus.[75] Van Wees thinks that the original pamphlet by Pausanias might have contained more portions of the *Eunomia* of Tyrtaeus than just the part cited by Diodorus,[76] but no source from antiquity, not even that of Pausanias, can be shown to have engaged with both versions *at the same time*. Even if there was a dispute about the addressee of the oracle, neither writer took pains to find its origin in the different versions of the poem by Tyrtaeus. Plutarch and Diodorus make interpretations on the basis of the poem before them, and do not discuss the different versions or interpretive traditions, and none of the other participants in the discussion (Hellanicus, Xenophon, Aristotle, Plato, or Ephorus) seems to do so, as far as we can tell from the extant evidence.

So, although textual variants may seem important to us today, they may not have been so important to ancient historiographers. They based their interpretations on the texts they had before them, and, at least in the case of Plutarch, we can demonstrate that his interpretation was rather loosely connected to the actual words of the poem—and there is no reason to suppose otherwise for Diodorus or other historiographers. A reconstruction of the poem in which both versions are combined may bring us closer to the text as Tyrtaeus composed it in the archaic period, and render service to those who research Tyrtaeus' poetry for its language, martial imagery, or connection to Homeric battle scenes. But it may just as likely deceive the reader who presumes that this was *the* text of Tyrtaeus as it was read throughout antiquity, for at least Plutarch and Diodorus had no problem with quoting different versions. By looking at the poet's versions as separate entities, we may get a better sense of how Tyrtaeus' poetry was continuously read and re-interpreted in antiquity. For both

---

73 Strabo 8.5.5. The passage is corrupt due to a damaged manuscript, which has led to much dispute about its title ('about' or 'against' Lycurgus) and contents; see Ducat (2006) 42–44.
74 Ephorus *BNJ* 70 fr. 118, with additional information on Sparta's constitution in frr. 148–149.
75 Nafissi (2010) 101.
76 Van Wees (1999) 16. On pp. 14–22 he reconstructs the complete fourth-century debate.

authors, the poem of Tyrtaeus is not *a version of* a poem, but a poem. For both authors, moreover, the poem of Tyrtaeus is not poetry, but history.

References

Andrewes, A. 1938. Eunomia. *CQ* 32.2: 89–102.
Bergk, T., ed. 1882. *Poetae Lyrici Graeci. Pars II Poetae Elegiaci et Iambographi.* 4th edn. Leipzig.
Boissevain, U.P., ed. 1906. *Excerpta Historica iussu imp. Constantini Porphyrogeniti confecta Vol. IV. Excerpta de Sententiis.* Berlin.
Cartledge, P. 2001. *Spartan Reflections.* London.
Chamoux, F., Bertrac, P. and Vernière, Y., eds. 1993. *Diodore de Sicile Bibliotheque Historique. Livre I.* Paris.
Cohen-Skalli, A., ed. 2012. *Diodore de Sicile Bibliotheque Historique. Fragments Tome 1: Livres VI–X.* Paris.
Diehl, E. ed. 1922. *Anthologia Lyrica Graeca. Vol. I fasc. 1: Poetae Elegiaci.* 2nd edition. Leipzig.
Ducat, J. 2006. *Spartan Education: Youth and Society in the Classical Period.* Swansea.
Fontenrose, J. 1978. *The Delphic Oracle. Its Responses and Operations, with a Catalogue of Responses.* Berkeley.
Gentili, B. and Prato, C., eds. 1988–2002. *Poetarum elegiacorum Testimonia et Fragmenta.* 2nd edn. Leipzig.
Gerber, D.E., ed. 1999. *Greek Elegiac Poetry*, Cambridge MA.
Kim, L. 2007. The Portrait of Homer in Strabo's *Geography*. *CPh* 102.4: 363–388.
Kim, L. 2010. *Homer between History and Fiction in Imperial Greek Literature.* Cambridge.
Koier, E. 2013. *Interpreting Particles in Dead and Living Languages: A Construction Grammar Approach to the Semantics of Dutch* ergens *and Ancient Greek* pou. LOT 321. Utrecht. [PhD Dissertation].
Koning, H.H.H. 2010. *Hesiod, the Other Poet: Ancient Reception of a Cultural Icon.* Leiden and Boston.
Link, S. 2000. *Untersuchungen zur spartanischen Staatsbildung im 7. und 6. Jahrhundert v. Chr. Pharos: Bd. 13.* Katharinen.
Link, S. 2003. Eunomie im Schoß der Rhetra? Zum Verhältnis von Tyrt. frgm. 14W (*sic*) und Plut. Lyk. 6,2 und 8. *Göttinger Forum für Altertumswissenschaft* 6: 141–150.
Luther, A. 2004. *Könige und Ephoren. Untersuchungen zur Spartanischen Verfassungsgeschichte.* Frankfurt.
Martindale, C. 1993. *Redeeming the Text: Latin Poetry and the Hermeneutics of Reception.* Cambridge.

Manfredini, M. and Piccirilli, L., eds. 1980. *Le vite di Licurgo e di Numa / Plutarco*. Milan.

Meier, M. 1998. *Aristokraten und Damoden: Untersuchungen zur inneren Entwicklung Spartas im 7. Jahrhundert v. Chr. und zur politischen Funktion der Dichtung des Tyrtaios*. Stuttgart.

Meier, M. 2002. Tyrtaios fr. 1^B G/P bzw. fr. 14 G/P (= fr. 4W) und die große Rhetra—kein Zusammenhang? *Göttinger Forum für Altertumswissenschaft* 5: 65–87.

Mercati, I. and Franchi de' Cavalieri, P. 1923. *Codices Vaticani Graeci Tomus I: 1–329*. Rome.

Nafissi, M. 2010. The Great *Rhetra* (Plut. *Lyc.* 6): A Retrospective and Intentional Construct? In *Intentional History: Spinning Time in Ancient Greece*, ed. L. Foxhall, H.J. Gehrke, and N. Luraghi, 89–119. Stuttgart

Ogden, D. 1994. Crooked Speech: The Genesis of the Spartan Rhetra. *JHS* 114: 85–102.

Oldfather, C.H. ed. 1939. *Diodorus of Sicily III: Books IV (continued)–VIII*. Cambridge MA.

Parke, H.W. and Wormell, D.E.W. 1956. *The Delphic Oracle. I: The History. II: The Oracular Responses*. 2nd edn. Oxford.

Pelling, C.B.R. 2002. *Plutarch and History: Eighteen Studies*. Swansea.

Prato, C., ed. 1968. *Tyrtaeus*. Rome.

Sacks, K.S. 1990. *Diodorus Siculus and the First Century*. Princeton.

Sacks, K.S. 1994. Diodorus and his Sources: Conformity and Creativity. In *Greek Historiography*, ed. S.J. Hornblower, 213–232. Oxford.

Sulimani, I. 2011. *Diodorus' Mythistory and the Pagan Mission: Historiography and Culture-heroes in the First Pentad of the* Bibliotheke. Leiden.

Tigerstedt, E.N. 1965. *The Legend of Sparta in Classical Antiquity. Vol. I*. Stockholm.

Van Wees, H. 1999. Nothing to do with the Great Rhetra. In *Sparta: New Perspectives*, ed. S. Hodkinson and A. Powell, 1–41. London.

Van Wees, H. 2002. Gute Ordnung ohne Große Rhetra. Noch einmal zur Tyrtaios' Eunomia. *Göttinger Forum für Altertumswissenschaft* 5: 89–103.

Vogel, F. ed. 1888–1906. *Diodori Bibliotheca historica. Post I. Bekker et L. Dindorf recognovit Fr. Vogel*. Leipzig.

Wade-Gery, H.T. 1943–1944. The Spartan Rhetra in Plutarch Lycurgus VI, A: Plutarch's Text, B: The Eynomia of Tyrtaios, C: What is the Rhetra? *CQ* 37.1–2: 62–72; *CQ* 38.1–2: 1–9; *CQ* 38.4: 115–126.

West, M.L. 1974. *Studies in Greek Elegy and Iambus*. Berlin.

West, M.L., ed. 1989–1992. *Iambi et elegi Graeci ante Alexandrum cantati*. 2nd edn. Oxford.

Wilamowitz-Moellendorff, U. von. 1900. *Die Textgeschichte der griechischen Lyriker*. Berlin.

Ziegler, K. ed. 1973. *Plutarchi Vitae Parallelae Vol. III Fasc 2*. Leipzig.

PART 2

Canons

∴

CHAPTER 4

On the Shaping of the Lyric Canon in Athens

Gregory Nagy

1   Introduction

This chapter is about the Lyric Canon as studied by Ulrich von Wilamowitz-Moellendorff in his *Textgeschichte der griechischen Lyriker* (1900). The nine poets of this canon were Alcman, Stesichorus, Ibycus, Sappho, Alcaeus, Anacreon, Simonides, Pindar, and Bacchylides, as we read in *Greek Anthology* 9.184 and 9.571;[1] also in the Scholia for Dionysius Thrax (*Grammatici Graeci* 1.3 ed. Hilgard 21 lines 17–19) and in Life of Pindar texts (ed. Drachmann 11). I will hereafter refer to the canonical grouping of these poets simply as the Lyric Nine, paraphrasing the expression *ennea lurikoi* 'nine lyric poets' as used in the Life of Pindar texts (Drachmann 10–11).

But now the question is, how did such a canon take shape? Or, to say it in a more technical way, how do we trace the canon-formation here? In searching for an answer, we need to keep in mind the fact that the earliest historical context for such a canon can be located in Athens and dated to the classical period starting around the middle of the fifth century BCE. This fact needs to be contrasted with two other facts: (1) curiously, the poets known as the Lyric Nine were all non-Athenian, and (2) even more curiously, they were all non-classical, dating back to the so-called archaic period that ended around the middle of the fifth century BCE.

The actual dates of the Lyric Nine extend from around 450 BCE as far back as 650 BCE or so. For classical Athens, then, the "classics" of their Lyric Canon were non-classical because they were pre-classical. And when I say "classics", I have in mind songs that were not only well known but also supposedly well loved, as we see from some telling references in sources stemming from classical Athens, especially in comedies.[2]

On the basis of such evidence, then, for an Athenian reception of the Lyric Nine, the canon-formation of lyric can be explained by arguing that it originated in contexts where lyric songs were reperformed for and by Athenian elites

---

1 Wilamowitz (1900) 5–6.
2 Wilamowitz (1900) 12–14. On references to lyric poets in Aristophanic comedy, see Calame's contribution to this volume.

participating in private symposia.³ To cite just one example of such contexts, I quote the wording of Aristophanes F 235 KA: ᾆσον δή μοι σκόλιόν τι λαβὼν Ἀλκαίου κἈνακρέοντος (sing me some drinking-song [*skolion*], taking it from Alcaeus or Anacreon).

But this explanation, which concentrates on the idea of reperformances at private symposia in Athens, needs to be broadened. Another fact to consider, I argue, is that the songs of the Lyric Nine were also reperformed at public concerts organized by the Athenian State for the seasonally recurring occasion of a grand civic festival known as the Panathenaia. I propose that these public concerts, known as *mousikoi agōnes* (competitions in song), were foundational for the creation of the Lyric Canon.⁴

I add here in passing that the book of Wilamowitz on the Lyric Canon nowhere even mentions the Panathenaia, except for a fleeting reference to the tradition of the Panathenaic procession as it survived in the fifth century BCE, where he expresses the opinion that such a tradition was no longer a venue for performing songs composed by the likes of Pindar or Isyllos.⁵

2   Citharodes, Aulodes, and Rhapsodes

At the seasonally recurring festival of the Panathenaia, there were separate competitions of *rhapsōidoi* (rhapsodes), of *kitharōidoi* (citharodes = *kitharā*-singers), of *aulōidoi* (aulodes = *aulos*-singers), of *kitharistai* (citharists = *kitharā*-players), and of *aulētai* (auletes = *aulos*-players), as we learn from an Athenian inscription, *IG* II² 2311, dated at around 380 BCE, which records Panathenaic prizes.⁶ We learn about these categories of competition also from Plato's *Laws* (6.764d–e), where mention is made of rhapsodes, citharodes, and auletes, and where the wording makes it clear that the point of reference is the Panathenaia. At this festival, the competing rhapsodes were performing epic while the competing citharodes and aulodes were performing lyric. From here on, I concentrate on the citharodes and the aulodes, keeping in mind the rhapsodes as a point of comparison.

Whereas the Lyric Canon was purely a textual tradition for Wilamowitz, for me such a Lyric Canon was also a performative tradition, both citharodic and

---

3   See the relevant remarks in Wilamowitz (1900) 13, 18.
4   For background on the *mousikoi agōnes* at the Panathenaia, see Kotsidu (1991).
5   Wilamowitz (1900) 11.
6   The portion of the inscription that deals with rhapsodes is lost, but it is generally accepted that rhapsodic competitions were mentioned in this missing portion; see Shear (2001) 367.

aulodic, stemming from the repertoire of citharodic and aulodic competitions of the *mousikoi agōnes* held at the festival of the Panathenaia in Athens. And, in terms of my overall argumentation, there existed separate categories of competition in performing citharodically and aulodically.

3   A Transition from Athens to Alexandria

For the moment, let us take as a given my argument that the *mousikoi agōnes* (competitions in song) at the Panathenaia in the classical period involved performances of songs from the Lyric Canon in separate competitions among citharodes and among aulodes. This argument, as we will now see, can help us make more sense of what happened to the Lyric Nine in the Hellenistic period. Our starting point is the well-known fact that the texts of these nine poets were preserved and edited by learned experts at the Library of Alexandria, founded in the late fourth century BCE, near the beginning of the Hellenistic period.[7] It is thanks to these Alexandrian experts that we even know about the term *ennea lurikoi*, or Lyric Nine, as preserved in Life of Pindar texts (ed. Drachmann 10–11). So, given this fact, the question is: how will my argumentation account for the transition of the Lyric Canon from classical Athens to Hellenistic Alexandria?

I start with the cumulative testimony of Aristotle and his Peripatetic followers Dicaearchus and Chamaeleon in the fourth and early third centuries BCE. This testimony shows that the Peripatetics were already working on texts of poets belonging to the Lyric Nine, such as Sappho and Anacreon.[8]

In general, it can be said that the work of researchers in Athens during the fourth and the early third centuries BCE extended into the work of the Alexandrians on the "classic" texts of the Nine. And such research in Athens involved the texts of other "classics" as well: an important example is the editorial work of the Peripatetics on the texts of two epics: the Homeric *Iliad* and *Odyssey*.[9] Another similarly important example in the late fourth century was the initiative taken by the statesman Lycurgus in actually legislating the massive project of producing new editions, to be stored and consulted in the state archives, of the tragedies composed by the canonical triad of Aeschylus, Sophocles, and Euripides—only those three (['Plutarch'] *Lives of the Ten Orators* 841f).[10]

---

7   Wilamowitz (1900) 16–17.
8   Wilamowitz (1900) 15.
9   Nagy (1996) ch. 7 187–206.
10   Commentary on the text of 'Plutarch' in Nagy (1996) 175.

In the case of all these examples, I posit a continuity of transmission from classical Athens to Hellenistic Alexandria. What would be most remarkable about such a posited continuity between Athens and Alexandria is that the Athenian side of the continuum would still have had access to the performance traditions that had led to the text traditions, whereas the Alexandrian side had direct access only to the text traditions.

4   On the Testimony of Aristotle's *Poetics*

In this chapter, I have been focussing on the performance traditions of the Lyric Nine in Athens, but now I must widen the lens to include the parallel performance traditions of epic and tragedy in Athens. We find a most central piece of relevant evidence at the very beginning of the *Poetics* of Aristotle (1447a13–15). There he lists in the following order the forms of composition in verbal art: epic or *epopoiiā* (which means literally 'the making of *epos*'), tragedy, comedy, dithyramb, and compositions involving performance on the *aulos* (reed) or the *kitharā* (lyre). All these forms as listed there at the beginning of Aristotle's *Poetics* correspond to forms of composition that were actually performed at the two major festivals of the Athenians:

(1)   The Panathenaia, featuring (a) epic recitation by *rhapsōidoi* (rhapsodes), accompanied by no musical instrument, (b) lyric singing by *aulōidoi* (aulodes) accompanied by the *aulos* (reed), (c) lyric singing by *kitharōidoi* (citharodes) accompanied by the *kitharā* (lyre), (d) instrumental music played by *aulētai* (auletes) on the *aulos*, without words, (e) instrumental music played by *kitharistai* (citharists) on the *kitharā*, without words.

(2)   The City Dionysia, featuring (a) tragedy, (b) comedy, (c) dithyramb, and (d) satyr drama.

In Aristotle's account, he ostentatiously pairs the composition of epic with the composition of tragedy (the wording is *epopoiiā ... kai hē tēs tragōidiās poiēsis*, which means literally 'the making of *epos* and the making of tragedy'). Elsewhere, he says that he views these two particular forms of composition— epic and tragedy—as cognates (*Poetics* 1449a2–6). In the works of Plato as well, epic is viewed as a cognate of tragedy; more than that, Homer is represented as a proto-tragedian (*Theaetetus* 152e; *Republic* 10.595c, 598d, 605c, 607a).

This pattern of associating tragedy with epic, and epic with tragedy, reflects an institutional reality. The genre of epic, as performed by *rhapsōidoi* at the festival of the Panathenaia, actually shaped and was shaped by the genre of tragedy as performed by actors and choruses at the festival of the City Dionysia.

In Athens, ever since the sixth century BCE, these two genres were 'complementary forms, evolving together and thereby undergoing a process of mutual assimilation in the course of their institutional coexistence'.[11]

On the basis of what we find, then, at the beginning of Aristotle's *Poetics*, we can see clearly a parallelism between Homer and tragedy. But we can see also a parallelism here between Homer and the Lyric Canon, once we recognize that compositions involving the *aulos* and the *kithara*, as highlighted by Aristotle, were meant to be performed at the Panathenaia.

5   Primary Venue, Secondary Venue

At this point, we come to a vital convergence of epic and lyric traditions. In terms of my overall argument, the festival of the Panathenaia in Athens was the primary venue for the traditions of performing both Homer and the Lyric Nine, and it was from these performance traditions that the text traditions of the Epic Canon and the Lyric Canon were derived.

Considering the centrality of the Panathenaia in the public life of Athens, I have argued so far that this festival was the primary "locus of diffusion", as linguists would call it, for the songs of the Lyric Nine as performed in the classical period. And here I return to the second part of my argument, introduced already at the beginning of this chapter: correspondingly, the performances of these songs at private symposia would be only a secondary "locus of diffusion". In other words, from the standpoint of my overall argument, the texts of the Lyric Nine as edited in Alexandria would have originated primarily from a centralized reception in contexts of public performances at the Panathenaia and only secondarily from a decentralized reception in contexts of performances at private symposia.

6   Positing Four Phases of Transmission

For the transmission of the Lyric Nine, I posit four phases, extending from the sixth century to somewhere around the middle of the fourth: 'Phase 1' is the era of the Pisistratidae, retrospectively described as tyrants who dominated the civic life of Athens in the sixth century; 'Phase 2' is the pre-classical era of the early democracy in the first half of the fifth century; 'Phase 3' is the classical

---

11   Nagy (1996) 81.

era of Athens as exemplified by Pericles; and 'Phase 4' is the post-classical era around the first half of the fourth century.

6.1   Phase 1

To illustrate 'Phase 1', I quote a passage from a text about Hipparchus, son of Pisistratus. In this passage, Hipparchus is credited with introducing the performance traditions of Homeric poetry in Athens, and in this same context he is also credited with introducing the lyric songs of Anacreon and Simonides in Athens. What I find most remarkable about this passage is the parallelism that is drawn between epic and lyric performance traditions.

> ... Ἱππάρχῳ, ὃς ἄλλα τε πολλὰ καὶ καλὰ ἔργα σοφίας ἀπεδέξατο, καὶ τὰ Ὁμήρου ἔπη πρῶτος ἐκόμισεν εἰς τὴν γῆν ταύτην, καὶ ἠνάγκασε τοὺς ῥαψῳδοὺς Παναθηναίοις ἐξ ὑπολήψεως ἐφεξῆς αὐτὰ διιέναι, ὥσπερ νῦν ἔτι {c} οἵδε ποιοῦσιν, καὶ ἐπ' Ἀνακρέοντα τὸν Τήιον πεντηκόντορον στείλας ἐκόμισεν εἰς τὴν πόλιν, Σιμωνίδην δὲ τὸν Κεῖον ἀεὶ περὶ αὑτὸν εἶχεν, μεγάλοις μισθοῖς καὶ δώροις πείθων· ταῦτα δ' ἐποίει βουλόμενος παιδεύειν τοὺς πολίτας, ἵν' ὡς βελτίστων ὄντων αὐτῶν ἄρχοι, οὐκ οἰόμενος δεῖν οὐδενὶ σοφίας φθονεῖν, ἅτε ὢν καλός τε κἀγαθός.

> [I am referring to] Hipparchus, who accomplished many beautiful things in demonstration of his expertise [*sophiā*], especially by being the first to bring over [*komizein*] to this land [= Athens] the verses [*epos* plural] of Homer, and he forced the rhapsodes [*rhapsōidoi*] at the Panathenaia to go through [*diienai*] these verses in sequence [*ephexēs*], by relay [*ex hupolēpseōs*], just as they [= the rhapsodes] do even nowadays. And he sent out a state ship to bring over [*komizein*] Anacreon of Teos to the city [= Athens]. He also always kept in his company Simonides of Keos, persuading him by way of huge fees and gifts. And he did all this because he wanted to educate the citizens, so that he might govern the best of all possible citizens. He thought, noble as he was, that he was obliged not to be stinting in the sharing of his expertise [*sophiā*] with anyone.
>   'Plato' *Hipparchus* 228b–c

The use of the word *sophiā* (expertise) in this passage is archaic: it expresses the idea that Hipparchus demonstrates his expertise in poetry by virtue of sponsoring poets like Homer, Anacreon, and Simonides, who are described as the ultimate standards for measuring expertise in poetry. In the overall logic of the narrative, Hipparchus makes this kind of gesture because he wants to demonstrate to the citizens of Athens that he is not 'stinting with his *sophiā*' (σοφίας φθονεῖν 228c), since he provides them with the poetry and songmaking of Homer, Anacreon, and Simonides; by implication, his *sophiā* is the key to the performance traditions of all these three poets in Athens.[12]

In the case of Homeric poetry, Hipparchus is being credited here not only with the regulation of Homeric performances at the Panathenaia, as we may infer from other passages (for example, Dieuchidas of Megara *FGH* 485 F 6 via Diogenes Laertius 1.57: this version credits Solon for such regulation). More than that, Hipparchus is credited with the far more basic initiative of actually introducing Homeric performances in Athens.

It is in this same context that Hipparchus is also credited with the initiative of introducing the lyric performances of Anacreon and Simonides in Athens. In the case of Anacreon, for example, the wording of the narrative shows that Hipparchus undertook a veritable rescue operation in transporting from Samos to Athens this master of lyric. In Samos, Anacreon had been a court poet of the Panionian maritime empire of Polycrates. Here I recall briefly a relevant story told by Herodotus about the final days of Polycrates, who was soon to be captured and executed by agents of the Persian Empire (3.125. 2–3). Right before that bitter end, we get a glimpse here of happier times: Polycrates is pictured as reclining on a sympotic couch and enjoying the company of that ultimate luminary of Ionian lyric poetry, Anacreon (3.121.1). In the logic of this narrative, the Ionian lyric tradition represented by Anacreon had to be rescued from the Persians once the old Panionian maritime empire of Polycrates of Samos had collapsed, soon to be replaced by the new Panionianism of the Pisistratidae of Athens. Once the rescue operation had succeeded, it could now be Hipparchus in Athens, not Polycrates in Samos, who got to enjoy the sympotic company of lyric celebrities such as Anacreon.

In terms of this narrative, Hipparchus accomplished something far more than simply inviting lyric poets for ad hoc occasions of performance at, say, symposia: what he also accomplished, as I will now argue, was to institutionalize the competitive performing of their songs at public concerts that were prominently featured at the festival of the Panathenaia.

Such a Panathenaic context for the performance of songs composed by these lyric poets can be reconstructed, I propose, by way of analyzing more closely the narrative about the accomplishments of Hipparchus. In the logic of this narrative, Hipparchus had a primary motive in introducing both Homeric and lyric performances to the Athenian people. I repeat here the original Greek wording: ταῦτα δ' ἐποίει βουλόμενος παιδεύειν τοὺς πολίτας, ἵν' ὡς βελτίστων ὄντων αὐτῶν ἄρχοι (And he did all this because he wanted to educate the citizens, so

---

12 This paragraph, and the next four, draw on Nagy (2009|2010) 26–28.

that he might govern the best of all possible citizens). The educating of the body politic, as the wording here makes clear, requires the reception of lyric song, not only of Homeric poetry. That is why I can argue that Hipparchus accomplished something far more than simply inviting lyric poets for ad hoc occasions of performance at symposia. After all, performances at private symposia for the elite would hardly contribute to the education of the citizens at large.

The narrative about the accomplishments of Hipparchus makes it clear that the initiative of Hipparchus in introducing the performance of Homeric poetry was parallel to his initiative in introducing the performances of lyric songs composed by the most celebrated poets in his era—figures such as Anacreon and Simonides. The use of the word *komizein* (228b) in expressing the idea that Hipparchus 'brought over' to Athens the *epē* (verses = *epos* plural) of Homer is parallel to the use of the same word *komizein* (228c) in expressing the idea that Hipparchus also 'brought over' to Athens the poet Anacreon—on a state ship, from the island of Samos. In terms of my interpretation, the parallelism implies that the songs of Anacreon were meant to be performed at the festival of the Panathenaia in the same way that the poetry of Homer was meant to be performed.

In the case of Homer, however, Hipparchus transported not the poet Homer but Homer's notional descendants, called the *Homēridai*; further, in contrast with the case of Anacreon, Hipparchus brought the *Homēridai* over to Athens not from the island of Samos but from the island of Chios.[13]

In terms of this narrative, then, there are two parallel accomplishments being attributed to Hipparchus: through his initiatives, it was not only the poetry of Homer that could now be performed in public concerts at the Panathenaia in Athens but also the Ionian lyric songs of poets such as Anacreon of Teos, and the Dorian lyric compositions of poets such as Simonides of Keos.

6.2 *Phase 2*

Moving now from 'Phase 1' to 'Phase 2' of the Panathenaia in Athens, we come to the era of the early democracy in the first half of the fifth century BCE. In this era, the songs of Anacreon were evidently well known in Athens, as we see most clearly from the evidence of vase paintings that show Anacreon himself (the adjacent lettering identifies him) in the act of singing while accompanying himself on a string instrument that is pictured as a barytone lyre or *barbitos* and

---

13   For arguments in support of this formulation, see Nagy (2009|2010) 28, 54–55, 57–66, 328.

occasionally as a concert lyre or *kithara*. For an admirable analysis of this iconographic evidence, I recommend the relevant comments in a book by Timothy Power.[14]

While the Anacreontic paintings point to the symposium as the immediate context to be visualized for the singing of songs attributed to Anacreon, both during and after his lifetime, I argue that the ultimate context would be the re-enactment of such sympotic singing in the context of public concerts at the Panathenaia, where the *kitharōidos* who re-enacts Anacreon would accompany himself either on the *barbitos* or on the more conventional *kithara*.

I also argue that the songs of Sappho, as channelled by the singing of Anacreon almost a century later, could likewise be re-enacted not only in a stylized symposium but also in a spectacular Panathenaic setting. We can see the picturing of such a Panathenaic spectacle in a vase painting dated around 480 or 470 BCE (Munich, Antikensammlungen no. 2416). The painting shows Sappho and Alcaeus (the adjacent lettering identifies them) in the act of singing a "duet" while both are accompanying themselves on the *barbitos*. Such a visual "duet" is matched by a verbal "duet" that is actually quoted by Aristotle (*Rhetoric* 1.1367a). In the wording of this "duet", which is conventionally but unsatisfactorily assigned to Sappho alone (F 137), the male and the female speakers are expressing in Aeolic song what the male and the female figures in the painting express by way of their visualized body language.[15] According to the formulation of Power, it is as if Sappho and Alcaeus, whom he describes in this context as 'amateur monodists *par excellence*', were being represented as 'professional agonists', that is, as *kitharōidoi* who are competing in the *mousikoi agōnes* at the Panathenaia.[16] It is perhaps unnecessary for me to add that such a visual representation would be simply an exercise in artistic imagination, since citharodic competitions would have required individual performances. In other words, the conventional format here is monodic. By contrast, our vase painting imagines two competing performers who are interacting in one scene. In a real Panathenaic scene, the two parts in the interaction would both be sung by one and the same monodic citharode.

Taking a broader look at the citharodic medium, I need to make a disclaimer at this point. I do not mean to say that all songs attributed to figures like Sappho or Anacreon would at all times be formally suitable for inclusion in the repertoire of citharodic songs to be performed at the Panathenaia. From reading

---

14 Power (2010) 413, 466, 470, 510; also recommended in general is Price (1990).
15 Nagy (2007) 233–237, 246–252, 255–260.
16 Power (2010) 413n275.

carefully Power's book on the evolution of citharodic performances at the Panathenaia and at symposia, I have learned to be more consistent about keeping in mind this basic argument as advocated by him: not all lyric forms were necessarily compatible with the citharodic forms that eventuated in the context of the Panathenaia.[17] Accordingly, I heed the reservations of Power concerning the historical possibilities of fitting lyric forms into a citharodic medium.[18] As we trace the citharodic medium forward in time, it seems that the metrical and the melodic formalities of this medium became increasingly constrained, so that we cannot in the end expect all lyric forms to fit into the narrower frame of the citharodic medium. That said, however, I maintain that this citharodic medium had been far more flexible in earlier stages of its evolution, and I think it was at such an earlier stage that lyric forms first made their massive entry into the citharodic medium as it evolved in the context of the Panathenaia. Most accommodating, in any case, were lyric forms that could readily convert from frames that were stanzaic to frames that were stichic (verse-by-verse), since the evolution of citharodic forms evidently gravitated away from strophic configurations. In the case of monodic songs attributed to Sappho, the composition known as *The Wedding of Hector and Andromache* (F 44) is an ideal example of a lyric form that suits the narrower requirements of the citharodic medium in its later configurations. I might add that, in terms of my argumentation, this kind of composition could readily be expanded in length, and such a formal capacity for expansion would be another feature that made such monodic singing especially suitable for citharodic performance.

I started my overview of 'Phase 2' by arguing that the songs of Anacreon, who was personally brought to Athens by Hipparchus, were integrated into the canonical repertoire of citharodic performances at the Panathenaia. Now I turn to the songs of Simonides. He too, as we saw in the same passage that mentioned Anacreon, was personally brought to Athens by Hipparchus. And now I will argue that the songs of Simonides were likewise integrated into the repertoire of performances at the Panathenaia. In this case, however, at least some of his songs were integrated into the repertoire of aulodic rather than citharodic performances.

Here I return to a specific argument I presented at a conference of the Network for the Study of Archaic and Classical Greek Song held in the summer of 2012 in Washington, DC, on which occasion I proposed that the Plataea Elegy of Simonides (fr. 11 West), celebrating the victory of the Hellenes who

---

17 Power (2010).
18 Power (2010) 262–263n187.

fought the Persian forces at the battle of Plataea in 479 BCE, had become part of the repertoire of the Lyric Canon.[19] In support of my proposal, I cited the work of Ewen Bowie on the performative traditions of archaic Greek elegy, expressing my agreement with his view that (1) elegiac compositions in the archaic and classical periods were conventionally sung to the accompaniment of the *aulos*, and (2) there were two basic social contexts for the singing of elegy by men, namely, the *symposium* and the *public festival*.[20] Accordingly, I argue that the performing of elegy at the Panathenaia belonged to competitions in the category of *aulōidiā* (singing to the accompaniment of the *aulos*).

This is not at all to say, however, that elegy was the only form of *aulōidiā* to be performed at the Panathenaia. Besides the stichic form of elegy, I leave room for the possibility that non-stichic forms of *aulōidiā* also existed in at least the earlier phases of the Panathenaia, just as I have left room for non-stichic forms of *kitharōidiā* 'singing to the accompaniment of the *kitharā*'.

I must also note here the possibility that aulodic performances could be interchangeable with citharodic performances, as well as the other way around. A case in point is Aristophanes' comedy *Women at the Thesmophoria*; here the tragic poet Agathon is depicted as wearing a turban and a woman's *khitōn*—matching the costume of the lyric poet Anacreon as depicted by the Cleophrades Painter (Copenhagen MN 13365).[21] In the comedy of Aristophanes, the stage Agathon even says that his self-staging replicates the monodic stagings of Ibycus, Anacreon, and Alcaeus (verses 159–163). This reference suggests, I argue, that Agathon, as a master of tragic poetry, was strongly influenced by the monodic performance traditions of lyric song, both citharodic and aulodic, as performed at the Panathenaia.[22]

I should emphasize in this context the fact that aulodic compositions were appropriate not only for performance at the competitions of aulodes at the Panathenaia but also for the competitions of choruses who were singing and dancing in the dramas of Athenian state theater at the city Dionysia and at other dramatic festivals, since the singing and dancing of the songs of drama was conventionally sustained by the accompaniment of a single *aulos*. So, my point about Agathon is that he was experimenting with compositions in his dramas that would have sounded like aulodic performances by aulodes com-

---

19 On Simonides fr. 11, see Boedeker and Sider (2001).
20 Bowie (1986) 14–21, 34; also Nagy (2010) 38.
21 Price (1990) 169, with further bibliography.
22 Nagy (2007) 245–246, following Bierl (2001) 160–163; on Agathon as a stage Anacreon, see Bierl (2001) 158n137, 165.

peting with each other at the Panathenaia. Going even further, Agathon experimented even with citharodic compositions in his dramas.

In short, I propose that the compositions of the Lyric Nine were suitable for both citharodic and aulodic performances at the *mousikoi agōnes* in at least the earlier phases of the Panathenaia.

6.3   Phase 3

Moving now from 'Phase 2' to 'Phase 3' of the Panathenaia in Athens, we come to the classical era of Athens, by which I mean the age of Pericles as a prime promoter of both the democracy and the so-called Athenian Empire. I pose here a most relevant question: where in this era did the competitions of *kitharōdoi* and *aulōidoi* take place on the occasion of the Panathenaia? The question extends of course also to the performances of the non-singing instrumentalists who likewise competed at the Panathenaia, namely, the *kitharistai* and the *auletai*. More importantly, the question extends even to the performances of the *rhapsōidoi*, who were competing as well as collaborating with each other in the act of reciting Homeric poetry at the same *mousikoi agōnes* of the Panathenaia. And here is the answer: the venue for the *mousikoi agōnes* of the Panathenaic festival in this era was the *Ōideion* (Odeum) of Pericles, built probably between 447 and 443 BCE.[23]

I draw special attention to some surviving details about the building of this Odeum, since they are relevant to what we know about the organization of an *agōn* (competition) at the Panathenaia in the context of the Odeum as the setting for this competition. I quote here a most relevant passage from Plutarch:[24]

{9} τὸ δ' Ὠιδεῖον, τῇ μὲν ἐντὸς διαθέσει πολύεδρον καὶ πολύστυλον, τῇ δ' ἐρέψει περικλινὲς καὶ κάταντες ἐκ μιᾶς κορυφῆς πεποιημένον, εἰκόνα λέγουσι γενέσθαι καὶ μίμημα τῆς βασιλέως σκηνῆς, ἐπιστατοῦντος καὶ τούτῳ {10} Περικλέους. διὸ καὶ πάλιν Κρατῖνος ἐν Θρᾴτταις παίζει πρὸς αὐτόν·

ὁ σχινοκέφαλος Ζεὺς ὅδε προσέρχεται τὠδεῖον ἐπὶ τοῦ κρανίου ἔχων, ἐπειδὴ τοὔστρακον παροίχεται.

---

23   Relevant to my chapter here is work done by Athanassaki (2012) concerning possible references to the Odeum in the *Ion* of Euripides. Such references to the Odeum, as collected and analyzed by Athanassaki, shed light on the evolution of the Lyric Canon.

24   The translation is mine, and the comments that I add are summarized from Nagy (2008| 2009) 4 §§174–176.

{11} φιλοτιμούμενος δ' ὁ Περικλῆς τότε πρῶτον ἐψηφίσατο μουσικῆς ἀγῶνα τοῖς Παναθηναίοις ἄγεσθαι, καὶ διέταξεν αὐτὸς ἀθλοθέτης αἱρεθείς, καθότι χρὴ τοὺς ἀγωνιζομένους αὐλεῖν ἢ ᾄδειν ἢ κιθαρίζειν. ἐθεῶντο δὲ καὶ τότε καὶ τὸν ἄλλον χρόνον ἐν Ὠιδείῳ τοὺς μουσικοὺς ἀγῶνας.

{9} As for the Odeum,[25] which was designed to have many seats and columns on the inside,[26] and the roofing of which had a steep slope from the peak downward,[27] they say it was a visual imitation of the Great King's[28] Tent [*skēnē*]—and {10} Pericles was supervising [*epistateîn*] this building project as well.[29] That is the point of reference when Cratinus— I quote him again—in his *Thracian Women* [F 73] playfully alludes to him:

This squill-head Zeus, this Pericles, is approaching, wearing the Odeum on top of his skull as his [head-]wear,[30] now that the time for ostracism has come and gone.

---

25 Stadter (1989) 172: 'Pericles' [Odeum] was on the south slope of the Acropolis, east of the theater of Dionysus. [Plutarch] knew only a reconstruction of the building, which had been burned by the Athenians in 86 [BCE], to prevent its wood from being used by Sulla to besiege the Acropolis' (Appian *Mithridateios* 6.38; see also Vitruvius 5.9.1; Pausanias 1.20.4). As Stadter continues: 'According to Vitruvius [as cited] the masts and spars of the Persian ships [from Salamis] were used to construct the roof' (173). Meiggs (1982) 474 notes that 'the roof beams would have been enormous, more than 70 feet (21.3 meters) long.'
26 Stadter (1989) 173: 'The forest of columns would have been similar to the [*Telestērion*] at Eleusis but covered an even larger area.'
27 Stadter (1989) 173: 'Apparently the roof was pyramidal, sloping on four sides.'
28 That is, the King of Kings of Persia: see also Plutarch *Pericles* 10.5.
29 Pericles is called the *epistatēs* (supervisor) of the Parthenon and of the *Telestērion* (Strabo 9.1.12 C395) and of the statue of Athena Parthenos (Philochorus *FGH* 328 F 121) and of the Lyceum (Philochorus F 37 via Harpocration s.v.); see Stadter (1989) 174.
30 Stadter (1989) 174: 'Pericles seems to be wearing the [Odeum] (or its pointed roof) as he did the helmet in the Cresilaus portrait: perhaps Cratinus thought that the pyramidal roof of the [Odeum], with its sharp peak, would be suitable for Pericles' head.' So the joke is inspired by the shape of the roof of the Odeum, with its sharp peak, and by the shape of the head of Pericles. The metonymic identification of Pericles with the Odeum—a major source of prestige for the statesman—has been comically turned into a metaphoric identification of the 'peak' of Pericles with the 'peak' of the Odeum. What I say here, which is an abbreviated version of what I say in Nagy (2008|2009) 4 §174, is not necessarily at odds with what is argued by Rusten (2013). I take his point that the direct referent in this passage from Cratinus is a stage-Zeus, who is imagined as wearing on top of his head a stylized *polos* in the sense of a 'celestial axis'. But my point remains that the indirect referent is still Pericles, whose own celestial axis is the Odeum that he built.

{11} It was then for the first time that Pericles, ambitious as he was, got a decree passed that there should be a competition [*agōn*] in *mousikē* at the Panathenaia,[31] and he set up the rules [*diatassein*], having been elected as an *athlothetēs* [= organizer of the *athloi* 'contests'] for those who were competing [*agōnizesthai*]—rules for them to follow about the *aulos*-playing and the singing and the *kitharā*-playing. At that point in time and in other periods of time as well, it was in the Odeum that people used to be spectators [*theâsthai*] of competitions [*agōnes*] in *mousikē*.

PLUTARCH *Pericles* 13. 9–11

As I infer from this passage, Pericles in the fifth century BCE initiated legislation reforming the *mousikoi agōnes* at the Panathenaia, including the competition of citharodes and aulodes. Plutarch leaves it unspecified whether the *agōnes* included rhapsodic performances, but we do see a specific reference attested in the ancient dictionary ascribed to Hesychius. In this dictionary we read under the entry ōideion: ᾠδεῖον· τόπος, ἐν ᾧ πρὶν τὸ θέατρον κατασκευασθῆναι οἱ ῥαψῳδοὶ καὶ οἱ κιθαρῳδοὶ ἠγωνίζοντο (Odeum: the place where, before the Theater [of Dionysus] was configured for this purpose, the rhapsodes and the citharodes used to engage in competition [*agōnizesthai*]).[32] It follows that Plutarch's elliptic reference to '*aulos*-playing, singing, and *kitharā*-playing' does in fact include the 'singing' of rhapsodes.[33]

The idea of the Odeum as a visual imitation of the *skēnē* or 'tent' of the Great King of the Persian empire, as we have just seen it described in Plutarch's *Pericles*, is a most fitting expression of imperial prestige.[34] The Odeum, as the "scene" for the monumental Panathenaic performances of Homer in the age of Pheidias, was monumental in its own right. On the inside, its 'forest of columns' matched the spectacular effect achieved at the *Telestērion* or Great Hall of Ini-

---

31 I take it that τότε πρῶτον (at that point for the first time) refers not to the establishing of an *agōn* in *mousikē* but to the fact that there was a formal decree involved. See Stadter (1989) 175 for citations of documentation for earlier phases of competitions in *mousikē* in Athens. The *mousikē* (craft of the Muses) as practiced at the Panathenaia includes the *tekhnē* (craft) of rhapsodes, not only of citharodes, citharists, aulodes, and auletes. Supporting evidence comes from Aristotle *Constitution of the Athenians* (60.1), Plato *Ion* (530a), and Isocrates *Panegyricus* (4.159).

32 On the use of the Theater of Dionysus for Homeric performances in the late fourth century BCE, see Athenaeus 14.620b–c and my relevant commentary in Nagy (1996) 158–163.

33 Nagy 2008|2009 4§175. The verb *āidein* (sing), formant of the derivative nouns *kithar-ōidos* and *rhaps-ōidos*, is actually used with reference to the performances of rhapsodes: see Plato *Ion* 535b and my relevant commentary in Nagy (1996) 26–27.

34 Nagy (2008|2009) 4 §178.

tiation at Eleusis.[35] In fact, the Odeum was even more spacious than the Great Hall, and the enormous seating capacity of such a monumental building made it a most fitting venue for spectacular events of state, including juridical and political assemblies.[36]

The macrocosm of the Odeum is metonymically—and comically—evoked by the visualization of a microcosm sitting on top of the head of Pericles. On top of his comically pointy head is a perfect fit, which is a pointy 'hat'. That pointy 'hat' is the magnificent Odeum, culminating in its magnificent peak. As the most public of all public figures in Athens, Pericles the monumental statesman is wearing his 'hat' as the primary organizer of the Panathenaia, which as we have seen featured the spectacular performances of epic as represented exclusively by Homer and of lyric as represented mainly by the Lyric Nine.

6.4 Phase 4

Moving now from 'Phase 3' to 'Phase 4' of the Panathenaia in Athens, we come to what I have already described as the post-classical era. By now we see a drastic decrease in evidence for any continued existence of a Lyric Canon as performed and then textualized in Athens. Conversely, we begin to see a marked increase in evidence for the textualization of this canon in Alexandria.

By now the repertoire of performable lyric songs in the *mousikoi agōnes* of the Panathenaia may have become so restricted in scope as to exclude most kinds of song that may have been transmitted in earlier phases of the performance traditions that had evolved in the context of this festival. In both the citharodic and the aulodic competitions, the repertoire could have been narrowed down to stichic songs that were readily expandable in length. In the case of the citharodic competitions, the form of monodic singing was known as the *kitharōidikos nomos* (citharodic nome = song sung to a tune), the generic protocols of which are admirably documented by Power (2010), and in the case of the aulodic competitions, the corresponding form would have been the elegiac couplet as analyzed by Bowie (1986).

Meanwhile, lyric songs composed in a far greater variety of metres and tunes would have survived as texts already in Athens, thanks especially to the Peri-

---

35 I refer to the mention of the *Telestērion* in Plutarch *Pericles* 13.7, as analyzed in Nagy (2008|2009) 4 § 174.

36 Stadter (1989) 173 cites Aristophanes *Wasps* 1108–1109 regarding the use of the Odeum as 'a court.' Citing the testimony of Xenophon *Hellenica* 2.4.9, 24, Stadter adds: 'The Thirty used it [the Odeum] as an assembly point when they were defending their rule in winter 404/3.' Immediately after citing these primary sources, Stadter cites a critical mass of secondary sources.

patetics, and the proliferation of such texts would have led to a large-scale project of collecting and editing as undertaken by the researchers working at the Library of Alexandria. Further, the impetus for finding texts of the Lyric Nine would easily have led to a widening in the scope of inquiry. That is how the Library of Alexandria acquired a vast array of lyric texts that had never been part of the textual tradition for the original Athenian Lyric Nine. A prime example, I suggest, is the case of Corinna. While retaining the nomenclature of *ennea lurikoi* (nine lyric poets), the Alexandrians added her as a tenth poet, as we see in the Scholia for Dionysius Thrax (21 line 19), where Corinna of Boeotia is described as the *dekatē* (tenth).[37] She was not a member of the original Lyric Nine because her songs were not part of a Panathenaic repertoire.

References

Athanassaki, L. 2012. A Magnificent Birthday Party in an Artful Pavilion: Lifestyle and Leadership in Euripides' *Ion* (on and off stage). In *Donum Natalicium Digitaliter Confectum Gregorio Nagy Septuagenario a Discipulis Collegis Familiaribus Oblatum. A Virtual Birthday Gift Presented to Gregory Nagy on Turning Seventy by his Students, Colleagues, and Friends*, ed. V. Bers, D. Elmer, D. Frame, and L. Muellner. Available online at https://chs.harvard.edu/CHS/article/display/4606.

Bierl, A. 2001. *Ritual und Performativität (unter besonderer Berücksichtigung von Aristophanes' Thesmophoriazusen und der Phalloslieder fr. 851 PMG)*. Munich.

Bierl, A. 2007. *Ritual and Performativity: The Chorus in Old Comedy* (tr. A. Hollmann). Cambridge MA. http://nrs.harvard.edu/urn-3:hul.ebook:CHS_Bierl.Ritual_and_Performativity.2009

Boedeker, D. and Sider, D., eds. 2001. *The New Simonides: Contexts of Praise and Desire*. Oxford.

Bowie, E.L. 1986. Early Greek Elegy, Symposium and Public Festival. *JHS* 106:13–35.

Kotsidu, H. 1991. *Die Musischen Agone der Panathenäen in Archaischer und Klassischer Zeit*. Munich.

Meiggs, R. 1982. *Trees and Timber in the Ancient Mediterranean World*. Oxford.

Miller, M. 1997. *Athens and Persia in the Fifth Century BC*. Cambridge.

Nagy, G. 1990. *Pindar's Homer: The Lyric Possession of an Epic Past*. Baltimore. http://nrs.harvard.edu/urn-3:hul.ebook:CHS_Nagy.Pindars_Homer.1990.

Nagy, G. 1996. *Poetry as Performance: Homer and Beyond*. Cambridge. http://nrs.harvard.edu/urn-3:hul.ebook:CHS_Nagy.Poetry_as_Performance.1996.

---

37 See also Wilamowitz (1900) 21.

Nagy, G. 2002. *Plato's Rhapsody and Homer's Music: The Poetics of the Panathenaic Festival in Classical Athens*. Cambridge, MA. http://nrs.harvard.edu/urn-3:hul.ebook:CHS_Nagy.Platos_Rhapsody_and_Homers_Music.2002.

Nagy, G. 2004. Transmission of Archaic Greek Sympotic Songs: From Lesbos to Alexandria. *Critical Inquiry* 31:26–48. http://nrs.harvard.edu/urn-3:hlnc.essay:Nagy.Transmission_of_Archaic_Greek_Sympotic_Songs.2004.

Nagy, G. 2007. Did Sappho and Alcaeus Ever Meet? In *Literatur und Religion: Wege zu einer mythisch-rituellen Poetik bei den Griechen. MythosEikonPoiesis* 1.1. ed. A. Bierl, R. Lämmle, and K. Wesselmann, 1:211–269. Berlin. Revised and updated version in http://nrs.harvard.edu/urn-3:hlnc.essay:Nagy.Did_Sappho_and_Alcaeus_Ever_Meet.2007.

Nagy, G. 2008|2009. *Homer the Classic*. Online | Printed version. http://nrs.harvard.edu/urn-3:hul.ebook:CHS_Nagy.Homer_the_Classic.2008 | Hellenic Studies 36. Cambridge MA.

Nagy, G. 2009|2010. *Homer the Preclassic*. Online | Printed version. http://nrs.harvard.edu/urn-3:hul.ebook:CHS_Nagy.Homer_the_Preclassic.2009 | Berkeley.

Nagy, G. 2010. Ancient Greek Elegy. In *The Oxford Handbook of the Elegy*, ed. K. Weisman, 13–45. Oxford. http://nrs.harvard.edu/urn-3:hlnc.essay:Nagy.Ancient_Greek_Elegy.2010.

Power, T. 2010. *The Culture of Kitharōidia*. Hellenic Studies 15. Cambridge MA. http://nrs.harvard.edu/urn-3:hul.ebook:CHS_Power.The_Culture_of_Kitharoidia.2010.

Price, S.D. 1990. Anacreontic Vases Reconsidered. *GRBS* 31:133–175.

Rusten, J.S. 2013. 'The Odeion on His Head': Costume and Identity in Cratinus' Thracian Women fr. 73, and Cratinus' Techniques of Political Satire. *Classical Studies E-Books Online. Mnemosyne Supplements* 353: 279–290. http://booksandjournals.brillonline.com/content/books/b9789004245457_016

Shear, J.L. 2001. *Polis and Panathenaia: The History and Development of Athena's Festival*. PhD dissertation, University of Pennsylvania.

Stadter, P.A. 1989. *A Commentary on Plutarch's Pericles*. Chapel Hill.

Wilamowitz-Moellendorff. U. von. 1900. *Textgeschichte der griechischen Lyriker*. Berlin.

CHAPTER 5

Melic Poets and Melic Forms in the Comedies of Aristophanes: Poetic Genres and the Creation of a Canon

Claude Calame, translated from the French by Jane Burkowski

1   Introduction

Throughout his extant comedies, Aristophanes cites by name "lyric" poets such as Alcaeus, Anacreon, and Pindar, and refers to specific forms of ritual melic poetry, including the paean, the dithyramb, and even the partheneion. The aim of this chapter is to examine the question of whether the names of the poets mentioned by Aristophanes correspond to particular poetic genres, as I was able to assert for Herodotus in an earlier study.[1] Consideration will, further, be given to the question of whether they reflect an early canon of poets (comparable with the πραττόμενοι of the Alexandrian period?) and a corresponding select list of poetic genres. That will entail, moreover, examination of the role played by Attic comedy in the formation and transmission of the tradition of Panhellenic melic poetry and the functions played, in their dramatic contexts, not only of Aristophanes' quotations from and allusions to μέλος, but also of the "lyrics" composed and dramatized by Aristophanes himself.

As a sort of initial *captatio benevolentiae*, allow me to note that, with the advancing years, a scholar is increasingly compelled to cite his own works. However, though it may become tedious, reference to one's own past works need not consist of straightforward and complacent repetition. It helps to limit the reiteration of ideas that are, after all, representative not so much of a cumulative mass of knowledge as of an application of one's theories to different objects of study, each in turn. Sounding out new terrain, meanwhile, cannot help but reorient one's initial perspectives as well as the instrumental concepts that necessarily directed and spurred one's enquiries.

---

1   Calame (2004b).

2   'What Is an Author?'

Michel Foucault, in the late 1960s, asked the question, 'What is an author?'. He sought to replace the traditional identification of the author with a specific individual, viewed in the context of his or her biographical reality and creative talents, with a new concept: that of the "author-function" (*fonction-auteur*). The author, according to this scheme, is a figure constructed to suit a particular form of discourse. In short, Foucault is noting that the function of an author's name is essentially a classificatory one; it allows us to establish connections between different texts (on the level of diction as well as theme), based on their shared features and shared origins, and even to establish their authenticity. The name of the author encourages a mode of reception for his discourse, while attributing to it a certain status and (I would add) a certain authority, for a readership with a shared social and cultural understanding. Thus the name of an author, far from calling up a real individual, complete with his biographical and historical identity, 'is a manifestation of a particular type of discourse, and refers to the status held by this discourse in a given society and culture'. The name of an author thus refers to an "author-function", which places a text within a defined form of discourse.[2] I would add, in the specific case of ancient Greece, that these forms of discourse are characterized by the formal features of each genre, such as characteristic word forms, or specific performance contexts, the latter being determined, for each form of discourse, by the rules of acceptability in a particular political, religious, and cultural situation.[3]

Thus, as I have at various points attempted to demonstrate,[4] the poetic *I*, viewed in its spatial and temporal context, refers not to the psycho-social identity or historical person of the poet, but instead to a figure of discourse, to a verbal figure. Linked as it is to its context of utterance, the *I*'s position of verbal authority can, through performance, be held by different speakers; it is a figure with many faces, manifesting itself in a polyphony that has only an indirect relation to the poet who composed the text. This is no doubt what Foucault is implying when, in connection with novels narrated in the first person, he asserts that the narrative *I* is a sort of *alter ego*. It is a "fictional speaker", and the "author-function" is born of the very schism between the real-life writer and this figure of discursive and performative authority.

What we know of the literary development of archaic and classical Greece makes clear that the names of authors could readily be attached to poetic

---

2   Foucault (1994 [1969])) 798–804, at 798.
3   For this brief definition of (poetic) genre, cf. Calame (1998) 87–92. In a different perspective, see also now on the notions of "genre" and of "author" Maslov (2015) 62–77.
4   These studies have been gathered together in one volume, Calame (1986/2000) [1995].

genres, or to specific forms of discourse: Homer for epic poetry, Arion of Methymna for dithyramb, Pindar for epinician, Sophocles for tragedy, etc. These associations, of course, are not exclusive. In old comedy too, the tragic poet, and the names of particular tragic poets, fulfil a well-defined "author-function": the tragedian is thought of as a διδάσκαλος (to use the Greeks' own term); he is the educator of the civic community.[5] But an examination of the 'signatures' attested in the Greek poetic fragments that have come down to us, from Hesiod to Thucydides, via Alcman, Theognis, Hecataeus, and Herodotus, suggests that the convention of the σφραγίς constitutes an acknowledgement on the part of authors themselves of the power of the "author-function". These 'signatures' are programmatic declarations, which reify the discourse that they introduce, and grant it a poetic (or prosaic) authority. My parallel study of references to poets in Herodotus led to two conclusions: first, that the primary reason to cite a poet by name is to reinforce the authority of the voice uttering the discourse; and second, that the name of a poet (Homer, for example) refers not so much to an individual, with his personal and historical identity, as to a poetic form: to a particular type of discourse and a particular poetic tradition—in the case of Homer, to the tradition of heroic epic.[6]

3   The Names of Melic Poets and the "Author-Function"

How does Aristophanes fit into this scheme? Even if the answer must remain a partial one, given the truncated nature of the corpus of Aristophanic comedies that has come down to us (we have only eleven of the forty-four comedies that were edited in Alexandria), the question is an important one. References to the names of "lyric" poets and melic verse-forms in comedy are evidence of their wider reception in classical Athens. Having in its turn become a 'song culture', on the pattern of those in Sparta, Lesbos, and Thebes, the poetic and musical culture of fifth-century Athens is an essential link in lyric poetry's chain of transmission, leading to Alexandria. A recent study of the tradition of Sappho's works produced several indications of the role that the poetic culture of classical Athens played both in the creation of the dominant ancient view of the poet of Lesbos and in the transmission of her poems, especially where the iconography of red-figure pottery is concerned. The knowledge of the poems

---

5 See, for example, the famous exchange between Aeschylus, Euripides, and Dionysus in Aristophanes *Frogs* 1004–1062, together with the fine commentary offered by Bouvier (2004).
6 On the convention of the σφραγίς, especially in Theognis, I may cite my own article ([2004b] 13–21), along with the various documents cited therein.

of Alcman, and especially of his *partheneia*, that Aristophanes displays similarly allows us to conjecture that the Spartan poet's songs were sung at Athenian symposia.[7] We should also take into consideration the extant fragments of the other poets of old comedy. The present study, however, will limit itself to notes on selected passages, in order to offer (with the help of Aristophanes) a modest contribution to the history of the reception of lyric poetry in antiquity.

3.1   Attitudes of the Poets of Sympotic Verse

The first passage from Aristophanes to be examined in terms of the references it makes to the names of lyric poets is a well-known one. At the opening of the *Thesmophoriazusae*, the tragic poet Agathon appears before Euripides and a relation of his. Dressed as a woman, Agathon is intoning a choral song, alternately taking on the roles of the *koryphaios*, and of the chorus—which is, naturally, made up of a choir of young girls (κοῦραι, line 102). Their song is a choral celebration of Apollo, who bestows the sacred prize 'in honour of the Muses'; there follows an invocation of Artemis, the virgin huntress, and an address to Leto, who is associated with the harmonious rhythms of the Phrygian Graces, and with the cithara, the 'mother of songs' (μάτερ' ὕμνων, line 124) sung by men. This melic song ends in the manner of a hymn, with a prayer that Apollo, son of Leto, might rejoice in the musical offering that has been made to him (χάριν, line 127; χαῖρε, line 129).

In typically Aristophanic fashion, Euripides' relative responds to this μέλος (line 130) with erotically charged comments, and with a series of questions about the sexual identity of the androgynous poet. Agathon defends himself by explaining that one's dress must match one's frame of mind, and that the poet must adopt attitudes appropriate to the *drámata* that he intends to compose (ποιεῖν, line 150). If the drama is feminine in nature, the poet's body must follow suit: it is simply a case of μίμησις (line 156). When Euripides' relative suggests that he would like to be transformed into an ithyphallic satyr so that he can participate sexually in the joint composition (συμποιῶ) of a satyr play, Agathon responds by rejecting this 'unmusical' (ἄμουσον, line 159) image of a savage, hairy poet; by way of contrast, the tragedian cites the example of Ibycus, Anacreon, and Alcaeus. These poets knew how to follow the principle of equivalence between musical composition and bodily attitude: they were able to 'season' their melodies (ἁρμονίαν, line 162) while maintaining an 'Ionian' gait—that is, a graceful one, or even (comedy being what it is) a languid and effeminate one.[8]

---

7   Cf. Yatromanolakis (2007) 51–164; on Alcman, see Carey (2011) 446–456.

8   Aristophanes, *Thesmophoriazusae* 101–167; the allusion to 'Ionian attitudes' is here no doubt

Why bring up these associations by means of allusions to three melic poets (all three of whom also appear in the Alexandrian canon of nine πραττόμενοι)? All three are traditionally associated with sympotic poetry. Based on the few fragments of Ibycus and Anacreon that survive, and on what we know of the παιδικά of Alcaeus, I would suggest that the works that Aristophanes is alluding to are, more specifically, their love poems, depicting the homoerotic relationship between ἐρώμενος and ἐραστής. Thus in response to Euripides' relative's implication that he would like to engage in adult homosexual relations, by having anal sex with Agathon, the tragedian sets up an alternative picture; it is based on the educational homoerotic relationship between adult poet and adolescent boy, as illustrated, in the context of the symposium, by the majority of the elegiac verses anthologized as the second book of the *Theognidea*.[9]

But that is not all there is to this passage. On the heels of these three melic poets, with their Ionian dispositions, comes a reference to the tragic poet Phrynichus, a predecessor of Aeschylus; Phrynichus is cited to illustrate the connection between poetic composition (ποιεῖν, line 167) and the nature (φύσις) of the poet: with masculine beauty and fine clothes, Agathon explains, come beautiful tragedies! Phrynichus is placed in contrast with three other, more obscure contemporary tragic poets; they are cited by Euripides' relative, who has by now understood the relationship between the body of the poet and the nature of his compositions: the hideous Philocles, who writes hideously awful plays; the ill-tempered Xenocles, who writes nasty plays; and the cold fish Theognis, who writes lifeless ones (in all three cases, the verb used is *poieîn*, lines 168–170).[10]

It should be noted that the relationship here established between the body of the poet and the characteristics of his verse, both in terms of form and of style, is by no means unique in Greek literary criticism. Aristotle, in his *Poetics*, defines tragedy as the representation (μίμησις) of noble actions through the

---

twofold in its referents: the allusion to Ionian harmonies is perhaps, on the one hand, a reference to Ionian dance, which is placed in contrast with austere Dorian harmonies (cf. scholia ad loc.), and, on the other, a reference to Ionian effeminacy (cf. Xenophanes, fr. 3 Gentili-Prato). See the commentary of Prato (2001) 188–189, which deals with the textual problem presented by διεκίνων, which is to be emended to διεκλῶντ(ο), and Trédé (2003) 173–174, who sees Agathon's song as a paean. On the concept of "seasoning", see below, n. 11.

9 I have, as others have before me, argued for the importance of distinguishing between homoerotic relationships and what we would call homosexual relationships; see Calame (2009) 119–145. On the παιδικά attributed to Alcaeus, see Vetta (1982).

10 On the three tragic poets, more or less contemporary with Aristophanes, at whom he aims his critiques, see the texts cited by Prato (2001) 189–190.

medium of 'well-seasoned' language—that is, language with rhythm, harmony, and melody (μέλος); by this reckoning, melic passages (μελοποιία) are the most strongly 'seasoned' (ἡδύσματα), in that they are endowed with the features of poetry best equipped to induce pleasure. So, they keep with the universal goal of Greek poetry: to charm the listener. At the opening of the *Rhetoric*, though, Aristotle associates the persuasive quality of a speech with the character (ἦθος) of the orator—albeit less with his own disposition than with the character of the speaker that is constructed through the speech itself. As far as the connection between the authenticity and formal beauty of a song and the character of the singer is concerned, however, our earliest surviving literary reference comes from the *Odyssey*'s Alcinous, who, at the court of the Phaeacians, notes that Odysseus has narrated his various adventures just as a bard would have done; the beauty of the hero's speech, born of his own experience, is witness to the virtue of his heart, in contrast to the lies crafted by those who aim to dissemble.[11]

There is one further indication that the three lyric poets cited as colleagues of the tragedian Agathon are viewed as belonging to a specific field of discourse. Far from being references to their biographical reality, the poets' names are cited in order to suggest the poetry of erotic praise sung at symposia, illustrated for us by the homoerotic *Theognidea*, as well as by the encomia and scolia of Pindar. A short fragment of the *Banqueters* of Aristophanes may be taken to support this interpretation, inasmuch as it associates the names of Alcaeus and Anacreon with the scolion, which is a poetic form associated with symposia.[12]

3.2 *Simonides and Poetic Forms*

Of the nine future πραττόμενοι, however, there is no doubt that it was Simonides who most attracted Aristophanes' attention.

First of all, there is the debate, in the final scene of the *Clouds*, between the elderly farmer Strepsiades and his irreverent son Pheidippides, moderated by the chorus. A disagreement has arisen during a symposium: Strepsiades asked Pheidippides to take up his lyre and perform a song (μέλος) of Simonides, but his son replied that playing the lyre and singing (κιθαπίζειν, ᾄδειν) while drinking was old hat (ἀρχαῖον)—and anyway, he added, Simonides is a terrible poet.

---

11   Aristotle, *Poetics* 6.1149b24–31; *Rhetoric* 1.1356a4–13; Homer, *Odyssey* 11.362–372. On the (erotic) charm exerted by poetry, in its various forms, see the texts cited in the study by Calame (2009): 56–60.

12   Aristophanes fr. 235 *PCG*, quoted at Athenaeus 15.693f, in a passage devoted to the definition of the poetic genre of the scolion; on this poetic form, see Fabbro (1995) vii–xix, and Robbins (2014).

The scholia on this passage quote the opening verses of the epinician ode to which Strepsiades alludes in his request to his son. Composed for the (probably Olympic) victory of an Aeginetan athlete who had been captured by the Spartans and delivered to Athens in the period preceding the Persian Wars, this celebratory song seems to have turned on a play on words, punning on the name of the victor, who is referred to as a 'ram' (Κριός) who has been 'sheared' upon his arrival at the sanctuary of Zeus; Aristophanes adopts precisely the same play on words.[13] The passage is of interest not only because it associates Simonides' name with the genre of epinician, and places the recital of his poetry in the context of an Athenian symposium, but also because, in place of a song by the lyric poet, Strepsiades suggests substituting a passage from Aeschylus. Faced with the renewed objections of his son, who denounces the tragedian as bombastic, incoherent, and pompous, he has no choice but to propose a monologue from Euripides, which turns out to describe the rape of a young girl by her own brother (the son of Aeolus). And yet, to Pheidippides, in a heavily ironic use of the word, Euripides is the 'wisest' (σοφώτατος) of poets![14]

Whether speeches or choral "lyrics", the verses of tragic poets are thus shown to have been recited at symposia, just as the sung compositions of melic poets were. The relevant poets, whether melic or tragic, are associated with an old-fashioned style of banqueting, characterized by traditional musical entertainment; the younger generation go out to symposia of a new type, no doubt characterized instead by sophistic debates.[15]

Though in this case it is not associated with any specific form of song, the same tendency to equate lyric poets with tragic poets is illustrated by a passage from the *Peace*. The former state of the city, before Eirene turned her back on it, is associated with the name of Sophocles. Sadly, in his old age, the poet has now become as stingy as Simonides. The scholiast on this passage adds that Simonides was the first poet to write a song for pay.[16] The same passage makes mention of the 'wise' (σοφός) Cratinos, a comic poet whom Aristophanes, as his rival, often ridicules for his drunkenness. Elsewhere, in the *Wasps*, by way of (insincere) reconciliation with a baker that he has jostled, Philocleon cites the

---

13 Aristophanes, *Clouds* 1345–1362, alluding to Simonides fr. 507 Page = 16 Poltera; cf. scholia ad 1356a and b (I, 3.1, p. 238 Koster); the story of the imprisonment of Krios of Aegina is told by Herodotus, 6.49–50, 73. See the commentary of Poltera (2008) 306–311.
14 Aristophanes, *Clouds* 1363–1379.
15 On the various forms of the symposion, see the bibliography commented on by Murray (1990).
16 Aristophanes, *Peace* 694–700, with scholia ad 697b (pp. 107–108 Holwerda) = Simonides test. 74 Poltera; see also Pindar, *Isthmian* 2.9, with scholia ad loc. (vol. iii, p. 214 Drachmann) = Simonides test. 68a Poltera; cf. Yatromanolakis (2007) 226.

rivalry between Simonides and his contemporary, Lasus of Hermione, who was famed for his hymns and dithyrambs. He asserts that during a singing contest—and the verb associated with such contests is the same as that referring to the staging of comedies (διδάσκειν, with the prefix ἀντι- added to suggest the competitive element)—Lasus said to Simonides that 'it mattered little to him' (ὀλίγον μοι μέλει), probably with a pun on the word μέλος.[17] In the same passage, a tragedian is referred to yet again: in this case, Euripides. Although, in a sense, Aristophanes is here yielding to a biographical tendency in his joke at the expense of Simonides, who was known for his sensitivity where κέρδος was concerned, the passage gives precedence to the "author-function" once again, relating, no doubt, to dithyramb as a poetic and musical genre.

On the subject of the reputation of Simonides in late fifth-century Athens, we must not forget that, in Plato's *Protagoras*, he is the poet cited by the sophist in counterargument to Socrates, to demonstrate the role that poetry plays in education. His famous poem in praise of Scopas is cited and discussed, as a means of examining whether virtue can be taught.[18]

4   Poet-Figures and Lyric Forms

It is, however, Aristophanes' comedy devoted the utopian city of the birds that offers the finest example of correspondence between individual melic poets and melic genres. Like all contemporary states, Cloudcuckooland is to be founded on a 'song and dance culture'. Following the establishment of new gods and heroes, who are celebrated in processions accompanied by song (προσόδια) and propitiated with sacrifices, the next order of business is to celebrate the new city itself. It is at this juncture that a poet comes forward, invoking the Muse and her songs of praise (τεαῖς ἐν ὕμνων ἀοιδαῖς). Asked to identify himself, the anonymous poet describes himself not only as a singer of (epic) verses 'sweet as honey', but also as a 'dedicated servant of the Muses'. In doing so, he explicitly cites the authority of Homer: the title he gives himself recalls the words of the poet of *Homeric Hymn* 32, to Selene, in which singers are self-referentially described in the same terms, as Μουσάων θεράποντες.[19] By echoing this poetic

---

17   Aristophanes, *Wasps* 1403–1413; cf. Simonides test. 65 Poltera (with some bibliographical information).

18   Plato, *Protagoras* 338e–347a, in allusion to Simonides fr. 542 Page = 260 Poltera (see also test. 25 Poltera); on this subject, see also Poltera's commentary, Poltera (2008) 454–467 (together with its plentiful bibliography!).

19   Aristophanes, *Birds* 846–884 and 895–921; cf. *Homeric Hymn* 32.19–20.

phrase, the state poet of the newly founded city of the birds assigns to these servants of the Muses the same "author-function" that Aristophanes, in the *Frogs*, assigns to tragic poets: they are διδάσκαλοι, the educators of the community.

At this point the poet lists the lyric poems (μέλη) that he has composed (a form of the verb ποιεῖν) for Cloudcuckooland: κύκλια, partheneia, and poems in the style of Simonides. The poet also states that 'for ages' he has been celebrating 'this city here' (τήνδε πόλιν—a kind of deictic double reference, at the same time denoting the utopian state that is being constructed on stage, and the city of Athens, on which the spectators are gazing). The word πάλαι, which he uses twice, no doubt refers to the 'old days'—the time of traditional genres of sung poetry. The first of the genres he lists is the dithyramb, which, in its Athenian incarnation, we know to have been sung at the Greater Dionysia, but also at other festivals, such as the Thargelia. The poet also includes songs intended for choruses of young girls, as composed by Alcman for the city of Sparta (an ancient commentator names Alcman as the creator of παρθένια σοφά). Last, there are the poems 'in the style of Simonides', which may be a reference either to epinician odes, or to the Coan poet's scolia.[20] In contrast to these varied poetic forms, which all consist of praise for the citizens and their future wives, the state poet of the birds' city remains unidentified.

But there is more. Once a sacrifice has marked the official foundation of the new state, it is time for the city to be "baptized". It is at this point that the poet offers a parody of the opening of a hyporchema that Pindar sent to Hieron, the tyrant of Syracuse, at the same time as his second Pythian ode, in celebration of the victory of Hieron's four-horse chariot at the Delphic Games. Just as in the Pindaric poem (the first lines of which are quoted by a scholiast) the eulogistic address to the founder of the colonial city of Aetna, quoted by Aristophanes, contains an etymological pun: Hieron's name is associated with the holy rites (ζαθέων ἱερῶν ὁμώνυμε; in Pindar, ἐπώνυμε), and the tyrant's will is thus implicitly compared to that of Zeus.[21] In order to rid himself of this 'wise poet'

---

20 On the use of the word κύκλια (μέλη, line 918: see also line 1403: κυκλιοδιδάσκαλος; cf. below, n. 24) to refer to dithyrambs, see Ieranò (2013) 381–383 (see also, in the same volume— dedicated to the dithyramb 'in its context' [Kowalzig and Wilson (2013)]—the contributions of Ceccarelli, D'Alessio, and Fearn); for a description of partheneia, and on the features of the genre, see Calame (1977) 149–176, as well as Alcman fr. 13 Page-Davies = fr. 8 test. IV, 9 Calame, cf. also below, note 32. According to the scholiast on Aristophanes, *Birds* 919c (p. 144 Holwerda) = Simonides test. 24 Poltera, the songs 'in the style of Simonides' refer to a category of poems that includes hymns, paeans, prosodies, etc.; see the commentary of Dunbar (1995) 531.

21 Aristophanes, *Birds* 922–930, parodying Pindar, fr. 105 (a); see the scholia to Pindar, *Pythian* 2.127.

(τῷ ποιητῇ τῷ σοφῷ!), Peisthetairos offers him a cloak, to keep out the cold (whether alluding to a poem of Hipponax, or to the 'cold' tragic poet Theognis).[22] The poet responds in his turn with three lines containing dialect forms found in Pindar, and sung in "dactylo-epitrites": the Muse accepts the gift, and the poet advises his interlocutor to remember the word, or the verse, of Pindar (Πινδάρειον ἔπος). The poet, again parodying Pindar's hyporchema for Hieron (via a reference to the nomadic Scythians), concludes by quoting its introductory line: 'Understand my words' (σύνες ὅ τοι λέγω). The 'word of Pindar' thus refers to this opening appeal on the part of a poet who addresses himself only to those who understand (συνετοί). The poet of Thebes expresses a similar sentiment in a famous passage from his second Olympian ode, in which the vocal talents of the poet are reserved for those who can appreciate them.[23] Finally, the state poet of the newly founded city agrees to leave, but not without quoting further melic verses; his use of obscure compound adjectives to describe an icy city surrounded by snow-covered plains suggests imitation of a dithyramb, and the metre once again evokes the works of Pindar.[24]

5 Dramatic Reorientations of Lyric Forms

Dithyramb and partheneion are not the only lyric genres to be mentioned in Aristophanes' comedies, but the dithyramb does hold pride of place. In the *Birds*, among the applicants to enrol as citizens of the birds' city in the sky, Aristophanes includes Cinesias, a contemporary of his, who seems to have been known for his dithyrambs. After having sung a few lines of Anacreon, describing the poet's flight to Olympus (transposing the original from an erotic context to a poetic one), Cinesias sings of his own desire to become a sweet-voiced nightingale. In verses that play in a highly sophisticated way on the various avian metaphors that lyric poets use to describe the qualities of their own songs, this representative of the contemporary dithyramb claims for his genre of lyric a winged nature, like the air in the sense that it is at once foggily obscure and shining. The poet then sings a few verses playing on the image of the flight of

---

22   On 'cold Theognis', cf. above (Aristophanes, *Acharnians* 138–140).
23   Aristophanes, *Birds* 931–945; cf. Pindar fr. 105 (b), with the scholia on Aristophanes, *Birds* 941b (Holwerda); for a full breakdown of the passage, see Dunbar (1995) 534–538 (527–528 on the metre); for συνετός in the sense of 'initiate', cf. Pindar, *Olympian* 2.83–85 and *Pythian* 5.107–108, as well as the famous φρονέοντι συνετὰ γαρύω of Bacchylides 3.85. Pindar numbers himself both among poets and among τέκτονες σοφοί: *Pythian* 3.112–115.
24   Aristophanes, *Birds* 946–955, again to be read with the help of Dunbar (1995) 528 and 538–540.

birds, parodying either Euripides or Cinesias himself. The passage alludes to the technique of the poet-σοφός (with a play on ἐσοφίσω and σοφά) as much as to poetic performance, understood as a type of διδάσκειν (with another play on words, as the poet sees himself as a κυκλιοδιδάσκαλος).[25] If there is a single lyric poet's name that Aristophanes associates with a poetic genre as well as with an "author-function", then, it is certainly that of his Athenian contemporary, Cinesias!

In the *Clouds*, Socrates denounces all the charlatans fed by the chorus of clouds: sophists, soothsayers, quack doctors, long-haired σφραγίς experts, and the 'turners of strophes for cyclic choruses' who compose music for the clouds. Strepsiades responds with a series of phrases filled with rich imagery, drawn from dithyrambs; one of these quotations is taken from a dithyramb by Philoxenus of Cythera and, judging by its allusion to the complex modulations of dithyrambic choruses, the object of Aristophanes' mockery is, no doubt, once again dithyrambs of the contemporary style.[26] In the *Peace*, too, a reference to the souls of two or three 'masters of dithyramb' (διθυραμβοδιδάσκαλοι) gliding through the air explicitly evokes the figure of the lyric and tragic poet Ion of Chios, and alludes to the 'morning star' with which one of his dithyrambs opened. Finally, in the parabasis of the *Frogs*, a trader is accused of humming cyclic choruses while defiling statues of Hecate, and of cutting into poets' wages because he had been mocked in a comedy put on as part of the 'ancestral mysteries performed for Dionysus'.[27]

Alongside these numerous references to partheneion and dithyramb, it would not be surprising to see Aristophanes stage at least one hymenaion. The final scene of the *Birds* depicts the reception of Peisthetairos, accompanied by his bride, Basileia; and sure enough, to celebrate the occasion, the chorus sings and dances a hymenaion, which is twice explicitly described as such, and which contains the famous ritual refrain, Ὑμὴν ὦ, Ὑμέναι' ὦ. The description of the bridegroom as the happiest of men, the formal praise of the bride as the consort of Zeus, and the evocation of the role played by Eros in presiding over the exemplary marriage of Hera and Zeus are all drawn from the varied tradi-

---

25   Aristophanes, *Birds* 1373–1409; cf. Ieranò (2013) 368–383, and above, note 19. On the metre of the parodic verses, and the evidence for Cinesias' poetic career, see Dunbar (1995) 660–673.
26   Aristophanes, *Clouds* 330–339, to be read with the commentary of Dover (1968) 144–146; cf. scholia ad 335, which attributes one of the phrases to Polyxenus of Cyrene, who is named in fr. 953 *PCG*; on complex melodies as a feature of new dithyramb, see Franklin (2013) 213–231 (on the *aulos* music that would have accompanied it), and Ieranò (2013) 383–386.
27   Aristophanes, *Peace* 828–836 (see Platnauer [1964] 138–139) and *Frogs* 363–367.

tion of this lyric genre, of which Sappho is the most famous representative.[28] This charming marriage-song, at the close of the comedy, becomes the choral song of the exodos, which leads the protagonists of this final scene offstage in a ritual procession, with the refrain of 'paean'.

The *Peace* draws to its conclusion in a similar way. The ritual celebration of the return of agricultural plenty and of women's fertility that ends the play takes the form of a marriage-song, celebrating the union of Trygaios and Opora. The traditional refrain of the hymenaion is taken up by the chorus, who engage the hero in an amoebaean song, in Aeolian metre. Punctuated by the refrain Ὑμήν, Ὑμέναι' ὤ, this marriage-song begins with the familiar trope of the makarismos, and ends with an appeal to the audience to join in the culinary and erotic pleasures of the marriage feast of Summer.[29] In short, just as in the exodos of the *Birds*, the hymenaion sung at the end of the *Peace*, with its ritualized elements, owes its shape as much to the plot of the play as to the ritual celebration that it enacts through the medium of musical performance; and it does so in terms of form as much as content, incorporating as it does the humorous elements demanded by comedy, as a poetic genre intended to honour Dionysus.

With these two hymenaia, we have strayed from the citation by name of "lyric" poets and melic genres into the full-scale dramatization of lyric poetry, enacted both musically and ritually in the orchestra. As in tragedy, then, this raises the issue of the imitation and enactment in Aristophanes' comedies of different types of traditional song, and of melic genres in particular. Of significance in this regard is the cultic genre of the paean, which calls to mind lyric poets such as Pindar. Though it is named as a poetic genre only once in the comedies of Aristophanes, this verse form makes several appearances in the course of the action of his plays, even if only in the form of the ritual cry Ἰὴ Παιών. Thus, in the *Thesmophoriazusae*, Euripides' relative takes on the role of Andromeda, who addresses her fellow παρθένοι in song; in place of a 'marriage paean', Andromeda intends to sing a song of lamentation for her own sufferings.[30] Elsewhere, as for example when an ἰὴ παιών accompanies the cry of victory that sets a seal on the *Birds*; when the refrain is integrated into the Athenian song that ends the *Lysistrata*, together with an address to victory, and

---

28 Aristophanes, *Birds* 1720–1742, 1748–1765; the features characteristic of a hymenaion that punctuate the song are listed by Dunbar (1995) 745–770; on the song's train of thought, see Calame (2004a) 176–181.
29 Aristophanes, *Peace* 1320–1359; see Calame (2004a) 172–176.
30 Aristophanes, *Thesmophoriazusae* 1034–1037; on the several parodic allusions to the tragedies of Euripides contained in this song, see Prato (2001) 190–191.

a repeated cry of 'euhoe', invoking the presence of Dionysus (as also at the end of the *Ecclesiazusae*); when, in the *Thesmophoriazusae*, the same ritual cry is repeated three times to conclude a prayer to Demeter and Kore, that the people of Athens might prosper; and when, in the *Peace*, the refrain is jokingly referred to in a play on words, punning on παιών in the sense of 'paean' and in the sense of 'striking', calls of 'paean' in Aristophanes generally appear within the context of a melic, choral form of song.[31] In an ode sung by the chorus of the *Knights*, the ritual cry of 'paean' even inspires the coinage ἰηπαιωνίζειν (on the pattern of βακχέβακχον ᾆσαι!).[32]

Be that as it may, a full treatment of the reformulations and 'repurposings' represented by these secondary melic and poetic creations, inserted into the fictional dramatic action, would require a monograph. These are not simple 'allusions' to traditional melic forms; they could easily provide matter for a separate enquiry, treating, for example, the two Laconian choral songs, on the style partly of hymns and partly of Spartan partheneia, which, as a sort of κῶμος, conclude both the dramatic action and the musical ritual performance that is the *Lysistrata*.[33]

6 Conclusion: Falling Short of Classification into Poetic Genres

Is this to say, then, that the canon of nine πραττόμενοι had been sketched out in fifth-century Athens? In those plays of Aristophanes that remain extant, four of these melic poets fail to secure a mention by name: Stesichorus, Bacchylides, Sappho, and Alcman—though the last is perhaps present in spirit in the striking Laconian song that opens the exodos of the *Lysistrata*, and the epithalamia of Sappho (of which a few lines survive) are echoed in the numerous wedding songs dramatized by Aristophanes. On the other hand, in a fragment of the *Helots*, Eupolis, a contemporary of Aristophanes, does cite poems by Stesichorus, Alcman, and Simonides as examples of an older style of song (ἀρχαῖον ἀείδειν).

---

31 Aristophanes, *Birds* 1763 (see Dunbar [1995] 769), *Lysistrata* 1291–1294, *Thesmophoriazusae* 310–311, *Peace* 453–455. On the forms and the sense of this ritual cry, which is not necessarily restricted to the poetic and ritual genre of paean, see Käppel (1992) 65–70; Ford (2006) 286–289.

32 Aristophanes, *Knights* 407–408. For the verb παιανίζειν, 'to chant a paean', see *Knights* 1318 and *Peace* 555.

33 Aristophanes, *Lysistrata* 1248–1272 and 1296–1320; cf. Calame (2004a) 162–172, with the points suggested by Bierl (2009). The similarity of these passages to the partheneia of Alcman was noted by Wilamowitz, (1900) 88–96, who attributes it to imitation on Aristophanes' part.

Another comedy by the same Eupolis depicted Socrates at a symposium, chanting a song of Stesichorus' to the tune of the lyre (while stealing an oinochoe?).[34] If we take these few fragmentary verses by comic poets other than Aristophanes into account, Bacchylides would be the only poet left uncited. Lasus of Hermione, meanwhile, is cited by Aristophanes though he is not part of the Hellenistic canon, as are Aristophanes' contemporaries, Cinesias the Athenian and Philoxenus of Cythera, both composers of dithyrambs.[35]

On the subject of poetic genres and melic forms, and to conclude, in a sort of ring composition, by returning to my remarks on the old age of the scholar, I would draw the reader's attention to an article now almost forty years old. As described in a fragment of a dirge by Pindar, five melic genres seem to have been implicitly recognised in the archaic period: the paean, the dithyramb, the hymenaion, the threnos, and, no doubt, the citharoedic nome (though the name was coined later); a few other sources attest to this categorization, notably the Homeric poems, which encourage us to add hymn (in the Platonic, restricted sense of the word) to the 'catalogue' provided by Pindar.[36]

On the one hand, this list, which is in no sense canonical, might encourage us to take into account all the forms of cletic hymns and cultic songs that Aristophanes has reinvented and inserted into the action of his comedies, for practical dramatic reasons, without labelling them with the name of any particular poetic genre. This applies, for example, to the numerous hymnic forms that punctuate the *Frogs*, enlivening the ritualized action of the comedy through addresses to the various deities of Eleusis; it equally applies to the ode sung by the female chorus of the *Thesmophoriazusae* which, as a performative utterance, constitutes the celebration of the 'holy rites' (ὄργια σεμνά) in honour of the two goddesses at the title festival. In each case, it is possible to associate these forms of ritual song with plausible *ad hoc* labels; the processional song addressed to Phales sung by Dicaeopolis at the opening of the *Acharnians*, for example, could be called a φαλλικόν.[37]

---

34   Eupolis fr. 148 and 395 *PCG*; for a likely allusion to Pindar, see also fr. 398 *PCG*.
35   On Lasus, cf. above, note 16, as well as Wilamowitz (1900) 7–8; at *Acharnians* 1150, the *koryphaios* also mentions a certain Antimachus, a composer of μέλη, now unknown; see also *Clouds* 1022.
36   Pindar, fr. 128c; cf. Plato, *Laws* 700a–b. See the textual and bibliographical notes in my 1974 article.
37   Aristophanes, *Thesmophoriazusae* 947–1000 and *Acharnians* 263–279; see the commentary on these two songs offered by Bierl (2001) 83–125 and 314–325, who focusses on their performative nature and their ritual function. On the hymnic forms and ritual elements that enliven the dramatic action of the *Frogs*, see the text with commentary of Furley and Bremer (2001) 963–971.

On the other hand, the group of poetic forms that were identified by specific labels early on does not include, for example, the banqueting song later known as the scolion. Nonetheless, the famous 'song of Harmodius' is described as such in the *Wasps*, in which two lines of the song are parodied. One line of this song—which Hesychius lists under the lemma Ἁρμοδίου μέλος, describes as a σκόλιον, and attributes to the poet Callistratus (who probably served as διδάσκαλος for some of Aristophanes' comedies)—is also incorporated into the *Lysistrata*. The 'song of Harmodius' (ὁ Ἁρμόδιος) is also mentioned in a sympotic context by the chorus of the *Acharnians* and, lastly, is labelled as the Ἁρμοδίου μέλος in a fragment of the *Pelargoí*.[38] Furthermore, iambic and elegiac poems might reasonably be added to the list of forms belonging to the larger category of μέλος. The difficulty associated with the generic classification of these two forms is a familiar one, as they are defined by their characteristic metres, but present highly varied content, and are associated with a number of different performance contexts.[39]

There is, then, no canon of nine πραττόμενοι to be found in late fifth-century Athens. Instead, we see a variety of prominent figures, organized into a 'Panhellenic' network of melic forms; these poetic forms relate to the individual 'song cultures' that grew out of each developing state, and the most well-known poems would often be recited, usually at symposia. There is even less evidence for a canonical list of fixed poetic forms that we can treat as poetic genres. Far from the more rigorous and systematic generic categorization that was made necessary by the editorial task of the Alexandrian philologists, we see flexible forms of sung and ritualized poetry, unrestricted by the regularities imposed by a long tradition of musical poetry, and adapted to suit a wide variety of performance contexts and degrees of creative competence. In tragedy and comedy, these ritual actions have been broadened, and shaped into those performed in the orchestra of the theatre-sanctuary, in a manner befitting a given fictional and dramatic context. Thence come the new melic forms, songs at once cultic and fictional, that are the choral odes of tragedy and comedy, with functions relating both to the dramatic situation being enacted and to the cultic and musical worship of Dionysus.

---

38 Aristophanes, *Wasps* 1222–1228, *Lysistrata* 630–635, *Acharnians* 978–981, fr. 444 *PCG*; cf. *carmina conuiualia* 893 and 894 Page = 10 and 11 Fabbro; cf. Hesychius, s.v. Ἁρμοδίου μέλος (*A* 7317 Latte).

39 On the ancient category of μέλος, as contrasted with the modern category of 'lyric', and in relation to iambic and elegy, cf. Calame (1998), as well as Budelmann (2009) 2–13. See also Bartol's contribution to this volume, pp. 131–134.

References

Bierl, A. 2009. *Ritual and Performativity: The Chorus of Old Comedy*, Washington, DC.

Bierl, A. 2011. Alcman at the End of Aristophanes' *Lysistrata*: Ritual Interchorality. In *Archaic and Classical Choral Song: Performance, Politics and Dissemination*, ed. L. Athanassaki and E. Bowie, 415–436. Berlin.

Bouvier, D. 2004. "Rendre l'homme meilleur" ou quand la comédie interroge la tragédie sur sa finalité: à propos des *Grenouilles* d'Aristophane. In *Poétique d'Aristophane et langue d'Euripide en dialogue.Études des lettres* 4, ed. C. Calame, 9–26. Lausanne.

Budelmann, F. 2009. Introducing Greek Lyric. In *The Cambridge Companion to Greek Lyric*, ed. F. Budelmann, 1–18. Cambridge.

Calame, C. 1974. Réflexions sur les genres littéraires en Grèce archaïque. *QUCC* 17: 113–128.

Calame, C. 1977. *Les chœurs de jeunes filles en Grèce archaïque* ii. *Alcman*. Rome.

Calame, C. 1998. La poésie lyrique grecque, un genre inexistant? *Littérature* 111: 87–110. (Translated into English as: Greek Lyric Poetry, a Non-Existent Genre?, in *Greek Lyric*, ed. I.C. Rutherford, Oxford, 2019, 35–60.)

Calame, C. 1995. *The Craft of Poetic Speech in Ancient Greece*. Ithaca, NY and London. (Translation of Calame [2000]).

Calame, C. 2000. *Le récit en Grèce ancienne. Énonciations et représentations de poètes*. 2nd edn. Paris (1st edn. 1986). (Translated into English as Calame [1995]).

Calame, C. 2004a. Choral Forms in Aristophanic Comedy: Musical Mimesis and Dramatic Performance in Classical Athens. In *Music and the Muses: The Culture of Mousike in the Classical Athenian City*, ed. P. Murray and P. Wilson, 157–184. Oxford.

Calame, C. 2004b. Identités d'auteur à l'exemple de la Grèce classique: signatures, énonciations, citations. In *Identités d'auteur dans l'Antiquité et la tradition européenne*, ed. C. Calame and R. Chartier, 11–39. Grenoble.

Calame, C. 2009. *L'Éros dans la Grèce antique*. 3rd edn. Paris. (Translated into English as *The Poetics of Eros in Ancient Greece*, 1999, Princeton.)

Carey, C. 2011. Alcman: From Laconia to Alexandria. In *Archaic and Classical Choral Song: Performance, Politics and Dissemination*, ed. L. Athanassaki and E. Bowie, 437–460. Berlin.

Ceccarelli, P. 2013. Circular Choruses and the Dithyramb in the Classical and Hellenistic Period: A Problem of Definition. In Kowalzig and Wilson 2013: 153–170.

Dover, K.J., ed. 1968. *Aristophanes* Clouds. Oxford.

Dunbar, N., ed. 1995. *Aristophanes* Birds. Oxford.

Fabbro, E., ed. 1995. *Carmina convivalia attica*. Rome.

Ford, A. 2006. The Genre of Genres: Paeans and paian in early Greek poetry. *Poetica* 38: 277–296.

Foucault, M. 1994 [1969]. Qu'est-ce qu'un auteur? In *Dits et écrits, 1954–1988*, vol. I, 789–821. Paris, 1994.

Franklin, J.C. 2013. "Songbenders of Circular Choruses": Dithyramb and the 'Demise of Music'. In Kowalzig and Wilson 2013: 213–236.

Furley, W.D. and Bremer, J.M. 2001. *Greek Hymns* ii. *Greek Texts and Commentary*. Tübingen.

Ieranò, G. 2013. "One who is Fought over by all Tribes". The Dithyrambic Poet and the City of Athens. In Kowalzig and Wilson 2013: 368–386.

Käppel, L. 1992. *Paian. Studien zur Geschichte einer Gattung*. Berlin.

Kowalzig, B. and Wilson, P., eds. 2013. *Dithyramb in Context*. Oxford.

Maslov, B. 2015. *Pindar and the Emergence of Literature*. Cambridge.

Murray, O. 1990. Sympotic History. In *Sympotica. A Symposium on the* Symposion, ed. O. Murray, 3–13. Oxford.

Platnauer, M. 1964. *Aristophanes* Peace. Oxford.

Poltera, O., ed. 2008. *Simonides Lyricus. Testimonia und Fragmente*. Basle.

Prato, C., ed. 2001. *Aristofane. Le donne alle Tesmoforie*. Milan.

Robbins, E. 2014. Skolion. In *Brill's New Pauly*. http://referenceworks.brillonline.com/entries/brill-s-new-pauly/skolion-e1115220

Trédé, M. 2003. Présence et image des poètes lyriques dans le théâtre d'Aristophane. In *La poésie grecque antique*, ed. J. Jouanna and J. Leclant, 169–183. Paris.

Vetta, M. 1982. Il *P. Oxy*. 2506 fr. 77 e la poesia pederotica di Alceo. *QUCC* n.s. 10: 7–20.

Yatromanolakis, D. 2007. *Sappho in The Making: The Early Reception*, Washington, DC.

Wilamowitz-Moellendorf, U. 1900. *Die Textgeschichte der griechischen Lyriker*. Berlin.

CHAPTER 6

Structuring the Genre: The Fifth- and Fourth-Century Authors on Elegy and Elegiac Poets

Krystyna Bartol

Let me begin with the obvious point that the early ancient testimonies concerning Greek lyric poetry constitute evidence concerning its reception.* Reception dates in fact from the first response a piece of poetry receives. This applies to all types of poems and elegy is no exception. So the sources from the fifth and fourth century BCE are crucial, as we might well expect, to an assessment of claims about poetry we now call elegy. One must of course be aware that there were differences between the conceptualization of genre in archaic oral culture and that which was developed in times of written poetic production.[1] It must also be realized that the performance-oriented reception of poetry very often—or indeed mostly—does not perfectly match its reception by readers, and that the concept of genre changes over time.[2] The sources from the classical period are, however, a special case. They were generated in a textual culture in which the remains of performance-based culture still strongly persisted. So, they reflect the important (and for us today fascinating) stage in the reception of lyric when poetry was experienced in both modes—(still) orally and (already) readerly. Examining sources from the classical period can help to uncover the connections between these two different modes of reception.[3]

---

* I would like to thank the organizers of the conference for their hospitality and participants for their comments. In particular, I am grateful to Ewen Bowie for his response, from which I have greatly benefited. I also wish to thank Bruno Currie for his help and support with the preparation of this chapter.
1 We are reminded of this problem in Depew's, Obbink's, and others' enquiry into matrices of genre in the oral and the textual phases of Greek culture; see Depew and Obbink (2000), esp. 1–6.
2 See Ercolani (2014) 12, 16.
3 The classical period can be regarded as an interim time between two phases of cultural phenomenon of conceptualizing literary genres. Ercolani (2014) 17 defines the early phase as a period 'in which events were decided by the particular dynamics of orality and occasion' and the later phase as one 'in which such factors gradually ceased to be relevant, eventually to become wholly insignificant.'

When Aristotle in the *Poetics* (1447b14) states that there is no common name for the form of 'imitation' (*mimesis*) produced in elegiacs, the centre of his interest is—as Else rightly observes—not the existence or otherwise of the elegiac art, but the namelessness of it and/or its subdivisions.[4] Aristotle's aim was to protest against describing elegy (and other kinds of 'imitations') only by means of the verse type used by its 'makers', as opposed to its true generic trait, i.e. 'imitation'.[5] He seems to have in mind the inadequacy of the generic terminology existing in his times. His diagnosis of the popular usage of the elegiac verse-name as the elegiac genre-name in the mid-fourth century BCE and his seemingly negative attitude to such a definition suggests that treating elegy as a purely metrical category could in those times be regarded as an act of misinterpretation. Modern scholars would recognize in his remark the traces of a quarrel between two approaches towards defining literary genres, the historical and the theoretical, the former being the result of an observation of literary reality, the latter emerging from the classificatory efforts of thinkers.[6]

It is obvious that Aristotle's attempt to formulate a grammar of genres, based on thematic, stylistic and formal criteria, which did not always match 'what we can know of the archaic and (at least partially) classical systems',[7] is the first harbinger of new heuristic approaches at a time when the performance culture of archaic and early classical Greece was slowly drawing to a close;[8] a culture in which certain kinds of poems were discerned as belonging to a category identifiable on the basis of performance discriminators. The lack of concern about the theoretical structuring of the genres in the archaic epoch, astutely subsumed by Rossi under the label *leggi non scritte, ma rispettate*, which aptly suggests the existence of immanent quasi-generic rules capable of being apprehended by audiences at this time, quickly underwent radical changes in the classical period, which redefined the status of the generic taxonomy, making it a theoretical and often also normative tool for determining the particular

---

4 Else (1957) 41. Generally, Aristotle pays scant attention to the poetic genres that are non-dramatic; see Halliwell's comment on the issue: Halliwell (1987) 74: 'A[ristotle] would have had great difficulty in reconciling most of the works in these categories with his basic principle that the poet is a "maker of plot-structures."'
5 See Halliwell (1987) 50.
6 See Rotstein (2012) 99, who instructively sketches the problem of defining genres. For the usage of Todorov's terminology with reference to the ancient literary culture, see Rotstein (2012) 99. She points also to other cognate conceptual frameworks, in which the two approaches are called respectively ethnic and analytical; see her remarks, 98–99.
7 Riu (2003) 21.
8 On the performance culture of archaic and early classical Greece, see Carey (2009) 22.

categories of songs and recitations.[9] According to Rossi,[10] the classical age of Greece was the time when generic rules were written and respected (*leggi scritte e rispettate*), but it does not seem right to keep this order of epithets (i.e. *scritte, rispettate*), since a set of written rules—in other words, a theoretical understanding of a genre—took its shape as a derivative of performance experiences, not vice-versa. Giulio Colesanti, when recently 're-reading Rossi's article', considers these two principles determined by 'il nostro Chico' to be fundamental to interpreting early Greek culture (together with the third principle concerning the later epoch when 'the laws were written, but not respected'), but imposes some limitations on them and argues that this binary opposition is not valid in the field of elegy.[11] To his distrust of the existence of elegiac 'laws written and respected' in the classical period I will return later in this chapter.

Elegy, indeed, forms a distinct body of Greek poetry. It made use of a great variety of themes, but the medium established for their presentation was uniform and simple: the couplet consisting of a dactylic hexameter followed by two *hēmiepē*. This pattern of verse-composing appears to have been for the early Greeks sufficiently distinctive to generate in their minds an idea of a separate category. Although the elegiac couplet as the simplest pattern of strophic poetry was sung with musical accompaniment,[12] elegy was recognized as divergent from melic in the archaic as well as in the classical epochs.[13]

That at the end of the fourth century BCE the genre of elegy was conceptualized in opposition to melic emerges from a Peripatetic source:[14] this contrast is implied by Clearchus (fr. 34 Wehrli, in Athenaeus 13.597a = Antimachus Test. 10 Matthews) in his *Erotica*, where he said that two poets, Antimachus and

---

9   Rossi (1971) 52–71. This does not mean, however, that the laws began to be written in the form of manuals. The presence of the metapoetic passages in various types of lyric may be treated as the proof of poets' awareness of such laws.
10 Rossi (1971) 52–71.
11 Colesanti (2012) 261–275 ('il nostro Chico', 264).
12 Simplest pattern of strophic poetry: Dale (1963) 46–50, who points out that some patterns of early Greek poetry present (47) 'the stanza-form': stanza used κατὰ στίχον, which are sung verses. Colesanti (2012) 265 calls the elegiac couplet '*strofa epodica.*' Faraone (2008) treats this feature the basic constituent of elegiac poems, making five-couplet 'strophes' the most important features of an elegiac composition.
13 In the poetic remains of elegiac poets, the only instance of the marked term μέλος (*Theognidea* 761) is not self-referential, as Budelmann and Power (2013) 5 have recently pointed out. See further below at n. 26 for their denial that the performance of elegy was properly melic.
14 The elegiac genre was not, however, as vigorous at this time as it had been earlier; compare West's extreme diagnosis, that 'the first quarter of the fourth century BC saw an almost complete drying-up' of this genre (West [1974] 1).

a certain Lamynthius of Miletus, shared love themes and composed poems entitled *Lyde*, the former ἐν ἐλεγείοις, the latter ἐν μέλει.[15] The contrast does not seem to emphasize the division between spoken and sung poetry, since other testimonies from that and a slightly later period prove the presence of musical accompaniment during elegiac performance.[16] It must be then something else that makes the ἐλεγεῖα differ from μέλος. The same opposition is found in the so-called Echembrotus inscription dated to 586 BCE (in Paus. 10.7.5–6). We are informed here that the Arcadian aulode won the Pythian contest singing μέλεα καὶ ἐλέγους.[17] Pausanias' definition of the latter (as mournful lament) is probably a later development,[18] and the inscription itself does not tell us anything about the content of *elegoi*. But even if the *elegos* (the derivative of which might be the ἐλεγεῖον) was a threnodic type of elegy,[19] the juxta-

15 ἀλλὰ (...) ἄνδρες φίλοι, ἐξελαθόμην ὑμῖν εἰπεῖν τήν τε Ἀντιμάχου Λυδήν, προσέτι δὲ καὶ τὴν ὁμώ-νυμον ταύτης ἑταίραν Λυδὴν ἣν ἠγάπα Λαμύνθιος ὁ Μιλήσιος. ἑκάτερος γὰρ τούτων τῶν ποιητῶν, ὥς φησι Κλέαρχος ἐν τοῖς Ἐρωτικοῖς, τῆς βαρβάρου Λυδῆς εἰς ἐπιθυμίαν καταστὰς ἐποίησεν ὁ μὲν ἐν ἐλεγείοις, ὁ δ' ἐν μέλει ('But I nearly forgot, my friends, to mention Antimachus' Lyde to you, as well as the courtesan Lyde who shared her name, and whom Lamynthius of Miletus was sweet on. For both poets, according to Clearchus in his *Erotica*, became infatuated with the barbarian Lyde and wrote poems entitled *Lyde*, the former in elegiacs, the latter in lyric meters,' translated by Olson [2011] 15–17).
16 Cf. Chamaeleon fr. 24 Steffen (ap. Ath. 14. 620c), Philochorus, 328 F 216 (ap. Ath. 14. 330c). On this subject, see Bartol (1987) 261–278.
17 Ἐχέμβροτος Ἀρκὰς | θῆκε τῶι Ἡρακλεῖ νικήσας τόδ' ἄγαλμα | Ἀμφικτυόνων ἐν ἄθλοις, | Ἕλλησι δ' ἀείδων | μέλεα καὶ ἐλέγους ('Echembrotus the Arcadian dedicated this gift to the glory of Heracles, having been victorious at the contests of the Amphictyons, where he sang songs and *elegoi* [Campbell translated: laments] to the Greeks').
18 Bowie (1986) 23 is right in saying: 'Too much reliance has been placed upon Pausanias' statement that the suspension of aulodic competitions at the Pythian games of 586 BC was due to the lugubrious quality of elegy sung to the *aulos*.' One must agree with his conclusion concerning Pausanias: 'The text is worthless as evidence of the nature of early elegy.' Pausanias continues the interpretation that might have started to be popular in the fifth century BCE. On this issue, see Lulli (2011) 20: '*I due generi letterari del* threnos *e dell'elegia, dunque, hanno avuto proprio l'*aulos *quale caratteristica commune. L'accompagnamento dell'*aulos, *strumento considerato dagli antichi il più adatto all'espressione del sentimento del dolore e del lutto, rappresenta così un possibile elemento catalizzatore dell'equivalenza stabilità tra* threnos *ed elegia, prima nella produzione drammatica attica del v sec. a. C., e in sequito nella tradizione erudita fino all'età bizantina.*' See also Gerber (1999) 1–2: 'We have an inscription commemorating the victory in the Pythian games of 586 won by Echembrotus of Arcadia "singing songs and elegies", but we are not told of the content of these elegies.' Campbell (1991) 201, however, insists on threnodic connotations of Echembrotus' *elegoi*. The inscription attracted Bowie's attention again more recently: see Bowie (2014) 39–55.
19 The problem of the character of *elegos* has been recently revisited by Nagy (2011) 13–45. He assumes (35) that the formation of elegy as a monodic genre takes its origin from the

position with μέλεα may point to a difference either in the character of the melodic accompaniment or in the metrical form, not to different themes[20] or moods of these compositions.[21] The binary pair expressed by the polarized phrases: μέλεα—ἐλέγους and ἐν μέλει—ἐν ἐλεγείοις appears to reflect the opposition between the highly varied and flexible lyric/melic metres and the relatively regular elegiac pattern,[22] based on one rhythmical dactylic sequence only.[23] This way of identifying the main characteristics of the two categories of poetic compositions may suggest that the performative difference between melic (usually sung with the accompaniment played, according to the occasion, on various instruments)[24] and elegy (performed to the accompaniment of the wind-instrument, the *aulos*) was decisive in the process of conceptualization of the elegiac genre in the archaic and classical periods.[25] What is fundamental to interpreting the meaning of both terms is the awareness of the idea of full-scale song embedded in them.[26] The relationship between melic

---

decontextualization of mournful emotions expressed in the form of choral performance, i.e. from the transferring such emotions into the context of the symposium and competitive monodic singing at public festivals.

20 See Gentili (1968) 51: '*la forma elegiaca non era ritenuta esclusiva del* threnos *ma coincidentalmente idonea ad altri differenti tipi di composizioni poetiche. Perciò* elegeion ... *non riguardò il contenuto trenodico del carme, ma soltanto il metro.*'

21 It seems, however, that the singing of a lament or expressing sorrows was only one item within the elegiac thematic repertoire. The form of funeral elegy might have flourished in the Peloponnese. The issue has been recently re-examined by Nobili (2011) 26–48.

22 I here use "lyric" in the narrow sense (= melic).

23 See Neri (2011) 16: '[*elegia*] *era scandita sempre dallo stesso metro, il distico elegiac.*'

24 Although in this particular case Echembrotus' *melea* belong to the aulody, it does not mean that in another context the same poetic text was not performed as a *kitharoidia* or was not treated rhapsodically. For 'alternative treatments of the same poetic texts,' see Ford (1988) 303 n. 25. See also Rotstein (2012) 117, who classifies some genres performed at the musical competitions as a group that 'could have been performed within different categories' (cf. 118, Fig. 4).

25 The agonistic context of performance as a primary "genre-defining" factor in the archaic Greece has been recently revisited by Rotstein (2012). She argues that 'by enacting taxonomies, either strengthening or weakening the specificity of traditional types, institutionalized poetic and musical competitions contributed to the ancient conceptualization of literary genres' (92). See also Cancik (2003) 130: 'Contest, including musical, epic, lyric, and dramatic contests, implies rules and standards; it requires judges, a large number of participants and an open, public space.'

26 But see Budelmann and Power's (2013) approach to the problem of elegiac sympotic performance. They have developed—in sharp contrast with other scholars—the notion of 'inbetweenness' of sympotic elegy. Having downplayed the musical element in presenting elegies at feasts, they argued that elegy situated itself between speech and song. See also Sbardella (2018) 7–16.

and elegy in their original cultural setting is then, paradoxically, better seen in their affinity (the shared musical environment) than in their otherness (different melodic patterns and degree of their complexity).[27] The understanding of the elegiac genre's relation to *melos* seems to have changed over time and shifted from being unified with it by the strong presence of the musical element to being definitively separated from it by the absence of melody during elegiac performance. When Pseudo-Plutarch (*De musica* 1134a) comments on a testimony of Hipponax (fr. 153 = 146 Degani) concerning Mimnermus' musical performance, he explains that at first (ἐν ἀρχῆι) the aulodes sang elegiac verses set to music.[28] He uses the phrase ἐλεγεῖα μεμελοποιημένα the meaning of which is approximately equivalent to 'elegies sung to a musical accompaniment'. The explanation suggests that in the post-classical time elegy was not regarded as sung and was consequently distinguished from melic. Elegy was then refused entry into the class of melic on the grounds of its assumed lack of musical character. Whatever one may think of the judgement of the post-classical critics,[29] it seems evident that in the archaic and classical periods a specific type of melody, related to specific metrical units, was one of the performance criteria for calling something an elegy or calling something a melic poem.

The early authors who exhibited an interest in exploring works of poets now called 'elegiac' tagged the type of poetry composed by them with three terms: ἔλεγος, ἐλεγεῖον, and ἐλεγεία.[30] Various attempts to explain the primary significance attached to these words and to clarify the relationship between them have been made by modern scholars. Although their thorough treatments offered of this problem are of great help in determining the terms' essential meanings, they do not let us draw decisive conclusions.[31] The main reason to feel gloomy about the conceptualization of genre expressed by the terms mentioned above

---

27   Affinity of melic and elegy: Vara Donado (1982) 433–453. Otherness: Barron and Easterling (1989) 87: 'Distinctions of genre are often clearer musically than metrically. Elegy was normally accompanied on the pipe, and is therefore quite distinct from the epic, which was chanted to the deep-voiced *cithara*, and from lyric, sung to the *lyra* or *barbitos*.'

28   Καὶ ἄλλος δ' ἐστὶν ἀρχαῖος νόμος καλούμενος Κραδίας, ὃν φησιν Ἱππῶναξ Μίμνερμον αὐλῆσαι. ἐν ἀρχῆι γὰρ ἐλεγεῖα μεμελοποιημένα οἱ αὐλωιδοὶ ἦιδον. ('There is another ancient nome called Cradias, which Hipponax says Mimnermus performed on the *auloi*; for at first singers to the *auloi* sang elegiac verse set to music'; translation by B. Einarson, P.H. De Lacy.)

29   See Bartol (2013) 401–416, esp. 414.

30   Compare Aloni (2011) 168–169, who points out that these three terms were used with reference to elegy 'at different times and in different ways.'

31   See, among others, West (1974) 1–4; Bowie (1986) 25–26; Gerber (1997) 94–96; Gerber (1999) 1–3; Bartol (1993) 18–30.

is the fact that early texts that include these terms are neither numerous nor extensive. Moreover, statements contained in the extant sources without a full context may be confusing or misleading.

Of the three terms ἔλεγος, ἐλεγεῖον, and ἐλεγεία, ἔλεγος seems to be the earliest. It is probable that it had two meanings: a later meaning reconstructed as sung lament, attested in the classical period by Euripides' plays performed after 415 (*Trojan Women* 119, *Iphigenia among the Taurians* 146, *Helen* 185, *Orestes* 968, *Hypsipyle* 1 III 9) and by Aristophanes *Birds* 217, and the original one, not necessarily related to lament. That the term ἔλεγος did not have to denote aspects of the content at all is suggested by the Echembrotus inscription (I have already mentioned the unreliability of Pausanias' comment on it), dated to 586 BCE, which might have polarized the melodic patterns of *melea* and ἔλεγοι, not their content. It is tempting to suspect that the term ἔλεγος in its original context denoted a certain fixed melodic pattern,[32] which corresponded to the metrical scheme of the couplet consisting of hexameter and two *hēmiepē*.[33] The fact that Pseudo-Plutarch in his treatise *On Music* (1132D), when enumerating names of *nomoi* and relying on Heracleides' list,[34] mentions ἔλεγοι as the name of an aulodic nome,[35] may support the hypothesis that melodic pattern, i.e. a performance feature, constituted one of its defining marks at the earliest stage of conceptualizing the elegiac genre.[36] The linking of ἔλεγος and lament, which started to appear in the late fifth century, was, as Bowie rightly argues,[37] partly the result of the regular usage of the metrical pattern hexameter plus two *hēmiepē* for sepulchral inscriptions.

The term ἐλεγεῖον, which must be derived from ἔλεγος, appears first about the end of the fifth century.[38] The two earliest instances of its usage are extremely interesting since they show that people of this time came close to an awareness of an elegiac genre and that the criteria for its definition were expanded, includ-

---

32   Not, more generally, 'a song sung to aulos', as Bowie (1986) 26 suggests.
33   But see Budelmann and Power (2013) 13, for whom 'a further facet of the complex ... semantics of ἔλεγος was ... the actual and conceptual inbetweenness typical of the genre.' See also: 'The associations of elegy that Euripides exploits here do not just include whatever connection the genre had with lament but also its intermediate place on the scale from speech to music' (14).
34   On Pseudo-Plutarch's sources, see Bartol (2013) 411–412.
35   Cf. Neri (2011) 15: '*primi ἔλεγοι, inni cantati con l'accompagnamento di un aerofono ad ancia detto "aulo"* (νόμοι *aulodici*).'
36   See Bartol (1993) 76.
37   Bowie (1986) 25.
38   See Bowie (1986) 25: 'the uses show that ἐλεγεῖον had been coined by the last decade of the fifth century, and suggest that the coinage may have been recent'.

ing now—besides melodic or metrical features—also theme, social appeal, and mode of communication.[39] I here refer to Critias fr. 4 W. and Pherecrates' *Chiron* (fr. 162.11–12 K.-A.), both composed around 410 BCE. In the case of Critias' two couplets:

καὶ νῦν Κλεινίου υἱὸν Ἀθηναῖον στεφανώσω
   Ἀλκιβιάδην νέοισιν ὑμνήσας τρόποις·
οὐ γάρ πως ἦν τοὔνομ' ἐφαρμόζειν ἐλεγείωι,
   νῦν δ' ἐν ἰαμβείωι κείσεται οὐκ ἀμέτρως

And now I shall crown the Athenian son of Cleinias, Alcibiades, with a song in a new manner. For it was not possible in any way to fit the name into elegiac verse; now it will lie, not unmetrically, in an iambic line

trans. D.A. GERBER

Here, he declares that he will crown Alcibiades with a song in a new manner, since it is not possible to fit his name into elegiac verse the name will be put in an iambic line (ἐν ἰαμβείωι κείσεται), the meaning of ἐλεγεῖον may seem to denote metrical features only, additionally stressed by using ἰαμβεῖον as its opposite. Such a sense of ἐλεγεῖον has been assumed by the majority of modern scholars who treat Critias' statement as—to use Colesanti's words— 'a technical remark on metrical choices'.[40] The metrical implication, made fully explicit by Critias, seems, however, to invite a further interpretation that goes beyond this "technical" surface. I am inclined to share with some Italian scholars the conviction that the poet, when polarizing two terms which apparently have purely metrical meanings, ἐλεγεῖον and ἰαμβεῖον, actually intended to adduce the framework within which a distinction between two different kinds (genres?) of poetry has been made, namely the elegiac *epainos* and iambic *psogos*.[41] Elegiac metre, he seems to say, is appropriate for an elevated praise whereas iambic is suitable for low themes and invective. The insertion of iambic rhythm into the dactylic sequence is then a signal indicating the real character of the whole poem,[42] which includes, not the praise, but the criti-

---

39   But see also Thucydides (1.132.2–3), who at about the same time used ἐλεγεῖον to mean 'elegiac couplet' (on the dedicatory inscription).
40   Colesanti (2012) 270: '*l'osservazione tecnica sulle scelte metriche*.' Cf. West (1974) 3; Bowie (1986) 25. See also Bartol (1993) 20.
41   Lapini (1995) 1–23; Ianucci (2002) 38–44; Ianucci (2003) 31–42.
42   If the problem with the name of Alcibiades was only of prosodical nature, Critias would have had various ways to solve it. See Lapini (2002) 3–4, and Ianucci (2003) 33: '*per*

cism of Alcibiades.[43] Critias' parodic play with the genre of elegiac *epainos* (its transformation into iambic *psogos*, a completely different form of poetry),[44] coupled with the audience's supposed experience in recognizing the poet's joke,[45] proves that in the last decade of the fifth century BCE elegy was treated as a category determined by features both of form and of content.

Pherecrates' (fr. 162. 10 K.-A.) hexameter parody of one and a half (non-consecutive) lines of an elegiac poem (ἐλεγεῖα) that might be by Euenus (fr. 8a W. = *Theognidea* 467–496),[46] as Bowie convincingly suggests,[47] incorporated into comic comment on unfriendly behaviour towards uninvited guests,[48] test-

---

    nomi prosodicamente incompatibili ai metra *dattilici erano infatti disponibili varie soluzioni alternative alla modifica del metro ... Crizia poteva ricorrere alla sinizesi ... o escogitare altri espedienti, ammesso che non fosse sufficente l'espressione Κλεινίου υἱόν.*

43 Cf. Lapini (2002) 4: '*l'inserzione di metri giambici in un tessuto epico presuppone* un intento ludibundus'.

44 Although, as Degani (1987) 1010, points out: '*giambo poteva anche essere ... i possibili contatti con l'elegia—una presa di posizione, più o meno risentita, su eventi contemporanei, su temi di ordine morale e politico*', the way of presenting themes, in some cases similar, was different in the two genres. The exception is perhaps Archilochus' elegiac production; on this issue see the recent remarks made by Nikolosi (2013) 21. She calls elegy '*genere per statuto serio*' and comments on Archilochus' elegies: '*l'aspetto scherzoso e l'habitus scoptico, nonché la* Stimmung *seriocomica, dovevano contraddistinguere tutta la sua produzione*.' The distinction between particular genres did not, however, result in constructing a hierarchy between genres in archaic or—at least partially—classical Greece, as Riu (2012) 249–282 convincingly argues.

45 The audience consisted of the symposiasts: see Neri (2011) 16: '*In età classica (V–IV secolo), la sempre più marcata destinazione simposiale portò l'elegia a specializzarsi come mezzo di comunicazione politica (con l'ambigua figura di Crizia), di gioco e relax conviviale ... di* ludus parodico.' One can treat Critias' joke as an example of generic interplay, a poetic procedure popular in the last quarter of the fifth century, as Foley (2008) 15–36, points out. Critias' elegy is an example of his high poetic self-consciousness. It shows that the scholars who deny classical elegists such an attitude to their own production, are wrong. See Murray (2010) 107–108: 'There is a tendency among modern scholars of early elegy to privilege the poetic form of the Archaic period as stable and fixed prototypes devoid of any self-consciousness, and to regard any subsequent variation as an illegitimate degeneration ... In fact ... the early elegists can be shown to be self-consciously negotiating the boundaries of the genre of their poetry in gestures that have come to associate only with Hellenistic poets.' On the problem of the boundaries of genres, see also Bartol (2017) 155–157.

46 *Theognidea* 467 and 469: μηδένα τῶνδ' ἀέκοντα μένειν κατέρυκε παρ' ἡμῖν, and μηδ' εὕδοντ' ἐπέγειρε, Σιμωνίδη ('Don't hold back anyone of these so that he remain with us against his will' and 'don't waken from his sleep, Simonides'; translated by D.E. Gerber).

47 Bowie (1997) 57; Bowie (2012) 129.

48 Fr. 162. 11–12 K.-A.: μηδένα μήτ' ἀέκοντα μένειν κατέρυκε παρ' ἡμῖν μηθ' εὕδοντ' ἐπέγειρε, Σιμωνίδη ('And neither hold back anyone who is unwilling to remain with us, nor wake the man who is asleep, Simonides'; translated by S.D. Olson).

ifies to the popularity of elegiac production in the last quarter of the fifth century,[49] independently of how it was diffused, whether still orally or as texts.[50] The passage parodied is strongly paraenetic (it contains sympotic precepts), and it seems that this very feature of elegy was perceived as equally characteristic of its content. In the classical period the didactic element in elegiac poetry is stressed by Isocrates (*To Nicocles* 42–43), who calls Theognis and Phocylides, apart from Hesiod, 'the best givers of advice' (ἀρίστους ... συμβούλους), and calls their poems 'instructions' (ὑποθῆκαι). Later, Lycurgus (*Against Leocrates* 106) says that Tyrtaeus' ἐλεγεῖα 'teach manliness' (παιδεύονται πρὸς ἀνδρείαν) and locates the main function of elegy in its paideutic effects. Demosthenes (*On the Embassy*, 19.254–256), quoting, as he says, τὰ τοῦ Σόλωνος ἐλεγεῖα, stresses that the poet's words show his hate for some people.[51] He understands, then, Solon's elegies as poems presenting the poet's attitude towards some persons and situations.[52] These attitudes concerning particular people and situations, repeated in a new context, become general.[53] So in a way, Demosthenes highlights the general character of elegiac statements. It seems that this factor played an important role in defining elegy in his time.

The term ἐλεγεία, which seems to be a later coinage,[54] is found for the first time in Aristotle (*Constitution of the Athenians* 5.2, 5.10). Originally it could have been a feminine form of the adjective ἐλεγεῖος, -α, -ον,[55] and could have acted as an attributive to a noun, for instance, ποίησις, but already the earliest surviving testimonies show a form that is undoubtedly a noun. No distinct tendency is observed in the choice of either term, ἐλεγεῖον or ἐλεγεία, in Aristotle. The usage of the singular or plural form depends on the context: when he intends to quote the beginning of a particular poem (as in the case of citing Solon's fr. 4a and 4b), he uses the singular ἐλεγεία, whereas noting (*Rhetoric* 1405a31)

---

49   Another example of elegy being alluded to by the classical authors is the passage from the parabasis of Aristophanes' *Peace* (734–740) staged in 421 BCE. Line 736 has been identified by the scholia as a Simonidean allusion (παρὰ τὰ Σιμωνίδου ἐκ τῶν ἐλεγείων) to his elegiac, not epigramatic, production. See Rawles (2013) 178–183.

50   Orally diffused: Colesanti (2011). Diffused as texts: Bowie (1997) 58. For the process of changing the way of transmitting elegies, from oral to that in written form, see Vetta (1983) lviii–lix.

51   Λέγε δή μοι λαβὼν καὶ τὰ τοῦ Σόλωνος ἐλεγεῖα ταυτί, ἵν' εἰδῆθ' ὅτι ὁ Σόλων ἐμίσει τοὺς οἵους ... ἀνθρώπους ('Please take and read these elegiac verses of Solon [fr. 4], so that you may know that Solon too hated such men'; translated by D.E. Gerber).

52   Elegy is, as Irvin (2005) 2 rightly says, 'intersection of archaic poetics and politics'.

53   For this characteristic of the archaic elegy, see Hunter (2012) 72.

54   See Bowie (1986) 25.

55   The existence of the adjective is proven by Aelian (*V.H.* 1.17: ἐλεγεῖος δίστιχος). See Zacher (1898) 10; Bartol (1993) 22.

that Dionysius Chalcus calls poetry 'the scream of Calliope' he says: προσαγορεύει ... ἐν τοῖς ἐλεγείοις κραυγὴν Καλλιόπης τὴν ποίησιν ('[Dionysius Chalcus'] who in his elegies calls poetry the scream of Calliope'). It seems that he had in mind one particular line of Dionysius' poem (fr. 7), and one might expect that he would employ the term ἐλεγεία, as in the case of quoting Solon's pieces. But he did not. This may mean that in Aristotle's time there were no clear semantic differences between ἐλεγεῖον and ἐλεγεία—that both terms were interchangeably used with reference to poems composed in elegiac couplets. The authors made use of them to indicate a class of poems with which the recipients of their works appeared to be familiar. So they had no need to explain in detail the criteria for distinguishing this class of poetry. The elegiac genre had already been constructed in the minds of the members of classical society, perhaps not very carefully, and at some points even inconsistently, but it is almost certain that an average consumer of culture in classical Athens knew how to use terms such as ἔλεγος, ἐλεγεῖον, and ἐλεγεία.

The notion of the elegiac genre must have been fixed quite early. The tangible proof of the classical Greeks' ability to negotiate the boundaries of this genre is the creation of the collections of early elegiac poetry. It is reasonable to suppose that thinking about what elegy was and was not by the end of the fifth century BCE was directly linked with judicious selective reading of the mass of poetic material at hand and, consequently, gathering, or compiling excerpts that seemed to be suitable for an anthology. One should therefore take issues of genre together with those of transmission,[56] since the definition of elegy, understood as a set of ideas clustered around the terms ἐλεγεῖον, ἐλεγεία, must have influenced the selection and then assembly of poetic pieces into an anthology by a compiler. We have some undisputed testimony, recently thoroughly treated by Ewen Bowie,[57] which indicate that the idea of gathering goes back at least to the late fifth century BCE. Furthermore, the process of the creation of the elegiac collection transmitted as *Theognidea* 'Book One' and 'Book Two' might have happened, as Bowie convincingly argues, in Athens late in the fifth century.[58] So it must be asked, what makes these sympotic pieces, which display a variety of subject and styles, distinctively elegiac.

The presumed sympotic context of their presentation could not be said to be a distinctive essence of the components of these two collections, since the

---

56 Cf. Swift and Carey's programmatic statement in their introduction to the recent book on iambus and elegy: Swift and Carey (2016) 6.
57 Bowie (2012) 125–127.
58 The process of the creation of the collection has been discussed by many scholars. See West (1974) 40–64; Selle (2007) 8; Colesanti (2011); Bowie (2012) 121–148.

same kind of context also applies to the genre of other *Commersbücher* circulating in Greece as early as the beginning of the fifth century BCE and never referred to as elegiac.[59] It appears that—in a process of selecting excerpts from poets' sympotic output—the key for demarcating what 'counted' for inclusion in an elegiac collection was both metre (the elegiac couplet) and the applicability of the content of a sympotic piece to moral aristocratic education.[60] It is reasonable to assume that the metre together with the topic that provides hearers / readers with moral and intellectual benefit were sufficient to mark the elegiac identity of a text and make it suitable for an elegiac collection. It also seems that those poems composed in elegiac couplets that exhibited purely (meta-) sympotic or erotic themes (e.g. *Theognidea* 261–269, 993–1002 and the whole of *Theognidea* 'Book 2') by including a coherent set of social ideas bearing upon the lifestyle of the archaic Greek aristocracy, thereby satisfied elegy's requirement for themes of "sympotic education" or at least an "educative register". By combining conventional elements of sympotic entertainment with the emotional experience of an individual they mirrored the group ethos of the élite circle and might therefore be understood as a part of the process of formation of the young *aristoi*. The elegiac *sylloge* thus resembles—in respect of its purpose—the gnomic anthology that aimed at giving lessons to the reader rather than the poetic *stephanos* woven first of all for a reader's pleasure. If we adopt John Barns' position regarding the existence of two different types of early anthologies (i.e. these compiled for mere pleasure and those aimed at teaching),[61] we will see that the early elegiac *syllogai* fit perfectly the early sophists' study of poetry and reflect the anthological or selective methods in literary education promoted by the sophists.[62] Barns' investigations, primarily concerned with the sophistic interest in poetic *gnomai*, particularly as an aid of teaching, and the proposal put forward recently by Bowie that we should see Euenus of Paros, the sophist, as a compiler putting together the elegiac collection 'for use by his wealthy young pupils that combined the light and metasympotic with the politically and morally improving' admirably converge on the point of the purpose of

---

59   Represented today by the remains of the collection of the Attic *scolia*. On this collection see Fabbro (1995) xlii, who calls the collection '*corpus che si formò probabilmente nel V o al piú tardi nel IV secolo*' and says (xxv) that '*la raccolta … riproduce uno dei numerosi* Commersbücher *circolti sin dall'ultimo scorcio del VI secolo ad uso dei simposiasti.*'
60   Demarcating what 'counted': I adopt here the neat formula of Swift and Carey (2016) 6.
61   Barns (1950) 134.
62   Barns (1951) 4–9.

making a collection.⁶³ This fact additionally inspires confidence in Bowie's claims concerning the identification of the creator of two early elegiac *syllogai*.⁶⁴

I think it is also noteworthy that the emergence of the couplets known to us as a part of the *Theognidea*, or allusions to them, in works of some classical authors supports the conception of elegiac verses as educative poems, and suggests that elegies were considered quintessentially gnomic and as offering authoritative advice concerning the area of aristocratic moral expertise. Of course it would be a mistake to insist that the authors in the fifth and fourth century took the quotations directly from the *syllogai* (they could simply repeat verses preserved in their memory, since poetry sung at symposia was still a common phenomenon). Nevertheless, their interest in moral standards and in precepts on the conduct of a noble man enjoined by elegiac pieces prove that didactic quality was recognized as the most important feature of the elegiac genre. When Plato makes Socrates (*Meno* 95d) quote elegiac verses, known to us as 33–36 of the Theognidean 'Book One', calling on young people to drink, dine, and sit with the noble, for from them they will learn noble things, he locates elegy among the paideutic genres. Three or four decades earlier,⁶⁵ the Aristophanic Peisetairos (*Av.* 1362–1363) seemed to be motivated by the same logic of elegiac definition, when alluding to the *Theognidea* 27–28 since he declares to give his son not bad advice (οὐ κακῶς ὑποθήσομαι) which he learned from noble men when he was still a child. A tendency on the part of poets to understand elegy as poetry whose character was akin to that of gnomic literature is also visible in fourth-century comedy.⁶⁶ In Theophilus' *Neoptolemus* gnomic elegiac couplets from the *Theognidea* (457–460) exploring the thought that a young wife is not suitable for an old husband were transformed into iambic trimeters while retaining the witty comparison of a woman to a boat (fr. 6 *PCG*).⁶⁷ Although the accounts linking the early elegiac poems and prob-

---

63   Bowie (2012) 131.
64   In a similar way to Bowie's proposition regarding Euenus as a redactor of an early Theognidean collection, Aloni and Ianucci (2016) 155–173 have recently suggested that Critias 'should be held responsible for an analogous *syllogē* including some of his own songs and other poems, traditionally performed and perceived as Solonian within a sympotic group to which he referred' (173). They date the collection to about 450 BCE. It should be pointed out that if one accepts the proposed identity of the author of this *syllogē*, also this example may serve to illustrate the sophistic environment's influence on the origin of elegiac compilations.
65   Plato's dialogue was written c. 382 BCE, Aristophanes' *Birds* were staged in 415 BCE.
66   For the reception of the *Theognidea* in Attic Comedy, see Kugelmeier (1996) 125–127.
67   On this fragment, see Papachrysostomou (2008) 263–268. On the relationship between

ably also the elegiac collections to educative purposes are largely Athenian and come from the classical period, this conception of the elegiac genre does not seem by any means to be a local phenomenon. Establishing a connection between sympotic songs composed in small stanzas and the paideutic purpose of moral and political issues presented in them must have taken place as early as in the archaic period. The universalizing educative tone of elegiac precepts must have opened up infinite possibilities of their territorial expansion all over the Greek world.[68] If we accept Colesanti's proposal to date a century before 420 BCE the creation of a Megarian ὑπόμνημα of elegiac sympotic poetry, which was transported to Athens circa 420 and which, used and re-used orally at symposia, became the basis for the collection known to us as the *Theognidea*,[69] we have to assume that the conception of the elegiac genre as a means of education was deep-rooted as early as the archaic epoch,[70] and that the symposium was recognized the occasion for presenting these paideutically oriented poetic pieces.[71]

From what has been said above one can draw the conclusion that elegy was treated as a separate literary genre in the archaic as well as in the classical period. In the archaic period elegy, sharing contextual factors (occasion of presentation), with other types of lyric, was recognized as a separate category

---

the *Theognidea* 457–460 and Theophilus' Fr. 6, see also Ferrari (1989) 146 and Gambato (2001) 1411, who writes that the passage from Theophilus' play '*costituisce una consapevole imitazione dei versi teognidei*.'

68   Their Panhellenic recognition is suggested by Theognis (237–254) who expects his poems to gain the spread across the Greek world (it is tempting to refer the expression καθ' Ἑλλάδα γῆν ... ἠδ' ἀνὰ νήσους, 247 [throughout the land of Greece and among the islands (translated by Gerber)] as much to his elegiac gnomology to Cyrnus as to Cyrnus himself, as the term στρωφώμενος might imply); see Wecowski (2014) 10.

69   See Colesanti (2011) 329–330: '*Nell'ultimo quarto del V secolo a. C. nei simposi ateniesi si esequivano soprattutto poesie di riuso ... In questo contesto guinge ad Atene dalla vicina Megara, non dopo il 429 a. C., anche l' ὑπόμνημα redatto più diu un secolo prima nell'eteria megarese, e le sue elegie, acconto a molti altri carmi di diversa provenienza, vengono eseguite come riusi nei simposi ... Ma l'ὑπόμνημα viene interpretato come la raccolta scritta delle poesie di un unico poeta*.'

70   If one accepts his proposal one must assume that the hypothetical collection of 520 BCE had a social or political bias.

71   The question concerning the circumstances of performing early elegy has long absorbed classicists, e.g. Reitzenstein (1893); West (1974) 10–13; Bowie (1986) 13–35; Bartol (1993) 51–57. See also Colesanti's remarks (2012) 265 on the sympotic embedding of elegy. He treats '*prassi simposiale—inserimento di una composizione elegiaca in una sequenza di interventi (la cosidetta "catena simposiale")*' as the main generic feature of elegy. See also Budelmann and Power (2013) 2–5, who argue that sympotic elegiac pieces might have turned into public elegy presented at public events.

through its being a paraenetic or paideutic song sung to a fixed melody and played on the *aulos*, which accompanied the singer's voice. That was enough for a poem to be called elegy. In the classical period this musical feature that determined the genre was "translated" into the rhythm of the text (i.e. was transformed from a melodic generic feature into a metrical one), which from then on became of greatest importance in defining the genre. This primary factor, supported by other characteristics (sympotic setting, paraenetic content, etc., some found also in another lyric types), determined the essence of the elegiac genre.

It is indeed surprising, however, that the earliest ancient views that we have about elegy as a poetic category definitely privilege the sympotic short poems composed in elegiac couplets, and that the classical authors do not devote any space to the issue of longer narrative pieces publicly performed at festivals,[72] perhaps indeed in cultic settings.[73] The existence of long, narrative elegies, incorporating foundation tales (as, for instance, Mimnermus' *Smyrneis*, Xenophanes' *Foundation of Colophon*) or including mythological, perhaps selfstanding narratives (such as Archilochus' Telephus elegy) as well as celebrating great historical events (for example, Simonides' Plataea elegy), established by testimonies and now by papyrus texts, forces us to confront one of the difficulties related to elegy's reception and at the same time this genre's conceptualization in the classical period. The fact that classical authors chose to refer to sympotic pieces and passed over narrative long poems in their construction of the genre seems to be the expression of a particular interpretation of these sympotic poems exclusively as vehicles of enjoyable instruction. Given that one cannot now find classical texts in which the nouns ἔλεγος, ἐλεγεῖον, or ἐλεγεία are used in connection with what we would call narrative elegy,[74] the lack of reference to long narrative poems might imply that the dominant way of thinking about archaic elegy in the classical epoch was that which treated it as a paraenetic or paideutic statement situated in a sympotic setting. Such an approach seems to lead classical authors to reduce the definition of elegy to a sympotic genre and hence to consider sympotic poems as elegy's "canonical exponents", in spite of the poetic *praxis* of the archaic and classical periods, when narrative pieces composed in elegiac couplets were quite popular and present in the Greek cultural life. The expansion of the concept of archaic elegy, that is the

---

72 See Bowie (1986) 13–35.
73 As Bowie has recently argued: Bowie (2016) 15–32.
74 Echembrotus' dedication cited by Paus. 10.7.5–6 is an exception, but it is pre-classical. Aristotle (*Pol.* 1306b36) calls Tyrtaeus' *Eunomia* ποιήσεως τῆς καλουμένης Εὐνομίας.

inclusion of the narrative species in the conceptualization of the elegiac genre, must have made its appearance, it seems, in later times.

I will finish by saying that in their writings, classical authors acknowledged the existence of the elegiac laws. These laws were written not in the form of a manual intended for junior trainees apprenticed to a master,[75] but functioned in classical authors' works as a descriptive device that—through the references to literary practice—sketched outlines of the elegiac genre and shaped the scope of its operation. So, in the classical epoch, elegiac laws were, contrary to Colesanti,[76] 'respected and written'. We must resist the temptation to reject Rossi's diagnosis.[77]

References

Aloni, A. 2011. Elegy. Forms, Functions and Communication. In *The Cambridge Companion to Greek Lyric*, ed. F. Budelmann, 168–188. Cambridge.

Aloni, A. and Ianucci, A. 2016. Writing Solon. In *Iambus and Elegy: New Approaches*, ed. L. Swift and C. Carey, 155–173. Oxford.

Barns, J. 1950. A New Gnomologium: With Some Remarks on Gnomic Anthologies. I. *CQ* 44: 126–137.

Barns, J. 1951. A New Gnomologium: With Some Remarks on Gnomic Anthologies. II. *CQ* n.s. 1: 1–19.

Barron, J.P. and Easterling, P.E. 1989. Early Greek Elegy: Callinus, Tyrtaeus, Mimnermus. In *The Cambridge History of Classical Literature*, Vol. I, Part I: *Early Greek Poetry*, ed. P.E. Easterling and B.M.W. Knox, 87–95. Cambridge.

Bartol, K. 1987. Litterarische Quellen der Antike und das Problem des Vortragens der frühgriechischen Elegie. *Eos* 75: 261–278.

---

[75] The presence of a manual is, in Colesanti's opinion, the prerequisite for applying to elegy the scheme *leggi scritte e rispettate*. See Colesanti (2012) 266: '*dobbiamo notare che, seper l'età arcaica risulta valido per l'elegia lo schema rossiano delle "leggi non scritte ma rispettate" (non abbiamo alcun manuale dedicato all'elegia in quest'epoca) ... per l'età classica non è invece applicabile lo schema delle "leggi scritte e rispettate": se è vero che le leggi sono rispettate anche in quest'epoca ... nessuno però le codifica per iscritto*', 267 '*Nel caso dell'elegia dobbiamo escludere l'"apprendistato di bottega" teorizzato da Rossi.*'

[76] Colesanti (2012) 266: '*Possiamo quindi dire che, per quanto riguarda le leggi dell'elegia ..., esiste un lungo periodo di "leggi non scritte e rispettate" che copre sia l'età arcaica sia l'età classica.*'

[77] Rossi (1971) 76: '*in questa seconda epoca le leggi sono rispettate, come già nella prima*', but '*diversamente dalla prima, tendono a fissarsi per iscritto, pur con variabile grado di sistematicità*'.

Bartol, K. 1993. *Greek Elegy and Iambus: Studies in Ancient Literary Sources*. Poznań.
Bartol, K. 2013. The Structure of Lysias' Speech in Pseudo-Plutarch's *On Music*. *Hermes* 141: 401–416.
Bartol, K. 2017. In the Borderlands Between Genres: Notes on a Recent Volume of Studies on Greek Iambus and Elegy. *Exemplaria Classica* 21: 151–159.
Bowie, E.L. 1986. Early Greek Elegy, Symposium and Public Festival. *JHS* 106: 13–35.
Bowie, E.L. 1997. The *Theognidea*: A Step Towards a Collection of Fragments? In *Collecting Fragments*, ed. G.W. Most, 53–66. Göttingen.
Bowie, E.L. 2012. An Early Chapter in the History of the *Theognidea*. In *Approaches to Archaic Greek Poetry*, ed. X. Riu and J. Pòrtulas, 121–148. Messina.
Bowie, E.L. 2014. Rediscovering Sacadas. In *Patterns of the Past: Epitedeumata in the Greek Tradition*, ed. A. Moreno and R. Thomas, 39–55. Oxford.
Bowie, E.L. 2016. Cultic Contexts of Elegiac Performance. In *Iambus and Elegy: New Approaches*, ed. L. Swift and C. Carey, 15–32. Oxford.
Budelmann, F. and Power, T. 2013. The Inbetweenness of Sympotic Elegy. *JHS* 133: 1–19.
Campbell, D.A. 1991. *Greek Lyric*, vol. III. Cambridge, MA.
Cancik, H. 2003. Standardization and Ranking of Texts in Greek and Roman Institutions. In *Homer, the Bible, and Beyond: Literary and Religious Canons in the Ancient World*, ed. M. Finkelberg and G.G. Stroumsa, 11–130. Leiden.
Carey, C. 2009. Genre, Occasion and Performance. In *The Cambridge Companion to Greek Lyric*, ed. F. Budelmann, 21–38. Cambridge.
Colesanti, G. 2011. *Questioni Teognidee. La genesi simposiale di un* corpus *di elegie*. Rome.
Colesanti, G. 2012. Rileggendo un saggio di Luigi Enrico Rossi: leggi non scritte e rispettate (con alcune eccezioni) nell'elegia arcaica e classica. *Studi Romani di Cultura Greca* n.s. 1: 261–275.
Dale, A.M. 1963. Stichos and Stanza. *CQ* 56: 46–50.
Degani, E. 1987. Giambici poeti. In *Dizionario degli scrittori Greci e Latini*, ed. F. della Corte, 1005–1035. Milan.
Depew, M. and Obbink, D. 2000. *Matrices of Genre: Authors, Canons, and Society*. Cambridge, MA.
Else, G.F. 1957. *Aristotle's Poetics: The Argument*. Cambridge, MA.
Ercolani, A. 2014. Defining the Indefinable: Greek Submerging Literature and Some Problems of Terminology. In *Submerged Literature in Ancient Greek Culture: An Introduction*, ed. G. Colesanti and M. Giordano, 7–18. Berlin.
Fabbro, E. 1995. *I carmi conviviali attici*. Rome.
Faraone, C. 2008. *The Stanzaic Architecture of Early Greek Elegy*. Oxford.
Ferrari, F., ed. 1989. *Teognide. Elegie*. Milan.
Foley, H.P. 2008. Generic Boundaries in Late Fifth-Century Athens. In *Performance, Iconography, Reception: Studies in Honour of Oliver Taplin*, ed. M. Revermann and P. Wilson, 15–36. Oxford.

Ford, A. 1988. The Classical Definition of ῥαψῳδία. *CPh* 83: 300–307.
Gambato, M.L. 2001. Commentary on Athenaeus' *Deipnosophists*, book 13. In *Ateneo. I Deipnosofisti. I dotti a banchetto*, ed. L. Canfora, Vol. 3., 1393–1581. Rome.
Gentili, B. 1968. Epigramma ed elegia. In *L'Épigramme grecque. Fondation Hardt, Entretiens sur l'antiquité classique* 14: 37–81.
Gerber, D.E. 1997. Elegy. In *A Companion to the Greek Lyric Poets*, ed. D.E. Gerber, 89–128. Leiden.
Gerber, D.E. 1999. *Greek Elegiac Poetry: From the Seventh to the Fifth Centuries BC*, Cambridge, MA.
Halliwell, S. 1987. *The Poetics of Aristotle: Translation and Commentary*. London.
Hunter, R.L. 2012. *Plato and the Traditions of Ancient Literature: The Silent Stream*. Cambridge.
Ianucci, A. 2002. *La parola e l'azione. I frammentu simposiali di Crizia*, Bologna.
Ianucci, A. 2003. Una "corona di giambi". Ipotesi di lettura del fr. 2 Gent.-Pr. di Crizia. *Seminari Romani di Cultura Greca* 6.1: 31–42.
Irvin, E. 2005. *Solon and Early Greek Poetry*. Cambridge.
Kugelmeier, C. 1996. *Reflexe früher und zeitgenössischen Lyrik in der Alten attischen Komödie*. Stuttgart.
Lapini, W. 1995. I frammenti alcibiadei di Crizia: Crizia amico di Alcibiade?. *Prometheus* 21: 1–23.
Lulli, L. 2011. *Narrare in distici. L'elegia greca arcaica e classica di argomento storico-mitico*. Rome.
Murray, J. 2010. Hellenistic Elegy: Out from Under the Shadow of Callimachus. In *A Companion to Hellenistic Literature*, ed. J.J. Clauss and M. Cuypers, 106–116. London.
Nagy, G. 2011. Ancient Greek Elegy. In *The Oxford Handbook of Elegy*, ed. K. Weisman, 13–45. Oxford.
Neri, C. 2011. *Lirici greci. Età arcaica e classica*. Rome.
Nikolosi, A., ed. 2013. *Archiloco. Elegie*. Bologna.
Nobili, C. 2011. Threnodic Elegy in Sparta. *GRBS* 51: 26–48.
Olson, S.D. 2011. *Athenaeus: The Learned Banqueters*. Vol. vii. Cambridge, MA.
Papachrysostomou, A. 2008. *Six Comic Poets: A Commentary on Selected Fragments of Middle Comedy*. Tübingen.
Rawles, R. 2013. Aristophanes' Simonides: Lyric Models for Praise and Blame. *In Greek Comedy and the Discourse of Genres*, ed. E. Bakola, L. Prauscello, and M. Telò, 178–183. Cambridge.
Reitzenstein, R. 1893. *Epigramm und Skolion*. Giesen.
Riu, X. 2003. Sobre los géneros literarios en la literatura griega. *Myrtia* 18: 21–56.
Riu, X. 2012. On the Reception of Archilochus and Invective Poetry in Antiquity. In *Approaches to Archaic Greek Poetry*, ed. X. Riu, and J. Pòrtulas, 249–282. Messina.
Rossi, L. 1971. I generi letterari e le loro leggi scritte e non scritte. *BICS* 18: 52–71.

Rotstein, A. 2012. Mousikoi Agones and the Conceptualization of Genre in Ancient Greece. *Classical Antiquity* 31: 92–127.

Sbardella, L. 2018. Aulodes and Rhapsodes: Performance and Forms of Greek Elegy from Mimnermus to Hermesianax. *Aitia. Regards sur la culture hellénistique au XXIe siècle* 8.1 (*Hellenistica Posnaniensia: Faces of Hellenistic Lyric*), https://journals.openedition.org/aitia/2247 (accessed 19 December 2018).

Selle, H. 2008. *Theognis und die Theognidea*. Berlin.

Swift, L. and Carey, C., eds. 2016. *Iambus and Elegy: New Approaches*. Oxford.

Vara Donado, J. 1982. Melos y Elegia. *Emerita* 50: 433–453.

Vetta, M. 1983. Poesia simposiale nella Grecia arcaica e classica. In *Poesia e simposio nella Grecia antica*, ed. M. Vetta, pp. xiii–lx. Rome.

Wecowski, M. 2014. *The Rise of the Greek Aristocratic Banquet*. Oxford.

West, M.L. 1974. *Studies in Greek Elegy and Iambus*. Berlin.

Zacher, K. 1898. Beiträge zur griechischen Wortforschung. *Philologus* 57: 8–23.

PART 3

Lyric in the Peripatetics

∴

CHAPTER 7

The Peripatetics and the Transmission of Lyric

Theodora A. Hadjimichael

1   Introduction*

The scale and nature of the Peripatetic works involving Greek literature and its representatives have turned them into one of the most important chapters in the history of criticism and transmission.[1] The entire corpus of the Peripatetics proves that the philosophers had a broad range of interests from the beginning of the foundation of the school until the late Hellenistic period, and the surviving titles and fragments of their treatises indicate a holistic curiosity and a focus on antiquarianism with an effort at historical documentation.[2] The broad range of interests of the philosophers covered most of the areas of human life—politics, education, ethics, literature, music, culture, poetry, philosophy, and science—and the body of knowledge displayed exemplifies, in some sense, the science of phenomenology.[3] It also demonstrates a peculiar kind of empiricism that involved the systematic collection of information, mainly from written records, as well as the collection of views of earlier scholars.[4] Both these features led to the establishment of encyclopaedic knowledge.[5]

---

*   This chapter is a shorter version of Chapter 4 from my monograph *The Emergence of the Lyric Canon* (Oxford, 2019), which is here reproduced by permission of Oxford University Press. The chapter was prepared for publication while I held a post-doctoral research fellowship at Ludwig-Maximilians-Universität München, which was funded by the DFG Exzellenzinitiative. The financial support for my research is gratefully acknowledged. Many thanks are due to Chris Carey for his comments on earlier versions of this chapter, to the audience at the conference in Reading for their valuable feedback, as well as to the two editors of the volume and the anonymous reviewer for their helpful suggestions. All remaining errors are my own.

1   Podlecki (1969) is one of the few studies exclusively devoted to the value of the Peripatetics as literary critics.

2   Montanari (2012) 349–350. The Peripatetics were also interested in mathematics, medicine, botany, political history, and the natural world. The main sources of the Peripatetic fragments are Athenaeus, who often refers to them by name in connection with the title of their treatises, as well as Stobaeus, Diogenes Laertius, and the scholiastic tradition.

3   Cf. Arist. *EN* 1145b2–6.

4   Aristotle outlines the methodology of his "research" in *Top.* 105a34–b19, where he clarifies how propositions and opinions should be collected and grouped together (προτάσεις ἐκλεκτέον, δόξας), while written acquisitions should also be used as sources of information (ἐκλέγειν δὲ χρὴ καὶ ἐκ τῶν γεγραμμένων λόγων).

5   Gibson (2005) 29. Strabo uses the verb ἀριστοτελίζειν (13.1.54, p. 609C.14 Radt) as probably

The aim of this chapter is to show that the Peripatetics can justifiably be considered a watershed in Greek literary criticism, especially in connection with the nine canonical lyric poets. For this reason, attention will primarily be given to those treatises that were associated with social and cultural themes. An outline of the principles with which the philosophers worked for the creation of their treatises will allow us to employ the designation "Peripatetic project" in order to describe the scholarly activity of the Peripatetic philosophers. Such an inclusive description is essential, as it encapsulates the complete dearth of the Peripatetic works in the Lyceum of Aristotle. As will be demonstrated, the Peripatetics were actively involved in the transmission and canonization of lyric poetry.[6] This role of the Peripatos as one of the mediators for lyric poetry creates connections both with the Platonic and comic views on specific poetic genres and with the Hellenistic attitude towards the classical melic poetry and the New Music.[7]

2   The Peripatetic Project

The Peripatos is renowned for its so-called biographies.[8] The treatises under question, however, were not solely biographical works or even exclusively dis-

---

   an indication that the development of a systematic empiricism was Aristotle's achievement.
6 A note should be made with reference to the term "lyric." I use the term in the narrow sense for poetry that was composed by the nine canonical lyric poets, which will often be interchanged with the term "melic" that will be applied when I refer to orally performed poetry. It will be indicated in the main text when the term "lyric" is used in a broader sense, in order to include not only melic but also elegiac and iambic poetry.
7 The edition used for the Peripatetic fragments is that of Wehrli (second and revised edition), whose numbering I follow, and where needed, I give the relevant numbering of the volumes. The edition of Athenaeus is that of S.D. Olson (2007–2012) in the Loeb Classical Library, and in most cases I follow Olson's text rather then Wehrli's when citing lyric fragments. A note is made when the text varies. All titles of the Peripatetic treatises are transliterated.
8 Hägg (2012) 70 emphasizes the importance of the second half of the fourth century for the history of ancient biography, and argues that 'the professionalization of biography production in the late fourth century is no doubt closely linked to the Peripatos'. In this he follows Dihle (1956) 57–87 and (1998) 130–131, 138, and Momigliano (1993) 84, who see a continuation between the Peripatetic and Hellenistic practice, as well as Arrighetti (1987) 162–163, Brugnoli (1995) 80, and Gallo (1995) 20–22 and (2005) 23, who point out that the Peripatos developed the techniques that later resulted in "true" biography. Similarly, Bing (1993) refers to 'the *bios*-tradition' and notes that, whilst it was prominent in the fourth century, it fully flourished in the Hellenistic era. On the other hand, Cooper (2002) 317 suggests that 'the important issue is not whether the Peripatetics actually wrote biography or even imagined they were writing biography but whether later readers regarded their writings as *bioi*'. McGing and Moss-

cursive works devoted to the poetic corpus, of the kind that we find in the Hellenistic period. They were mixed works that had to do with genre, the content of poetry, language, style, lexicographical issues, and the poetic corpus of a specific poet, as well as biographical details.[9] The entire literary project of the Peripatos could be perceived as an attempt to register and memorialize Greek social and cultural history. The philosophers investigated consistently musical festivals and competitions, which had been in existence throughout the fifth century and had also by their time expanded beyond Athens. Poetry— epic, tragedy, and lyric—as a cultural phenomenon of the Archaic and Classical period was thus incorporated in a broader cultural and musical context. It therefore became an object of discussion not only in treatises that were about specific poetic genres, poets, or poems but also in works that focussed on broader themes including presumably poetry, e.g. the *Peri Melopoiias* by Aristoxenus (frr. 92–93), the *Peri Mousikōn Agōnōn* by Dicaearchus (frr. 73–89), or the *Synagōgē tōn en mousikē ⟨dialapsantōn⟩* by Heraclides Ponticus (frr. 157– 163). As the titles in connection with poetry reveal, some treatises explored cultural and musical issues, such as erotic and sympotic contexts of performance (and behaviour), whereas others tackled large generic contexts, such as tragedy, comedy, the Homeric epics, and finally specific poets. Generic works are to be expected, since this is the period when ideas of genre were in the process of becoming fixed. Homer and Pindar had already used generic lyric terms in their work and had listed occasions for performances of lyric genres,[10] and fifth-century comedy also shows an explicit awareness of generic tendencies.[11] Be that as it may, it is in the fourth century that we can detect explicit and more systematic interest in poetic genres. The great interest of the Peripatetics

man (2006) ix–xi draw attention to the slippery nature of the term "biography": the genre of ancient biography was not *biographia* and those whom we would consider as ancient biographers wrote *bioi* (*lives*) not biographies.

9   With special reference to the work of Demetrius of Phalerum Montanari (2000) 397 notes how the Peripatetic treatises were grounded on interpretation of texts and showed a 'close relationship between hermeneutic and literary criticism'. Biographical details are the focus of a number of Peripatetic fragments, e.g. Chamaeleon *Peri Pindarou* fr. 32a–b on the story on Pindar and the honeycomb at Helicon, *Peri Simonidou* fr. 33 on Simonides' avidity, *Peri Kōmōidias* fr. 43 on Anaxandrides' aggressiveness and appearance, while directing a dithyramb in Athens, Hieronymus of Rhodes *Peri Poiētōn* fr. 31 on Sophocles' piety.

10 Hom. *Il.*1.472–474, *Il.*22.391–392—paean (παιήονα); *Il.*18.492–493—*hymenaios* (ὑμέναιος); *Il.*24.719–722—*thrēnos* (θρήνων, ἐθρήνεον); Pind. fr. 128c—paean and *hymenaios* (παιάνιδες, Ὑμέναιον/ ἐν γάμοισι); cf. Archil. fr. 120 W—dithyramb (διθύραμβον).

11 See Calame's contribution to this volume.

in Greek culture has to be related to the need to retain, infuse, and transmit Greek culture and Greek identity during a period of immense change, not only geographically but also culturally.[12]

With reference to lyric poetry, it is striking that, though we have works dealing with specific lyric poets, we have no other general and generic work for melic poetry or for kinds of melic poetry, except perhaps for Aristoxenus' *Symmikta Sympotika* (frr. 122–127) and the *Erōtika* (frr. 21–35) of Clearchus of Soli. The few surviving fragments from these two general treatises are explicit about their context. They reveal that the theme of discussion was not so much poetry *per se* as customs at the symposia and behavioural issues concerning erotic or musical matters, what I called above cultural history or more precisely antiquarianism. Fragments from Aristoxenus' *Symmikta Sympotika* reveal that in a number of passages Aristoxenus was concerned with customs relating to the symposium and other celebratory contexts,[13] in other fragments he expressed his views on the proper type of *mousikē* and *harmoniai* that were meant to accompany the drinking of the symposiasts in order to mitigate the power of wine,[14] while he also set out his beliefs on the psychagogic power of music and on its ability to affect the *ēthos* of people.[15] With reference to individual poets and their compositions, it is uncertain how far specific lyric poems, genres, or named lyric poets were discussed or mentioned in any of the other broader Peripatetic works. Nonetheless, a number of fragments suggest that lyric poets were often named in treatises that may not have had a direct connection with lyric poetry. The text of Athenaeus suggests that Sappho and Anacreon were mentioned in the extract from Clearchus on erotic and Locrian poems.

Κλέαρχος δὲ ἐν δευτέρῳ Ἐρωτικῶν τὰ ἐρωτικά φησιν ᾄσματα καὶ τὰ Λοκρικὰ καλούμενα οὐδὲν τῶν Σαπφοῦς καὶ Ἀνακρέοντος διαφέρειν.

Clearchus in the second book of the *Erōtika* claims that the erotic songs and the so-called *Lokrika* are no different from those of Sappho and Anacreon.

CLEARCHUS *Erōtika* fr. 33 = Ath.14.639a

---

12   Grayeff (1974) 26–41 and Anagnostopoulos (2009) 2–13 on how the political situation in Greece at the time affected Aristotle's life and the Lyceum.
13   E.g. Aristoxenus fr. 125 = *Suda* s.v. σχολιόν [σ 643 Adler] on marital contexts.
14   E.g. Aristoxenus fr. 122 = [Plut.] *De mus.* 1146c 436.
15   E.g. Aristoxenus fr. 123 = Strabo 1.2, pp. 15C–16C.12 Radt.

Clearchus takes for granted that Sappho and Anacreon were known, and the ease with which both names are introduced suggests that these names would recall the poetry he has in mind. Their poems are in some sense employed as a yardstick in order to define the erotic songs that were called Locrian. The poems of Sappho and Anacreon are thus recalled as a parallel in Clearchus' attempt to explain the nature of these songs, and this suggests that the two named lyric poets were probably thought of as paradigms of erotic song compositions. In another fragment from the *Erōtika*, the assimilation works the other way round. Clearchus presumably attempted to explain a specific verse in Sappho's fr. 122 by positioning it within a cultural and anthropological context. In fr. 122 Sappho draws attention to a girl collecting flowers.

> Κλέαρχος δ' ὁ Σολεὺς ἐν τοῖς Ἐρωτικοῖς διὰ τί, φησί, μετὰ χεῖρας ἄνθη καὶ μῆλα καὶ τὰ τοιαῦτα φέρομεν; [...] ἢ δυοῖν χάριν ταῦτα περιφέρουσιν; ἀρχή τε γὰρ ἐντυχίας καὶ παράδειγμα τῆς βουλήσεως αὐτοῖς γίνεται διὰ τούτων, αἰτηθεῖσι μὲν τὸ προσαγορευθῆναι, δοῦσι δὲ ⟨τὸ⟩ προυπογράφειν ὅτι δεῖ καὶ αὐτοὺς μεταδιδόναι τῆς ὥρας. ἡ γὰρ τῶν ὡραίων ἀνθῶν καὶ καρπῶν αἴτησις εἰς ἀντίδοσιν τῆς τοῦ σώματος ὥρας προκαλεῖται τοὺς λαβόντας. ἢ τὴν τούτων ὥραν παραψυχὴν καὶ παραμυθίαν τῆς ἐπὶ τῶν ἐρωμένων ὥρας ταῖς ἐπιθυμίαις χαίροντες ἔχουσιν αὑτοῖς· ἐκκρούεται γὰρ ὑπὸ τῆς τούτων παρουσίας ὁ τῶν ἐρωμένων πόθος. εἰ μὴ ἄρα τοῦ περὶ αὐτοὺς κόσμου χάριν καθάπερ ἄλλο τι τῶν πρὸς καλλωπισμὸν συντεινόντων ἔχουσί τε ταῦτα καὶ χαίρουσιν αὑτοῖς· οὐ γὰρ μόνον στεφανουμένων τοῖς ὡραίοις ἄνθεσιν, ἀλλὰ καὶ μετὰ χεῖρας ἐχόντων τὸ πᾶν εἶδος ἐπικοσμεῖται. τάχα δ' ἴσως διὰ τὸ φιλοκάλους εἶναι· [...] φυσικὸν γὰρ δή τι τὸ τοὺς οἰομένους εἶναι καλοὺς καὶ ὡραίους ἀνθολογεῖν. ὅθεν αἵ τε περὶ τὴν Περσεφόνην ἀνθολογεῖν λέγονται, καὶ Σαπφώ φησιν ἰδεῖν
> ἄνθε' ἀμέργοισαν παῖδ' ἄγαν ἀπάλαν.[16]

Clearchus of Soli says in his *Erōtika*: for what reason do we carry in our hands flowers, apples, and the like? ... Or do they carry them around for two reasons? Because through them it is possible to initiate an encounter and to show what they want; for those who would like to be greeted and for those who offer gifts, their indicating in advance that others need to share their youthful beauty (*hōra*). For the request of flowers and fruits that are in season (*hōraia*) invites those who accept them as gifts to offer

---

16 I reproduce in the above passage the Sapphic line as given in Olson's edition of Athenaeus, who follows Lobel and Page (fr. 122 *PLF*) and Voigt (Sappho fr. 122 Voigt). Wehrli's edition of Clearchus (vol. iii) gives ἄνθε' ἀμέργουσαν παῖδ' ἄγαν ἀπαλάν, whereas Campbell gives Sappho's fr. 122 as ἄνθε' ἀμέργοισαν παῖδ' † ἄγαν † ἀπάλαν.

the youthful beauty (*hōra*) of their body in return. Or perhaps they cling to them enjoying their desires as a consolation and as a relief from the youthful beauty of their beloved. The longing of their objects of love is disturbed by the presence of such items. Unless perhaps they hold these items and enjoy them because they make them more attractive, just like anything else that serves to the attractiveness of someone. Because the appearance in general is made to look more attractive not only when they wear garlands of flowers that are in season (*hōraiois*) but also when they hold them in their hands. It might also perhaps be because they are fond of beauty and elegance ... for it is natural for those who believe that they are handsome and full of youthful beauty (*hōraious*) to gather flowers. For this exact reason the girls who accompanied Persephone are described as gathering flowers, and Sappho claims that she saw

'a very delicate girl collecting flowers'.
CLEARCHUS *Erōtika* fr. 25 = Ath.12.553e–554b

Clearchus' explanatory notes on the theme of youthful beauty, on the way in which people use the seasonal gifts of nature and on the manner in which individuals attract and desire each other position Sappho's fragment in an interpretative frame with three poles: (i) the girl, who is called delicate by Sappho, collects flowers because it is natural for those who are young and beautiful to gather flowers; (ii) Sappho draws attention to the collecting of flowers because it is a sign of the girl's wish to be observed, perhaps of her desire to initiate a meeting, and most importantly a sign of her beauty; (iii) Sappho gazes at beauty, more specifically at the beauty of the object of her desire, but her lust is both calmed and distracted by the beautiful flowers in her hands. The focus in the passage of Clearchus is obviously not Sappho's verse and its interpretation but the beauty of both humans and nature, as well as the behaviour of those who know they are beautiful and desirable. The verse, however, is employed as literary evidence, one may say, of a certain kind of human behaviour and of Clearchus' comments on the beautiful and luxurious way of life.[17]

This preference of the Peripatetics for sympotic and erotic contexts of poetry suggests that they were interested in themes of behavioural ethics. Evidence of this interest is Dicaearchus' reference in his treatise *Peri Mousikōn Agōnōn* (fr. 88) to the three kinds of *skolia* which were sung at a symposium (= *Suda* s.v. σκολιόν [σ 643 Adler]). Dicaearchus uses the term *skolion* to denote a type

---

17 Cf. Clearchus' fr. 41 *Peri Biōn* (= Ath. 15.187a) where Sappho's fr. 58.25–27 is employed in the treatise as evidence that Sappho herself did not dissociate honour from luxury.

of song as well as a generic label of a song (ὃ δὴ καλεῖσθαι διὰ τὴν τάξιν σκολιόν), and he comments predominantly on the performative features of that specific song: context of performance and performers. *Skolia* were songs sung at symposia (ἡ παροίνιος ᾠδή) and they were of three types (τρία γένη ἦν ᾠδῶν): one type was sung by all the participants (ὑπὸ πάντων ᾀδόμενον), another type by each individual (καθ' ἕνα ἑξῆς), and a third type by those who have been judged as the wisest (ὑπὸ τῶν συνετωτάτων ὡς ἔτυχε τῇ τάξει). Most importantly, this focus of the Peripatetics on performative contexts is suggestive of the continuing role of the symposium that may have given a longer life to songs of an erotic nature or songs with an ethical character in connection to sympotic behaviour. This interest is also at the same time suggestive of the survival of the song-culture at the time of the Peripatos, and of the continuous performance of lyric songs in a number of private and public occasions. A number of passages from Aristotle's *Politics* support the conclusion that the song-culture was still vibrant at the time of the Peripatos. Aristotle appears to be as sensitive as Aristoxenus to the question of the *harmoniai* that should be employed by the type of *mousikē* that was meant for relaxation and amusement (*Pol.*1339b10–42, 1340a12–14). We can additionally conclude from epigraphic evidence that a great deal of religious song and dance was still in performance in the late fifth and early fourth centuries. A number of poems that are preserved on stone are predominantly religious, a convention that recalls the public character of songs that were framed by a ritual and were meant to be performed by communities often as communal offerings.[18]

A number of passages further suggest that references to lyric genres or even names of lyric poets were plausibly mentioned in treatises with a general character. Aristoxenus in his *Peri Mousikēs* refers to a poem by Stesichorus (fr. 277), in which a woman called Καλύκη prays to Aphrodite for the love of a young man.[19] From this song, he claims, originated a custom where women perform the particular poem that has been given as a label the name of this woman.

---

18   LeVen (2014) 283–329 discusses in their performative context the hymn to Health by Ariphron of Sicyon, the paean to Asclepius, Aristonous' hymns to Hestia and Apollo, Isyllus' paean to Asclepius, and the paean to Dionysus by Philodamus of Scarphea, all of which were inscribed on stone.

19   Cf. the love story of Sappho and Phaon: Men. *Leucad.* fr. 258 Körte (= Strabo 10.2.9, p. 452C.19–22 Radt), *Suda* s.v. Σαπφώ (σ 108 Adler). LeVen (2014) 228–230 raises the possibility that the Stesichorus mentioned by Aristoxenus was a second Stesichorus of Himera, whose victory the Parian Marble dates to the early fourth century BCE (*Marm. Par. FGrH* 2.B 239 A 73). This debate concerning *Kalykē*'s authorship is already expressed in Rose (1932). As the performers of the poem are characterized as women of the past (αἱ ἀρχαῖαι γυναῖκες), I am of the opinion that the poem was composed by the classic poet Stesichorus.

Ἀριστόξενος δὲ ἐν τετάρτῳ Περὶ Μουσικῆς, ᾖδον, φησίν, αἱ ἀρχαῖαι γυναῖκες Καλύκην τινὰ ᾠδήν. Στησιχόρου δ' ἦν ποίημα, ἐν ᾧ Καλύκη τις ὄνομα ἐρῶσα Εὐάθλου νεανίσκου εὔχεται τῇ Ἀφροδίτῃ γαμηθῆναι αὐτῷ· ἐπεὶ δὲ ὑπερεῖδεν ὁ νεανίσκος, κατεκρήμνισεν ἑαυτήν. ἐγένετο δὲ τὸ πάθος περὶ Λευκάδα. σωφρονικὸν δὲ πάνυ κατεσκεύασεν ὁ ποιητὴς τὸ τῆς παρθένου ἦθος, οὐκ ἐκ παντὸς τρόπου θελούσης συγγενέσθαι τῷ νεανίσκῳ, ἀλλ' εὐχομένης εἰ δύναιτο γυνὴ τοῦ Εὐάθλου γενέσθαι κουριδία ἢ εἰ τοῦτο μὴ δυνατόν, ἀπαλλαγῆναι τοῦ βίου.

Aristoxenus says in the fourth book of his *Peri Mousikēs*: women of old days were singing a song called *Kalykē*. This was a poem by Stesichorus, in which someone named Kalykē, who was in love with a young man called Euathlus, prays to Aphrodite, asking to marry him. When the young man showed no interest in her, she threw herself over a cliff. This misfortune took place in Leucada. The poet presented the girl as extremely chaste, for under no circumstances did she want to have sex with the young man, but prayed that it might be possible to become Euathlus' bride or, if that was impossible, that she may die.

ARISTOXENUS *Peri Mousikēs* fr. 89 = Ath.14.619d–e

Stesichorus' poem is paraphrased and not cited in the passage, presumably because Aristoxenus' interest was not the poem itself, but this custom of women singing that song called *kalykē*. It is especially worth commenting in this case how Aristoxenus relates the gender of the performers (αἱ ἀρχαῖαι γυναῖκες) to the story narrated in Stesichorus' poem and how he connects the name of the woman in the poem (Καλύκη) with what had presumably been identified as a quasi-generic label in subsequent performances (Καλύκην τινὰ ᾠδήν). Stesichorus' poem therefore is perceived as the *aition* of a ritual that may still have been practiced at Aristoxenus' time. This aetiological connection between the poem and the ancient custom, moreover, reveals specific contexts and characteristics of its performance—female performers performing the same song at regular intervals presumably in front of the community audience—but most importantly, it reveals the poem's continuous reperformance. It lastly suggests that the *Peri Mousikēs* of Aristoxenus included ethnographical material that was interpreted aetiologically.[20]

Beyond generic and performative contexts for lyric poetry, a number of poets received individual works by the Peripatetics, and the titles of these works

---

20 Cf. Aristoxenus' fr. 129 from his *Abbreviated Commentaries* (Ath. 14.619e5–9) on the origin of the name *Harpalykē* for a singing contest between maidens.

bore the poet's name. Of the lyric poets, Anacreon, Sappho, Lasus, Simonides, Pindar, and Stesichorus received a treatise by Chamaeleon, and Alcaeus by Dicaearchus.[21] If we broaden the meaning of lyric to include elegy and iambus, Hermippus of Smyrna supplemented this list with a treatise on Hipponax, a work presumably with lexicographical features,[22] while Heraclides Ponticus coupled Archilochus with Homer, and his work, which was apparently a treatise on language and style, is classified by Diogenes Laertius as grammatical. Evidently the project on poets and poetry of the past was a priority for the Peripatetic philosophers, since evidence of their focus can be traced to the school's foundation. The principal philosophers involved—Heraclides Ponticus, Dicaearchus, Chamaeleon,[23] and Praxiphanes who worked on a number of other poets[24]—lived broadly in the same period (second half or end of the fourth century BCE) and belonged to the second generation of Peripatetics at the Lyceum when Theophrastus was the head of the school.[25] The school apparently flourished under Theophrastus (317–307 BCE), and the period of his headship constitutes the most significant period in its development: empirical studies were further extended, and as the surviving titles suggest the works at the Lyceum became gradually specialized and monographic in character.[26]

---

21   Momigliano (1993) 70 stresses that, although Dicaearchus' works were full of references to details (true or imaginary) of the poet's life, they 'do not appear to have been biographies', and he emphasizes that 'no biography is quoted as coming from his pen' (71).

22   Bollansée (1999) 428 characterizes Hermippus' work on Hipponax as lexicographical, whereas Degani (1984) 23, 35 identifies it (with no evidence) as a biography. Bollansée (1999) 428–430 rightly emphasizes that the resemblance of the title to those that were often in connection with a clear-cut biography is not helpful for the establishment of the character of the treatise.

23   Momigliano (1993) 73 and Bollansée (1999) 430 call the *peri*-works of Chamaeleon on poets "commentaries", whereas Gallo (2005) 25 suggests that his treatises were works closer to biographies. Montanari (2012) 412 argues that Chamaeleon's *peri tou deina* treatises were biographies in the ancient sense of the word, that is 'exegetical and literary historical treatises in which biographical aspects also played a role'. On Chamaeleon's method, see the contribution of Bouchard to this volume, pp. 189–194

24   Praxiphanes probably worked on Sophocles and also studied Homer and Hesiod individually. Poets, other than those already mentioned in the main text, who received separate treatises were Homer and Hesiod by Heraclides Ponticus, who also produced a grammatical work on Homer and Archilochus, Thespis, Aeschylus by Chamaeleon, and Euripides by Hermippus of Smyrna.

25   Montanari (2012) 354 considers Praxiphanes and Chamaeleon as those who awarded the study of literature a significant place in the Peripatos.

26   Sollenberger (1992) 3851. The works of Theophrastus' most famous students/associates prove the simultaneous expansion of the work of the school and the specialization in certain areas of expertise: Aristoxenus the *mousikos* introduced the science of musicology, Eudemus of Rhodes wrote a history of geometry, arithmetic, and astronomy, and Demet-

With reference to the treatises on lyric poets in particular, the existing titles reveal the complementary character of the Peripatetic project. Chamaeleon was the scholar who worked predominantly on the lyric poets and he may plausibly be considered the first who initiated this kind of work. Yet he did not produce a treatise on Alcaeus. This is supplemented by Dicaearchus, who did not attempt to duplicate Chamaeleon's work on the other lyric poets but to fill in the gaps in his list. He thus produced only a treatise on Alcaeus.

The hierarchy of poetic and musical interests of the early Peripatos seems to reflect, to some extent, Platonic views. Plato was renowned for his hostility towards the musical experimentations of the late fifth and early fourth century BCE that led to a new type of music and poetry that followed no rules; lyric genres became indistinct and musical *harmoniai* were mixed, and this led to the liberated and chaotic New Music (Pl. *R*.398d, *Lg*.700d–e). This remains for the Peripatetics the boundary they never cross when they consider lyric poetry. The same hierarchy also shows the influence of Aristotle's attempts to reassert specific poetic issues addressed in Plato. Tragedy, the poetic genre that Plato had dismissed, is re-established and gets back to the table not only in Aristotle's *Poetics* but also within the broader frame of the Lyceum. A number of Peripatetics work on the three tragedians, either as a group or individually, they collect information on the *didaskaliai* of tragedies, and they write *hypotheseis* for specific plays.[27] The project as a whole suggests that the approach of the Lyceum to literary issues was conservative, and this in turn determined the scale and sequence of cataloguing and explicating. The project is always backward-looking, and for tragedy and lyric poetry the rules were already set before the time of the Peripatos. Tragedy is one of those "fixed" literary fields. For the Peripatetics the clock stops at the end of the fifth century: only fifth-century tragedians are included in the Peripatetic project (with the exception of Thespis as *prōtos heuretēs*), and only the big three receive a monograph. In the case of lyric, we are obviously dealing with a closed list; the chronological development of the Peripatetic corpus omitted the new poetic and musical achievements. The striking absence of separate or even collective treatments devoted to the New Music and to individual New Poets suggests that (as far as we can see) the Peripatetics had no interest in the New Music.[28] We can observe

---

rius of Phalerum had various interests in a number of fields. See also Sharples (1999) 148 for a list with the interests of those Peripatetics who produced works based on their specializations.

27 E.g. Dicaearchus fr. 78 on *hypotheseis* of Euripides and Sophocles, fr. 79 on Sophocles' *Aias*, fr. 80 on Sophocles' *OT*, fr. 81 on the *hypothesis* of *Rhesus*.
28 The obsession with an idealized past is also evident in the musical treatises of Aristoxenus

the persistence of this silence right down to Hermippus of Smyrna, whose work on Hipponax confirms the complementary as well as the conservative character of the Peripatetic project. This is contrary to what we know of the popular reception at the time.[29] The Peripatetic scholarly tradition evidently ignored the contemporary performative culture and was at odds with fourth-century popular taste. The influence of pre-Aristotelian conservative agendas—the comic poet Aristophanes (and Old Comedy in general) and Plato—is evident in this.

Chamaeleon himself worked on comedy (*Peri Kōmōidias* frr. 43–44) and his familiarity with the surviving comedies probably influenced his interpretation of poets and literary works, as well as his views on literary history and criticism.[30] A fragment from Chamaeleon's *Peri Aeschylou*, for example, shows how comedy was used as source of information for the Peripatetic treatises:

> Χαμαιλέων γοῦν πρῶτον αὐτόν φησι σχηματίσαι τοὺς χοροὺς ὀρχηστοδιδασκάλοις οὐ χρησάμενον, ἀλλὰ καὶ αὐτὸν τοῖς χοροῖς τὰ σχήματα ποιοῦντα τῶν ὀρχήσεων, καὶ ὅλως πᾶσαν τὴν τῆς τραγῳδίας οἰκονομίαν εἰς ἑαυτὸν περιιστᾶν. ὑπεκρίνετο γοῦν μετὰ τοῦ εἰκότος τὰ δράματα, Ἀριστοφάνης γοῦν—παρὰ δὲ τοῖς κωμικοῖς ἡ περὶ τῶν τραγικῶν ἀπόκειται πίστις—ποιεῖ αὐτὸν Αἰσχύλον λέγοντα·
> τοῖσι χοροῖς αὐτὸς τὰ σχήματ' ἐποίουν ...

Chamaeleon in any case says that he [*sc.* Aeschylus] was the first to have formed choruses without the help of dance teachers, but he instead prepared the dance figures for the choruses himself and in general that he took the entire management of the tragedy upon himself. It seems there-

---

of Tarentum. Power (2012) 129–133 notes that, although Aristoxenus writes after the end of the cultural politics in which the New Music had developed, he still attacks on its performative novelties that, according to the philosopher, denoted barbarization and degeneration at the specific historical moment in the later fifth century (e.g. fr. 124). Aristoxenus' work is endowed with melancholic nostalgia, as we get the 'sense of a profound disconnection between Aristoxenus' elitist conservatism and the demotic experience of music in the later fourth century polis' (131).

29 E.g. Polybius 4.20.8–9, where it is stated that Timotheus and Philoxenus were included in the school curriculum in Arcadia in the second century BCE; Pausanias 8.50.3 and Plutarch *Philop*.11.1 record how Timotheus' poems were still performed in the second century BCE.

30 Athenaeus mentions Chamaeleon's work on comedy in two passages, and he does so differently—'in the sixth [book] *Peri Kōmōidias*' (ἐν ἕκτῳ Περὶ Κωμῳδίας Ath. 9.373f–374a) 'in the sixth [book] *Peri tēs Archaias Kōmōidias*' (ἐν ἕκτῳ Περὶ τῆς Ἀρχαίας Κωμῳδίας Ath. 9.406e)—while he also cites extracts from the two treatises where specifically a poet of Middle Comedy in the first case (Anaxandrides) and a poet of Old Comedy in the latter

fore very likely that he participated in his own plays. Indeed, Aristophanes (for comic playwrights are credible concerning tragic playwrights) portrays Aeschylus saying:

I myself created the dance figures for the choruses
CHAMAELEON *Peri Aeschylou* fr. 41 = Ath.1.39.21d–f

Although the comment on the reliability of Aristophanes and of the comic genre in general as sources for the representation of the tragic poets is probably Athenaeus', it is, nonetheless, a conclusion drawn from the fragments of Chamaeleon. Apparently, Aristophanes portrayed Aeschylus (either in a lost redaction of *Frogs* or in *Gērytadēs*) saying how he himself composed the movements of the choruses (Ar. fr. 696 *PCG*), and it is on this portrayal that Chamaeleon maps his representation of Aeschylus as skilful choreographer.[31] Comedy is also used as a source for the Peripatetic treatises on the lyric poets. Chamaeleon in his *Peri Simonidou* describes a scene where Simonides dines at the court of Hieron in order to portray Simonides as greedy.

Περὶ δὲ λαγῶν Χαμαιλέων φησὶν ἐν τῷ Περὶ Σιμωνίδου ὡς δειπνῶν παρὰ τῷ Ἱέρωνι ὁ Σιμωνίδης, οὐ παρατεθέντος αὐτῷ ἐπὶ τὴν τράπεζαν καθάπερ καὶ τοῖς ἄλλοις λαγωοῦ, ἀλλ᾽ ὕστερον μεταδιδόντος τοῦ Ἱέρωνος, ἀπεσχεδίασεν·
οὐδὲ γὰρ ⟨...⟩ εὐρύς περ ἐὼν ἐξίκετο δεῦρο[32]
ὄντως δ᾽ ἦν ὡς ἀληθῶς κίμβιξ ὁ Σιμωνίδης καὶ αἰσχροκερδής, ὡς Χαμαιλέων φησίν. ἐν Συρακούσαις γοῦν τοῦ Ἱέρωνος ἀποστέλλοντος αὐτῷ τὰ καθ᾽ ἡμέραν λαμπρῶς πωλῶν τὰ πλείω ὁ Σιμωνίδης τῶν παρ᾽ ἐκείνου πεμπομένων ἑαυτῷ μικρὸν μέρος ἀπετίθετο. ἐρομένου δέ τινος τὴν αἰτίαν· "ὅπως," εἶπεν, "ἥ τε Ἱέρωνος μεγαλοπρέπεια καταφανὴς ᾖ καὶ ἡ ἐμὴ κοσμιότης."

About hares Chamaeleon says in his treatise *Peri Simonidou* that when Simonides was dining by the side of Hieron and the hare was not served to him at the table as it was to the others but was instead offered to him later by Hieron he extemporized,

---

(Hegemon) become objects of discussion. This could suggest that Chamaeleon produced two treatises on comedy, one on the comic genre *in toto* and a second separate treatise exclusively on Old Comedy.

31   According to Kaibel (Γηρυτάδης Catal. Fab. [test. 2a14] *PCG*), fr. 696 *PCG* could belong to the play *Gērytadēs*, where Aeschylus himself speaks about his tragic art: '*de altera parte iudicarem, si fr. 696 ad Gerytaden referendum esse constaret, ubi ipse Aeschylis de sua arte disserens inducitur.*' See also *PCG* III.2, p. 358. Cf. Chamaeleon fr. 42 (= Ath. 14.628d–e), where the play *Skeuais* either by Aristophanes or by the comic Plato is mentioned as a source.

32   Both Wehrli (vol. ix) and Campbell supplement the lacuna with ⟨οὐδ᾽⟩.

THE PERIPATETICS AND THE TRANSMISSION OF LYRIC 163

> It is indeed broad, but it has not reached here
> Simonides was in fact truly skinflint and greedy, as Chamaeleon claims. For in Syracuse, although Hieron provided his daily needs handsomely, Simonides sold most of what was sent by him and kept for himself only a small part. When he was asked of the reason, he said, 'so that Hieron's magnificence and my propriety may be manifested clearly'.
> CHAMAELEON *Peri Simonidou* fr. 33 = Ath.14.656c–e

Although Chamaeleon bases his conclusion on a joke that is presented as being wittily fabricated by Simonides (eleg. 7) and on an anecdote about him selling Hieron's gifts, which he may well have invented, the figure of Simonides as a miser was well established before the Peripatos.[33] The biographical anecdotes and Simonides' proverbial attitude for money are recorded in a number of sources.[34] Aristotle himself even contributed with a number of anecdotal stories to the development of Simonides' image as a scandalous figure of miserliness and as a court-poet associated with wealthy tyrants.[35] But the first source to portray him as a figure of avarice was Aristophanes in his *Peace*. In this passage, Trygaeus wants to depict Sophocles in advanced age and to characterize him as greedy for money. He thus selects for his representation in this passage the poetic figure whose main characteristic denoted the information needed at that particular instance in the passage: avidity and old age.

> Τρ.   Ἐκ τοῦ Σοφοκλέους γίγνεται Σιμωνίδης.
> Ερ.   Σιμωνίδης; πῶς;
> 698 Τρ.   Ὅτι γέρων ὢν καὶ σαπρὸς
>   κέρδους ἕκατι κἂν ἐπὶ ῥιπὸς πλέοι.
>
> T: From Sophocles he becomes Simonides.
> H: Simonides? How so?
> T: He is very old, but he would still go to sea on wicker-work to make profit.
> ARISTOPHANES, *Peace* 694–699

---

33 The supposed verse of Simonides is ironically built on Hom. *Il*.14.33.
34 Schol. Ar. *Pax* 697c–e = Xenophanes fr. 21 W, on which Rawles (2018) 157–160; [Pl.] *Hipp.* 228c1–2; Arist. *EN* 1121a4–7, *Rh*.1405b23–34; schol. Pind. *Isthm.* 2.9a Drachmann; Callim. fr. 222 Pfeiffer; Ael. *VH* 8.2.9–10. For a summary of Simonides' features on which the biographers focussed, see Lefkowitz (2012) 55–60 and recently Rawles (2018) ch. 4.
35 Arist. *EN* 1121a4–7 on how money matters according to Simonides; *Rh*.1390b32–1391a14 on how for Simonides wealth is more important and powerful than wisdom; *Rh*.1405b23–28 on how Simonides' poetic rhetoric depends on the payment he receives.

Simonides brought with him invaluable connotations of avarice that were largely connected with his role as the first freelance poet who was paid by his patrons.[36] Chamaeleon sketches a scene with the three features of the commissioning process: poet (Simonides), patron (Hieron), and payment (hospitality, food, and gifts). Nonetheless, this picture of the greedy Simonides is not established by Chamaeleon himself. He most likely follows a long anecdotal tradition that was already at work in the fifth century and probably established Simonides as *the* greedy poet *par excellence*. It is both on this tradition, presumably initiated by Aristophanes, that this portrayal of Simonides is built.

The only exception to the picture presented above with reference to the silence surrounding the New Music in the Peripatos is Aristoxenus' life of Telestes, *Bios Telestou* (fr. 117), a dithyrambic poet at the end of the fifth century BCE. The one surviving fragment that is reported in Apollonius' *Marvellous Stories* 40 reveals the difference in character between this treatise and those of Chamaeleon that were devoted to the classical lyric poets.

Ἀριστόξενος ὁ μουσικὸς ἐν τῷ Τελέστου βίῳ φησίν, ᾧπερ ἐν Ἰταλίᾳ συνεκύρησεν, ὑπὸ τὸν αὐτὸν καιρὸν γίγνεσθαι πάθη, ὧν ἓν εἶναι καὶ τὸ περὶ τὰς γυναῖκας γενόμενον ἄτοπον· ἐκστάσεις γὰρ γίγνεσθαι τοιαύτας, ὥστε ἐνίοτε καθημένας καὶ δειπνούσας ὡς καλοῦντός τινος ὑπακούειν, εἶτα ἐκπηδᾶν ἀκατασχέτους γιγνομένας καὶ τρέχειν ἐκτὸς τῆς πόλεως. μαντευομένοις δὲ τοῖς Λοκροῖς καὶ Ῥηγίνοις περὶ τῆς ἀπαλλαγῆς τοῦ πάθους εἰπεῖν τὸν θεόν, Παιᾶνας ᾄδειν ἐαρινοὺς [δωδεκάτης] ἡμέρας ξ', ὅθεν πολλοὺς γενέσθαι παιανογράφους ἐν τῇ Ἰταλίᾳ.

Aristoxenus the music theorist says in his *Life of Telestes* that misfortunes were afoot at around the time when Telestes visited Italy, of which one was this untoward thing that befell the women: there were such frenzies that sometimes when they were sitting at dinner they would hear somebody as if calling them and then in an unrestrainable state would jump to their feet and run out of the city. When the Locrians and the Rhegians consulted an oracle on how to get rid of the misfortune, the god responded that they should sing [twelve] springtime Paeans for sixty days. For this reason there are so many writers of paeans in Italy.

ARISTOXENUS *Bios Telestou* fr. 117

---

36 Bell (1978) 29, 71–72.

Both the title and the fragment suggest that Aristoxenus' work was indeed biographical. The title is telling, as it explicitly states that it is a *Life* (Βίος). This comes in marked contrast to the treatises on the nine lyric poets, wherein the preposition περί is used in the title in conjunction to their names. Fragments from these *peri*-works, a number of which have been discussed above, indicate their varied character. The focus of each treatise may have been the lyric poet, but the focus of the discussion was not always the poet as such or events related to his life. Aristoxenus was renowned for his biographies, and especially for his polemical judgements in them, and he has been seen as the writer who initiated the writing of literary biographies and influenced the formation of the genre.[37] The fragment informs us about the frenzy of Italian women and about paeans in Italy, but attention is drawn to details from Telestes' life and not to his own compositions. His travels to Italy seemingly give rise to the comments related to these two anthropological and ethnographical characteristics of the Italian landscape. It is not possible to know whether any of Telestes' poems were discussed in this treatise, but if we are to judge from this one source, the focus presumably fell on Telestes' life and on information related to or derived from events in his *vita*.[38]

We may reasonably conclude that the Peripatetic agenda on lyric poetry seems to converge around the judgement (aesthetic, perhaps also moral and ethical) of Aristophanes, as illustrated in a number of his comedies, and of Plato. They both distinguished explicitly in their works between the representatives of classical lyric poetry and the New Music, a distinction that is also a crucial feature of Old Comedy in general. Although one should be cautious about generalizing comments, both Plato and Aristophanes seem to treat the New in lyric poetry with apparent condemnation, an attitude that shows that the classicizing process is already evident in their works. The Peripatetic agenda is

---

37 Plut. *Ne suaviter quidem vivi posse sec. Epicuri decreta* 10.1093b, Hieronymus *De viris illustribus* Praefatio (fr. 10a–b). Leo (1901) 102–103 recognises that Aristoxenus' method influenced the writing of literary biographies, a view that is further developed in Momigliano (1993) 76 who points out that Aristoxenus was perhaps the first to have made anecdotes an essential part of biography. Momigliano stresses that 'unless Dicaearchus' περὶ βίων was a collection of biographies, Aristoxenus had no rival as a biographer in the first generation of the Peripatos' (79); Sonnabend (2002) 70–71 argues that Aristoxenus initiated the use of biography as a means for both criticising and praising the person to which it was devoted; Hägg (2012) 93 states that Aristoxenus was 'the leading man in the process that made biography a recognizable literary form in the late fourth century BC'. See Schorn (2012b), who attempts to define the character of Aristoxenus' biographies and reappraise Aristoxenus both as biographer and as historical source.

38 On Aristoxenus' biography of Telestes, Power (2012) 132n5; LeVen (2014) 14–15.

also a classicized agenda; even with the existence of Aristoxenus' biographical work on Telestes, the philosophers are concerned predominantly with poets and poetry that had been established as classic by the time of Aristotle and the Peripatos.

3   The "Lyric" Library of the Peripatos

The Aristotelian approach to phenomenology and the doxographical tradition that Aristotle initiated define the nature of the Peripatetic project. Aristotle's method of empirical inquiry and doxography, which the Peripatetics employed, allows us to conclude that the philosophers were principally compilers;[39] their common task was to gather the opinions of others mainly from written records and to retain what seemed valid by adding their own commentary.[40] This observation is also confirmed by the fragments; the philosopher producing a specific treatise often states explicitly the opinion of others usually by using the verb φησίν, or offers the source for the information he includes in his work.[41] Following Aristotle's method, the Peripatos created learned compilations, while it also accumulated writings of the past.[42] The activity in the Lyceum subsequently led to the formation of the Peripatetic library, the 'first comprehensive collection of books in history'.[43] It appears therefore that the scholars of the Lyceum were working with written texts and presumably with (collected) poems of individual poets. The comments of the Peripatetics in a number of treatises have the actual text as a starting point. Fragments of Praxiphanes' works are probably the best evidence in favour of the existence of poetic texts in the Peripatetic library.

---

39   The term "doxography" is a modern fabrication from the Latin neologism "doxographi" introduced by Hermann Diels in order to characterize the method that was followed in the Aristotelian school. One of the main methodologies of Aristotle was to record and list the views that had been held by various people in order to reach the truth. Diels used the term to indicate the authors of a rather strictly specified type of literature that he studied and edited in his *Doxographi Graeci* of 1879.

40   Grayeff (1974) 64.

41   E.g. Chamaeleon in *Peri Methēs* fr. 10 (= Ath. 10.427b) φασὶν οἱ Λάκωνες ('the Spartans claim'), in *Peri Sapphous* fr. 26 (= Ath. 13.599c) λέγειν τινάς φησιν ('he says that some claim'), fr. 25 (= Ath. 13.600f–601a) Ἀρχύτας δ' ὁ ἁρμονικός, ὥς φησι Χαμαιλέων ('according to Chamaeleon, Archytas the harmonist [states that]'), fr. 42 (= Ath. 14.628e) διὸ καὶ Ἀριστοφάνης ἢ Πλάτων ἐν ταῖς Σκευαῖς, ὡς Χαμαιλέων φησίν, εἴρηκε οὕτως ('for this reason Aristophanes or Plato in the *Skeuais*, according to Chamaeleon, said the following').

42   Lynch (1972) 105.

43   Grayeff (1974) 40. Ath. 1.3a, Strabo 13.1.54, p. 608C. 31–33 Radt. It should perhaps be cla-

Μοῦσαι Πιερίηθεν: ἰστέον ὅτι Ἀρίσταρχος καὶ ἕτεροι ὀβελίζουσι τὸ προοίμιον, καὶ Πραξιφάνης ὁ μαθητὴς Θεοφράστου, λέγων ἀπροοιμιάστῳ βιβλίῳ ἐντυχεῖν, ἀρχομένῳ ἐντεῦθεν· οὐκ ἄρα μοῦνον ἔην Ἐρίδων γένος.

Muses from Pieria: It must be known that Aristarchus and others obelize the proem, as does Praxiphanes the student of Theophrastus, who says that he came upon the book without a proem and that it began from this: there is not after all just one kind of strife.

    TZETZES In Hesiodi Opera commentarii = PRAXIPHANES fr. 22b *Commentary on Hesiod*

Tzetzes couples Praxiphanes with Aristarchus in his commentary, and this ultimately places both of them on similar ground; they both dealt with or commented upon poems as those appeared as physical texts, and their observations shared a number of features. The fragment suggests not only that Praxiphanes is in a position to make a remark on the missing proem because he had Hesiod's text of the *Work and Days* at hand but also that Aristarchus' comment on the proem reflects and reacts to that of Praxiphanes'.[44] In other words, matters of emendation and interpolation already concerned the Peripatetic school at the end of the fourth century, and especially Praxiphanes, who was thought to be the first grammarian in antiquity.[45]

With reference to lyric poetry, a number of fragments also validate the assumption that the Peripatetics were working with texts. Chamaeleon in his treatise *Peri Sapphous* refers to a possible erotic relationship between Anacreon and Sappho, which appears to be based on two of their fragments. Athenaeus refers to an opinion recorded in Chamaeleon that Anacreon composed his fr. 358 for Sappho and that she equally replied with one of her poems (T8).[46] Athenaeus refers specifically to the content of the treatise.

---

    rified that the term "library" does not imply public use of a library by those who did not belong to the school. It denotes the collection of written works for private and scholarly use within the Peripatos that can be thus characterized as a textual community, to use a phrase coined by Woolf (2013) 12–13.

44 With reference to the word βιβλίον in the fragment, Wehrli (1969e) 114 points out that we should refrain from identifying the copy of Hesiod's *Works and Days* that Praxiphanes presumably had with the main book-roll of the work.

45 Clem. Al. *Strom.* 1.16.79.3–4. See also the other fragments of Praxiphanes that share features with the Hellenistic commentaries, Praxiphanes apparently dealt with the meaning of words (fr. 21), interpolations, and emendations (fr. 22a–b), and with what we would today call literary explanations of poems or poetic passages (fr. 20).

46 Cf. Arist. *Rh*.1367a5–15 on a similar biographical reading of Sappho's fr. 137 with note by Campbell ad loc.

Χαμαιλέων δ' ἐν τῷ Περὶ Σαπφοῦς καὶ λέγειν τινάς φησιν εἰς αὐτὴν πεποιῆσθαι
ὑπὸ Ἀνακρέοντος τάδε·
    σφαίρῃ δηὖτέ με πορφυρῇ[47]
    βάλλων χρυσοκόμης Ἔρως
    νήνι ποικιλοσαμβάλῳ
    συμπαίζειν προκαλεῖται·
    ἣ δ', ἐστὶν γὰρ ἀπ' εὐκτίτου
    Λέσβου, τὴν μὲν ἐμὴν κόμην,
    λευκὴ γάρ, καταμέμφεται,
    πρὸς δ' ἄλλην τινὰ χάσκει
καὶ τὴν Σαπφὼ δὲ πρὸς αὐτὸν ταὐτά φησιν εἰπεῖν·
    κεῖνον, ὦ χρυσόθρονε Μοῦσ', ἔνισπες
    ὕμνον, ἐκ τᾶς καλλιγύναικος ἐσθλᾶς
    Τήϊος χώρας ὃν ἄειδε τερπνῶς
    πρέσβυς ἀγαυός.
ὅτι δὲ οὔκ ἐστι Σαπφοῦς τοῦτο τὸ ᾆσμα παντί που δῆλον· ἐγὼ δὲ ἡγοῦμαι παίζειν
τὸν Ἑρμησιάνακτα περὶ τούτου τοῦ ἔρωτος. καὶ γὰρ Δίφιλος ὁ κωμῳδιοποιὸς
πεποίηκεν ἐν Σαπφοῖ δράματι Σαπφοῦς ἐραστὰς Ἀρχίλοχον καὶ Ἱππώνακτα.

Chamaeleon in *Peri Sapphous* claims that some say that Anacreon composed the following for her:
> Once again golden-haired Erōs strikes me with a purple ball
> and challenges me to play with the maiden of the embroidered sandal.
> But she, for she is from beautifully built Lesbos,
> mocks my hair, for it is white, and gazes at another

and he claims that Sappho said the following in response to him:
> golden-throned Muse,
> you evoked that hymn from Teos,
> the noble land of beautiful women,
> which the glorious old man sang pleasantly.

That this poem is not by Sappho is evident to all; **but I think** that Hermesianax jokes about this love affair. For the comic poet Diphilus also portrayed Archilochus and Hipponax as Sappho's lovers in his play *Sappho*.

    CHAMAELEON *Peri Sapphous* fr. 26 = Ath.13.599c–d

---

47 The text of Wehrli (1969e) in the first line of Anacreon's fragment is σφαίρῃ δεῦτέ με πορφυρέῃ.

That Chamaeleon included the two poems in his treatise and that the quotation from his book runs between Χαμαιλέων and δῆλον is evident in the revelation of Athenaeus' persona (ἐγὼ δὲ ἡγοῦμαι) with which his commentary on the issue of the contemporaneity between the two poets starts.[48] Chamaeleon after all is not concerned with the period at which the two poets lived, but with the content of their poems as well as with the erotic context in which they were composed. The pronouns τάδε and ταῦτα in Athenaeus also provide evidence for close attention to detail in the Peripatetic treatise, especially on matters of morphology and vocabulary.[49] This would only have been possible if the lyric fragment was included in the treatise. Similarly, in his treatise *Peri Anakreontos* Chamaeleon apparently cited (προθείς) a specific poem by Anacreon (fr. 372).

Χαμαιλέων δ' ὁ Ποντικὸς ἐν τῷ Περὶ Ἀνακρέοντος προθεὶς τὸ
    ξανθῇ δ' Εὐρυπύλῃ μέλει
ὁ περιφόρητος Ἀρτέμων,
τὴν προσηγορίαν ταύτην λαβεῖν τὸν Ἀρτέμωνα διὰ τὸ τρυφερῶς βιοῦντα περιφέρεσθαι ἐπὶ κλίνης. καὶ γὰρ Ἀνακρέων αὐτὸν ἐκ πενίας εἰς τρυφὴν ὁρμῆσαί φησιν ἐν τούτοις·
    πρὶν μὲν ἔχων βερβέριον, καλύμματ' ἐσφηκωμένα
    καὶ ξυλίνους ἀστραγάλους ἐν ὠσὶ καὶ ψιλὸν περὶ
        πλευρῇσι ⟨...⟩ βοός,[50]
    νήπλυτον εἴλυμα κακῆς ἀσπίδος, ἀρτοπώλισιν
    κἀθελοπόρνοισιν ὁμιλέων ὁ πονηρὸς Ἀρτέμων,
        κίβδηλον εὑρίσκων βίον,
    πολλὰ μὲν ἐν δουρὶ τιθεὶς αὐχένα, πολλὰ δ' ἐν τροχῷ,
    πολλὰ δὲ νῶτον σκυτίνῃ μάστιγι θωμιχθείς,
        κόμην πώγωνά τ' ἐκτετιλμένος·
    νῦν δ' ἐπιβαίνει σατινέων χρύσεα φορέων καθέρματα
    †παῖς Κύκης† καὶ σκιαδίσκην ἐλεφαντίνην φορεῖ[51]
    γυναιξὶν αὔτως ⟨– ⏑ –⟩.

---

48 Martano (2012) 231; Schorn (2012a) 423n51.
49 Cf. Chamaeleon fr. 39 *Peri Aeschylou* where Athenaeus uses the pronoun ταῦτα in connection with παρέθετο ('cited') after citing Aeschylus (Ath. 9.375f); Clearchus' fr. 41 *Peri Biōn* where Sappho's fr. 58.25–26 is introduced with the phrase λέγουσα ὧδε ('putting it thus').
50 Olson in his Athenaeus edition and Page (fr. 388 *PMG*) do not supplement the lacuna; Campbell gives πλευρῇσι ⟨δέρμ' ἧει⟩ βοός in his Loeb edition; while Martano, the most recent editor of Chamaeleon, supplements with ⟨δέρριον⟩.
51 I reproduce Olson's text in his Athenaeus edition who, like Campbell in his Loeb edition, follows Page (fr. 388 *PMG*), whereas Martano gives πάϊς Κύκης, καὶ σκιαδίσκην ἐλεφαντίνην φορέει in his edition of Chamaeleon. Campbell also adds ⟨ἐμφερής⟩ at the very end of the fragment.

Chamaeleon of Pontus **having quoted** in his treatise *Peri Anakreontos* the
blond Eurypyle
is in love with litter-borne Artemon,
explains that Artemon got this name because he lived luxuriously and was
borne about in a litter. For even Anacreon says in these lines that he leapt
from poverty to luxury:
he used to go about in a shabby garment, a waspy hood,
and wooden earrings in his ears as well as having a hairless oxhide
around his ribs,
the unwashed wrapping of a poor shield, that wretch Artemon,
conversing with bread-women and willing prostitutes,
devising a life of fraud,
at times putting his neck on the pillory, at times on the wheel,
at times being flogged in the back with a leather strap,
his hair and beard being plucked.
But now he rides in a carriage wearing gold earrings,
†the son of Cyce†, and an ivory sunshade,
just like the ladies.

CHAMAELEON *Peri Anakreontos* fr. 36 = Ath.12.533e–534b

Schorn discusses the above passage in order to draw conclusions on the nature of Chamaeleon's work, especially on whether his treatises were commentaries or not.[52] He observes that Athenaeus employs in his work the participle προθείς with different meanings: 'it can mean "to write under a lemma (in a commentary)", but also "to set first" and "to quote before",'[53] and he concludes that the participle in Athenaeus 'can mean any kind of mention, account, or quotation that comes before an explanation or addition'.[54] This conclusion has a bearing on the issue raised above relating to the existence of poetic citations in Chamaeleon's work, as well as on the existence of lyric texts in the Peripatetic library. The participle in the above passage from Athenaeus refers specifically to the format Chamaeleon used in his treatise on Anacreon: he apparently first cited the verses of Anacreon's fr. 372 and subsequently explained the reason why Artemon, who was of low status, was portrayed in the poem as living luxuriously. This explanation once again rests on Anacreon's poetry (fr. 388), a

---

52 Both Leo (1960) 369–370 and Schorn (2012a) 420–421 use the above passage and the participle to draw conclusions on the nature of Chamaeleon's work, i.e. whether his treatises were commentaries or not.
53 Schorn (2012a) 420nn39–41 for examples from Athenaeus' text.
54 Schorn (2012a) 420.

tendency that shows that any interpretation offered was based on the poem itself and was derived from within the poetic corpus. In general, Chamaeleon's approach suggests that the poems included in the Peripatetic treatises were often employed as interpretative tools.[55]

Both the above passages are suggestive of the existence of poetic quotations in the treatises of Chamaeleon on Anacreon and Sappho presumably in order to make use of the passages as the basis for discussion. Nonetheless, the poems themselves and their interpretation were not always the subject of the discussion. Athenaeus' references (*passim*) to Chamaeleon's work suggest that the philosopher often used information deduced from individual poetic fragments to prove or reinforce claims in favour of the existence of specific customs and rituals. As we have already seen with the case of Stesichorus and the poem *kalykē*, Pindar's *enkomion* to Xenophon (fr. 122) and Simonides' epigram XIV are also employed by Chamaeleon in his treatise *Peri Pindarou* (fr. 31 = Ath.13.573c) with a short reference to the first two lines of Pindar's *Olympian* 13. This is done in order to report on the existence of a Corinthian custom and ritual at which the city included prostitutes every time its citizens prayed to Aphrodite.[56] The extract from Chamaeleon's *Peri Pindarou* is included in a long discussion in Athenaeus on the theme of courtesans, in the course of which Athenaeus offers information derived from a number of sources. These sources are explicitly mentioned in his narrative.[57] I do not cite the Pindaric fr. 122 in the extract below.

νόμιμόν ἐστιν ἀρχαῖον ἐν Κορίνθῳ, ὡς καὶ Χαμαιλέων ὁ Ἡρακλεώτης ἱστορεῖ ἐν τῷ Περὶ Πινδάρου, ὅταν ἡ πόλις εὔχηται περὶ μεγάλων τῇ Ἀφροδίτῃ, συμπαρα-

---

[55] Cf. Heraclides Ponticus fr. 60 *Peri Hēdonēs* where Plutarch (*Pericles* 27) points out that Heraclides used the poems of Anacreon to draw conclusions on Artemon's luxury (ἐλέγχει τοῖς Ἀνακρέοντος ποιήμασιν).

[56] On the connection between the Pindaric narrative and such Corinthian rituals, see among others Calame (1989); Kurke (1996); Budin (2008b) 112–152 with criticism by Pirenne-Delforge in her review (*BMCR* 2009.04.28). On the specifics of Simonides' epigram, particularly the problematic δαιμονίᾳ in the second line, and for an analysis of its three preserved versions, see (very selectively) van Groningen (1956); Page (1981) 207–211; Brown (1991); Budin (2008a).

[57] Ath. 13.571c–573c: Apollodorus *Peri Theōn FGrH* 2.B 244 F112, Sappho fr. 160 and fr. 142, Menander *Parakatathēkē* fr. 287 *PCG*, Ephippus *Empolē* fr. 6 *PCG*, Eubulus *Kampyliōn* fr. 41 *PCG*, Antiphanes *Hydria* fr. 210 *PCG*, Anaxilas *Neottis* fr. 21 *PCG*, Alexis *Hypnos* fr. 244 *PCG*, Ephippus *Sappho* fr. 20 *PCG*, Aeschines *Against Timarchus* 1.75, Philetaerus *Kynēgis* fr. 8 *PCG*, Hegesander *en Hypomnēmasi FHG* 4, p. 418 fr. 25, Pamphilus fr. 29 Schmidt, Neanthes *Mythika FGrH* 2.A 84 F9, Alexis *Hōrai Samiakai FGrH* 3.B 539 F1, Eualces *Ephesiaka FGrH* 3.B 418 F2, Clearchus *Erōtika* fr. 29, [Demosthenes] *Against Neaira* 59.122, Aeschylus fr. 313a *TGrF*.

λαμβάνεσθαι πρὸς τὴν ἱκετείαν τὰς ἑταίρας ὡς πλείστας, καὶ ταύτας προσεύχεσθαι τῇ θεῷ καὶ ὕστερον ἐπὶ τοῖς ἱεροῖς παρεῖναι. καὶ ὅτε δὴ ἐπὶ τὴν Ἑλλάδα τὴν στρατείαν ἦγεν ὁ Πέρσης, ὡς καὶ Θεόπομπος ἱστορεῖ καὶ Τίμαιος ἐν τῇ ἑβδόμῃ, αἱ Κορίνθιαι ἑταῖραι εὔξαντο ὑπὲρ τῆς τῶν Ἑλλήνων σωτηρίας εἰς τὸν τῆς Ἀφροδίτης ἐλθοῦσαι νεών. διὸ καὶ Σιμωνίδης ἀναθέντων τῶν Κορινθίων πίνακα τῇ θεῷ τὸν ἔτι καὶ νῦν διαμένοντα καὶ τὰς ἑταίρας ἰδίᾳ γραψάντων τὰς τότε ποιησαμένας τὴν ἱκετείαν καὶ ὕστερον παρούσας συνέθηκε τόδε τὸ ἐπίγραμμα·

αἵδ᾽ ὑπὲρ Ἑλλήνων τε καὶ εὐθυμάχων πολιητᾶν
ἐστάθεν εὔχεσθαι Κύπριδι δαιμονίᾳ·
οὐ γὰρ τοξοφόροισιν ἐμήσατο δῖ᾽ Ἀφροδίτα
Πέρσαις Ἑλλάνων ἀκρόπολιν προδόμεν.

καὶ οἱ ἰδιῶται δὲ κατεύχονται τῇ θεῷ τελεσθέντων περὶ ὧν ἂν ποιῶνται τὴν δέησιν ἀπάξειν αὐτῇ καὶ τὰς ἑταίρας. ὑπάρχοντος οὖν τοῦ τοιούτου νομίμου περὶ τὴν θεὸν Ξενοφῶν ὁ Κορίνθιος ἐξιὼν εἰς Ὀλυμπίαν ἐπὶ τὸν ἀγῶνα καὶ αὐτὸς ἀπάξειν ἑταίρας εὔξατο τῇ θεῷ νικήσας. Πίνδαρός τε τὸ μὲν πρῶτον ἔγραψεν εἰς αὐτὸν ἐγκώμιον, οὗ ἡ ἀρχή·

τρισολυμπιονίκαν
ἐπαινέων οἶκον,

ὕστερον δὲ καὶ σκόλιον τὸ παρὰ τὴν θυσίαν ᾀσθέν, ἐν ᾧ τὴν ἀρχὴν εὐθέως πεποίηται πρὸς τὰς ἑταίρας, αἳ παραγενομένου τοῦ Ξενοφῶντος καὶ θύοντος τῇ Ἀφροδίτῃ συνέθυσαν. διόπερ ἔφη·
[Pind. fr. 122.17–20]
ἤρξατο δ᾽ οὕτως τοῦ μέλους·
[Pind. fr. 122.1–9]
ἀρξάμενος δ᾽ οὕτως ἑξῆς φησιν·
[Pind. fr. 122.10–15]
δῆλον γὰρ ὅτι πρὸς τὰς ἑταίρας διαλεγόμενος ἠγωνία ποῖόν τι φανήσεται τοῖς Κορινθίοις τὸ πρᾶγμα. πιστεύων δέ, ὡς ἔοικεν, αὐτὸς αὑτῷ πεποίηκεν εὐθέως·
[Pind. fr. 122.6]

An old custom exists in Corinth, as Chamaeleon of Heraclea reports in his *Peri Pindarou*, that, whenever the city prays to Aphrodite about important matters they include in their supplication as many prostitutes as possible and that they [sc. the prostitutes] also pray to the goddess and later attend the sacrifices. Indeed, when the Persian led the expedition against Greece, as Theopompus reports and also Timaeus in his seventh book, the Corinthian prostitutes prayed for the safety of the Greeks by going to the temple of Aphrodite. For this reason, when the Corinthians set up a plaque to the goddess, which remains there even now, and wrote down

individually the names of the prostitutes who made the supplication and were later present at the sacrifices, Simonides composed this epigram here:
> These women stood in prayer to heavenly Kypris
> on behalf of the Greeks and their fair-fighting fellow citizens,
> for divine Aphrodite did not plan to betray
> the acropolis of the Greeks to the arrow-bearing Persians.

Individuals also pray privately to the goddess and promise that they will bring to her prostitutes, if what they make their request about is fulfilled. As this custom existed in connection with the goddess, Xenophon of Corinth, when he went to Olympia for the competition, promised that he would also bring prostitutes to the goddess, if he won. And in the first place Pindar wrote an encomium for him, the beginning of which is,
> I praise a house
> that was thrice victorious at Olympia.

and he later wrote a *skolion* that was sung at a sacrifice, the beginning of which he immediately addressed to the prostitutes who joined the sacrifice when Xenophon was on hand and sacrificing to Aphrodite. He thus said:
> [Pind. fr. 122.17–20]

And he began the song in this way
> [Pind.fr. 122.1–9].

Having begun in this way, he then continues
> [Pind.fr. 122.10–15].

For it is obvious that in addressing the prostitutes he was concerned about how the whole thing would look to the Corinthians. But with confidence in himself, as it seems, he thereafter wrote:
> [Pind. fr. 122.6]

CHAMAELEON *Peri Pindarou* fr. 31 = Ath.13.573c–574b

It is clear that Chamaeleon's narrative on the worship of Aphrodite in Corinth was created by combining data from both Simonides' epigram and the Pindaric *skolion*, as Chamaeleon calls the *enkomion* to Xenophon.[58] One may say that Chamaeleon interprets the poems historically or that he attempts to deduce information on customs that may (or may not) have been in practice at the time of the poems' composition.[59] The narrative from his treatise probably does not

---

58 Van Groningen (1960) 16–17, 46–50 for the suggestion that Pindar's fr. 122, which he characterizes as a *skolion* rather than as *enkomion*, was performed at the symposium.
59 Schorn (2012a) 431 on autopsy as an important factor in Chamaeleon's method of histor-

break off with the reference to Theopompus and Timaeus in Athenaeus (καὶ ... νεών). Although Chamaeleon explains the custom of the Corinthian prostitutes differently—the prostitutes are invited as suppliants to Aphrodite every time Corinth prays for important matters—he might still have brought in the testimonies of Theopompus and Timaeus on the role of prostitutes in prayers to Aphrodite at the time of the Persian invasion to support his claim on the existence of the custom.[60] Simonides' epigram was in all probability included in the narrative of either of the two historians, and was consequently included in that of Chamaeleon in his *Peri Pindarou*.

The method of Athenaeus in the entire discussion about prostitutes may be helpful in concluding whether Simonides' epigram and Pindar's encomium to Xenophon (fr. 122) were included in the treatise. The narrative on prostitutes in Athenaeus is actually formed by accumulating sources related to the theme. Athenaeus does not interpret the sources nor does he comment on them extensively. It is enough for him to present them in his work by introducing the name of the author and by citing the passage relevant to the discussion. In this sense, the name of the author functions as a heading, since it becomes clear that the source changes only when another author is introduced. In the extract from Chamaeleon's *Peri Pindarou* therefore the phrases with which the compositions of Simonides and Pindar are introduced were in all probability in the actual work of Chamaeleon and these were followed by the quotations included in Athenaeus' text: συνέθηκε τόδε τὸ ἐπίγραμμα for Simonides' epigram; ἐγκώμιον, οὗ ἡ ἀρχή for lines 1–2 of Pindar's *Olympian* 13; ὕστερον δὲ καὶ σκόλιον τὸ παρὰ τὴν θυσίαν ᾀσθέν, ἐν ᾧ τὴν ἀρχὴν, ἤρξατο δ' οὕτως τοῦ μέλους, αὐτὸς αὑτῷ πεποίηκεν εὐθέως for introducing piecemeal Pindar's encomium for Xenophon.

It should be stated that the existence of lyric texts in the Peripatetic library does not imply that the Peripatos possessed the complete corpus of the lyric poets, even of any one lyric poet, or that the philosophers created editions of their work.[61] The surviving titles of their treatises and the nature of the fragments are strong evidence that the Peripatetics did not organize, classify, or

---

ical research; cf. Budin (2008) 347–349 who argues that Chamaeleon invented the Corinthian custom in order to explain Pindar's encomium and Simonides' epigram.
60 Theopompus *FGrH* 3.B 115 F285 (cf. schol. Pind. *Ol*.13.32b Drachmann), Timaeus *FGrH* 3.B 566 F10.
61 Commenting on Chamaeleon's *Peri Pindarou*, Schorn (2012a) 422 concludes that 'the book was a commented edition, and not a commentary', a conclusion that is based on Chamaeleon's fr. 31 but cannot be inferred from other fragments. Schorn, nonetheless, does not imply that the Peripatetic treatises were edited works in the Alexandrian sense or that they included the whole corpus of a poet. His comments on both Chamaeleon's fr. 31, where Pindar's verses are not cited in their original order, and on the nature of his other

edit the text of lyric. With the exception of Clearchus' *Erōtika* that plausibly included references to some poets and poems with an erotic nature, no title reveals a generic categorization of lyric poetry or any other form of classification. The work of the Peripatos on lyric poetry was ultimately work on the lyric poets, since the name of the poet was often the criterion for the compilation. The act of classification is closely related to the need to organize texts, which the Peripatetics did not do; it is left to the Alexandrians to classify.

We are left with some intriguing lacunae in the Peripatetic project and some striking gaps in the study of lyric that merit further discussion here. Interest in classic lyric poets in the Peripatos does not take account of Alcman, Ibycus, and Bacchylides. We have no evidence for monographs on Bacchylides and Ibycus, and Alcman receives a Peripatetic treatise chronologically late compared to the other classic lyric poets.[62] Alcman is undeniably mentioned as the pioneer of love song, and Chamaeleon is explicit as to the authority of the information.

Ἀρχύτας δ' ὁ ἁρμονικός, ὥς φησι Χαμαιλέων, Ἀλκμᾶνα γεγονέναι τῶν ἐρωτικῶν μελῶν ἡγεμόνα καὶ ἐκδοῦναι πρῶτον μέλος ἀκόλαστον, ὄντα καὶ περὶ τὰς γυναῖκας καὶ τὴν τοιαύτην μοῦσαν εἰς τὰς διατριβάς. διὸ καὶ λέγειν ἔν τινι τῶν μελῶν·

"Ἔρως με δηὖτε Κύπριδος ϝέκατι[63]
γλυκὺς κατείβων καρδίαν ἰαίνει

Archytas the theorist of musical harmonies, as Chamaeleon says, claimed that Alcman became the leading figure in erotic songs and that he was the first to have prepared a licentious song, as he would spend his time being occupied with women and with that sort of muse. For this reason he says in one of his songs;
Once again for Kypris' sake Erōs
flows sweet and melts my heart
CHAMAELEON fr. 25 = Ath.13.600f

---

fragments suggest that he employs the phrase "commented edition" in order to discard the characterisation "commentary" that Leo attached to Chamaeleon's works.

62 Wehrli (1969e) 79 and Hinge (2006) 308 record that Alcman eventually receives a monograph at the time of Callimachus' *Pinakes*; Philochorus, a Hellenistic scholar-historian (c. 340–263/2 BCE) is the first to produce a *Peri Alkmanos*—*FGrH* 3.B 328 T1 (= *Suda* s.v. Φιλόχορος [φ 441 Adler]) ἔγραψεν ... Περὶ Ἀλκμᾶνος ('he wrote ... a *Peri Alkmanos*'). Hinge (2006) 310 also mentions that Sosibios produced a work entitled as such—Ath. 14.646a Σωσίβιος ἐν τρίτῳ περὶ Ἀλκμᾶνος ('Sosibios in the third [book] *Peri Alkmanos*').

63 Wehrli (1969e) gives Ἔρως με δηὖτε Κύπριδος ⟨ϝ⟩έκατι.

Athenaeus, however, does not specify in which work Chamaeleon makes that claim.⁶⁴ This silence of Athenaeus comes in marked contrast to the manner in which he refers to these kinds of works for other lyric poets. One can discern a pattern; for all the treatises on lyric poets Athenaeus is very precise: he refers to the actual work. Thus: ἐν τῷ Περὶ Σαπφοῦς (fr. 26 = Ath.13.599c), ἐν τῷ Περὶ Πινδάρου (fr. 31 = Ath.13.573c), ἐν τῷ Περὶ Στησιχόρου (fr. 28 = Ath.14.620c), ἐν τῷ Περὶ Σιμωνίδου (fr. 33 = Ath.13.656c, fr. 34 = Ath.10.456c, and fr. 35 = Ath.13.611a), ἐν τῷ Περὶ Ἀνακρέοντος (fr. 36 = Ath.12.533e), ἐν τῷ περὶ αὐτοῦ τοῦ Λάσου (fr. 30 = Ath.8.338b), ἐν τῷ Περὶ Ἀλκαίῳ (fr. 95 = Ath.15.668e).⁶⁵ This suggests that Chamaeleon probably produced no work dedicated to Alcman and that he mentions Alcman either in a work dedicated to music or lyric poetry or in a discussion devoted to the origin of certain lyric genres or poetic modes.⁶⁶ Information of this sort could have derived from Alcman's established reputation as a poet composing erotic songs and from reperformances of his poetry, including sympotic poetry.⁶⁷

These lacunae raise tantalizing questions about the pace of textualization, and the nature and scale of collected works of poets. If indeed, as suggested, texts were necessary for the kind of analysis the Peripatetics pursued, one possible reason for absences or late appearance of treatises is that they did not possess the texts of the poets in question, at least until the end of the third century BCE. We should not assume that the shift to the written word as the primary medium of preservation meant that all texts were readily available even in a major cultural centre such as Athens. We possess no evidence that the lyric poets were ever edited in Athens. Thus, in the case of lyric poetry, it is likely that the scholars of the Peripatos were dependent on texts obtained from abroad. The Peripatetics themselves were not Athenians in origin. They may have brought with them texts as soon as they joined Aristotle's school, and these texts could plausibly have arrived either from the native town of each

---

64   Cf. Chamaeleon fr. 24 (= Ath. 9.389f–390a).
65   Wehrli does not capitalize the first letter of the preposition περί in his edition of Chamaeleon and puts in brackets [τοῦ Λάσου] (fr. 30), whereas Olson capitalizes the first letter of Περί with the exception of περὶ αὐτοῦ τοῦ Λάσου (Ath. 8.338b).
66   Cf. Martano (2012) 229.
67   Cf. Eupolis fr. 148 PCG on no longer singing Alcman. Hinge (2006) 304 claims that by the end of the archaic period some of Alcman's poetry was written down. His assumption is based on Ath. 14.632f–633a, where it is stated how Spartans preserved their music most faithfully (διετήρησαν τὴν μουσικήν). Athenaeus' passage, however, does not provide any evidence in favour of the development of a written poetic tradition in Sparta, as Hinge would wish. It rather suggests that songs of Spartan poets continued to be reperformed. On reperformance of Alcman's poetry, Carey (2011) 433–434.

philosopher, or from other nearby towns. If the silence of our sources about Peripatetic works on Ibycus and Bacchylides reflects the absence of a treatise, it may be the case that the Peripatos did not possess their text or at least not a good text. The complete picture of the Peripatetic treatises reveals their broad knowledge of Greek culture, literature, and prose, and their great interest in musical matters and festivals. It is therefore difficult to assume that they did not know of or at least had not heard of these two lyric poets. Thus, although they were presumably aware of their existence, lack of a (good) text did not allow them practically to analyse either the poets or their poetry. Ibycus' presence in the Athenian landscape but his absence from the Peripatos reinforces this assumption. Ibycus is mentioned by Agathon together with Anacreon and Alcaeus in Aristophanes' *Thesmophoriazusae* (159–163), while in Plato's *Parmenides* the aged Parmenides cites Ibycus' fr. 287 (136e9–137a4), a poem that he identifies by the phrase τὸ τοῦ Ἰβυκείου ἵππου, and Socrates cites his fr. 310 in the *Phaedrus* (242c6–b1). It is obvious that, even in the cases of pure biographies or biographical anecdotes, the starting point of any assumption was the text of the poet and conclusions were often drawn from his poetry.[68] The attitude of these philosophers towards the rest of the nine, particularly Alcman, and also Hipponax, as well as the timing of the production of a treatise for each one of them supports the above argument. The fact that both Ibycus and Bacchylides receive no treatise even later in the Hellenistic era could suggest not only that their text was unavailable in the Peripatetic library but also that it reached Alexandria at a time when editions became more important than monographs. An alternative is that they were purposely neglected in the Peripatos in favour of the witty and playful poetry of Anacreon in the case of Ibycus, and of the work of Pindar and Simonides in the case of Bacchylides.

The move towards textuality has important implications. The use of a physical text as the raw material means that the text itself now becomes the focus, and consequently the poetry itself and the poet. This is a radical shift of focus. Although one can frequently find in Plato's dialogues quotations, paraphrases, and discussions of lyric poetry or of specific passages of lyric poetry, the most substantial of which is Simonides' Ode to Scopas in the *Protagoras*, their employment is made for the sake of the Platonic argument. The same applies at times to Aristotle. Aristotle often uses the lyric poets as historical or political sources—a practice that we have also detected in Chamaeleon's *Peri Pindarou* and *Peri Stesichorou*—he refers to them as paradigms of his rhetorical

---

68 Fairweather (1974) 232–239; Lefkowitz (2012) 2. Momigliano (1993) 70 emphasizes that the inclination of the Peripatetics to infer personal details from the poetic text contributed to the technique of biographical research.

instructions, and he also frequently cites selected lyric works.[69] He, nonetheless, gradually paves the way for the Peripatetic approach. The lyric poems *per se* now become an object of discussion by the Peripatetics, and their attempts to explicate and analyse focus on details available only because of the existence of books and texts.[70] When it comes to the Peripatetic project, poetry itself was the starting point for a treatise. We have entered an era of literary study. In this sense, as well as in the Peripatetic prioritization of texts for study, the Peripatetics set the agenda for Alexandria.

References

Anagnostopoulos, G. 2009. Aristotle's Life. In *A Companion to Aristotle*, ed. G. Anagnostopoulos, 3–13. Chichester.

Arrighetti, G. 1987. *Poeti, eruditi e biografi. Momenti della riflessione dei Greci sulla letteratura*. Pisa.

Bell, J.M. 1978. Κίμβιξ καὶ σοφός: Simonides in the Anecdotal Tradition. *QUCC* 28: 29–86.

Bing, P. 1993. The *Bios*-Tradition and Poets' Lives in Hellenistic Poetry. In *Nomodeiktes. Greek Studies in Honor of Martin Ostwald*, ed. R. Rosen and J. Farrell, 619–631. Michigan.

Bollansée, J. 1999. *Hermippos of Smyrna = Die Fragmente der Griechischen Historiker Continued*. IV.A: *Biography and Antiquarian Literature*, ed. G. Schepens. Leiden.

Brown, C.G. 1991. The Prayers of the Corinthian Women (Simonides, *Ep*. 14 Page, *FGE*). *GRBS* 32: 5–14.

Brugnoli, G. 1995. Nascita e sviluppo della biografia romana: aspetti e problemi. In *Biografia e autobiografia degli antichi e dei moderni*, ed. I. Gallo and I. Nicastri, 79–108. Naples.

Budin, S.L. 2008a. Simonides' Corinthian Epigram. *CP* 103(4): 335–353.

---

69 Quotations of lyric poets in Aristotle that are accompanied by the name of the poet are found in: *Rh*.1401a17 (quotation of Pindar's *Partheneion* 1 on false enthymeme); *Rh*.1367a5–15 (Alcaeus and Sappho on what is noble, with Campbell's note on Sappho's fr. 137); *Rh*.1394b34–1395a2 and *Rh*.1412a22–24 (Stesichorus' T17 on using maxims and witty apophthegms); *Rh*.1363a15 (Aristotle cites Simonides' fr. 572 on deliberation), *Rh*.1367b20 (Simonides' Epigr.26(a).3 is cited in the section on things noble and praiseworthy), *Rh*.1405b16–27 (quotation of Simonides' fr. 515 on the use of metaphors drawn from beautiful words); *H.A*.542b4–10 (Simonides' fr. 508 is cited as part of Aristotle's definition of the halcyon days); *Pol*.1285a31–b3 (the reference to Alcaeus' exile from Mytilene accompanied by a quotation of his fr. 348 both as examples of cases where tyrants were chosen by the people).

70 Pfeiffer (1968) 62 also suggests that the Academy and the Peripatos used books.

Budin, S.L. 2008b. *The Myth of Sacred Prostitution in Antiquity*. Cambridge.
Calame, C. 1989. Entre rapports de parenté et relations civiques: Aphrodite l'Hétaïre au banquet politique des hetaîroi. In *Aux sources de la Puissance. Sociabilité et parenté*, ed. F. Thélamon, 101–111. Rouen.
Carey, C. 2011. Alcman: From Laconia to Alexandria. In *Archaic and Classical Choral Song*, ed. L. Athanassaki and E.L. Bowie, 423–446. Berlin.
Cooper, C. 2002. Aristoxenos, Περὶ Βίων and Peripatetic Biography. *Mouseion* 2: 307–339.
Degani, E. 1984. *Studi su Ipponatte*. Bari.
Dihle, A. 1956. *Studien zur griechischen Biographie*. Göttingen.
Dihle, A. 1998. Zur antiken Biographie. In *La Biographie Antique: Huit Exposés Suivis de Discussions*, ed. S.M. Maul and W.-W. Ehlers, 119–140. Geneva.
Fairweather, J. 1974. Fiction in the Biographies of Ancient Writers. *Ancient Society* 5: 231–275.
Fortenbaugh, W.W. and Schütrumpf, E. eds. 2001. *Dicaearchus of Messana. Text, Translation, and Discussion*. New Brunswick.
Gallo, I. 1995. Nascita e sviluppo della biografia greca: aspetti e problemi. In *Biografia e autobiografia degli antichi e dei moderni*, ed. I. Gallo and L. Nicastri, 7–22. Naples.
Gallo, I. 2005. *La Biografia Greca. Profilo Storico e breve Anthologia di testi*. Soveria Manelli.
Gibson, S. 2005. *Aristoxenus of Tarentum and the Birth of Musicology*. New York.
Grayeff, F. 1974. *Aristotle and his School: An Inquiry into the History of the Peripatos with a Commentary on Metaphysics Z, H, L and Q*. London.
Hägg, T. 2012. *The Art of Biography in Antiquity*. Cambridge.
Hinge, G. 2006. *Die Sprache Alkmans: Textgeschichte und Sprachgeschichte*. Wiesbaden.
Kurke, L. 1996. Pindar and the Prostitutes, or Reading Ancient "Pornography". *Arion* 4(2): 49–75.
Lefkowitz, M.R. 2012. *The Lives of the Greek Poets*. London.
Leo, F. 1901. *Die griechisch-römische Biographie nach ihrer litterarischen Form*. Leipzig.
Leo, F. 1960. Satyros Βίος Εὐριπίδου. In *Ausgewählte Kleine Schriften II*, ed. E. Fränkel, 365–383. Rome.
LeVen, P.A. 2014. *The Many-Headed Muse. Tradition and Innovation in Late Classical Greek Lyric Poetry*. Cambridge.
Lobel, E. and Page, D., eds. 1955. *Poetarum Lesbiorum Fragmenta*. Oxford.
Lynch, J.P. 1972. *Aristotle's School: A Study of a Greek Educational Institution*. Berkeley.
Martano, A. 2012. Chamaeleon of Heraclea: The Sources, Text, and Translation. In *Praxiphanes of Mytilene and Chamaeleon of Heraclea: Text, Translation, and Discussion*, ed. A. Martano, E. Matelli and D. Mirhady, 157–228. New Brunswick.
McGing, B. and Mossman, J. 2006. Introduction. In *The Limits of Ancient Biography*, ed. B. McGing and J. Mossman, 1–12. Swansea.

Momigliano, A. 1993. *The Development of Greek Biography*. Cambridge, MA.

Montanari, F. 2000. Demetrius of Phalerum on Literature. In *Demetrius of Phalerum: text, translation, and discussion*, ed. W.W. Fortenbaugh and E. Schütrumpf, 391–411. New Brunswick.

Montanari, F. 2012. The Peripatos on Literature. Interpretation, Use and Abuse. In *Praxiphanes of Mytilene and Chamaeleon of Heraclea*, ed. A. Martano, E. Matelli, and D. Mirhady, 339–358. New Brunswick.

Olson, S.D. 2007–2012. *Athenaeus: The Learned Banqueters*. I–VIII. Cambridge, MA.

Page, D.L. 1981. *Further Greek Epigrams*. Cambridge.

Pfeiffer, R. 1968. *History of Classical Scholarship: From the Beginnings to the End of the Hellenistic Age*. Oxford.

Podlecki, A.J. 1969. The Peripatetics as Literary Critics. *Phoenix* 23(1): 114–137.

Power, T. 2012. Aristoxenus and the "Neoclassicists". In *Aristoxenus of Tarentum. Discussion*, ed. C.A. Huffman, 129–154. New Brunswick.

Rawles, R.J. 2018. *Simonides The Poet: Intertextuality and Reception*. Cambridge.

Rose, H.J. 1932. Stesichoros and the Rhadine-Fragment. *CQ* 26.2: 88–92.

Schorn, S. 2012a. Chamaeleon: Biography and Literature *Peri tou deina*. In *Praxiphanes of Mytilene and Chamaeleon of Heraclea. Text, Translation, and Discussion*, ed. A. Martano, E. Matelli, and D. Mirhady, 411–444. New Brunswick.

Schorn, S. 2012b. Aristoxenus' Biographical Method. In *Aristoxenus of Tarentum: Discussion*, ed. C.A. Huffman, 177–221. New Brunswick.

Sharples, R.W. 1999. The Peripatetic School. In *Routledge History of Philosophy, vol. II From Aristotle to Augustine*, ed. D. Furley, 147–187. London.

Sollenberger, M.G. 1992. The Lives of the Peripatetics: An Analysis of the Contents and Structure of Diogenes Laertius' "*Vitae Philosophorum*" book 5. *ANRW* 36(6): 3793–879.

Sonnabend, H. 2002. *Geschichte der antiken Biographie. Von Iokrates bis zur Historia Augusta*. Stuttgart.

van Groningen, B.A. 1956. Théopompe ou Chamaeléon? À propos de Simonide 137 B, 104 D. *Mnemosyne* 9(1): 11–22.

van Groningen, B.A. 1960. *Pindare au Banquet. Les fragments des scolies édité avec un commentaire critique et explicatif*. Leiden.

Wehrli, F. 1967a. *Die Schule des Aristoteles. Texte und Kommentare: I Dikaiarchos*. Basel.

Wehrli, F. 1967b. *Die Schule des Aristoteles. Texte und Kommentare: II Aristoxenos*. Basel.

Wehrli, F. 1968a. *Die Schule des Aristoteles. Texte und Kommentare: IV Demetrios von Pharenon*. Basel.

Wehrli, F. 1968b. *Die Schule des Aristoteles. Texte und Kommentare: VI Lykon und Ariston von Keos*. Basel.

Wehrli, F. 1969a. *Die Schule des Aristoteles. Texte und Kommentare: III Klearchos*. Basel.

Wehrli, F. 1969b. *Die Schule des Aristoteles. Texte und Kommentare*: V *Straton von Lampsakos*. Basel.

Wehrli, F. 1969c. *Die Schule des Aristoteles. Texte und Kommentare*: VII *Herkleides Pontikos*. Basel.

Wehrli, F. 1969d. *Die Schule des Aristoteles. Texte und Kommentare*: VIII *Eudemos von Rhodos*. Basel.

Wehrli, F. 1969e. *Die Schule des Aristoteles. Texte und Kommentare*: IX *Phainias von Eresos, Chamaileon, Praxiphanes*. Basel.

Wehrli, F. 1969f. *Die Schule des Aristoteles. Texte und Kommentare*: X *Hieronymos von Rhodos, Kritolaos und Seine Schüler, Rückblick: Der Peripatos in Vorchristlicher Zeit, Register*. Basel.

Wehrli, F. 1974. *Die Schule des Aristoteles. Texte und Kommentare: Supplementband I Hermippos der Kallimacher*. Basel.

Wehrli, F. 1978. *Die Schule des Aristoteles. Texte und Kommentare: Supplementband II Sotion*. Basel.

Woolf, G. 2013. Introduction: Approaching the Ancient Library. In *Ancient Libraries*, ed. J. König, K. Oikonomopoulou, and G. Woolf, 1–20. Cambridge.

CHAPTER 8

The Self-Revealing Poet: Lyric Poetry and Cultural History in the Peripatetic School

Elsa Bouchard

1   Introduction*

Unlike modern scholars, ancient readers of poetry were almost unanimously unaware of the possible use by poets of a literary persona. The poets who composed in genres pervaded by first-person utterances were invariably believed to be giving a straightforward expression to their own individual thought. Critias' account of Archilochus (Critias B 44 DK = Ael. *VH* 10.13) is a famous illustration of this tendency: he rebuked the iambic poet for 'speaking ill of himself' by revealing to all Greece that he was born to a slave named Enipô, that he was an indigent exile, slanderous towards both friends and enemies, lecherous, and a coward. Each one of these "autobiographical" details can indeed claim support from the relatively small corpus of the preserved fragments or in general features of Archilochean iambic. As a matter of fact, the ancient readers' reflex was to look for clues about the poet's age, education, moral character, political opinions, etc., even when the author composed epic or dramatic poetry.[1] In the case of Old Comedy, this kind of reading might have been encouraged by the presence of a parabasis, but the same holds true for the authors of tragedy. For instance, the scholia to Euripides make repeated claims about how his characters and choruses make transparent remarks betraying the poet's personal ideas.[2]

The identification of the first-person narrator with the author was so natural to the ancients that if some external evidence caused one to reject it, this exceptional phenomenon appeared worthy of mention. Hence the following comment from Democritus, one of Athenaeus' 'sophists at dinner':

---

* I give my thanks to the editors of this volume and organizers of the conference, Ian Rutherford and Bruno Currie, as well as to Claude Calame, for their useful comments on an earlier draft of this chapter.
1 Cf. Clay (1998) 12; Nünlist (2009) 132–133. Lefkowitz (2012) characterizes the biographical tradition on poets as directly derivative of their works.
2 Cf. Elsperger (1907) 127–154, esp. 152–154; Lord (1908) 9–17.

ἄτοπος δὲ ὁ Ἀνακρέων ὁ πᾶσαν αὑτοῦ τὴν ποίησιν ἐξαρτήσας μέθης· τῇ γὰρ μαλακίᾳ καὶ τῇ τρυφῇ ἐπιδοὺς ἑαυτὸν ἐν τοῖς ποιήμασι διαβέβληται, οὐκ εἰδότων τῶν πολλῶν ὅτι νήφων ἐν τῷ γράφειν καὶ ἀγαθὸς ὢν προσποιεῖται μεθύειν οὐκ οὔσης ἀνάγκης.

Anacreon, who connected all his poetry to drunkenness, is an unusual case; he is maligned for surrendering himself to effeminate luxury in his poetry, but most people are unaware that he was sober when he composed, and merely pretended to be drunk, despite being a decent person, when there was no need to do so.[3]

Anacreon is strange not only because he creates a false impression about himself but also because this image, that of a drunkard, is a negative one. As Democritus points out, Anacreon's persona was bound to be taken as historically accurate by most of his readers—which is indeed what happened to Archilochus, whose voluntary self-depreciation provoked Critias' outraged reaction. Democritus' final remark to the effect that nothing compelled Anacreon to act this way is paralleled by Critias' surprise before Archilochus' unabashed exhibitionism, without which 'we would not know' (οὐκ ἂν ἐπυθόμεθα ἡμεῖς) of his shameful lineage and deeds; this unnecessary revelation of distasteful details about himself, rather than Archilochus' behaviour *per se*, seems to be the main reason for Critias' blame.[4] Athenaeus' text is probably the single most explicit testimony of an ancient reader acknowledging the existence of a literary persona in a poet's work, and its formulation strongly suggests that Anacreon is the exception that proves the rule.[5]

---

3 Athenaeus 10.429b. Throughout this chapter I use the text and translation of S.D. Olson's Loeb edition of Athenaeus.
4 Cf. Rankin (1975); Ford (1993) 68. Rotstein (2007) 144–145 suggests that Critias was being disingenuous regarding the biographical value of Archilochus' poems, since he was 'doubtless familiar with poets and performers adopting fictional personalities' (144), but I see no compelling reason to believe so.
5 Of course, an interest in the relationship between poet and work can be traced back much earlier than Athenaeus, most clearly in Aristophanes' playful treatment of the fallacious principle according to which one composes 'in conformity with their nature' (*Thesm.* 167; cf. Ar. fr. 694 *PCG*, and Aeschylus' and Euripides' simultaneously professional and *ad hominem* attacks in the *Frogs*). Still, Aristophanes' ironical stance on this principle is not quite equivalent to a straightforward recognition of the essential distinction between author and characters. As a matter of fact, most commentators take him at face value and ascribe him an authentic belief in *'l'inseparabilità della persona e dell'opera'* (Paduano [1996] 95); cf. Arrighetti (2006) 296. For a more balanced view, see Muecke (1982); Wright (2012) 123–125.

As we shall see presently, there are reasons to think that Aristotle's poetic theory was at odds with the generalized biographical reading of poets. That being said, this theory almost completely ignores lyric, as well as iambic and elegiac poetry. By contrast, Aristotle's pupil Chamaeleon is the author of numerous monographs on such poets as Alcman, Pindar, and Sappho. The remnants of these texts suggest that Chamaeleon considered these authors' work in light of the available details of their biography, and vice versa. This exegetical approach, although ubiquitous among ancient readers, is regularly referred to as 'Chamaeleon's method' by modern scholars.

This chapter will argue in favour of a continuity, albeit with a change of emphasis, between Aristotle and other Peripatetics as regards the status of lyric poetry. In the first place, I shall contend that Aristotle ignores lyric genres because they clash with his mimetic conception of poetry as it is expounded in the *Poetics*. Next, I will look at the "method of Chamaeleon" and its application to one particular case, that of Alcman. Finally, I will adduce a number of other testimonies from various members of the Lyceum in order to demonstrate that Peripatetic work on lyric poetry did not result from an interest in literary theory and criticism *per se*, such as that displayed in Aristotle's, Dicaearchus', or Chamaeleon's works on Homeric poetry.[6] The school's treatises on lyric poets seem rather to have been concerned with anthropological, historical, and ethical issues related to the origins and development of *mousikê*. Thus one should be cautious when speaking of a 'Peripatetic' influence upon ancient scholarship on lyric poetry:[7] the Alexandrians made unprecedented efforts to describe the formal features of early lyric (classification into genres, metrical analysis, etc.);[8] nothing of the sort is attested in the works of the Peripatetics.

2 Aristotle on the Lyric Poets

Aristotle, arguably the most enlightened literary critic of his time, might be an exception to the generalized biographical fallacy of ancient readers, at least as far as non-lyrical genres are concerned. Not only does he refrain from offering

---

6 For a recent review of Peripatetic scholarship on Homer, see Montanari (2012).
7 Barbantani (2009) 298: 'the Peripatetic school ... had a great influence on the study of early lyric, and in the collection of biographical material on lyric poets; see for instance the works of Chameleon'.
8 See Färber (1936) for a review of ancient taxonomies of lyric poetry. Calame (1974) 115 rightly describes Färber's reconstruction as reflecting a theoretical framework that does not go back earlier than the Alexandrian period.

biographical readings of Homer and the tragedians, but he also dismisses *in principle* the intervention of the poet's personal voice in the poem:

> Ὅμηρος δὲ ἄλλα τε πολλὰ ἄξιος ἐπαινεῖσθαι καὶ δὴ καὶ ὅτι μόνος τῶν ποιητῶν οὐκ ἀγνοεῖ ὃ δεῖ ποιεῖν αὐτόν. αὐτὸν γὰρ δεῖ τὸν ποιητὴν ἐλάχιστα λέγειν· οὐ γάρ ἐστι κατὰ ταῦτα μιμητής. οἱ μὲν οὖν ἄλλοι αὐτοὶ μὲν δι' ὅλου ἀγωνίζονται, μιμοῦνται δὲ ὀλίγα καὶ ὀλιγάκις· ὁ δὲ ὀλίγα φροιμιασάμενος εὐθὺς εἰσάγει ἄνδρα ἢ γυναῖκα ἢ ἄλλο τι, καὶ οὐδέν' ἀήθη ἀλλ' ἔχοντα ἦθος.

> Homer deserves praise for many other qualities, but especially for realizing, alone among epic poets, the place of the poet's own voice. For the poet should say as little as possible in his own voice, as it is not this that makes him a mimetic artist. The others participate in their own voice throughout, and engage in mimesis only briefly and occasionally, whereas Homer, after a brief introduction, at once 'brings onto stage' a man, woman, or other figure (all of them rich in character).[9]

This text has been variously understood by readers of the *Poetics*, but the most convincing case that can be made is that Aristotle is referring to Homer's well-known discretion as a narrator: the poet successfully retreats behind his poem to the point of being forgotten by the auditors.[10] This he accomplishes by creating characters endowed with a substantial and autonomous personality. The underlying meaning of the last part of the passage is that the fact that Homeric characters possess true *êthos* secures the poet's disappearance behind them. Indeed, were they to be deprived of character (ἀήθη), they might end up being mere spokesmen for Homer's personal statements.[11]

What then of these 'others' who are disadvantageously compared to Homer in that they keep 'putting themselves on stage throughout' (δι' ὅλου ἀγωνίζονται)? Aristotle literally says that Homer is the 'only' poet (μόνος τῶν ποιητῶν) to make a proper use of mimesis. Since this judgement appears excessive, and considering that chapter 24 of the *Poetics* is largely concerned with epic, translators and commentators limit the meaning of τῶν ποιητῶν to 'the epic poets', as Halliwell does here. According to this reading, the 'others' who speak too much with their own voices are the so-called cyclic poets, a term that covers the

---

9   *Poet.* 24.1460a5–11; transl. Halliwell.
10 See de Jong (2005), who appropriately refutes the view that Aristotle is speaking of the relative proportion of direct speech in Homer.
11 Cf. Lallot (1976).

largely anonymous crowd of the rivals of Homer.[12] Although our knowledge of the cyclic poets is very limited, especially as regards narrative technique, what we do know about them is certainly hard to reconcile with Aristotle's remark.[13] How can these authors be said to 'stage themselves' all the way through their work? A famous study on the content and style of the cyclic poets concludes that the latter were, on the contrary, boringly 'dispassionate' and 'uninterested' narrators.[14]

Whoever these epic poets are, Aristotle's indictment of them suggests that he should be all the more critical of the lyric poets for the apparent lack of mimetic value of their work. As a matter of fact, we should seriously consider the possibility that the contrast drawn by Aristotle here is not between Homer and the other epic poets, but rather between Homer and the other 'ancient poets' in general—that is to say, poets that Aristotle might have dated more or less to the generation of Homer, such as Archilochus and other early authors exemplifying the pre-dramatic forms of encomium and blame.[15] In chapter 4 of the same treatise, Homer was similarly singled out from his contemporaries:

> καὶ ἐγένοντο τῶν παλαιῶν οἱ μὲν ἡρωικῶν οἱ δὲ ἰάμβων ποιηταί. ὥσπερ δὲ καὶ τὰ σπουδαῖα μάλιστα ποιητὴς Ὅμηρος ἦν (μόνος γὰρ οὐχ ὅτι εὖ ἀλλὰ καὶ μιμήσεις δραματικὰς ἐποίησεν), οὕτως καὶ τὰ τῆς κωμῳδίας σχήματα πρῶτος ὑπέδειξεν, οὐ ψόγον ἀλλὰ τὸ γελοῖον δραματοποιήσας.

> Of the older poets some became composers of epic hexameters, others of iambic lampoons. Just as Homer was the supreme poet of elevated sub-

---

12 So Gudeman (1934) 408; Else (1957) 619–621; Lucas (1968) 226 (who also suggests Antimachus); Dupont-Roc and Lallot (1980) 380. Although Hesiod has been frequently understood to give an autobiographical account of himself in his poems, along with a fair number of personal moralizing statements, it seems unlikely that Aristotle would use him to make a contrast with Homer in this context; on Aristotle's references to Hesiod, which are all concerned with the didactic value (scientific or moral) of his poems, see Koning (2010) 151–152.
13 Aristotle's own explicit critique of the cyclic poets is that they compose stories containing too many parts about a single person and a single period (cf. 1459a36–b2, on the authors of the *Cypria* and the *Little Iliad*; 1451a16–22, on the authors of poems on Heracles and Theseus). The subject matter of the poems is relatively well known thanks to Proclus' summaries. There is roughly 120 preserved lines of the Cycle.
14 These epithets are the ones used by Jasper Griffin in his seminal article on the epic cycle (1977).
15 In a text that likely derives from Aristotle's lost dialogue *On Poets*, Archilochus is named along with Mimnermus and Callinus as a possible inventor of the elegiac couplet, whose name is etymologized from the fact that the elegiac lament (ἔλεγος) was used to *eulogize* (εὖ λέγειν) the dead (Arist. *On Poets* fr. 31b Janko).

jects (for he was preeminent not only in quality but also in composing dramatic mimesis), so too he was the first to delineate the forms of comedy, by dramatising not invective but the laughable.[16]

Just as in 1460a5, the meaning of μόνος in the latter text seems not so much to be 'the only one' as 'the only one of his time', viz. 'the first one'. In this historically oriented chapter of the *Poetics* Homer is placed at a crucial point in the development of poetry, that is when some poets turned from encomium and invective to poetry proper, and from historical figures as objects of their poems to fictional characters. The passage about Homer in chapter 24 draws a very similar contrast between mimetic and non-mimetic poetry, but it focuses on the issue of the presence or the absence of the author in his work. According to this reading, the separation between the poet and his work is an essential requisite to Aristotle's notion of poetic mimesis, at least in the full sense of the word.[17] This narrowly defined concept of mimesis would explain why lyric poetry is so conspicuously absent from the *Poetics*, except as a foil to the artistic accomplishment of Homer.[18]

It is remarkable that when Aristotle cites lyric poets, their verses are always subjected to a biographical reading. For instance, in the sole passage where Aristotle refers to verses from either Sappho or Alcaeus,[19] he presents these verses as part of an ongoing conversation between the two poets allegedly engaged in a love affair. Archilochus also provides a good example. Only twice does Aristotle comment on some of his verses, and in both cases he reads them as personal utterances, albeit oblique rather than explicit. One of these passages is in the *Politics*, where Archilochus is adduced as a witness in a rejection of Plato's portrait of the city-guardians as men who are gentle to friends but harsh to enemies:

ὁ θυμός ἐστιν ὁ ποιῶν τὸ φιλητικόν· αὕτη γάρ ἐστιν ἡ τῆς ψυχῆς δύναμις ᾗ φιλοῦμεν. σημεῖον δέ· πρὸς γὰρ τοὺς συνήθεις καὶ φίλους ὁ θυμὸς αἴρεται μᾶλλον ἢ

---

16   *Poet.* 1448b34–1449a2.
17   In its original form, mimesis is a simple human reflex, according to Aristotle's anthropological model (cf. *Poet.* 1448b38). This is why, at an early stage, poetry was divided according to the ethos, serious or petty, of its practitioners (1448b19–27). This need not (and indeed should not) be the case in the fully developed compositions of historical times.
18   The neglect of lyric poetry in the *Poetics* has been variously explained; see e.g. Halliwell (1986) 276–285; Bolonyai (1998); Calame (1998) 108–109; Stabryla (2000) 48–49; Rotstein (2010) 69–71.
19   *Rh.* 1.1367a7–15.

πρὸς τοὺς ἀγνῶτας, ὀλιγωρεῖσθαι νομίσας. διὸ καὶ Ἀρχίλοχος προσηκόντως τοῖς φίλοις ἐγκαλῶν διαλέγεται πρὸς τὸν θυμόν· σὺ γὰρ δὴ παρὰ φίλων ἀπάγχεαι.

The *thymos* is what produces love, for this is the faculty of the soul by which we love. Here is a proof: when one feels that he has been scorned, the *thymos* revolts more strongly against parents and friends than against strangers. That is why Archilochus, at the moment when he rightly accuses his friends, talks to his *thymos*, saying: 'For it is by friends you are being strangled'.[20]

Aristotle's point here is that people endowed with a fair share of *thymos* are just as likely, or even more likely, to revolt against friends as against enemies when they feel they have been wronged. The citation of Archilochus should be considered more than a convenient poetic ornament to a philosophical argument: it looks like a reaction to the disparaging biographical tradition about Archilochus to which the Critias fragment mentioned above belongs.[21] Indeed, one of Critias' charges was that Archilochus attacked his friends just as harshly as his enemies, an attitude for which Aristotle here provides an ethical justification.

The only other Aristotelian citation of Archilochus is in a passage of the *Rhetoric*, which K.J. Dover identifies as the *locus classicus* for the problem of Archilochus' 'assumed personality':[22]

εἰς δὲ τὸ ἦθος, ἐπειδὴ ἔνια περὶ αὑτοῦ λέγειν ἢ ἐπίφθονον ἢ μακρολογίαν ἢ ἀντιλογίαν ἔχει, καὶ περὶ ἄλλου ἢ λοιδορίαν ἢ ἀγροικίαν, ἕτερον χρὴ λέγοντα ποιεῖν, ὅπερ Ἰσοκράτης ποιεῖ ἐν τῷ Φιλίππῳ καὶ ἐν τῇ Ἀντιδόσει, καὶ ὡς Ἀρχίλοχος ψέγει· ποιεῖ γὰρ τὸν πατέρα λέγοντα περὶ τῆς θυγατρὸς ἐν τῷ ἰάμβῳ χρημάτων δ' ἄελπτον οὐθέν ἐστιν οὐδ' ἀπώμοτον, καὶ τὸν Χάρωνα τὸν τέκτονα ἐν τῷ ἰάμβῳ οὗ ἀρχὴ οὔ μοι τὰ Γύγεω, καὶ ὡς Σοφοκλῆς τὸν Αἴμονα ὑπὲρ τῆς Ἀντιγόνης πρὸς τὸν πατέρα ὡς λεγόντων ἑτέρων.

As regards character, since saying some things about oneself brings about either envy, prolixity or contradiction, and speaking of another is insulting or vulgar, one must make somebody else speak, which is what Isocrates does in the *Philip* and the *Antidosis*, and which is the way Archilochus engages in invective: for in an iambic poem he makes the father talk

---

20 *Pol.* 1327b40–1328a5 (Archilochus fr. 129).
21 Cf. Rankin (1977) 168.
22 Dover (1964) 206. Dover rightly questions Aristotle's reading of Archilochus' poem as 'employing a literary device for the expression of *his own* views' (209) (Dover's emphasis).

about his daughter saying 'Nothing is unexpected nor declared impossible on oath' and he introduces Charon the carpenter in an iambic poem which begins 'The wealth of Gyges is nothing to me'. And as Sophocles does, making Haemon talk about Antigone to his father as if others were saying it.[23]

Archilochus along with Isocrates and Sophocles' Haemon are cited as examples of the rhetorical expedient consisting of putting one's own ideas into somebody else's mouth. Here the use by Archilochus of what we would call a literary persona is presented as a mere rhetorical manoeuvre such as that used by the famous orator Isocrates. There is no doubt that according to Aristotle, it is still Archilochus speaking in this poem, and that he is simply using the mask of a character in order to protect himself.

Of Aristotle's works the *Constitution of the Athenians* is undoubtedly the one in which a 'lyric' poet is the most extensively cited. Indeed, the whole section reporting Solon's political measures is based on the legislator's elegies, which Aristotle consistently adduces to support his claims. Graziano Arrighetti identifies the *Constitution of the Athenians* as an Aristotelian precedent to what he calls the method of Chamaeleon, which consists of extracting biographical data from poetic works.[24] But it is plain that Aristotle thinks of Solon as a legislator rather than as a poet, and likely that he would have considered Solon's use of a metrical form a purely accidental feature of his expression. His case would then be comparable to that of Empedocles, whom Aristotle explicitly brands 'a naturalist rather than a poet' despite his use of the hexameter.[25] When it comes to those he considers fully fledged poets, such as Homer or Euripides, Aristotle makes no attempt to correlate their works with biographical data.

3   Chamaeleon's Method and the Origins of Song

Aristotle's implicit rejection of lyric from the realm of "genuine" (that is, mimetic) poetry might *prima facie* appear to be contradicted by the work of his pupils, among whose fragments and attested book titles can be found such items as Dicaearchus' *On Alcaeus*, and especially Chamaeleon's monographs on Pindar, Sappho, Stesichorus, Lasus, Simonides, and Anacreon. The variety

---

23   *Rh.* 3.1418b23–32. The citation of Archilochus corresponds to the first line of fr. 122.
24   See Arrighetti (1987) 170–176; cf. Leo (1901) 106; Majoli (1993) 28–30.
25   *Poet.* 1447b18–20. Cf. Laurenti (1987) i.255.

of Chamaeleon's literary works,[26] which also included books on non-lyrical poetry—including Aeschylus, Homer, comedy, and satyr-play—makes him an ideal case study for an assessment of the Peripatetics' stance toward lyric. Chamaeleon's works on poets focussed on two main elements, namely their artistic innovations and their character traits—these elements being typical, respectively, of Peripatetic interest in literary history and ethical biography.

Although the intertwining of biographical data and literary criticism is a feature of nearly all the ancient biographies of Greek poets,[27] Arrighetti has pointed to Chamaeleon as the most prominent exponent of the method. This seems to be due to the fact that Chamaeleon's fragments allegedly contain two explicit enunciations of the principles upon which this method is based. These "programmatic" statements, which are both found in citations from his book *On Aeschylus*, have recently been submitted to some well-deserved reassessments that significantly qualified their value.[28] Suffice it to say for now that the evidence for Chamaeleon's use of the method that bears his name is much more prominent in the case of lyric poets than in any other.[29]

Indeed, 'Chamaeleon's method' is really Chamaeleon's when it comes to lyric poetry. The fact that all of his books on this topic are named after individual poets suggests that he had no comprehensive category of 'lyric' as a genre or of any of its sub-genres. Moreover, many of his reported comments on the lyric poets show a biographical interest. For instance, in fr. 28 he examines an opinion held by certain people according to which Anacreon wrote some verses for Sappho.[30] Chamaeleon seems to have rejected this opinion on the grounds that Sappho and Anacreon were not contemporaries, which is confirmed by the fact that a comic poet (Diphilus) made her a contemporary of Archilochus and Hipponax.[31] In frr. 35 and 37 he locates poems by Simonides and Pindar within the historical contexts where they were composed, showing his awareness of the topical and performative nature of their compositions.

---

26 For a review of Chamaeleon's work on poetry, see Scorza (1934); Podlecki (1969) 120–124.
27 Compare Schorn (2012) 426.
28 See Mirhady (2012); Schorn (2008, 2012); Bouchard (2016) 224–233.
29 An exception is found in fr. 47 which concerns the poet Hegemon, believed to be the inventor of the genre of parody. Chamaeleon reports that the parodist was nicknamed 'Lentil soup' and then cites two groups of verses in which Hegemon refers to himself with that name. Outside the fragments of his treatises on lyric poetry, that is the only text that testifies to Chamaeleon's use of a poet's verses as evidence for his life.
30 Chamaeleon's fragments are referred to following the numbering of the latest edition by Martano, Matelli, and Mirhady (2012).
31 Compare Martano, Matelli, and Mirhady (2012) 231n1.

I will now focus on two fragments regarding Alcman that provide the clearest evidence of a biographical interpretation of a lyric poet as well as of the ethical stance of Chamaeleon's reading.[32] The first is fragment 27:

Ἀρχύτας δ' ὁ ἁρμονικός, ὥς φησι Χαμαιλέων, Ἀλκμᾶνα γεγονέναι τῶν ἐρωτικῶν μελῶν ἡγεμόνα καὶ ἐκδοῦναι πρῶτον μέλος ἀκόλαστον, ὄντα καὶ περὶ τὰς γυναῖκας καὶ τὴν τοιαύτην μοῦσαν εἰς τὰς διατριβάς. διὸ καὶ λέγειν ἔν τινι τῶν μελῶν·
Ἔρως με δηῦτε Κύπριδος ϝέκατι
γλυκὺς κατείβων καρδίαν ἰαίνει.[33]

According to Chamaeleon, the music-theorist Archytas claims that Alcman invented erotic lyrics and was the first person to publish a depraved song, since he liked to spend his time around women and that kind of music. This is why he says in one of his songs: 'When sweet Eros, at Cypris' bidding, floods my heart and warms it'.[34]

The passage is textually problematic (a governing verb is missing in the first sentence) and lends itself to various interpretations.[35] For instance, it is unclear whether ἀκόλαστον is an attribute of μέλος or a predicate of Ἀλκμᾶνα (in which case the comma should be put after μέλος), but the first option gives a more satisfactory sense.[36] The identity of Chamaeleon's source, Archytas, is also a matter of contention: he could be either the Pythagorean philosopher Archytas of Tarentum (the most popular option) or the musician Archytas of Mytilene. In his recent edition of Archytas of Tarentum Huffman attributes our fragment to the Mytilenian on the grounds that 'we have no other evidence that Archytas of Tarentum engaged in analysis of poetry'.[37] But the passage is not so much

---

32 Contra Scorza (1934) 8–9, these fragments are probably not derived from an unattested Περὶ Ἀλκμᾶνος, but are more likely to be attributed either to Chamaeleon's work *On Pleasure* or to his writings on ethical and musical matters.
33 It is unclear who the subject of λέγει is in Athenaeus' next sentence: λέγει δὲ καὶ ὡς τῆς Μεγαλοστράτης οὐ μετρίως ἐρασθείς [...]. I adopt a conservative stance and consider that what can be safely attributed to Chamaeleon stops after the first citation of Alcman.
34 Ath. 13.600f (Alcman fr. 59a).
35 A discussion of textual matters can be found in Marzullo (1964).
36 For other occurrences of ἀκόλαστον as applied to songs or types of music see Ar. *Lys.* 398; Philod. *De musica* IV 20. 3 and 98.41 (ed. Delattre). If ἀκόλαστον is predicated of Alcman, then the text makes a strange connection between the poet's character and the action of publishing a 'song' *tout court*.
37 Huffman (2005) 27.

about literary analysis as about the ethical tenor of a kind of music, a topic that is quite appropriate to a Pythagorean—and just as much in its place in the work of a Peripatetic, for that matter.[38]

It seems then that Chamaeleon, following Archytas, made two kinds of connection between Alcman and his poems. First, a thematic correspondence between moral character and poetic genre: Alcman's innovation in composing love songs is explained by his own erotic dispositions.[39] The remark has the value of an aetiology of a poetic genre in psychological terms: this linking of the emergence of a genre with a moral trait is strongly reminiscent of a section of Aristotle's history of poetry in the *Poetics*,[40] where he attributes the invention of serious and comic poetry to the corresponding types of men. Although the correlation between a poet's character and his work is a comic trope,[41] the aetiologically minded version of this notion, which focuses on the historical moments of poetic innovation, is a distinctly "scientific" novelty of Peripatetic anthropology. The second connection in Chamaeleon's text is between moral character and some specific verses, which are cited to confirm an impression about Alcman's personality. Ironically, modern scholars usually view these verses as part of a *partheneion*, and thus as having been originally assumed by the singing voice of a group of maidens.[42]

Fragment 26 provides yet another kind of correspondence, one between a supposed historical event in Alcman's life and the seal (*sphragis*) of one of his poems:

καλοῦνται δ' οἱ πέρδικες ὑπ' ἐνίων κακκάβαι, ὡς καὶ ὑπ' Ἀλκμᾶνος λέγοντος οὕτως·

ϝέπη τάδε καὶ μέλος Ἀλκμὰν
εὗρε γεγλωσσαμέναν
κακκαβίδων ὄπα συνθέμενος,

σαφῶς ἐμφανίζων ὅτι παρὰ τῶν περδίκων ᾄδειν ἐμάνθανε. διὸ καὶ Χαμαιλέων ὁ Ποντικὸς ἔφη τὴν εὕρεσιν τῆς μουσικῆς τοῖς ἀρχαίοις ἐπινοηθῆναι ἀπὸ τῶν ἐν

---

38   The musicologist Aristoxenus, a contemporary of Chamaeleon and a fellow Peripatetic, wrote a biography of Archytas of Tarentum with a strongly eulogizing bent; cf. Momigliano (1993) 75–76; Rocconi (2012) 73; Provenza (2012) 95–96.
39   Alcman's innovation: there is no doubt that ἡγεμόνα means not only 'premier' but also 'inventor'. Cf. the Suda's entry on Alcman: ὢν ἐρωτικὸς πάνυ εὑρετὴς γέγονε τῶν ἐρωτικῶν μελῶν.
40   1448b24–27.
41   See n. 7 above.
42   Calame (1983) 558; contra Carey (2011) 447–448, who deems the fragment to be monodic.

ταῖς ἐρημίαις ᾀδόντων ὀρνίθων· ὧν κατὰ μίμησιν λαβεῖν στάσιν τὴν μουσικήν. οὐ πάντες δ' οἱ πέρδικες, φησί, κακκαβίζουσιν.

Some authorities, however, refer to partridges as *kakkabai*. Alcman, for example, says the following:
'Alcman invented these
verses and articulate song
by arranging the sound made by partridges',
making it clear that the partridges taught him how to sing. This is why Chamaeleon of Pontus claimed that people in ancient times discovered how to make music by listening to the birds sing in deserted places; music developed through imitating them. But not all partridges, he claims, say '*kakkabê*'.[43]

Reading Alcman's verses as an autobiographical statement, Chamaeleon used this testimony to support an anthropological theory on the invention of music by imitation of birds. The reference to 'ancient times' suggests that his reading of Alcman was part of a philosophical enquiry on the origins and development of *mousikê*. Interest in these matters is well attested among other figures of the Peripatos.[44]

By comparing frr. 26 and 27, one might wonder what Chamaeleon's idea of Alcman's poetic inspiration was after all. Did it come from his frequentation of women or from that of birds? From his own inner erotic disposition or from outer nature? Chamaeleon's account of the origin of Alcman's poetry is not as contradictory as it looks if we take into account the peculiarity of Alcman's choosing partridges as his poetical model instead of the more conventional and dignified swans or nightingales.[45] The Greeks thought of partridges as salacious birds,[46] and this reputation was documented in Peripatetic ornithology. Indeed, Aristotle's zoological treatises abound in references to the strong sexual

---

43 Ath. 9.389f–390a (Alcman fr. 39). Chamaeleon's paradoxical combination of the ideas of 'discovery' (εὕρεσιν) and 'invention' (ἐπινοηθῆναι) is in fact consistent with the ancient prevailing view of poetic composition: see Gentili (1971).

44 See e.g. Demetrius of Phaleron frr. 144 and 146 SOD, about poets and singers from the mythical past; Heraclides Ponticus fr. 114 Schütrumpf.

45 On human imitation of swans and nightingales, see Democritus B 154 DK; on birds as images of differing poetic "programs" throughout Greek literature, see Steiner (2007). According to Calame (1983) 483, Alcman's reference to partridges would have been at home in a *partheneion*, since these birds were associated with femininity.

46 Cf. Sirna (1973) 31.

proclivity of partridges, but also to the fact that the singing of birds occurs especially during the mating season.⁴⁷ The erotic context in which Alcman's birds have taught him music is also hinted at by the expression 'in remote places' (ἐν ταῖς ἐρημίαις): this expression is consistently and exclusively used in Aristotle to talk about the 'remote places' where different species of animals go to copulate.⁴⁸ Chamaeleon's knowledge of Aristotelian zoology, particularly of the details about the sexual customs of partridges, is not in doubt, since the final reference to the different cries of the partridges is also paralleled in Aristotle's *History of Animals*.⁴⁹ In Chamaeleon's understanding, the music of the partridges that Alcman heard can only have been a rudimentary form of a μέλος ἀκόλαστον, a licentious song. Thus what is indeed a programmatic statement of Alcman's on one of his own compositions is given a wider meaning as hinting at the foundation of a whole genre: that of erotic poetry.⁵⁰

4   Lyric Poetry and Antiquarian Research in the Lyceum

Chamaeleon's account of Alcman's invention of song is a paradigmatic example of Peripatetic research in cultural anthropology and in the natural origins of mimesis.⁵¹ A similar aetiology for another kind of song was proposed by his fellow Peripatetic Clearchus:

> Κλέαρχος δ' ἐν πρώτῳ Ἐρωτικῶν νόμιον καλεῖσθαί τινά φησιν ᾠδὴν ἀπ' Ἠριφανίδος, γράφων οὕτως· Ἠριφανὶς ἡ μελοποιὸς Μενάλκου κυνηγετοῦντος ἐρασθεῖσα ἐθήρευεν μεταθέουσα ταῖς ἐπιθυμίαις· φοιτῶσα γὰρ καὶ πλανωμένη πάντας τοὺς ὀρείους ἐπεξῄει δρυμούς, ὡς μῦθον εἶναι τοὺς λεγομένους Ἰοῦς δρόμους· ὥστε μὴ μόνον τῶν ἀνθρώπων τοὺς ἀστοργίᾳ διαφέροντας, ἀλλὰ καὶ τῶν θηρῶν τοὺς ἀνημερωτάτους συνδακρῦσαι τῷ πάθει, λαβόντας αἴσθησιν ἐρωτικῆς ἐλπίδος. ὅθεν ἐποίησέ τε καὶ ποιήσασα περιῄει κατὰ τὴν ἐρημίαν, ὥς φασιν, ἀναβοῶσα καὶ ᾄδουσα τὸ καλούμενον νόμιον, ἐν ᾧ ἐστιν· μακραὶ δρύες, ὦ Μενάλκα.

---

47 See e.g. *Hist. an.* 488b, 564b, 613b; *Gen. an.* 746a.
48 See e.g. *Hist. an.* 540a, 607a.
49 536b.
50 On the programmatic nature of *sphragides*, see Calame (2004) 13–19.
51 This secular approach to poetry is opposed to traditional stories about the divine origins of song and is inherited from fifth-century rationalistic accounts of cultural history; see Kleingünther (1933) 135–143; Ford (2002) 139–152; Ford (2011) 352–354.

Clearchus in Book I of the *Erotica* reports that a certain pastoral song got its name from Eriphanis. He writes as follows: The lyric poetess Eriphanis fell in love with Menalces when he was out hunting, and she began to hunt herself, as a way of pursuing her desires; for she visited all the mountain thickets in her travels and her wanderings, making Io's so-called courses an empty story by comparison. As a consequence, not only did people known for their cold temperament weep at her suffering, but even the most savage beasts did, when they recognized her erotic longing. This is what inspired her poetry, and after she composed it, they say, she wandered through the wilderness, shouting and singing her so-called pastoral song, which includes the words: The oaks are tall, Menalcas![52]

Just like Chamaeleon's, Clearchus' story ascribes to an enamoured lyric composer the invention of a type of song and places this invention in a remote and rural setting (κατὰ τὴν ἐρημίαν, cf. Chamaeleon's ἐν ταῖς ἐρημίαις above). Both human beings and animals (μὴ μόνον τῶν ἀνθρώπων [...], ἀλλὰ καὶ τῶν θηρῶν) are involved in the poet's original inspiration, as was the case for Alcman. Other fragments from Clearchus' *Erotica* attribute the origin of lyric compositions to poets in love, or else use lyric poets to make various points on moral matters.[53]

Peripatetic work on lyric poets appears to have been narrowly connected to a field of study that was ubiquitous in the school, namely antiquarian research in the mores and cultural achievements of people of old.[54] Sympotic practices were a prominent hobbyhorse, as is evinced by Aristotle's, Theophrastus', and Chamaeleon's treatises *On Drunkenness* and other related titles. Noteworthy in this regard are the fragments from Dicaearchus' *On Musical Contests* and *On Alcaeus*, which include erudite comments on the σκόλιον, explained to be a drinking song, on the game of *kottabos*, and on various ancient customs relating to the symposium.[55] This properly antiquarian interest that lies behind the Peripatetic study of lyric poetry can account for the "conservative" corpus of authors that were the object of the treatises: indeed it seems that none of them had been devoted to any author of, or posterior to, the so-called "New Music" movement.[56]

---

52 Clearchus fr. 32 Wehrli = Ath. 14.619c–d.
53 Frr. 22, 24, 25, 33, 34 Wehrli. Cf. Aristoxenus frr. 89 and 129 Wehrli (on two kinds of song named after girls who died from unreciprocated love).
54 This field of study was initiated by Aristotle himself: Pfeiffer (1968) 79–84.
55 See frr. 89, 90, 91, 105, 106, 107, 108, 109 Mirhady.
56 See Hadjimichael's contribution to this volume, who stresses the connections between what she calls 'the Peripatetic project' and the classicizing process already at work in fifth-century BCE assessments of poetry.

As far as Chamaeleon is concerned, it is clear that his treatment of the lyric poets cannot be severed from the generally ethical import of his writings.[57] The overwhelming majority of Chamaeleon's fragments and book titles belong either to literary or ethical contexts, and among the latter many are about the emotional and therapeutic effects of music, in line with the Peripatetics' special concern with the phenomenon of musical catharsis. A tantalizing passage of Philodemus involving the ethical component of lyric poetry makes a reference to Chamaeleon:

```
............ ⌊πρὸς ψυχα⌋-‖
‖γωγίαν ἰδίαι περιειλῆφ⟦α⟧θα[ι
παρά [γ]ε τοῖς μελοποιοῖς ὅσοι
χρ]ησίμως πεφιλο{ι}μουσή-
κ]ασιν· μὴ γὰρ κακῶς ἐπιση-
μ]αίνεσθαι χαμαιλέοντα τὸ
τοιοῦτόν τι τοὺς κωμικοὺς
α[ἰ]νίττεσθαι περὶ τῶν ποη-
τῶν προσηγορίαις μὲν χρω-
μ]ένους ταῖς τῶν βρωτῶν
καὶ ποτῶν, πα|ριστάντας δὲ
τὴν ἰδιότητα | [τ]ούτων *. Ἔχειν
δέ τι καὶ πρὸς φ|[ι]λίαν οἰκεῖον·
ἐπει`δὴ´ γὰρ πρὸς ἔρω|[τ]' ἐδείχθη, κα[ὶ
πρὸς τὸ τέλος αὐτοῦ | [λ]όγον αἱ- ✳
ρεῖν *· ἔτι δ', ἐπεὶ πρὸς [τὰ συμ]|π[ό-
σια, καὶ ⌜π⌝`ρ`⌜ὸ⌝[ς] τὸ τέλος [αὐτῶν
φαίνεσθα[ι π]άλι, φιλο⌊φροσύ⌋-
νην· εἰ δὲ [πρ]ὸς ταύτ[ην, οὐδὲ
πρὸς φιλίαν ἄλλως [ἔχειν, ὅτι
τὴν [ψυχὴ]ν ἀνίησιν [καὶ ἀφι-
λαροῖ καὶ ἡμ]ᾶς διαλ[υτικοὺς
ποιεῖ......]
```

Having *psychagôgia* as a particular function music was included, at least by lyric poets who took advantage of their love of music. For Chamaeleon

---

57 Chamaeleon's sole reference to Alcaeus in the preserved fragments (fr. 13) seems in fact to have been made in his treatise *On Drunkenness*; see Scorza (1934) 38–39 and Fortenbaugh (2012) 381–382.

was not wrong to think that comic poets expressed such a thing enigmatically when they used words of food and drink to refer to the poets, thus revealing their particular character. And music is adapted to friendship. Indeed, considering that this has been demonstrated for love, it is logical that it be the case for what is the goal of love. Moreover, since it is appropriate to banquets, it is once again appropriate to their end, that is friendliness. And if it is appropriate to friendliness, it is not different as regards friendship, because music relaxes and cheers the soul and makes us prone to reconciliation.[58]

The context of the passage is Philodemus' criticism of the poetics of Diogenes of Babylon, who had made use of Chamaeleon while exposing his theory. Judging by the thematic elements present in this text, Chamaeleon had discussed lyric poetry and music and their association to personal character and to ethical dispositions, adducing the testimony of the comic poets to support his claim. This text finds a close parallel in another Philodeman passage from the same treatise where a reference is made to Dicaearchus:

Ἐξ ὧν δὲ παρατίθετ[αι
Δ|[ικ]αιάρχου λάβοι τις ἂν ὅ- ※
σ' ἂν κ]αὶ πρὸς τὴν ἐνεστηκυ[ῖ-
αν] ὑπόθεσιν ἦ[ι]· τὸ τοὺς πα-
λα]ιοὺς καὶ σοφὸν τὸν ᾠδὸν
νο]μίζειν, ὡς εἶναι δῆλον
ἐπὶ] τοῦ παρὰ τῆι Κλυταιμή-
στραι κατ]αλειφθέντος· καὶ
........] 'γ'νῶναί φασιν ὅ{δ}'ς'
ἂν τ]ούτων ἀκούσῃ[ι], δι' οὗ τε-
........]φωνεῖται καὶ πλείο-
να .....]τα· [κ]αὶ τὸ πρὸ⟨ς⟩ ταῖς ἄλ-
λαις δυνάμ]εσιν τὸ μέλος καὶ
στάσεων κ]αὶ ταραχῶν εἶ- ※
ναι κ]αταπ[α]υστικόν, ὡς ἐπὶ
τῶν ἀνθρώ]πων καὶ τῶν ζώι-
ων φαίνε]σθαι καταπραϋνο-
μένω]ν ※· διὸ καὶ τὸν Ἀρχίλο-

---

58 Chamaeleon fr. 6 = Phld. *De musica* col. 46.45–47.22. I cite Philodemus from Delattre's edition of *De musica*.

χον λ]έγειν· κηλ⌈έε¹ται δ' ὅτις
βροτ]ῶν ἀοιδαῖς.

⟨From Diogenes' citations⟩ of Dicaearchus we may retain whatever is relevant to the present discussion. The ancients believed that the singer was also wise, as is obvious with the one who was left in the company of Clytemnestra. And they say that whoever listens to these things knows by what means [text corrupt] … and that apart from its other powers, song can appease strife and trouble, as is shown by men and animals who are brought to tranquillity. That is why Archilochus says 'Any mortal is charmed by songs'.[59]

Although the final citation of Archilochus might go back to Diogenes rather than to Dicaearchus,[60] there is no doubt to be cast on the Dicaearchan origin of the previous lines. These report ancient beliefs regarding the therapeutic potential of music and the social status of singers in the heroic age. (The example of Clytemnestra's "chaperone" seems to have been a *topos* in the Peripatetic circle.[61]) Another Dicaearchan fragment mentions a certain Tellen as a piper and composer of 'unruly' songs,[62] while in yet another, Dicaearchus is reported to have made an interpretation of an Alcaean poetic *griphos* involving the 'witlessness' of people blowing into a wind-instrument.[63] As far as can be gathered, Dicaearchus' engagement with the lyric poets seems to have been just as much 'opportunistic'—that is, primarily concerned with ethics in an antiquarian context, not with lyric poetry *per se*—as the other members of the Peripatos.[64]

---

59   Dicaearchus fr. 39 Mirhady = Phld. *De musica* col. 49.20–39 (Archilochus fr. 253).
60   Cf. Delattre (2007, vol. 2) 376; *contra*, Gigante (1993) 8. Gigante (1999) 108–109 thinks that Diogenes took this citation from a book of *Homeric Questions*, but no such title is attested among Dicaearchus' writings.
61   See Rispoli (1992) who traces the use of this Homeric *paradeigma* in Aristoxenus, Dicaearchus, and Demetrius of Phaleron.
62   αὐλητὴς καὶ μελῶν ἀνυποτάκτων ποιητής (fr. 97 Mirhady). Cf. fr. 98, probably about the same Tellen.
63   See fr. 110 Mirhady and West's commentary (1990) 6, superseding the analysis of Slater (1982) 337–340.
64   Hadjimichael's chapter in this volume contains further examples of Peripatetic derivation of historical information from lyric poets.

5 Conclusion

Although the Peripatetic school may be considered an important intermediary in the transmission of archaic lyric down to the Hellenistic age, one should recall that the school has in fact played this role in an almost accidental way. In Aristotle's view lyric poetry was not much more than a preliminary step in the early development of the τέχνη ποιητική. But for his immediate successors, it also had a historical value, as a testimony to the original context of poetical inventions. Being replete with first-person narrators apparently making a free disclosure of their own ethos both in their words and in their music, the lyric corpus understandably became a privileged field of study for Peripatetic thinkers: with their seemingly autobiographical comments, the ancient lyric poets showed themselves to be convenient sources for an enquiry into the historical and psychological conditions that gave rise to poetry and music. The case of Alcman's seal is exemplary: although the poet does not use the first person and talks about himself as a third-person narrator, the fact that he gives his proper name conveys an impression of historical truthfulness and objectivity. Chamaeleon and his fellow Peripatetics were more than willing to accept a story like that of his learning music from the birds as a genuine account of an early stage of human mimesis.

References

Arrighetti, G. 1987. *Poeti, eruditi, biografi. Momenti della riflessione dei Greci sulla letteratura.* Pisa.
Arrighetti, G. 2006. *Poesia, poetiche e storia nella riflessione dei Greci.* Pisa.
Barbantani, S. 2009. Lyric in the Hellenistic Period and Beyond. In *The Cambridge Companion to Greek Lyric*, ed. F. Budelmann, 297–318. Cambridge.
Bolonyai, G. 1998. Lyric Genres in Aristotle's *Poetics*. AAntHung 38(1): 27–39.
Bouchard, E. 2016. *Du Lycée au Musée. Théorie poétique et critique littéraire à l'époque hellénistique.* Paris.
Calame, C. 1974. Réflexions sur les genres littéraires en Grèce archaïque. *QUCC* 17: 113–128.
Calame, C. 1983. *Alcman.* Rome.
Calame, C. 1998. La poésie lyrique grecque, un genre inexistant? *Littérature* 111: 87–110.
Calame, C. 2004. Identités d'auteur à l'exemple de la Grèce classique: signatures, énonciations, citations. In *Identités d'auteur dans l'Antiquité et la tradition européenne*, ed. C. Calame and R. Chartier, 11–39. Grenoble.
Carey, C. 2011. Alcman: From Laconia to Alexandria. In *Archaic and Classical Choral*

Song: Performance, Politics and Dissemination, ed. L. Athanassaki and E. Bowie, 437–460. Berlin.

Clay, D. 1998. The Theory of the Literary Persona in Antiquity. *MD* 40: 9–40.

Delattre, D. 2007. *Philodème de Gadara. Sur la musique, Livre IV*. Paris.

Dover, K.J. 1964. The Poetry of Archilochos. In *Archiloque. Fondation Hardt, Entretiens sur l'antiquité classique 10: 181–222*. Geneva.

Dupont-Roc, R. and Lallot, J., eds. 1980. *Aristote, La Poétique*. Paris.

Else, G.F. 1957. *Aristotle's Poetics: The Argument*. Cambridge.

Elsperger, W. 1907. Reste und Spuren antiker Kritik gegen Euripides gesammelt aus den Euripidesscholien. *Philologus Supplementband* XI: 1–176.

Färber, H. 1936. *Die Lyrik in der Kunsttheorie der Antike*. Munich.

Ford, A. 1993. L'inventeur de la poésie lyrique: Archiloque le colon. *Mètis* 8: 59–73.

Ford, A. 2002. *The Origins of Criticism: Literary Culture and Poetic Theory in Classical Greece*. Princeton.

Ford, A. 2011. Dionysos' Many Names in Aristophanes' *Frogs*. In *A Different God? Dionysus and Ancient Polytheism*, ed. R. Schlesier, 343–355. Berlin.

Fortenbaugh, W.W. 2012. Chamaeleon on Pleasure and Drunkenness. In *Praxiphanes of Mytilene and Chamaeleon of Heraclea: Text, Translation, and Discussion*, ed. A. Martano, E. Matelli, and D.C. Mirhady, 359–386. New Brunswick.

Gentili, B. 1971. I frr. 39 e 40 P. di Alcmane e la poetica della mimesi nella cultura greca arcaica. In *Studi filologici e storici in onore di V. de Falco*, 57–67. Naples.

Gigante, M. 1993. Filodemo e Archiloco. *Cronache ercolanesi* 23: 5–10.

Gigante, M. 1999. *Kepos e Peripatos: contributo alla storia dell'aristotelismo antico*. Naples.

Griffin, J. 1977. The Epic Cycle and the Uniqueness of Homer. *JHS* 97: 39–53.

Gudeman, A. 1934. *Aristoteles Περὶ ποιητικῆς*. Berlin.

Halliwell, S. 1986. *Aristotle's Poetics*. Chapel Hill.

Huffman, C.A. 2005. *Archytas of Tarentum: Pythagorean, Philosopher, and Mathematician King*. Cambridge.

Janko, R. 2010. *Philodemus, On Poems Books 3–4, with the Fragments of Aristotle, On Poets*. Oxford.

Jong, I.J.F. de 2005. Aristotle on the Homeric Narrator. *CQ* 55(2): 616–621.

Kleingünther, A. 1933. *ΠΡΩΤΟΣ ΕΥΡΕΤΗΣ: Untersuchungen zur Geschichte einer Fragestellung*. Leipzig.

Koning, H.H. 2010. *Hesiod, the Other Poet: Ancient Reception of a Cultural Icon*. Leiden.

Lallot, J. 1976. La mimesis selon Aristote et l'excellence d'Homère. In *Écriture et théorie poétiques. Lectures d'Homère, Eschyle, Platon, Aristote*, 15–25. Paris.

Laurenti, R. 1987. *Aristotele, I frammenti dei dialoghi* i–ii. Naples.

Lefkowitz, M.R. 2012. *The Lives of the Greek Poets*. 2nd edn. Baltimore.

Leo, F. 1901. *Die griechisch-römische Biographie nach ihrer literarischen Form*. Leipzig.

Lord, L.E. 1908. *Literary Criticism of Euripides in the Earlier Scholia and the Relation of this Criticism to Aristotle's* Poetics *and to Aristophanes*. Göttingen.

Lucas, D.W. 1968. *Aristotle Poetics*. Oxford.

Majoli, A. 1993. Le iscrizioni archilochee di Paro e il metodo di Cameleonte. *Vichiana* 4: 28–37.

Martano, A., Matelli, E., and Mirhady, D.C., eds. 2012. *Praxiphanes of Mytilene and Chamaeleon of Heraclea: Text, Translation, and Discussion*. New Brunswick.

Marzullo, B. 1964. Alcman fr. 59 P. *Helikon* 4: 297–302.

Mirhady, D.C. 2012. Something to do with Dionysus: Chamaeleon on the Origins of Tragedy. In Martano, Matelli, and Mirhady 2012: 49–71.

Momigliano, A. 1993. *The Development of Greek Biography*. Cambridge, MA.

Montanari, F. 2012. The Peripatos on Literature: Interpretation, Use and Abuse. In Martano, Matelli and Mirhady 2012: 339–358.

Muecke, F. 1982. A Portrait of the Artist as a Young Woman. *CQ* 32: 41–55.

Nünlist, R. 2009. *The Ancient Critic at Work: Terms and Concepts of Literary Criticism in Greek Scholia*. Cambridge.

Paduano, G. 1996. Lo stile e l'uomo: Aristofane e Aristotele. *SCO* 46: 93–101.

Pfeiffer, R. 1968. *History of Classical Scholarship from the Beginning to the End of the Hellenistic Age*. Oxford.

Podlecki, A.J. 1969. The Peripatetics as Literary Critics. *Phoenix* 23(1): 114–137.

Provenza, A. 2012. Aristoxenus and Music Therapy: Fr. 26 Wehrli Within the Tradition on Music and Catharsis. In *Aristoxenus of Tarentum: Discussion*, ed. C.A. Huffman, 91–128. New Brunswick.

Rankin, H.D. 1975. Μοιχός, λάγνος καὶ ὑβριστής. Critias and his Judgement of Archilochus. *Grazer Beiträge* 3: 323–334.

Rankin, H.D. 1977. Aristotle on Archilochus. *AC* 46: 165–168.

Rispoli, G.M. 1992. Fragilità della virtù (PHerc 424, fr. 4–1572 fr. 2). *Vichiana* 3: 88–97.

Rocconi, E. 2012. Aristoxenus and Musical *Ethos*. In *Aristoxenus of Tarentum: Discussion*, ed. C.A. Huffman, 65–90. New Brunswick.

Rotstein, A. 2007. Critias' Invective against Archilochus. *CPh* 102(2): 139–154.

Rotstein, A. 2010. *The Idea of Iambos*. Oxford.

Schorn, S. 2008. Chamaileonstudien. In *Dona sunt pulcherrima: Festschrift für Rudolf Rieks*, ed. K. Herrmann and K. Geus, 51–81. Oberhaid.

Schorn, S. 2012. Chamaeleon: Biography and Literature *Peri tou deina*. In Martano, Matelli, and Mirhady 2012: 411–444.

Scorza, G. 1934. Il peripatetico Cameleonte. *RIGI* 18: 1–48.

Sirna, F.G. 1973. Alcmane εὑρετὴς τῶν ἐρωτικῶν μελῶν. *Aegyptus* 53: 28–70.

Slater, W.J. 1982. Aristophanes of Byzantium and Problem-Solving in the Museum. *CQ* 32(2): 336–349.

SOD: *see* Stork, van Ophuijsen, and Dorando (2000).

Stabryla, S. 2000. The Notion of the Lyric as a Literary Genre in the Greek Theory. In *Studies in Ancient Literary Theory and Criticism*, ed. J. Styka, 41–52. Cracow.

Steiner, D.T. 2007. Feathers Flying: Avian Poetics in Hesiod, Pindar, and Callimachus. *AJPh* 128(2): 177–208.

Stork, P., van Ophuijsen, J.M. and Dorando, T., eds. 2000. Demetrius of Phalerum: The Sources, Text and Translation. In *Demetrius of Phalerum: Text, Translation and Discussion*, ed. W.W. Fortenbaugh and E. Schütrumpf, 1–310. New Brunswick.

West, M.L. 1990. Notes on Sappho and Alcaeus. *ZPE* 80: 1–8.

Wright, M. 2012. *The Comedian as Critic: Greek Old Comedy and Poetics*. London.

PART 4

Early Reception

∴

CHAPTER 9

Lyric Reception and Sophistic Literarity in Timotheus' *Persae*

David Fearn

1   Introduction

Timotheus' *Persae* presents an extraordinarily rich and diverse array of poetic and cultural thinking, which invites a range of questions about meaning, interpretation, and audience response. This text's diverse indebtedness to fifth-century literary culture (not only lyric, tragedy, and comedy, but also sophistic rhetoric) invites serious scrutiny, and, in recent scholarship is finally receiving some deserved attention. I here set out some of my own interpretations of and responses to Timotheus' dazzling and at times perplexing literary talent.

Impetus for this study comes from three main directions: my own interest in Bacchylidean and Pindaric lyric and its reception; a greater willingness among scholars of recent years to think more deeply and with greater sophistication about the nature of dithyramb (in all its variety);[1] and new-found critical interest in the New Music: work by Eric Csapo,[2] Tim Power,[3] and most recently the excellent and path-finding new treatments by Pauline LeVen and Felix Budelmann of the poetics of the New Music.[4]

A good deal of work has been done in recent years, particularly by Pauline LeVen, to explore intertexts in *Persae*, and to add fresh insight to our understanding of the particular stylistic characteristics of the New Music. I will restrict my own commentary to new observations and thoughts about stylistic, structural, and intertextual factors not covered by LeVen, especially with reference to affinities between Timothean and Bacchylidean lyric style; and to cases where her analyses have inspired my own further thoughts.

---

1 In particular, Kowalzig and Wilson (2013); my own discussions of Bacchylidean dithyramb in context in Fearn (2007).
2 Csapo (2004, 2011); see also Csapo (1999–2000); D'Angour (2006); Csapo and Wilson (2009).
3 Power (2010), particularly fine on New Musical *kitharôidia*.
4 LeVen (2014); Budelmann and LeVen (2014). For recent critical interest in the text of Timotheus' *Persae*, see in particular Hordern (2002) and Sevieri (2011); Budelmann (2018).

After some preliminary discussion of historical reasons for a lack of interest in the lyric pedigree of the New Music, my discussion will be in three main sections. In the first part I outline some structural thoughts about *Persae*, both as a celebratory narrative lyric poem with a specific fifth-century dithyrambic pedigree, and as a piece of self-consciously stylized poetic rhetoric. In the second, I pay specific attention to the similarities and differences between Timothean diction and more traditional, and particularly Bacchylidean, lyric, building on some of the structural observations I made earlier. I also examine some further intertexts, an element now recognized as an important feature of Timothean poetics.[5] In the final section, I discuss the challenges of literary interpretation posed by Timothean lyric, especially as a cultural form informed by and indeed a part of the sophistic movement, with specific reference to Gorgias.

2 Preliminaries: 'New' and 'Old' Fifth-Century Lyric in Modern Scholarship

Any investigation of the possible relations between Timotheus and earlier lyric poetry will soon discover that there has been virtually no scholarship on this topic since the Timotheus papyrus came to light. Perhaps this should not surprise, given the general antipathy of modern scholars towards the New Musical output, and an implicit contrast between the New Music and the canonical masterpieces of fifth-century lyric before the New Music arrived on the scene.

Scholarship on earlier fifth-century lyric has also not helped matters because of its general unwillingness to think too far beyond its own immediate circumstances of performance: work on the fifth-century reception of lyric poetry is still in its relative infancy. Until very recently, the general lack of interest in the New Music, or even its literary background, by scholars of Greek lyric poetry has been exacerbated by the dominance of Pindar within studies of fifth-century lyric, as well as a complicity—sometimes tacit, sometimes open—with Platonic reactionism. In the face of these complicating factors, it is perhaps no surprise that no work has been done to investigate the potential similarities between Bacchylides and the poetic style of the New Music.[6]

---

[5] e.g. Firinu (2009); Budelmann and LeVen (2014) esp. 201 for the way intertexts in Timotheus provide structural support for his often-outlandish images and metaphors; also Gurd (2016) 118; Budelmann (2018) 233.

[6] See, though, Gurd (2016) 120 on the links with the choral lyric tradition in terms of rhythmic complexity.

If we turn to the possible literary affinities between Timotheus and Bacchylides, both these poets—both notable papyrological discoveries within a few years of each other—received relatively short shrift from scholarship in the century after their discoveries.[7] General antipathy towards Timotheus as a New Musical lyric poet worked on the back of implicit contrast with Pindar's elevated genius, and in a direct line back to Platonic reactionism.

The scholarly reaction to both Timotheus and Bacchylides in the early years after their discoveries is coloured to an interesting degree by broader issues of ideology and taste, with an implied contrast and competitiveness between Britain (the owner of the Bacchylides papyrus) and Germany (owner of the Timotheus papyrus). The original reception of Bacchylides was somewhat encouraging, though at one particularly charged point—the last year of World War I—markedly in opposition to that of Timotheus:

> Timotheus … is as complete a contrast to Bacchylides as can be imagined. Burne Jones once said, à propos of the Pergamum sculptures now at Berlin: 'Truth is, and it is a scientific induction, that whenever Germans go forth to dig and discover, their special providence provides for them and brings to the surface the most depressing, heavy, conceited, dull products of dead and done-with Greece; and they ought to be thankful, for that it is what they like'. I do not make myself responsible for the permanent truth of this *obiter dictum*, and it is not to be denied that, if the Germans have not hitherto had the fortune to acquire any of the great new literary treasures, they have at least known how to make good use of those which have fallen into the hands of others; but Timotheus might have been made expressly to illustrate Burne Jones' law.[8]

But, as is well known, beyond the flourishing critical industry on the text in the years immediately following the discovery of the Bacchylides papyrus, very little attention was paid to his work; for Bacchylides the limited approval and overt contrast with Pindar offered by Longinus continued to wield considerable authority.[9]

Jebb in his magisterial commentary positions Bacchylides alongside Pindar in the opening excursus on the fifth-century literary history of lyric poetry, stating at one point indeed that '[t]he seventeenth poem of Bacchylides, a dithy-

---

7 For an overview regarding the New Music, see LeVen (2014) 1–8, and Csapo and Wilson (2009) 278–279 on Timotheus.
8 Kenyon (1918) 7; Fearn (2010) 171.
9 Stern (1970); Pfeijffer and Slings (1999); [Long.] *De subl.* 33.5.

ramb in the form of a dialogue, shows no trace of those faults which disfigure the diction and style of a later school. Bacchylides also maintains the tradition that a dithyramb should be composed in strophes.'[10] For Jebb, Bacchylides is the very last of the great lyric poets before (and Jebb follows Plato very closely here) the outrageous decadence of Timotheus and the other New Musicians:

> But, in the latter part of the fifth century, one form of choral song, the dithyramb, received a new development, fraught with far-reaching consequences to the whole lyric art. That development was beginning just as the life of Bacchylides must have been drawing to an end.[11]

For Jebb, Timotheus simply won't do: commenting on two notable excerpts of *Persae*, he finds himself bewildered:

> The absurdity, alike, of style and of matter, could scarcely be exceeded: but the poet is serious. In a later passage, however, he seems to be designedly comic. A Phrygian prisoner, bewailing himself, speaks fourteen verses of broken Greek.[12]

Jebb concludes his overview as follows:

> Lastly, we have sought to elucidate the principal causes which, immediately after the time of Bacchylides, led to the rapid and final decay of Greek lyric art; thus enabling us to understand why his name is the last in the series of those Greek lyric poets who attained to classical rank.[13]

Clearly, Timotheus was shocking, and scholarship endeavoured to protect earlier lyric from his dangerously vapid charms. We need, then, to be a little suspicious about the neatness of Jebb's cut-off between Bacchylides and the New Music. Literary history does not generally conform to such clean breaks. Jebb's own private concerns about the literary merits of Bacchylides are also evident: at times it seems that Jebb wished that Bacchylides had been better, perhaps just a bit more like Pindar, and Jebb's noisy antipathy to Timotheus' recent publication may hide his private concerns about his own poet.[14]

---

10   Jebb (1905) 46: general excursus, 27–55, and on dithyramb in particular, 45–55.
11   Jebb (1905) 45.
12   Jebb (1905) 49.
13   Jebb (1905) 55.
14   See here A.W. Verrall's comments in Lady Caroline's biography of her husband (Jebb, C.

There is, however, rather more to say about the literary relationship between Bacchylides and Timotheus; their obvious differences notwithstanding, their similarities and affinities may also be enlightening.[15]

Much more recently, Eric Csapo found that a lack of scholarly understanding of the literary and cultural history of fifth-century dithyramb, and as a consequence his own doubts about where to situate Bacchylides within this, precluded a fully blown literary-historical examination of the lyric heritage of Euripides' so-called dithyrambic stasima:

> One problem with this characterization of Euripides' "dithyrambic style" is that there is nothing particularly dithyrambic about "self-contained ballad-like narratives", barring the oddity of Bacchylides, whose "dithyrambs" are not certainly dithyrambs, and who in any case represents a style normally opposed to New Dithyramb.[16]

Csapo's important paper opts instead for detailed discussion of the distribution of music sung by professional actors in a survey of Euripides' place within the New Music. In the light of more recent scholarship on the development of dithyramb in fifth-century Greece, and Athens in particular, and its relation to the circular choral performance form, we may in fact now find reason to agree with Kranz against Csapo and say that there may, in fact, be something characteristically—even if not exclusively—dithyrambic about self-contained lyric narrative in Euripidean New Music.[17] As I have argued elsewhere, the predominance of contextually flexible mythological narrative in earlier fifth-century dithyramb might have worked together with its mode of performance to provide a twin authority for this cultural form. The contextual flexibility of circular choruses (that is, appropriate for both Dionysus and Apollo, at least)

(1907) 474): 'The disinterred pieces of Bacchylides are a precious addition to a miserably defective chapter in the history of literature; one or two of them are notable works of art; but, if they were modern and familiar, five pages, instead of five hundred, would be enough to bestow upon them. "One does wish," as I heard Jebb say, with a sigh, in the midst of his labour, "that the man were just a little better."'

15 For further more detailed discussion about Bacchylides' place in the history of fifth-century lyric and the new music, see Fearn (2007) 163–337; cf. Fearn (2017) 248–254. For more recent work on the whole history of dithyramb, including Bacchylides as well as the New Music, see Power (2010); Kowalzig and Wilson (2013), including in particular D'Alessio (2013), Fearn (2013a), Franklin (2013), and Power (2013). For more on the varied complexities of narrative and experience in Greek lyric, see Fearn (forthcoming).

16 Csapo (1999–2000) 408, critiquing Kranz (1933); Kranz 254 for 'völlig absolut stehende balladeske Erzählung' in Euripidean neo-dithyrambic lyric.

17 See also Battezzato (2013).

could work together with the plasticity of mythological narrative, to ensure the form's appropriateness to a wide range of festival contexts in which it could be both performed and reperformed.[18]

Although Timotheus' *Persae* is technically a kitharodic nome, it will be argued here that there are pointed stylistic, intertextual, and structural connections between Bacchylides and Timotheus that reveal the extent to which earlier fifth-century narrative dithyramb was an important source of inspiration for the later poet. This shows the extent to which literary history is an important strand in the story of the reception of lyric poetry, in that the connections implicit in poetic reception provide a different kind of insight into lyric transmission.[19]

3   Structural Dithyrambic Intertextuality

The parodies of the modishness of the New Music to be found in ancient sources such as Aristophanes and Plato mean that modern scholars have tended to overlook the extent to which these later fifth-century authors were themselves indebted to the earlier lyric tradition in order to mark out their innovations. In the case of Timotheus' *Persae*, dependence upon texts such as Aeschylus' *Persians* are now well known, but the New Musical inheritance from earlier lyric poetry still warrants further discussion. In what follows I will pick up two specific examples that may have had an important structural bearing on Timotheus' sense of his poem within the lyric tradition: first, the opening intertext with the beginning of a well-known Pindaric dithyramb

---

18   See Fearn (2013a), esp. 146–148 for the possibility of both a Dionysiac and an Apolline presence in Bacchylides 17 on the basis of both linguistic and narrative detail, and of contextual flexibility of performance. This is one way of explaining the significance of Bacchylidean narrative dithyramb; it must also be said that scholarly worries about the oddity of the Bacchylidean form founder on the lack of evidence for what exactly other earlier fifth-century dithyrambs, even those by Pindar, actually looked like, and Bacchylidean dithyramb may not in fact have been atypical. See e.g. Pind. *Dith.* 2 (*Herakles or Kerberos*) for a dithyramb with a mythological title along the model of titles in the Hellenistic edition of Bacchylides' *Dithyrambs*; also discussion of Pindar's treatment of the myth of Orion in dithyrambic form (Lavecchia [2000] 273–278): in these cases at least, mythological narrative would surely have had a prominent role. The relation between dithyramb and narrative set out by Plato at *Rep.* 3.394b–c should not, I think, be taken to relate exclusively to New Musical dithyramb, even if there remain doubts about the applicability of Plato's statement to all earlier fifth-century dithyramb (Peponi [2013] 355–356).

19   For the close links between Timothean kitharoidic nome and dithyramb, see esp. Power (2010) 503–505; Power (2013).

composed for performance in Athens, fragments 76–77; second, a deeper structural indebtedness to Bacchylides 17.

In the opening line of the hexameter *prooimion* of *Persae* Timotheus praises Athens, or the Greek victory at Salamis (or, perhaps less likely, Themistocles) as follows:[20]

κλεινὸν ἐλευθερίας τεύχων μέγαν Ἑλλάδι κόσμον

Fashioning a famous and great adornment of freedom for Greece.
fr. 788

I will have more to say about this line in the final section of this discussion, but here it is worth emphasizing not only the extent of Timothean allusion to a variety of significant earlier fifth-century lyric texts, but also the effects of these points of contact in combination, and the particular significance of the Pindaric reference.[21] As has been emphasized recently by both LeVen and Power, Timotheus is pointing here towards at least three noteworthy fifth-century lyric texts, all of which relate directly to the Persian Wars.[22] In the marked use of the language of *kosmos* in the context of military celebration, we are directed to Simonides' Plataea elegy (~ τόνδ[ε μελ]ίφρονα κ[όσμον ἀο]ιδῆς, fr. 11.23 W²), and Simonides *PMG* 531 (261 Poltera) for the Spartan war-dead at Thermopylae (~ ἀρετᾶς μέγαν λελοιπὼς | κόσμον ἀέναόν τε κλέος, lines 7–8). And with the combination of an architectural metaphor and the reference to freedom, Timotheus recalls Pindar's dithyramb for Athens, which opened with praise of the city as a Hellenic bulwark against Persian enslavement in the aftermath of Artemision, fragments 76–77:

Ὦ ταὶ λιπαραὶ καὶ ἰοστέφανοι καὶ ἀοίδιμοι, Ἑλλάδος ἔρεισμα, κλειναὶ Ἀθᾶναι, δαιμόνιον πτολίεθρον.

ὅθι παῖδες Ἀθαναίων ἐβάλοντο φαεννάν
κρηπῖδ' ἐλευθερίας.

---

20   First line of proem: Hordern (2002) 127–128; see Power (2010) 530–531 for the alternative, though perhaps more doubtful, suggestion that this is the first line of the poem proper.
21   Here I build on some of the observations made by Power (2010) 530–532. See also LeVen (2014) 90–92, 193–195, with 219–220 for the narrative model provided by Simonides' *Plataea Elegy*, from the poem's opening right through to the *sphragis*; Bassett (1931) 155 picks out the Pindaric allusion; cf. also Budelmann (2018) 236.
22   Cf. Hordern (2002) 121, 128–129.

> O gleaming and violet-crowned and celebrated in song,
> bulwark of Greece, glorious Athens, divine city.
>
> [Artemision,] where the sons of the Athenians laid down
> a shining foundation of freedom.
>   trans. RACE

The latter intertext generates a sense that Pindaric dithyramb was a classic mode for civic praise of Athens, particularly with reference to her military prowess. Of course, though, the sense that this might by now already be a rather hackneyed trope is captured in the parodic allusion to this poem by Dikaiopolis in Aristophanes' *Acharnians*.[23]

Timotheus picks up the Pindaric phrase and extends and modifies it in line with his practice elsewhere in *Persae* when dealing with other intertextual material, building on, developing, and extending previous usage.[24] Timotheus, I believe, takes Pindar's material-cultural metaphor, with the vehicle κρηπῖδα in the general sense of architectural foundation or statue-base, and reworks and enlarges it in a specifically sculptural direction, filling out Pindar's image of the base or foundations of freedom that the Athenians provided with a statement figuring the fashioning of freedom as, not simply a base, but the aesthetic object of admiration supported on such a base.[25] If we are able to read Timotheus metapoetically here, his intertextual self-fashioning is itself figured as an act of standing proudly on solid Pindaric foundations, as well as the lavishing of even more praise onto the Greek victory in the Persian Wars.[26]

The non-extant grammatical subject of this opening sentence of Timotheus' poem has been the matter of a great deal of discussion, but, as Power has suggested, we should probably assume the subject to have taken the form of a general reference to Greek military prowess, rather than some over-specific reference to a particular historical individual.[27] Moreover, with the carefully chosen language of craft, Timotheus points programmatically to the aesthetic-

---

23 Ar. *Ach.* 637 with Σ; cf. also Ar. *Equ.* 1329; Kugelmeier (1996) 102–107; cf. also Ἑλλάδος ἔρεισμα at Soph. *OC* 54–58; Fearn (2013a) 136–159.
24 See further LeVen (2014) 205–218; Budelmann and LeVen (2014) 201, 204–205.
25 LSJ s.v. κρηπίς II; Hordern (2002) 121.
26 As LeVen (2014) takes great pains to set out throughout, we should not be worried about New Musical lyric exhibiting this degree of intertextual self-consciousness, both formally and ideologically; see also e.g. Firinu (2009). Timotheus is also cueing himself in to a fifth-century lyric tradition obsessed with material-cultural metaphor; I will have more to say about this below, p. 213.
27 Power (2010) 531–533; cf. Budelmann (2018) 236 (especially not to Themistocles himself).

ally arresting effects of his own lyric composition at the same time as showering praise on Greek military achievement.[28]

In an important recent study, Elena Firinu has suggested that Timothean intertextuality with the first ('dithyrambic') stasimon of Euripides' *Iphigenia at Tauris* in *Persae* is marked by a reworking and combining of separate Euripidean images into original new forms with greater complexity and obscurity.[29] Elsewhere, as Budelmann and LeVen also show, Timotheus' dexterity with figurative complexity often has the potential to disorientate audiences; or, as LeVen herself puts it separately (commenting on New Musical compound neologisms), to defamiliarize audiences, allowing them the opportunity—if, at least, they can take it, given the dazzling speed with which Timothean imagery often operates—to reflect self-consciously on the language itself.[30] This pronounced literary self-consciousness, which is felt down to the level of the intertextual resonances and metaphorical potential of individual words, seems highly distinctive and original, especially given the programmatic quality of it here at the outset of Timotheus' poem. Moreover, Timotheus is drawing us in to the materiality or objecthood of his own linguistic exposition and inviting reflection upon the dazzling surface of his text.[31]

Timotheus' use of Pindaric dithyramb may be one of a number of significant intertextual pointers directing us to a specifically Athenian contextualization for the language and literarity of *Persae*, despite the text's own notorious failure to explicitly specify a performance context for itself.[32] The lack of contextual specificity, together with the intertextual openness of *Persae*, both to Athenian dramatic and lyric texts and to Spartan lyric, also presents an ideological and hermeneutic challenge, especially taken together with the attention devoted to Sparta explicitly by name in the *sphragis* (line 207). We can agree with Power that the coyness with which Timotheus raises issues of context and ideological pointedness with this poem is of a piece with his own kitharoidic itinerant pro-

---

28   With τεύχων here picked up again with νεοτευχῆ in the *sphragis* at line 203: LeVen (2014) 90.
29   Firinu (2009).
30   Budelmann and LeVen (2014); LeVen (2014) 162, with Arist. *Rhet.* 1406a35–36 and [Dem.] *Eloc.* 91; cf. Gurd (2016) 120.
31   Of itself, this shows Timotheus' affinities with pre-existing lyric tropes of self-consciousness, which I have explored for Alcaeus in Fearn (2018); perhaps even more obvious are the links to the later choral lyric poets, and Pindar in particular here: cf. Fearn (2017), e.g. 116–118 with Pind. *Nem.* 8.15–16; cf. (again) Sim. *PMG* 531 (261 Poltera) line 8 with Fearn (2013b) 235–239; Budelmann (2018) 214 ad loc. I will return below, p. 232, to this point with specific reference to affinities between Timotheus and Gorgias.
32   Discussed in detail in Power (2010) 522–533.

fessionalism.[33] But we might go further to say that this is also a marker of the new distinctive challenges of the micro-mechanisms of Timotheus' intertextual literacy. Whom precisely this poem is for, and why, is a question that *Persae* may be posing right from its opening line. There, if we accept the Pindaric and Simonidean intertextuality, we have an opening statement about working within and developing the Spartan and Athenian lyric tradition of praise for Hellenic military prowess. Yet the text's surface provides us with a general statement relating to the fifth-century past and the Persian Wars. It does not seem to specify outright any more specific contemporary contextual or ideological pointedness.[34] What we seem to have, then, is a literary puzzle about encomiastic referentiality.

The lack of contextual specification in the performative *deixis* of lines 237–238, ἁγνὰν ... τάνδε πόλιν ('this holy city'), should also be considered in this light. It is more than simply a nod to established encomiastic convention within the lyric tradition, for which a wide variety of scholarly reactions are themselves still available;[35] I would prefer to see this lack of explicit grounding as a final question to audiences about the appropriateness or ideological pointedness of this text, in whatever context it is being performed.[36] This could be in Athens—as the traditionally ['old-']dithyrambic and almost clichéd use of 'holy city' might suggest[37]—or elsewhere, especially in conjunction with the closing words about *eunomia*, which might, or might not, suggest Sparta.[38] This is especially important since the fundamental question of what it might mean at the end of the fifth century to compose a lyric poem in honour of the battle of Salamis would surely have admitted of a wide variety of contextually and ideologically dependent responses at the time. Timotheus seems to be stretching this issue of contextual appropriateness by putting even more pressure on the assumed closeness of the connection between content, form, and perform-

---

33 Power (2010) 525–526; cf. Budelmann (2018) 234: 'The likelihood of an Athenian premiere makes it noteworthy that nothing in the text points explicitly to Athens.'
34 Cf. Hordern (2002) 129 ad loc.
35 See, e.g. the papers in Felson (2004); also Agocs (2012) esp. 219.
36 Cf. Budelmann (2018) 252 'τάνδε πόλιν could be applied to any city in which the nome was reperformed'.
37 'Holy city' as an earlier Athenian dithyrambic motif: Pind. fr. 75.4, Bacch. 18.1, Bacch. 23.1, Fearn (2013a) 136–137; Budelmann (2018) 252; cf. e.g. Soph. *Aj.* 1221–1222, Ar. *Equ.* 1319. Here Timotheus perhaps surprises with the unexpected simplicity of this traditional noun-epithet combination, but interpretative issues may be more difficult to unravel—(atypical) simplicity of noun-epithet phraseology may in this instance itself be a barrier to fully understanding the significance of the reference.
38 For Spartan overtones in the reference here in the context of potentially Spartan *eunomia*, see LeVen (2014) 101. Cf. Power (2010) 537–539 with esp. 539n355; Budelmann (2018) 252.

ance contextualization, already challenged distinctively by Pindar in poems such as *Nemean* 8, the deictic complexity of which I have explored in detail elsewhere.[39] Again, this is a point to which I return in the final section.

I now turn to Bacchylides 17. A starting point may be provided by the first stasimon of Euripides' *Iphigenia in Tauris*, which Firinu has argued is alluded to throughout *Persae*.[40] As Eric Csapo has pointed out, later Euripidean lyric is extremely fond of images and phrases that point to dithyramb—the number of instances of mythical choral projection, with groups (of sometimes 50) dancing in circles, is noteworthy.[41] Of particular interest here are those that involve dancing Nereids and dolphins: *Electra* 434 (Nereids and Dolphins dancing in a circle); *Iphigenia at Tauris* 427–429 (fifty Nereids dancing in a circle); *Iphigenia at Aulis* 1055–1057 (Nereids dancing in a circle); and especially the passage from *Iphigenia at Tauris*. The language which Euripides uses to advertise his dithyrambic choral projection is noteworthy: first, the reference to Amphitrite, whose reappearance in *Persae* Firinu picks up; second, the beginning of the ode.

In lines 392–406, the chorus ask who these strangers are who have arrived from overseas, in a peculiar and rather pointed way:

κυάνεαι κυανέας σύνοδοι θαλάσσας,
ἵν' οἶστρος †ὁ πετόμενος Ἀργόθεν†
ἄξενον ἐπ' οἶδμα διεπέρασε ⟨πόντου⟩
Ἀσιήτιδα γαῖαν Εὐρώπας διαμείψας·
τίνες ποτ' ἄρα τὸν εὔυδρον δονακόχλοον
λιπόντες Εὐρώταν ἢ ῥεύματα σεμνὰ Δίρκας
ἔβασαν ἔβασαν ἄμεικτον αἶαν, ἔνθα κούρᾳ
Δίᾳ τέγγει
βωμοὺς καὶ περικίονας
ναοὺς αἷμα βρότειον;

Dark confluences of the dark sea,
where the gadfly that flew from Argos
passed over the wave of the Hostile Sea
to Asia's land, leaving Europe behind:
who can they be then who left the reeds and plentiful water
of the Eurotas or the august streams of Dirce

---

39   Fearn (2017).
40   Firinu (2009).
41   Csapo (1999–2000) 418–424 with fig. 3a.

and came, came, to the savage land where for the maiden
daughter of Zeus
the altars and colonnaded temples are drenched
in human blood?
> trans. KOVACS

If we ask why Euripides presents the geographic tableau in the opening of this ode in the way he does, an answer may arrive from a rather unexpected quarter. It is worth considering the possibility that Euripides is gesturing towards the literary history of the dithyramb, setting out a kind of metatextual literary landscape involving seafaring and Greek myth which points us to Bacchylides, and to two of his Athenian dithyrambs in particular: Bacchylides 17 (*Youths or Theseus*) and perhaps also Bacchylides 19 (*Io, for the Athenians*). The opening polyptoton κυάνεαι κυανέας in line 392 may indeed serve as a metatextual marker.[42] We are invited to pause, if we can, to consider the poetic quality and resonance of the diction. It may in fact pick up the opening word of Bacchylides 17, with its focus on the dark-blue prow of Minos' ship, cleaving the waves of the Aegean on his way back from Athens to Knossos:

κυανόπρωιρα μὲν ναῦς μενέκτυ[πον
Θησέα δὶς ἑπτ[ά] τ' ἀγλαοὺς ἄγουσα
κούρους Ἰαόνω[ν
Κρητικὸν τάμνε⟦ν⟧ πέλαγος·

The ship with the blue-black prow, as it carried Theseus, steadfast in the battle din, and the twice seven splendid youths and maidens of the Ionians, was cleaving the Cretan sea.
> trans. RACE

The later reference in lines 427–429 to a chorus of fifty Nereids dancing in circles may reinforce the allusion: the dancing Nereids whom Theseus watches in Bacchylides 17 (lines 101–108) may have been among the more well-known literary depictions in earlier Athenian poetry, especially given the Athenian ideological flavour this choral vision may have had.[43] In addition, the reference to Io in the next lines may itself pick up the depiction of Io's plight in Bacchylides

---

42 For the place of polyptoton within the range of devices that New Musical poetry uses as part of a self-conscious attitude towards its own literarity, see LeVen (2014) 165–167 discussing Melanippides and Licymnius, and Gorgianic style.
43 For which see Fearn (2013a) 139–146.

19, and in particular the paradigm this text provides for a Greek mythological heroine travelling overseas to the ultimate benefit of Athens (in Bacchylides' text, Io gives birth in Egypt to Epaphos, ultimate ancestor of Dionysus). The myths of both these texts involve unfortunate individuals heading off on voyages they would rather not be making, but that will turn out unexpectedly successfully for them; these might, then, have provided Euripides with a neat, dithyrambically inspired, rationale for his own self-consciously innovative late fifth-century take on the Orestes myth in this play.

Now that we are beginning to familiarize ourselves with readings of late fifth-century lyric, which make room for this kind of intertextual sophistication, we might now consider the extent of material from earlier 'classic' dithyramb in these later-fifth-century New Musically 'dithyrambic' compositions.[44]

If we return now to Timotheus' *Persae*, one of the most obvious parallels between Timotheus' text and Bacchylides' dithyrambic style most notable in Bacchylides 17 is the use of a series of extended but in themselves relatively simple paratactic narrative tableaux, with a simple syntax and where the use of numerous epithets relating to colour, beauty, and form, add to a heightened pictorial quality.[45] What is so different about Timotheus is, as we shall see in the next section, the different effects of the use of compound adjectives; but on the level of narrative style, there are clear points of similarity—in *Persae* Timothean narrative style is, at base, Bacchylidean, and self-consciously so.

While the use of a nautical narrative does not of course by itself suggest any direct relation, there are three details within Timotheus' treatment of it that

---

44   What is again noteworthy is the possibility of a structural kind of intertextuality pointedly relating to opening words or lines of well-known texts, something that we have been trained to expect only in Hellenistic poetry and later. I raise the possibility that the later fifth-century Athenian book-trade (whose effects appear visible elsewhere in Aristophanic and Euripidean drama, for instance) may have allowed for more sustained engagement with the materiality of literary texts than had been generally possible in earlier decades—as thematized, for instance, in Aristophanes, *Frogs*. In the next section on poetic style I will go on to compare and contrast the kinds of intertextuality that we can see in Bacchylides and Timotheus.

45   Hordern (2002) 50–55; in particular, Budelmann and LeVen (2014) 203: 'Timotheus avoids intricately embedded chronological sequences that characterize, for example, the style (and challenge) of Pindar's odes; rather, the narrative shifts laterally between a series of tableaux, with no prolepsis or analepsis. The surviving section of *Persians* moves from sea, to shore, to land, before finally focusing on the king's tent.' For Budelmann and LeVen the point of this simplicity is to draw attention to linguistic and figurative complexity, though I suggest in addition that such simplicity of syntax and narrative style may also be intertextually resonant and pointed.

suggest that Bacchylides 17 provided enough interest of detail and structure to provide Timotheus with an empowering narrative model.

First, the interesting use of Amphitrite as, in part, a grandiloquent periphrasis for the sea (*Persae* lines 37–39) responds to the important role of the sea-goddess Amphitrite within the narrative structure of Bacchylides' poem of Theseus' heroic exploits (Bacch. 17.109–116).

Second is an amusing (or perhaps grotesque, depending on your sensibility) intertextual parallelism between the two most famous swimmers in Greek literature after Odysseus.[46] For the description, and speech, of Timotheus' hapless Persian drowning in the waves as the Persian fleet rushes on in flight (lines 60–87) involves in part an ironic reversal and narrative antitype to the successful Theseus, whose dive into the sea in Bacchylides 17 is anything but hapless, and whose unexpected return from the waves comes despite Minos' unwillingness to stop for him: Timotheus transforms the narrative tableau invented by Bacchylides. Note in particular the use of the same verb to describe the passing of the ships in both versions, leaving our hero and antihero behind in the water: in Bacchylides, line 90 has ἵετο δ' ὠκύπομπον δόρυ, 'the swiftly moving vessel sped on'; in Timotheus' version this becomes φυγᾷ δὲ πάλιν ἵετο Πέρ- | σης στρατὸς βάρβαρος ἐπισπέρχων, 'in flight and backwards the barbarian Persian army sped on, rushing along', lines 86–87, where the backwards direction of Timotheus' Persians in retreat may serve as a metatextual marker of the reversal of the Bacchylidean triumphal trope.[47]

Third, the performative or mimetic slippage in the segue between historical narrative and the opening of the *sphragis* in *Persae* may not only pay homage to a distinctive Bacchylidean narrative technique, but also direct us nicely to the close of Bacchylides 17.[48] In *Persae*, the slip between the historical Greeks singing their paean when erecting their trophies and the voice of Timotheus the poet calling on Apollo as his *epikouros* (with its concomitant allusion to Simonides fr. 11.21 W²) takes as its principal model the close of Bacchylides 17, where the triumphal performance of Theseus and the *ēitheoi* segues into the performance of Bacchylides' poem by its chorus of Keians. Compare *Persae* lines 196–205 and Bacchylides 17.124–132:

---

46 Cf. Hall (1993), updated in Hall (2006b).
47 It is interesting to note that the form ἵετο is relatively frequent in the *Iliad* as a verb of emotion and of physical assault; it is not used in the *Odyssey* of seafaring, and is in fact only so used in extant archaic and classical texts in the two passages under consideration here.
48 See also Bacch. 3.9–22, with discussion by Carey (1999) 19–20, noting the characteristically Bacchylidean and un-Pindaric quality of the technique. Power (2010) 533 notes the referential ambiguity here but misses the Bacchylidean overtone; similarity with Bacch. 17.128–132 is noted by Budelmann (2018) 243 without further comment.

οἱ δὲ τροπαῖα στησάμενοι Διός
ἁγνότατον τέμενος, Παιᾶν'
 ἐκελάδησαν ἰήϊον
ἄνακτα, σύμμετροι δ' ἐπε-
 κτύπεον ποδῶν
ὑψικρότοις χορείαις.
ἀλλ' ὦ χρυσεοκίθαριν ἀέ-
 ξων Μοῦσαν νεοτευχῆ,
ἐμοῖς ἔλθ' ἐπίκουρος ὕ-
 μνοις ἰήϊε Παιάν·

But the Greeks, setting up trophies to Zeus to be the holiest of sanctuaries, called upon Paean the healer lord, and keeping in time stamped out their high-pounding dances with their feet. Come, you who foster the golden-lyred, new-fashioned Muse, come as ally to my songs, healer Paean.

 ἀγλαό-
θρονοί τε κοῦραι σὺν εὐ-
 θυμίαι νεοκτίτωι
ὠλόλυξαν, ἔ-
 κλαγεν δὲ πόντος· ἠΐθεοι δ' ἐγγύθεν
νέοι παιάνιξαν ἐρατᾶι ὀπί.
Δάλιε, χοροῖσι Κηΐων
 φρένα ἰανθείς
ὄπαζε θεόπομπον ἐσθλῶν τύχαν.

and the splendid-throned girls cried out in new-found joy, and the sea rang out; nearby the youths sang a paean with lovely voice. Delian, with your mind warmed by choruses of Keians, grant a fortune of blessings conveyed by god.

This use of Bacchylidean technique and allusion is one of the final intertextual notes in *Persae*. Timotheus fuses the Panhellenic prestige of the Greek victors at Salamis with his own poetic claims to lyric stardom;[49] and by using Bacchylides' famous poem to achieve this, Timotheus may be weighing down his own text with some final Athenian ideological baggage, using the poetic

---

49   Cf. Power (2010) 533.

pedigree of earlier fifth-century culturally imperialist Athenian dithyramb to generate his own fresh claims to authority and significance.[50]

The acknowledged range of lyric texts that Timotheus points towards in *Persae* is generally associated with the Persian Wars—Simonides' Plataea elegy and eulogy of the Spartan war-dead from Thermopylae; Pindar's dithyrambic celebration of Athenian success at Artemision. The addition of Bacchylides 17 sheds new light onto later fifth-century lyric reception, revealing Timotheus' interest in Bacchylides 17 as itself another ideologically charged text from the general Persian Wars period (or at least reasonably soon after, as is the most likely dating of Bacchylides 17). As has been plausibly suggested elsewhere, the depiction of Minos in Bacchylides' poem has distinctively Persian overtones, and Theseus' triumph represents the ideological triumph of Athens as Ionian protectors of the Aegean.[51] Timotheus picks up the political symbolism and ideological suggestiveness of Bacchylides' limpid narrative snapshot of an extraordinary mythical event, and redirects its energies into his own non-mythological lyric narrative.

4 Stylistics

In this section I discuss the similarities and differences between Timothean and Bacchylidean lyric style. I use the intertextual relation between Bacchylides' and Timotheus' Amphitrite as my starting point.

The description of the sea in *Persae* has been the focus of attention in some important work.[52] Here I build on this—in particular the discussion by Firinu—by factoring in Bacchylides' own Amphitrite in *Dithyramb* 17, and using the comparison and contrast between the two poets' visions to add more detail on the stylistic characteristics of both poets.

In the opening extant verses of *Persae* the first reference to the sea, ἅλμας (line 19), lacks further poetic colouring. This quickly changes, however, with the highly elaborate description of the following section, lines 31–39:

σμαραγδοχαίτας δὲ πόν-
τος ἄλοκα ναΐοις ἐφοι-
νίσσετο σταλά[γμασι,
κρ]αυγᾷ βοᾷ δὲ [συ]μμι[γ]ὴς κατεῖχεν·

---

50 Bacchylides 17 and Athenian cultural (and choral) imperialism: Fearn (2013) esp. 139–152.
51 Castriota (1992) 60–61; Calame (1996); Fearn (2007); Calame (2009) 175.
52 LeVen (2014) 150–152 and 180; Firinu (2009) 123–124.

ὁμοῦ δ[ὲ] νάϊος στρατός
βάρβαρος ἄμμι[γ' αὖτις
ἀντεφέρετ' ἐ[π' ἰχ]θυ[ο]-
 στεφέσι μαρμαροπ[τύχ]οις
κόλποισιν ['Ἀμφιτρί]τας.

And the emerald-haired sea was reddened in its furrows by the drops from the ships, and shouts mingled with shrieking prevailed. And together the barbarian naval army was borne back upon the fish-wreathed bosom of Amphitrite with its shining folds.

In her discussion of this passage, LeVen notes in particular the jarring juxtapositions:

> part of the passage's effect resides in the violent juxtaposition of colors and in the poignant antithesis of personification of the sea, bejewelled with emerald and wreath, and the crudeness of the battle with its blood and shrieks.[53]

She also draws attention to the Homeric intertextuality inherent in the language Timotheus chooses to figure the sea.[54] Here I will add the issue of Timothean engagement with lyric precedent for a fuller sense of the passage's distinctiveness.

Firinu suggests that Timotheus draws on the reference to Amphitrite in the first stasimon of Euripides' *Iphigenia at Tauris* (ἐπ' Ἀμφιτρί- | τας ῥοθίῳ, 'by the billows of Amphitrite', 425–426).[55] Firinu has excellent and insightful things to say then about what the effects of Timotheus' new vision of Amphitrite are. Not only are we here faced with the clash between the serenity of Amphitrite's abode and the blood and destruction of an ensuing sea battle: we are actually being presented with a cognitive challenge of interpretation, since Timotheus' language of the sea can be interpreted as, alternatively, both enargically hyper-vivid and concrete, and also highly anthropomorphic. Ultimately, Timotheus is posing questions about the nature of the sea, and the extent to which lyric diction can help to articulate its essence, whether an elemental substance, a divinity, or perhaps both at once. The semantic density of Timotheus' Amphitrite/sea involves the audience or reader in a game about

---

53   LeVen (2014) 151.
54   LeVen (2014) 180 with Hom. *Od.* 3.91, 5.122, 12.60, 12.97; *Il.* 18.140, *Od.* 5.52–53.
55   Firinu (2009) section 2.2.

the nature of lyric referentiality, since the language is drawing us here to pay attention to both the glittering surface of water and the potential anthropomorphism of the sea-deity, whether in epiphanic terms or statue-form: both these interpretations may be supported by the expression μαρμαροπ[τύχ]οις κόλποισιν (with the glittering folds of its troughs / her bosom); σμαραγδοχαίτας (emerald-haired) and ἰχ]θυ[ο]στεφέσι (fish-wreathed) might also both point in both enargeic and anthropomorphic directions at once.[56]

We may accept with LeVen that the effects here are jarring, and that ultimately Timotheus' language is defamiliarizing, or at least that it takes us away from our more straightforward everyday encounters with the world through language in a challenging way. But let us now explore what happens when we factor Bacchylides' Amphitrite into Timotheus' description. I suggest that Timotheus uses a Bacchylidean intertextual frame to add further dithyrambic narrative structure to his text, and also draws attention to his extraordinarily ornate style, and in so doing invites us to reflect on the nature of lyric expression and particularly the limits of description through comparison with Bacchylides.

Theseus' encounter with Amphitrite comes in lines 109–116 of Bacchylides 17:

> εἶδέν τε πατρὸς ἄλοχον φίλαν
> σεμνὰν βοῶπιν ἐρατοῖ-
>   σιν Ἀμφιτρίταν δόμοις·
> ἅ νιν ἀμφέβαλλεν ἀϊόνα πορφυρέαν,
>
> κόμαισί τ' ἐπέθηκεν οὔλαις
> ἀμεμφέα πλόκον,
> τόν ποτέ οἱ ἐν γάμωι
> δῶκε δόλιος Ἀφροδίτα ῥόδοις ἐρεμνόν.

And he saw his father's dear wife, stately ox-eyed Amphitrite, in the splendid house; she wrapped him in a purple cloak, and placed upon his thick hair an immaculate garland, the one which once on her wedding day crafty Aphrodite had given her, dark with roses.

---

56 Firinu (2009) 123–124. Compare also the insightful comments of LeVen (2014) 172–174 on the description of Health in Licymnius *PMG* 769. I will take some of these points further in the final section.

This is the most sustained and vivid encounter with Amphitrite in all extant Greek lyric poetry, and it presents interesting points of comparison with Timotheus' passage. This encounter is focalized through the eyes of Theseus, and although most of the language is visually evocative, with reference to colours, textures, and objects in particular, the peculiar thing to note is that, although in this instance Amphitrite is the recipient of a string of adjectives, none of them is very much use for communicating a sense of what Amphitrite actually looks like. The only term here that is in any sense visual is βοῶπιν (ox-eyed), which, rather than being straightforwardly if at all visual, is surely used to evoke Homeric divinities and to add some epic weight to Amphitrite's divine majesty.[57] Timotheus and Bacchylides both use a build-up of adjectives to characterize their lyric style, but whereas Bacchylides often adds emotional depth, colour, or charm to his characters and narratives in this way, Timotheus compresses so many different effects into his piling up of noun-epithet combinations that his style seems deliberately provocative and challenging, inviting us all the time to pause, think, and consider what the words mean and their relation to Greek literary history.[58] In the case of Amphitrite, if Timotheus has led us to one of the most well-known and extensive passages about this deity in the tradition, the point ultimately may be the recognition of a lyric irony, that even Bacchylidean *enargeia* cannot fully reveal the nature of divinity: Timotheus explores the limits of lyric description through not only the aesthetic challenges posed by his own piling up of vivid pictorial diction, but also by virtue of allusion to one of the acknowledged masters of lyric vividness.[59] This is, again, an intensification of issues surrounding lyric *enargeia* already inherent in the lyric history of narrative and description taking us back through Simonides (as well as Bacchylides) to Stesichorus.[60]

---

57 Cf. also Bacch. 5.98–99 and 11.37–39 for comparable build-ups of epithets referring to Artemis; in the first instance (inside a myth) the epithets there do help to create the visual impression of an anthropomorphic deity, but the beauty of the colours there jars markedly and deliberately with the rage of the goddess against the neglectful mortal Oeneus.

58 On Bacchylides' use of epithets, see classically Segal (1976), e.g. 101: 'Bacchylides' lyric style atomizes this coherent, well-integrated universality and comprehensiveness [sc. of the Homeric epithet]. It renders the content of the epic world, but broken down into discrete scenes and moments. These are, on the one hand, part of the epic tradition; but on the other hand they are totally separate from it because the poet's special perceptions and art have endowed them with a new individuality, vibrancy, and intensity of emotion.' See also further below.

59 Compare here Torrance (2013) ch. 2 on Euripidean intertextual ekphrasis.

60 For Simonides, cf. esp. *PMG* 543 (271 Poltera) with Fearn (2017) 229–248; for comparison between Stesichorus and Bacchylides, see Fearn (forthcoming).

We might draw a similar conclusion from Theseus' underwater vision of the dancing Nereids moments before in this same passage: the Nereids' 'liquid feet' (ὑγροῖσι ποσ⟨σ⟩ὶν line 108) is a charming expression precisely because of its slippage between potentially concrete and metaphorical signification— Timothean intertextuality draws us into the lyric history of the critique of the relation between narrative description and stylized expression.[61]

It is also worth pausing here with Timotheus' Amphitrite to note the quasi-Bacchylidean quality of the effects of the language of colour: in lines 31–33 the colour-clash between the emerald green of Amphitrite's locks and the red of the sailors' blood is emotionally charged and evocative, and it picks up and continues a Bacchylidean interest in colour contrasts and combinations, especially with the language of blood. In the Iliadically inspired narrative of the myth of Bacchylides 13, Hector's slaughter of the Achaeans is described through the clash of the colours of blood and earth, which itself picks up and develops Homeric usage:

ἐναρίζ[ο]μ[έν]ων
[δ' ἔρ]ευθε φώτων
[αἵμα]τι γαῖα μέλα[ινα]
['Ἕκτορ]έας ὑπὸ χει[ρός]

and the black earth was red with the blood of men slain by the hand of Hektor.

BACCHYLIDES 13.151–154

Bacchylides flaunts his enargeic lyric artistry by being able to use the redness of blood and the blackness of earth in the same phrase, whereas Homeric formulaic expression only has black earth and black blood; blood in the *Iliad* is only red when it mixes with water.[62] In these terms Timotheus' clash of green hair and red blood is highly Bacchylidean, but in the broader context of Timotheus' visual and significatory challenges, it may be more extreme and pointed, and becomes distinctively Timothean.

---

61 Cf. e.g. Kirkwood (1980) 160: '[I]n Bacchyl. 17.108 the feet of the Nereids are undoubtedly wet, yet the basic element in ὑγροῖσι ποσσίν is the liquid suppleness of these dancing feet.' Also Maehler (2004) 185 ad loc., going further than Maehler (1997) 203 ad loc. with Burnett (1985) 22; note, by contrast, the disapproval of Jebb (1905) 387 ad loc.: 'The use of the word [ὑγρός] in reference to Nymphs of the *sea* is not very felicitous.'

62 Most closely paralleled by Hom. *Il.* 15.713–715; red blood in water: Hom. *Il.* 21.21; Fearn (2007) 137.

The affinities between Bacchylidean and Timothean lyric style are still, though, worth further investigation. With Bacchylides, we are again in a literary environment heavily reliant upon the potentially multiplicitous referentiality of lyric epithets to engage audiences. In the passage I cited earlier, LeVen speaks of the 'violent juxtaposition' and 'poignant antithesis' between elements of Timothean diction; yet such a description might be a neat way of figuring Bacchylides' own style of lyric narrative, and indeed Segal comes very close to this in his brilliant observations on the language of Bacchylides 13.121–123:

ἀλλ' ὅτε δὴ πολέμοιο
λῆξεν ἰοστεφάνου
   Νηρῆιδος ἀτρόμητος υἱός ...

But when the untrembling son of the Nereid violet-crowned ceased from war ...

'Untrembling warrior' stands in strong contrast with 'Nereid violet-crowned'. 'Violet-crowned' is so placed that it looks as if it might go with 'war' and 'Nereid'. The colometry, in fact, encourages us initially to translate 'war violet-crowned ...' We correct this 'mistake' at once when we read (or hear) the next line, but we may wonder whether this invitation to misconstrue may not be deliberate. In any event it creates not merely a pathetic collocation of opposites, but a violent fusion and interpenetration of antithetical realms of experience.[63]

To conclude this section, then, looking at Bacchylides both as an intertextual source for Timotheus and as a means of stylistic comparison is insightful in a number of respects. It allows us to see with more clarity the affinities as well as differences between Timotheus and more traditional lyric narrative: we should be prepared to emphasize continuities as much as discontinuities; one further advantage is that comparisons of this kind allow us also to reassess our views of Bacchylides and the significance of his own style of composition.

---

63 Segal (1976) 130; Fearn (2007) 133–134; Fearn (forthcoming) for critique of the claim by Segal that Bacchylides' Achilles is a lyric simplification of Iliadic complexity: not a simplification but an intense specification of lyric difference. As I suggest there, the focus on Achilles' desire for Briseis' alluring body ('with longing in her limbs', ἱμερογυίου, Bacch. 13.137) both intensifies Homeric narrative and potentially prefigures our own mesmerization by lyric's own special mythological narrativity.

5 Timotheus the Sophist

I turn now to a consideration of the wider cultural and intellectual context of the late fifth century, and the sophists in particular. LeVen has highlighted a number of affinities between the poets of the New Music and the sophists, and I would like to follow her lead by making one specific observation about Timotheus' *Persae*, but also to offer a slightly different assessment of the sophistic nature of New Musical poetic rhetoric. For LeVen, the defamiliarizing nature of New Musical diction is an aspect that Timotheus and his colleagues shared with the sophists.[64] The sophistic rhetoricians and sophistic poets together appeal to the mind and senses in new and challenging ways by inviting close scrutiny of the surface of their extraordinary texts, and provoking a range of responses.[65]

As we have seen through the previous discussion, Timothean diction seems to pose deliberate challenges at the individual lexical level, and, as I have suggested, involving specific intertextual games; one of LeVen's most important insights is to see this as sophistic, because of the defamilarizational properties inherent in the linguistic and stylistic flair of the New Musical 'dithyrambic' style in common with contemporary sophistic rhetoric. According to LeVen, this is part of a broader quest for truth: 'Any poet or prose writer, of course, exploits the aural and musical potential of language, but what connects neo-dithyrambists and sophists is their apparent interest in finding *truth* in language, which leads them to pursue the logic of language and its expressive possibilities, and playing with (and discussing) the "material" elements of language.'[66]

I want to build upon, but modify, LeVen's insights by focussing on two key elements of sophistic thought; taken together these are important starting points for the fuller appreciation being outlined here not only of the self-conscious literarity of Timothean lyric style, but also its significance and point. These are: 'the turn to *nomos* and *phusis*, convention/law and nature, as explanatory categories' and what I would term 'the shock of *logos*'.[67]

---

64 LeVen (2014) 161–167, and 164 in particular with Dion. Hal. *Lys.* 3 (= Gorg. 82 A 4 D-K) for the similarities between Gorgianic rhetoric and dithyramb.
65 For the view of the sophists as a fascinatingly egregious and diverse group of thinkers associated particularly with late fifth-century Athens, see Goldhill (2002) 47–48; for a sophistic Euripides see Conacher (1999) (though justifiably critiqued by Goldhill [1999]); Allan (1999–2000). There is still more work to be done on relations between fifth-century literary and sophistic rhetoric, even with Euripides.
66 LeVen (2014) 166.
67 Borrowing the first and developing the third of Goldhill's four signposts: Goldhill (2002)

Goldhill sets out clearly the significance of the turn to *nomos* and *phusis*:

> One the one hand, the opposition of 'nature' and 'culture' is itself a sign and symptom of the rapid cultural change of the classical city ... The contest over what is natural (proper, right) and conventional (arbitrary, open to change, debateable) marks the conflict and worry of social change ... [T]he turn to *nomos* and *phusis* as explanations repeatedly seeks to understand specific events, attitudes, projects as signs of abstract and general principles—which is one of the foundational strategies of science, philosophy, and the other self-reflexive disciplines.[68]

'The shock of logos' figures the ways in which sophistic language unsettles and challenges, inviting us both to pay attention to the surface glitter of the literally self-consciousness of the writing, and also by tempting us to delve further within and to attempt to find further insight, or indeed truths, beyond the surface. It also involves the self-conscious attention drawn to language itself, and thus to rhetoric, as a suitable and effective form of communication.

What I would like to focus on is, first, a sense that through this degree of self-consciousness in the building-up of poetic form out of intertextually resonant, and aesthetically and cognitively jarring diction, Timotheus shares with the sophists, and Gorgias in particular, a deep-seated fascination with *logos* itself. *Logos*, first, in terms of poetic language, partly through the literary inheritance of the Greek literary tradition of lyric and epic. And *logos*, second, in terms of *reason*, particularly in relation to how language, and its most preeminent practitioners, affect the ways we interpret the world.

48–53: for *nomos* and *phusis*, Goldhill (2002) 48–49; classically, Guthrie (1969) ch. 4. My 'shock of *logos*' is an extension of Goldhill's choice of 'reversal and paradox' (2002) 50–51 (Goldhill's other two signposts are 'the argument from probability', 49, and 'teaching virtue', 51–53). 'Shock' here is a way of figuring *ekplêxis*, 'snatching people out of their senses', which is intended to capture the double-edged nature of audience response with sophistic rhetoric in particular: classically, Diodorus' account of the Athenians' first reactions to Gorgias (Diod. Sic. 12.53.2–4), with *ekplêxis* double-edged in terms of not only wonderment and captivation, but also bewilderment and the risk even of madness. Cf. Lada (1993) esp. 97–98, with e.g. Ar. *Ran.* 961–962 (Euripides critiquing Aeschylus), Pl. *Ion* 535b–e (the rhapsode on audience captivation), Polyb. 2.56.11 on tragedy and the captivation of the soul. In Gorgias himself (*Hel.* 16) *ekplêxis* is presented as psychological trauma, interpreted as 'the deep turmoil of the soul inextricably interwoven with confused judgement (wrong evaluation of circumstances) and resulting in non-rational behaviour' (Lada (1993) 127 n. 28); also Thuc. 7.42.3, with Hunter (1986) 418 for 'shock'.

68 Goldhill (2002) 48.

Second, it is important to investigate the ways in which this sophistic interest in language relates to a broader intellectual interest in the relation between *nomos* and *phusis*. Rather than being interested straightforwardly in any quest for 'truth', I would suggest that the sophists, and Gorgias in particular, are posing questions about the relation between language and reality. They are testing and challenging the assumptions their audiences/readers naturally make, exploring the ways values and identities are in part shaped by being grounded in traditions of a variety of kinds, including perhaps most importantly literary traditions. Gorgias does this by challenging readers to confront what they think they know about Helen, and on what terms, also thus challenging them to confront the persuasive complicity of the language of literary tradition as it shapes opinions, attitudes, and values.

In the shaping of attitudes and values, Gorgias, and Timotheus too, are tapping in to the ways earlier lyric had itself already done this.[69] Yet the shock of Timothean lyric/musical professionalism in *Persae* and of Gorgianic sophistic rhetoric in *Helen*, in turn, is these texts' very awareness and implicit critique of the basic association between tradition and cultural value. For Timotheus, this might shed further light on the significance of the text's final word. If we are to identify a pun on two senses of *nomos* in *eunomia*, the poem finishes with a word which pre-circumscribes, enacts, and also universalizes the appropriateness of performance-context on the basis of audience receptivity to Timotheus' own professional lyric superstardom: 'a community with εὐνομία is a community that has good nomes, and [Timotheus'] prayer for this community is a further prayer for his own music and a further self-advertisement.'[70] This use of a final pun that radically re-associates the appropriateness of lyric to setting could, then, for some at least, also mark the collapse of ethics, politics, and music together that Plato so detested about the New Musicians at *Laws* 3.700a–701a; the projection of a warm welcome for Timotheus' *Persae* by a setting already configured on the basis of New Musical receptivity would work as a hyper-extension of the lyric trope of encomiastic *kleos* familiar from at least as early as Ibycus and the end of S151;[71] and, fundamentally, this pun would operate as a final, radical, and sophistic reconstitution of culture itself (*nomos*) according to the measure of Timothean music (*nomos*).

---

69 As I have argued in Fearn (2017) 13 and 48 (and more widely) on Pindar, with Felski (2015) 159–160 on literature and culture more broadly.
70 Budelmann (2018) 252 on line 240; cf. Gurd (2016) 123.
71 Following e.g. Spelman (2018) 164–166: 'The "Polycrates Ode", like so many Pindaric epinicians, presents itself as the product of a celebrated author and anticipates being remembered as such' (166).

We can already sense how the literary multiplicities of Timotheus' *Persae* provoke a range of reactions on a number of diverse grounds. The text can draw audiences to feel shocked (whether positively or negatively) by the surface effects of its linguistic plays; captivated by the potentially engrossing narrative; intrigued by Timotheus' intertextual games; or outraged or astonished by the tonal uncertainties of what results.[72] We should entertain the possibility that many of the different elements that make up Timotheus' extraordinarily rich literature will clash with one another. The ornate compound adjectives and the intertextuality may draw audiences and readers away from the narrative account of the sea battle. Their attentiveness to the narrative may even be interrupted by the allure of the specifics of the language itself, and/or of the intertexts.[73] Indeed, as I have already suggested, it may be that some of those lyric intertexts have the potential to raise questions about the very limits of narrativity.

In addition, the very diversity of the intertextual plays that Timotheus offers raises interpretative paradoxes and difficulties of its own; intertexts may provide jarring shifts in diction or produce clashes of tonal register with the surrounding narrative. I refer back here to Jebb's initial shock at being unable to work out a consistency of tone in Timotheus' handling of the Persian characters in this text.[74] Yet we too might justifiably wonder what to make of a text

---

72 On the aesthetics of literary shock, see Felski (2008) 130–131: 'Shock thus teeters precariously between the threat of two forms of failure, caught between the potential humiliation of audience indifference and the permanent risk of outright and outraged refusal. An aesthetic that assaults our psyches and assails our vulnerabilities turns out to be all too vulnerable to the vagaries of audience response.' Where 'indifference' figures nicely a century and more of scholarly avoidance of Timotheus and 'refusal' nicely captures Platonic outrage (as well as that of the early modern critics of Timotheus we encountered earlier), recuperating aesthetic shock as a self-conscious act of recognizing lyric *thelxis* is a quintessential response to Timothean lyric; and it also helps us to appreciate the astonishing (?) ability of Timotheus to wow original and subsequent ancient audiences. For a different orientation of Felski on aesthetic shock to ancient lyric narrative with reference to Anacreon, see Fearn (forthcoming).

73 Again, these are extensions of affective qualities and challenges already inherent in earlier lyric narrative, perhaps especially that of Stesichorus, on which see Fearn (forthcoming), discussing in particular the interpretative challenges of *Geryoneis* S15 (fr. 19 Finglass).

74 See above, p. 208. Moreover, such shock at the tonal complexity of Timotheus' focus on Persian characters is of a piece with the broader sense of 'exoticism' detectable more widely across *Persae* (on which see further Gurd (2016) 118 for a reading of the language and sonic effect of the *sphragis* at lines 209–210 that has Timotheus potentially figure himself as a defeated Persian in the way the Spartan censure is described); exoticism is also a well-known characteristic of the ancient reception of the sophist Gorgias, for which e.g. Diodorus 12.53.2–4.

which alludes not only to Simonidean, Pindaric, and Bacchylidean lyric, but also to Aeschylus' *Persians* and *Oresteia* (in making, for instance, his own Xerxes speak in line 178 like the chorus of Aeschylus' *Choephoroe* line 50),[75] to a range of Euripidean (and other tragic)[76] and even Aristophanic passages;[77] and when we finally—and perhaps exhaustedly—reach the *sphragis* after listening to Xerxes' lament, we are, I suppose, left to wonder about the nature of our emotional reaction: are we to laugh, or cry?[78]

The nature of interpretative response to a glittering text is perhaps nowhere more markedly at stake than in the most famous extant piece of sophistic rhetoric, Gorgias' *Encomium of Helen*. This is the most obvious contemporary piece of writing to challenge conventional wisdom, inviting audiences to assess and reassess their own worldviews and their underpinnings, via a thoroughgoing re-evaluation of the relation between language, persuasion, and the

---

[75] Cf. Budelmann (2018) 241 ad loc.: the effect is jarring, disconcerting, and seemingly inappropriate. On Aeschylus in Timotheus' *Persae*, see esp. LeVen (2014) 182–183, 206–210; also Rosenbloom (2006) 151.

[76] For Euripides, see most notably Firinu (2009) on *IT*; LeVen (2014) 210–211 for links to the opening of *Medea* and also to lines 386–388; for the question of the relation between Timotheus' Phrygian and the Phrygian slave in Euripides' *Orestes*, LeVen (2014) 215.

[77] On Aristophanes, LeVen (2014) 214 and Hall (2006b) 279; Budelmann (2018) 245 for the intriguing suggestion that the *sphragis* also resembles Aristophanic parabases.

[78] In addition to the intertextual links with Euripides suggested by others, I would also point to possible links with other major tragic themes and passages, particularly in the Persian lamentations of lines 121 ff.: I suggest that Ἰλιοπόρος κακῶν λυαί- | α μόνα γένοιτ' ἄν (A crossing to Ilion would be the only release from ills) provides, first, a metatextual pointer to a Trojan, and specifiably tragic and Homeric, literary domain, and also an ironic reversal of wishes evoked about that space: ideas about what it might be like in future with Troy left behind, as evoked in, for instance, Aeschylus' *Oresteia* from its opening line, and more specifically in the sense of choral isolation, remoteness, and wish-fulfillment inherent in passages like Soph. *Aj.* 1185–1222 and esp. Eur. *Tro.* 190–229. The concluding phrase of the speech, ἔνθα κείσομαι οἰκτρός, ὀρ- | νίθων ἔθνεσιν ὠμοβρῶσι θοίνα (and here I shall lie, pitiable, a feast for the flesh-eating tribes of birds), lines 137–138, leaves us with a deictic that doesn't refer to Troy, but that provides a final intertextual cue to the Trojan (tragic and Homeric) literary landscape. Such Timothean intertextual games reverse the chain of tragic causation and wish-fulfillment, but also pay homage to contemporary tragedy, and in particular Euripides. What the effects of these intertextual plays and concomitant tonal shifts and disjunctions are, is, as often with Euripides, difficult to definitively evaluate (do we, for instance, want to pity this Persian?)—and I would suggest that this is a function of the sophistic density of Timotheus' interventions in *logos*. Intellectual challenges of this sort with Trojan and Persian subject-matter have been with us since at least as far back as Aeschylus' *Persae*, but with Timotheus the literary density of reference makes question of tone and interpretative response even more challenging and insistent.

poetic tradition.[79] With Gorgias, the glaring implausibility of the arguments put across about Helen's blamelessness is far more than a simple and ultimately pointless or insignificant ruse, because of the way Gorgias, through his strangely new encomiastic vehicle, makes audiences and readers think about the potential connections between power, persuasion, and language, and the ways that (literary) tradition, and thus convention, may condition us to behave and think.

What is also very important for Gorgias is a basic and indeed metaphysical question about the nature of reality, in terms of the relation between the surface effects of language and convention, and the existence of any ulterior structure that might convey truth: this basic issue is posed by the opening sentence of *Helen*:

Κόσμος πόλει μὲν εὐανδρία, σώματι δὲ κάλλος, ψυχῆι δὲ σοφία, πράγματι δὲ ἀρετή, λόγωι δὲ ἀλήθεια.

The adornment of a city is manpower,
of a body beauty,
 of a soul, wisdom,
  of an action, virtue,
   of a speech, truth.[80]

Kosmos here is the key term, delicately poised as it is between superficiality and deep structure. Robert Wardy teases out some of the intricacies of this opening:

> Since he immediately assures us that 'one should honour with praise what is worthy of praise, but attach blame to the unworthy', the purpose of the opening sentence is evidently to enumerate across a wide range of cases what might properly be the subject of an encomium. If so, then Gorgias' abstract designation of what deserves admiration is *kosmos*. But '*kosmos*' was, we will remember, a key-word in Parmenides: although the core-meaning of the word is 'order' or 'harmony', it extends to cover *speciously* attractive, imposed arrangements ... And does *alêtheia* here, the *kosmos* of *logos*, signify unvarnished 'truth', with the implication that Gorgias' *Encomium* in particular can achieve the excellence of *logos* only if it tells is a

---

79 Among key modern work on Gorgias' *Helen* I would highlight especially Wardy (1996) and Porter (2010) 276–298, though much more remains to be done.
80 Trans. Dillon, preserving the quasi-poetic quality of Gorgias' parallelisms with an ornate layout cleverly reminiscent of Nisetich's well-known translation of Pindar.

true story? If *kosmos* can regularly connote ornamentation and artifice, the danger is that a cosmetic *logos* may disguise rather than represent reality.[81]

Our anticipation that Gorgias may be building towards some deeper theory of truth is, of course, notoriously dashed, with the joke on us provided by the sting in the tail of Gorgias' avowedly self-indulgent *paignion* (§ 21).[82] Gorgias only leaves us with doubts about the possibility that there is in fact anything more to reality than a dependency on the dangerous instabilities of language and *nomos*, and the major challenges of getting beyond the superficialities of *kosmos* to an understanding of something beyond.[83]

As Wardy observes, the language of *kosmos* here is both traditionally encomiastic and philosophically suggestive.[84] We now need to recall that, within Timotheus' renegotiation of Pindaric material-cultural metaphor in what is likely to have been the opening of the *prooimion* of *Persae*, Timotheus himself uses the word *kosmos*, both to heap praise on the historical subject matter of his composition, and, implicity, figuring his own work:

κλεινὸν ἐλευθερίας τεύχων μέγαν Ἑλλάδι κόσμον.

Fashioning a famous and great adornment of freedom for Greece.
    fr. 788

Earlier I pointed towards two obvious lyric intertexts for this use of *kosmos*, both from Simonides. But if we are happy enough to acknowledge Timotheus' affiliations with sophistic thought more generally, we might like at least to countenance the possibility that Timotheus is also picking up Gorgias' usage (and if so this would be one more instance of a structural reference to the way another text opens, in addition to the presence of Pindar frr. 76–77 here). If so, Timotheus is perhaps discovering a fresh appropriateness in the conventional

---

81 Wardy (1996) 29–30, with 153n8 critiquing MacDowell's relatively flat interpretation of *kosmos* here (MacDowell [1982] 28 ad loc.); cf. Goldhill (2002) 54–59.
82 Wardy (1996) 50.
83 Cf. Porter (2010) 297–298.
84 See also Worman (2002) 157 on the Pindaric background to Gorgianic *kosmos*: 'the notion of appropriate adornment is also a Pindaric *topos* and most particular to praise speech. This epinician technique serves to establish the authority of the poet by demonstrating in visualizing terms his grasp of the proper order of things.' Also Worman (2002) 24, though her references are garbled; Slater (1969) s.v. for Pind. *Pyth.* 2.10, *Ol.* 3.13, 8.83, and 11.13, *Nem.* 2.8 and 3.31, *Isthm.* 6.69 and fr. 194.1; also *Pyth.* 3.82 for the adverbial sense 'fittingly'.

figurative language of traditional encomiastic praise when now seen through a contemporary Gorgianic filter.

If we take this possibility seriously, we may be able to make more of the peculiar appropriateness of picking up Gorgias' *kosmos*—delicately poised, as that clever usage is, between a sense of ordered structure and a potentially deceptive superficiality[85]—within the broader literary strategies of Timotheus' text. I suggested earlier that Timothean claims to *kosmos* for both his subject and his own poem are a programmatic statement of intent. If we now factor in Gorgias, it may be possible to sense in the usage an additional programmatic self-consciousness concerning a systematic tension, for the recipients of this poetry, between surface and structure, and between appearance and truth.

We might think, first, of an opposition between the dazzling and often perplexing charms of the linguistic surface of the text, and the possibilities of narrative absorption: here there are methodological similarities with the tension between 'absorption' and 'erudition' which is now seen as an important way in to thinking about classical visual art.[86]

We might also think in associated ways about Timotheus' attitude towards divinity, which, as we have seen in the case of Amphitrite may raise both representational and theological questions; we know independently that Euripides also took an interest in such issues, especially since he promotes a naturalistic and proto-euhemeristic theological outlook of the sophist Prodicus at *Bacchae* 274–285. Perhaps Timotheus is again making a virtue of contemporary sophistic theorizing here.[87]

And finally, we might ask broader questions about the kinds of response appropriate to a complex poetics of this nature. If Timotheus' *Persae* is itself a kind of encomium, what is its point, and to what extent is it, in any sense, true? How meaningful for a late fifth-century audience (of whatever kind) is Timotheus' extraordinarily stylized and at times bizarrely narrated praise of an historical event and its participants which, though highly significant, have

---

85 Cf. also Goldhill (2002) 55.
86 For which see Newby (2009), further elaborated by Platt (2011); ultimately Fried (1980). This is a tension I have explored heuristically for the complexities of earlier lyric: for Pindar in Fearn (2017) esp. ch. 2; additionally in relation to Anacreon, Stesichorus, and Bacchylides in Fearn (forthcoming); cf. also Felski (2008) 76, concluding a discussion of the importance of literary enchantment: 'Once we face up to the limits of demystification as a critical method and a theoretical ideal, once we relinquish the modern dogma that our lives should become thoroughly disenchanted, we can truly begin to engage the affective and absorptive, the sensuous and somatic qualities of aesthetic experience.'
87 On Prodicus see Guthrie (1971) 279 and 238–241, citing the Euripides passage; also Lloyd (1987) 48. Cf. Whitmarsh (2014) on the Sisyphus fragment.

now stagily become rather remote and objectified, and even mythologized or fictionalized—especially after, for instance, Aeschylus' *Persians*, Herodotus' *Histories*, and the representations of barbarians in late fifth-century tragedy and comedy?[88]

These are very difficult questions to answer, but I suggest that Timotheus' highly stylized lyric is raising them, in part to highlight the distinctiveness and creativity of his own talent, inspired both by the lyric tradition and by a broader sense of fifth-century literary history down to the sophists.

In this sense, we can appreciate afresh why paying attention to Timothean poetics matters. It helps us to reassess the extent to which important texts of fourth-century Greek literary / performance culture were already concerned with their own status and pedigrees. In our case, this goes well beyond Timotheus' surface foregrounding of lyrical innovation, the Spartan tradition, and Terpander in lines 202–233. He provides further evidence for the deeper intellectual sophistication and self-consciousness of the New Music, especially in its connections with sophistic rhetoric.

This provides a sense of the importance of the continuities within lyric literary history. Timothean lyric not only reminds us of the links with the earlier archaic and classical lyric tradition, but is also a sign of what was to follow in the Hellenistic period, especially in the mixing of intellectual/philosophical and literary-historical concerns within Greek poetics.[89] As well as a stunning, perplexing, and (originally at least) immensely successful piece of popular culture, Timotheus may usefully be read as a lyric test-bed, a sign of broader poetic and cultural self-reflection on the nature of language and the issue of literary referentiality: that is, lyric's place in the world.

---

88 For the latter, Hall (1989, 2006a); Croally (1994) 103–115. For important recent work on fictionality in Old Comedy, see Ruffell (2011), esp. 35–43. For questions about the identification and significance of a first performance context for *Persae*, see e.g. Power (2010) 526, with 410 BCE as a suggested date: '[A]fter the victory of the Athenian fleet at Cyzicus in the spring of 410 over combined Peloponnesian and Persian forces, which was followed shortly by the collapse of the oligarchic government in Athens, it would have been heard too as an epinician celebration of Athenian naval success: Salamis would stand as a kind of heroic exemplar for current victories, echoing them on a grand mythic historic stage;' alternatively see the very different position of Rosenbloom (2006) 149, for whom a first performance in Ephesus in 394 is preferred; Gurd (2016) 118 thinks of Miletus; Budelmann (2018) 234 suggests Athens (though circumspectly). My own feeling, outlined here, is that the highly sophisticated literary and tonal complexity of *Persae* makes references across to performance context as a bridge to explanation of the text's point or function rather moot.

89 On Callimachus especially, see scholarly trends discussed in e.g. Acosta-Hughes and Stephens (2012); cf. Lightfoot (2013) 156–157.

References

Acosta-Hughes, B. and Stephens, S.A. 2012. *Callimachus in Context: From Plato to the Augustan Poets*. Cambridge.

Agocs, P. 2012. Performance and Genre: Reading Pindar's κῶμοι. In *Reading the Victory Ode*, ed. P. Agocs, C. Carey, and R. Rawles, 191–223. Cambridge.

Allan, W. 1999–2000. Euripides and the Sophists: Society and the Theatre of War. *ICS* 24(5): 145–156.

Bassett, S.E. 1931. The Place and Date of the First Performance of the *Persians* of Timotheus. *CPh* 26: 153–165.

Battezzato, L. 2013. Dithyramb and Greek Tragedy. In Kowalzig and Wilson 2013: 93–110.

Budelmann, F. ed. 2018. *Greek Lyric: A Selection*. Cambridge.

Budelmann, F. and LeVen, P.A. 2014. Timotheus' Poetics of Blending: A Cognitive Approach to the Language of the New Music. *CPh* 109: 191–210.

Burnett, A.P. 1985. *The Art of Bacchylides*. Cambridge, MA.

Carey, C. 1999. Ethos and Pathos in Bacchylides. In *One Hundred Years of Bacchylides: Proceedings of a Colloquium Held at the Vrije Universiteit Amsterdam on 17 October 1997*, ed. I.L. Pfeijffer and S.R. Slings, 17–29. Amsterdam.

Calame, C. 1996. *Thésée et l'Imaginaire Athénien: Légende et culte en Grèce antique*. 2nd rev. edn. Lausanne.

Calame, C. 2009. Apollo in Delphi and Delos: Poetic Performances between Paean and Dithyramb. In *Apolline Politics and Poetics*, ed. L. Athanassaki, R. Martin, and J.F. Miller, 169–197. Athens.

Castriota, D. 1992. *Myth, Ethos and Actuality: Official Art in Fifth-Century B.C. Athens*. Madison.

Conacher, D.J. 1998. *Euripides and the Sophists*. London.

Croally, N. 1994. *Euripidean Polemic:* The Trojan Women *and the Function of Tragedy*. Cambridge.

Csapo, E. 1999–2000. Later Euripidean Music. *ICS* 24(5): 399–426.

Csapo, E. 2004. The Politics of the New Music. In Murray and Wilson 2004: 207–248.

Csapo, E. 2011. The Economics, Poetics, Politics, Metaphysics and Ethics of the "New Music". In *Music and Cultural Politics in Greek and Chinese Societies. Volume I: Greek Antiquity*, ed. D. Yatromanolakis, 65–131. Cambridge, MA.

Csapo, E. and Wilson, P. 2009. Timotheus the New Musician. In *The Cambridge Companion to Greek Lyric*, ed. F. Budelmann, 277–294. Cambridge.

D'Alessio, G.B. 2013. "The Name of the Dithyramb": Diachronic and Diatopic Variations. In Kowalzig and Wilson 2013: 113–132.

D'Angour, A. 2006. The New Music—So What's New? In *Rethinking Revolutions through Ancient Greece*, ed. S. Goldhill and R. Osborne, 264–283. Cambridge.

Fearn, D.W. 2007. *Bacchylides: Politics, Performance, Poetic Tradition*. Oxford.

Fearn, D.W. 2010. Imperialist Fragmentation and the Discovery of Bacchylides. In *Classics and Imperialism in the British Empire*, ed. M. Bradley, 158–185. Oxford.

Fearn, D.W. 2013a. Athens and the Empire: The Contextual Flexibility of Dithyramb and its Imperialist Ramifications. In Kowalzig and Wilson 2013: 133–152.

Fearn, D.W. 2013b. *Kleos* v stone? Lyric Poetry and Contexts for Memorialization. In *Inscriptions and their Uses in Greek and Latin Literature*, ed. P. Liddel and P. Low, 231–253. Oxford.

Fearn, D.W. 2017. *Pindar's Eyes: Visual and Material Culture in Epinician Poetry*. Oxford.

Fearn, D.W. 2018. Materialities of Political Commitment? Textual Events, Material Culture, and Metaliterarity in Alcaeus. In *Textual Events: Performance and the Lyric in Early Greece*, ed. F. Budelmann and T. Phillips, 93–113. Oxford.

Fearn, D.W. forthcoming. The Allure of Narrative in Greek Lyric Poetry. In *Under the Spell of Stories: Experience, Narrative and Criticism in Ancient Greece*, ed. J. Grethlein, L. Huitink and A. Tagliabue. Oxford.

Felski, R. 2008. *Uses of Literature*. Malden, MA.

Felski, R. 2015. *The Limits of Critique*. Chicago.

Felson, N., ed. 2004. *The Poetics of Deixis in Alcman, Pindar, and Other Lyric. Arethusa* Special Issue, 37(3).

Firinu, E. 2009. Il primo stasimo dell'*Ifigenia Taurica* euripidea e i *Persiani* di Timoteo di Mileto: un terminus post quem per il nomos? *Eikasmos* 20: 109–131.

Franklin, J.C. 2013. "Songbenders of Circular Choruses": Dithyramb and the 'Demise of Music.' In Kowalzig and Wilson 2013: 213–236.

Fried, M. 1980. *Absorption and Theatricality: Painting and Beholder in the Age of Diderot*. Berkeley.

Goldhill, S. 1999. Review of D. Conacher *Euripides and the Sophists. BMCR* 1999.01.18.

Goldhill, S. 2002. *The Invention of Prose*. Oxford.

Gurd, S.A. 2016. *Dissonance: Auditory Aesthetics in Ancient Greece*. New York.

Guthrie, W.K.C. 1969. *A History of Greek Philosophy Volume Three: The Fifth-Century Enlightenment*. Cambridge.

Guthrie, W.K.C. 1971. *The Sophists*. Cambridge.

Hall, E. 1989. *Inventing the Barbarian*. Oxford.

Hall, E. 1993. Drowning by Nomes: The Greeks, Swimming, and Timotheus' *Persians*. In *The Birth of European Identity: the Europe-Asia Contrast in Greek Thought 490–322 B.C.*, ed. H.A. Khan, 44–80. Nottingham.

Hall, E. 2006a. Recasting the Barbarian. In *The Theatrical Cast of Athens: Interactions between Ancient Greek Drama and Society*, ed. E. Hall, 184–224. Oxford.

Hall, E. 2006b. Drowning Act: The Greeks, Swimming, and Timotheus' *Persians*. In *The Theatrical Cast of Athens: Interactions between Ancient Greek Drama and Society*, ed. E. Hall, 255–287. Oxford.

Hordern, J.H. 2002. *The Fragments of Timotheus of Miletus*. Oxford.

Hunter, V. 1986. Thucydides, Gorgias, and Mass Psychology. *Hermes* 114: 412–429.
Jebb, C. 1905. *Bacchylides: The Poems and Fragments*. Cambridge.
Jebb, C. 1907. *Life and Letters of Sir Richard Claverhouse Jebb*. Cambridge.
Kenyon, F.G. 1918. Greek Papyri and their Contribution to Classical Literature: A Paper Communicated to the Leeds Branch of the Classical Association at its Fourth Annual Meeting, 26 January 1918.
Kirkwood, G.M. 1980. Review of M.R. Lefkowitz, *The Victory Ode: An Introduction*. *CPh* 75: 158–160.
Kowalzig, B. and Wilson, P., eds. 2013. *Dithyramb in Context*. Oxford.
Kranz, W. 1933. *Stasimon: Untersuchungen zu Form und Gehalt der griechischen Tragödie*. Berlin.
Kugelmeier, C. 1996. *Reflexe früher und zeitgenössicher Lyrik in der Alten attischen Komödie*. Stuttgart.
Lada, I. 1993. "Empathetic Understanding": Emotion and Cognition in Classical Dramatic Audience-Response. *PCPhS* 39: 94–140.
Lavecchia, S. 2000. *Pindari dithyramborum fragmenta*. Rome.
LeVen, P.A. 2014. *The Many-Headed Muse: Tradition and Innovation in Late Classical Greek Lyric Poetry*. Cambridge.
Lightfoot, J. 2013. Review Article: Callimachus. *JHS* 133: 147–157.
Lloyd, G.E.R. 1987. *The Revolutions of Wisdom: Studies in the Claims and Practice of Ancient Greek Science*. Berkeley.
MacDowell, D. 1982. *Gorgias: Encomium of Helen*. Bristol.
Maehler, H. 1982/1997. *Die Lieder des Bakchylides, I Die Siegeslieder; II Die Dithyramben und Fragmente*. *Mnemosyne* Supplements 62 and 167. Leiden.
Maehler, H. 2003. *Bacchylidis carmina cum fragmentis*. 11th edition. Munich.
Maehler, H. 2004. *Bacchylides: A Selection*. Cambridge.
Murray, P. and Wilson, P., eds. 2004. *Music and the Muses: The Culture of "Mousikē" in the Classical Athenian City*. Oxford.
Newby, Z. 2009. Absorption and Erudition in Philostratus' *Imagines*. In *Philostratus*, ed. E.L. Bowie and J. Elsner, 322–342. Cambridge.
Peponi, A.-E. 2013. Dithyramb in Greek Thought: The Problem of Choral Mimesis. In Kowalzig and Wilson 2013: 353–367.
Platt, V.J. 2011. *Facing the Gods: Epiphany and Representation in Graeco-Roman Art, Literature and Religion*. Cambridge.
Pfeijffer, I.L. and Slings, S.R. 1999. One Hundred Years of Bacchylides: An Introduction. In *One Hundred Years of Bacchylides: Proceedings of a Colloquium Held at the Vrije Universiteit Amsterdam on 17 October 1997*, ed. I.L. Pfeijffer and S.R. Slings, 7–15. Amsterdam.
Porter, J.I. 2010. *The Origins of Aesthetic Thought in Ancient Greece: Matter, Sensation, and Experience*. Cambridge.

Power, T. 2010. *The Culture of Kitharôidia*. Washington, DC.
Power, T. 2013. Kyklops *Kitharoidos*: Dithyramb and Nomos in Play. In Kowalzig and Wilson 2013: 237–256.
Rosenbloom, D.S. 2006. *Aeschylus Persians*. London.
Ruffell, I.A. 2011. *Politics and Anti-realism in Athenian Old Comedy: The Art of the Impossible*. Oxford.
Segal, C.P. 1976. Bacchylides Reconsidered: Epithets and the Dynamics of Lyric Narrative. *QUCC* 22: 99–130.
Sevieri, R., ed. 2011. *Timoteo: I Persiani*. Milan.
Slater, W.J. 1969. *Lexicon to Pindar*. Berlin.
Spelman, H. 2018. *Pindar the Poetics of Permanence*. Oxford.
Stern, J. 1970. An Essay on Bacchylidean Criticism. In *Pindaros und Bakchylides. Wege der Forschung* Band 134, ed. W.M. Calder and J. Stern, 290–307. Darmstadt.
Torrance, I. 2013. *Metapoetry in Euripides*. Oxford.
Wardy, R. 1996. *The Birth of Rhetoric: Gorgias, Plato and their Successors*. London.
Whitmarsh, T. 2014. Atheistic Aesthetics: The Sisyphyus Fragment, Poetics and the Creativity of Drama. *PCPhS* 60: 109–126.
Worman, N. 2002. *The Cast of Character: Style in Greek Literature*. Austin.

CHAPTER 10

"Total Reception": Stesichorus as Revenant in Plato's *Phaedrus* (with a New Stesichorean Fragment?)

Andrea Capra

1   Introduction*

ἐμοὶ μὲν οὖν, ὦ φίλε, καθήρασθαι ἀνάγκη· ἔστιν δὲ τοῖς ἁμαρτάνουσι περὶ μυθολογίαν καθαρμὸς ἀρχαῖος, ὃν Ὅμηρος μὲν οὐκ ᾔσθετο, Στησίχορος δέ. τῶν γὰρ ὀμμάτων στερηθεὶς διὰ τὴν Ἑλένης κακηγορίαν οὐκ ἠγνόησεν ὥσπερ Ὅμηρος, ἀλλ᾽ ἅτε μουσικὸς ὢν ἔγνω τὴν αἰτίαν, καὶ ποιεῖ εὐθὺς

οὐκ ἔστ᾽ ἔτυμος λόγος οὗτος,
οὐδ᾽ ἔβας ἐν νηυσὶν εὐσέλμοις,
οὐδ᾽ ἵκεο Πέργαμα Τροίας

καὶ ποιήσας δὴ πᾶσαν τὴν καλουμένην Παλινῳδίαν παραχρῆμα ἀνέβλεψεν. ἐγὼ οὖν σοφώτερος ἐκείνων γενήσομαι κατ᾽ αὐτό γε τοῦτο· πρὶν γάρ τι παθεῖν διὰ τὴν τοῦ Ἔρωτος κακηγορίαν πειράσομαι αὐτῷ ἀποδοῦναι τὴν παλινῳδίαν, γυμνῇ τῇ κεφαλῇ καὶ οὐχ ὥσπερ τότε ὑπ᾽ αἰσχύνης ἐγκεκαλυμμένος

So I, my friend, must purify myself, and for those who offend in the telling of stories there is an ancient method of purification, which Homer did not understand, but Stesichorus did. For when he was deprived of his sight because of his slander against Helen, he did not fail to understand, like Homer; because he was a true follower of the Muses, he knew the cause, and immediately composed the verses: 'This is not a genuine *logos*, / you made no journey in the well-decked ships / Nor voyaged to the citadel of Troy'. And after composing the whole of the so-called Palinode he at

---

* I have presented part of this chapter at the Research Symposium of the Harvard Center for Hellenic Studies in April 2012 ('Socrates Plays Stesichorus'; see http://www.chs-fellows.org/2012/05/09/socrates-plays-stesichorus-2/ [last accessed: 22/09/2019]). Warm thanks to the audience for their support and precious feedback and warm thanks, also, to Lucia Floridi and George Gazis, who found the time to read the chapter and comment on it. In ch. 1 of Capra (2014) I further develop Plato's engagement with Stesichorus, in a perspective that, in contrast to the present contribution, pursues the relevant implications for Platonic studies.

once regained his sight. So I shall follow a wiser course than Stesichorus and Homer in just this respect: I shall try to render my palinode to Love before anything happens to me because of my slander against him, with my head bare, and not covered as it was before for shame … for you see how shameless the speeches were, this second one and the one which was read from the book.

Phaedrus 243a–c, trans. ROWE, modified

This chapter argues that Plato's reception of Stesichorus' Helen in the *Phaedrus* amounts to a multifaceted re-enactment and somehow "resurrects" Stesichorus' Helen performance. As such, as we shall see, it bears on all of the three main areas of the present volume: transmission, canonization, and paratext. My conclusion will focus on Plato's appropriation of Stesichorus from a *performative* point of view, which can be construed as a form of comprehensive, "total", reception.

1.1 A Stesichorean Pastiche?

Socrates' three-line quote from Stesichorus is the culmination of a poetic climax, whereby Socrates presents himself as an inspired poet.[1] Socrates' inspiration is not limited to his famous palinode, which the quoted passage introduces, but concerns also his first, impious speech, which requires 'purification'. This first speech begins with a curious invocation to the Muses:

ἄγετε δή, ὦ Μοῦσαι, εἴτε δι' ᾠδῆς εἶδος λίγειαι, εἴτε διὰ γένος μουσικὸν τὸ Λιγύων ταύτην ἔσχετ' ἐπωνυμίαν, 'ξύμ μοι λάβεσθε' τοῦ μύθου

Come then, you Muses, clear-voiced (*ligeiai*), whether you are called that for the nature of your song, or whether you acquired this name because of the musical nature of the Ligurians, 'take part with me' in the myth.

Phaedrus 237a, trans. ROWE, modified

After this extravagant beginning, which made Dionysus of Halicarnassus jump out of his skin,[2] this same speech ends on an equally poetic note, that is with some kind of epic verse, although there are philological complications and (at least) two different texts are possible (a and b):[3]

---

1 References to Socrates' inspiration are listed below, n. 50.
2 Dion. Hal. *Dem.* 7.9 ff.
3 I discuss the text below, pp. 242–244.

(a) ὡς λύκοι ἄρνας ἀγαπῶσιν, ὡς παῖδα φιλοῦσιν ἐρασταί
(b) ὡς λύκοι ἄρν' ἀγαπῶσ', ὡς παῖδα φιλοῦσιν ἐρασταί

just as wolves love the lamb, so is lovers' affection for a boy.
Phaedrus 241d, trans. ROWE[4]

A bit further, Socrates claims that he is beginning to deliver *epē* (ἤδη ἔπη φθέγγομαι).[5] Scholars construe *epē* as 'hexameter verses', which is why, as we shall see, they tend to favour text (b), a more obviously hexametrical line. However that may be, Socrates' first speech is marked by a poetic beginning as well as by a poetic close, and as such it matches his palinode, which Socrates himself explicitly describes as a poetic achievement.[6] In this respect, we may conclude that Socrates, like Stesichorus, launches into both "ode" and "palinode". As is clear from Socrates' extensive quotation, Stesichorus is a model for Socrates' pious palinode. However, to what extent, if any, is he a model for Socrates' impious "ode"?

Let me begin with a point of vocabulary, namely the strange poetic beginning of Socrates' first speech, as he summons the Muses in the passage quoted above. One striking feature is surely the epithet *ligeiai*: this is the only place in extant classical prose to feature this adjective. In archaic poetry, the form *ligeia* usually modifies the *phorminx*. Only occasionally does it modify the Muse(s):[7] no individual Greek poet seems to have more than one such instance.[8] The one exception seems to be Stesichorus, who apparently uses it *twice* to refer to the Muses:

δεῦρ' ἄγε Καλλιόπεια λίγεια[9]

ἄγε Μοῦσα λίγει' ἄρξον ἀοιδᾶς ἐρατωνύμου
Σαμίων περὶ παίδων ἐρατᾷ φθεγγομένα λύρᾳ[10]

---

4 On balance, Rowe favours text a. See Rowe (1986), ad loc.
5 *Phdr.* 241e ('By now I'm uttering *epe*').
6 *Phdr.* 257a, quoted below.
7 E.g. Hom. *Od.* 24.62, Pind. fr. 520.32.
8 That is, if we discard the *Homeric Hymns*, in which the epithet is relatively frequent. Alcman, however, comes very close: see frr. 14 (the adjective modifies a Muse) and 30 (it modifies a Siren).
9 Fr. 240 (= 177 Finglass) 'Come hither, clear-voiced Calliopeia' (trans. Campbell).
10 Fr. 278 (= 327 Finglass) 'Come clear-voiced Muse, begin your song of lovely repute about the Samian children, saying to your lovely lyre' (trans. Campbell. The poem is classified among the *Spuria*, but is in fact likely to be authentic. See below, n. 39).

The analogy with Socrates' invocation is apparent: note the verb *ago*, and note also that the subject of the second fragment is paederotic. Accordingly, Socrates seems to be summoning a "Stesichorean" Muse.

Another strange feature of Socrates' invocation is his strange request for cooperation as opposed to full inspiration (ξύμ μοι λάβεσθε). This reminds one of Stesichorus' *Oresteia* as quoted in Aristophanes' *Peace*, which also have the same exceptional 'with me' motif:

Μοῖσα σὺ μὲν πολέμους ἀπωσαμένα πεδ' ἐμεῦ[11]

In sum, one might begin to suspect that Socrates' invocation is a Stesichorean pastiche, containing snatches of genuine Stesichorus.[12] Its culmination, I argue, comes at the conclusion of Socrates' first speech quoted above in two different versions. It is now time to delve into this problematic text.

At the end of Socrates' first speech the manuscripts feature a quasi-hexameter (ὡς λύκοι ἄρνας ἀγαπῶσιν, ὡς παῖδα φιλοῦσιν ἐρασταί), which is what one reads in Burnet's venerable OCT edition. Yet more recent editors and commentators tend to print a different text, resulting in a full hexameter line (ὡς λύκοι ἄρν' ἀγαπῶσ', ὡς παῖδα φιλοῦσιν ἐρασταί).[13] The grounds alleged for emending the text are the following: first, there is some support from the indirect tradition, as Hermogenes and Hermias of Alexandria testify to the existence of ancient variants featuring a full hexameter line;[14] second, as we have seen, Socrates claims he is uttering *epē*: accordingly, Cambridge "Yellow-and-Green" commentator Harvey Yunis goes as far as to say that 'it is certain that Plato composed a hexameter verse for this spot';[15] third, the hexameter restored by Yunis and other editors is slightly irregular, in that it violates Hermann's bridge, just like an equally irregular hexameter verse that Socrates will utter later.[16] Accordingly,

---

11   Fr. 210.1 (= 172.1 Finglass) 'Muse, thrust aside wars and with me'.
12   Hunter (2015) 146–151, discusses this passage as an example of rhetorical sweetness. While he does not pinpoint the Stesichorean features of the passage, he mentions it in a context devoted to 'sweetness' and to 'sweet' Stesichorus, which results in the suggestion that the 'invocation to the Muse at 237a was not generally "lyric" but specifically Stesichorean' (151).
13   See e.g. Hackforth (1952); de Vries (1969) with further bibliography; Yunis (2011).
14   See the *Belles Lettres* apparatus by Claudio Moreschini: ἄρν'ἀγαπῶσ' HERMIAS 61,26 Bekker ἄρνα φιλοῦσιν HERMIAS 61,7 Stephan. ἄρνα φιλεῦσ' HERMOG. (Moreschini [1985]. Note that Moreschini prints the mss. text, while the *note complémentaire ad* 61,7 does not rule out the text given by Hermias).
15   Yunis (2011), ad loc.
16   *Phdr.* 252b–c; see below, p. 243.

nobody less than Jules Labarbe, a major expert on "Plato's Homer", interpreted the violation as Plato's jocular signature, designed to mark verses of his own making: on this view, the very irregularity of the hexameter line, somewhat paradoxically, is turned into an argument against the non-hexametric text of the manuscripts.[17]

In my opinion, none of these arguments is persuasive. First, the indirect tradition is clearly inconsistent: Hermias has two different hexameters, both differing from that found in Hermogenes, while both authors explicitly connect Socrates' claim to epic with the crafting of the hexameter. This seems to reflect three independent attempts at creating a full hexameter line so as to confirm Socrates' claim to epic inspiration, which is precisely the agenda of modern editors keen on correcting the medieval manuscripts. While it is understandable that ancient readers and copyists could be tempted to alter the text so as to create a full hexameter verse, the reverse scenario—a full hexameter came to be corrupted in the tradition—is very unlikely, because the metre tends of course to protect the original wording. Second, *epē* does not have to mean 'hexameter lines', but can refer equally well to the quasi-epic verse of Stesichorus, as both Pausanias and Plato's pupil Heraclides Ponticus attest.[18] To be sure, Plato's usage of *epē* is flexible enough to accommodate even lyric poetry, as is clear from the *Protagoras*, in which the word refers to a song by Simonides.[19] Third, the parallel with Socrates' quotation from the Homeridae simply backfires. Let us have a look at the relevant passage:

λέγουσι δὲ οἶμαί τινες Ὁμηριδῶν ἐκ τῶν ἀποθέτων ἐπῶν δύο ἔπη εἰς τὸν ἔρωτα,
ὧν τὸ ἕτερον ὑβριστικὸν πάνυ καὶ οὐ σφόδρα τι ἔμμετρον· ὑμνοῦσι δὲ ὧδε
  τὸν δ' ἤτοι θνητοὶ μὲν ἔρωτα καλοῦσι ποτηνόν,
  ἀθάνατοι δὲ Πτέρωτα, διὰ πτεροφύτορ' ἀνάγκην.

I think some of the Homeridae cite two verses from the less well-known poems, the second of which is quite outrageous and not very metrical: they celebrate him like this:
  'We mortals call him Mighty Love, a winged power of great renown,
  Immortals call him Fledgeling Dove—since Eros' wings lack down'.
    Phaedrus 252b, trans. ROWE, modified

---

17 See Labarbe (1994). 'Plato's Homer' echoes the title of his famous book, Labarbe (1949).
18 Paus. 9.11.2, Heraclid. Pont. 109.23.
19 338e.

By assigning them to the Homeridae in a dialogue that so fiercely criticizes Homer, Socrates is likely to be discrediting these two lines. He openly comments on the shameless irregularity of the second one, and the violation of Hermann's bridge found in the first one might be part of the same derogatory game.[20] In sum, the third argument is as unconvincing as the first two.

As I hope to have made clear, there is nothing wrong with the manuscripts and we should retain their non-hexametric reading, i.e. ὡς λύκοι ἄρνας ἀγαπῶσιν, ὣς παῖδα φιλοῦσιν ἐρασταί. What are we left with, then? In my view, Socrates' very last words *do* form a complete verse anyway, as should be clear from the following outline:

(a) ὣς παῖδα φιλοῦσιν ἐρασταί   (*Phdr.* 241d1, final words of Socrates' first speech)
− − ∪ ∪ − ∪ ∪ − ×

≈ (b) Οὐκ ἔστ' ἔτυμος λόγος οὗτος   (192.1, i.e. line 1 of palinode according to Plato)[21]
≈ (c) οὐδ' ἵκεο Πέργαμα Τροίας   (192.3, i.e. line 3 of palinode according to Plato)
≈ (d) Δεῦρ' αὖτε θεὰ φιλόμολπε   (193, *incipit* of palinode 1, given by Chamaeleon)[22]
≈ (e) Χρυσόπτερε πάρθενε ⟨- x⟩[23]   (193, *incipit* of palinode 2, given by Chamaeleon)

I have no intention of venturing through metrical technicalities, as my point is a straightforward one: Socrates' final words (ὣς παῖδα φιλοῦσιν ἐρασταί) amount to precisely the type of verse we find in Stesichorus' palinode. To begin with, they scan exactly like two of the three verses that Socrates quotes from Stesichorus' palinode to introduce his second speech (b and c). Even more importantly, they scan like the very beginning of Stesichorus' twofold palinode as quoted by Chamaeleon (d and e). To the ears of Plato's original audiences, then, Socrates' final words, by conforming to Stesichorus' metre, *announced the rhythm of the palinode*. This is why Socrates claims he is uttering *epē*, a term that in this context we should refrain from rendering with 'hexameter lines'.

I have discussed a sample of lexical, philological, and metrical factors, but the main point is that Socrates' quotation of Stesichorus is in fact much more than a quotation, as it involves a number of interrelated dimensions and suggests that both speeches of Socrates are remarkably "Stesichorean". I will now

---

20   Otherwise we should conclude that the first line was not problematic to Plato's ears, as Cantilena (2007) plausibly argues. This would be just as fatal to Labarbe's argument.
21   192 *PMG* = 91a Finglass; 193 *PMG* = 90 Finglass.
22   I am of course referring to P.Oxy 2506 fr. 26 col. I, where Chamaeleon famously refers to two palinodes by Stesichorus. See below, p. 252.
23   ⟨Μοῖσα⟩ suppl. West. Quite possibly a Siren: see Cerri (1984–1985).

develop this point and test it against three main perspectives, namely transmission, canonization, and paratexts.

2 The Transmission through Antiquity

The transmission of poetry through antiquity entails a dynamic relationship between individual authors and groups of performers, most famously in the case of Homer and the Homeridae. Similarly, can lyric personae be understood as performance traditions? As Jesús Carruesco has recently noticed, 'the fact that Stesichorus is nominally cited alongside Homer in a poem by Simonides confirms the role assigned to him as the paramount representative of a poetic tradition', a foundational status that 'is also suggested by the change of his name in the biographical tradition, from Tisias to Stesichorus'.[24] This provides a convenient starting point for the present paragraph.

As a preliminary move, it is important to note that both Homer and the Homeridae are mentioned in the *Phaedrus*. Moreover, the opposition between Stesichorus and Homer has to do with the former's ability to correct himself: insofar as he is *mousikos*, Stesichorus, unlike Homer, made amends and regained his sight, and Socrates closely follows in his footsteps. By adopting the persona of Stesichorus, Socrates can compare unfavourably the fixed impersonal discourse of Homer with the flexible personal speech of the lyric poet, who can 'know the cause'—note the philosophical touch—and adapt his song accordingly. This implicit tension between "lyric" and "rhapsodic" forms of discourse becomes quite explicit towards the end of the dialogue, when Socrates makes a strange comparison in order to describe his ideal writer:

> Ὁ δέ γε ἐν μὲν τῷ γεγραμμένῳ λόγῳ περὶ ἑκάστου παιδιάν τε ἡγούμενος πολλὴν ἀναγκαῖον εἶναι, καὶ οὐδένα πώποτε λόγον ἐν μέτρῳ οὐδ' ἄνευ μέτρου μεγάλης ἄξιον σπουδῆς γραφῆναι οὐδὲ λεχθῆναι, ὡς οἱ ῥαψῳδούμενοι ἄνευ ἀνακρίσεως καὶ διδαχῆς πειθοῦς ἕνεκα ἐλέχθησαν, ἀλλὰ τῷ ὄντι αὐτῶν τοὺς βελτίστους εἰδότων ὑπόμνησιν γεγονέναι … οὗτος δὲ ὁ τοιοῦτος ἀνὴρ κινδυνεύει, ὦ Φαῖδρε, εἶναι οἷον ἐγώ τε καὶ σὺ εὐξαίμεθ' ἂν σέ τε καὶ ἐμὲ γενέσθαι.

> But the man who thinks that there is necessarily much that is merely for amusement in a written speech on any subject, and that none has ever yet been written, whether in verse or in prose, which is worth much seri-

---

24   Carruesco (2017) 181. The reference is to Simonides 564 *PMG*.

ous attention—or indeed spoken, in the way the rhapsodes speak theirs, to produce conviction without questioning or teaching, but that the best of them have really been a way of reminding people who know ... this is likely to be the sort of man, Phaedrus, that you and I would pray that we both might come to be.

PLATO *Phaedrus* 277e–278b, trans. ROWE

This ideal writer, who does not take writing too seriously and who prefers 'genuine *logoi*' (*gnesious*) is of course the philosopher, as Socrates promptly remarks.[25] The 'genuine' discourse of lyric-philosophy is thus contrasted with the 'spurious' (*ouk etymos*) discourse of rhapsody-rhetoric.

Socrates identifies fixed discourse, i.e. current rhetoric, with static Homeric rhapsodies, and in so doing he adopts the persona of 'musical' Stesichorus as opposed to that of non-musical Homer, i.e. to the fixed text of Homer as monumentalized and recited by rhapsodes. This is highly significant from a cultural point of view, in that it builds on the historical opposition 'Rhapsodes versus Stesichorus', the title of a seminal article by Walter Burkert.[26] In the sixth century, the rivalry revolved around, or even resulted in, highly musical performances of Stesichorus' songs as opposed to the rhapsodes' abandoning of 'the element of *music* and the element of improvisation in favour of a fixed text'. Thus the rhapsodes were 'ousted from the field of music', and reacted by sticking to a fixed text to be recited, thus promoting the first ever 'separation of performer and author'.[27] The opposition between 'Homer' and 'Stesichorus', then, is by and large one between two rival poetic traditions as embodied in two distinct poetic personae: contrast the Homeric rhapsode, who in the *Hymn to Apollo* famously emphasizes blindness, with Stesichorus' regained sight in the Palinode. All of this is especially significant in an Athenian context: not only did the Panathenaea regularly stage the rhapsodic performances of the Homeridae, but, as Ewen Bowie has recently suggested, Stesichorean performances seem to have had a major role in Athens from an early age.[28] The two traditions probably evolved side by side, but one may imagine that in the long run the gradual shift from orality to literacy proved more favourable to Homer's "fixed" and less "musical" text.

25 *Phdr.* 278d.
26 Burkert (1987). Further discussion in Sbardella (2012) 223–244.
27 Burkert (1987) 53 and 55. Cassio (2012) argues that Stesichorus reworked Homer's text, one that—he claims—was already relatively fixed.
28 Bowie (2015).

2.1 Canonization and Its Victims

Canonization is of course a matter of choosing, as the success of canonized texts is only possible insofar as other texts are left behind. As we have seen, Socrates revives the quarrel between Stesichorus and the rhapsodes. Both parties could lay claim to canonization, but it would have been impossible to deny Homer the status of a canonical author and to strip him entirely of his Athenian and Panhellenic honours, except of course in Plato's dream-city: indeed, Plato notoriously ousts Homer from his *kallipolis*. The *Phaedrus*, however, is firmly rooted in Athenian society and culture: although Homer is unfavourably compared with Stesichorus, the radical solution put forth in the *Republic* is in fact unavailable here. This does not rule out the possibility of *staging* the very process of canonization, even though, predictably, the ultimate victim cannot be Homer himself, if not indirectly. Yet Plato has a brilliant solution in store.

Socrates' palinode closes with a strange apotropaic prayer, which is meant to remind the reader of Stesichorus' averted blindness:

> Αὕτη σοι, ὦ φίλε Ἔρως, εἰς ἡμετέραν δύναμιν ὅτι καλλίστη καὶ ἀρίστη δέδοταί τε καὶ ἐκτέτεισται παλινῳδία, τά τε ἄλλα καὶ τοῖς ὀνόμασιν ἠναγκασμένη ποιητικοῖς τισιν διὰ Φαῖδρον εἰρῆσθαι. ἀλλὰ τῶν προτέρων τε συγγνώμην καὶ τῶνδε χάριν ἔχων, εὐμενὴς καὶ ἵλεως τὴν ἐρωτικήν μοι τέχνην ἣν ἔδωκας μήτε ἀφέλῃ μήτε πηρώσῃς δι' ὀργήν, δίδου τ' ἔτι μᾶλλον ἢ νῦν παρὰ τοῖς καλοῖς τίμιον εἶναι. ἐν τῷ πρόσθεν δ' εἴ τι λόγῳ σοι ἀπηχὲς εἴπομεν Φαῖδρός τε καὶ ἐγώ, Λυσίαν τὸν τοῦ λόγου πατέρα αἰτιώμενος παῦε τῶν τοιούτων λόγων.

> This, dear Eros, is offered and paid to you as the finest and best palinode of which I am capable, especially given that it was forced to use somewhat poetical language because of Phaedrus. Forgive what went before and regard this with favour; be kind and gracious—do not in anger **take away or maim the erotic expertise** which you gave me, and grant that I be valued still more than now by the beautiful. If in our speech Phaedrus and I said anything harsh against you, blame Lysias as the father and **make him cease from speeches** of this kind.
>
> PLATO *Phaedrus* 257b–c, trans. ROWE, modified

With its sole Platonic instance of the verb 'to maim' (*pēroō*), the prayer expresses Socrates' concern for his elusive *ars amatoria*. The maiming refers back to the blinding of Stesichorus, and in fact it is certainly possible that Socrates' prayer echoes a now lost invocation in Stesichorus' palinode, in which the poet would have addressed Helen and asked her to restore his sight.[29] Yet this is not the whole story: Socrates also alludes to the archetypal incident of this kind. I am thinking of Thamyris, the Thracian poet who was notoriously maimed by the Muses and who became a very popular subject in classical Athens.[30]

In the *Iliad*, the poetic "termination" of Thamyris—included as it is in the emphatically Muse-inspired Catalogue of ships—seems to provide a negative foil for "Homer" himself.[31] Homer's blindness was synonymous with inspiration, as if blindness were the price he had to pay for his prodigious song (one thinks of Demodocus in the *Odyssey*).[32] By contrast, Thamyris is trapped in an unexpected lose-lose situation, for after suffering physical damage he is *also* deprived of his song.[33] It is worth revisiting the relevant passage in the *Iliad*:

> ἔνθά τε Μοῦσαι
> ἀντόμεναι Θάμυριν τὸν Θρήϊκα **παῦσαν ἀοιδῆς**
> Οἰχαλίηθεν ἰόντα παρ' Εὐρύτου Οἰχαλιῆος·
> στεῦτο γὰρ εὐχόμενος νικησέμεν εἴ περ ἂν αὐταὶ
> Μοῦσαι ἀείδοιεν κοῦραι Διὸς αἰγιόχοιο·
> αἳ δὲ χολωσάμεναι **πηρὸν θέσαν**, αὐτὰρ ἀοιδὴν
> θεσπεσίην **ἀφέλοντο** καὶ ἐκλέλαθον κιθαριστύν

> ... where the Muses
> met Thamyris the Thracian and **made him cease from his song**
> as he was journeying from Oechalia, from the house of Eurytus the Oechalian:
> for he vaunted with boasting that he would conquer, were the Muses themselves

---

29 See Rozokoki (2009–2010) 427.
30 Plato mentions Thamyris three times: *Ion* 533b, *Republic* 620a, and *Laws* 829e. Thamyris became very popular in fifth-century Athens, probably because Sophocles dedicated an early tragedy to him, the *Thamyras* (see Meriani [2007] and Wilson [2009]), in which, according to *Vita Sophoclis* 4.5, he also performed as an actor. In the fourth century, Antiphanes' *Thamyris* (fr. 104 *PCG*) was dedicated to him, and he also featured importantly in the *Rhesus* (921–925). By then, the myth had been accrued with a number of erotic details that suit the *Phaedrus* very well.
31 See e.g. Ford (1992) 97; Martin (1989) 229–230; Nagy (1990) 376.
32 *Odyssey* 8.62–64. See Graziosi (2002) 143–144.
33 *Iliad* 599 αὐτὰρ ἀοιδὴν would seem to 'introduce a contrast' that is a compensation, but such expectations are belied: see Wilson (2009) 50.

to sing against him, the daughters of Zeus that bears the Aegis;
but they in their wrath **maimed him, and took away**
his wondrous song, and made him forget his minstrelsy.

HOMER, *Iliad* 2.594–600, trans. MURRAY

The verbal similarities with Socrates' prayer are striking. Socrates implicitly depicts himself as a potential Thamyris.

Unlike Thamyris, Socrates wishes to retain both his art *and* his integrity, which would make him superior to both Homer and Stesichorus—not to mention poor Thamyris. This amounts to a sort of ranking, with Thamyris in the last position, preceded by Homer, Stesichorus, and the winner of the implicit contest, i.e. Socrates. As I anticipated at the beginning of the present section, this may be construed as Plato's way of staging and stylizing the very process of canonization, which in his view should be based on a markedly religious criterion (compare pious Socrates with impious Thamyris). In order to give some credibility to his placing Stesichorus before Homer, moreover, Plato resorts to what was possibly the only ace he had up his sleeve: Stesichorus' three lines from the palinode were a highly canonized text, which must have been very popular in Attic symposia and apparently gave birth to the expression 'the three of Stesichorus', i.e. Stesichorus' quintessential verse.[34] Such an expression perfectly encapsulates the notion of canonization, and of course Plato's *Phaedrus* further enhanced the success of these three lines, to the expense of other texts (including Stesichorus' own).

3 The Blurred Boundaries of (Para)texts and a New Fragment

A third important area of interest concerns paratexts, i.e. the various forms of texts in which lyric quotations are embedded, such as commentaries, scholia, and the biographical tradition: how indissolubly linked are poetic text and paratext? Is it ever possible to dissociate the former from the latter? Must the paratext always be seen as secondary to the poetic text? We have seen that the biographical tradition of Stesichorus, as well as that of his epic "rivals" Homer and Thamyris, is integral to the dialogue and to the quotation of the three lines from the Palinode, as well as to the implicit anti-paradigm provided by Thamyris. Accordingly, it is surely interesting to consider the complex relationship between text and biographical paratext in the *Phaedrus*.

---

34 I discuss below, p. 251, the expression τὰ τρία Στησιχόρου.

Socrates' quotation of Stesichorus, I have argued, amounts to a full re-enactment, something that entails lexical, metrical, and structural elements. Interestingly, the two speeches are preceded by Phaedrus' attempt to question the credibility of traditional myths. On the way to the plane-tree, Phaedrus mentions the story of Oreithyia, who was supposedly abducted by Boreas on the banks of the Ilissus.[35] Socrates famously replies that he has no time for the rationalization of myth, and that in such matters he prefers to stick to tradition. With characteristic pompousness,[36] Phaedrus refers to the story of Oreithyia as a 'piece of mythology' (μυθολόγημα), a rare word probably drawn from some kind of rationalistic jargon:[37]

ἀλλ' εἰπὲ πρὸς Διός, ὦ Σώκρατες, σὺ τοῦτο τὸ μυθολόγημα πείθῃ ἀληθὲς εἶναι;

But by Zeus, Socrates: do you believe this **piece of mythology** to be **true**?
PLATO *Phaedrus* 229c

It seems to me that Phaedrus' question(ing) foreshadows the Stesichorean quotation 'this story isn't true', with a significant reversal: whereas Phaedrus questions the truth of mythology, Socrates questions the truth of rationalism and rehabilitates a traditional story following in the footsteps of Stesichorus, who, like a revenant, looms large on the horizon of the dialogue.

Socrates' identification with Stesichorus is so strong that he utters a verse—ὡς παῖδα φιλοῦσιν ἐρασταί—that sounds like Stesichorus' Palinode and is designed to announce its metre. Whose verse is this, however? Interestingly, Socrates' words recall a proverb that, according to the relevant Homeric scholia, underlies *Iliad* 22.263.[38] As such, the line has Homeric credentials, but the same is true for most of Stesichorus' production, which was by and large a reperformance of epic themes and apparently included erotic and paederotic motifs.[39]

---

35 *Phdr.* 229b–c.
36 Phaedrus is subtly presented as an opinionated *maître à penser* throughout the dialogue: see e.g. Griswold (1986) 37.
37 There are only two more instances of the word μυθολόγημα in pre-CE literature (Pl. *Leg.* 663e and Philoch. F 3b 328 F *FGrH* = Plut. *Thes.* 14.2) and in all three cases the context is one in which the credibility of a story is put to the test.
38 A few scholia (263b) give the proverb in metrical form as follows: ἄρνα φιλοῦσι λύκοι, νέον ὡς φιλέουσιν ἐρασταί.
39 The poem *Daphnis* (279) shared with the *Kalyke* and *Rhadine* (277 and 278) a romantic subject. In my view, Lehnus (1975) convincingly defends Stesichorus' authorship. See now Ornaghi (2013) and Rutherford (2015), with further bibliography. Rutherford makes the important point that these poems, whether authentic or not, may have been regarded

In fact, one could go so far as to maintain that Socrates' verse reproduces, or at least closely reflects, Stesichorus', which would result in a new "Stesichorean" fragment.

At this point one may wonder why Plato felt the need to ventriloquize the voice of Stesichorus, and in fact the biographical tradition of Socrates himself may perhaps provide a credible answer. In his excellent edition of Stesichorean testimonia, Marco Ercoles argues persuasively that 'the three of Stesichorus', as found in the proverb 'you don't even know the three of Stesichorus',[40] originally referred to the Palinode's best known three verses as sung in symposia, i.e. those quoted by Socrates in the *Phaedrus*.[41] Furthermore, Ercoles believes that the mocking proverb goes back to some Attic comedy: presumably, an uneducated character was ridiculed precisely for his inability to sing the three lines Socrates quotes in the *Phaedrus* and to take active part in the symposium. If this is so, it is not hard to see why Plato has Socrates quote precisely these three lines. Besides providing the *Phaedrus* with a touch of realism (it is natural enough that Socrates knows by heart such a famous piece as 'the three of Stesichorus'), this choice is in essence apologetic, in that it seems to be designed to counter the accusation, voiced by Aristophanes in the *Clouds* and in the *Frogs*, that Socrates was ultimately 'unmusical' and hostile to the traditional *paideia* based on music.[42]

As we have seen, the biographical tradition of both Stesichorus and Socrates is of paramount importance for understanding the quotation from the Palinode and its rationale. Plato's appropriation of Stesichorus is so profound that the link between text and paratext is indeed inextricable. It is hardly possible to dissociate them, and it is even less advisable to try and establish which of the two is primary or secondary.

4   Total Reception: Reperforming Stesichorus

The ancient reception of lyric poetry often takes the form of brief quotations embedded in a series of largely fictional anecdotes. This prompts a number

---

as Stesichorean in the fourth century BCE, which would be sufficient for my own argument.

40 First attested in Diogenianus (n. 14 Οὐδὲ τὰ τρία Στησιχόρου γινώσκεις), the expression τρία Στησιχόρου is found 14 times in Greek literature (TLG count).
41 Ercoles (2013) 533–534. Pitotto (2015), while agreeing with Ercoles, argues that a connection with the triadic structure of Stesichorus' verse may have coexisted with the reference to the Palinode's three lines right from the beginning.
42 *Nub.* 1314–1315, *Ran.* 1491–1499. See Capra (2014) 149–155.

of questions that, while not being strictly related to its main three areas, take centre stage in the present volume. To choose but one, one may ask the following: are the relevant anecdotes entirely fictional? And how can we tell?

Stesichorus' Helen is a notorious conundrum: how many (palin)odes were there? A number of sources refer to Stesichorus' *Helen* and *Palinode*, which used to be construed as two different poems composed at different times. The already complicated relationship between these two supposedly distinct poems was made even more elusive in 1963, with the publication of a papyrus that has the Peripatetic Chamaeleon referring to as many as two *Palinodiai*, complete with different beginnings.[43] Needless to say, I cannot address this question here. Let me just mention a recent critical trend, according to which there was after all just *one* poem about Helen, as David Sider and others have argued.[44] In a highly charged *performance*, the poet would first denigrate Helen, which results in his notional blindness. At a later stage of the performance, he would move to a second and possibly to a third section of the song (palinodes 1 and 2) and rehabilitate Helen against the epic tradition.[45] At this point, the performer would pretend to regain his sight as a result of his recantation. Centuries later, when reading replaced performance, the different sections of the song were construed, and possibly began to circulate, as independent poems, which is why our late sources seem to refer to the *Helen* and *Palinode*(s) as different poems. In sum, the succession of different moments within one and the same performance was wrongly taken to reflect two distinct moments in the life of Stesichorus, who was credited with different poems composed at different times.

The "spectacular" scenario envisaged by Sider and others is all the more promising in that it fits very well the *Phaedrus*.[46] Some years ago, Marian Demos drew attention to Socrates' strange "acting" in the *Phaedrus*. Socrates covers his head before delivering his first, impious speech, only to uncover

---

43 P.Oxy 2506 fr. 26 col. i. The relevant material is now usefully collected and discussed in Davies and Finglass (2014) 121–126 and 299–343.
44 Sider (1989); Arrighetti (1994); Kelly (2007); Carruesco (2017). This view is not discussed in Davies and Finglass (2014) and some scholars keep debating the possible venue of the first performance of Stesichorus' different Helen poems (in the plural), see e.g. Grossardt (2012) ch. 4. However, this reconstruction has made its way into standard accounts of the Helen myth. See Edmunds (2016) 136–138.
45 The performance possibly included an explicit reference to Homer's blindness, as Schollmeyer (2014) plausibly suggests.
46 As well as Isocrates' *Helen* 64–65, the other classical source that cites Stesichorus' Palinode. Isocrates' passage features a number of performative elements, which I cannot discuss here. See Sider (1989).

it when he launches into his palinode (γυμνῇ τῇ κεφαλῇ). Demos makes the important point that 'the legend that Stesichorus lost his sight because of his defamation of Helen is analogous to Socrates' lack of vision during the speech he delivers with his head covered'.[47] Once we replace 'legend' with 'performance' this makes perfect sense: Socrates' delivering of his two speeches is clearly analogous to Stesichorus' putative performance, and Socrates goes so far as to ask Phaedrus for directions: as if he were a blind man, he asks 'where's my boy, the one I was talking to?' and Phaedrus promptly reassures him 'He's here'.[48] This strongly suggests that a performative element is crucial to Socrates' identification with Stesichorus. In turn, this provides additional evidence in favour of the performative interpretation put forth by Sider and others.

Socrates' two speeches are conceptualized as a single, evenly inspired speech act: not only does Socrates refer to them as one and the same process divided into two halves and capable of 'moving (μεταβῆναι) from censure to praise,'[49] but references to Socrates' inspiration are scattered throughout the dialogue and clearly point to *both* speeches.[50] Thus it is possible that on embarking on a speech act divided into equally inspired "ode" and "palinode" Socrates is somehow reproducing the pattern of Stesichorus' performance. From this point of view, it is significant that Socrates, just before delivering his palinode, draws attention to his *daimonion*, which has prevented him from leaving the scene before 'making expiation' (ἀφοσιώσωμαι) towards the god.[51] As we know from [Plutarch] (*On Music*), singers of hymns 'made expiations (ἀφοσιωσάμενοι) to the gods as they wished' and then 'would move immediately (ἐξέβαινον εὐθύς)' to the poetry of Homer and other poets.[52] This squares well with the putative "performance" of Socrates, who makes expiation and then, at the beginning of the palinode proper, adopts the persona of Stesichorus, who, says Socrates, 'being *mousikos* immediately (εὐθύς) composed the verses' of the palinode. In other words, on adopting Stesichorus' persona, Socrates appropriates a transitional formula that was typical of sung hymns, and it is remarkable that Conon

---

47   Demos (1999) 70. Compare Hunter (2015) 151.
48   *Phdr.* 243e ΣΩ: ποῦ δή μοι ὁ παῖς πρὸς ὃν ἔλεγον; ἵνα καὶ τοῦτο ἀκούσῃ, καὶ μὴ ἀνήκοος ὢν φθάσῃ χαρισάμενος τῷ μὴ ἐρῶντι. ΦΑ: οὗτος παρά σοι μάλα πλησίον ἀεὶ πάρεστιν, ὅταν σὺ βούλῃ.
49   ἀπὸ τοῦ ψέγειν πρὸς τὸ ἐπαινεῖν ἔσχεν ὁ λόγος μεταβῆναι (*Phdr.* 265b; cf. 264e ff. for Socrates' way of referring to his two speeches as two symmetrical parts, exploring the two opposing sides of eros).
50   See *Phdr.* 235c, 237a, 238d, 241d, 242d–243b, 245a, 258e–259d, 262c–d, 263d.
51   Plato has Socrates use this verb only here and in *Phd.* 60e–61a.
52   Plut. [*De mus*] 1133b–c τὰ γὰρ πρὸς τοὺς θεοὺς ὡς βούλονται ἀφοσιωσάμενοι, ἐξέβαινον εὐθὺς ἐπί τε τὴν Ὁμήρου καὶ τῶν ἄλλων ποίησιν. δῆλον δὲ τοῦτ᾽ ἐστὶ διὰ τῶν Τερπάνδρου προοιμίων. Compare Power (2010) 187.

refers to the Palinode precisely as a composition of hymns.[53] This transition between different parts of the same performance reinforces the interpretation put forth by Kelly, whose main argument is that Stesichorus devoted to Helen a single composition, possibly divided into 'two hymnodic "segments"' in the rhapsodic manner.[54]

In the end, we may conclude that the anecdote surrounding Stesichorus' palinode in the *Phaedrus* is entirely fictional, although in an unexpected way: the story about the blinding and healing of Stesichorus ultimately depends on the performance of one and the same poem, which in turn informs Socrates' "performance" in Plato's *Phaedrus*. Socrates re-enacts and resurrects Stesichorus' performative persona in (some of) its most minute details. As we have seen, these include lexical, metrical, and even acting features, which in turn bear on the present volume's main areas of interest, namely transmission, canonization, and paratexts. Thus Plato's reviving of Stesichorus' amounts to an intriguing example of what may be referred to as "total reception".

References

Arrighetti, G. 1994. Stesicoro e il suo pubblico. *MD* 32: 9–30.

Bowie, E.L. 2015. Stesichorus at Athens. In *Stesichorus in Context*, ed. P.J. Finglass and A. Kelly, 111–124. Cambridge.

Burkert, W. 1987. The Making of Homer in the Sixth Century B.C.: Rhapsodes versus Stesichorus. In *Papers on the Amasis Painter and his World*, 43–62. Malibu.

Cantilena, M. 2007. Due versi di Platone. *QUCC* 85: 143–149.

Capra, A. 2014. *Plato's Four Muses: The Phaedrus and the Poetics of Philosophy*. Washington, DC.

Carruesco, J. 2017. The Invention of Stesichorus: Hesiod, Helen, and the Muse. In *Authorship and Greek Song: Authority, Authenticity, and Performance*, ed. E.J. Bakker, 178–196. Leiden.

Cassio, A.C. 2012. Epica orale fluttuante e testo omerico fissato: riflessi su Stesicoro (PMGF 222b 229 e 275). *SemRom* I 2: 253–260.

Cerri, G. 1984–1985. Dal canto citarodico al coro tragico: la *Palinodia* di Stesicoro, l'*Elena* di Euripide e le sirene, *Dioniso* 55: 157–174.

Davies, M. and Finglass, P.J. 2014. *Stesichorus. The Poems: Edited with Introduction, Translation and Commentary*. Oxford.

---

53   *FGrH* 26F = Ta30a Ercoles.
54   Kelly (2007) 1.

Demos, M. 1999. *Lyric Quotation in Plato*. Lanham.
Edmunds, L. 2016. *Stealing Helen: The Myth of the Abducted Wife in Comparative Perspective*. Princeton.
Ercoles, M. 2013. *Stesicoro: le testimonianze antiche*. Bologna.
Ford, A. 1992. *Homer: The Poetry of the Past*. Ithaca.
Graziosi, B. 2002. *Inventing Homer*. Cambridge.
Griswold, C.L. 1986. *Self-Knowledge in Plato's Phaedrus*. New Haven.
Grossardt, P. 2012. *Stesichoros zwischen kultischer Praxis, Mythischer Tradition und eigenem Kunstanspruch: zur Behandlung des Helenamythos im Werk des Dichters aus Himera*. Tübingen.
Hackforth, R., ed. 1952. *Plato's Phaedrus*. New York.
Hunter, R.L. 2015. Sweet Stesichorus. Theocritus 18 and the *Helen* Revisited. In *Stesichorus in Context*, ed. P.J. Finglass and A. Kelly, 145–163. Cambridge.
Kelly, A. 2007. Stesikhoros and Helen. *MH* 64: 1–21.
Labarbe, J. 1949. *L'Homère de Platon*. Paris.
Labarbe, J. 1994. Socrate épique dans le *Phèdre* de Platon. *AntClass* 63: 225–230.
Lehnus, L. 1975. Note stesicoree. I poemetti minori (frr. 277–279 PMG). *SCO* 24: 191–196.
Martin, R. 1989. *The Language of Heroes: Speech and Performance in the Iliad*. Ithaca.
Meriani, A. 2007. Il *Thamyras* di Sofocle. In *Musica e generi letterari nella Grecia di età classica*, ed. P. Volpe Cacciatore, 37–70. Naples.
Moreschini, C. 1985. *Platon*, Phèdre, *notice de L. Robin, texte établi par C. Moreschini et traduit par P. Vicaire*. Paris.
Nagy, G. 1990. *Pindar's Homer: The Lyric Possession of an Epic Past*. Baltimore.
Ornaghi, M. 2013. Stesicoro, Teocrito, Epicarmo e i padri della poesia bucolica. *SIFC* 11: 42–81.
Pitotto, E. 2015. Notes on Stesichorus' Proverbial τρία. *Mnemosyne* 68: 1–10.
Power, T. 2010. *The Culture of Kitharôidia*. Washington, DC.
Rowe, C., ed. 1986. *Plato, Phaedrus: Edited with an Introduction, Translation and Notes*. Oxford.
Rozokoki, A. 2009–2010. The Evidence in Plato's *Phaedrus* for the Stesichorean Palinode. *Δωδώνη* 38–39: 425–432.
Rutherford, I.C. 2015. Stesichorus the Romantic. In *Stesichorus in Context*, ed. P.J. Finglass and A. Kelly, 98–108. Cambridge.
Sbardella, L. 2012. *Cucitori di canti. Studi sulla tradizione epico-rapsodica greca e i suoi itinerari nel VI secolo a.C.* Rome.
Schollmeyer, J. 2014. Homer und Stesichorus in Platons *Phaidros* 243a3–b3. *RhM* 157: 239–250.
Sider, D. 1989. The Blinding of Stesichorus. *Hermes* 117: 423–431.
Vries, G.J. de, ed. 1969. *A Commentary on the Phaedrus of Plato*. Amsterdam.

Wilson, P. 2009. Thamyris the Thracian: The Archetypal Wandering Poet? In *Wandering Poets in Ancient Greek Culture. Travel, Locality and Pan-Hellenism*, ed. R.L. Hunter and I.C. Rutherford, 46–79. Cambridge.

Yunis, H., ed. 2011. *Plato,* Phaedrus. Cambridge.

CHAPTER 11

Indirect Tradition on Sappho's *kertomia*

Maria Kazanskaya

1   Introduction*

The story of Charaxus' romantic attachment to a Naucratite hetaera and Sappho's poetic reaction to it is a well-known episode of the poetess's biography, recounted or alluded to in Herodotus (2.134–135), Posidippus (*Epigram* 122 Austin-Bastianini), Strabo (17.1.33), Ovid (*Heroides* 15.63–68), Athenaeus (13.596b–d), and P.Oxy. 1800 (fr. 1.7 f. = Sappho 252).[1] These sources agree in the general outline of the story. Charaxus, while on business in Naucratis, fell in love with a courtesan who was a slave at that time and paid a large sum of money to set her free; but once freed, the girl left Charaxus and continued to exercise her profession independently; Charaxus then returned to Mytilene and Sappho wrote a poem on the affair. There is however significant divergence in details. The name of the girl is given as Doricha (Posidippus *Epigram* 122.1; Athenaeus 13.596b–c; Strabo 17.1.33) or alternatively Rhodopis (Herodotus 2.134–135; Strabo 17.1.33). The tone of Sappho's poem is characterized as taunting by Herodotus (ἐν μέλεϊ Σαπφὼ πολλὰ κατεκερτόμησε, Herodotus 2.135) and as malign by Athenaeus (διὰ τῆς ποιήσεως διαβάλλει, Athenaeus 13.596b), while Posidippus' qualification of Sappho's verses as φίλη ᾠδή suggests a positive poetic reaction, and Ovid speaks of an 'admonition' (*monui bene multa fideliter*, Ovid *Heroides* 15.67; compare 68 *pia lingua*). The most significant divergence concerns the target of Sappho's poem: Herodotus' text seems to indicate that Sappho's κερτομία was directed against Charaxus,[2] while Athenaeus states specifically that she wrote against Doricha.[3]

---

* I would like to thank Bruno Currie and André Lardinois for their comments on the first draft of this chapter. I am also grateful to Dirk Obbink, Ewen Bowie, Lucia Athanassaki, Deborah Boedeker, Glenn Most, André Lardinois, and Hans Bernsdorff for the discussion of my paper during the conference on the reception of Greek lyric poetry hosted by Reading University in 2013. I am infinitely grateful for Ian Rutherford for his suggestions on my chapter, as well as for his kindness and support.
1   The relationship is also mentioned in the lexicographical tradition (*Suda*, ρ 211 Adler; Photius *Lex.* s.v. Ῥοδώπιδος ἀνάθημα; *App. Prov.* 4.51).
2   Χάραξος δὲ ὡς λυσάμενος Ῥοδῶπιν ἀπενόστησε ἐς Μυτιλήνην, ἐν μέλεϊ Σαπφὼ πολλὰ κατεκερτόμησέ μιν. Ῥοδώπιος μέν νυν πέρι πέπαυμαι (Hdt. 2.135).
3   Δωρίχαν τε, ἣν ἡ καλὴ Σαπφὼ ἐρωμένην γενομένην Χαράξου τοῦ ἀδελφοῦ αὐτῆς κατ' ἐμπορίαν

Among Sappho's fragments several concern Charaxus' trip to Naucratis, namely the 'Prayer to the Nereids' for a brother's safe return home (fr. 5),[4] the final stanza of fr. 15 mentioning Doricha's name, and now the 'Brothers' poem' that speaks directly of Charaxus' expected return from a trading trip.[5] It is clear that Sappho wrote a series of poems in connection with Charaxus' voyage that the biographical tradition reconstructed into an account of Charaxus' love affair in Naucratis. The poem mentioned by Herodotus, Athenaeus, and Strabo cannot be identified with the extant fragments, and despite numerous allusions to the story, frustrating lacunas remain both in the indirect tradition and between the indirect tradition and Sappho's fragments. This article proposes to examine the evidence on this poem, focusing on three questions: (a) the tonality of the poems on Charaxus' love affair; (b) the object of Sappho's disapproval; (c) the name of the hetaera. It will be shown that in some points the different accounts in the indirect tradition can be reconciled in a way that gains support from the extant fragments.

2   Tone of the Poem(s)

There is a consensus among scholars, based on Herodotus' and Athenaeus' evaluation, that the tone of Sappho's poem (or poems) on her brother's affair mentioned by the indirect tradition was derogatory. This follows the qualification of the poem in the two fullest accounts—Herodotus' and Athenaeus'. Herodotus, who is our earliest source for this story, concludes his account by the following words: Χάραξος δὲ ὡς λυσάμενος Ῥοδῶπιν ἀπενόστησε ἐς Μυτιλήνην, ἐν μέλεϊ Σαπφὼ πολλὰ κατεκερτόμησέ μιν (Once Charaxus after freeing Rhodopis returned to Mytilene, Sappho in her song strongly berated μιν) (Herodotus 2.135).[6] Here the negative nuance of κερτο-

---

    εἰς τὴν Ναύκρατιν ἀπαίροντος διὰ τῆς ποιήσεως διαβάλλει ὡς πολλὰ τοῦ Χαράξου νοσφισαμένην (Athenaeus 13.596b).

4 See Obbink (2016) 22–23 for a new reconstruction of this fragment, based on the new papyrus fragments published in 2014.

5 Obbink (2014). Other fragments that are cited with reference to this story are frr. 3, 7, 9 and 20. Rosenmeyer (2006) 24 adds fr. 26. Such words as ὄνειδος, ἄσαιο, κακότατο[ς in fr. 3 and ἀγερωχία in fr. 7 clearly indicate a disapprobatory tone; furthermore, Doricha's name has been reconstructed by Lobel in fr. 7.1, but only on the evidence of]χας where χ is uncertain. In view of the poor state of the text it is, unfortunately, not easy to use these fragments. On their possible connection with the story of Charaxus' love affair, see in particular Burris, Fish, and Obbink (2014) 16; Ferrari (2014) 10; Lardinois (2016) 170–172.

6 For the moment I leave μιν without translation. In the course of this chapter, I either quote extant translations (the translator is always specified) or give my own.

μέω[7] is reinforced by the prefix κατα- and the adverbial πολλά. And Athenaeus, whose rendering of this story is indebted to Herodotus (see below), uses the verb διαβάλλω implying a deliberate attack on Doricha's character: Δωρίχαν τε, ἣν ἡ καλὴ Σαπφὼ ἐρωμένην γενομένην Χαράξου τοῦ ἀδελφοῦ αὐτῆς κατ' ἐμπορίαν εἰς τὴν Ναύκρατιν ἀπαίροντος διὰ τῆς ποιήσεως διαβάλλει ὡς πολλὰ τοῦ Χαράξου νοσφισαμένην ([among them] Doricha, who became the mistress of Charaxus, brother of the beautiful Sappho, when he came to Naucratis on business, and whom Sappho abused in her poetry for extracting a big sum of money from him) (Athenaeus 13.596b). The use of the verb διαβάλλω in Athenaeus and of the expression πολλὰ κατεκερτόμησέ μιν in Herodotus show that the poet's criticism must have been harsh indeed. This characterization is also confirmed by the negative tone of Sappho fr. 15.9–12 that mentions Doricha's name.[8] More generally Sappho's negative reaction to Charaxus' love affair fits in neatly with the tradition of Sappho the *iambopoios*:[9] the fact that Sappho wrote "iambic" poetry (iambic probably in tone, rather than in metre) is mentioned by Emperor Julian (*Epist.* 10 Bidez-Cumont), the biographical entry in the *Suda* (σ 107 Adler = Test. 235 Voigt), and most importantly Philodemus (*de Poem.* 2 Janko fr. 117): οἱ γ[ὰρ ἰ]αμβοποιοὶ τραγικὰ ποιοῦσιν, καὶ οἱ τραγῳδοποι|οἱ πάλιν ἰαμβικά, καὶ Σαπφώ τινα ἰαμβικῶς ποιεῖ, καὶ Ἀρχίλοχος οὐκ ἰαμβικῶς (for the iambographers compose tragic verses, and the tragic poets compose iambic verses in their turn, and Sappho composes some poems in the iambic manner, and Archilochus—in a manner that is not iambic).

Thus a large part of the indirect and direct tradition is in agreement; the question of Sappho's attitude with regard to her brother's affair is worth examining, as the tone of the poem is qualified very differently in Posidippus and Ovid. Admittedly, in both cases we are dealing with poetic reactions that allow for a greater freedom in handling the facts than the prose of a historian or an

---

7 The verb κερτομέω itself is ambiguous: its etymology is uncertain (see Chantraine, s.v. κέρτομος; Beekes, s.v. κέρτομος), and some of its early usages are confusing: cf. especially *Il.* 24.649 where the authorial description of Achilles' tone as ἐπικερτομέων clashes with his general conduct towards Priam. For a discussion of the semantics of the verb in this passage and elsewhere in Homer see Hooker (1986) 33–36; Jones (1989); Clay (1999); Lloyd (2004); Gottesmann (2008). However, in Hdt. 2.135 the prefix κατα- is important, and the comparison of this passage with the description of Harpagus' mockery over the fall of Astyages (ἐόντι δὲ αἰχμαλώτῳ τῷ Ἀστυάγεϊ προσστὰς ὁ Ἅρπαγος κατέχαιρέ τε καὶ κατεκερτόμεε) shows that in the *Histories* the verb κατακερτομέω with the prefix denoting hostility indicated a berating tone.

8 Κύ]πρι κα[ί σ]ε πι[κροτ.]αν ἐπεύρ[οι / μη]δὲ καυχάσ[α]|το τόδ' ἐννέ[ποισα / Δ]ωρίχα τὸ δεύ[τ]ερον ὡς πόθε[ννον / εἰς] ἔρον ἦλθε (Sapph. fr. 15.9–12). Lidov (2002) 203 argues that the letter before -ρίχα cannot be ω, but this is disputed by Yatromanolakis (2007) 331.

9 See, among others, Tsomis (2001) 222; Rosenmeyer (2006); Dale (2011); Martin (2016).

erudite scholar, but it is worth considering why their qualification is so different from the main tradition.

(1) Posidippus. The epigram addressed to Doricha (*Epigram* 122 Austin-Bastianini) is regularly evoked in studies dedicated to the interplay of Hellenistic poetry with its lyric predecessors.[10] It was probably intended as an epigraph for a real or imaginary monument for Doricha.[11]

> Δωρίχα, ὀστέα μὲν †σ' ἀπαλὰ κοιμήσατο δεσμῶν †
> χαίτης ἥ τε μύρων ἔμπνοος ἀμπεχόνη,
> ᾗ ποτε τὸν χαρίεντα περιστέλλουσα Χάραξον
> σύγχρους ὀρθρινῶν ἥψαο κισσυβίων.
> Σαπφῷαι δὲ μένουσι φίλης ἔτι καὶ μενέουσιν
> ᾠδῆς αἱ λευκαὶ φθεγγόμεναι σελίδες.
> οὔνομα σὸν μακαριστόν, ὃ Ναύκρατις ὧδε φυλάξει,
> ἔστ' ἂν ἴῃ Νείλου ναῦς ἐφ' ἁλὸς πελάγη.[12]

Doricha, your bones fell asleep long ago ... the bands of your hair, and the perfume-breathing shawl in which you once wrapped the handsome Charaxus, and joining him to your flesh, grasped the wine cup in the small hours. But the white ringing pages of Sappho's dear song abide and will still abide. Happy your name, which Naucratis will preserve thus as long as a ship from the Nile goes upon the wide salt sea.

trans. D.A. CAMPBELL, citing the epigram as Sappho, Test. 15

The first verse of the epigram is severely damaged, and several other emendations have been introduced at the end of the poem.[13] As a rule, the epigram is

---

10 Thus, Acosta-Hughes and Barbantani (2007) 439; Gutzwiller (2007) 45–46; Acosta-Hughes (2010) 2–3.
11 Thus, Gabathuler (1937) 51–52; Angiò (1999) 154; Gow and Page (1965) ii.498; and others.
12 The text is printed as it appears in Page (1975) lines 1650–1657.
13 The majority of divergent readings and proposed emendations are not important for the present discussion, as they concern above all v. 1–2 and 8. The question of printing a point at the end of v. 6 (thus, Gow and Page; Campbell; Gulick; Scheiweiler [1958] 95; Angiò [1999] 153–154) or allowing the sentence to run over into the fourth distich (thus, Schott; Austin and Bastianini; Zanetto, Pozzi, and Rampichini; Olson) will have a bearing on the following. The separation of the third and fourth distich is to be preferred, as the hemistich φθεγγόμεναι σελίδες (v. 7) is clearly modelled on the pentameter ending first found in Theognis (φθεγγόμενος στόματι, Theogn. 1230) and recurring several times with slight modifications in the *Palatine Anthology* (6.10, 5.135, 7.12, 7.641; *A.P. App. ep. did.* 291; *carm. sep.* 167). In all these passages the participle φθεγγόμενος means 'resounding' and is

discussed independently of Athenaeus, its only source, and the interpretation, apart from the textual difficulties, varies little. The poem is usually divided in two equal parts, with verses 1–4 describing Doricha's long-gone beauty and the poignancy of her and Charaxus' love, and verses 5–8 speaking of her enduring fame (but Sappho's poems remain, and the city of Naucratis shall preserve Doricha's name as long as it itself lasts).[14] This opposition between human mortality and the immortality of poetry would indeed be the natural way to understand the progression of ideas, if nothing but this epigram survived. It implies, however, that Sappho's poem presented Doricha in positive light; and the expression φίλη ... ᾠδή is particularly difficult to reconcile with Herodotus' and Athenaeus' testimony concerning Sappho's critical reaction.[15] The idea of Sappho's poetry assuring Doricha's continuing fame has been explained as irony on Posidippus' part,[16] or as a variation of the motif of the immortalizing power of poetry,[17] and often commentators' remarks testify to a sense of paradox that is difficult to explain.[18] The distribution of roles in preserving Doricha's fame between Sappho's verses and Naucratis is also problematic: it has been suggested that Naucratis might have contributed as a centre of trade and that the ship mentioned in verse 8 may be carrying papyri with Sappho's poetry.[19]

---

not accompanied by accusative, and Posidippus' use is likely to conform to this model. For a full discussion, see Kazanskaya (2016a) 33–38.

14 Compare Lidov (2002) 222–223 'Whatever the difficulties of the reading in the first couplet, the motif, or topos, is clear enough: the body is gone, but the fame will live on the page.'

15 Gow and Page (1965) ii.498 note that the choice of φίλη is unexpected, as in this context ᾠδή must refer to Sappho's poem on Doricha. Scheidweiler (1958) 95 suggested altering its form, so as to transform it into a vocative: φίλη, σ' (this unnecessary emendation is not retained by editors). The suggestion advanced by Angiò (1999) 153 that φίλη might allude to the fact that Sappho wrote love poetry is not convincing.

16 Thus, Wilamowitz (1913) 19–20n1 'Sehr geschickt und auf wissende Leser berechnet ist es, daß er so aussieht, als hätte Sappho die Liebe ihres Bruders gefeiert, die sie gescholten hatte'; cf. Yatromanolakis (2007) 327. Lidov (2002) 223n46 opposes this idea.

17 Thus, Klooster (2011) 29 'The *pointe* of the epigram is therefore that immortality can only be achieved by (becoming the subject of) poetry, no matter how powerful charm may be—and no matter what this poetry precisely states.' Cf. Bing (2009) 262; Acosta-Hughes and Barbantani (2007) 439. Zanetto, Pozzi, and Rampichini in their commentary (ad loc.) combine the two interpretations.

18 Compare Zanetto, Pozzi, and Rampicchini (ad loc.): '*Forse Posdippo sceglie di sviluppare il tema della poesia eternatrice ... in modo originale e quasi straniante.*'

19 This was first suggested in a passing remark by Rosenmeyer (1997) 132 and Rosenmeyer (2006) 24; it has also been accepted by Acosta-Hughes (2003) 45; Yatromanolakis (2007) 327n184; Bing (2009) 262–263; Klooster (2011) 29n48.

A different construction of the poem seems more likely. Verses 1–6 present the obstacles to the just appreciation of Doricha (the fact that she is dead, and that Sappho's criticism on the contrary survives), whereas the last distich presents a positive solution:[20] Naucratis, the city where the courtesan became famous, will preserve her memory and do her justice. The expression φίλη ... ᾠδή is used generically of Sappho's poetry, and not specifically of the poem on Doricha.[21] Placed in a hyperbaton, φίλη emphasizes that the general admiration for Sappho's poetry, as well as the enduring nature of her poems (μένουσι ... ἔτι καὶ μενέουσιν), is yet another hindrance to the just appreciation of Doricha. Thus Posidippus in this epigram rivals Sappho, helping to restore Doricha's name that Sappho had attacked. According to this reading, there was no contradiction between Posidippus' view of Sappho's poem on Doricha with what Herodotus and Athenaeus tell us. It also gains implicit support from the fact that Athenaeus, when quoting this epigram (596b–d), saw no contradiction between his own words διὰ τῆς ποιήσεως διαβάλλει and the way Sappho's poetic reaction was presented by Posidippus.

(2) Ovid.[22] Although the treatment of Sappho's relationship with her brother in *Heroides* 15 is vague, and certain traits were surely invented by Ovid,[23] it probably also incorporates details that would have resonated with Ovid's readers familiar with Sappho's poetry. In particular, the passage on the quarrel

---

20 It should be noted (although it is only a tendency and by no means a law) that the asymmetrical structure '3 + 1 distichs' is found in most Posidippus' epigrams of the same length: eight of the twelve poems comprising eight verses share the '3 + 1' division (*Ep.* 8, 15, 33, 36, 37, 39, 56, 57, 95, 121, 140 Austin and Bastianini). In this group, *Ep.* 140 with its first three stanza listing toasts to lovers and poets, and the last stanza separated by the same asyndeton is particularly close to *Ep.* 122.

21 The noun ᾠδή can be used of a single poem or of poetry in general, but λευκαὶ φθεγγόμεναι σελίδες point to a poetry-book rather than a single poem. In that case, the epithet φίλη must also refer to Sappho's poetry in general, rather than specifically to the poem on Doricha.

22 The authorship of *Epistula Sapphous* is debated: see Tarrant (1981); Murgia (1985); Knox (2002) 134. I follow Dörrie (1975) in accepting the poem as Ovid's.

23 Thus Charaxus taunting Sappho spitefully with her daughter (117–120) is probably an Ovidian invention. The allusion to the 'bad way of earning money' (*quasque male amissit nunc male quaerit opes*, 66) that Charaxus fell into after his separation from Doricha is very vague. It has been assumed that *male* (taken together with *agili peragit freta caerula remo*, in the previous verse) refers to piracy, but as Knox (1995) 292 in his note to *Her.* 15, 66 points out, Ovid could have inserted *male* for stylistic repetition. Dale (2011) 68–69 compares this attitude to Hesiod's disapproval of the seafaring in general, and Morgan (2016) 300–301 suggests that it might be explained by a negative view of trade.

between Sappho and Charaxus has a bearing on the issue of the tone of Sappho's poem(s) on his love affair:

> arsit iners frater meretricis captus amore
>   mixtaque cum turpi damna pudore tulit;
> factus inops agili peragit freta caerula remo,
>   quasque male amisit, nunc male quaerit opes.
> me quoque, quod monui bene multa fideliter, odit;
>   hoc mihi libertas, hoc pia lingua dedit.

> My untaught brother was caught in the flame of harlot love, and suffered loss together with foul shame; reduced to need, he roams the dark blue seas with agile oar, and the wealth he cast away by evil means once more by evil means he seeks. As for me, because I often warned him well and faithfully, he hates me; this has my candour brought me, this my duteous tongue.
>   OVID *Heroides* 63–68, trans. G. SHOWERMAN

The phrase *monui bene multa fideliter* must refer to Sappho's poems addressed to Charaxus, an allusion that Ovid's readers would have recognized. The choice of words suggests an admonition that had Charaxus' interest at heart, even if he was not able to accept with good grace,[24] and her language is qualified as 'frank' and 'pious' (*hoc mihi libertas, hoc pia lingua dedit*). It is thus very different from Herodotus' πολλὰ κατεκερτόμησέ μιν and Athenaeus' διαβάλλει. But two passages from Sappho's own poetry can give an idea how such admonition might have sounded: cf. ὄσσα δὲ πρ]όσθ' ἄμβροτε πάντα λῦσα[ι / καὶ φίλοισ]ι ϝοῖσι χάραν γένεσθαι ... (and all that he has done wrong, may he atone for it and become a pleasure to his friends) from the "Prayer to the Nereids" speaking of Charaxus (Sapph. fr. 5), and αἴ κε ϝὰν κεφάλαν ἀέρρη / Λάριχος καὶ δή ποτ' ἄνηρ γένηται ... (if Larichus raises his head and ever becomes a man) of her second brother, Larichus, in the 'Brothers' poem' (vv. 21–22).[25] Both expressions contain an element of reproach that could cause bitterness, but do not have the malice that Herodotus' κατακερτομέω implies (Herodotus 2.135). A very differ-

---

24 Compare Page (1955) 50: 'The Ovidian "epistle of Sappho" makes a natural inference: Charaxus resented his sister's public admonitions.'
25 The text is quoted from Obbink (2016) 26. On this passage, see Obbink (2014) 34; Ferrari (2014) 9; Stehle (2016) 288–292; Martin (2016) 121–124. The interpretations of the phrase vary from the 'crowning insult' (Stehle [2016] 290) to 'well-wishing to Larichos, that he grow up to be a settled member of the leisured, aristocratic class' (Obbink [2014] 34).

ent tone, however, is suggested by the verses 63–64, and especially by the word that designates the woman Charaxus fell in love with. *Meretrix*, here emphasized by the hyperbaton, is an untypically harsh word with vulgar connotations; it belongs to the low style and does not appear in other *Heroides*.[26] Such a qualification could well appear in an invective that Herodotus and Athenaeus speak of.

While it is important not to overstate the case, the passage in the *Epistula Sapphous* suggests that there might have been a difference of tone when Sappho wrote about Charaxus' unwise choice and when she dealt with the girl he fell in love with. It is important to stress that Ovid's *monui bene multa fideliter*, *libertas*, and *pia lingua* certainly characterize the tone of the poems addressed to Charaxus.

To sum up, Herodotus' and Athenaeus' testimony that Sappho's poetic reaction to her brother's love affair was negative is not contradicted by Posidippus (*Epigram* 122 Austin and Bastianini) and Ovid (*Heroides* 15.63–68). Posidippus' epigram presents itself as an inscription on a real or imaginary monument for Doricha seeking to re-establish the name of the woman that Sappho had spoken ill of; and Ovid's wording suggests that Sappho's verses addressed to Charaxus resembled an admonition, whereas her tone was much harsher when she spoke of the hetaera.

3 The Object of Sappho's κερτομία

The question of who was it that Sappho targeted in the poem(s) that Herodotus and Athenaeus speak of is a vexed one. Athenaeus states clearly that Sappho's invective was directed against the courtesan, not Charaxus (Δωρίχαν τε, ἣν ἡ καλὴ Σαπφώ ... διὰ τῆς ποιήσεως διαβάλλει ὡς πολλὰ τοῦ Χαράξου νοσφισαμένην, Athenaeus 13.596b). But Herodotus' wording at the end of his digression on Rhodopis, Χάραξος δὲ ὡς λυσάμενος Ῥοδῶπιν ἀπενόστησε ἐς Μυτιλήνην, ἐν μέλεϊ Σαπφὼ πολλὰ κατεκερτόμησέ μιν, has generally been understood as referring to an attack on Charaxus.[27] Most scholars accept the version of events based

---

26 Ov. *Am.* 1.10.21, 1.15.18, 3.14.9; *A.A.* 1.435; *Ep. ex Pont.* 2.3.20; *Tr.* 2.303; for the discussion of the word *meretrix* in Augustan poetry, see Tränkle (1960) 120. It should also be mentioned that by making his Sappho refer to the girl as *meretrix*, Ovid cleverly eschews the issue of the double name Rhodopis/Doricha (see below).

27 This reading goes back as far as Lorenzo Valla's translation of Herodotus and Angelo Poliziano's commentary on *Epistula Sapphus*; see Gronovius and Valla (1715) 140; Poliziano (1971) 60.

on this reading and dismiss Athenaeus' testimony,[28] some claiming that he had misunderstood Herodotus,[29] others trying to reconcile his account with Herodotus' by suggesting that while the main censure concerned Charaxus, the courtesan must also have had her share of the blame in Sappho's poem.[30] Different reasons have also been suggested for the harshness of Sappho's reaction to her brother's conduct. Smyth and Bowra suggested that Sappho's disapproval of Charaxus' liaison with Rhodopis was a proof of her own high moral standards.[31] Page, noting that the majority of the testimonia mention money,[32] explained it by the size of the sum that Charaxus spent on his mistress.[33] Gomme, calculating that Charaxus cannot have been young when he got entangled with Rhodopis,[34] suggested that Sappho might have criticized him for making a fool of himself at an advanced age.[35] Lidov, taking as his basis the information provided by the *Suda*, Χάραξος ὁ ἀδελφὸς Σαπφοῦς ἔλαβε γυναῖκα καὶ ἐξ αὐτῆς γεννᾷ 'Charaxus, Sappho's brother, married her and had children with her' (*Suda* αι 334, s.v. Αἴσωπος), suggested that Sappho wrote a lascivious

---

28 Among older scholars there was a certain *vir doctus*, mentioned by Baehrs (1856) 739 in his commentary (ad loc.), who suggested that μιν in Hdt. 2.135 referred to Rhodopis (I have not been able to trace this reference), and Smyth (1900) 252 also suggested that Athenaeus' testimony should be followed.

29 Compare Larcher's note (ad loc.): '*Il y a dans le grec μιν qui peut se rapporter à Charaxus ou à Rhodopis. Je me suis déterminé pour le premier parce qu'il est le sujet de la phrase... Il est très vraisemblable que c'est [Athénée] qui se trompe.*'

30 Thus, Page (1955) 49: 'Athenaeus says that Doricha herself had a share of hard words in Sappho's verse', probably independently of Rawlinson (1862) on Hdt. 2.135: 'It is probable that both [Charaxus] and Rhodopis were lampooned by Sappho, since in Herodotus the word μιν seems to refer to the former, while Athenaeus says that it was Rhodopis.' Conversely, Martin (2016) 120 has suggested that Sappho's invective against the hetaera could have been perceived by readers as an attack on Charaxus' as well.

31 Smyth (1900) 252; Bowra (1936) 229; the formulation in the second edition of *Greek Lyric Poetry* (Bowra [1961] 209–211) is more prudent.

32 Thus, ἐλύθη χρημάτων μεγάλων in Herodotus (2.135), πλεῖστα κατεδαπάνησεν (P. Oxy. 1800); *factus inops* in the *Epistula Sapphus* (*Her.* 15.65); πολλὰ νοσφισαμένην in Athenaeus (13.569b).

33 Page (1955) 50–51. Saake (1968) 106–107 is critical of this idea.

34 If we trust Herodotus' information that Charaxus fell in love with Rhodopis and that Rhodopis flourished in the time of Amasis we are presented with an unexpected timeline: Sappho herself would have been around fifty at the time. On this see di Benedetto (1982) 226–229; Boardman (1994) 142.

35 See Gomme (1957) 259; his conclusion, however, is cautious: '[Sappho] may, in the lost stanzas, for all we know, have mocked him and his white hairs, as Anakreon laughed at his own; but it is better to take warning from the past and not guess, but confine ourselves to what we can read.'

song for Charaxus' wedding with Rhodopis, a poem so full of sexual innuendo that it was mistaken by later biographers for an invective.[36]

And yet, Athenaeus' account, based on a comparison of several sources (Herodotus, Cratinus, and Posidippus are mentioned and cited explicitly) demands a more serious consideration, not to mention the fact that as a native of Naucratis, he would have read Sappho's poem about the famous courtesan from his city. Following the discovery of the 'Brother's poem', Obbink and Ferrari have suggested that πολλὰ κατεκερτόμησέ μιν in Herodotus 2.135 can actually refer to Rhodopis,[37] and in what follows I would like to review the arguments in favour of this solution.

The sentence mentioning Sappho's poem occurs at the very end of a long digression on the famous hetaera from Naucratis, Rhodopis. Herodotus' main purpose in this section of his narrative is to prove that the pyramid of Mycerinus could not be Rhodopis' tomb, for although famous and wealthy for a woman of her profession, her dedication of spits at Delphi shows that she was not wealthy enough to have constructed a pyramid for herself; however, the historian uses this opportunity to introduce some piquant biographical details. Herodotus concludes his digression stating that Naucratis was particularly famous for the charms of its hetaerae (in particular, Rhodopis and Archedike who lived after her), evoking Charaxus' return and Sappho's κερτομία and finally marking the end of his digression with a capping phrase:

> Τοῦτο μὲν γὰρ αὕτη, τῆς πέρι λέγεται ὅδε ὁ λόγος, οὕτω δή τι κλεινὴ ἐγένετο ὡς καὶ οἱ πάντες Ἕλληνες Ῥοδώπιος τὸ οὔνομα ἐξέμαθον, τοῦτο δὲ ὕστερον ταύτης ⟨ἑτέρη⟩ τῇ οὔνομα ἦν Ἀρχιδίκη ἀοίδιμος ἀνὰ τὴν Ἑλλάδα ἐγένετο, ἧσσον δὲ τῆς προτέρης περιλεσχήνευτος. Χάραξος δὲ ὡς λυσάμενος Ῥοδῶπιν ἀπενόστησε ἐς Μυτιλήνην, ἐν μέλεϊ Σαπφὼ πολλὰ κατεκερτόμησέ μιν. Ῥοδώπιος μέν νυν πέρι πέπαυμαι.

On one hand, this hetaira (the one of whom this story is told) became so famous that all Greeks learnt Rhodopis' name; on the other hand, another courtesan by name of Archedike, later became subject of song, although she was less subject of gossip than Rhodopis. Once Charaxus after freeing Rhodopis returned to Mytilene, Sappho in her song strongly berated μιν. And now I have said enough about Rhodopis.

HERODOTUS 2.135

---

36   Lidov (2002) 230–233.
37   Obbink (2014) 41 and Ferrari (2014) 10–11. This was also the point I made in the paper read at the conference at Reading in 2013.

From the point of view of syntax, the emphatic position of Charaxus' name at the very beginning of the sentence (Χάραξος δὲ ὡς ...) is in favour of μιν referring to him.[38] Other details, however, seem to be in favour of Rhodopis being meant. The pronoun μιν is placed between two mentions of Rhodopis' name (in the subordinate clause ὡς λυσάμενος Ῥοδῶπιν and in the capping phrase Ῥοδώπιος μέν νυν πέρι), and, if she was the target of Sappho's invective, Herodotus would have been obliged to replace her name with a pronoun, as it was preferable for it to appear in the phrase that caps the digression.[39] Furthermore, the expression ἐν μέλεϊ [...] πολλὰ κατεκερτόμησέ μιν corresponds to περιλεσχήνευτος used in the comparison of Archedike's and Rhodopis' notoriety in the preceding sentence.[40] Finally, the progression of thought in this final part of the digression is smoother if we assume that μιν referred to Rhodopis: the courtesan did become well known in Greece, though also a subject of gossip, and Sappho, after her brother's return, contributed to Rhodopis' notoriety by her censure. The emphatic placement of Charaxus' name before ὡς allows Herodotus to indicate that he is picking up the story about the way Rhodopis obtained her freedom—an episode that he had spoken of a while before. This reading of the passage has the advantage of avoiding the brusqueness of transitions that we find in the traditional interpretation.

The idea that μιν refers to Rhodopis as the central figure of the digression in Herodotus 2.135, gains support from Herodotus' evocation of lyric poetry

38 In particular, Lardinois (2016) 170 stresses the importance of the position of Charaxus' name: 'Charaxus' name is prominently placed as topic at the front of the whole sentence, outside the subordinate clause to which it syntactically belongs. In other sentences in Herodotus which are structured in this way, such a topic always returns in the main clause either as subject or object'. Unfortunately, Lardinois cites only examples where the word placed before the conjunction of the subordinate clause is the subject of the main clause and which are not accurate parallels to Χάραξος δὲ ὡς ... Σαπφὼ πολλὰ κατεκερτόμησέ μιν. Besides, there are counterexamples to the principle as formulated by Lardinois: e.g., Κῦρος δὲ ὡς ἀπίκετο καὶ ἀντεστρατοπεδεύσατο Κροίσῳ, ἐνθαῦτα ἐν τῇ Πτερίῃ χώρῃ ἐπειρῶντο κατὰ τὸ ἰσχυρὸν ἀλλήλων (Hdt. 1.76.3). Observations from functional grammar can give a useful insight into the text, but can only be cited as tendencies, not laws; cf. the admirable discussion of topic with relation to oral strategies in Herodotus' narrative in Slings (2002).
39 For similar capping sentences that conclude narrative sections and digressions, cf. Νείλου μέν νυν πέρι τοσαῦτα εἰρήσθω (Hdt. 2.35); τοσαῦτα μὲν θηρίων πέρι ἱρῶν εἰρήσθω (2.67); καὶ περὶ μὲν τοὺς ἰχθῦς οὕτως ἔχει (Hdt. 2.93); "Ομηρος μέν νυν καὶ τὰ Κύπρια ἔπεα χαιρέτω (2.117); τὸ μὲν δὴ ἱρὸν τοῦτο οὕτως ἔχει (Hdt. 2.138); etc.
40 Note in particular how Herodotus uses περιλεσχήνευτος and ἀοίδιμος to highlight the difference in Rhodopis' and Archedike's reputation. Yatromanolakis (2007) 325 takes a step further when he suggests that 'the syntagmatic contiguity of the final reference to Kharaxos with the emphatic περιλεσχήνευτος and its sociocultural associations indicates that the story about Kharaxos should be viewed as part of the chats and singing about the courtesan that took place in male gatherings.'

in other passages of his *Histories*. It has been noticed that the reference to Sappho at Herodotus 2.135 resembles four other references which share the same constituent elements, position, and function in the narrative.[41] Herodotus mentions Archilochus at the end of the story of Candaules' murder by Gyges (Herodotus 1.12, referring in all probability to Archil. fr. 19); Alcaeus at the end of the account of the struggle over Sigaeum between Athens and Mytilene (Herodotus 5.95; the reference is to Alcaeus fr. 401 B that tells of Alcaeus' escape from the battle with the Athenians); Simonides' praise of Eualcides who fell in the battle of Ephesus (Herodotus 5.102; no fragment survives); and Solon's praise of Philocyprus, the tyrant of Cyprus, when narrating the death of his son Aristocyprus in the battle of Cyprus (Herodotus 5.113; a fragment has been preserved by Plutarch, see Solon fr. 19). In each case, Herodotus refers, without quoting it, to a poem that bears witness to an eminent historical figure (Gyges) or an important historical event (the war over Sigeum, the battle of Ephesus, the battle of Cyprus). He mentions the name of the poet and his birthplace and indicates the genre of the poem (either the metre or the type of the poem, or both, as in Sappho's case, ἐν μέλεϊ [...] πολλὰ κατεκερτόμησε). In each case, the reference marks a break in the narrative, as is the case in Herodotus 2.135, though not necessarily a complete change of subject. It is characteristic of all five passages that the reference leaves the impression of being "exterior" to the body of the narrative, as if it could be easily omitted. For example, the reference to Solon in Herodotus 5.113 appears all the more out of place, as Aristocyprus had not even been mentioned in the previous narrative, and that Solon's poem concerned his father, Philocyprus.[42] This first impression, however, disappears on closer examination of the context. The references transmit a personal point of view or an evaluation of the person or event, that is central to Herodotus' narrative at that moment: to use the same example, in the case of Philocyprus, the praise of the tyrant by the democrat Solon (ἐν ἔπεσι αἴνεσε τυράννων μάλιστα) reflects on his son, and the mention of this praise in the context of the battle allows Herodotus to emphasize of the greatness of the Cypriotes' loss.[43] Herodotus refers his readers to these lyric poems as to personal testimonies

---

41 See in particular Verdin (1977) 63–65; Rotstein (2010) 194–196; Kazanskaya (2016b). The closeness of these five passages has also been emphasized by Yatromanolakis (2007) 328 in order to show that 'the ethnographer [*sc.* Herodotus] does refer to actual poems'.

42 It is perhaps this reason that gave doubts as to authenticity of the passages to some scholars: thus, How and Wells (1989), Asheri, Lloyd and Corcella (2007) in their respective commentaries on Herodotus express their doubts as to the authenticity of the reference to Archilochus; similarly, Sploesteter (1911) had suspected Hdt. 5.113 of being an interpolation.

43 For full argumentation, see Kazanskaya (2016b) 237–244, especially 240–242 on Hdt. 5.113.

concerning historical figures or events,[44] thereby also admitting into his narrative a poetic voice that either resonates with his account or opposes it.

The uniformity of method in these five passages allows us to make several inferences with regard to the evocation of Sappho's κερτομία in Herodotus 2.135. Despite the absence of quotation, Herodotus was alluding to a precise poem that his audience knew (as in Herodotus 1.12, 5.95, and 5.113), and the reference must have concerned the figure central to this part of his narrative. I agree with Martin that Herodotus must be speaking of a specific poem.[45] It is also clear that this poem cannot be identified with the existing fragments of Sappho. However, it was certainly part of the cycle of poems on Sappho's family[46] in particular the group of poems on Charaxus' trip and his misadventure in Naucratis. To conclude, both syntax and observations on Herodotus' approach to lyric poetry suggest that the poem, evoked in Herodotus 2.135, criticized Rhodopis who is the central figure of the digression (cf. τῆς πέρι λέγεται ὅδε ὁ λόγος), not Charaxus.[47]

4 The Name of the Hetaera

The third question concerns the name of Charaxus' beloved. Herodotus (2.134–135), Strabo (17.1.33), Suda (δ 1466; ρ 211 Adler) and Photius (Lex. s.v. 'Ροδῶπις) call her Rhodopis (all but Herodotus also mention that Sappho called her Doricha); Athenaeus, on the other hand, insists that Doricha and Rhodopis were two different women, and that the woman that Charaxus fell in love with was Doricha. It has been noted that both Δωρίχα and 'Ροδῶπις can be used as personal names and as nicknames. On one hand, Δωρίχα is formed on the basis of Δωρίς with the use of the diminutive suffix -ιχ-, so that the name means 'the little Dorian'.[48] While this suffix does not seem to have been very productive in most dialects, it is well attested in Aeolic and Boeotian (incidentally, the name of Sappho's other brother's name, Λάριχος, has the same formation). On

---

44 Compare Verdin (1977) 64: 'tout en se rendant compte de l'élément subjectif que peuvent contenir les écrits, [Hérodote] a pris surtout en considération le caractère direct de ces témoignages qui se rapportaient à des réalités vécues par les auteurs.' See also Kazanskaya (2016b) 250–251.
45 Martin (2016) 120.
46 Obbink (2014) 35.
47 Compare Raaflaub (2016) 129: 'If Rhodopis stood out as the best in her category, Charaxos owes his mention in Herodotus to her and not to his own achievements. The historian does not even tell us why he went to Naucratis.'
48 See Chantraine (1933) 404 and Bechtel (1982) 558 for a list of proper names.

the other hand, Ῥοδῶπις finds parallels in other proper names (especially slave names) with a similar structure and resembling epithets. It is usually assumed that Doricha was the courtesan's real name, whereas Rhodopis was her 'professional' name.[49] This explanation, while it does account for the transmission of the double name, is not completely satisfactory. If Sappho called the courtesan Doricha, why did Herodotus identify her as Rhodopis known from other stories, especially the offering of ox-spits at Delphi? And why was Athenaeus so certain that this identification was wrong and that Doricha was not the same woman as Rhodopis?

Identification of Doricha with Rhodopis is problematic from the point of view of chronology. If Rhodopis lived during the reign of Amasis (i.e. after 570 BCE), as Herodotus tells us, Sappho would have been over fifty, and Charaxus, although we do not know the age difference between them, would have been even older. It is thus best to accept Athenaeus' claim that they were two different women.[50] Concerning the distribution of names, it can be pointed out that the name Doricha never appears independently of the Sappho-Charaxus story (whereas Rhodopis is mentioned in the Aesopic tradition, and the Delphic tradition, and finally in the pyramid story);[51] the name also preserves its Aeolic form, Δωρίχᾱ, without undergoing the phonetic change to *Δωρίχη which would be expected, had the name circulated independently in the Attic dialect or the κοινή. It seems safe to assume that Sappho gave the name of her brother's mistress as Δωρίχᾱ (cf. fr. 15.11) and only Doricha. However, given the controversy between Athenaeus and Herodotus, we can conjecture that there was something in Sappho's text that allowed Herodotus to identify the woman with Rhodopis. It might, of course, have been some specific detail about Charaxus' lover that resonated with Rhodopis' biography (given that both came from Naucratis and were women of loose morals). But it is equally possible that in the invective poem of which Herodotus and Athenaeus speak, Sappho

---

49   Thus, Page (1955) 55; Lloyd (1988) 86; Boardman (1994) 142n13. Legrand (in his note to Hdt. 2.135 n. 1) amusingly characterizes the name Ῥοδῶπις as '*un nom de guerre, une épithète louangeuse prise pour surnom.*' The fact that Sappho preferred to call the girl Doricha and not Rhodopis has been explained as a wish to avoid advertising her name: thus, di Benedetto (1982) 229, '*se Rhodopis era un vezzeggiativo, è comprensibile che Saffo evitasse di usarlo nelle sue poesie data la sua ostilità contro l'amante del fratello*'; cf. Palmer (*ad Ov. Her.* 15.63); Page (1955) 49 n. 1; etc. Dörrie (1975) 112n35 is sceptical of this explanation.
50   Cf. Ferrari (2014) 9.
51   On the pyramid story, see Hall (1904); van de Walle (1934); Coche-Zivie (1972). Lloyd in his commentary on Hdt. 2.134–135 provides a useful overview of works and opinions on the story of the pyramid. Add to this list Scobie (1977) 17–18 who analyses Strabo's account as the earliest attested version of the Cinderella story.

had refrained from mentioning Doricha's name but designated her instead by the word ῥοδῶπις, but not as a name, but as an epithet 'rosy-faced':[52] there is one example of deliberate omission of the name of the criticized person in Sappho—fr. 55, where she condemns to obscurity an unnamed woman. In that case the epithet could have been mistaken by Herodotus and other readers for an allusion to the famous hetaera. But if ῥοδῶπις did suggest the connection to Herodotus, why did Athenaeus not only fail to see it, but also contradict Herodotus so vehemently (Ἡρόδοτος δ' αὐτὴν Ῥοδῶπιν καλεῖ, ἀγνοῶν ὅτι ἑτέρα τῆς Δωρίχης ἐστὶν αὕτη)?

I would like to suggest that there was an important detail in which the text of the poem that Athenaeus had before him differed from one Herodotus knew. If the assumption concerning the use of ῥοδῶπις as an epithet is correct, in Athenaeus' times it would have been written as *βροδῶπις. Although neither the exact rules that determine the spelling βρ- for word-initial ῥ- nor the approximate date when this spelling came to be universalized for Aeolic texts is known, the ancient grammarians' remarks show that in late antiquity it came to be regarded as a specific mark of the Aeolic dialect.[53] Word-initial βρ- is consistent in βρόδον and its derivatives: note βρόδοισι (Sappho fr. 2.6); βροδόπαχυν Αὔων (fr. 58.19); βροδο[(fr. 74a.4); βροδοδάκτυλος σελάννα (96.8); βρόδα (fr. 96.13); cf. ἴων καὶ βρ[όδων (fr. 94.12–13).[54] The discrepancy between the Aeolic and the Ionian-Attic (or κοινή) form would have presented no difficulty in the case of a personal name: thus, although Sappho calls herself Ψάπφω,[55] the spelling raised no question among readers who knew her under the name Σαπφώ. However, if ῥοδῶπις appeared in Sappho as an epithet, and not as a name, the spelling *βρόδωπις would have weakened the association with the famous courtesan. We can also add that it would have suited Athenaeus' purposes in this passage to distinguish

---

52   The epithet ῥοδῶπις is not frequent, although it does appear in Nonnus (10.176, 11.487, 13.350, 33.19, 42.237, 42.428). Its rarity may be due to the fact that compound epithets with the second root -ωψ tend to be used to characterize the eyes, rather than the face; see Maxwell-Stuart (1981) 157–163.

53   The *Etymologicum Magnum* cites the authority of Herodian and Choeroboscus (*Et. M.* 210.42); cf. Priscianus (1.23 and 25); Johannes Grammaticus, *Comp.* 11; Eustath. *Comm. in Hom. Il.* 1.252. The question of the rendering of the digamma before -ρ- in Aeolic literary texts, of its approximate dating and rules, has been analyzed by M. Parry (1934) 142–143; Hooker (1977) 27–30; Bowie (1981) 80–84; Sowa (2011) 166–172. See also Lobel (1925) xxix–xxx.

54   I have excluded βρόδων in Sappho fr. 55.2 and βροδοπάχεες Χάριτες in fr. 53: in both cases the word-initial βρ- is an emendation, as the manuscripts read ῥόδων and ῥοδοπάχεες respectively.

55   Sapph. frr. 1.20, 65.5, 94.5, 133.2.

Rhodopis and Doricha, as it augmented the list of famous Naucratite courtesans, confirming the claim φιλεῖ γάρ πως ἡ Ναύκρατις, ὡς ὁ Ἡρόδοτός φησιν, ἐπαφροδίτους ἔχειν τὰς ἑταίρας (Athenaeus 13.596d).[56]

5 Conclusions

The study of these questions (the tone of the poem dealing with Charaxus' lover, the main target of Sappho's κερτομία, and the reasons behind the identification of Doricha with Rhodopis) throws light on the poem that we know only from references in later writers. This poem must have been part of the cycle that spoke of the poet's family (and in particular, of her brothers' affairs); criticism of Doricha's conduct was the main subject of this poem (although in such a context Charaxus himself would not have appeared in a flattering light), and Sappho must have been harsh on the girl, if Herodotus and Athenaeus describe her tone by the terms πολλὰ κατεκερτόμησε (Herodotus 2.135) and διὰ τῆς ποιήσεως διαβάλλει (Athenaeus 596b). Finally, the identification of Doricha with Rhodopis could be due to Sappho's choice to omit the girl's name in this poem (although she did name her in other poems, cf. fr. 15), as she also did in fr. 55 with regard to another criticized woman: if she replaced the name with the epithet ῥοδῶπις, it could explain the identification of Charaxus' Naucratite mistress with the famous hetaera from Naucratis. However, this last assumption remains purely conjectural.

References

Acosta-Hughes, B. 2003. Alexandrian Posidippus: On Rereading the GP Epigrams in Light of P. Mil. Vogl. VIII 309. In *Laboured in Papyrus Leaves: Perspectives on an Epigram Collection Attributed to Posidippus (P. Mil. Vogl. VIII 309)*, ed. B. Acosta-Hughes, E. Kosmetatou, and M. Baumbach, 42–56. Cambridge, MA.

Acosta-Hughes, B. 2010. *Arion's Lyre: Archaic Lyric into Hellenistic Poetry*. Princeton.

Acosta-Hughes, B. and Barbantani, S., ed. 2007. Inscribing Lyric. In *Brill's Companion to Hellenistic Epigram*, ed. P. Bing and J.S. Bruss, 429–457. Leiden.

Angiò, F. 1999. Posidippo di Pella, l'ep. XVII Gow-Page e l'Αἰθιοπία. *MH* 56: 150–158.

Asheri, D., Lloyd, A., and Corcella, A., eds. 2007. *A Commentary on Herodotus, Books I–IV*, ed. O. Murray and A. Moreno. Oxford.

---

56 More generally on the role of Naucratis in Athenaeus' *œuvre*, see Thompson (2000) 81–82.

Baehrs, J.C.F. 1856. *Herodoti Halicarnassensis Musae*. Vol. 1. Leipzig.
Bechtel, F. 1982. *Die historischen Personnennamen des Griechischen bis zur Kaiserzeit.* Hildesheim.
Beekes, R. 2010. *Etymological Dictionary of Greek*, with the assistance of L. van Beek. Vols. 1–2. Leiden.
Bierl, A. and Lardinois, A., eds. 2016. *The Newest Sappho: P. Sapph. Obbink and P.GC inv. 105, frs. 1–4*. Leiden.
Bing, P. 2009. *The Scroll and the Marble: Studies in Reading and Reception in Hellenistic Poetry*. Ann Arbor.
Boardman, J. 1994. Settlement for Trade and Land in North Africa: Problems of Identity. In *The Archaeology of Greek Colonisation: Essays Dedicated to Sir John Boardman*, ed. G.R. Tsetskhladze and F. de Angelis, 137–149. Oxford.
Bowie, A.M. 1981. *The Poetic Dialect of Sappho and Alcaeus*. New York.
Bowra, C.M. 1936. *Greek Lyric Poetry from Alcman to Stesichorus*. Oxford.
Burris, S., Fish, J., and Obbink, D. 2014. New Fragments of Book 1 of Sappho. *ZPE* 189: 1–28.
Chantraine, P. 1968–1977. *Dictionnaire étymologique de la langue grecque: Histoire des mots*. Vols. 1–4. Paris.
Chantraine, P. 1933. *Formation des noms en grec*. Paris.
Clay, J.S. 1999. Iliad 24.649 and the Semantics of κερτομέω. *CQ* 49: 618–621.
Coche-Zivie, C. 1972. Nitocris, Rhodopis et la troisième pyramide de Giza. *BIFAO* 72: 115–138.
Dale, A. 2011. Sapphica. *HSCPh* 106: 47–74.
di Benedetto, V. 1982. Sulla biografia di Saffo. *SCO* 32: 217–230.
Dörrie, H. 1975. *P. Ovidius Naso: Der Brief der Sappho an Phaon mit literarischem und kritischem Kommentar im Rahmen einer motivgeschichtlichen Studie*. Munich.
Ferrari, F. 2014. Saffo e i suoi fratelli e altri brani del primo libro. *ZPE* 192: 1–19.
Gabathuler, M. 1937. *Hellenistische Epigramme auf Dichter*. Basle.
Gomme, A.W. 1957. Interpretations of Some Poems of Alkaios and Sappho. *JHS* 77: 255–266.
Gottesman, A. 2008. The Pragmatics of Homeric κερτομία. *CQ* 58: 1–12.
Gow, A.S.F. and Page, D.L., ed. 1965. *The Greek Anthology*, vol. 1: *Hellenistic Epigrams*. Cambridge.
Gutzwiller, K.A. 2007. *A Guide to Hellenistic Literature*. Malden.
Hall, H.R. 1904. Nitokris-Rhodopis. *JHS* 24: 208–213.
Hooker, J.T. 1977. *The Language and Text of the Lesbian Poets*. Innsbruck.
Hooker, J.T. 1986. A Residual Problem in *Iliad* 24. *CQ* 36: 32–37.
How, W.W. and Wells, J. 1989. *A Commentary on Herodotus, with Introduction and Appendices*. Vols. 1–2. Oxford.
Jones, P.V. 1989. Iliad 24.649: Another Solution. *CQ* 39: 247–250.

Kazanskaya, M. 2016a. Posidippus 122 (Austin-Bastianini): Composition and Structure. *Philologia Classica* 11: 31–41.

Kazanskaya, M. 2016b. Références à la poésie lyrique en tant que source historique dans les *Histoires* d'Hérodote. *LALIES* 34: 233–259.

Klooster, J. 2011. *Poetry as Window and Mirror: Positioning the Poet in Hellenistic Poetry*. Leiden.

Knox, P.E. 2002. The *Heroides*: Elegiac Voices. In *Brill's Companion to Ovid*, ed. B. Weiden Boyd, 117–140. Leiden.

Lardinois, A. 2016. Sappho's Brothers Song and the Fictionality of Early Greek Lyric Poetry. In Bierl and Lardinois 2016: 167–187.

Lidov, J.B. 2002. Sappho, Herodotus, and the *Hetaira*. *CPh* 97: 203–237.

Lloyd, M. 2004. The Politeness of Achilles: Off-Record Conversation Strategies in Homer and the Meaning of κερτομία. *JHS* 124: 78–89.

Martin, R.P. 2016. Sappho, Iambist: Abusing the Brother. In Bierl and Lardinois 2016: 110–126.

Maxwell-Stuart, P.G. 1981. *Studies in Greek Colour Terminology*. Vol. 1. Leiden.

Morgan, L. 2016. The Reception of Sappho's Brothers Poem in Rome. In Bierl and Lardinois 2016: 293–301.

Murgia, C.E. 1985. Imitation and Authenticity in Ovid, *Met.* 1, 477 and *Her.* 15. *AJPh* 106: 456–474.

Obbink, D. 2014. Two New Poems by Sappho. *ZPE* 189: 32–49.

Obbink, D. 2016. The Newest Sappho: Text, Apparatus Criticus, and Translation. In Bierl and Lardinois 2016: 13–54.

Page, D.L. 1955. *Sappho and Alcaeus: An Introduction to the Study of Ancient Lesbian Poetry*. Oxford.

Parry, M. 1984. The Traces of the Digamma in Ionic and Lesbian Greek. *Language* 10: 130–144.

Pârvulescu, A. 1986. Grk. κέρτομος 'Mocking'. *Emerita* 54: 299–301.

Perpillou, J.-L. 1986. De 'couper' à 'insulter'. In *O-o-pe-ro-si: Festschrift für Ernst Risch zum 75. Geburtstag*, ed. A.M. Etter, 72–84. Berlin.

Poliziano, A. 1971. *Commento inedito all'epistola ovidiana di Saffo a Faone*, ed. E. Lazzeri. Florence.

Raaflaub, K.A. 2016. The Newest Sappho and Archaic Greek-Near Eastern Interactions. In Bierl and Lardinois 2016: 127–147.

Rosenmeyer, P.A. 1997. Her Master's Voice: Sappho's Dialogue with Homer. *MD* 39: 123–149.

Rosenmeyer, P.A. 2006. Sappho's Iambics. *Letras clásicas* 10: 11–36.

Rotstein, A. 2010. *The Idea of Iambos*. Oxford.

Saake, H. 1968. *Zur Kunst Sapphos: Motiv-analytische und kompositionstechnische Interpretationen*. Bochum.

Scheidweiler, F. 1958. Zwei Epigramme. *RhM* 101: 91–95.
Scobie, A. 1977. Some Folk-Tales in Graeco-Roman and Far-Eastern Sources. *Philologus* 121: 1–23.
Slings, S.R. 2002. Oral Strategies in the Language of Herodotus. In *Brill's Companion to Herodotus*, ed. E.J. Bakker, I.J.F. de Jong and H. van Wees. 53–77. Leiden.
Smyth, H.W., ed. 1900. *Greek Melic Poets*. London.
Sowa, W. 2011. Griechische Dialekte, dialektalen Glossen und die antike lexikographische Tradition. *Glotta* 87: 159–183.
Sploesteter, M. 1911. *De Solonis carminum civilium compositione*, Diss. Königsberg.
Stehle, E. 2016. Larichos in the Brothers Poem: Sappho Speaks Truth to the Wine-Pourer. In Bierl and Lardinois 2016: 266–292.
Tarrant, R.J. 1981. The Authenticity of the Letter of Sappho to Phaon (*Her.* XV). *HSCPh* 85: 133–153.
Thompson, D. 2000. Athenaeus in His Aegyptian Context. In *Athenaeus and His World: Reading Greek Culture in the Roman Empire*, ed. D. Braund and J. Wilkins, 77–84. Exeter.
Tränkle, H. 1960. *Die Sprachkunst des Properz und die Tradition der lateinischen Dichtersprache*. Wiesbaden.
Tsomis, G. 2001. *Zusammenschau der frühgriechischen monodischen Melik (Alkaios, Sappho, Anakreon)*. Stuttgart.
van de Walle, B. 1934. La 'quatrième pyramide' de Gizeh et la légende de Rhodopis. *AntCl* 3: 303–312.
Verdin, H. 1977. Les remarques critiques d'Hérodote et de Thucydide sur la poésie en tant que source historique. In *Historiographia antiqua: Commentationes Lovanienses in honorem W. Peremans septuagenarii editae*, 54–65. Louvain.
Wilamowitz-Moellendorff, U. von 1913. *Sappho und Simonides: Untersuchungen über griechische Lyriker*. Berlin.
Yatromanolakis, D. 2007. *Sappho in the Making: The Early Reception*. Washington, DC.

Editions Cited

Austin and Bastianini: *Posidippi Pellaei quae supersunt omnia*, ed. C. Austin and G. Bastianini. Milan, 2002.
Campbell: *Greek Lyric*, vol. 1: *Sappho and Alcaeus*, ed. D.A. Campbell. Cambridge, MA, 1990.
Gabathuler, M. 1937. *Hellenistische Epigramme auf Dichter*. Basle.
Gow and Page: *The Greek Anthology*, vol. 1: *Hellenistic Epigrams*, ed. A.S.F. Gow and D.L. Page. Cambridge, 1965.
Gronovius–Valla: *Herodoti Halicarnassei Historiarum libri IX, Musarum nominibus inscripti*, ed. J. Gronovius and L. Valla. Lugduni Batavorum, 1715.
Gulick: *Athenaeus, The Deipnosophists*, vols. 1–7. ed. C.B. Gulick. Cambridge, MA, 1950.

Knox: *Ovid, Heroides: Select Epistles*, ed. P.E. Knox. Cambridge, 1995.

Larcher, P.H. (1802). *Histoire d'Hérodote: traduite du grec, avec des remarques historiques et critiques, un essai sur la chronologie d'Hérodote, et une table géographique.* Vols. 1–9. Paris.

Legrand: *Hérodote, Histoires*, vol. 1–9, ed. P.-E. Legrand. Paris, 1932–1954.

Lloyd, A.B. (1988). *Herodotus Book II. Commentary 99–182.* Leiden, New York, Copenhagen, and Cologne.

Lobel and Page: *Poetarum lesbiorum fragmenta*, ed. E. Lobel and D. Page. Oxford, 1955.

Lobel: Σάπφους μέλη: *The Fragments of the Lyrical Poems of Sappho*, ed. E. Lobel. Oxford, 1925.

Olson: *Athenaeus, The Learned Banqueters*, vol. 1–8, ed. S.D. Olson. Cambridge, MA, 2006–2012.

Page: *Epigrammata graeca*, ed. D.L. Page. Oxford, 1975.

Palmer: *P. Ovidi Nasonis Heroides, with the Greek translation of Planudes*, ed. A. Palmer. Oxford, 1898.

Rawlinson, G. 1862. *History of Herodotus: A New English Version.* London.

Schott: *Posidippi Epigrammata*, ed. P. Schott. Diss. Berolinensis, 1905.

Voigt: *Sappho et Alcaeus. Fragmenta*, ed. E.-M. Voigt. Amsterdam, 1971.

West: *Iambi et elegi graeci ante Alexandrum cantati*, vol. 1–2, ed. M.L. West. Oxford, 1971–1972.

Zanetto, Pozzi, and Rampichini: *Posidippo, Epigrammi*, ed. G. Zanetto, S. Pozzi, and F. Rampichini. Milan, 2008.

PART 5

Reception in Roman Poetry

∴

CHAPTER 12

Alcaeus' *stasiotica*: Catullan and Horatian Readings

Ewen Bowie

1   Introduction

This chapter addresses two points in the long, complex, and fascinating story of the relation of Latin lyric poetry to the songs of the seventh/sixth century poet of the Mytilenean elite, Alcaeus. The first concerns Catullus, and departs radically from the current *communis opinio*. The second concerns Horace's interpretation of Alcaeus' ship poems, and may be judged to be less iconoclastic.

2   Catullus

      Furi et Aureli comites Catulli,
      siue in extremos penetrabit Indos,
      litus ut longe resonante Eoa
          tunditur unda,
5   siue in Hyrcanos Arabesue molles,
      seu Sagas sagittiferosue Parthos,
      siue quae septemgeminus colorat
          aequora Nilus,
      sive trans altas gradietur Alpes,
10   Caesaris uisens monimenta magni,
      Gallicum Rhenum horribile aequor ulti-
          mosque Britannos,
      omnia haec, quaecumque feret uoluntas
      caelitum, temptare simul parati,
15   pauca nuntiate meae puellae
          non bona dicta.
      cum suis uiuat ualeatque moechis,
      quos simul complexa tenet trecentos,
      nullum amans uere, sed identidem omnium
20   ilia rumpens;
      nec meum respectet, ut ante, amorem,

> qui illius culpa cecidit uelut prati
> ultimi flos, praetereunte postquam
> > tactus aratro est.

> Furius and Aurelius, Catullus's companions, whether he makes his way even to the furthest Indians, where the shore is beaten by the far-resounding Eastern wave, or to the Hyrcanians and soft Arabians, or to the Sacae and arrow-bearing Parthians, or to those plains whose colour the sevenfold Nile changes, or whether he will tramp across the high Alps, viewing the memorials of great Caesar, the Gaulish Rhine, the dreadful sea, and the Britons, remotest of men—O my friends, ready as you are to encounter all these things with me, whatever the will of the gods above shall bring, take a few words, not kind words, to my girl. Bid her live and flourish with her adulterous lovers, three hundred of whom she holds at once in her embrace, not loving one of them truly, but again and again breaking the thighs of them all. And let her not cast her eye, as before, on my love, which by her fault has collapsed like a flower on the meadow's edge, after it has been touched by the passing plough.
> > CATULLUS 11; trans. F. WARRE CORNISH, revised by G.P. GOOLD, modified[1]

In this well-known and much-discussed poem, Catullus addresses as *comites* two contemporaries who also appear 'separately or together' in six other poems (15, 16, 21, 23, 24, 26) in most of which 'the tone is abusive'.[2] He asks them to convey to his *puella* a message whose language constructs his relationship with Lesbia as one of marriage and presents him as using the formal Roman divorce procedure *per nuntium*—let her live with her countless adulterous lovers, taking no heed of his own passion which, by her actions, has toppled like a flower struck by a passing plough.[3]

I think it is fair to say that most scholars subscribe to some version of Fordyce's assessment in 1961:

---

1 The text is that reproduced by Mynors (1958) and Thomson (1978, 1998), i.e. accepting Haupt's conjecture *horribile aequor* for the reading of the Veronensis, *horribilesque*. Acceptance of the (to my mind less persuasive) conjecture *horribiles vitro* (McKie [1984]) would in no way affect my argument.
2 Fordyce (1961) 124. I share the view that these other sceptic poems do not prevent Furius and Aurelius being considered genuine *comites* of Catullus (cf. Thomson [1998]), certainly at the time of this particular poem's composition. For the sceptic tradition in Greek sympotic poetry see esp. Pellizer (1990).
3 Divorce *per nuntium*: Mayer (1983).

For his final repudiation of Lesbia Catullus deliberately returns to the form of poem 51, the lines translated from Sappho, in Sappho's own metre, in which he had addressed her in the early days of their love.[4]

I do not want to challenge the strong presence of Sapphic elements in poem 11, the only one among the polymetrics other than 51 to be written in the metre that by Catullus' day was being called 'Sapphic' by metricians, and the metre in which the whole of the first book of the Alexandrian edition of Sappho was composed—though of course it is not the only metre that Catullus shares with Sappho. One important Sapphic intertext was not picked out by Fordyce, but it had already been noted by Ellis:[5] the closing simile evokes one from a Sapphic epithalamion, Sappho fr. 105(c),[6] which compares a bride to a hyacinth trampled down by shepherds:

οἴαν τὰν ὐάκινθον ἐν ὤρεσι ποίμενες ἄνδρες
πόσσι καταστείβοισι, χάμαι δέ τε πόρφυρον ἄνθος ...

like the hyacinth that in the mountains shepherd men
trample down with their feet, and on the ground its dark-red flower ...

We know these lines of Sappho from their quotation by the essay περὶ ἑρμηνείας (*de elocutione*) 106, an essay ascribed to Demetrius of Phalerum but written in the late Hellenistic or early Roman period, and one that might conceivably have been known to Catullus. Given Catullus' manifest interest in Sappho, however, he will probably have known the lines from a complete edition or from a selection of her poems.[7] It is especially poignant that he alludes to a Sapphic wedding poem at the close of a poem terminating his relationship with his *puella*.

---

4 Fordyce (1961) 124. Compare e.g. Wiseman (1969); Wiseman (1974) 108–109.
5 Ellis (1889) 43. It is hinted at by Kroll's cross-reference in Kroll (1959) 26 (ad loc.) to Catullus 62.39 (also in an *epithalamium*!), but in commenting on that line Kroll (1959) 127 does not follow through the Sapphic ancestry of 62.39–48 (*ut flos in saeptis secretus nascitur hortis ... nec pueris iucunda manet, nec cara puellis*) that can be established by comparison with Longus, *Daphnis and Chloe* 3.33.4–34: for a detailed exploration, see Bowie (2013) 187–191.
6 I quote Sappho and Alaceus from Campbell (1982), a text both more up-to-date and user-friendly than Voigt (1971), and one its publishers have both kept in print and now made available online (unlike that of Voigt).
7 The new Cologne fragments of Sappho (P. Köln 21351 and 21376) have in my view made it clear that the poems of Sappho circulated in more than one edition in the Hellenistic and Roman periods; see Lardinois (2009).

Nor, in this context, do I want to explore at length the difference between a poem which uses the name Lesbia and one, like this and several others, which uses simply the term *puella*. But I do want to stress that one marker Catullus might have chosen to brand this poem as a descendant of Sappho's poetry, the name Lesbia, has *not* been employed.

I turn, now, to the grandiloquent opening three stanzas of the poem—its first half—in which Catullus lists the remote lands and peoples to which his *comites* Furius and Aurelius are supposedly (presumably on the basis of previous asseverations of loyal friendship) willing to accompany him: Indians, Hyrcanians, Arabs, Sacae, Parthians, and the Nile in the East; the Alps, Gaul, and Britain in the north-west.

There is nothing Sapphic about these exotic names. Sappho's surviving poetry has some mentions of nearby Lydia, as a place from which luxury accessories may be acquired (fr. 98a) or to which one of her girls has departed (fr. 96); in mythical contexts she refers to Troy (*nominatim* fr. 16.9); in connection with her brother's relationship with a *hetaira* from Naucratis she seems likely to have mentioned Naucratis and Egypt (fr. 202);[8] and in connection with Aphrodite she names Cyprus, Paphos, and a Panormos (fr. 35). But by comparison with melic contemporaries and near-contemporaries—Alcaeus, Stesichorus, Ibycus—her poetry draws little on exotic places and their names.

In this matter Alcaeus is different. He too mentioned Egypt, and according to Strabo went there (Strabo 1.2.30 = Alcaeus fr. 432); in central Greece he mentioned Coronea (fr. 325) and Delphi (fr. 307); in the northern Aegean Thrace and the river Hebrus (fr. 45); and much further afield Ascalon (fr. 48), and, in two different poems, Babylon (frr. 48.10 and fr. 350)—in one of these, Babylon is represented as located at the end of the world: ἦλθες ἐκ περάτων γᾶς ... ('you have come from the ends of the earth ...,' fr. 350.1); Scythians (fr. 354); Hyperboreans (fr. 307); and the other, western end of the world, bounded by the Ocean: ὄρνιθες τίνες οἴδ' Ὠκεάνω γᾶς ἀπὺ πειράτων ('what are these birds of the Ocean, from the ends of the earth,' fr. 345.1).

It might be reasonable to think, then, that in a poem written in a Lesbian metre also used by Alcaeus (e.g. in fr. 42), and in some ancient scholars' view actually invented by Alcaeus,[9] the catalogue of exotic places to which his

---

8 Naucratis is also the implied location of her brother Charaxus in the recently discovered 'Brothers song', for the best text of which see Obbink (2016) 25–26, but here too the exotic toponym is eschewed. For the probable Egyptian connection of fr. 189 (νίτρον / natron) see Bowie (2016) 162–163.
9 Marius Victorinus, *Ars grammatica* 6.161 Keil.

comites might be ready to accompany him might evoke Alcaeus rather than Sappho. Catullus' references, of course, are contemporary and relate closely to the military ambitions of the first triumvirate—he could not have achieved the effects at which he aimed by simply repeating exotic toponyms that Alcaeus' activities, and those of his brother, had made relevant to him and his Lesbian audiences.

Another reason for Catullus' readers to associate his poem with Alcaeus is precisely its fourth word, *comites*. Sappho does indeed use the term ἔταιραι ('companions') of her female friends to whom she might sing (fr. 160) and of the divine friends Leto and Niobe (fr. 142). She also seems to have used it in the singular of a friend, perhaps in a sexual context, in fr. 126, δαύοις ἀπάλας ἐτάρας ἐν στήθεσιν ('may you sleep on the breasts of your tender companion'). But there is no evidence that for Sappho the term had the same ideological charge as ἔται- ροι ('comrades') seems to have had for Alcaeus, to judge from the solemnity and passion with which Alcaeus claims in fr. 129 that he and his ἔταιροι (fr. 129.16) swore mutual loyalty, oaths of which Pittacus took no thought: κήνων … οὐ διε- λέξατο | πρὸς θῦμον ἀλλὰ βραιδίως πόσιν | ἔμβαις ἐπ' ὀρκίοσι … ('he did not have dialogue with these men's hearts, but he heedlessly trampled with his feet upon the oaths …,' fr. 129.21–23).

Alcaeus can be imagined asking his ἔταιροι to follow him to the ends of the earth; Sappho can hardly be imagined asking her ἔταιραι to do so.

I now turn to a further reason for seeing the opening of Catullus 11 as evoking Alcaeus. We have clear testimony to the survival of a poem of Alcaeus in which he addressed a *comes* and asked him to convey a message: fr. 428, set in the context of the struggle between Athens and Mytilene for control of Sigeum in the Troad in the years immediately preceding 600 BCE:

> παντοῖα καὶ ἄλλα ἐγένετο ἐν τῇσι μάχῃσι, ἐν δὲ δὴ καὶ Ἀλκαῖος ὁ ποιητὴς συμ- βολῆς γενομένης καὶ νικώντων Ἀθηναίων αὐτὸς μὲν φεύγων ἐκφεύγει, τὰ δέ οἱ ὅπλα ἴσχουσι Ἀθηναῖοι καί σφεα ἀνεκρέμασαν πρὸς τὸ Ἀθήναιον τὸ ἐν Σιγείῳ. ταῦτα δὲ Ἀλκαῖος ἐν μέλεϊ ποιήσας ἐπιτιθεῖ ἐς Μυτιλήνην ἐξαγγελλόμενος τὸ ἑωυτοῦ πάθος Μελανίππῳ ἀνδρὶ ἑταίρῳ.

> Among the various incidents of this war, one in particular is worth mention; in the course of a battle in which the Athenians had the upper hand, Alcaeus the poet took to flight and escaped, but his armour was taken by the Athenians and hung up in the temple of Athena at Sigeum. Alcaeus wrote a poem about this and sent it to Mytilene. In it he relates his own misfortune to his friend Melanippus.
>
> HDT. 5.95, trans. A.D. GODLEY

ὅτε καὶ Ἀλκαῖός φησιν ὁ ποιητὴς ἑαυτὸν ἔν τινι ἀγῶνι κακῶς φερόμενον τὰ ὅπλα
ῥίψαντα φυγεῖν. λέγει δὲ πρός τινα κήρυκα, κελεύσας ἀγγεῖλαι τοῖς ἐν οἴκωι
   Ἄλκαος σάος †ἄροι ἐνθάδ' οὐκυτον ἀληκτορὶν †
   ἐς Γλαυκώπιον ἶρον ὀνεκρέμασσαν Ἄττικοι

> it was indeed at this time that the poet Alcaeus says that when he was being worsted in a conflict he threw away his weapons and fled. And he says to a herald, telling him to take the message to the people at home:
>   Alcaeus is safe but his (?shield?)
>   the men of Attica have hung up in the temple of the Grey-eyed goddess
>
> STRABO 13.1.38 600C = ALCAEUS fr. 428

Meineke, following Kramer, believed that the sentence concerning Alcaeus, which is certainly corrupt, had crept into the text from a marginal note, and was not written by Strabo. Recent editors do not delete it,[10] and, by whomever it was written, it *seems* to preserve a fragment of Alcaeus, a fragment that is very likely to be from the poem mentioned by Herodotus.

I take this poem to have been addressed to Melanippus (who is also the addressee of the meta-sympotic poem fr. 38A), and to have asked him to act as a κᾶρυξ, and to carry to Mytilene the news of Alcaeus' loss of his armour to the Athenians. Alcaeus envisages two audiences, Melanippus, and doubtless other *hetairoi*, in the *hic et nunc* of the Mytileneans' base in the Troad, and then other, remote Mytileneans back home, where civic *symposia* and sympotic singing by older men doubtless continued while the city's νέοι were fighting and dying in the Troad. We have no evidence that Melanippus was asked to take a written version, nor that he was in any official sense or capacity a herald. Alcaeus is simply playing with the role of heralds in archaic Greece, as did Solon about the same time when he presented himself as a herald from the island of Salamis.[11] Such a game with the notion of a herald had already been played in the middle of the seventh century by Archilochus (fr. 185). Alcaeus' game is different, but since this poem is often claimed to be re-working the elegiac song of Archilochus on the loss of *his* shield, fr. 5, it may be that here Alcaeus is *also* showing that he can play the herald card differently from Archilochus fr. 185. Whether or not that is so, Alcaeus, in a world where certain formal commu-

---

10 E.g. Radt (2004) 578.
11 αὐτὸς κῆρυξ ἦλθον ἀφ' ἱμερτῆς Σαλαμῖνος κόσμον ἐπέων ᾠδὴν ἀντ' ἀγορῆς θέμενος ('I have come myself a herald from desirable Salamis, setting forth an adornment of verses, a song, instead of a speech,' Solon fr. 1.1–2).

nications were conducted by heralds and not by letters, telegrams, or emails, exploits the idea that his poem might be a formal communication to his *polis* Mytilene. The poem will first have been sung in the presence of Melanippus and others in the Mytilenean encampment near Sigeum, then later have circulated around the *symposia* of Mytilene. We have no right to suppose that Melanippus actually set off for Mytilene the morning after, though equally, perhaps, we have no right to deny that he might have done.

If Herodotus and perhaps Strabo knew Alcaeus' herald poem, Catullus, the aficionado of Lesbian melic poetry, most probably knew it too, and might reasonably have viewed it as a charter-text in the development of quasi-epistolary poetry.

For these reasons I suggest that Catullus expected the opening of his poem 11, whether an audience or reader encountered it on its first publication as a self-standing text or performance or whether a reader encountered it later in a collection (not necessarily in the position in that collection in which we find it in ours), to be read primarily against Alcaeus, not primarily against Sappho. For three stanzas Catullus casts himself and his *comites* as Alcaeus-like warriors, ready, like Alcaeus' brother Antimenidas, to go to the ends of the earth (fr. 350.1). But the poem the stanzas most evoke, fr. 428, was one in which Alcaeus confronted military humiliation, the loss of his ὅπλα, weapons. Catullus and his readers probably knew that Alcaeus' response was dismissive, like that of Archilochus (fr. 5) before him—though since we do not have the text of the poem such a stance is conjectural. Perhaps it was even a 'farewell to arms'— 'soon I shall be back among *symposia* and with my *hetairoi*'. If something like that were so, the intertext would prepare the reader for a move from grandiloquence to something quite different.

It will not, however, have prepared the reader for a sudden thematic switch from distant and exciting military adventures (in some sense Catullus' world of *negotium*) to the decisive and painful rupture in the poet's relations with his *puella* (his tangled and messy world of *otium*).[12] At that point an educated reader might have perceived an intertextual migration from the world of Alcaeus to that of Sappho, who seems not to have spared her rivals for the attention of her young *puellae*, whatever we suppose her relation to these *puellae* to have been (note the invective of frr. 55, 57, 133).[13] It is, however, a migration that does not involve total abandonment of the Alcaic *persona* of lines 1–12. The all-consuming rage and hurt that are so vehemently expressed in lines 13–16

---

12   I am grateful to Lucia Athanassaki for drawing my attention to this contrast.
13   See further on this question the contributions of Cacciagli and Schlesier to this volume.

are characteristic more of Alcaeus than of Sappho; and the dismissive suggestion that that the *puella* need no longer 'cast her eye on' (*respectet*) the poet's *amor* is analogous to Alcaeus' outrage that Pittacus took no heed of the stasiotic group's oaths: κήνων ὁ φύσγων οὐ διελέξατο | πρὸς θῦμον ἀλλὰ βραιδίως πόσιν ἔμβαις ... (fr. 129.21–22, quoted and translated above).

In the year 55 BCE, or early in 54 BCE, Catullus has offered his Roman readers a brilliant collage drawing *both* on Alcaeus *and* on Sappho.

3 Horace

My second proposal concerns Horace's understanding of Alcaeus' ship poems —a small issue in the very large and much-discussed question of Horace's refashioning of Alcaeus' poetry, both (meta-)sympotic and (meta-)stasiotic.

My starting point is *Odes* 1.14:

> O nauis, referent in mare te noui
> fluctus. O quid agis? Fortiter occupa
>   portum. Nonne uides ut
>   nudum remigio latus,
>
> 5   et malus celeri saucius Africo
>   antemnaeque gemant ac sine funibus
>   uix durare carinae
>   possint imperiosius
>
>   aequor? Non tibi sunt integra lintea,
> 10 non di, quos iterum pressa uoces malo.
>   Quamuis Pontica pinus,
>   siluae filia nobilis,
>
>   iactes et genus et nomen inutile:
>   nil pictis timidus nauita puppibus
> 15   fidit. Tu, nisi uentis
>   debes ludibrium, caue.
>
>   Nuper sollicitum quae mihi taedium,
>   nunc desiderium curaque non leuis,
>   interfusa nitentis
> 20   uites aequora Cycladas.

O ship! Will new waves carry you out to sea
again? O, what are you doing? Get boldly
   to harbour. Don't you see how
      your side is sheered of its oars,

your mast is crippled by the swift African wind,
and its yardarms are groaning, and without ropes
   the hull has little chance of holding out
      against the ever more tyrannical

waters? Your sails are unsound,
so too the gods you call upon again in dire distress.
   Though you are a Pontic pine,
      daughter of a well-born forest,

and boast your useless ancestry and name,
the frightened sailor puts no trust
   in painted sterns. Unless the winds
      are owed some sport by you, watch out!

Not long ago you were a worry and a weariness for me,
and now a longing and a no slight concern.
   So steer clear of the waters that swirl
      between the shining Cyclades.
         HORACE, *Odes* 1.14; trans. DAVID WEST, adapted[14]

It is almost a *communis opinio* that Horace's ship is an allegory for the *res publica*.[15] That was observed a century after its composition by Quintilian 8.6.44: *navem pro re publica, fluctus et tempestates pro bellis civilibus, portum pro pace atque Concordia dicit*, and was accepted by Nisbet and Hubbard among many other scholars.[16] Nisbet and Hubbard also note that the poem clearly relates

---

14 The text is that of Garrod (1901).
15 As Bruno Currie has pointed out to me, a strong case can also be made for a meta-poetic reading of *Odes* 1.14. I do not think the same holds for the Alcaeus fragments, so I do not pursue this issue here.
16 Nisbet and Hubbard (1970) 179. So, albeit with various *caveats* and degrees of caution, Jocelyn (1982); Nisbet (1995) 416–418; Syndikus (2001) 162n13; Cucchiarelli (2004, 2005); Strauss Clay (2010) 139–140; Mayer (2012) 136–137. *Contra* Knorr (2006); Kruschwitz (2007). The allegory of the ship of state has of course also been extensively discussed with rela-

not simply to one but to two songs of Alcaeus, fr. 6 and 326 Lobel and Page = 208 Voigt / Campbell.

> τόδ' αὖ]τε κῦμα τὼ π[ρ]οτέρ[ω †νέμω
> στείχει, παρέξει δ' ἄ[μμι πόνον π]όλυν
> ἄντλην ἐπ]εί κε νᾶ[ος ἔμβαι
> [   ].όμεθ' ἐ[
>
> 5   [   ]..[..]·[
>   [   ]
>   φαρξώμεθ' ὡς ὤκιστα [
> 8   ἐς δ' ἔχυρον λίμενα δρό[μωμεν,
>
> καὶ μή τιν' ὄκνος μόλθ[ακος
> λάβηι· πρόδηλον γάρ· μεγ[
> μνάσθητε τῶ πάροιθε γ[
> 12 νῦν τις ἄνηρ δόκιμος γε[
>
> καὶ μὴ καταισχύνωμεν[
> 14 ἔσλοις τόκηας γᾶς ὔπα κε[ιμένοις
>   ..] τᾶνδ[
>   τὰν πο[

> This wave in turn (like?) the previous one,
> advances, and it will give us much trouble
>   to bale out when it enters the ship's ...
>
> Let us strengthen (the ship's sides) as quickly as possible,
> 8   and let us race into a secure harbour;
>
> and let soft fear not
> seize any of us; for a great (ordeal) stands clear before us.
>   Remember the previous (hardship):
>   now let every man show himself steadfast.

---

tion to Alcaeus, e.g. recently by Brock (2013). See also Nunns (2010) (I am grateful to Bruno Currie for drawing my attention to this thesis).

> And let us not disgrace (by cowardice)
> 14 our noble fathers lying beneath the earth,
> who ...
> the city ... being
>
> ALCAEUS fr. 6 LOBEL and PAGE / VOIGT / CAMPBELL; trans. CAMPBELL

> ἀσυννέτημμι τῶν ἀνέμων στάσιν,
> τὸ μὲν γὰρ ἔνθεν κῦμα κυλίνδεται,
> τὸ δ' ἔνθεν, ἄμμες δ' ὂν τὸ μέσσον
> νᾶϊ φορήμμεθα σὺν μελαίναι
>
> 5 χείμωνι μόχθεντες μεγάλωι μάλα·
> πὲρ μὲν γὰρ ἄντλος ἰστοπέδαν ἔχει,
> λαῖφος δὲ πὰν ζάδηλον ἤδη,
> καὶ λάκιδες μέγαλαι κὰτ αὖτο,
>
> χόλαισι δ' ἄγκυ(ρ)ραι, τὰ δ' ὀή[ια ...

> I fail to understand the direction of the winds:
> one wave rolls in from this side,
> another from that, and we in the middle
> are carried along in company with our black ship,
>
> 5 much distressed in the great storm.
> The bilge-water covers the masthold;
> all the sail lets the light through now,
> and there are great rents in it;
>
> the anchors are slackening; the rudders ...
>
> ALCAEUS fr. 326.1–9 LOBEL and PAGE = 208.1–9 VOIGT / CAMPBELL; trans. CAMPBELL

Nisbet and Hubbard further observe that these poems of Alcaeus were read as allegorical by Heraclitus in his *quaestiones Homericae*, and pronounce this reading to be correct, seeing as decisive the presence in fr. 6 line 27 of the word μοναρχίαν and in lines 11–14 'an appeal to remember former toils and dead ancestors' (καὶ μὴ καταίσχυνωμεν [| ἔσλοις τόκηας γᾶς ὔπα κε[ιμένοις). Here they follow Page.[17]

---

[17] Page (1955) 184.

It has never seemed to me that these arguments put forward by Page *were* decisive, and I questioned them in an article that took shape in the early 1980s and was published in 1986. My main point is this: we can imagine—and Alcaeus could either recall or imagine—a situation where he and his political associates, his *hetairoi*, were engaged in a shipboard military operation where there was a choice between beaching the ship, and thus securing safety at the expense of their operation's success, or keeping going until they reached a port that was in friendly hands—fr. 6 line 8 ἐς δ'ἔχυρον λίμενα δρόμωμεν. That of course entails the belief that a Mytilenean sympotic singer of the late 7th or early 6th centuries might conjure up for his audience a storm-scene of a sort with which most or all of that audience will have been familiar—a procedure against which Page unleashed his characteristically hyperbolic rhetoric.

It may be that a non-allegorical interpretation was not envisaged by Alcaeus, but at least the points I have made seem to me to show that such an interpretation is possible. Furthermore, Horace's presentation of stormy Alcaic seas in another poem, *Odes* 1.32, indicate that he was aware of such an interpretation. Addressing his lyre (*barbite*), Horace describes it as one used by the bellicose Alcaeus to sing of Dionysus, the Muses, Venus, Cupid, and his dark-eyed ἐρώμενος Lycus, even in battle-contexts or when his storm-tossed ship had been moored on a wave-beaten beach:

> Poscimus, si quid uacui sub umbra
> lusimus tecum, quod et hunc in annum
> uiuat et pluris, age, dic Latinum,
>   barbite, carmen,
>
> 5 Lesbio primum modulate ciui,
> qui, ferox bello, tamen inter arma,
> siue iactatam religarat udo
>   litore nauem,
>
> Liberum et Musas Veneremque et illi
> 10 semper haerentem puerum canebat
> et Lycum nigris oculis nigroque
>   crine decorum.
>
> O decus Phoebi et dapibus supremi
> grata testudo Iouis, o laborum
> 15 dulce lenimen, mihi cumque salue
>   rite uocanti.

We beg, if ever at leisure with you in the shade
we have played a melody that may live for this year
and for more, come, sound a Latin
   song, my Greek lyre,

first tuned by a citizen of Lesbos,
who, fierce in war, yet in the time of battle,
or if he had tied up his battered ship
   on the wave-soaked shore,

would still sing of Bacchus and the Muses,
of Venus and the boy who is always clinging to her side,
and of Lycus, with his jet-black eyes and jet-black
   hair, gorgeous.

O glory of Phoebus, welcome at the feasts
of supreme Jupiter, tortoise-lyre, O my labours'
sweet assuager, grant me your aid whenever
   I solemnly call upon you.
      HORACE, *Odes* 1.32; trans. DAVID WEST, adapted[18]

The sequence *ferox bello, tamen inter arma, | siue iactatam religarat udo | litore nauem* is unambiguous: Alcaeus was a tough fighter, but even in the course of a war, or in a breathing space afforded by the beaching of a ship, he would sing *sympotica*: such a ship has been storm-tossed, *iactatam*, and the shore on which it is beached is wet, *udo*, because it too has been wave-beaten.

A similar sequence is found in *Odes* 2.13: after casting imprecations on the tree that fell and nearly killed him, and reflecting on the unpredictability of death, Horace imagines how in the underworld he nearly heard Sappho and Alcaeus performing, the latter singing of *dura nauis, dura fugae mala, dura belli*:

Quam paene furuae regna Proserpinae
et iudicantem uidimus Aeacum
   sedesque discriptas piorum et
      Aeoliis fidibus querentem

---

18   The text is based on that of Garrod OCT, but reading *poscimus* for his *poscimur* in line 1.

> 25 Sappho puellis de popularibus
> et te sonantem plenius aureo,
>   Alcaee, plectro dura nauis,
>   dura fugae mala, dura belli.
>
> How near did we come to having the realms of dark Proserpina
> and Aeacus sitting in judgement before our eyes,
>   and the seats of the holy set apart,
>   and, accompanied by her Aeolian strings, the plaints
>
> of Sappho about the girls of her community,
> and you, resonating in fuller tones, with a golden
>   plectrum, Alcaeus, the hardships of ship-life,
>   the tough hardships of exile, the hardships of war.
>
> HORACE *Odes* 2.13.21–28; trans. DAVID WEST, adapted

As Nisbet and Hubbard observed, in 2.13.27–28 *nauis* 'can hardly refer simply to politics'[19]—that is, Horace offers three different, albeit related, examples of *mala*: those to do with a ship, those to do with exile, and those to do with war.

Nisbet and Hubbard also remark (363): 'as well as writing about the ship of state (above, p. 179) Alcaeus seems to have written about a real ship, or at any rate Horace thought that he did'. But this observation on p. 363 had no impact on the argument of p. 179—doubtless partly because of the way in which Nisbet and Hubbard proceeded with their commentary, writing a draft commentary on each *Ode* separately, showing these drafts to each other, and then moving on to the next poem.

One may doubt that Horace assembled his first book of *Odes* in quite this way—indeed the artistry of the arrangement has been brought out by many scholars. So if at one point in his 38 poem-book he offers us a poem (14) that reads Alcaeus' ship—or ships—allegorically, and then at another point a poem (32) that reads Alcaeus' ship—or ships—literally, we are not entitled to assume that he knew some other ship poems of Alcaeus that were manifestly to be understood literally—poems that we simply happen to have lost, and about which Heraclitus misleadingly kept silent.

To me, at least, a more persuasive story is the following. Horace knew his Alcaeus well. He also, I suggest, knew Hellenistic scholarship on Alcaeus.[20] Such scholarship discussed the ship poems, and one branch of it appears in

---

19   Nisbet and Hubbard (1970) 363, commenting not on 2.13 but on 1.32.8.
20   Cf. Alcaeus fr. 305 and 306 (= *P.Oxy.* 2306 and 2307), commentaries written in the second

Heraclitus, who is hunting for allegories and very ready to accept an allegorical interpretation when one is on offer. But Horace knew that there was another view, and he displays himself as a *poeta doctus* by presenting his readers in the same book with two poems each of which implied a different reading of Alcaeus.

References

Bierl, A. and Lardinois, A., eds. 2016. *The Newest Sappho. P. Sapph. Obbink and P. GC inv. 105, frs. 1–4. Studies in Archaic and Classical Song 2 (Mnemosyne Supplement 392).* Leiden.

Bowie, E.L. 1986. Early Greek Elegy, Symposium and Public Festival. *JHS* 106: 13–35.

Bowie, E.L. 2013. Caging Grasshoppers: Longus' Materials for Weaving 'Reality.' In *The Construction of the Real and Ideal in the Ancient Novel*. Ancient Narrative *Supplementum* 17, ed. M. Paschalis and S. Panayotakis. 179–197. Groningen.

Bowie, E.L. 2016. How did Sappho's Songs Get Into the Male Sympotic Repertoire? In Bierl and Lardinois 2016: 148–164.

Brock, R. 2013. *Greek Political Imagery from Homer to Aristotle*. London.

Campbell, D.A. 1982. *Greek Lyric. Vol. 1. Sappho Alcaeus*. Cambridge, MA.

Cucchiarelli, A. 2004. La nave e lo spettatore. Forme dell' allegoria da Alceo ad Orazio I. *SIFC*[4] 2: 189–206.

Cucchiarelli, A. 2005. La nave e lo spettatore. Forme dell' allegoria da Alceo ad Orazio II. *SIFC*[4] 3: 30–72.

Davis, G., ed. 2010. *A Companion to Horace*. Chichester.

Ellis, R. 1889. *A Commentary on Catullus*. 2nd edn. Oxford.

Fordyce, C.J. 1961. *Catullus: A Commentary*. Oxford.

Garrod, H.W., ed. 1901. *Q. Horati Flacci opera*. Oxford.

Greene, E. and Skinner, M.B., eds. 2009. *The New Sappho on Old Age: Textual and Philosophical Issues. Hellenic Studies 38*. Washington, DC.

Jocelyn, H.D. 1982. Boats, Women, and Horace *Odes* 1.14. *CPh* 77: 330–335.

Knorr, O. 2006. Horace's Ship Ode (*Odes* 1.14) in Context: A Metaphorical Love-triangle. *TAPhA* 136: 149–169.

Kroll, W. 1959. *C. Valerius Catullus*. 3rd edn. Stuttgart.

Kruschwitz, P. 2007. *Fluctuat nec mergitur*: Überlegungen zu Horaz' Ode 1, 14. *Hyperboreus: Studia Classica* 13: 151–173.

---

century CE, but very probably drawing on Hellenistic scholarship: fr. 305(b) relates precisely to fr. 208.

Lardinois, A. 2009. The New Sappho Poem (P. Köln 21351 and 21376). Key to the Old Fragments. In Greene and Skinner 2009: 41–57.

Mayer, R.G. 1983. Catullus' divorce. *CQ* 33: 297–298.

Mayer, R.G. 2012. *Horace. Odes Book 1.* Cambridge.

McKie, D. 1984. The Horrible and Ultimate Britons: Catullus 11.11. *PCPhS* 208 (n.s. 30): 74–78.

Murray, O., ed. 1990. *A Symposium on the* Symposion. Oxford.

Mynors, R.A.B., ed. 1958. *C. Valerii Catulli carmina.* Oxford.

Nisbet, R.G.M. 1995. *Collected Papers on Latin Literature*, ed. S.J. Harrison. Oxford.

Nisbet, R.G.M. and Hubbard, M. 1970. *A Commentary on Horace:* Odes *Book One.* Oxford.

Nunns, L. 2010. Nature, Imagery and Alcaeus. DPhil thesis, Oxford.

Obbink, D. 2016. The Newest Sappho: Text, Appartus Criticus, and Translation. In Bierl and Lardinois 2016: 13–33.

Page, D.L. 1955. *Sappho and Alcaeus.* Oxford.

Pellizer, E. 1990. Outlines of a Morphology of Sympotic Entertainment. In Murray 1990: 177–184.

Radt, S. 2004. *Strabons Geographika: mit Übersetzung und Kommentar*, Vol. 3. Göttingen.

Strauss Clay, J. 2010. Horace and Lesbian lyric. In Davis 2010: 128–146.

Syndikus, H. 2001. *Die Lyrik des Horaz: eine Interpretation der Oden.* 3rd edn. Darmstadt.

Thomson, D.F.S. 1978. *Catullus. A Critical Edition.* Chapel Hill.

Thomson, D.F.S. 1998. *Catullus: Edited with a Textual and Interpretative Commentary.* Toronto.

Voigt, E.-M. 1971. *Sappho et Alcaeus.* Amsterdam.

Wiseman, T.P. 1969. *Catullan Questions.* Leicester.

Wiseman, T.P. 1974. *Cinna the Poet and other Roman Essays.* Leicester.

CHAPTER 13

Pindar, Paratexts, and Poetry: Architectural Metaphors in Pindar and Roman Poets (Virgil, Horace, Propertius, Ovid, and Statius)

Gregor Bitto

1   Introduction*

'One might indeed almost say that Latin literature owed its origin to "grammar".' Thus runs M.L. Clarke's conclusion concerning the influence of Alexandrian philology on Latin literature. Accordingly, for Livius Andronicus' translation of Homer's *Odyssey*, the first work of Latin poetry, Hermann Fränkel can detect traces of Alexandrian exegesis.[1] And the same has successfully been done for later authors as well, such as Ennius, Catullus, and Virgil.[2]

However, this influence of philology is not limited to literary works. For example, in a letter to Dolabella dating to 45 BCE, Cicero uses Greek technical terms in order to refer to a conflict where he acted as arbiter between a friend of Dolabella's, Nicias, and his opponent Vidius:

> profert alter, opinor, duobus uersiculis expensum Niciae, alter Aristarchus hos ὀβελίζει; ego tamquam criticus antiquus iudicaturus sum utrum sint τοῦ ποιητοῦ an παρεμβεβλημένοι.

---

* Clarke (1971) 19. I want to thank the organizers of the conference, Ian Rutherford and Bruno Currie, for the wonderful possibility to present my ideas to such an inspiring audience. Furthermore, I have to thank Professor Bardo Gauly for reading several versions of this chapter and for making very helpful suggestions for its improvement. Last, but not least I want to thank the anonymous reviewer and the editor Bruno Currie for their corrections and supplements.

The word paratext is used here in the broad sense as it was employed in the conference's concept (in the sense of scholarly paratexts as e.g. commentaries, biographies etc.). For a concise overview of theoretical issues of paratextuality, see Jansen (2014) 3–9.

The following editions have been used: for Horace Shackleton Bailey's Teubner; for Propertius Heyworth's OCT; for Ovid Tarrant's OCT; for Statius Courtney's OCT; for Virgil Mynors' OCT; for the scholia to Pindar Drachmann's Teubner.

1   Fränkel (1932) 306–308.
2   See e.g. for Ennius: Lennartz (1994) and Bitto (2013); for Catullus: Zetzel (1978); for Virgil: Schlunk (1974) and Schmit-Neuerburg (1999). See now, too, Bitto and Ginestí Rosell (2019).

The one, as I see it, has a record of two little lines concerning money loaned to Nicias, the other obelizes them as a second Aristarchus, whereas I am to decide like an ancient critic whether they are authentic or interpolated.[3]

CICERO, *Ad Familiares*, 9.10.1; my translation

Nicias, being not only a friend of Dolabella's but also a grammarian,[4] triggered this witty wordplay. But, apart from being funny, this quotation also shows that Cicero can safely assume that his addressee is familiar with Greek philological terminology. Moreover, we find such philological wordplay not only in private correspondence: also in the speech *In Pisonem* Cicero alludes to Aristarchus as a philologist *par excellence*.[5]

Two factors are of importance in order to explain the omnipresence of philology. The first is that a commentary is necessary and the second is that one is inescapable. Therefore, literature was not just read in schools, but it was also studied with philological tools and methods. Thus a philological approach to literature became the primary reading mode.[6]

That some sort of help with grammar, vocabulary, *realia*, and historical background, among other things, was needed is easy to imagine.[7] But, taking an Alcaeus papyrus as an example, Oliver Lyne stated:

---

3 Cicero refers several times to Aristarchus as the embodiment of textual and literary criticism: see *Fam.* 3.11.5 and *Att.* 1.14.3. In the last passage, Atticus is called Cicero's Aristarchus because he emends Cicero's writing (cf., too, *Att.* 15.14.4 and 16.11.1). Although some of these references are made jokingly, the humour is not on Aristarchus as though *antiquus criticus* might suggest a dated or defunct critical activity. It arises from the contradiction between Aristarchus's high standing and the mundane context. Cicero's calling Atticus his Aristarchus supports this. In general, the view on Aristarchus in antiquity is very positive and in later antiquity even enthusiastic; see Pfeiffer (1968) 232.
4 For Nicias, see Herzog (1922) 190–216 (for Cicero's letter, see 199–200) and Christes (1979) 55–56. Suetonius also quotes Cicero's letter to Dolabella in his account of Nicias (*Gram.* 14).
5 *Pis.* 73.
6 For the role of γραμματική in ancient education, see Morgan (1998) 152–189. For an exemplary study concerning education in Hellenistic and Roman Egypt, see Cribiore (2001), esp. 185–219 for topics and approaches.
7 Compare Porro (1994) 23, on Horace and Alcaeus: '*pure sembra ragionevole pensare che ai carmi, quasi certamente nell'edizione aristarchea, fosse affiancato un hypomnema che agevolasse l'interpretazione: anche se la conoscenza del greco da parte del Venosino è fuor di discussione, e indubbio che la lingua di Alceo offrisse non meno motivi di oscurità ad Orazio che a Demetrio Lacone o a Dionigi di Alicarnasso.*' And in general Barchiesi (2002) 114: 'If Horace ... was reading the learned editions of Pindar and other Greek masters, he would be in a position similar to our own, that of trying to imagine a distant universe through written testimonia.'

> It is educational to see ... how inescapable commentary in some texts was ... The way such 'scholia' are now relegated to the apparatus gives a misleading impression of the impact commentary might have made.[8]

Furthermore, commentaries on Greek poets became a stimulus for emulation. According to Tilman Schmit-Neuerburg, Virgil does not depend on Homeric scholarship, but consciously adapts its ideas and wants his audience to consider him to be a learned *Homerus Romanus*.[9] Thus Virgil uses the Alexandrian Homeric exegesis as 'a stimulation and above all as a projection screen for his own poetic ideas and concepts'.[10] Seen in this light, parallels between a Roman author and Alexandrian exegesis are to be interpreted neither as unrelated phenomena nor as intellectual dependency, but as conscious references.

So, when I turn now to the reception of Pindaric philology in Rome, I assume the same thing. I do not want to imagine, for example Horace cobbling together lines from Pindar and certain commentaries.[11] Rather, I think that knowing a poet and his work implies for a (Roman) Hellenistic *poeta doctus* knowing the accompanying commentary tradition as well. So, it is not the necessity of a commentary, which I want to stress. It is, rather, a certain trait of Roman poetry I want to illustrate, a poetry that gains part of its appeal from this philological reflection on its predecessors. In a profound pun, Alessandro Barchiesi has termed Horace's *carmina* 'secondary lyric', with all the implications of this *callida iunctura*.[12]

For Pindar, we are in the fortunate position of possessing not only four almost complete books of poetry transmitted through manuscript tradition, but also of benefitting from the fact that these manuscripts contain valuable extracts from ancient commentaries.[13] Thus Pindar is the only lyric poet for whom we are able to trace the reception of his poetry and its accompanying commentary tradition in antiquity to a great extent.[14]

---

8   Lyne (2005) 543n6.
9   Schmit-Neuerburg (1999) 4.
10 Schmit-Neuerburg (1999) 353 ('*als Anregung, vor allem aber auch als Projektionsfläche eigener dichterischer Ideen und Konzepte*').
11 For a fuller discussion of the methodological problems, see Bitto (2012) 18–23. For a short overview about the reception of Pindar in Rome, see Bitto (2012) 41–44.
12 Barchiesi (2009) 326.
13 For a short history of the textual transmission of the Pindaric scholia, see Bitto (2012) 50–60. For the Alexandrian Pindar edition(s), see Negri (2004) and Lowe (2007). For a 'diachronic' reading of ancient interpretations of Pindar that includes the scholia see Phillips (2016).
14 For other lyric poets, only papyrus fragments remain. For Alcaeus, Alcman, and Bac-

Pindar was known to the late republican audience at least by name and had a certain reputation as a canonical writer as we can assume from several mentions in Cicero's rhetorical and philosophical writings.[15] Cicero himself seems to have possessed an intimate knowledge of Pindar, as we can see from three quotations in letters to Atticus, dating from 45 BCE.[16] But, when dealing with Pindar's reception in Roman poetical texts, one faces a paradoxical situation. The two poets named by Horace and Ovid[17] as the foremost Pindaric poets of the day, Titius and Rufus, are completely lost. So, ironically Horace, the poet who in *Odes* 4.2 appears to advise against Pindaric imitation,[18] is for us the one who became the benchmark for the Roman reception of Pindar.

Thus Horace is the starting point of my analysis.[19] As an exemplary case, I take the reception of two famous metaphoric passages from Pindar in which a building and its physical existence are used for metapoetic statements. For the first passage, we will move chronologically from Horace to Statius.

2   Horace

In the now proverbial opening lines of *Odes* 3.30, the final ode of the first collection, Horace places his poetic achievement above buildings such as the pyramids because what he has accomplished is immune to rain, wind, and time:

> Exegi monumentum aere perennius
> regalique situ pyramidum altius,
> quod non imber edax, non Aquilo inpotens
> possit diruere aut innumerabilis
> annorum series et fuga temporum.

> I have completed a monument more lasting than bronze / and higher than the decaying Pyramids of kings, / which cannot be destroyed by the gnaw-

---

chylides see the first volumes in the *Commentaria et lexica Graeca in papyris reperta* series.

15   *Or.* 4; *Fin.* 2.115.
16   *Att.* 10.10.3: fr. 105; *Att.* 12.5.1: *Nem.* 1.1; *Att.* 13.38.2: fr. 213.
17   Hor. *Ep.* 1.3.9–14; Ov. *Pont.* 4.16.28.
18   For *Carm.* 4.2 and its *recusatio*, see the convincing interpretations of Harrison (1995) and Becker (1963) 124–134, as well as Athanassaki (2016) on the importance of the (irreproducible) performance context of a Pindaric ode as a main difference between Horace and Pindar.
19   The following section is taken from Bitto (2012) 253–255 (with alterations).

ing rain / nor wild north wind, or by the unnumbered / procession of the years and flight of time.
> HORACE, *Odes* 3.30.1–5, trans. DAVID WEST

In Pindar's sixth *Pythian* we find a similar comparison, in which a treasure-house of a Pythian victor serves as an analogy for Pindar's epinician ode.[20]

Πυθιόνικος ἔνθ' ὀλβίοισιν Ἐμμενίδαις
ποταμίᾳ τ' Ἀκράγαντι καὶ μὰν Ξενοκράτει
ἑτοῖμος ὕμνων θησαυρὸς ἐν πολυχρύσῳ
Ἀπολλωνίᾳ τετείχισται νάπᾳ·
τὸν οὔτε χειμέριος ὄμβρος, ἐπακτὸς ἐλθών
 ἐριβρόμου νεφέλας
στρατὸς ἀμείλιχος, οὔτ' ἄνεμος ἐς μυχούς
ἁλὸς ἄξοισι παμφόρῳ χεράδει
τυπτόμενον.

[...] where at hand for the fortunate Emmenidai / and for Akragas on its river, yes, and for Xenokrates, / a Pythian victor's/treasure house of hymns / has been built in Apollo's valley rich in gold, / one which neither winter rain, coming from abroad / as relentless army / from a loudly rumbling cloud, nor wind shall buffet / and with their deluge of silt carry into the depths / of the sea.
> PINDAR, *Pythian* 6.5–14; trans. WILLIAM RACE

Both poets share a set of three elements with environmental conditions that are detrimental to physical objects. These two sets are similarly, but not identically structured. Pindar has a dicolon with an apposition, Horace a tricolon.

Two elements are analogous, but with a variation. Pindar and Horace begin with the rain, but choose different attributes: *edax* (gnawing) in Horace, χειμέ-

---

20 I concentrate here on one point of comparison. For other approaches, see e.g. Lowrie (1997) 70–76.
  Several other intertexts have been offered, especially Simonides, see e.g. Nisbet and Rudd (2004), 365–366 and the notes to lines 1–4. This has led Cavarzere (1996) 239 to read 3.30 as announcement of a different poetic programme for Book IV, one that combines Pindar and Simonides, in contrast to the Aeolic programme of Books I–III. But I hope to show that the Pindaric intertext and the further receptions of Horace's treatment of Pindar create a meaningful nexus of interrelated allusions.
  For Simonides and Horace, see e.g. Harrison (2001), for an overview 261–262, and 263–264 for *Carm.* 3.30. For Simonides in Horace's fourth book of odes, see Barchiesi (1996).

ριος (hibernal) in Pindar. With the wind-element that both poets share, too, we can discern a change from generalization to specification: from simple ἄνεμος in Pindar to the north wind in Horace, which has an attribute attached to it (*Aquilo inpotens*).

Horace's third element has no counterpart in Pindar. Apart from rain and wind, Pindar's second element, the cloud army (νεφέλας στρατός), is a metaphorical apposition to the rain that has been severely criticized in the scholia. Pindar is said to have used an austere metaphor in a dithyrambic manner (σκληρᾷ μεταφορᾷ χρησάμενος διθυραμβωδῶς).[21] It seems that Horace approves of this criticism and thus has avoided adopting Pindar's metaphor. Or, if we want to rephrase this, Horace has been inspired by this criticism to look for a different third element, one that is closer to the world of thoughts of his own odes. Horace's tricolon is completed by the idea of time. Yet, this very idea is prefigured in the scholia. Another scholion[22] explains the treasure-house in the following way: 'this is the hymn: because it is treasured for all time' (ὁ ὕμνος· θησαυρίζεται γὰρ παντὶ τῷ χρόνῳ). This idea of time treasuring the hymn is not part of Pindar's ode but was added by the commentator. And this must have seemed a fitting supplement for Horace who shows himself in many odes as being interested in the topics of time and transitoriness.[23] Accordingly, this idea is put at the end of the tricolon and expressed in a very emphatic way: *innumerabilis annorum series* and *fuga temporum*.

3   Propertius

Now we turn to Propertius. The third book's opening cycle of five elegies has been interpreted as a reaction to the Roman odes, the opening cycle of Horace's third book of *Odes*.[24] The second elegy has an especially strong intertextual relationship with Horatian odes. J.F. Miller, for example, has convincingly demonstrated these multiple Horatian references and their interrelation.[25] For the present purpose I will limit myself to the intertextual references to *Odes* 3.30.[26]

---

21   Schol. *Pyth.* 6.11 (Drachmann ii.195).
22   Schol. *Pyth.* 6.4 (Drachmann ii.194).
23   Cf. e.g. *Carm.* 1.4, 1.9, 1.11, 2.16, 4.7.
24   See e.g. Nethercut (1970) 386–387, and for a fuller treatment see Cremona (1987).
25   Miller (1983).
26   For these cf. Solmsen (1948) 106–107; Miller (1983) 295–298; Mader (1993), 330–340, although Mader differs from my interpretation in his conclusions concerning the *ingenium* (cf. 339–340): according to Mader, Propertius wants to separate his *ingenium* from Cynthia and achieve an equal level with Horace.

In 3.2 Propertius writes about the power of poetry and especially of the power of his own poetry. The short elegy closes with the following lines:

> fortunata meo si qua es celebrata libello:
>   carmina erunt formae tot monumenta tuae.
> nam neque pyramidum sumptus ad sidera ducti,
> 20   nec Iouis Elei caelum imitata domus,
> nec Mausolei diues fortuna sepulcri
>   mortis ab extrema condicione uacant.
> aut illis flamma aut imber subducet honores,
>   annorum aut tacito pondere uicta ruent.
> 25   at non ingenio quaesitum nomen ab aeuo
>   excidet: ingenio stat sine morte decus.

> Happy you who are celebrated in my book, if any woman is: my every poem will be a monument to your beauty. For neither the extravagance of the pyramids raised to the stars, nor the heaven-imitating house of Jupiter at Olympia, nor the rich treasure of the tomb of Mausolus is free from the final state of death. Either flame or rain will take away their glories, or they will crumble conquered by the silent weight of years. But never in all eternity will the name acquired by a poet's talent perish: through poetry honour persists without end.
>   PROPERTIUS 3.2.17–26, trans. S.J. HEYWORTH

Already at first glance the verbal references to Horace become apparent. The Horatian *monumentum* (3.30.1) is echoed in *formae tot monumenta tuae* (18). Both poems have a comparison with Egyptian pyramids (3.30.2 versus 3.2.19). Both poets elude death via their poetry (3.30.6–7 versus 3.2.22) and both poems have a tricolon of detrimental influences. At the same time, emulative strategies emerge. While Horace contents himself with the pyramids as objects of reference, Propertius introduces two more buildings, namely Zeus' temple at Elis and the tomb of Mausolus. In addition, the Propertian pyramids, in contrast to the Horatian ones, reach the sky (*ad sidera ducti*).

Flach (1967) devotes a thematically structured monograph to the literary relationship between Propertius and Horace and discusses the motif of literary fame (97–108). Juhnke (1963) offers a kind of parallel interpretation of Horace's and Propertius' metapoetic poems. In his treatment of Propertius 3.2, though, he refers to Horace *Carm.* 3.30 only in passing (454–458).

A fitting complement to the emulative intentions of 3.2 would be an allusion to Horace's point of reference, namely Pindar. And indeed, praising someone else (note *celebrata* in line 17) and the mention of the Olympic temple at Elis (line 20) seem to work exactly towards a reference to the epinician poet Pindar. So, the reader could assume that Propertius now would not only point to Horace, but to Pindar and to Pindaric philology as well.

But the elegy continues in a quite different way. In Propertius, we find a tricolon of fire, rain, and time, not the Horatian combination of rain, wind, and time. So Propertius deviates from his model by introducing *flamma*, and at the same time he calls special attention to this deviation by remaining otherwise quite close to Horace. He retains the word *imber*, and the genitive *annorum* also appears at the beginning of a line. Introducing a new element to the tricolon would have been an opportunity for a nod towards Pindar or the commentaries. But this is exactly what Propertius avoids. To be sure, one has to be careful with conclusions *ex negativo*, and the remaining scholia are only a tiny portion of the original commentaries. But I think there is a metapoetic explanation for Propertius' move in 3.2 so that avoiding Pindar and by doing so avoiding the commentary tradition as well, becomes a meaningful gap in the emulation of a Horatian ode. Stressing the *ingenium* in the last couplet seems to me an ironic confirmation of this avoidance. Propertius' *ingenium* looks out for other ways, different from those that led Horace to Pindar. It is a Pindaric argument, the *ingenium*, that is used here to dissociate Propertius from Pindar. The primacy of the *ingenium* is seen by the commentators on Pindar as especially Pindaric. The scholia present ample evidence of this.[27] Even passages that could be seen as combining *ars* and *ingenium* as an ideal have been interpreted as confirming the preconception of the primacy of the *ingenium*.[28] And, it may be safe to assume that not only did the commentators read Pindar this way but readers of Propertius, too. Propertius himself hints at this by identifying Pindar with the high style in the ode to Bacchus 3.17.[29] Here, we find the only instance in Propertius where Pindar is referred to explicitly by name:

> haec ego non humili referam memoranda coturno,
>   qualis Pindarico spiritus ore tonat.

---

27 See Bitto (2012) 82–84.
28 See e.g. schol. *Nem.* 3.134a (Drachmann iii.61).
29 I concentrate on only one aspect of 3.17. For a fuller interpretation taking the general development of Propertian elegy in book III into account, see Mader (1994).

I shall tell these themes to be celebrated in the elevated buskin, with such breath as thundered from the mouth of Pindar.

PROPERTIUS 3.17.39–40, trans. S.J. HEYWORTH

Interestingly, this reference to Pindar is mediated through a Horatian intertext, namely his ode to Bacchus, *Odes* 3.25.[30] But in 3.17 we can also observe a comic distancing from Pindar.[31] The elegy begins with two distichs where Bacchus is summoned not to inspire praise as in Horace,[32] but to distract the lover from his sorrows.[33] At the end, directly after the Pindar-distich, the poem concludes with a further appeal for relief from sorrows.[34]

Propertius reaffirms this distancing in the Actium elegy 4.6. A poem that commemorates[35] the battle of Actium could have easily been ornamented with references to Pindar's epinician odes or even stylized as a Pindaric epinician. Instead, not Pindar but two Hellenistic poets, namely Callimachus and Philitas, are evoked at the beginning.[36] Thus Propertius explicitly aligns himself with a Hellenistic tradition rather than a Pindaric one.[37]

---

30 See especially lines 17–18: *nil paruum aut humili modo,/nil mortale loquar* ('let me say nothing/small or in lowly tone,/nothing mortal'); also see Miller (1991) 78–80. As Bruno Currie rightly adds, the Pindaric closural poem of Horace's first collection is present here, too: cf. *Carm.* 3.30.12 *ex humili potens* ('from humble beginnings I had the power').

31 Cf. Lyne (1980) 138. Miller (1991) also argues for a distancing from the contemporary poets Horace and Tibullus.

32 See *Carm.* 3.25.3–6.

33 3.17.1–4 (without Heyworth's transposition of lines 7 f. after line 2): *Nunc, o Bacche, tuis humiles aduoluimur aris:/da mihi pacato uela secunda, pater./tu potes insanae Veneris compescere fastus,/curarumque tuo fit medicina mero* ('Now, Bacchus, we prostrate ourselves humbly at your altar: make me calm and give me sails set fair, father. You can restrain the blasts of mad Venus; in your wine there is a cure for passion').

34 3.17.41–42: *tu modo seruitio uacuum me siste superbo,/atque hoc sollicitum uince sopore caput* ('Do you only set me free from my servitude from an arrogant woman, and overcome this troubled mind with sleep').

35 I pass over the question of Propertius' alleged Augustan development. For a sound approach, see Kennedy (1993) 35–37. For a general interpretation of 4.6 in different perspectives (structure, genre, occasion etc.), see Cairns (1984).

36 4.6.1–4: *sacra facit uates: sint ora fauentia sacris;/et cadat ante meos icta iuuenca focos./serta Philiteis certet Romana corymbis,/et Cyrenaeas urna ministret aquas.* ('The holy man is sacrificing; voices should be silent for the sacrifice; let the heifer be struck and fall before my altar. Let a Roman garland vie with Philitean ivy berries, and the pitcher provide Cyrenean water.') See Pillinger (1969) 189–198 for Callimachean influences in 4.6.

37 This is what Richard Thomas has argued for the proem to *Georgics* 3, see below. The climactic battle sequence in Prop. 4.6, though, seems to be adorned with two references to choral lyric. At 4.6.60 the deified Caesar looks down from heaven to Octavian and says:

To return to 3.2, Propertius' *ingenium* is quite different from Pindar's, so that the Propertian argument is Pindaric and un-Pindaric at the same time. Propertius' *ingenium* is the result of his love for his *puella*: 'my girl creates my talent' (*ingenium nobis ipsa puella facit*), we read at the beginning of the opening elegy of book two (2.1.4). And, without Cynthia, he confesses at the end of 2.30 that his *ingenium* would be nothing (*nam sine te nostrum non ualet ingenium*). So, avoiding Pindar is a strategy to secure elegiac identity, by remaining at equal distance from lyric in particular and from lofty poetry in general.

Furthermore, the newly introduced *flamma* may also be a metapoetic hint, since this word is used metaphorically also for love and thus can point to love poetry. For example, in 2.34 the poet Varro of Atax is called *Leucadiae maxima flamma suae* (greatest lover of his Leucadia, 2.34.86).

This staging of avoiding Pindar in 3.2 as part of a larger scheme of emulating Horace can be corroborated with a further reference to Horace's *Odes* 3.30 in Ovid.[38]

4 Ovid

At the end of the *Metamorphoses* there is a famous *sphragis* in which Ovid promises a long life for his work:

> Iamque opus exegi, quod nec Iouis ira nec ignis
> nec poterit ferrum nec edax abolere uetustas.
> cum uolet, illa dies, quae nil nisi corporis huius
> ius habet, incerti spatium mihi finiat aeui;
> 875   parte tamen meliore mei super alta perennis

---

sum deus: est nostri sanguinis ista fides ('I am a god: this is proof of our bloodline'). Hutchinson (2006) 165 contrasts in his commentary ad loc. a passage from Pindar where Zeus addresses Polydeuces: ἐσσί μοι υἱός ('You are my son,' *Nem.* 10.80) and points out the main difference: 'He [Caesar in Propertius 4.6] rather affirms his own deity, as if it had been uncertain to him until Augustus proved it.' Bruno Currie links the following joy of the sea gods in Prop. 4.6.61–62 to Bacchylides 17.124–128. In Bacchylides the joy results from Theseus having proven his divine ancestry. So, both passages, the one from Pindar and the one from Bacchylides, serve to highlight the moment of divine kinship in Propertius. But just as important is the difference pointed out by Hutchinson that looks like a typically Alexandrian twist and adds a further encomiastic aspect to the portrayal of Augustus in 4.6.

38   For a general discussion of Ovid's intertextual relationship to Horace, see Korenjak (2007).

astra ferar, nomenque erit indelebile nostrum;
quaque patet domitis Romana potentia terris
ore legar populi, perque omnia saecula fama
(siquid habent ueri uatum praesagia) uiuam.

And now my work is done, which neither the wrath of Jove, nor fire, nor sword, nor the gnawing tooth of time shall ever be able to undo. When it will, let that day come which has no power save over this mortal frame, and end the span of my uncertain years. Still in my better part I shall be borne immortal far beyond the lofty stars and I shall have an undying name. Wherever Rome's power extends over the conquered world, I shall have mention on men's lips, and, if the prophecies of bards have any truth, through all the ages shall I live in fame.
Metamorphoses 15.871–879, trans. FRANK JUSTUS MILLER

As in Propertius, the references to Horace are clear. After an enumeration of detrimental influences, a statement of the poet's immortality through his work follows.[39] Furthermore, this reference to the immortality of the work, which in Horace is linked to the temporal existence of the Empire,[40] is echoed in the spatially connected reference to Rome.[41] But, there is an important difference, too. Ovid has expanded the tricolon into a tetracolon. Horatian is *opus exegi* and the *edax uetustas*, Propertian *ignis*, Ovidian *Iovis ira* and *ferrum*.[42] So it would seem. But, in a retroactive reading, *ira* and *ignis* can be seen as martial metaphors when looking back from *ferrum*.[43] In doing this, Ovid recalls the metaphorical Pindaric cloud army and expands the martial metaphoric context of the Pindar passage. Like Horace, he seems to agree with the criticism of

---

39 Cf. Also the verbal references: *parte tamen meliore mei* (15.875)—*multaque pars mei* (3.30.6); *perennis* (15.875)—*perennius* (3.30.1); *legar* (15.878)—*dicar* (3.30.10).

40 *Carm.* 3.30.8–9: **dum Capitolium / scandet cum tacita virgine pontifex** ('while the priest/climbs the Capitol with a silent virgin').

41 *Met.* 15.877: **quaque patet domitis Romana potentia terris**. For further structural and syntactical parallels, see Korenjak (2007) 242. A detailed discussion of Ovid's reception of Horace's *Carm.* 3.30 is offered by Einberger (1960) 17–22. In contrast to the opinion advanced here, Einberger sees only marginal Pindaric influence in Horace *Carm.* 3.30.

42 The phrase *Iouis ira* is used several times in the exile poetry for Augustus' verdict against Ovid (*Tr.* 1.5.78; 3.11.62). This has led some scholars to believe that the *sphragis* was added after the relegation. But see Spahlinger (1996) 47–48n69 for a critical assessment of this question.

43 Cf. *OLD* s.v. *ferrum* 5 for the metaphorical use and 5c for the phrase *ferrum et ignis*.

this particular metaphor but, in an Alexandrian manner, he points not only to Horace but also to his model Pindar and the accompanying commentary tradition. Furthermore, the phrase *Iouis ira* can be seen as an intratext within the *Metamorphoses* themselves. It occurs in the context of the destructive flood in book one and thus creates a kind of ring composition.[44] Moreover, through this intratext, Ovid hints at wind and water as detrimental influences that are not only present in book one,[45] but are also present in Horace and Pindar, and partly in Propertius, too. But they are not mentioned explicitly in the *sphragis*.

It is not only Pindar as of one Horace's models that Ovid points to. With the last distich he alludes to Ennius' famous epitaph *uolito uiuos per ora uirum* (Var. 17 ²Vahlen). In Horace, there are no verbal references, but there is a close relationship to Ennius in thought. The verb *dicar* (3.30.10) echoes the orally transmitted fame Ennius claims for his poetry. Horace alludes to Ennius' name in the opening line with the comparative *per-ennius*.[46] Ovid, on the other hand, occludes this allusion and reverses the comparative to the positive form *perennis* (15.875), but remains verbally closer to Ennius: *ore* (15.878)—*per ora*; *uiuam* (15.879)—*uiuos*. At the same time, Ovid uses exactly this verbal closeness in order to distance himself from the rustic[47] Ennius: *ore legar* may echo Ennius's *uolito per ora*, but Ovid's poetry is, in contrast to Ennius's claim, explicitly *read*. Thus Ovid undercuts the fiction of orality that Horace tries to maintain in *Odes* 3.30, even though the monument he speaks of may imply a physical object.[48] For Ovid, for a work of literature to be an ever-living *opus* it requires to be written. This is exactly what the ancient commentaries sometimes openly, sometimes tacitly assume for Pindar. They see him as a writing poet since they have his written works before them. Thus Pindar's claims for immortality seem to be justified via his work's status as written literature.[49]

---

44   *Met.* 1.274; I owe this reference to Prof. Gauly.
45   Cf. directly before: *Met.* 1.262–273.
46   For the pun on Ennius' name with the adjective *perennis*, see Gale (2001) 168n1.
47   Cf. Ovid *Tr.* 2.424: *Ennius ingenio maximus, arte rudis*.
48   In the first collection of odes Horace presents himself as a singer, an oral composer; in the fourth book this changes, especially in 4.9. For this lyrical fiction of orality see e.g. Lowrie (1997) 55–70, and for the wider Augustan context Lowrie (2009).
49   See Bitto (2012) 75–76 in general on this point, and 363–365 on schol. *Nem.* 4.10a (Drachmann iii.65) and its successive reinterpretation of Pindar's ῥῆμα δ' ἐργμάτων χρονιώτερον βιοτεύει (*Nem.* 4.6) moving via several paraphrases from oral to written poetry. One of these paraphrases runs as follows: τὰ μὲν γὰρ ἔργα τῷ γεγονέναι παρήκει, τὰ δὲ γραφόμενα αἰώνια παραδίδοται ('deeds come to end when they are done, but what is written remains forever'). To give another example: schol. *Ol.* 1.48a (Drachmann i.32) explains Pindar's χάρις (grace, *Ol.* 1.30) as χάρις τῆς ποιητικῆς γραφῆς ('grace of poetic writing').

Another poet follows on Ovid's way from Horace back to Pindar and this takes us to Statius.

5   Statius

In his epicedion to his father, Statius claims that those who have been educated by his father have gained a broad knowledge of literature.[50] This education included not only Homer and Hesiod but also, besides Hellenistic poets like Callimachus and Lycophron, the lyric poets as well: mirroring his special canonical status,[51] Pindar opens the sequence of lyric poets including in addition the names of Ibycus, Alcman, Stesichorus, and Sappho.[52] Elsewhere, Statius makes the canonical status of his work explicit by calling Pindar *regnator lyricae cohortis*.[53] Interestingly, the wording in *Silvae* 5.3 emphasizes a technical aspect: [*discere*], *qua lege recurrat / Pindaricae uox flexa lyrae* ('[to learn] what law governs the recurring voice of Pindar's winding harp').[54] His learned father, *genitor praedoctus*, as he is called,[55] introduced his pupils—and one may assume his son as well—to just that aspect of Pindar's lyrical poems that Horace presented as not measurable.[56]

---

50   *Silv.* 5.3.146–158. In his commentary, Gibson (2006a) 321 discerns four categories of literary knowledge in *Silv.* 5.3.146–158: plot, effects, metre, exegesis. For a discussion of this account and the intellectual background of Statius' father, see McNelis (2002). According to McNelis the curriculum of Statius' father 'is consistent with the known activity of grammatikoi' (83). For the social relevance of knowing Greek poetry, see 86–90. Holford-Strevens (2000) argues for situating Statius more in the Greek literary background and takes the catalogue of authors in *Silv.* 5.3 taught by his father as one piece of evidence.

51   See Färber (1936) I 26 that Pindar is often singled out in the lyrical canon, e.g. in Quintilian, Statius' contemporary (*Pindarus princeps lyricorum*, 8.6.71; *novem vero lyricorum longe Pindarus princeps*, 10.1.61). For the testimonia see Färber (1936) ii.22–25.

52   *Silv.* 5.3.151–155.

53   *Silv.* 4.7.5.

54   *Silv.* 5.3.151–152; translation by D.R. Shackleton Bailey.

55   *Silv.* 5.3.3.

56   *Carm.* 4.2.11–12: [*Pindarus*] *numeris fertur/lege solutis*. Holford-Strevens (2000) 41–42 argues that Statius read Horace's statement about Pindaric metre as referring to 'rules of internal responsion' and that he 'corrected' Horace on this point. Holford-Strevens offers the following paraphrase of Statius' lines: 'thanks to my father, I know what Horace (for all *his* father's care over his schooling) did not know, how Pindaric metre works, by what law, from which he is not free, the strophic sound of his lyre does not run wild but returns to its starting point, *qua lege recurrat Pindaricae vox flexae lyrae*' (42).

The first *Silvae* of the first book[57] already seems to validate this claim regarding the knowledge of Pindar.[58] At the end of *Silvae* 1.1 Statius promises a long life for the equestrian statue of Domitian erected around 90 CE on the forum:[59]

> Non hoc imbriferas hiemes opus aut Iouis ignem
> tergeminum, Aeolii non agmina carceris horret
> annorumue moras; stabit, dum terra polusque,
> dum Romana dies.

> This work fears not rainy winters [nor Jupiter's threefold fire] nor the troops of Aeolus' dungeon nor the long-drawn years; it shall stand as long as earth and heaven and Roman day.
> STATIUS, *Silvae* 1.1.91–94, trans. D.R. SHACKLETON BAILEY; in square brackets my supplement for the missing translation of *aut Iouis ignem tergeminum*

As we will see, Statius outdoes Ovid. He, too, presents a tetracolon, but his contains winter rain, lightning, wind, and time. References are made clear: *imbriferas* recalls the Horatian *imber*, *annorum* is again at the beginning of a line, and *Iovis ignem* seems like a contraction of the Ovidian phrase, *nec Iovis ira nec ignem*.[60] But the reference to Pindar is made even more obvious than in Ovid. The Pindaric cloud army is not only evoked by the martial context as in Ovid, but is explicitly mirrored in Statius' wind army in the form of a mythologically enhanced periphrasis, *Aeolii agmina carceris*. As Alex Hardie observes, Statius added 'more epic flavour with the hyperbolic description of the winds, taken from Virgilian vocabulary'.[61]

---

57 *Silvae* 1.1 has been interpreted quite differently in Statian scholarship. See Ahl (1984) 91–102 for a subversive interpretation, Geyssen (1996) for an affirmative one, Newlands (2002) 46–73 for an approach that seeks to avoid these clear cut distinctions, and especially Nauta (2002) 424–426 for more general thoughts on subversive interpretations in panegyrical poems like *Silvae* 1.1. For a structural overview of 1.1 see Cancik (1965) 95, and Rühl (2006) 314–328 for the *Silvae* in connection to the imperial building program, and Dewar (2008) for the *equus* being the central part of the Flavian conception of the *Forum Romanum*.

58 By name Pindar is evoked in *Silv.* 1.3.101 concerning the poetic activities of Manilius Vopiscus, and in *Silv.* 4.7.5–8, where Pindar is asked for a concession to write poetry in a lighter vein after having sung about his hometown in the *Thebaid*. In both places, Pindar is equivalent to high style.

59 For the dating of *Silvae* 1.1 see Geyssen (1996) 31n4 and Nauta (2002) 422n141.

60 So, too, Hardie (1983) 155.

61 Hardie (1983) 155. Hardie compares Verg. *Aen.* 1.82 (*uenti uelut agmine facto*) and 1.141 (*Aeolus et clauso uentorum carcere regnet*). Further echoes of the Virgilian phrases corroborate this idea of epic flavor, cf. Ovid's *Fast.* 2.455–456 (*sex reserata diebus/carceris Aeolii*

Exactly that metaphorical element that was criticized as excessive in the commentary, was avoided by Horace, and was only implicitly hinted at by Ovid now features prominently in Statius.[62] This fits into the hyperbolic frame of the whole poem. Right at the beginning in the first three lines, Statius talks about the colossal appearance of the statue that encompasses the whole forum[63] and seems to be a work that has fallen from heaven.[64]

But there is an important difference, as Alex Hardie has indicated. In Statius, it is a real monument, Domitian's equestrian statue, that is praised as immune against detrimental environmental conditions. It is not poetry as in Pindar, Horace, Propertius, and Ovid, for whom a real building is just a point of reference. Rather, Statius ascribes a Pindaric-Horatian eternal life to the *equus Domitiani* that normally only poetry can claim to possess.[65] In contrast, Statius' *Silvae* are ephemeral works, according to the preface of the first book written in a day or two.[66] Thus the monument can rightly possess what Statius' poetry cannot. This is of course a metapoetical joke that at the same time has a panegyrical character. In a poem that is published, as in *Silvae* 1.1, the *equus Domitiani* will live on and *within* the poem, it is immune to environmental influences.[67] At the same time, its *physical* existence has caused Statius' poem to exist as it offered the *materia* for the poem.[68] This, then, is the point where Statius comes closer to Pindar than Horace or Ovid, who praise themselves or rather their own achievement, while Pindar and Statius offer their poetic

---

ianua lata patet) and Lucan 5.609–611 (*non imbribus atrum/Aeolii iacuisse Notum sub carcere saxi/crediderim*). For interactions with epic in the *Silvae*, see Gibson (2006b) and van Dam (2006).

62 See, too, Bitto in Bitto and Ginestí Rosell (2019) for Statius' *Achilleid*, where a similar handling of Alexandrian Homeric criticism is displayed.
63 *Silv.* 1.1.2: *Latium complexa forum*.
64 *Silv.* 1.1.2–3: *caelone peractum/fluxit opus?*
65 Hardie (1983) 155.
66 1 *praef.* 11–12. For the *equus* poem Statius maintains in the *praefatio* that it was handed to the emperor the day after the dedication (*postero die quam dedicauerit opus tradere ausus sum*, 1 *praef.* 18–19). As evidence for his ability to compose poems in a short amount of time he refers to the epithalamium to his fellow poet Stella (*Silvae* 1.2) which was written in two days although being three times as long as *Silvae* 1.1 (1 *praef.* 19–23). For the quickness of composition in relation to the poetics of the *Silvae*, see Gibson (2006a) xviii–xxviii.
67 Geyssen (1996) 121–123 also argues that Statius promises longevity for the statue through the longevity of his work.
68 Already in the prefatory epistle there is an oblique allusion to Horace and the immortalizing poetry in *Carm.* 3.30 which will figure more prominently in the following *Silva*: Right after referring to his compositional speed regarding 1.1 and 1.2 he talks about the addressee of 1.3, Manilius Vopiscus, a Pindarizing poet (cf. 1.2.101), who saves literature from decaying: *uindicat a situ litteras iam paene fugientes* (1 *praef.* 24–25)—cf. *situ* in Hor. *Carm.* 3.30.2.

ability in order to praise someone else. But Statius presents himself as more humble than Pindar or Propertius, who claim their poetry much more openly to be extraordinarily fit for praise.[69] Carole Newlands has succinctly summarized this paradoxical situation:

> Although he [Statius] does not openly claim ... that his own poem is superior to the work of art, in a sense he appropriates the statue by shaping it with his own poetic values. As the statue tests the limits of imperial art with its colossal scale, so the poet tests the limits of imperial panegyric.[70]

6 Virgil

After having examined Roman poetical monuments that look back to Pindar's sixth *Pythian*, I would like to turn at the end to Virgil who took *Olympian* 6 and its commentary tradition as an inspiration for the proem to the third book of the *Georgics*:

13 et uiridi in campo templum de marmore ponam
    ...
16 in medio mihi Caesar erit templumque tenebit:
    ...
26 in foribus pugnam ex auro solidoque elephanto
    Gangaridum faciam uictorisque arma Quirini,
    atque hic undantem bello magnumque fluentem
    Nilum ac nauali surgentis aere columnas.
    ...
34 stabunt et Parii lapides, spirantia signa,
    Assaraci proles demissaeque ab Ioue gentis
    nomina, Trosque parens et Troiae Cynthius auctor.

and I'll erect a marble temple in a grassy meadow by the waters ... At its centre I'll place Caesar, master of the shrine ... on its doors I will have carved in gold and solid ivory / images of battle, of the Ganges, and the

---

69 For the different self-presentations of Statius in the *Silvae* see Nauta (2008), esp. 144–150 for poems addressed to the emperor. In his conclusion, Nauta states that 'the role in which he addresses his addressees is mostly that of the praise poet' (173).
70 Newlands (2002) 73.

all-conquering regiments of Romulus, / and, yes, the mighty Nile in the full flood of war, / and columns springing up and decorated with bronze prows of battleships …

Then I'll set up, cut in stone from Paros, statues standing in relief so true to life / they seem to breathe, the scions of Assaracus, famous race of Jupiter, / the founding father Tros, and he who set up Troy, Apollo.

VIRGIL, *Georgics* 3.13 / 16 / 26–29 / 34–36, trans. PETER FALLON

That Virgil does not want to become a real temple builder is quite obvious. Rather, he alludes to the opening lines of *Olympian* 6:[71]

Χρυσέας ὑποστάσαντες εὐ-
τειχεῖ προθύρῳ θαλάμου
κίονας ὡς ὅτε θαητὸν μέγαρον
πάξομεν· ἀρχομένου δ' ἔργου πρόσωπον
χρὴ θέμεν τηλαυγές.

Let us set up golden columns to support/the strong-walled porch of our abode/and construct, as it were, a splendid/palace; for when a work is begun, it is necessary to make/its front shine from afar.

PINDAR, *Olympian* 6.1–4, trans. WILLIAM RACE

Richard Thomas states that '[t]here is overall little pure Pindar in Virgil. But Pindar does matter to Virgil.'[72] Accordingly, Thomas expresses doubts that Virgil is directly or mainly influenced by Pindar and draws instead attention to an epinician fragment from Callimachus's *Aetia*.[73] All the other elements in the proem to *Georgics* III that previous scholars have identified as Pindaric are traced back by Thomas to Hellenistic and especially Callimachean epinician poetry.[74]

In contrast, Ryan Krieger Balot has convincingly argued that *Olympian* 6 is a central model for Virgil's proem and he has shown the tightly woven nexus

---

71   There are, of course, other important Pindaric intertexts: cf. *Nem.* 4.80–85 and *Nem.* 7.77–79. Since my aim is here not to discuss the Pindaric intertexts in Virgil as such but to focus on the interaction with the commentary tradition I concentrate on *Ol.* 6 where the extant commentary material allows such an investigation. For the ancient commentaries on the passages from the *Nemeans*, see Bitto (2012) 146–147.
72   Thomas (1998) 120.
73   Thomas (1998) 106, drawing on Thomas (1983) 92–101.
74   Thomas (1998) 108. For Hellenistic receptions of epinician poetry, see Barbantani (2012), and especially for Callimachus, see Fuhrer (1992).

of Pindaric motifs.[75] I want to pick out one point of his thorough discussion, concerning the architectural metaphors, about which Balot says:

> Thomas has argued that Pindar's architectural metaphors are too brief to be considered legitimate parallels for Virgil's elaborate treatment of the image, but there is no reason why Virgil could not have elaborated an image that was already present, albeit in smaller scope, in Pindar.[76]

A glance into the scholia can confirm Balot's assumption. A scholion to *Olympian* 6.1 explicates the allegory: the poet is said to speak figuratively (ἀλληγορεῖ) and then all the essential elements of the allegory are contrasted with their poetical counterparts: building the house corresponds to writing the epinician ode, the gateway corresponds to the proem, the whole house to the hymn, and the builder to the poet.[77] Thus the commentator surpasses Pindar in the explicitness of the allegorical details. Some lines later Pindar says that we have to open the gates of song for the victorious mules.[78] A scholion to this line stresses the continuity of the image (ἐνέμεινε τῇ τροπῇ).[79] At first, this refers to the immediate context. The charioteer is called to harness the mules and prepare them for the return home. But, it can easily be expanded in its range to refer back to the architectural metaphors of the opening lines. So, the commentators offer exactly what Thomas misses in the ode itself in order to see *Olympian* 6 as a model for Virgil. Furthermore, it could have been an inspiration for Virgil that Pindar, in another scholion to this passage,[80] is explicitly commended for his encomiastic image of the gates of song because, with this image, he shows the magnitude of the praise and his own ability to praise.

---

[75] Balot restates the case made by Wilkinson (1970) against Thomas, arguing for the prime importance of Pindar.

[76] Balot (1998) 86, referring to Thomas (1983) 97. But compare the more inclusive approach of Gale (2000) 14: 'the Pindaric, Callimachean, Ennian and Lucretian echoes are formed into a harmonious whole.' For a different approach to the proem not concentrating on epinician intertexts of any kind, see Meban (2008).

[77] Schol. *Ol.* 6.1a (Drachmann i.154): ἀλληγορεῖ ὁ ποιητής, ὡς ἐπὶ οἰκίας μεγαλοπρεποῦς κατασκευαστὴς τὸν ἐπίνικον διατεθειμένος. παραβάλλει δὲ προπυλαίῳ μὲν τὸ προοίμιον, τῷ δὲ ὅλῳ οἴκῳ τὸν ὕμνον, ἑαυτὸν δὲ τῷ κατασκευάζοντι.

[78] *Ol.* 6.27: χρὴ τοίνυν πύλας ὕ-/μνων ἀναπιτνάμεν αὐταῖς.

[79] Schol. *Ol.* 6.44e (Drachmann i.164).

[80] Schol. *Ol.* 6.44f (Drachmann i.164): εὖ δὲ τῇ παρασκευῇ παρίστησι τήν τε τοῦ ἐπαίνου μεγαλειότητα καὶ τὴν ἐν τῷ ἐπαινεῖν ἑαυτοῦ δύναμιν ὁ ποιητής.

7 Conclusion

We have seen that Horace gained two important points for his remodelling of Pindar from the commentaries: the exclusion of an excessive metaphor and a substitute for the completion of the tricolon, namely the idea of time as an important factor. In contrast, Propertius stages a kind of elaborate evasive manoeuvre regarding Pindar and Pindaric philology. He approaches Horace while at the same time calling attention to the fact that he is not referring back to Pindar. Ovid addresses Horace and Propertius but implicitly hints at Pindar and the commentary tradition in order to show his independence from Horace. The criticism of a certain excessive use of metaphor does not result in an exclusion and substitution as in Horace but in a moderated form of metaphorical surrounding that alludes to the original metaphor. Closer to Pindar again, but also different, is Statius' approach. He does not substitute nor moderate an excessive metaphor, but uses it. Furthermore, by adding a mythological periphrasis, he expands it. In order to fit his Pindaric intertext even more into a hyperbolic praise poem Statius takes the criticism the other way round, so as to become a kind of super-Pindar and to praise the emperor appropriately.

Finally, Virgil uses the Pindaric commentaries as a starting point also to expand Pindar. But, Statius and Virgil work in opposite directions. Statius reverses negative aesthetic criticism turning it into panegyric, while Virgil develops explanations and specifications in the commentary in accordance with the commentator's aesthetic ideals. So, like Horace and the Alexandrian philologists, Virgil adheres to the principle of πρέπον. His aim is not a super-Pindar as it is with Statius, but a refined one, a *Pindarus deductus*.

All the poets examined here have one thing in common concerning Alexandrian philology. They agree on its assessment of Pindar's poetry, but they employ the aesthetic comments to their individual ends. Thus they create a spectrum that ranges from adherence to subversion. Furthermore, this usage of Alexandrian philology was shown to be part of a larger set of emulative strategies, especially for Propertius, Ovid, and Statius. In an almost paradoxical way, this emulation is not limited to a Greek predecessor. Rather, Greek literary criticism serves as a means to emulate a Roman author as well.

References

Ahl, F. 1984. The Rider and the Horse: Politics and Power in Roman Poetry from Horace to Statius. *ANRW* II 32(1): 40–124.

Athanassaki, L. 2016. Pindarum quisque studet aemulari: Greek and Roman Civic Performance Contexts in Pindar's Fourth and Fifth Pythians and Horace's Odes 4.2. In *Le poète lyrique dans la cité antique*, ed. B. Délignon, N. Le Meur, and O. Thévenaz, 131–158. Lyon.

Balot, R.K. 1998. Pindar, Virgil, and the Proem to Georgic 3. *Phoenix* 52: 83–94.

Barbantini, S. 2012. Hellenistic Epinician. In *Receiving the Komos: Ancient and Modern Receptions of the Victory Ode*, ed. P. Agócs, C. Carey, and R. Rawles, 37–55. London.

Barchiesi, A. 1996. Poetry, Praise, and Patronage: Simonides in Book 4 of Horace's 'Odes'. *ClAnt* 15: 5–47.

Barchiesi, A. 2002. The Uniqueness of the Carmen saeculare and its Tradition. In *Traditions and Contexts in the Poetry of Horace*, ed. T. Woodman and D. Feeney, 107–123. Cambridge.

Barchiesi, A. 2009. Lyric in Rome. In *The Cambridge Companion to Greek Lyric*, ed. F. Budelmann, 319–335. Cambridge.

Bitto, G. 2012. *Lyrik als Philologie. Zur Rezeption hellenistischer Pindarkommentierung in den Oden des Horaz*. Rahden.

Bitto, G. 2013. Beobachtungen zur Ennius als Euripides-Übersetzer. *Hermes* 141: 227–232.

Bitto, G. and Ginestí Rosell, A., eds. 2019 *Philologie auf zweiter Stufe. Literarische Rezeptionen und Inszenierungen hellenistischer Gelehrsamkeit*. Stuttgart.

Cairns, F. 1984. Propertius and the Battle of Actium (4.6). In *Poetry and Politics in the Age of Augustus*, ed. T. Woodman and D. West, 129–168. Cambridge.

Cancik, H. 1965. *Untersuchungen zur lyrischen Kunst des P. Papinius Statius*. Hildesheim.

Cavarzere, A. 1996. *Sul limitare. Il motto e la poesia di Orazio*. Bologna.

Christes, J. 1979. *Sklaven und Freigelassene als Grammatiker und Philologen im antiken Rom*. Wiesbaden.

Clarke, M.L. 1971. *Higher Education in the Ancient World*. London.

Cremona, V. 1987. Emulazione e polemica: Properzio III, 1–5: Orazio III, 1–6. *Euphrosyne* 15: 247–256.

Cribiore, R. 2001. *Gymnastics of the Mind: Greek Education in Hellenistic and Roman Egypt*. Princeton.

van Dam, H.-J. 2006. Multiple Imitations of Epic Models in the Silvae, In *Flavian Poetry*, ed. R.R. Nauta, H.-J. van Dam, and J.J.L. Smolenaars, 185–205. Leiden.

Dewar, M. 2008. Statius' Ecus Maximus Domitiani Imperatoris and the Flavian Forum. In *The Poetry of Statius*, ed. J.J.L. Smolenaars, H.-J. v. Dam, and R.R. Nauta, 65–83. Leiden.

Einberger, R. 1960. *Die Behandlung gleicher Motive bei Horaz und Ovid*. Heidelberg.

Fallon, P. 2006. *Virgil* Georgics. Oxford.

Färber, H. 1936. *Die Lyrik in der Kunsttheorie der Antike*. Munich.

Flach, D. 1967. *Das literarische Verhältnis von Horaz und Properz*. Marburg.

Fränkel, H. 1932. Griechische Bildung in altrömischen Epen. *Hermes* 76: 303–311.
Fuhrer, T. 1992. *Die Auseinandersetzung mit den Chorlyrikern in den Epinikien des Kallimachos*. Basle.
Gale, M. 2000. *Virgil on the Nature of Things: The Georgics, Lucretius, and the Didactic Tradition*. Cambridge.
Gale, M. 2001. Etymological Wordplay and Poetic Succesion in Lucretius. *CPh* 96: 168–172.
Gibson, B. 2006a. *Statius. Silvae 5*. Oxford.
Gibson, B. 2006b. The Silvae and Epic. In *Flavian Poetry*, eds. R.R. Nauta, H.-J. van Dam, and J.J.L. Smolenaars, 163–183. Leiden and Boston.
Hardie, A. 1983. *Statius and the* Silvae. Liverpool.
Harrison, S.J. 1995. Horace, Pindar, Iullus Antonius, and Augustus: Odes 4.2. In *Homage to Horace*, ed. S.J. Harrison, 108–127. Oxford.
Harrison, S.J. 2001. Simonides and Horace. In *The New Simondes: Contexts of Praise and Desire*, ed. D. Boedeker and D. Sider, 261–271. Oxford.
Heyworth, S.J. 2007. *Cynthia*. Oxford.
Herzog, R. 1922. Nicias und Xenophon von Kos. *Historische Zeitschrift* 125: 189–247.
Holford-Strevens, L. 2000. In Search of Poplios Papinios Statios. *Hermathena* 168: 38–54.
Hutchinson, G.O. 2006. *Propertius Elegies Book IV*. Cambridge.
Jansen, L. 2014. Introduction: Approaches to Roman Paratextuality. In *The Roman Paratext: Frame, Text, Readers*, ed. L. Jansen, 1–18. Cambridge.
Juhnke, H. 1963. *Das dichterische Selbstverständnis des Horaz und Properz*. Kiel.
Kennedy, D.F. 1993. *The Arts of Love: Five Studies in the Discourse of Latin Elegy*. Cambridge.
Korenjak, M. 2007. Von den Metamorphosen zum Brief an Augustus: Ovids 'horazische Periode'. In *Ovid. Werk-Kultur-Wirkung*, ed. M. Janka, U. Schmitzer, and H. Seng, 239–256. Darmstadt.
Lennartz, K. 1994. *Non verba, sed vim. Kritisch-exegetische Untersuchungen zu den Fragmenten archaischer römischer Tragiker*. Stuttgart.
Lowe, N.J. 2007. Epinician Eidography. In *Pindar's Poetry, Patrons, and Festivals*, ed. S. Hornblower and C. Morgan, 167–176. Oxford.
Lowrie, M. 1997. *Horace's Narrative Odes*. Oxford.
Lowrie, M. 2009. *Writing, Performance, and Authority in Augustan Rome*. Oxford.
Lyne, R.O.A.M. 1980. *The Latin Love Poets: From Catullus to Horace*. Oxford.
Lyne, R.O.A.M. 2005. Horace Odes Book 1 and the Alexandrian Edition of Alcaeus. *CQ* 55: 542–558.
Mader, G. 1993. Architecture, Aemulatio, and Elegiac Self-Definition in Propertius 3.2. *CJ* 88: 312–340.
Mader, G. 1994. Propertius' Hymn to Bacchus (3.17) and the Poetic Design of the Third

Book. In *Studies in Latin Literature and Roman History 7*, ed. C. Deroux, 369–385. Brussels.

Meban, D. 2008. Temple Building, Primus Language, and the Proem to Virgil's Third Georgic. *CPh* 103: 150–174.

McNelis, C. 2002. Greek Grammarians and Roman Society During the Early Empire: Statius' Father and his Contemporaries. *ClAnt* 21: 67–94.

Miller, F.J. 1984. *Ovid* Metamorphoses, *Book IX–XV*. Cambridge, MA. Revised 2nd edn. by G.P. Goold.

Miller, J.F. 1983. Propertius 3.2 and Horace. *TAPhA* 113: 289–299.

Miller, J.F. 1991. Propertius' Hymn to Bacchus and Contemporary Poetry. *AJPh* 112: 77–86.

Morgan, T.J. 1998. *Literate Education in the Hellenistic and Roman Worlds*. Cambridge.

Nauta, R. 2002. *Poetry for Patrons: Literary Communication in the Age of Domitian*. Leiden.

Nauta, R. 2008. Statius in the Silvae. In *The Poetry of Statius*, ed. J.J.L. Smolenaars, H.-J. v. Dam, and R.R. Nauta, 143–174. Leiden and Boston.

Negri, M. 2004. *Pindaro ad Alessandria*. Brescia.

Nethercut, W.R. 1970. The Ironic Priest. Propertius' Roman Elegies, III,1–5: Imitations of Horace and Vergil. *AJPh* 91: 385–407.

Newlands, C. 2002. *Statius' Silvae and the Poetics of Empire*. Cambridge.

Nisbet, R. and Rudd, N. 2004. *A Commentary on Horace: Odes. Book III*. Oxford.

Pfeiffer, R. 1968. *History of Classical Scholarship: From the Beginning to the End of the Hellenistic Age*. Oxford.

Phillips, T. 2016. *Pindar's Library: Performance Poetry and Material Texts*. Oxford.

Pillinger, H.E. 1969. Some Callimachean Influences on Propertius, Book 4. *HSPh* 73: 171–199.

Porro, A. 1994. *Vetera Alcaica. L'esegesi di Alceo dagli Alessandrini all'età imperiale*. Milan.

Rühl, M. 2006. *Literatur gewordener Augenblick. Die Silven des Statius im Kontext literarischer und sozialer Bedingungen von Dichtung*. Berlin.

Shackleton Bailey, D.R. 2003. *Statius* Silvae. Cambridge, MA.

Schmit-Neuerburg, T. 1999. *Vergils Aeneis und die antike Homerexegese*. Berlin.

Schlunk, R. 1974. *The Homeric Scholia and the Aeneid*. Ann Arbor.

Solmsen, F. 1948. Propertius and Horace. *CPh* 43: 105–109.

Spahlinger, L. 1996. *Ars latet arte sua. Die Poetologie der Metamorphosen Ovids*. Stuttgart.

Thomas, R. 1983. Callimachus, the Victoria Berenices, and Roman Poetry. *CQ* 33: 92–113.

Thomas, R. 1998. Virgil's Pindar. In *Style and Tradition: Studies in Honor of Wendell Clausen*, ed. P.E. Knox and C. Foss, 99–120. Stuttgart.

West, D. 2002. *Horace* Odes *III*. Oxford.

Wilkinson, L.P. 1970. Pindar and the Proem to the Third Georgic. In *Forschungen zur römischen Literatur*, ed. W. Wimmel, 286–290. Wiesbaden.
Zetzel, J.E.G. 1978. A Homeric Reminiscence in Catullus. *AJPh* 99: 332–333.
West, D. 2002. *Horace* Odes *III*. Oxford.

PART 6

Second Sophistic Contexts

∴

CHAPTER 14

Sympotic Sappho? The Recontextualization of Sappho's Verses in Athenaeus

Stefano Caciagli

A turning point in studies about Sappho was reached around the year 2000, when a section of Anglo-Saxon scholarship, especially in North America, rejected the traditional understanding that this poet was a sort of schoolmistress.* According to these scholars, especially Parker and Stehle, all reconstructions of Sappho's audience in modern times stem from arguments of Welcker and of Wilamowitz: Sappho was a teacher surrounded by her pupils.[1] A crucial component of this reconstruction was the alleged age of Sappho's companions: in his seminal book, *Sappho von einem herrschenden Vorurtheil befreyt*, Welcker equated the μαθήτριαι and the ἑταῖραι of the *Suda* (σ 107 Adler), identifying them with persons younger than the poet: Sappho was an adult, the pupils παῖδες and παρθένοι.[2]

> ἑταῖραι δὲ αὐτῆς καὶ φίλαι γεγόνασι τρεῖς, Ἀτθίς, Τελεσίππα, Μεγάρα· πρὸς ἃς καὶ διαβολὴν ἔσχεν αἰσχρᾶς φιλίας. μαθήτριαι δὲ αὐτῆς Ἀναγόρα Μιλησία, Γογγύλα Κολοφωνία, Εὐνείκα Σαλαμινία.
>
> She had three companions and friends, Atthis, Telesippa and Megara, and she got a bad name for her impure friendship with them. Her pupils were Anagora of Miletus, Gongyla of Colophon, and Eunica of Salamis.
>
> *Suda* σ 107 Adler, trans. CAMPBELL

---

* I would like to thank Professor Claude Calame, Professor Alberta Lorenzoni, Professor Jim Marks, Dr Luna Martelli, Professor Camillo Neri, Dr Enrico Prodi, and Professor Renzo Tosi for their useful suggestions.
1 Parker (1993); Stehle (1997). Cf. Welcker (1816); Müller (1865) 364 ff.; Schmid (1912) 198–199; Wilamowitz (1913); Bowra (1936) 187–190 (who in the second edition of 1961 eliminates all references to the *thiasos* present in the first edition); Schadewaldt (1950) 11; Merkerbach (1957); Gentili (1966) = (2006) 138 ff.; Calame (1977) i.363–385, cf. Calame (1996); Lardinois (1994); compare Caciagli (2011) 299–303.
2 Welcker (1845) 97.

According to Stehle and Parker, this idea is based only on late *testimonia*, and does not go back to Sappho's *ipsissima uerba*.[3] Further, if several sources represent the poet as being surrounded by young women, it is likely that Sappho's poems were oriented towards at least two different contexts and, consequently, two audiences: one consisting of adult companions in communal meetings of women, the other consisting of the bride's young friends along with her family and its allies at wedding feasts. The equation made by Welcker of μαθήτριαι and ἑταῖραι would then be wrong; in the words of Parker:

> there is absolutely nothing ... to show that Sappho was an older woman (or) ... that her addressees were young children, or that they left her care for marriage. This latter wide-spread assumption seems to be built entirely on the fact that she wrote epithalamia—as if that were all she wrote ... On this slender basis has been erected the whole tower of Sappho Schoolmistress.[4]

So, if we restrict ourselves to Sappho's *ipsissima uerba* and dismiss the late *testimonia*, no young women surround the poet when she sang for her companions.[5] Of course, the epithalamic poems mention παῖδες, παρθένοι and νύμφαι, but it is impossible to say whether these women were members of Sappho's group. Indeed, a bride's family might commission Sappho to compose a wedding poem simply because she was a famous poet. However, according to Parker, the fragments that imply a female community refer not to young women, but to φίλαι and ἑταῖραι, one example being fr. 160 τάδε νῦν ἑταίραις / ταῖς ἐμαῖσι †τερπνὰ† καλῶς ἀείσω. When in a poem we find companions, we have to assume that the audience consisted of age-mates of the *persona loquens*, because the word ἑταῖρος in Greek seems to imply a relatively equal status between the companions.[6] By way of comparison it is never suggested that Archilochus' or Alcaeus' companions were young, so why would the situation be different, seeing that Sappho shares themes with such sympotic poets? At the conclusion of his essay, perhaps as a challenge, Parker even proposes a sympotic context for fr. 2, the famous garden poem, where Aphrodite is invoked to pour a libation.

---

3   Parker (1993); Stehle (1997) 262 ff.
4   Parker (1993) 322–323.
5   After Parker's and Stehle's publications, P.Oxy. 1787 (= Sapph. fr. 58) was joined to P. Köln 429+430: in this poem, as before as now, appears the word παῖδες. In my view, the new text does not change the question of the presence of young women in Sappho's community: in fact, it is difficult to say in which kind of context this song was performed.
6   Cf. Chantraine (1968–1980) 393; Calame (1977) i.76–77; Caciagli (2011) 93–96.

Parker's and Stehle's reading of the evidence deserves serious consideration, but it certainly goes too far. In the first place, the complete assimilation between Sappho and the male poets that they propose fails to take into account fundamental differences in ancient Greece between the social roles of men and women. Second, it is difficult to dismiss the presence of young women in Sappho's community and to eliminate the evidence of the *testimonia*: the sources, of course, report unlikely and imaginative elements, but may also embed pieces of information from lost poems. If the *testimonia* are to be treated as authentic primary source material, the kind of rigorous *Quellenforschung* that Welcker established at the beginning of the nineteenth century is called for:[7] instead of dismissing sources, it would be important to consider how, in what context, and for what reason a piece of evidence might have been fabricated in antiquity. In this way, it can be determined whether a *testimonium* stems from a text of a poet or is the product of mere speculation. Further, the idea that Sappho addressed herself to two different audiences—one consisting of female companions, the other nuptial—is hardly self-evident. If it is possible to assume that the poet composed wedding poems for her φίλαι—as I deduce from fr. 27—it is nevertheless true that a Sappho who composes for brides to whom she has no ties of φιλότης suggests the possibility of a professional role.[8] In my opinion, this professional role is difficult to demonstrate in archaic Greece at least until Anacreon and Polycrates' "court".[9]

Despite these problems, there is, to be sure, some truth in the criticism of "Sappho Schoolmistress". For this poet shares with others several themes; moreover, her audience shares structural similarities with the male communities of companions, both of which probably consisted of persons who came from the same family or alliance of families, i.e. from a sort of faction.[10] A poem such as fr. 71, in this context, is revealing, displaying as it does the direct relationship between a name of a family and the concept of φιλότης.

× – ⏑ ⏑ – – ⏑ ⏑ – – ⏑ ⏑]μις σε Μίκα
× – ⏑ ⏑ – –]ελα[‥ἀλ]λά σ' ἔγωὐκ ἐάσω
× – ⏑ ⏑ – –]ν φιλότ[ατ'] ἤλεο Πενθιλήαν

---

7   See Calder (1998) 64 ff.
8   See Caciagli (2009).
9   See Sappho fr. 213Ag and, further, Ferrari (2007) 50–52: in any case, I am sceptical about the possibility of a sort of professionalism of archaic poets until at least Anacreon: if it is difficult to define the status of Alcman in Sparta, poets such as Archilochus, Alcaeus, or Sappho seem to me to be the poetical voices of small groups, where real relationships of φιλότης bind their members: cf. Rösler (1976, 1980) 33–36; Caciagli (2011) 56 ff.
10   See Parker (1993) 343 ff.

... Mica ... you / ... but I shall not allow you / ... you chose the friendship of ladies of the house of Penthilus / ..., you villain, ...

SAPPHO fr. 71.1–4, trans. CAMPBELL

Here I cannot examine in depth the question of the composition of Lesbian feminine groups and their relationship with the aristocratic families of Lesbos, but I would like at least to sketch the outlines of the argument that Sappho's audience was likely a version of a ἑταιρεία, i.e. the female equivalent of the sort of male group that is well known in archaic and classical Greece.[11] Indeed, it seems likely to me that the members of Sappho's group were recruited from the female members of an alliance of Lesbian families, which surrounded a more influential one, perhaps the Cleanactidae.[12] In my view, these groups of ἑταῖραι and φίλαι represent the way that Lesbian society had "chosen" to organize the members of its aristocracy, divided in different factions: these communities were likely active in several contexts, domestic, public, and sacral. This reconstruction is not in contrast to the fact that some of Sappho's companions were not Lesbian, since the relationship of ξενία between the faction of the poetess and others from abroad can explain this situation, especially if all her family was involved in seaborne trade, as Charaxus was.[13] If we follow Parker in comparing Alcaeus' and Sappho's groups, we have to postulate that their audiences consisted of both young and adult members, at least in some contexts. In fact, Alcaeus' and Theognis' pederastic poetry testifies to the presence of young men—probably the relatives of ἑταῖροι—in the main meeting of ἑταιρεῖαι, i.e. the symposium, where they served as cupbearers.[14] On the other hand, when we consider together the evidence of Sappho's fr. 24a, the recurrence of the word ἑταίρα in her corpus generally, and a close reading of lines 199–202 of Ovid's fifteenth *Epistle*, it is possible to postulate the presence of adult women in addition to παῖδες and παρθένοι in Sappho's group.[15] If the structure of Sappho's group is similar to that of Alcaeus', there would seem to be significance

---

11 See Calhoun (1913); Sartori (1957); Ghinatti (1970); Rösler (1980); Welwei (1992); Caciagli (2018).
12 Caciagli (2011) 212 ff.
13 The Greek seaborne trade was based on ξενία in the Archaic Age: see Caciagli (2011) 261–262, 269–274.
14 On the link between ἑταιρεῖαι and symposium, cf. Murray (1983a, 1983b, 1983c, 1991); Schmitt-Pantel (1992) 17 ff. On pederastic poetry, see Buffière (1980); Vetta (1982): given the existence of Alcaeus' pederastic poetry, it is impossible to eliminate the presence of young men in Alcaeus' sympotic audience. On the identity of young men in the aristocratic symposium, see Caciagli (2011) 92 ff. and 169 ff.
15 See Caciagli (2011) 10 ff.

in the fact that some fragments of Sappho attest gestures that recall sympotic ones, like pouring wine in fr. 2 or wearing a crown in fr. 94.

So, if the emphasis on Sappho's *ipsissima uerba* seems to be unproblematic, we should not dismiss the *testimonia*, which should rather be evaluated through a study of their sources. However, the problem is not only the understanding of the sources, but also of the fragments: the latter could mislead, in the sense that the interpretation of a poem can be affected by the context of quotation. For example, the sympotic atmosphere that it is possible to detect in some of the fragments could be a consequence of their being quoted in a sympotic context. In this respect, my present discussion is a sort of self-criticism: my understanding of Sappho's community as a sort of female ἑταιρεία is in part based on fragments where the word ἑταίρα appears, fragments mostly attested by Athenaeus, who seems to hint at a sympotic tradition in his *Deipnosophistai*.

Given these considerations, it is first of all interesting to consider the concept of "companionship" in Sappho. The word ἑταίρα is attested three times in her work, as well as in a *testimonium* to fr. 2. Thus we find it in fr. 126, quoted in a lexicographic context for δαύω.

δαύω· τὸ κοιμῶμαι· Σαπφώ (fr. 126)· 'δαύοις ἀπάλας ἐτα(ί)ρας ἐν στήθεσιν' λέγει δὲ Ἡρωδιανὸς ὅτι ἅπαξ κεῖται ἡ λέξις παρὰ Σαπφοῖ

δαύω, 'sleep': Sappho: 'May you sleep on the bosom of your tender companion.' Herodian says that the word occurs once only in Sappho.
Etymologicum Genuinum AB [46 Calame] = *Etym. Magn.* 250.10–11, trans. CAMPBELL

Here, it is possible only to say that the addressee of the *persona loquens* is, at least, a παρθένος, because of her physical maturity. It is on the other hand difficult to identify the speaker owing to the easy confusion made by the sources between the *persona loquens* and the author of a poem.

The word ἑταίρα also figures in frr. 142 and 160, transmitted by Athenaeus in a passage to be analyzed presently. Sappho fr. 160 is essential for the reconstruction of Sappho's audience; the performative future ἀείσω and the audience consisting of companions promise a context that could recall a performance at symposium. This context is not so different from what we see in fr. 22, i.e. it is possible to postulate for Sappho a sort of domestic gathering very similar to male ones. Incidentally, Athenaeus uses ἑταῖρος when he finishes the quotation of Sappho's fr. 2: this poem, or better its quotation in *Learned Banqueters*, will also be analyzed below.

With regard to the use of word ἑταίρα and the audience that it implies, it is hardly a revelation that, in a work entitled *The Learned Banqueters*, Sappho would appear to be a sympotic poet: the manner in which her *ipsissima uerba* are excerpted from the original context and reworked in the new one could deeply affect their meaning. In addition, there is another problem, one that concerns the textual tradition of the Sapphic fragments quoted by Athenaeus. According to Nicosia, all of her fragments as well as those of Alcaeus that we know derive—directly or indirectly—from Alexandrian editions.[16] This interpretation holds generally, apart from P. Köln 429+430. However, we may also note that Athenaeus knows sympotic anthologies, such as the *Carmina conuiualia Attica*, which circulated from the sixth century for the use of symposiasts: the *Theognidea* may have the same origin.[17] The *Carmina conuiualia Attica* is of great interest in the context of the tradition of Aeolic poetry, because here a "quotation" of Alcaeus' fr. 249 appears,[18] with some variants in comparison with P.Oxy. 2298 fr. 1. As to the *Carmina conuiualia Attica*, we should imagine a sympotic tradition, especially if, as argued by Fabbro, these poems were probably collected during the fifth century, i.e. before the Alexandrian edition of Alcaeus.[19]

In any case, it is conceivable that, out of their original context, Sappho's poems have been seen as erotic ones suitable for the symposium: in fact, Plutarch (*Quaestiones conuiuales* 622c) and Aulus Gellius (19.9) seem to attest the presence of Sappho in the poetical *corpus* that was sung during symposia in Roman Age.[20] If we trust in the story handed down by Aelian (fr. 190 Domingo-Forasté),[21] it is also possible to postulate that the insertion of Sappho in a sympotic context was not only a Roman custom, for he relates that Solon listened to a boy singing a μέλος of Sappho during a symposium and wished to learn it by heart. Does this setting really come from a long tradition, one that begins

---

16   Nicosia (1976) 29 ff.
17   See Fabbro (1995) xxv and Colesanti (2011) 219–241.
18   *Carmina conuiualia*, 891 *PMG* = Ath. 15.695a (cf. Alc. fr. 249) ἐκ γῆς χρὴ κατίδην πλόον, / εἴ τις δύναιτο καὶ παλάμην ἔχοι. / ἐπεὶ δέ κ' ἐν πόντῳ γένηται, / τῷ παρεόντι τρέχειν ἀνάγκη.
19   Fabbro (1995) xlii.
20   Plut., *Quaest. conv.* 622c ἐζητεῖτο παρὰ Σοσσίῳ Σαπφικῶν τινων ᾀσθέντων, ὅπου καὶ τὸν Κύκλωπα "μούσαις εὐφώνοις ἰᾶσθαι" φησὶ "τὸν ἔρωτα" Φιλόξενος. Gell. 19.9 *ac posteaquam introducti pueri puellaeque sunt, iucundum in modum* Ἀνακρεόντεια *pleraque et Sapphica et poetarum quoque recentium* ἐλεγεῖα *quaedam erotica dulcia et venusta cecinerunt*.
21   Ael. fr. 190 Domingo-Forasté Σόλων ὁ Ἀθηναῖος Ἐξηκεστίδου παρὰ πότον τοῦ ἀδελφιδοῦ αὐτοῦ μέλος τι Σαπφοῦς ᾄσαντος, ἥσθη τῷ μέλει καὶ προσέταξε τῷ μειρακίῳ διδάξαι αὐτόν. ἐρωτήσαντος δέ τινος διὰ ποίαν αἰτίαν τοῦτο σπουδάσειεν, ὁ δὲ ἔφη "ἵνα μαθὼν αὐτὸ ἀποθάνω."

in Archaic Age? Is Athenaeus, in a sense, an inheritor of this long tradition? According to Yatromanolakis, the symposium was a fundamental moment for Sappho's tradition, maybe more than comedy, which is thought to be mainly responsible for the distorted image of this poet from Welcker onwards.[22] In any case, some vase paintings in the late sixth century testify to the presence of Sappho's poems in Attic symposia: these vases have a sympotic shape and represent a female figure with the label 'Sappho'.[23] Moreover, Sappho is not unique in this respect, for Anacreon is also represented on Attic pottery, interestingly during the period in which he lived in Athens. The earliest mentions of Sappho in Greek literature pose perhaps insoluble questions: in fact, if the mention of Sappho by Alcaeus (fr. 384) is far from being certain,[24] the origin of the story about Charaxus in Herodotus (2.135)[25] and the way in which Plato (*Phaedrus* 235c) knew her work are equally difficult to ascertain. The example of the former 'New Sappho' (P. Köln 429+430) is interesting in this regard, since it could show the insertion of our poet into a third-century BCE anthology, perhaps of sympotic origin.[26]

Although the elements are unclear and difficult to understand, it is likely that the symposium was an important moment of Sappho's tradition as it was of Alcaeus', Solon's, Mimnermus', or Anacreon's. If this hypothesis has merit, it is conceivable that this tradition has affected the manner in which Athenaeus quotes Sappho: it is possible that the manner of excision from the original poems itself assimilates her to sympotic poets. In view of the direct link between sympotic groups and ἑταιρεῖαι in the sixth and fifth centuries BCE, the assimilation of Sappho's audience to a ἑταιρεία suggested above could also be the last consequence of the reworking that turned Sappho into a sympotic poet. This being the case, Sappho's *ipsissima uerba* as quoted by Athenaeus would

---

22   Yatromanolakis (2007).
23   Cf. Yatromanolakis (2007) 63 ff.: the label 'Sappho' is on a *kalpis* (Warsaw, National Museum, inv. 142333: 510–500 BCE), on a *kalathos-psykter* (Munich, Staatliche Antikensammlungen, inv. 2416: 480–470 BCE), on a *krater* (Bochum, Ruhr-Universität, Kunstsammlungen, inv. S 508: 580–470 BCE), and on a *hydria* (Athens, National Archaeological Museum, inv. 1260: 440–430 BCE).
24   The reading Σάπφοι is problematic for linguistic reasons in Sappho fr. 384: cf. Liberman (1999) 169n339.
25   Cf. Lidov (2002). The so-called 'Brothers Poem', published by Obbink (2014, 2016), attests the presence of the name of Charaxus in her *corpus*, along with that of Larichus. Without accepting Lidov's scepticism about the story of Charaxus and Doricha, the new text doesn't allow a certain link between this new poem and Sappho frr. 5, 15, although I think that this link is very likely: cf. Caciagli (2011) 249 ff.
26   Cf. Aloni (2008) 154 ff.

be unreliable out of context, a point that is very important for the arguments of Parker and Stehle and—finally—for my own reconstruction of the social background of Sappho's poetry.

In what follows, I shall adduce three examples, from which it is possible to observe different ways in which Athenaeus reworks Sappho's poems. The first comes from the beginning of the thirteenth book of the *Deipnosophistai*, the topic of which is ἔρως and κάλλος.

> περὶ τῶν ὄντως ἑταιρῶν τὸν λόγον πεποίημαι, τουτέστιν τῶν φιλίαν ἄδολον συντηρεῖν δυναμένων, ἃς ὁ Κύνουλκος τολμᾷ λοιδορεῖν, ⟨τὰς⟩ μόνας τῶν ἄλλων γυναικῶν τῷ τῆς φιλίας ὀνόματι προσηγορευμένας [ἢ] ἀπὸ τῆς παρὰ τοῖς Ἀθηναίοις καλουμένης Ἑταίρας [τῆς] Ἀφροδίτης. περὶ ἧς φησιν ὁ Ἀθηναῖος Ἀπολλόδωρος ἐν τοῖς περὶ Θεῶν οὕτως. "Ἑταίραν δὲ τὴν Ἀφροδίτην τὴν τοὺς ἑταίρους καὶ τὰς ἑταίρας συνάγουσαν· τοῦτο δ᾽ ἐστὶν φίλας'. καλοῦσι γοῦν καὶ αἱ ἐλεύθεραι γυναῖκες ἔτι καὶ νῦν καὶ αἱ παρθένοι τὰς συνήθεις καὶ φίλας ἑταίρας, ὡς ἡ Σαπφώ (fr. 160)·
>
>> τάδε νῦν ἑταίραις
>> ταῖς ἐμαῖσι τερπνὰ καλῶς ἀείσω.
>
> καὶ ἔτι (fr. 142)·
>> Λατὼ καὶ Νιόβα μάλα μὲν φίλαι ἦσαν ἑταῖραι.

What I have described are instead actual courtesans, which is to say, women capable of maintaining a friendship not based on trickery, but whom Cynulcus dares to insult, even though they are the only women addressed as 'friendly', a name they get from the Aphrodite known in Athens as Hetaira ['the Courtesan']. Apollodorus of Athens in his *On the Gods* [*FGrH* 244 F 112] says the following about her: 'Aphrodite Hetaira, who brings together male and female companions [*hetairai*], that is to say female friends [*philai*]. Even today, at any rate, free women and girls refer to their friends and associates as *hetairai*, just like Sappho [fr. 160]: "I will now sing these / † pleasant † songs beautifully for my *hetairai*". Furthermore [Sappho fr. 142]: "Lato and Nioba were very close *hetairai*".'

ATHENAEUS 13.571c–d, trans. OLSON, adapted

After an introductory section, the *deipnosophistai* Myrtilus and Cynulcus engage in a debate. The first (563d) finds fault with the Stoics because they refuse relationships with women, but love young boys; afterwards, he praises the beauty of women and men. Cynulcus (566e) replies that Myrtilus' scholarship is not a real πολυμαθία, but πορνογραφία: he accuses him of spending his time in wine shops, not with his friends (ἑταίρων) but with courtesans (ἑταιρῶν).[27] Myrtilus retorts that he would like to discuss only the ἑταῖραι in the original sense of the word, linked to the concept of φιλία and companionship. It is for this reason that he quotes the two examples from Sappho because, like her, 'even today ... free women and girls refer to their friends and associates as *hetairai*' (trans. Olson). With these words, Myrtilus ultimately assimilates Sappho's group to Athenaeus' *deipnosophistai*, both consisting of companions, and so subverts the beginning of Cynulcus' speech about ἑταῖροι and ἑταῖραι.

Do the Sapphic fragments come from a sympotic tradition? Of course the subject of courtesans is typical of the symposium, but the structure of Myrtilus' speech seems to be related to a different tradition: the sophist explains the real meaning of ἑταίρα and gives several examples in a way that recalls a treatise. In any case, Athenaeus—or his source—could have reworked the *ipsissima uerba* of Sappho in such a way that it is now impossible to catch their original meaning and their audience. Out of context, for example, it is hard to determine the kind of performance hinted at in fr. 160 and the kind of relationship the companions have with Sappho; further, it is also difficult to say whether Sappho really is the *persona loquens* in this fragment or another woman. So, at least in this case, it is difficult to determine the context of the *ipsissima uerba*.

My second example comes from the fifteenth book of the *Deipnosophistai*.

ἐστεφανοῦντο δὲ καὶ τὰ στήθη καὶ ἐμύρουν ταῦτα, ἐπεὶ αὐτόθι ἡ καρδία. Ἐκάλουν δὲ καὶ οἷς περιεδέοντο τὸν τράχηλον στεφάνους ὑποθυμίδας, ὡς Ἀλκαῖος (fr. 362.1 f.) ἐν τούτοις·
    ἀλλ' ἀνήτω μὲν περὶ ταῖς δέραισι
    περθέτω πλεκτὰς ὑποθυμίδας τίς
καὶ Σαπφώ (fr. 94.15–16)·
    καὶ πολλαῖς ὑποθυμίδας
    πλεκταῖς ἀμπ' ἀπάλᾳ δέρᾳ.
καὶ Ἀνακρέων (397 *PMG*)·
    πλεκτὰς δ' ὑποθυμίδας περὶ στήθεσι λωτίνας ἔθεντο.
Αἰσχύλος δ' (frr. 202, 235 *TGrF*) ...
Σαπφὼ δ' ἁπλούστερον τὴν αἰτίαν ἀποδίδωσιν τοῦ στεφανοῦσθαι ἡμᾶς, λέγουσα τάδε (fr. 81.4–7)·

---

27 Ath. 13.567a σὺ δέ, ὦ σοφιστά, ἐν τοῖς καπηλείοις συναναφύρῃ οὐ μετὰ ἑταίρων ἀλλὰ μετὰ ἑταιρῶν, μαστροπευούσας περὶ σαυτὸν οὐκ ὀλίγας ἔχων καὶ περιφέρων αἰεὶ τοιαυτὶ βιβλία Ἀριστοφάνους καὶ Ἀπολλοδώρου καὶ Ἀμμωνίου καὶ Ἀντιφάνους, ἔτι δὲ Γοργίου τοῦ Ἀθηναίου, πάντων τούτων συγγεγραφότων περὶ τῶν Ἀθήνησι Ἑταιρίδων.

σὺ δὲ στεφάνοις, ὦ Δίκα, περθέσθ' ἐραταῖς φόβαισιν
ὄρπακας ἀνήτοιο συνέρραις ἀπαλαῖσι χερσίν.
εὐανθέα γὰρ πέλεται καὶ Χάριτες μάκαιραι
μᾶλλον προσόρην, ἀστεφανώτοισι δ' ἀπυστρέφονται.
ὡς εὐανθέστερον γὰρ καὶ κεχαρισμένον μᾶλλον τοῖς θεοῖς παραγγέλλει στεφανοῦσθαι τοὺς θύοντας.

> They put garlands around their chests as well, and covered them with perfume, since that is where the heart is located. They referred to the garlands they wrapped around their necks as *hypothymides*, as for example Alcaeus [fr. 362.1–2] in the following passage: 'But let someone place *hypothymides* woven of anise about our necks.' Also Sappho [fr. 94.15–16]: 'and many woven *hypothymides* around my soft neck'. And Anacreon [397 *PMG*]: 'They placed *hypothymides* made of *lôtos* about their chests.' And Aeschylus [frr. 202, 235 *TGrF*] … And Sappho [fr. 81.4–7] offers a simpler explanation of why we wear garlands, saying the following: 'Wrap anise shoots together into garlands, Dica, with your soft hands, and place them around your lovely hair; with fine flowers † for it is † and the blessed Graces more [corrupt], but turn away from those who wear no garlands.' For she recommends that people making a sacrifice wear garlands, because whatever has more flowers is more appealing to the gods.
>
> ATHENAEUS 15.674c–e, trans. OLSON

The book begins with a discussion of the sympotic game of *kottabos*; then Cynulcus (669c) proposes discussion of crowns, because the παῖδες are bringing crowns and unguents to the banqueters: it is the typical act that begins a symposium after a banquet. After a section about lovers with crowns and about the plant *agnus castus*, Democritus notices that it is possible to put crowns on the breast: these crowns have a particular name, ὑποθυμιάδες. In this regard, he quotes verses from Alcaeus (fr. 362.1), Sappho (frr. 81.4–7 and 94.15–16) and Anacreon (397 *PMG*), in which the actions represented are very similar: with Anacreon and Alcaeus, we are faced with a practice peculiar to a symposium. What about Sappho? We could think about an assimilation of the actions represented by Sappho to sympotic practices, in particular with regard to the acts that begin a symposium; in this regard, it is quite interesting that Sappho is quoted in this series. However, the original meaning of Sappho's fr. 94, from which the quotation is excerpted, has a context that can be hardly related to a symposium: in fact, the Sapphic ὑποθυμιάδες scene concludes with an erotic involvement on στρωμναί (21), which cannot be directly assimilated to sympotic κλῖναι, because στρωμνή means only "bed", i.e. a 'place where you lie down for the night'.[28] Furthermore, the wine is absent. On the contrary, it is likely that Sappho represents in this poem a female communal scene that leads to an erotic involvement in a—possibly—sacral or domestic atmosphere.[29] In any case, what is represented in Sappho's fr. 94 has several similarities with a sympotic scenario, with the hints at unguents, crowns, and στρωμναί, which are different from but—of course—recall sympotic κλῖναι: it is possible that these elements favour a reworking of these lines in a sympotic way.

Nevertheless, Athenaeus' passage in its entirety does not concern only the actions that characterize a symposium, but also sacral ones, related with a sort of sacrifice. In fact, when Democritus explains why human beings have to crown themselves he explains that gods look with favour on those who do it: on this subject, he quotes Sappho's fr. 81, identifying its context with a θυσία. If the context is clearly different from a sympotic one, the topic of fr. 81 is nevertheless consistent with the beginning of a symposium: in fact, a convivial male meeting was characterized by a sacral *aura*, as we infer from the *incipit* of the *Theognidea* or of the *Carmina conuiualia Attica*. In any case, this passage is probably similar to the previous example: the quotations of Anacreon, Sappho, and Alcaeus seem to be quoted by Athenaeus or his source for linguistic reasons, i.e. because the word ὑποθυμιάς appears here. So Athenaeus would not collect sympotic passages, following a thematic approach, but possibly used a source about crowns and ὑποθυμιάδες in general, maybe a σύγγραμμα, in which the verses of these poets were already connected.

The last example is from the eleventh book and is more remarkable than the previous ones. The *deipnosophistai* settle down on κλῖναι and one of them, Plutarchus, introduces the topic of the current symposium, i.e. the cups. As we are going to see below, the latter Sapphic excerpt seems to recall all the previous quotations and provide a good conclusion for Plutarchus' opening words. In what is quoted below, I have highlighted in bold the words that recall those of Sappho's fr. 2 at the end of the passage. Furthermore, it is important to note that the Sapphic quotation is not complete: I suspect that Athenaeus hints at what is omitted through passages that precede Sappho, especially though Xenophanes' poem. So I have italicized in the passages that precede the Sapphic quotation the words that appear in what Athenaeus omits of fr. 2.

---

28 See Page (1955) 79. Sappho fr. 94.14–23: ... π(ε)ρεθήκα(ο) / καὶ πόλλαις ὐπαθύμιδας / πλέκταις ἀμφ' ἀπάλᾳ δέρᾳ / ἀνθέων ἐ[– 6 –] πεποημμέναις / καὶ ... / ... / ... / καὶ στρώμν[αν ἐ]πὶ μολθάκαν / ἀπάλαν πα..[⏑ –]ογων / ἐξίης πόθο[ν – ⏑ νε]ανίδων (you ... and round your tender neck you put many woven garlands made from flowers and ... and on soft beds ... you would satisfy your longing for tender young women [trans. Campbell, adapted]).

29 See Ferrari (2003) 64; Caciagli (2011) 175 ff.

ὁρῶν οὖν ὑμῶν καὶ αὐτὸς τὸ συμπόσιον κατὰ τὸν Κολοφώνιον Ξενοφάνη πλῆρες ὂν πάσης θυμηδίας (fr. 1 Gentili and Prato)·

νῦν γὰρ δὴ ζάπεδον καθαρὸν καὶ χεῖρες ἁπάντων
καὶ **κύλικες**· πλεκτοὺς δ' ἀμφιτιθεῖ στεφάνους,
ἄλλος δ' εὐῶδες μύρον ἐν φιάλῃ παρατείνει·
κρατὴρ δ' ἕστηκεν μεστὸς εὐφροσύνης·
ἄλλος δ' οἶνος ἕτοιμος, ὃς οὔποτέ φησι προδώσειν,
μείλιχος ἐν κεράμοις, ἄνθεος ὀσδόμενος·
ἐν δὲ μέσοις ἁγνὴν ὀδμὴν λιβανωτὸς ἵησι·
ψυχρὸν δ' ἐστὶν ὕδωρ καὶ γλυκὺ καὶ καθαρόν.
πάρκεινται δ' ἄρτοι ξανθοὶ γεραρή τε τράπεζα
τυροῦ καὶ μέλιτος πίονος ἀχθομένη·
βωμὸς δ' ἄνθεσιν ἂν τὸ μέσον πάντῃ πεπύκασται,
μολπὴ δ' ἀμφὶς ἔχει δώματα καὶ **θαλίη**.
...
οὔτι μάχας διέπειν Τιτήνων οὐδὲ Γιγάντων
οὐδέ ⟨τι⟩ Κενταύρων, πλάσματα τῶν προτέρων,
ἢ στάσιας σφεδανάς, τοῖς οὐδὲν χρηστὸν ἔνεστι,
θεῶν ⟨δὲ⟩ προμηθείην αἰὲν ἔχειν ἀγαθόν.

καὶ ὁ χαρίεις δ' Ἀνακρέων φησίν (fr. eleg. 2 West)·

οὐ φιλέω ὃς κρητῆρι παρὰ πλέῳ οἰνοποτάζων
νείκεα καὶ πόλεμον δακρυόεντα λέγῃ,
ἀλλ' ὅστις Μουσέων τε καὶ ἀγλαὰ δῶρ' **Ἀφροδίτης**
συμμίσγων ἐρατῆς μνήσεται εὐφροσύνης.

καὶ Ἴων δὲ ὁ Χῖός φησιν (fr. 27 West = fr. 2 Valerio)·

χαιρέτω ἡμέτερος βασιλεύς, σωτήρ τε πατήρ τε·
ἡμῖν δὲ κρητῆρ' **οἰνοχόοι** θέραπες
κιρνάντων προχύταισιν ἐν ἀργυρέοις· ὁ δὲ **χρυσὸς**
οἶνον ἔχων χειρῶν νιζέτω εἰς ἔδαφος.
σπένδοντες δ' ἁγνῶς Ἡρακλέι τ' Ἀλκμήνῃ τε,
Προκλέι Περσείδαις τ', ἐκ Διὸς ἀρχόμενοι,
πίνωμεν ...

ἐποιοῦντο δὲ καὶ οἱ ἑπτὰ καλούμενοι σοφοὶ συμποτικὰς ὁμιλίας ... συνιοῦσι καὶ ἡμῖν ἐπὶ τὰς Διονυσιακὰς ταύτας λαλιὰς οὐδεὶς ἂν εὐλόγως φθονήσαι νοῦν ἔχων, κατὰ τοὺς Ἀλέξιδος Ταραντίνους (fr. 222 *PCG*),

οἳ τῶν πέλας
οὐδέν' ἀδικοῦμεν οὐδέν ...
ἔγνωκα γοῦν οὕτως ἐπισκοπούμενος
εἶναι μανιώδη πάντα τἀνθρώπων ὅλως,
ἀποδημίας δὲ τυγχάνειν ἡμᾶς αἰεὶ

τοὺς ζῶντας, ὥσπερ εἰς πανήγυρίν τινα
ἀφειμένους ἐκ τοῦ θανάτου καὶ τοῦ σκότους
εἰς τὴν διατριβὴν εἰς τὸ φῶς τε τοῦθ', ὃ δὴ
ὁρῶμεν. ὃς δ' ἂν πλεῖστα γελάσῃ καὶ πίῃ
καὶ τῆς Ἀφροδίτης ἀντιλάβηται τὸν χρόνον
τοῦτον ὃν ἀφεῖται, κἂν τύχῃ γ', ἐράνου τινός,
πανηγυρίσας ἥδιστ' ἀπῆλθεν οἴκαδε.
καὶ κατὰ τὴν καλὴν οὖν Σαπφώ (fr. 2.13–16)·

ἐλθέ, Κύπρι,
χρυσίαισιν ἐν κυλίκεσσιν ἁβρῶς
συμμεμιγμένον θαλίαισι νέκταρ
οἰνοχοοῦσα
τούτοις τοῖς ἑταίροις ἐμοῖς τε καὶ σοῖς (σοι Α[30]).

Since I can see for myself, then, that your party is full of happiness of every sort, as in the description offered by Xenophanes of Colophon [fr. 1 Gentili and Prato]: 'For now the floor is clean, as are everyone's hands and the **cups**. (One slave) places woven garlands around (our heads), while another offers us fragrant perfume in a bowl; and a mixing-bowl full of good cheer stands in the middle. Another type of **wine**, sweet as honey and smelling of flowers, is ready in the jars, and promises that we will never run out of it. In our midst is *frankincense* that produces a *sacred* scent; and the *water* is *cold*, delicious, and pure. Golden-brown loaves of bread have been set beside us, along with a table full of honor and heavy with cheese and dense honey. In the middle is an *altar* covered on all sides with flowers; song and dance and **celebration** fill the house ... But they ought not to spend their time describing battles fought by Titans, or Giants, or centaurs, stories our ancestors made up, or their violent quarrels; topics of this sort are worthless. Instead, they should always have good forethought for the gods.' So too the witty Anacreon says [eleg. fr. 2 West]: 'I dislike the man who talks of quarrels and war, which is full of tears, as he drinks wine beside a full mixing-bowl; better someone who **combines** the Muses glorious gifts with those of **Aphrodite**, and fixes his mind on the cheer we desire.' Ion of Chios [fr. 27 West] as well says: 'Hail to our king, savior and father! Let the servants who **pour the wine** mix up a bowl for us using silver pitchers (*prochutai*); † and the **gold** having **wine** of hands let it wash onto the floor! † Let us **pour** *holy* **libations** to

---

30 Cf. Bergk (1853) 669; Brunet (2003) 67.

Heracles and Alcmene, and to Procles and the descendants of Perseus, although we begin with Zeus; and let us drink ...' The so-called Seven Wise Men also held drinking parties ... when we gather for these Dionysiac conversations, 'no one with any sense would have reasonable grounds for resenting our behaviour', to quote Alexis' *Men of Tarentum* (fr. 222 *PCG*), 'since we're not hurting the people around us ... But I've thought about it, and I've come to the following conclusion: human existence is entirely, completely insane, and as long as we're alive, we're enjoying a reprieve, like going to a **festival**; we've been released from death and darkness and allowed to have a party in this light we see. And whoever laughs the most, and drinks the most, and grabs **Aphrodite** during the time he's released, or a dinner party if he gets the chance—he's the happiest when he goes home after the festival.' So to quote the lovely Sappho (fr. 2.13–16): '**Come, Cypris**, and daintily **pour nectar mixed** with **celebrations** into **gold cups** for these friends of yours and mine.'

ATH. 11.462c–463e, trans. OLSON

After a digression on the population of Kylikranes, Plutarchus assimilates the rejoicing of his companions with the banquet represented by Xenophanes in fr. 1 Gentili and Prato. The end of this poem, with a refusal to talk about wars, allows Plutarchus to quote Anacreon (fr. eleg. 2 West), where the poet rejects war and invites the audience to enjoy the banquet: these quotations permit a connection to be made between the *deipnosophistai* and the Seven Sages. Plutarchus says that there is no blame for the learned banqueters, if they enjoy the sympotic chat, because, according to Alexis, life is a sort of short journey far from the darkness of death: so, we have to seize the moment. Alexis' invitation to enjoy Aphrodite is the reason to quote a section of Sappho's fr. 2, where the poet requests the goddess to come and pour nectar in gold cups. This summary makes clear how greatly this example differs from previous ones: the link that connects the quotations here is not linguistic, but thematic. In a sense, we are at the beginning of a sort of sympotic chain that is based on picking up the words of previous poetical excerpts.[31] In fact, all the passages revolve not only around the joy of the banquet, but also around some words and their synonyms: κύλιξ, οἶνος, θαλία, σπένδειν, συμμίγνυμι, χεῖν, χρυσός and Ἀφροδίτη. These words represent the best way to have εὐφροσύνη, an element suitable for the symposia of the wise. In this context, Sapphic quotation is a fitting conclusion to Plutarchus' opening remarks, in that it picks up all the topics of his

---

31   See Vetta (1980); Colesanti (2011) 8ff.

speech. Plutarchus directly connects Sapphic quotation with Alexis, who offers the exhortation to grab Aphrodite. In any case, the Sapphic quotation also picks up all the previous passages: for Κύπρι, one may compare Anacreon; for χρυσίαισιν, Ion of Chios; for κυλίκεσσιν, Xenophanes; for συμμεμιγμένον, Anacreon; for θαλία, Xenophanes and Alexis; and for the act of pouring wine, Xenophanes and Ion. In this context, Sappho's verses are suitable for a hymn, which is characteristic of the beginning of a symposium.

If we have a glance at the other *testimonium* of Sappho's fr. 2,[32] the Florentine *ostrakon* (*PSI* 1300), we notice how Athenaeus—or his source—has possibly reworked Sappho's verses.

```
1a   – ᴗ – ᴗ – ᴗ ᴗ – ᴗ – ᴗ‖
2a   – ᴗ – ᴗ – ᴗ ᴗ – ᴗ – ᴗ‖
3a   – ᴗ – ᴗ – ᴗ ᴗ ἔλθε (?) – ×
4a   – ᴗ ᴗ – ᴗ‖‖
```

δεῦρύ μ' ἐκ ⟨Κ⟩ρήτας πρ[οσίοισ'] ἔναυ⟨λ⟩ον
ἄγνον, ὅππ[αι δὴ] χάριεν μὲν ἄλσος
μαλί[αν], βῶμοι δὲ ⟨τε⟩θυμιάμε-
4   νοι [λι]βανώτω⟨ι⟩·
ἐν δ' ὔδωρ ψῦχρον κελάδει δι' ὔσδων
μαλίαν, βρό⟨δ⟩οισι ⟨δ⟩ὲ παῖς ὀ χῶρος
⟨ἐ⟩σκίαστ', αἰθυσσομένων δὲ φύλλων
8   κῶμα κατέρρει·
ἐν δὲ λείμων ἰππόβοτος τέθαλε
ἠρίνοις⟨ιν⟩ ἄνθεσιν, αἰ ⟨δ'⟩ ἄηται
μέλλιχα πνέοισιν ⟨ᴗ – – ᴗ – ×⟩
12   ⟨– ᴗ ᴗ – ᴗ⟩·
ἔνθα δὴ σὺ †(.)υ.τ.[ ]† ἔλοισα, Κύπρι,
χρυσ⟨ί⟩αι⟨σι⟩ ἐν κυλίκεσσιν ἄ⟨β⟩ρως
⟨ὀ⟩μ⟨με⟩μείχμενον θαλίαισι νέκταρ
16   ⟨οἰ⟩νοχόαισα[ι].

Hither come to me from Crete, going to this holy haunt, in which is your delightful grove of apple-trees, and altars smoking with incense; therein cold water babbles through apple-branches, and the whole place is shadowed by roses, and from the shimmering leaves the sleep of enchantment

---

[32] The text of Sappho fr. 2 that I reproduce is the result of my reading of *PSI* 1300 in 2009: I discuss it in Caciagli (2015).

comes down; therein too a meadow, where horses graze, blossoms with spring flowers, and the winds blow gently ...; here, Cypris, taking ... pour gracefully into golden cups nectar that is mingled with our festivities.

SAPPHO, fr. 2, trans. CAMPBELL, adapted

In Plutarchus' speech, the reference to the natural landscape of fr. 2 has completely disappeared: it is in this 'garden' that the poetess invites Aphrodite to come and to pour nectar. The most important difference between the text of the *ostrakon* and Athenaeus' quotation is perhaps syntactical. With Sappho's words, Plutarchus summons Aphrodite through an imperative, ἐλθέ, on which οἰνοχοοῦσα depends. In the case of the *ostrakon*, on the other hand, we do not find ἐλθέ, but ἔλοισα: with this participle we lose the main verb in Athenaeus. What about οἰνοχοοῦσα? In line 16, the *ostrakon* presents the reading οινοχοαισα[, with the potsherd breaking just after *alpha*. The imperative οἰνοχόαισον that Lobel and Page have proposed is based on a mistaken reading;[33] but while the reading does not commend itself, these editors—in my opinion—have stumbled on the correct sense of the sentence, i.e. with an imperative at the end of the poem that is the main verb of lines 13–16 in the original version of Sappho's poem. Of course we also look for a main verb in the lacuna of line 13, but I think that the simplest solution is to interpret the *ostrakon* reading as οἰνοχόαισα[ι: this form could be an imperative middle or, perhaps better, an active infinitive of the aorist used imperatively.

If this reconstruction is correct, Athenaeus—or his source—will have completely reworked the syntactical construction of Sappho's sentence. Why? Plutarchus' aim is probably to invoke Aphrodite in order to perform a sympotic libation, as usual at the beginning of a symposium. The need to invoke Aphrodite probably entails Plutarchus quoting Sappho, given the strong relationship between this poetess and the goddess, but the invocation in fr. 2 does not fit with his speech: in fact, it does not imply a sympotic environment, because lines 2–12 seem to represent a τέμενος, an ἔναυλος or, more generally, a shrine in which it is possible to imagine a sort of sacrifice and to which the poetess summons the goddess.[34] Of course, a sanctuary does not rule out a symposium,

---

33 The signs on *PSI* 1300 line 17 seem to require the reading -αισα[: see Lanata (1960) 75; Ferrari (2000) 42–43; Caciagli (2011) 138–141.

34 In my view, the reading ναῦ{γ}ον proposed by Lobel is not suitable for description that follows it: the poetess describes a natural landscape that is not fenced (i.e. it seems not a τέμενος), but that simply has altars. In any rate, it is really inconceivable a temple where there is a grove, a meadow and—probably—a river: an ἔναυλος ('a dwelling in the open air') seems to me the best correction of ΕΝΑΥΓΟΝΑΓΝΟΝ in *PSI* 1300, but it is also pos-

which could be performed after a sacrifice in a ἑστιατόριον:[35] however, I suggest that this latter location is inconsistent with the natural landscape described by Sappho. As to the syntax, the entire relative clause, which begins in line 2, necessarily depends on a verb in line 1 (or in a previous line), where an imperative is probably required: it is very likely that this verb was one of movement, because δεῦρυ, ἐκ and ὄππ[α in line 1 seem to imply a movement from somewhere to the place where the *persona loquens* invokes the goddess; from line 13 a new sentence begins, possibly with another imperative (οἰνοχόαισα[ι?), linked to the previous sentence by ἔνθα, which, in a sense, resumes the description of the natural landscape in lines 1–12.

So then, in order to produce a sort of sympotic invocatory hymn, Athenaeus (or his source) eliminated all reference to the original context, which was not suitable for a banquet, and quoted only the end of the poem, where there is a libation that also suits a symposium. However, after the elimination of the beginning of Sappho's poem, the quotation has lost its invocatory verb. It is therefore tempting to imagine that Athenaeus (or his source) finds ἐλθέ in line 1 or in a previous line, so that we should maybe fill it somewhere in the *incipit* of fr. 2: he picks up it from here and puts it in line 13, where on the *ostrakon* there is a word with a similar sound to ἐλθέ, that is ἔλοισα. Because of the room in the lacuna of line 1 of the Florentine *ostrakon* and because of the metrical structure of this line, the verb cannot be ἔλθε if we would like to insert an invocatory verb in the lacuna of this line, but it could have been a compound of ἔρχομαι. Athenaeus (or his source) would thus also have simplified the compound, possibly playing with the poetical memory of his "audience", which knows that ἔλοισα has no preverb in the original context. Otherwise, we could also fill ἔλθε in the stanza that—in my opinion—has to be before line 1.[36] If this reconstruction finds its mark, it is possible to postulate that the need to pick up the imperative from the beginning of Sappho's poem implies the change of οἰνοχόαισαι into a participle for syntactical reasons.

In short, I suggest that we may be confronting an oral technique of composition that was characteristic of the symposium from the archaic age onwards.[37]

---

     sible that the right reading is ΕΝΑΥΛΟΝΑΓΝΟΝ (the letter between *upsilon* and *omikron* has the left stroke slightly curved).

35   See Caciagli (2014) 75–80.

36   In my view, it is difficult to see line 1 as the *incipit* of the poem: in fact, a prayer without an invocation at the beginning is very strange; further, the address in line 13 seems to require an invocation in *incipit*, if we consider the ring composition that characterizes texts similar to fr. 2: cf. e.g. Sappho frr. 1 and 5.

37   Pelling (2000) analyses the way Athenaeus introduces and reworks the quotations of the

A banqueter was able, by this technique, to rework "famous" poems in order to adapt them to new contexts. A good example of this phenomenon is the *Theognidea*, in which some elegies are connected to those that preceded them through a thematic or linguistic link, and some metrical or linguistic reworking to fit a famous poem to a new context is evident.[38] If this reconstruction is plausible, it is interesting that the learned banqueter's store of memorized poetry, which naturally includes Sappho's poems, can have played a role. In fact, several elements of Sappho's garden that have been eliminated by Athenaeus in order to fit his quotation to a sympotic context appear in Xenophanes' poem, i.e. the first of Plutarchus' quotations: ἄνθος, ἁγνός, λιβανωτός, ψυχρός, ὕδωρ, βωμός. So, when a learned reader arrives at Sappho's quotation, which ends the introduction to the 11th book, it is possible that he retrospectively reinterprets these elements as an allusion to the section of fr. 2 that Plutarchus-Athenaeus has had to eliminate for contextual reasons. Faced with this situation, it is impossible to say whether the reworking is by Athenaeus or by a source that he has used, but the significant point is that the final result is a speech that is suitable for a sympotic context.

To sketch a conclusion, Sappho's ἑταιρεία is a problematic concept, when Athenaeus is the main witness for the fragments that could support this idea. Of course, the presence of the word ἑταίρα in these lines is relevant, but Athenaeus could hint at a pre-existing sympotic tradition in which they were included (and dating from the sixth century BCE onwards) or he could be reworking the texts of the Alexandrian edition in order to emphasize sympotic themes. In a word, not only the *testimonia*, but also the *ipsissima uerba* may be unreliable since they can be reworked in contexts that are very different from the original one. In this regard, the words used by Athenaeus to conclude the quotation of Sappho fr. 2.13–16 are quite interesting. Scholars have discussed whether the sentence that ends this quotation—τούτοις τοῖς ἑταίροις ἐμοῖς τε καὶ σοῖς—stems from Sappho or Plutarchus, the character in the *Deipnosophistai*: in any case, it is possible to postulate that, in Athenaeus' representation, Sappho's group is obviously conceived—by analogy with the Learned Banqueters—as a sympotic community. Could this verse or *testimonium* point to a sort of Sapphic ἑταιρεία for which the gathering of female companions was assimilated to male institution of the symposium? Is Parker's idea of a sympotic context for fr. 2 appealing? The juxtaposition—at least in the last example analyzed—between

---

historians, adapting them to the context of learned symposia, in which the oral character of the communication was important.

38 See Colesanti (2011) 16ff. and 35ff.

Sappho's and Athenaeus' groups, which Athenaeus' readers could have made, is not really odd: in fact, lines 13–16 of fr. 2, which are suitable for a hymn at the beginning of a symposium, become sympotic in Plutarchus' speech.

I therefore conclude that a full appreciation of female ἑταιρεία cannot rest solely on Sappho's *ipsissima uerba*, which can be as misleading as the *testimonia* are purported to be. When the aim is to reconstruct the social and performative context of Sappho's audience, caution in the use not only of *testimonia*, but also of fragments does not necessitate rejection of the idea of a female ἑταιρεία. This hypothesis still seems to me the best one, because it is based not only on *testimonia* and fragments, but also on the comparison between Sappho and other poets, especially Alcaeus, who—despite the difference of gender and, consequently, of social role—happens to be her contemporary and from the same society. On the other hand, the concept of φιλότης expressed in fr. 1 is consistent with that of φιλότης and ἑταιρεία in Alcaeus (cf. e.g. frr. 70.2–5 and 129.14–20), i.e. the reciprocal relationship between the members of a specific social group.[39] Moreover, frr. 22 or 160 represent a musical performance not so different from those one could have found at a symposium. Thus we find in fr. 71, about the women of the Penthilidae, a society in which relationships of φιλότης were linked to familial relations in context of conflicts among different aristocratic factions, while in fr. 94 some activities of Sappho's group resemble those of Alcaeus or Anacreon.[40] All these poems, which probably come from the Alexandrian editions, offer an idea of Sappho's community that is not so different from that of Alcaeus, one based on familial links and relationships of φιλότης. But then, whether we should trust the text of the Alexandrian edition without understanding the ways in which it was reworked is another intriguing question.

References

Aloni, A. (2008), *Nuove acquisizioni di Saffo e della lirica greca: per il testo di P. Köln inv. 21351 + 21376 e P. Oxy. 1787*. Alessandria.
Bergk, T. 1853. *Poetae lyrici Graeci*. 2nd edn. Leipzig.
Bowra, C.M. 1936. *Greek Lyric Poetry from Alcman to Simonides*. 2nd edn. 1961. Oxford.
Brunet, P. 2003. Sappho au 'Banquet des savants'. In *La poésie grecque antique*, ed. J. Jouanna and J. Leclant, 63–76. Paris.

---

39 See Caciagli (2011) 49–52 (for Alcaeus) and 52–88 (for Sappho).
40 See Caciagli (2011) 175–185.

Buffière, F. 1980. *Eros adolescent. La pédérastie dans la Grèce antique*. Paris.

Caciagli, S. 2009. Sappho fr. 27 v.: l'unità del pubblico saffico. *QUCC* 91: 63–80.

Caciagli, S. 2011. *Poeti e società. Comunicazione poetica e formazioni sociali nella Lesbo del VII/VI secolo a.C.* Amsterdam.

Caciagli, S. 2014. Case di uomini, case di dèi. Per un contesto di Alc. fr. 140 v. *QUCC* 137: 57–92.

Caciagli, S. 2015. Per un nuovo testo di Sapph. fr. 2 v. *Eikasmós* 26: 31–52.

Caciagli, S. 2018. *L'eteria arcaica e classica*. Bologna.

Calame, C. 1977. *Les chœurs de jeunes filles en Grèce archaïque*. Vols. 1–2. Rome.

Calame, C. 1996. Sappho's Group: An Initiation into Womanhood. In *Reading Sappho: Contemporary Approaches*, ed. E. Greene, 113–124. Berkeley.

Calder III, W.M. 1998. *Men in Their Books: Studies in the Modern History of Classical Scholarship*. Hildesheim.

Calhoun, G.M. 1913. *Athenian Clubs in Politics and Litigation*. Austin.

Chantraine, P. 1968–1980. *Dictionnaire étymologique de la langue grecque*. Vols. 1–2. Paris.

Colesanti, G. 2011. *Questioni teognidee*. Rome.

Fabbro, E. 1995. *Carmina convivalia Attica*. Rome.

Ferrari, F. 2000. Due note al testo del fr. 2 di Saffo. *APapyrol* 12: 37–44.

Ferrari, F. 2003. Il pubblico di Saffo. *SIFC* 96: 43–89.

Ferrari, F. 2007. *Una mitra per Kleis: Saffo e il suo pubblico*. Pisa.

Gentili, B. 1966. La veneranda Saffo. *QUCC* 2: 37–62.

Gentili, B. 2006. *Poesia e pubblico nella Grecia antica*. 4th edn. (1st edn. 1984). Milan.

Ghinatti, F. 1970. *I gruppi politici ateniesi fino alle guerre persiane*. Rome.

Lanata, G. 1960. L'ostracon fiorentino con versi di Saffo. Note paleografiche ed esegetiche. *SIFC* 36: 64–90.

Lardinois, A. 1994. Subject and Circumstances in Sappho's Poetry. *TAPhA* 124: 57–84.

Liberman, G. 1999. *Alcée. Fragments*. Paris.

Lidov, J.B. 2002. Sappho, Herodotus, and the Hetaira. *CPh* 97(3): 203–237.

Merkelbach, R. 1957. Sappho und ihr Kreis. *Philologus* 101: 1–29.

Müller, O. 1865. *Histoire de la littérature grecque* i. 1st German edition, 1841. Paris.

Murray, O. 1983a. The Greek Symposion in History. In *Tria corda*, ed. E. Gabba, 257–272. Como.

Murray, O. 1983b. The Symposion as Social Organisation. In *The Greek Renaissance of the Eighth Century B.C.: Tradition and Innovation*, ed. R. Hägg, 195–199. Stockholm.

Murray, O. 1983c. Symposion and Mannerbund. In *Concilium Eirene 16*, ed. P. Oliva and A. Frolikova, 47–52. Prague.

Murray, O. 1991. War and the Symposium. In *Dining in a Classical Context*, ed. W.J. Slater, 83–103. Ann Arbor.

Nicosia, S. 1976. *Tradizione testuale diretta e indiretta dei poeti di Lesbo*. Rome.

Obbink, D. 2014. Two New Poems by Sappho. *ZPE* 189: 32–49.

Obbink, D. 2016. The Newest Sappho. Text, Apparatus Criticus, and Translation, in *The Newest Sappho, P. Sapph. Obbink and P. GC inv. 105, frs. 1–4*, ed. A. Bierl and A. Lardinois, 13–33. Leiden.

Parker, H.N. 1993. Sappho Schoolmistress. *TAPhA* 173: 309–351.

Pelling, C. 2000. Fun with Fragments. Athenaeus and the Historians. In *Athenaeus and his World*, ed. D. Braund and J. Wilkins, 171–190. Exeter.

Rösler, W. 1976. Die Dichtung des Archilochos und die neue Kölner Epode. *RhM* 99: 289–310.

Rösler, W. 1980. *Dichter und Gruppe*. Munich.

Sartori, F. 1957. *Le eterie nella vita politica ateniese del VI e V secolo a.C.* Rome.

Schadewalt, W. 1950. *Sappho: Welt und Dichtung in der Liebe*. Postdam.

Schmid, W. 1912. *Geschichte der Griechischen Litteratur*. Vol. 1. 6th edn. Munich.

Schmitt-Pantel, P. 1992. *La cité au banquet: histoire des repas publics dans les cités grecques*. Paris.

Stehle, E. 1997. *Performance and Gender in Ancient Greece*. Princeton.

Vetta, M. 1980. *Teognide. Elegie, libro II*. Rome.

Vetta, M. 1982. Il P.Oxy. 2506 e la poesia pederotica di Alceo. *QUCC* 39: 7–20.

Welcker, F.G. 1816. *Sappho von einem herrschenden Vorurtheil befreyt*. Göttingen. Reprinted in F.G. Welcker. 1845. *Kleine Schriften zur Griechischen Literaturgeschichte. Zweiter Theil* Bonn

Welwei, K.W. 1992. Polisbildung, Hetairos-Gruppen und Hetairien. *Gymnasium* 99: 481–500.

Wilamowitz-Moellendorff, U. von. 1913. *Sappho und Simonides*. Berlin.

Yatromanolakis, D. 2007. *Sappho in the Making*. Washington, DC.

CHAPTER 15

A Sophisticated *hetaira* at Table: Athenaeus' Sappho

Renate Schlesier

In the banqueters' debates dramatized in Athenaeus' *Deipnosophistae*,[1] Sappho looms large. She and her poetry are almost omnipresent in this work, being referred to in twelve of its fifteen books.[2] Only in book 3 (on appetizers) and in books 6 and 7 (on parasites, slaves, and fishes), is the poetess not mentioned. Altogether she is evoked and quoted in more than thirty contexts, the vast majority of them being located in the last six books of the work (books 10 to 15), devoted to the after-dinner symposion. Remarkably, the overwhelming amount of references to Sappho and quotations of her poetry are to be found in book 13, which focuses on courtesans (*hetairai*).

To my knowledge, this significant and specialized presence of Sappho in Athenaeus has, surprisingly, as yet not been studied systematically and comprehensively.[3] Therefore the following remarks can be just an outline,

---

1 For the better understanding of this work, Lukinovich (1990) provided subsequent scholarship with many pioneering insights, further developed especially in Braund and Wilkins (2000), McClure (2003), Jacob (2004), Danielewicz (2006), Lenfant (2007), and Paulas (2012). A detailed commentary is to be found in the lavishly furnished Italian edition of Canfora (2001), with a splendid introduction of which Jacob (2013) is an expanded English version. See also the new bilingual Loeb edition of Athenaeus: Olson (2006–2012). In my chapter, I am citing, and sometimes discussing, Olson's translation, if not otherwise stated. On the complex structure of the *Deipnosophistae*, see the reconstruction in Maisonneuve (2007). Cf. the short summary of the thematic arrangement in Jacob (2013) 35–36. My warmest thanks go to Bruno Currie and Ian Rutherford who invited me to present this topic at the conference on the reception of Greek lyric poetry organized by them in September 2013 at Reading University, and to Joshua Billings who kindly looked over my English formulations.
2 See the synopsis in the appendix. In the following, all fragments of Sappho quoted by Athenaeus and all references to her in the *Deipnosophistae* are presented and briefly analyzed with respect to the context in which they appear, from book 1 to 15. For convenience and in order to account for Athenaeus' technique of internal cross-references, the presentation according to the sequential order is in two instances replaced by a thematic one: this concerns the Sappho fragments on symposion vessels (book 2 with books 10 and 11) and on musical instruments (book 4 with book 14). Conversely, I reserve the discussion of the particular prominence of Sappho in book 13 for the last part of my chapter.
3 I only know of two rather short studies on this topic: Brunet (2003), and Bartol (2005). I am

combined with an attempt at sketching some conspicuous features and situating them in their particular context.[4]

The main impression one gets from passing through Athenaeus' references to Sappho is that she is considered by him and his fellow experts as an uncontested authority, although less for eating procedures and foodstuffs than for the symposion and its material paraphernalia—drinking vessels, musical instruments, garlands, perfumes—and for the luxury, erotics, and verbal ingenuity connected with a typical banquet. In this respect, Sappho is presented as an authority equivalent to or even more pertinent than other archaic poets. From a quantitative point of view, the number of her fragments quoted or summarized—twenty (along with several further testimonies)—is approximately the same as the number of quotations of Archilochus and Alcman, her predecessors, and Alcaeus, her contemporary, and only surpassed by those of her successor Anacreon (27 fragments). Other contemporary or later archaic poets are quoted significantly less often (Stesichorus: 14 fragments; Simonides and Hipponax: 13; Semonides: 12; Ibycus: 8; Theognis: 7; Solon: 6; Mimnermus: 2).[5]

Sappho's importance for Athenaeus is also stressed by the fact that all protagonists of his banquet of scholars betray by their quotations a deep knowledge of her poetry, first hand or second hand: Sappho's verses are easily remembered by Ulpian, the symposiarch, by the other grammarians Plutarch and Myrtilus, by the philosophers Democritus and Cynulcus, by the poet, musical and legal

---

grateful to Krystyna Bartol who called my attention to her article. Both however consider only parts of the corpus of quotations of Sappho fragments in Athenaeus (Brunet: 50%, Bartol 75%) and refrain almost completely from taking other references to Sappho in the *Deipnosophistae* into account, Brunet's scope being primarily philological, while Bartol aims at a summarizing overview (yet not acknowledging Brunet). Bowie (2000) exclusively treats elegiac and iambic poetry in Athenaeus.

4 On context as a particularly sophisticated, strategic feature in Athenaeus, see the apt remarks of Danielewicz (2006) 122: 'It appears, for example, that the citations as demonstrations of arguments are not to be taken every time at their face value; they must be reinterpreted in the light of what follows, occasionally even at some distance from the passage in question. The discourse organisation is sequentially emergent, i.e. imposing its own contexts; hence also the meanings of the inserted quotations must be continually adjusted.' And: 'the context appears, most typically, both retrospective and prospective' (128).

5 Cf. Bowie (2000) 125, with a different counting. Athenaeus quotes also 24 fragments of Pindar (apart from the *Epinikia*). For the statistics concerning the presence of Greek poetry in Athenaeus, see the comprehensive indices in Canfora (2001) and Olson (2006–2012). On potential allusions in the *Deipnosophistae* to further fragments of Sappho, in addition to the 20 fragments quoted, see below, n. 88.

expert Masurius, and also by the musician Alceides. Only the medical doctors (Daphnus, Dionysocles, Galen), other rather marginal figures (Magnus, the philosopher Pontianus, the lexicographer Palamedes) and equally less prominent grammarians (Aemilianus, Arrian, Leonidas, Varus, Zoilus) refrain from quoting Sappho's poetry. And it should be noted that the Roman host of the party, Larensius, although not furnishing a genuine fragment of Sappho, still quotes 21 verses from Antiphanes' fourth-century comedy *Sappho* featuring the poetess as posing a riddle to a man and herself offering its solution.

In fact, Athenaeus provided posterity with the largest amount of fragments of Sappho transmitted by a single ancient author.[6] Fuller versions of four very important fragments found later on an ostrakon (fr. 2), on papyri (fr. 44, and the Oxyrhynchus version of fr. 58), and on a parchment (fr. 94) can be confidently assigned to her thanks to Athenaeus' partial quotation and explicit attribution. Yet altogether, only some forty verses of Sappho are cited in the whole of Athenaeus' work (c. 5 per cent of her extant poetry). In general, the learned deipnosophists seem to presuppose in their debates that a short extract from a Sappho poem or a brief hint at it will be sufficient, as if each of them knows the whole poems very well or has even memorized much of the Alexandrian Sappho edition (which comprised c. 8000 verses).[7] They apply the same procedure, however, to their quotations of other archaic poets, equally, with rare exceptions, extending only from one word to six verses, as in the case of Sappho. But none of these male archaic poets appears in so many contexts and in so many books of the *Deipnosophistae* as she does. In particular, Sappho's conspicuous presence in book 13 is all the more significant since in this book Archilochus seems to be quoted just once and Alcaeus is not cited at all,[8] while Anacreon is only quoted twice, both times in connection with her.

---

6 Some of them are only transmitted by him: frr. 101, 122, 138, 142, 160. Bartol (2005) 50n6 also lists fr. 143, which however is transmitted as well in paraphrases by Eustathius. See the edition of Voigt (1971). Cf. Lobel and Page (1955) and Campbell (1982).

7 This does not seem to be far-fetched, since the library of Athenaeus' Roman patron Larensius is described as phenomenal (1.3a), implying, according to Braund (2000) 4, that the author of the *Deipnosophistae* 'had access to an outstandingly wide range of original texts.' On Athenaeus' focus of the banqueters' very precise bibliographical knowledge, see Jacob (2013) *passim*. This accounts for their decisions to cite less well-known authors and works more fully than the better-known ones (cf. e.g. 15.676f). Twice, books (II and V) of the Alexandrian Sappho edition are referred to: see below, nn. 14 and 31.

8 In 13.594d, Archilochus is quoted with his fr. 331, considered however as spurious by West (1989).

Against this background, the aim of my chapter is to ask the following questions: what are the thematic frames in which Sappho as a poet and quotations of her work appear? How is her peculiar prominence in book 13 to be explained, and what results from it? Why does Athenaeus cite Sappho in his 'banquet of words',[9] and why so often?

The first thematic frame in which a Sapphic quotation occurs in Athenaeus is the topic of elegant dressing style required for attractive urban people (in book 1, summarized by the epitomator: fr. 57.1/3):[10]

τίς δ' ἀγροιῶτις θέλγει νόον
οὐκ ἐπισταμένη τὰ βράκε' ἔλκειν ἐπὶ τῶν σφυρῶν;

What unsophisticated girl charms your mind,
one who does not know how to pull her robes over her ankles?

But already the next quotation, in book 2, has to do with the symposion. The epitomator quotes three verses of a fragment (fr. 141.1–3) that turns out to be the most frequently cited in the *Deipnosophistae* and happens to be familiar to some of its most versatile speakers:

ἀμβροσίας μὲν
κρατὴρ ἐκέκρατο,
Ἑρμᾶς δ' ἕλεν ὄλπιν θεοῖς οἰνοχοῆσαι.

---

9   = 1.1b (λογόδειπνον). On this feature, see Romeri (2000).
10 = 1.21c. According to Athenaeus, Sappho applied this phrase mockingly to Andromeda (a female personal name actually mentioned in Sappho's frr. 68a, 90, 131, 133a, none of them quoted in the *Deipnosophistae*). See also below, n. 77. The text is taken (here and elsewhere) from *TLG* online, reproducing the edition of Kaibel (1887–1890). Athenaeus typically replaced Aeolic forms with more common ones (kept by Kaibel and in the edition of Canfora [2001]). Olson (2006–2012) however follows the restoration of the Aeolic forms by twentieth-century editors of Sappho, e.g. Voigt (1971). On this philological method, see the criticism of Brunet (2003) 74: 'Corriger Athénée au nom de Sappho et réintroduire l'élément amendé dans Athénée serait faire preuve d'une grande désinvolture à l'égard d'un citateur qui possède ses stratégies, son art de citer, d'adapter et peut-être de récrire.' In the current Sappho editions, a line quoted by Maximus Tyrius (*Or.* 18.9) is inserted into fr. 57 as its v. 2 (ἀγροΐωτιν ἐπεμμένα στολήν 'dressed in country garb' [trans. Campbell])—a procedure castigated as illegitimate by Brunet (2003) 70: 'Il va de soi qu'il faut rapprocher les deux fragments, sans aller toutefois jusqu'à en faire un objet de rapiéçage qui n'a jamais existé, ni chez Athénée, ni chez Maxime de Tyr, ni chez Sappho.' On Maximus Tyrius' treatment of Sappho and all of her fragments cited by him, see Schlesier (2017).

A bowl of ambrosia
had been mixed up,
and Hermes picked up a vessel and poured wine for the gods.[11]

The quotation of these verses meets several objectives at once: it shows that the symposion has a divine prototype; that ambrosia is a divine drink analogous to wine; and that the god Hermes is a model of the human wine-pourers.[12] Already the verses quoted here contain the terms for two central symposion vessels (the *kratēr* and the jug, *olpis*). This Sappho fragment, therefore, is well-suited as an anticipation of the later discussion of such vessels, after the start of the symposion proper in book 10, when these verses are cited again and slightly more fully, as well as, in book 11, three further verses (attributed in scholarship to the same fragment) that contain a term (in the plural) for a special drinking cup under discussion (*karchēsion*):

κῆνοι δ' ἄρα πάντες
καρχησία ⟨τ'⟩ ἦχον
κἄλειβον· ἀράσαντο δὲ πάμπαν ἐσλὰ τῷ γαμβρῷ.

So they all
held *karchasia*
and poured a libation; and they prayed that everything good might
    come to the bridegroom.[13]

---

11   = 2.39a–b. This translation by Olson is less precise than one would expect: Sappho uses the terms *kratēr* ('mixing vessel') and *olpis* ('jug'). The same verses are also alluded to by the speaker Masurius in 5.192c (below, n. 26), and cited again by Ulpian, in a slightly fuller version, in 10.425c–d: κῆ δ' ἀμβροσίας μὲν / κρατὴρ ἐκέκρατο, / Ἑρμᾶς δ' ἔλεν ὄλπιν θεοῖς οἰνοχοῆσαι ('and there, a *kratēr* of ambrosia / had been mixed up, / and Hermes picked up an *olpis* in order to pour wine for the gods' [my translation]). Cf. Brunet (2003) 68–69.

12   Another divine wine-pourer, Aphrodite, although serving nectar, appears in Sappho's fr. 2.13–16, quoted later in book 11.463e. See below, n. 16. On the prominence of Aphrodite in Sappho's poetry, especially associated with claims of immortality, see Schlesier (2011, 2016).

13   = 11.475a (the speaker is Plutarch). Nowhere else in Athenaeus is a hint to be found that weddings might be a topic of Sappho's poetry. Note that here, as in fr. 44, this topic belongs to a narrative, though not necessarily of a divine banquet (as in fr. 141.1–3). Modern editors include this further Sappho quotation in fr. 141 (as vv. 4–6). Brunet (2003) 69 rejects the arbitrary juxtaposition of the two quotations as '*un monstre*' and convincingly argues that they should be edited as separate fragments. He rightly insists (*passim*) on the methodological problems connected with the handling of Athenaeus' text in current editions of Sappho.

It comes as no surprise, then, that in the context of the catalogue of symposion vessels presented in book 11, the speakers are keen to emphasize that Sappho uses also other terms for drinking cups, first *potērion* (in the plural: fr. 44.10):[14]

καὶ Σαπφὼ δ' ἐν τῷ β' ἔφη·
'πολλὰ δ' ἀνάριθμα ποτήρια καλαιφις'

Sappho as well said in Book 11 (fr. 44.10):
   'many countless *potēria* and ivory'

and then *kylix* (in plural: fr. 2.14),[15] mentioned in the context of four verses quoted from this poem:[16]

καὶ κατὰ τὴν καλὴν οὖν Σαπφώ·
               'ἐλθέ, Κύπρι,
χρυσίαισιν ἐν κυλίκεσσιν ἁβρῶς
συμμεμιγμένον θαλίαισι νέκταρ
οἰνοχοοῦσα'

So to quote the lovely Sappho (fr. 2.13–16):
   'Come, Cypris,
   and daintily pour

---

14   = 11.460d. Ulpian is keen to give the exact bibliographical reference (on another one, cf. below, n. 31). The last cited word, καλαιφις, has been marked by Kaibel (1890) as corrupt. Thanks to a papyrus found later, it could be restored to κἀλέφαις. See Lobel and Page (1955) and Voigt (1971), followed by Olson. Problems of philological method still remain, see Brunet (2003) 65.

15   Note that later in this book (11.487a), Athenaeus connects Sappho indirectly with a further symposion vessel, quoting Diphilus who in his comedy *Sappho* (fr. 70 *PCG*) mentions another drinking cup, *metaniptris*, in an address to the character 'Archilochus' (spoken by the character 'Sappho'?). See also below, n. 69.

16   = 11.463e. See also above, n. 12. Athenaeus (or rather the speaker Plutarch) seems to apply these verses directly to himself and his fellow-symposiasts, adding τούτοις τοῖς ἑταίροις ἐμοῖς τε καὶ σοῖς ('for these friends [*hetairoi*, masc.] of mine and yours'). While most modern scholars attribute this addition to Athenaeus, Campbell (1982) ad loc. suspects that '[t]his phrase may also have been in S[appho]'s poem'. According to Brunet (2003) 67, both intuitions may be correct. See also his discussion of the divergence of Athenaeus' quotation of fr. 2 from the evidence of the Florentine ostrakon found in the twentieth century. On the frequent use of *kalē* ('beautiful', not 'lovely', as Olson has it) as epithet of Sappho in the *Deipnosophistae* (four times), see also below, nn. 26, 32, and 59.

>   nectar mixed with celebrations
>   into gold cups'.

By this token, Athenaeus confers on Sappho's poetry a strong sympotic quality for which the most frequently quoted fragment of hers, fr. 141, receives an emblematic value as an unmistakable *leitmotiv*.

Still in book 2, Sappho is also referred to in relation to snacks, in this case chickpeas (fr. 143) and eggs (fr. 166 and 167). As for the phrasing of these short texts themselves, the aim of quoting Sappho does not, at first glance, seem to allude to her acquaintance with the institution of the drinking party, in contrast to the mentioning of symposion vessels in her poetry. But here, it is clearly the context that deliberately creates such a relationship: fr. 143,[17] containing chickpeas,

>   χρύσειοι ἐρέβινθοι ἐπ' ἀιόνων ἐφύοντο

>   golden chickpeas were growing on the shores

is quoted just after a fragment of Xenophanes which speaks of a man lying on a soft couch,[18] drinking wine and nibbling chickpeas, and just before a reference to Theophrastus calling some chickpeas *krioi* ('rams'),[19] followed by a quotation from comedy giving the 'ram chickpea' an obscene sense. Later on, the topic of eggs, which in the Sappho fragments is related to the birth of Helen (fr. 166),[20]

>   φασὶ δή ποτε Λήδαν ὤιον εὑρεῖν

>   they say that Leda once found an egg

as well as to a cunning rhetorical device,[21] a 'supra-superlative' (fr. 167),[22]

---

17   = 2.54 f. On the frequent use of the terminology of gold in Sappho's poetry, and its connection to the epic 'golden Aphrodite', see Schlesier (2014b).
18   Xenophanes, fr. 21 B 22 Diels-Kranz.
19   Theophr. *Hist. pl.* 8.5.1.
20   = 2.57d. Significantly, the figure born from this egg, polyandric Helen, is mentioned by Sappho conspicuously often, and never disparagingly. See fr. 16 and fr. 23; cf. fr. 161.
21   See Zellner (2006) and (2010) 11–17, on this device, very frequent in Sappho. For another example see the following note.
22   = 2.57d. Cf. Sappho fr. 156: χρύσω χρυσοτέρα ('more golden than gold'), with n. 17, above.

ὤίω πολὺ λευκότερον

much whiter than an egg

is contextualized by further sophisticated accounts, first Anaxagoras (fr. 59 B22 Diels-Kranz) and then others mainly from Attic comedy, a series interrupted by an iambic verse of Semonides—all of these accounts equally pointing to the connection of eggs with procreation and erotics.

In book 4, then, there first surfaces a topic that will especially be pursued in book 13, with an addendum in book 14: the relationship between Sappho and the emblematic sympotic poet, Anacreon. The musician Alceides, called upon by the symposiarch to talk about musical entertainment terminology, emphasizes that both Sappho (fr. 176) and Anacreon use the technical terms for two particular musical instruments, *barōmos* and *barbitos*:

τὸν γὰρ βάρωμον καὶ βάρβιτον, ὧν Σαπφὼ καὶ Ἀνακρέων μνημονεύουσι[23]

the *barōmos* and the *barbiton*, which Sappho (fr. 176) and Anacreon (472 *PMG*) mention.

This statement will be supplemented much later, in book 14, by further information: that some historians (Menaechmus, Aristoxenus) ascribe the invention of another stringed instrument, the *pēktis*—which is the same as the *magadis*—to Sappho being the first to use it, as a forerunner of Anacreon (cf. Sappho test. 247):[24]

Μέναιχμος δ' ἐν τοῖς περὶ Τεχνιτῶν τὴν πηκτίδα, ἣν τὴν αὐτὴν εἶναι τῇ μαγάδιδι, Σαπφώ φησιν εὑρεῖν.
[...] πηκτὶς δὲ καὶ μάγαδις ταὐτόν, καθά φησιν ὁ Ἀριστόξενος καὶ Μέναιχμος ὁ Σικυώνιος ἐν τοῖς περὶ Τεχνιτῶν καὶ τὴν Σαπφὼ δέ φησιν οὗτος, ἥτις ἐστὶν Ἀνακρέοντος πρεσβυτέρα, πρώτην χρήσασθαι τῇ πηκτίδι.

---

23 = 4.182e. Before, in 4.175e, Alceides however had attributed the invention of the *barbitos* exclusively to Anacreon. Barker (2000), in his chapter on music in Athenaeus, regrettably omits almost completely the topic, so prominent in the *Deipnosophistae*, of stringed instruments, and their relationship to archaic poetry and the symposion. On ancient stringed instruments, including those mentioned by Athenaeus with reference to Sappho: West (1992) 48–80. See also the following note.

24 = 14.635b and 635e (the speaker is Masurius). The term *pēktis* is actually used in several fragments of Sappho: fr. 22 and fr. 156, as well as in the new Sappho fragment transmitted by a Cologne papyrus, see e.g. Greene and Skinner (2009) 10. The *pēktis*, a kind of harp, was a typical instrument in Lydian and archaic Greek symposia: Power (2010) *passim*.

Menaechmus in his *On Artists* (*FGrH* 131 F4a) claims that Sappho (fr. 247) invented the *pēktis*, which he identifies with the *magadis*.

[...] A *pēktis* and a *magadis* are the same instrument, according to Aristoxenus (fr. 98 Wehrli) and Menaechmus of Sicyon in his *On Artists* (*FGrH* 131 F4b); the latter authority adds that Sappho, who is earlier than Anacreon, was the first person to play the *pēktis*.

Furthermore, the same polymath Masurius reminds his fellow-symposiasts that another historian, the Peripatetic Clearchus (in his *Erotica*, fr. 33 Wehrli) considers notoriously lascivious erotic songs like the *Lokrika* as equivalents to the love poetry of both Sappho and Anacreon.[25]

Apart from an additional hint in book 5 at the cup-bearer Hermes in Sappho's fr. 141,

παρὰ δὲ τῇ καλῇ Σαπφοῖ καὶ ὁ Ἑρμῆς οἰνοχοεῖ τοῖς θεοῖς

and in the noble Sappho Hermes pours wine for the gods,[26]

as well as, in book 8, the mocking of a man who is fond not of fish but of young male cithara-players, with a quotation from Timocles' comedy *Sappho* evoking Sappho's phraseology,[27] the next direct reference to a Sappho fragment comes in book 9. Here Aphrodite appears for the first time in the *Deipnosophistae* with

---

25 = 14.639a (Sappho test. 39 Campbell). An example (*carm. pop.* 853 *PMG*) for 'Locrian songs', designated as μοιχικαί ('having to do with lascivious sex' [my translation]), is given by Cynulcus at 15.697b–c. On the exact semantic value of such a terminological designation see Bogner (1941).

26 = 5.192c (the speaker is Masurius). Olson's translation of *kalē* by 'noble' does not seem justified to me (see also above, n. 16, and below, nn. 32 and 59). The translation '*leggiadra*' ('dainty') in Canfora (2001) doesn't fit well either. The same epithet is used for Sappho, in the context of other references to her poetry, also by the speakers Ulpian (fr. 203a = 10.424f–425a), Plutarch (fr. 2.13–16 = 11.463e), and Myrtilus (fr. 15 = 13.596b), translated there as 'lovely' by Olson, and, rightly, as '*bella*' ('beautiful') in Canfora. Elsewhere in Athenaeus, καλή is exclusively an epithet of named *hetairai* in the technical sense, e.g. Laïs and Phryne. This corresponds to the terminologically marked use of *kalē* inscriptions on Attic symposion vessels in the archaic and classical periods. See also Plato, *Phdr*. 235C, referring to Anacreon and Sappho as authorities of love poetry and designating her as *kalē*. One could argue that the epithet in Plato accounts for his analogical presentation, in Book 10 of the *Politeia*, of mimesis and poetry as a *hetaira*, boldly interpreted as an allusion to Sappho by Peponi (2012) 135 and *passim*.

27 Timocles *Sappho* fr. 32 *PCG* = 8.339c: ὁ Μισγόλας οὐ προσιέναι σοι φαίνεται / ἀνθοῦσι τοῖς νέοισιν ἠρεθισμένος ('Misgolas doesn't seem to be approaching you, / even though he gets excited by handsome boys').

regard to Sappho: in the context of birds as main courses is integrated a reference to the sparrows (*strouthoi*) in fr. 1,[28] the famous address to Aphrodite, quoted in full by Dionysius of Halicarnassus, an author however completely silenced in the debates of the deipnosophists. Athenaeus provides a playful sexy explanation:

οἱ στρουθοὶ δέ εἰσιν ὀχευτικοί· διὸ καὶ Τερψικλῆς τοὺς ἐμφαγόντας φησὶν στρουθῶν ἐπικαταφόρους πρὸς ἀφροδίσια γίνεσθαι. μήποτε οὖν καὶ ἡ Σαπφὼ ἀπὸ τῆς ἱστορίας τὴν Ἀφροδίτην ἐπ' αὐτῶν φησιν ὀχεῖσθαι·

sparrows are also highly sexed [*ocheutikoi*]; this is why Terpsicles claims that people who eat sparrows are prone to lust. Perhaps, therefore, this is the basis on which Sappho (fr. 1.9–10) reports that Aphrodite's chariot is drawn [*ocheisthai*] by sparrows.[29]

The relationship between the goddess and the poetess, which is certainly much emphasized in most of her transmitted poetry, is thus, in the *Deipnosophistae*, immediately connected with sex (*aphrodisia*). The trouble is that the traditional term *ocheisthai* ('to be drawn'), from which the metaphorical term *ocheutikos* ('salacious') was later derived, does not actually occur in Sappho's poem. But especially from this passage on, eroticism will become the most prominent of the poetess' characteristics in Athenaeus. Already a bit later in book 9, Sappho's privileged relationship to Aphrodite is evoked again: someone quotes Sappho (fr. 101), with precise reference to her Alexandrian edition (Book v), telling the goddess that towels (*cheiromaktra*) as women's head-clothes (a typical *hetairai*-offering) had been sent to one of her sanctuaries as a gift of honour:[30]

Σαπφὼ δ' ὅταν λέγῃ ἐν τῷ πέμπτῳ τῶν μελῶν πρὸς τὴν Ἀφροδίτην·
'χειρόμακτρα δὲ καγγόνων
πορφύρα καταυταμενάτατι
Μνᾶσις πέμψ' ἀπὺ Φωκάας
δῶρα τίμια [καγγόνων]',

---

28 Sappho fr. 1.9–10: ἄρμ' ὑπασδεύξαισα· κάλοι δέ σ' ἆγον / ὤκεες στροῦθοι περὶ γᾶς μελαίνας ('when you [Aphrodite] put a chariot under the yoke. And beautiful ones led you, / swift sparrows, over the black earth' [my translation]).

29 = 9.391 f. See the pertinent comment of Brunet (2003) 75: '*Ici, une allusion d'Athénée dévoile l'interprétation que les Anciens pouvaient avoir d'un poème de Sappho.*'

30 For a headdress as dedication to Aphrodite, see e.g. Nossis (= *Anth. Pal.* 6.275).

κόσμον λέγει κεφαλῆς τὰ χειρόμακτρα, ὡς καὶ Ἑκαταῖος δηλοῖ ἢ ὁ γεγραφὼς τὰς περιηγήσεις ἐν τῇ Ἀσίᾳ ἐπιγραφομένῃ· 'γυναῖκες δ' ἐπὶ τῆς κεφαλῆς ἔχουσι χειρόμακτρα'.³¹

When Sappho in Book v of her *Lyric Poems* (fr. 101) tells Aphrodite:
and towels [corrupt]
with purple [corrupt]
[corrupt] he sent from Phocaea
as a gift full of honour [corrupt],
she is using *cheiromaktra* to refer to something worn on one's head, as Hecataeus (or whoever wrote his *Tours*) makes clear in his work entitled *Asia* (*FGrH* 1 F358): 'Women wear *cheiromaktra* on their heads.'

Before the erotic dimensions of Sappho's poetry, but also of her personality, will be in full swing in book 13, their sympotic dimensions are stressed once more, i.e. at the very beginning of the drinking party in book 10. Just after the slaves bring the cups in and fill them, two references to Sappho are stated by the symposiarch in order to remind the banqueters that the office of the cup-bearer was traditionally not confined to slaves or females. Ulpian makes Sappho testify that her brother Larichus poured wine in the *prytaneion* of the Lesbian city of Mytilene (fr. 203a):

Σαπφώ τε ἡ καλὴ πολλαχοῦ Λάριχον τὸν ἀδελφὸν ἐπαινεῖ ὡς οἰνοχοοῦντα ἐν τῷ πρυτανείῳ τοῖς Μυτιληναίοις.

The lovely Sappho (fr. 203a) repeatedly praises her brother Larichus for pouring wine in the town-hall for the Mytileneans.³²

---

31 = 9.410d–e. In this Kaibel text, the name Mnasis is a conjecture of Wilamowitz (see the criticism of Brunet [2003] 71, who stresses the identity of the addressee, Aphrodite, and the absence of a name for the gift-giver in Athenaeus' quotation). The Codex Marcianus has μάσεις. In current Sappho editions, several parts of fr. 101 are considered as corrupt. Voigt (1971) prints (followed by Olson): χερρόμακτρα δὲ †καγγόνων† / πορφύραι †καταυταμενά-/τατιμάσεις† ἔπεμψ' ἀπὺ Φωκάας / δῶρα τίμια †καγγόνων†. The context in Athenaeus at least shows that the person who in the Sappho fragment is sending *cheiromaktra* to Aphrodite should be a woman, not a man, as in Olson's translation. Is the second-person address (to Aphrodite) τιμάσεις ('you will honour') or ἀτιμάσεις ('you will not honour') to be read in the text (vv. 2–3)?

32 = 10.424f–425a. Note that Olson here translates Sappho's epithet *kalē* by 'lovely'. See also above, nn. 16, 26, and below, n. 59. Bartol (2005) 50n12 lists evidence of the use of the epithet *kalos* in Athenaeus for ancient authors and for some of the deipnosophists themselves. Cf. also Phaon designated as *kalos*, in 13.596e, as lover of Sappho (below,

And he emphasizes once more, that according to Sappho, Hermes himself poured wine for the other gods (fr. 141.1–3).[33] Later, during an interruption of the drinking bout, Ulpian suggests taking up the question of riddles, a popular sympotic pastime. Here Sappho figures prominently, although not with a quotation from her poetry, but with a long extract, quoted by the host Larensius, from a comedy of Antiphanes named after her.[34] It is remarkable that in this passage, as in those from several other Attic comedies with the title *Sappho* quoted by Athenaeus, Sappho is never ridiculed. The person who in fact is ridiculed in the scene from Antiphanes is an old man unable to solve the riddle, who is ironically addressed by the character 'Sappho' as ὦ πάτερ. Larensius makes clear, however, what kind of social status this 'Sappho' had to represent, since he immediately continues with a reference to a comedy by Diphilus (*Theseus* fr. 49 *PCG* = 10.451b–c) in which three *hetairai* from Samos are posing, and obscenely solving, a riddle at a banquet during the Adonia— a further allusion to Sappho in whose work the first extant evocations of this festival occur.[35]

Apart from three Sappho fragments—containing terms for drinking vessels—in book 11, another one appears in book 12. Athenaeus, the only speaker in this book featuring lust (*hēdonē*), takes fr. 122,[36]

---

n. 63). Sappho's fr. 203a (actually only a paraphrase) has been taken by many modern scholars as a confirmation of the biographical hypothesis that Sappho comes from an aristocratic family. This conclusion does not seem self-evident to me. The personal name Larichus, hitherto attested, with regard to Sappho, only in Athenaeus, appears in a new Sappho poem recently published, although not being textually identified as brother of the poetess, *pace* Obbink (2014, 2015, 2016). On an alleged other brother, Charaxus, see below, n. 59.

33 = 10.425c–d. See above, n. 11.

34 Antiphanes *Sappho* fr. 194 *PCG* = 10.450e–451b. McClure (2003) 81 briefly points to this passage in the context of the 'tradition of females propounding riddles', and 'of prostitutes as riddle-tellers', although she apparently does not imply that the character 'Sappho' in Antiphanes represents a *hetaira*. Brunet (2003) 76 elusively notes: '*Athénée, en prenant chez Antiphane une Sappho souveraine en énigmes, livre à sa manière la clé de son statut et de son interprétation.*' On the prominence and the function of comedy for the *Deipnosophistae* in general, see Wilkins (2000), Anderson (2000).

35 See Sappho fr. 140 and fr. 168. Athenaeus however does not take Sappho's poetry into account when he repeatedly mentions Adonis, instead referring to comedy and to mythological accounts in prose (Adonis as beloved of Aphrodite: 2.69b–d, 4.174f, 10.456a–b, 13.566d, 13.575a).

36 = 12.554b. Instead of Olson's translation of ἄγαν by 'very' (cf. Canfora [2001]: '*davvero*', 'really'), 'too much' would be an alternative, perhaps more appropriate in Athenaeus' context.

ἄνθε' ἀμέργουσαν παῖδ' ἄγαν ἀπαλάν

a very delicate girl collecting flowers

as a testimony for the 'physical tendency' of persons (of either gender) interested in their own attractiveness, 'who believe that they are handsome and full of youthful beauty to gather flowers'.[37] This again points to Sappho's close relationship with eroticism that will soon be exhaustively reflected in book 13, especially in connection to Anacreon, while the more technical, musical points of contact between the two poets are relegated to book 14, resuming a topic already treated in book 4.[38]

Finally, the last book of the *Deipnosophistae* gives Sappho, once more contextually connected to Anacreon, a prominent place in the discussion of garlands and perfumes, especially with the quotation of four verses from fr. 94 at some distance,[39]

καὶ πολλαῖς ὑποθυμίδας
πλεκταῖς ἀμπ' ἀπαλᾷ δέρᾳ
   vv. 15–16

and many woven
upathumides around [a] soft neck

as well as

βρενθείω βασιληίω
   vv. 19–20

---

37   = 12.554b: φυσικὸν γὰρ δή τι τὸ τοὺς οἰομένους εἶναι καλοὺς καὶ ὡραίου ἀνθολογεῖν.
38   Sappho and Anacreon in book 4: above, n. 23; in book 14: above, nn. 24 and 25.
39   First quotation from fr. 94 = 15.674d. The Sappho verses (15–16) are quoted here by Democritus (after Alcaeus, fr. 362,1–2, and before Anacreon, fr. 397 *PMG*) as the second of three evidences for the word *hypothymides* ('perfumed garlands') in archaic sympotic poetry. In v. 16, Sappho is actually citing the *Hom. Hymn* 5.88; the context there is Aphrodite's tricky seduction of Anchises. Olson erroneously translates fr. 94.16 by 'around my soft neck'. The other quotation (by Masurius) from Sappho's fr. 94 (extracts from vv. 19–20) referring to precious and seductive perfumes—the last Sappho words cited in the *Deipnosophistae*—comes at 15.690e, after two quotations from comedy, mentioning *brentheios* perfume (Pherecrates fr. 105 *PCG*) and royal perfume (Crates fr. 2 *PCG*). See Brunet (2003) 72, on both excerpts from fr. 94. On the symposiastic, rhetorical, and erotic implications of this fragment of Sappho, see Schlesier (2015).

with *brentheios* ...
... with royal

Almost immediately after the verses 15–16 of this poem, the quotation of the four-verse fr. 81 is added,[40] referred to as explaining why symposiasts wear garlands:

σὺ δὲ στεφάνοις, ὦ Δίκα, περθέσθ' ἐραταῖς φόβαισιν
ὄρπακας ἀνήτοιο συνέρραις ἀπαλαῖσι χερσίν.
εὐανθέα γὰρ πέλεται καὶ Χάριτες μάκαιρα
μᾶλλον προσόρην, ἀστεφανώτοισι δ' ἀπυστρέφονται

Wrap anise shoots together into garlands, Dica,
with your soft hands, and place them around your lovely hair;
with fine flowers †for it is† and the blessed Graces
more [corrupt], but turn away from those who wear no garlands.

Furthermore, the only explicit quotation of Sappho by Cynulcus is to be found in the same last book of the *Deipnosophistae* (fr. 58.25–26):[41]

ἐγὼ δὲ φίλημ' ἀβροσύναν
καί μοι τὸ λαμπρὸν ἔρος ἀελίω καὶ τὸ καλὸν λέλογχε

But I love daintiness,
and in my opinion a longing for the sun implies what is bright and beautiful.[42]

---

40 = 15.674e. Note that the cult of the Charites (mainly associated to Aphrodite) seems to be evoked here. The speaker Democritus interprets the verses as pointing to people sacrificing. Cf. Brunet (2003) 72–74, about the manuscript lesson μάκαιρα (v. 3), reproduced by Kaibel (instead of μάκαιρα⟨ι⟩ in current editions, adopted by Olson), and against the addition of some lacunose papyrus lines to fr. 81.

41 = 15.687a–b. This quotation is part of a passage (15.687a–c), the whole of which being considered in scholarship as a long paraphrase of Clearchus' *On Lives* (fr. 41 Wehrli). However, when Cynulcus cites and discusses Sappho in the course of this passage, he does not directly refer to Clearchus. The verses 25–26 of fr. 58 are also transmitted on an Oxyrhynchus papyrus, cf. Voigt (1971) ad loc. After the discovery of the new Cologne Sappho papyrus, where the poem ends before these verses (missing in this papyrus) and a different poem follows, the verses quoted by Athenaeus could possibly (but need not) be assigned to another poem. See, e.g. the discussions in Greene and Skinner (2009).

42 Instead of Olson's translation of *habrosyne* by 'daintiness', I would prefer 'delicacy' or 'splendour'. Cf. '*eleganza*' in Canfora (2001). Yet (Canfora [2001]) 'vita' ('life') for ἀελίω and

These two verses associating delicacy (*habrosynē*), *eros*, the sun, brilliancy, and beauty are interpreted, by the Cynic philosopher, in a particularly biased way—surprisingly, as proof for Sappho's virtue (*aretē*), a word that is actually missing in the fragment cited. Thus Cynulcus introduces his quotation with a rhetorical question and an authoritative statement:

> ὑμεῖς δὲ οἴεσθε τὴν ἁβρότητα χωρὶς ἀρετῆς ἔχειν τι τρυφερόν; καίτοι Σαπφώ, γυνὴ μὲν πρὸς ἀλήθειαν οὖσα καὶ ποιήτρια, ὅμως ᾐδέσθη τὸ καλὸν τῆς ἁβρότητος ἀφελεῖν.

> Do you believe that daintiness, if divorced from virtue, contains anything resembling luxury? Yet Sappho, who was certainly a woman as well as a poetess, was nonetheless reluctant to distinguish beauty from daintiness.

In Cynulcus' reading, the verses now cited as reference are to be understood as follows:

> φανερὸν ποιοῦσα πᾶσιν ὡς ἡ τοῦ ζῆν ἐπιθυμία τὸ λαμπρὸν καὶ τὸ καλὸν εἶχεν αὐτῇ· ταῦτα δ' ἐστὶν οἰκεῖα τῆς ἀρετῆς.[43]

> making it apparent to everyone that her lust for life involved the bright and beautiful; these qualities are closely associated with virtue.

This sounds as if Athenaeus provides here a supplement to the quarrel between Cynulcus and Myrtilus in book 13, in other words, as if Cynulcus here defends the poetess against the presentation she formerly received.

As a matter of fact, in this earlier book—the only one with an extra title, *On women* (Περὶ γυναικῶν)—Sappho is obviously the most prominent issue in Myrtilus' encomium of courtesans, aimed at refuting Cynulcus' disparagement of these women.[44] Yet this prominence, almost completely overlooked

---

      '*onore*' ('honour') for τὸ καλὸν do not seem accurate to me either. Tentatively, I would suggest a translation differing from Olson's: 'But I love splendour, also for me Eros has obtained the bright of the sun and the beautiful.'

43 Cynulcus' interpretation of these Sappho verses seems to allude to her fr. 16, the famous priamel, especially vv. 5–6: πάγχυ δ' εὔμαρες σύνετον πόησαι / πάντι τοῦτ' ('It is perfectly easy to make this understood by everyone' [trans. Campbell]), as if the Cynic tries to outdo the poetess by emulating her sophisticated poetical techniques and (ironically?) claiming to follow her stance.

44 Remarkably, the naming of these protagonists of book 13 reproduces the same naming techniques that have been typically adopted by their controversial topic, the *hetairai*:

or at least downplayed in scholarship,[45] and sometimes even removed by textual emendation,[46] is displayed in a peculiar tricky way. First of all, even before the quarrel between Cynulcus and his opponent starts, Myrtilus quotes Sappho (fr. 138) in the context of his attack on Stoic philosophers as boy-lovers:[47]

στᾶθι κἄντα, φίλος,
καὶ τὰν ἐπ' ὄσσοις ἀμπέτασον χάριν.

Stand also opposite, dear one,
and spread wide the delight that is in your eyes.

Sappho is introduced here with an address of a male (*philos*) who is (and even quite ironically) summoned for his delightful glance no less than the beloved boys are in the homoerotic fragments of Anacreon and Pindar, quotations of which immediately follow.[48] It certainly did not escape the banqueters present in the narration (nor the ancient readers) that Sappho's term for the addressee, *philos*, is just the one that the male archaic poets (and analogously, Athenaeus' deipnosophists) regularly use in their addresses as a synonym of *hetairos*, a fellow-symposiast. This implies that a female who uses this address term is consequently to be identified as a *hetaira*, a figure who in the realm of a symposion is traditionally presented as rival of the *hetairoi* in their courtship of young men.[49]

Cynulcus ('Hound-Master') is the nickname of the deipnosophist identified in the end as Theodorus (15.669e and 692b), and Myrtilus, bearing a name with obscene innuendo, ominously disclosed by Cynulcus himself as the namesake of a comic poet, is mockingly addressed, with the Homeric epithet of Eos, transferred by Sappho (fr. 96.8) to Selene (see Schlesier [2018] 105–106), as not 'rosy-fingered' (13.566e–f) by the Cynic deipnosophist. On *hetairai* names, see below, n. 87.

45 McClure (2003), who did much to rescue book 13 of the *Deipnosophistae* from scholarly neglect, does not take Sappho's prominence in this book into account, nor in Athenaeus in general, for that matter. Sappho is even missing from McClure's index, although she mentions her on pages 12, 32, 51, 55, 81, 85. But throughout, McClure avoids asking the question why Sappho appears in Athenaeus in close connection to his bunch of 'courtesans at table', a central topic of the *Deipnosophistae*, and actually the title of McClure's book. On the structure of Athenaeus' book 13, see also Hawley (1993) 80–86; Sappho, however, is completely silenced in his account.

46 See below, n. 63.

47 = 13.564d. Note the male gender of the addressee, which disappears in Olson's translation.

48 = 13.564d–e: Anacreon, fr. 360 *PMG*, and Pindar, fr. 123.2–6.

49 Significantly, just before the quotation of Sappho's fr. 138, Licymnius of Chios' fr. 771 *PMG*

The next quotations of Sappho occur at the beginning of Myrtilus' apology for courtesans, in response to Cynulcus, who had armed himself with many quotations insulting prostitutes and had attacked his opponent as a *pornographos*.[50] Myrtilus' defence of courtesans proceeds in the rhetorically skilled manner of a juridical pleading in favour of a defendant. It starts with a sharp distinction between mere prostitutes and *hetairai*, the latter being defined as 'women capable of maintaining a friendship not based on trickery (*philia adolos*)'.[51] Myrtilus goes on to refer to Apollodorus of Athens' account (in his book *On the Gods*) of Aphrodite Hetaira 'who brings together male and female companions (*hetairai*), that is to say female friends (*philai*)',[52] with the comment that 'even today, at any rate, free women and girls refer to their friends and associates as *hetairai*'.[53] At this point, suddenly, Sappho comes in, with her fragments 160 and 142:[54]

ὡς ἡ Σαπφώ·
    τάδε νῦν ἑταίραις ταῖς ἐμαῖσι τερπνὰ καλῶς ἀείσω.
καὶ ἔτι·
    Λατὼ καὶ Νιόβα μάλα μὲν φίλαι ἦσαν ἑταῖραι.

(= 13.564c–d) is cited which makes the god Hypnos ('Sleep') a homoerotic lover of the mortal youth Endymion, whose most famous lover is female, Selene ('Moon'). This goddess' love for Endymion seems to have been a subject of Sappho's poetry (fr. 199). It is striking that loves of goddesses for mortal youths were one of Sappho's favourite topics (apart from Selene and Endymion, especially Aphrodite and Adonis, Eos and Tithonos); see Schlesier (2013a) 214.

50   = 13.567b. In an anachronistic manner and from a radical feminist point of view, Henry (1992) and (2000) denounces Athenaeus himself as a 'pornographer', even the 'Ur-Pornographer'.

51   = 13.571c: τουτέστιν τῶν φιλίαν ἄδολον συντηρεῖν δυναμένων. Is this an ironic hint at Sappho, fr. 94.1, where the speaker pronounces her will to be dead, 'without trickery' (ἀδόλως)? On the impact of this adverb, see Schlesier (2015) 305–306. A *philia adolos* of a *hetaira*, as in Myrtilus' encomium, is a paradox, since it would distance her from the patroness of *hetairai* and generally of lovers, Aphrodite, who is the leading expert at every kind of *dolos* in the service of physical love. Sappho, followed by later poets, defined this goddess as *doloplokos*, 'weaver of trickery' (fr. 1.2). For some traditional aspects of the connection between Aphrodite and *dolos* since Homer and Hesiod, see Bouchard (2015).

52   = 13.571c: [...] Ἑταίρας [τῆς] Ἀφροδίτης. περὶ ἧς φησιν ὁ Ἀθηναῖος Ἀπολλόδωρος ἐν τοῖς περὶ Θεῶν (FGrH 244 F 112) οὕτως. Ἑταίραν δὲ τὴν Ἀφροδίτην τὴν τοὺς ἑταίρους καὶ τὰς ἑταίρας συνάγουσαν· τοῦτο δ' ἐστὶν φίλας.

53   = 13.571c–d: καλοῦσι γοῦν καὶ αἱ ἐλεύθεραι γυναῖκες ἔτι καὶ νῦν καὶ αἱ παρθένοι τὰς συνήθεις καὶ φίλας ἑταίρας.

54   = 13.571d.

For example Sappho (fr. 160):
   I will now sing these pleasant songs beautifully for my *hetairai*.
Furthermore (Sapph. fr. 142):
   Lato and Nioba were very close *hetairai*.

This is a *coup-de-théâtre*: past and present, literature and reality are blurred here, as so often in Athenaeus,[55] when, most strikingly, Sappho's poetry is brought in as a testimony for what is done, and spoken, now. But Myrtilus adds: the same contemporary women also refer to women paid for sex as *hetairai*,[56] therefore implying, given the chronological mixture he used before, that this could apply to Sappho, too, as it applies to the comic dramatists of Hellenistic times he subsequently quotes as witnesses for the technical use of the term. In any case, paying with sex for attending a party can happen to young men as well, as Myrtilus soon illustrates with a quotation from Ephippus' comedy *Sappho*.[57]

Myrtilus does not quote further fragments of Sappho in the remaining course of his speech, although he later actually alludes to one. Yet he reserves most of the last large part (13.596b–605e) of his ensuing 'erotic catalogue' of famous courtesans to none other than Sappho, and to her appearance in the work of several later writers, be they historians, philosophers, lyric poets, or comic playwrights.[58] It should be noted that this is the most lengthy part of the *Deipnosophistae* in which the dominating feature is historical and literary criticism. And its object is Sappho the poetess. The author first challenged is Herodotus. His naming of the courtesan, who was the lover of Sappho's brother Charaxus, as Rhodopis is relentlessly refuted: her name was not Rhodopis but Doricha, and Herodotus just confounded two famous courtesans. Furthermore, the poetess did not attack her brother because of this woman, as the historian pretends, but the courtesan herself (cf. fr. 15):[59]

---

55 See e.g. the sensible remarks of Ceccarelli (2000) 273 and 278, about the 'fluidity of time' in Athenaeus and his deliberate confusing of 'the distance between present and past'. Note that in Sappho's poetry, the same feature is often to be found.

56 This is clear from the formulation καλοῦσι δὲ καὶ τὰς μισθαρνούσας ἑταίρας ('they also refer to women who work for pay as *hetairai*'), with which the speaker Myrtilus continues the sentence begun before the Sappho quotations, describing the linguistic habits of free women in remote times as well as in the present (see above, n. 53).

57 Ephippus *Sappho* fr. 20 *PCG* = 13.572c.

58 The term 'erotic catalogue' is used by Myrtilus in 13.599e (ἐρωτικὸν κατάλογον)—as a summarizing synthesis of what he has done up to now—just after having finished a learned discussion on Sappho and her potential male lovers.

59 = 13.596b–c. Note that here again, as three times before, Sappho is designated as *kalē* (see

[...] Δωρίχαν τε, ἣν ἡ καλὴ Σαπφὼ ἐρωμένην γενομένην Χαράξου τοῦ ἀδελφοῦ αὐτῆς κατ' ἐμπορίαν εἰς τὴν Ναύκρατιν ἀπαίροντος διὰ τῆς ποιήσεως διαβάλλει ὡς πολλὰ τοῦ Χαράξου νοσφισαμένην. Ἡρόδοτος δ' αὐτὴν Ῥοδῶπιν καλεῖ, ἀγνοῶν ὅτι ἑτέρα τῆς Δωρίχης ἐστὶν αὕτη.

[...] Doriche, who was a lover of Sappho's brother Charaxus, who sailed to Naucratis on a trading journey; the lovely [*kalē*] Sappho (fr. 254c; cf. fr. 15) abuses her in her poems for extracting a substantial amount of money from Charaxus. Herodotus (2.135.1) refers to her as Rhodopis, being unaware that this is a different person from Doriche.

On the other hand, Sappho did not only attack the courtesan Doricha, but also composed a friendly song (*philē ōdē*) for her, as is testified by a poem of Posidippus, quoted in full by Athenaeus, which ends with the following verses (vv. 5–8):[60]

Σαπφῷαι δὲ μένουσι φίλης ἔτι καὶ μενέουσιν
  ᾠδῆς αἱ λευκαὶ φθεγγόμεναι σελίδες
οὔνομα σὸν μακαριστόν, ὃ Ναύκρατις ὧδε φυλάξει,
  ἔστ' ἂν ἴῃ Νείλου ναῦς ἐφ' ἁλὸς πελάγη.

But the white columns of Sappho's lovely ode
  still endure and will endure, proclaiming
your [i.e. Doricha's] blessed name, which Naucratis will preserve
  so long as ships sail forth from the Nile into the sea.

Since in this epigram, as already in Herodotus, Naucratis is made the setting of the love affair of this courtesan, ambiguously connected with Sappho, further information is supplied about other famous courtesans from Athenaeus' native town. And here comes the next *coup-de-théâtre*: without any trans-

---

above, nn. 16, 26, 32): thanks to this label, she is furtively put on the same level as the *hetaira* Doricha. Charaxus—hitherto absent in Sappho's extant poetry—now appears, although not explicitly as her brother, *pace* Obbink (2014, 2015, 2016), in a new Sappho poem (see also above, n. 32, and below, n. 77).

60 Posidippus fr. 122 Austin and Bastianini = 13.596c–d. Is this quotation of Posidippus a stand-in for poems of Sappho, not quoted in the *Deipnosophistae*, which refer positively to the *hetaira* Doricha, even in a glorifying way? Since modern scholars consider this improbable, Posidippus' mentioning of Sappho's 'friendly song' for Doricha is generally understood as irony. Compare also Kazanskaya's contribution to this volume, pp. 260–262, with further arguments stressing the alleged improbability.

ition, another courtesan, this time from Lesbian Eresus, is immediately added, namely Sappho herself, who according to the historian Nymphis (or Nymphodorus?) loved the beautiful Phaon.[61] That the poetess is meant here, and not a "second Sappho" put forward by other ancient authors,[62] has however been obscured by modern philological intervention: Kaibel suggested, in a footnote to his 1890 edition, that the words *poētrias homōnymos* ('a namesake of the poetess') should be inserted in the text in which Sappho actually figures, without further ado, as a *hetaira*, and this insertion has been adopted even by Olson in his recent new edition:

καὶ ἡ ἐξ Ἐρέσου δὲ τῆς ἑταίρας ... Σαπφὼ τοῦ καλοῦ Φάωνος ἐρασθεῖσα περιβόητος ἦν[63]

Olson however translates:

So too the courtesan Sappho of Eresus, who shared a name with the poetess, was notorious for being in love with the handsome Phaon.

The second author who is challenged with regard to his treatment of Sappho is the Hellenistic poet Hermesianax. His long elegy that contains a catalogue of love affairs of poets and philosophers is quoted in full.[64] In this poem, both Alcaeus and Anacreon are presented as lovers of Sappho:[65]

---

61 Olson adopts Wilamowitz's opinion that Nymphodorus, not Nymphis, as in the Codex Marcianus, is meant. Elsewhere in Athenaeus (2.69d), Phaon is presented as Aphrodite's beloved, not Sappho's.

62 See Schlesier (2013b) 839–840, and *passim* on the tradition and the long-lasting debate about 'the courtesan' Sappho, from the fifth century BCE until the twentieth century CE.

63 = 13.596e. Olson prints καὶ ἡ ἐξ Ἐρέσου δὲ τῆς ⟨ποιητρίας ὁμώνυμος⟩ ἑταίρας Σαπφὼ τοῦ καλοῦ Φάωνος ἐρασθεῖσα περιβόητος ἦν—thus including the supplement from Kaibel's apparatus, but diverging from his replacement of the transmitted genitive ἑταίρας by the nominative ἑταίρα. Olson's translation is puzzling, since even with Kaibel's supplement, Olson's text would rather fit another rendering: 'So too the Sappho of Eresus, namesake of the poetess, a courtesan, was notorious for'. I concede that the transmitted text calls for some supplement, perhaps not necessarily Kaibel's. Canfora (2001) and Cavallini (2001) give ἡ ἐξ Ἐρέσου δὲ τῆς ποιητρίας ὁμώνυμος ἑταίρα Σαπφὼ without indicating that both the nominative ἑταίρα and ποιητρίας ὁμώνυμος are Kaibel's emendations. Hence Athenaeus is erroneously taken as testimony for a "second Sappho" (on which see Sappho, test. 256 Voigt), as e.g. McClure (2003) 85 does also.

64 Hermesianax fr. 7 Powell = 13.597b–599b.

65 Hermesianax fr. 7.47–56 Powell = 13.598b–c. Cf. Yatromanolakis (2007) 348–351 (see especially his discussion of some scholarly interpretations of the puzzling terms στελλομένην and ἄμμιγα in v. 52, that he renders by 'surrounded by, mingled with' [349]).

Λέσβιος Ἀλκαῖος δὲ πόσους ἀνεδέξατο κώμους,
    Σαπφοῦς φορμίζων ἱμερόεντα πόθον,
γινώσκεις. ὁ δ' ἀοιδὸς ἀηδόνος ἠράσαθ' ὕμνων
    Τήιον ἀλγύνων ἄνδρα πολυφραδίη.
καὶ γὰρ τὴν ὁ μελιχρὸς ἐφωμίλησεν Ἀνακρέων
    στελλομένην πολλαῖς ἄμμιγα Λεσβιάσι·
φοίτα δ' ἄλλοτε μὲν λείπων Σάμον, ἄλλοτε δ' αὐτὴν
    οἰνηρῇ δείρῃ κεκλιμένην πατρίδα,
Λέσβον ἐς εὔοινον· τὸ δὲ Μύσιον εἴσιδε Λέκτον
    πολλάκις Αἰολικοῦ κύματος ἀντιπέρας.

You know how many drunken wanderings Lesbian Alcaeus
    undertook, celebrating with his lyre his lovely desire
for Sappho. The bard loved the nightingale, and he caused grief
    for the man from Teos by the eloquence of his hymns.
For Anacreon, sweet as honey, also competed for her
    who was beautifully attired among Lesbos' many women.
Sometimes he left Samos, at other times his own fatherland
    nestled against a grapevine-covered ridge, and went
to wine-filled Lesbos; and often he gazed upon Mysian
    Lectus on the other side of the Aeolian wave.

The following comment stresses that this cannot be true for Anacreon, since he was much younger than the poetess.[66] What should be noted, however, is the fact that this argument does not concern Alcaeus. Therefore, Hermesianax' presentation of Alcaeus as Sappho's lover is in no way contested in Athenaeus.

The third author challenged for his account of Sappho is the Peripatetic philosopher Chamaeleon.[67] He is much more violently attacked than Hermesianax, since he pretends to give a serious biographical interpretation of Anacreon's fr. 358 *PMG*, quoted in full in Athenaeus. With the same chronological argument advanced against Hermesianax, Chamaeleon's assertion that Anacreon's "girl of Lesbos" was Sappho is rigorously refuted, and moreover,

---

66   = 13.599c (cf. 14.635e, above, n. 24): ἐν τούτοις ὁ Ἑρμησιάναξ σφάλλεται συγχρονεῖν οἰόμενος Σαπφὼ καὶ Ἀνακρέοντα, τὸν μὲν κατὰ Κῦρον καὶ Πολυκράτην γενόμενον, τὴν δὲ κατ' Ἀλυάττην τὸν Κροίσου πατέρα ('Hermesianax is in error in this passage, since he believes that Sappho [fr. 250] and Anacreon are contemporaries, whereas in fact Anacreon lived in the time of Cyrus and Polycrates, but Sappho lived in the time of Croesus' father Alyattes'). Danielewicz (2006) 127 is one of the few readers of Athenaeus to acknowledge that 'literary criticism' is at stake here.

67   = 13.599c–d.

Chamaeleon's attribution of another fragment he quotes to Sappho is denigrated as a proof of scholarly ignorance.[68] Myrtilus displays his historical and literary expertise even more distinctively when he stresses the differences between the philosopher and the poets despite a superficial resemblance in their treatment of Sappho: while Chamaeleon is just talking nonsense, Hermesianax is giving a playful account, as does Diphilus in his comedy *Sappho*, where he presents Archilochus and Hipponax as lovers of the poetess.[69] What is denied, then, in Athenaeus, is not that the historical Sappho had several male lovers, but only the attribution, against chronological probability, of some particular lovers to her.

This is not the end of Sappho's appearances in book 13. Just before Myrtilus finishes his praise of courtesans, she shows up once more: this time, voiced by a literary courtesan, a character in Epicrates' comedy *Antilaïs*,[70] who boasts of her memorizing of *erōtika*, in the first place Sappho's:

τἀρωτίκ' ἐκμεμάθηκα ταῦτα παντελῶς
Σαπφοῦς, Μελήτου, Κλεομένους, Λαμυνθίου.

[I] have systematically memorized this erotic poetry produced by Sappho, Meletus, Cleomenes, and Lamynthius.

---

68 Fr. 953 adesp. *PMG*.
69 Diphilus *Sappho* fr. 71 *PCG* = 13.599d. An address to the character 'Archilochus' in this comedy has been quoted before, with respect to a term for a drinking vessel, in 11.487a; see above, n. 15. Sappho actually seems to have alluded to Archilochus in her poetry, terminologically and thematically responding, by means of pride or of irony, to the earlier poet's contemptuous treatment of heterosexually promiscuous women and replacing his perspective with a positive one, from a self-confident female point of view (cf. e.g. fr. 1.18 and fr. 121), see Schlesier (2014a) 92–93. If this is the case, it does not come as a surprise that, in the realm of comedy, she has been playfully presented as a lover of Archilochus, as Athenaeus attests.
70 Epicrates *Antilaïs* fr. 4 *PCG* = 13.605e. Since Antilaïs seems to be a female personal name (of a *hetaira*), I assume that the passage in Athenaeus implies that the protagonist of this comedy is the speaker. The irony of this statement is especially underlined by the fact that Epicrates' courtesan has not only learned Sappho's poetry by heart (as *hetairai*, according e.g. to Philodemus *Anth. Pal.* 5.132, used to do), but that she had also memorized, like a particularly pedantic, polymath scholar, much less well-known authors, never quoted by Athenaeus, such as the tragic poet Meletus (mentioned in the *Deipnosophistae* just as part of still another quotation from comedy, 12.551c), the dithyrambic poet Cleomenes of Rhegium, whose work even the learned deipnosophist Democritus has only read a long time ago (9.402a), and the lyric poet Lamynthius of Miletus, whom Myrtilus mentioned earlier for his infatuation with the *hetaira* Lyde, but without a quotation from his poetry (13.597a).

And Myrtilus does not refrain from identifying himself with this *hetaira*, since he too, as he triumphantly emphasizes, has done the same.

What results from this treatment of Sappho in book 13, and, as it seems to me, in the same vein in the rest of the *Deipnosophistae*? Doubtless, Sappho is presented as having equal rights in the literary and cultural sphere of the banquet as the other archaic poets. But since only *hetairai* and female slaves are typically included in this sphere, her status ought by implication to be the same as the courtesans'. This is argued for by several factors: her privileged association with Aphrodite;[71] her use of stringed instruments mainly related to the symposion;[72] her expertise in symposion vessel terminology and in poetic *erōtika*;[73] her addressing of men as *philos*;[74] her addressing of women, including at least one *hetaira*, in a scornful but also in a friendly way;[75] her praising of females who try to be seductive by using perfumes and garlands of flowers, as testified by her poetry itself;[76] and not least the particular onomastic quality of the female personal names she uses, which are markers of a courtesan or slave status (Athenaeus mentions Andromeda and Dica).[77] This is supplemented and underlined by quotations taken from later tradition, which bear witness to the extensive knowledge of her poetry by courtesans,[78] as well as by male banqueters (including of course the deipnosophists themselves), and also by mentioning famous later courtesans who were namesakes of women Sappho addressed in her poetry (Archeanassa,[79] Eirana),[80] and in general, by

---

71 As exemplified e.g. by Athenaeus' quotations of fr. 1 and fr. 2 (above, nn. 29 and 16), representative of numerous other fragments where Sappho claims Aphrodite to be her divine companion or even her *alter ego*. See Schlesier (2011, 2016).

72 Above, nn. 23 and 24.

73 Symposion vessel terminology: above, nn. 11–16.

74 Sappho fr. 138 (above, n. 47). A further address of a *philos* is to be found in her fr. 121 (not cited by Athenaeus). On both fragments, typically neglected in scholarship, see Schlesier (2014a) 92–94.

75 Above, nn. 59 and 60.

76 Above, nn. 36 and 39.

77 Andromeda: Sappho fr. 57 (above, n. 10); Dica: Sappho fr. 81 (above, n. 40). On the marked onomastic value of female personal names in Sappho, see Schlesier (2013a). Sappho uses at least fourteen proper names of human females in her extant poetry. Male personal names (i.e. Charaxus and Larichus) only recently appeared in a new Sappho poem, Obbink (2014, 2015, 2016). See above, nn. 32 and 59.

78 See, for example, above, n. 70.

79 Archeanassa in Sappho: fr. 103c.4 and fr. 213.2–3 (not cited in the *Deipnosophistae*). In Athenaeus 13.589c (as elsewhere in late ancient tradition), this is the name of a *hetaira* from Colophon, concubine of Plato the philosopher; see Schlesier (2013a) 203–204.

80 Eirana, in Sappho: fr. 91 and fr. 135 (not cited in the *Deipnosophistae*). On the *longue durée* of the onomastic record for Eirana (and variations of this name) see Schlesier (2013a) 205;

associating her with courtesans' skills and several love affairs with men, in her unambiguous quality as a *hetaira* herself. It should be noted that hints at homoerotic aspects of Sappho's renown are possibly not completely missing in Athenaeus,[81] but they are treated very discreetly, and do not contradict the dominating heterosexual lascivious aspects pertaining especially to a courtesans' world.[82]

Conclusion

According to Athenaeus and his learned protagonists, Greek and Roman intellectuals of the second-century cosmopolitan Roman Empire, Sappho has much to say about what characterizes a traditional banquet, no less than the other poets that are quoted in the course of Athenaeus' work. And as in the case of those, her verses and the terms she uses are conspicuously integrated into the discursive travelling-through and merging of different times and places and libraries the banqueters perform.[83] By this token, her person as a poet as well as her voice is made a virtual participant in the banqueters' playful and cunning debates,[84] linking up with Hellenistic comedy, where Sappho appears as a

---

to the references listed there, the *hetaira* Eirenion (*Anth. Pal.* 5.194) should be added. In Athenaeus, two historical courtesans bear a similar name: Eirenis, a *hetaira* of fourth-century Athens, mentioned in an oration of Lycurgus (13.586f), and Eirene, the lover of a son of Ptolemy Philadelphus (13.593a–b).

[81] I am not sure that the Sappho fragments, quoted by Athenaeus, which address females, fr. 57 (above, n. 10) and fr. 81 (above, n. 40), or talk about females, fr. 122 (above, n. 36) and fr. 160 (above, n. 54), should necessarily be interpreted as allusions to female homoeroticism or exclusive female companionship, as it was generally understood in scholarship. One could ask, however, whether the quotation of seventeen lines from Chaeremon's tragedy *Oineus* (*TrGF* 71 F 14 = 13.608b–c), using some of Sappho's flowery vocabulary, alludes to female same-sex tenderness (of maenads?), witnessed by a man. At any rate, there is no trace in Athenaeus (and, in my reading, neither in Sappho's extant poetry) in support of the idea, predominating today, that Sappho educated adolescent girls by means of an initiatory circle, aimed at preparing them for respectable marriages.

[82] On the issue of homoeroticism of *hetairai* since the archaic period, regularly overlooked or even, oddly enough, disavowed as improbable by modern scholars, see Schlesier (2014a) 96–99, with nn. 58–60. Plato's neologism ἑταιρίστριαι as sub-category of women loving women (*Symp.* 191e) seems to refer to "lesbian" courtesans (but not to "masculine" tribades, as later in Lucian, *Dial. meret.* 5). See Boehringer (2007) 169 and *passim*, although she unconvincingly associates them with passivity. Pitts (2002) 205–206 however rightly stresses the activity linguistically marked by the term.

[83] See the illuminating remarks of Wilkins (2008) and Jacob (2013) *passim*.

[84] This is of course not an isolated case: Jacob (2013) 40 emphasizes the fact that the *Deipno-*

character who was obviously more prominent in this genre than any other lyric poet, with several comedies named after her and presenting her as a sophisticated woman inclined to heterosexual promiscuity.[85]

Even more specifically, her privileged expertise in erotic poetry, luxury, and sympotic practices makes her in the *Deipnosophistae*—*pace* the Cynic moralist Cynulcus—an obvious stand-in for the female musicians and witty *hetairai* whom Athenaeus, in the footsteps of Plato's *Symposium*,[86] has not included in his male company, although without excluding them from the speeches—letting them even speak in their own voice. And it should be added, that Athenaeus' choice of names for his scholars at dinner follows the model of a courtesans' procedure: e.g. the names Arrian, Democritus, Galen, Palamedes, and Plutarch are *noms-de-guerre*, that is, the deipnosophists adopt the names of famous predecessors or contemporaries as professional labels in the same way as did the historical courtesans Laïs, Leontion, and many others.[87] As a constantly evoked creative woman and much-quoted female poet,[88] Sappho is given an outstanding prominence that is comparable to that of Plato's Diotima

---

  sophistae 'deploy a complex polyphony, almost a dialogue of the dead', i.e. of authors from many times and genres, who 'converse through the medium of quotations'.

85 Yatromanolakis (2007) 312 and *passim* tried to extenuate this, in an attempt at "purification" of the poetess, in the footsteps of Wilamowitz (1913), typical for most modern scholars.

86 While in Plato's *Symposium* (176e) a female *aulos* player is explicitly expelled from the banquet and sent to the women in Agathon's house—not necessarily spouses—(although an *auletris* later comes in with Alcibiades, 212c–d), the catalogue of the banqueters at the beginning of the *Deipnosophistae* (1.1c–f) and the presentation of persons sharing their company over the course of the work implicitly exclude female entertainers. Plato is however referred to as serving only as a literary model: the epitomator states (1.1f) that 'Athenaeus dramatizes the dialogue with Platonic verve' [my translation] (δραματουργεῖ δὲ τὸν διάλογον ὁ Ἀθήναιος ζήλῳ Πλατωνικῷ, translated by Olson as 'Athenaeus imitates Plato in his dramatization of the dialogue'). On Athenaeus' use of citations from Plato and on his anti-platonist stance, see Romeri (2004, 2007).

87 On courtesans' names, nicknames, homonyms, professional and secondary names in Athenaeus, see the exhaustive account of McClure (2003) 59–78, although adopting a dogmatic Marxist bias (*hetairai* are mainly assessed as commodity 'fetishes' by her). She focusses, oddly enough with moralizing indignation, on the 'decontextualization' of those names and pays much less attention to their recontextualization and to Athenaeus' literary strategies (including the naming of the deipnosophists themselves). See above, n. 44. On Sappho's inventive use of female personal names, whose 'reality effect' especially points to *hetairai* names, see Schlesier (2013a).

88 Apart from the explicit quotations and paraphrases of fragments of Sappho, plenty of allusions to her vocabulary, themes, and poetic techniques are possibly to be detected in the *Deipnosophistae*. See e.g. above, nn. 10, 20, 24, 35, 43, 44, 49, 51, 60, 69. A closer study of such allusions would however exceed the scope of the present chapter.

in the *Symposium*. Like this expert in love, Sappho, in Athenaeus, is no less an authority.[89] But she possesses here, in contrast to Plato's fictitious priestess and philosophical teacher, a real poetic authority in uncensored sympotic language and cultural heritage, in other words, in the fields of knowledge and physical as well as intellectual pleasure that the deipnosophists are most interested in. And simultaneously, this seems to show that Athenaeus the independent thinker, the Anti-Platonist—who is not a Stoic or a Cynic either—creates, insinuatingly, a metaphorical analogy between the main stuff of his work, the quotations,[90] and one of its main topics, the courtesans, both possibly being abused, but, nevertheless, both tending to be on everyone's lips.

Appendix

1 *Fragments of Sappho (ed. Voigt) in Athenaeus*
1.1   Ordered by Fragment Number

fr. 1.9–10	9.391f
fr. 2.13–16	11.463e
fr. 15	13.596b–c
fr. 44.10	11.460d
fr. 57.1/3	1.21c
fr. 58.25–26	15.687a–b
fr. 81	15.674e

---

89 An explicit comparison between Sappho and Diotima has been advanced by Athenaeus' contemporary Maximus Tyrius (*Or.* 18.7 and 18.9). See Schlesier (2011) 2–4 and (2017) 145–147, 153–155, 160.

90 On quotations in Athenaeus as ludic performance, playfully put in new contexts, see Paulas (2012). Relying on Jacob (2004) and McClure (2003), he argues for a reading of the *Deipnosophistae* as a dramatization of reading itself, applying to it exclusively the features 'intertext' and 'intratext' and, strangely enough, denying it any encyclopaedic value (411–412). Yet without narrow theoretical biases, Athenaeus' 'virtuoso game' has been analyzed most brilliantly by Jacob (2013) 47, and especially 96: 'Extraction enables the segmentation of those materials and their archiving on a level different from the original text. It certainly answers a preoccupation of ergonomic order, since extraction is selection, but also subdivision of a continuous text into elements that are independent, objectivized, mobile, and such that they lend themselves to any sort of new combination. The procedure also has intellectual effects, since decontextualization cannot happen without a form of recontextualization, which produces specific meanings.' Jacob's apt metaphor for the *Deipnosophistae* and its 'art of weaving links' (103–108) is the term 'web'.

fr. 94.15–16	15.674d
fr. 94.19–20	15.690e
fr. 101	9.410d–e (fragment transmitted only in Athenaeus)
fr. 122	12.554b (fragment transmitted only in Athenaeus)
fr. 138	13.564d (fragment transmitted only in Athenaeus)
fr. 141.1–3	2.39a–b
fr. 141.1–3	10.425c–d
fr. 141.3	5.192c
fr. 141.4–6	11.475a
fr. 142	13.571d (fragment transmitted only in Athenaeus)
fr. 143	2.54f
fr. 160	13.571d (fragment transmitted only in Athenaeus)
fr. 166	2.57d
fr. 167	2.57d
fr. 176	4.182e
fr./test. 203a	10.424f–425a

1.2   Ordered by Book Number

1.21c	fr. 57.1/3	[two verses quoted]
2.39a–b	fr. 141.1–3	[three verses quoted]
2.54f	fr. 143	[one verse quoted]
2.57d	fr. 166	[one verse quoted]
2.57d	fr. 167	[one verse quoted]
4.182e	fr. 176	[two terms quoted]
5.192c	fr. 141.3	[paraphrase]
9.391f	fr. 1,9–10	[paraphrase]
9.410d–e	fr. 101	[four verses quoted]
10.424f–425a	fr. 203a	[paraphrase] [= test. 203a Voigt]
10.425c–d	fr. 141.1–3	[three verses quoted]
11.460d	fr. 44.10	[one verse quoted]
11.463e	fr. 2.13–16	[four verses quoted]
11.475a	fr. 141.4–6	[three verses quoted]
12.554b	fr. 122	[one verse quoted]
13.564d	fr. 138	[two verses quoted]
13.571d	fr. 160	[one verse quoted]
13.571d	fr. 142	[one verse quoted]
13.596b–c	fr. 15	[paraphrase] [= test. 254c Voigt]
15.674d	fr. 94.15–16	[two verses quoted]
15.674e	fr. 81	[four verses quoted]

15.687a–b	fr. 58.25–26	[two verses quoted]
15.690e	fr. 94.19–20	[two terms quoted from two verses]

2 Sappho in Athenaeus, with Reference to Other Ancient Authors
2.1 Comic Playwrights

8.339c	[Timocles *Sappho* fr. 32 *PCG*, two verses quoted]
10.450e–451b	[Antiphanes *Sappho* fr. 194 *PCG*, twenty-one verses quoted]
11.487a	[Diphilus *Sappho* fr. 70 *PCG*, two verses quoted]
13.572c	[Ephippus *Sappho* fr. 20 *PCG*, four verses quoted]
13.599d	[Diphilus *Sappho* fr. 71 *PCG*, paraphrase]
13.605e	[Epicrates *Antilaïs* fr. 4 *PCG*, two verses quoted]

2.2 Other Poets as well as Historians

13.596c	[Herodotus 2.135: paraphrase] [= Sappho, test. 254a Voigt]
13.596c–d	[Posidippus fr. 122 Austin and Bastianini]
13.598b–c	[Hermesianax fr. 7.47–56 Powell]
13.599c–d	[Chamaeleon fr. 26 Wehrli: paraphrase] [= Sappho, test. 250 Voigt]
14.635b/e	[Menaechmus *FGrH* 131 F4a and b: paraphrase] [= test. 247 Voigt]
14.635e	[Aristoxenus fr. 98 Wehrli: paraphrase]
14.639a	[Clearchus fr. 33 Wehrli: paraphrase] [= Sappho, test. 39 Campbell]

References

Anderson, G. 2000. The Banquet of Belles-Lettres: Athenaeus and the Comic Symposium. In Braund and Wilkins 2000: 316–326, 572–573.

Barker, A. 2000. Athenaeus on Music. In Braund and Wilkins 2000: 434–444, 586.

Bartol, K. 2005. Safona w *Uczcie Medrców* Atenajosa (= Acta Universitatis Wratislaviensis no. 2715). *Classica Wratislaviensia* 26: 49–56.

Boehringer, S. 2007. *L'homosexualité féminine dans l'Antiquité grecque et romaine*. Paris.

Bogner, H. 1941. Was heisst μοιχεύειν? *Hermes* 76: 318–320.

Bouchard, E. 2015. Aphrodite *philommêdês* in the *Theogony*. *JHS* 135: 8–18.

Bowie, E. 2000. Athenaeus' Knowledge of Early Greek Elegiac and Iambic Poetry. In Braund and Wilkins 2000: 124–135, 554.

Braund, D. 2000. Learning, Luxury and Empire: Athenaeus' Roman Patron. In Braund and Wilkins 2000: 3–22, 539.

Braund, D. and Wilkins, J., eds. 2000. *Athenaeus and His World: Reading Greek Culture in the Roman Empire*. Exeter.

Brunet, P. 2003. Sappho au Banquet des Savants. In *Colloque: La poésie grecque antique. Actes* (= Cahiers de la Villa Kérylos 14), ed. J. Jouanna and J. Leclant, 63–76. Paris.

Ceccarelli, P. 2000. Dance and Deserts: An Analysis of Book Fourteen. In Braund and Wilkins 2000: 272–291, 567–570.

Danielewicz, J. 2006. Poetic Quotations and Discourse Strategies in Athenaeus. *Eos* 93: 116–131.

Greene, E. and Skinner, M.B., eds. 2009. *The New Sappho on Old Age: Textual and Philosophical Issues*. Cambridge, MA.

Hawley, R. 1993. 'Pretty, Witty and Wise': Courtesans in Athenaeus' *Deipnosophistai* Book 13. *International Journal of Moral and Social Sciences* 8: 73–91.

Henry, M.M. 1992. The Edible Woman: Athenaeus's Concept of the Pornographic. In *Pornography and Representation in Greece and Rome*, ed. A. Richlin, 250–268. Oxford.

Henry, M.M. 2000. Athenaeus the Ur-Pornographer. In Braund and Wilkins 2000: 503–510, 590–591.

Jacob, C. 2004. La citation comme performance dans les *Deipnosophistes* d'Athénée. In *La citation dans l'Antiquité*, ed. C. Darbo-Peschanski, 147–174. Grenoble.

Jacob, C. 2013. *The Web of Athenaeus*. Cambridge, MA.

Lenfant, D., ed. 2007. *Athénée et les fragments d'historiens*. Paris.

Lukinovich, A. 1990. The Play of Reflections between Literary Form and the Sympotic Theme in the *Deipnosophistae* of Athenaeus. In *SYMPOTICA. A Symposium on the Symposion*, ed. O. Murray, 263–271. Oxford.

Maisonneuve, C. 2007. Les *Deipnosophistes* d'Athénée: Repères dans une structure complexe. In *Athénée et les fragments d'historiens*, ed. D. Lenfant, 387–412. Paris.

McClure, L. 2003. *Courtesans at Table: Gender and Greek Literary Culture in Athenaeus*. New York.

Obbink, D. 2014. Two New Poems by Sappho. *ZPE* 189: 32–49.

Obbink, D. 2015. Interim Notes on 'Two New Poems of Sappho'. *ZPE* 194: 1–8.

Obbink, D. 2016. The Newest Sappho: Text, Apparatus Criticus, and Translation. In *The Newest Sappho: P. Sapph. Obbink and P. GC inv. 105, frs. 1–4*, ed. A. Bierl and A. Lardinois, 13–33. Leiden.

Paulas, J. 2012. How to Read Athenaeus' *Deipnosophists*. *AJPh* 133: 403–439.

Peponi, A.-E. 2012. *Frontiers of Pleasure: Models of Aesthetic Response in Archaic and Classical Greek Thought*. Oxford.

Pitts, A.L. 2002. *Prostitute, Muse, Lover: The Biographical Tradition of Sappho in Greek and Roman Literature*. Diss. University of Wisconsin. Madison.

Power, T. 2010. *The Culture of Kitharôidia*. Cambridge, MA.

Romeri, L. 2000. The λογόδειπνον: Athenaeus between Banquet and Anti-Banquet. In Braund and Wilkins 2000: 256–271, 563–567.

Romeri, L. 2004. Platon chez Athénée. In *La citation dans l'Antiquité*, ed. C. Darbo-Peschanski, 175–188. Grenoble.

Romeri, L. 2007. Les citations de Platon chez Athénée. In *Athénée et les fragments d'historiens*, ed. D. Lenfant, 341–354. Paris.

Schlesier, R. 2011. Presocratic Sappho: Her Use of Aphrodite for Arguments about Love and Immortality. *Scientia Poetica* 15: 1–28.

Schlesier, R. 2013a. Atthis, Gyrinno, and other *hetairai*: Female Personal Names in Sappho's Poetry. *Philologus* 157: 199–222.

Schlesier, R. 2013b. s.v. Sappho. In *Historische Gestalten der Antike: Rezeption in Literatur, Kunst und Musik* (= Der Neue Pauly. Suppl. 8), ed. P. von Möllendorff, A. Simonis, and L. Simonis, 835–860. Stuttgart.

Schlesier, R. 2014a. Symposion, Kult und frühgriechische Dichtung: Sappho im Kontext. In *Medien der Geschichte: Antikes Griechenland und Rom*, ed. O. Dally, T. Hölscher, S. Muth, and R.M. Schneider, 74–106. Berlin.

Schlesier, R. 2014b. Gold as Mediator Between Divinities and Humans in Homer and in Sappho's Poetry. In *AURUM. Funzioni e simbologie dell'oro nelle culture del Mediterraneo antico*, ed. M. Tortorelli Ghidini, 291–301. Rome.

Schlesier, R. 2015. Unsicherheiten einer poetisch-erotischen Welt: Anreden und Konstellationen von Personen bei Sappho. In *Irritationen: Rhetorische und poetische Verfahren der Verunsicherung*, ed. R. Früh, T. Fuhrer, M. Humar, and M. Vöhler, 297–321. Berlin.

Schlesier, R. 2016. Loving, but not Loved: The new Kypris Song in the Context of Sappho's Poetry. In *The Newest Sappho: P. Sapph. Obbink and P. GC inv. 105, frs. 1–4*, ed. A. Bierl and A. Lardinois, 368–395. Leiden.

Schlesier, R. 2017. How to make Fragments: Maximus Tyrius' Sappho. In *Fragments, Holes, and Wholes: Reconstructing the Ancient World in Theory and Practice*, ed. T. Derda, J. Hilder, and J. Kwapisz, 141–162. Warsaw.

Schlesier, R. 2018. Sappho bei Nacht. In *La nuit. Imaginaire et réalités nocturnes dans le monde gréco-romain*, ed. A. Chaniotis, 91–121. Vandœuvres.

West, M.L. 1992. *Ancient Greek Music*. Oxford.

Wilamowitz-Moellendorff, U. von 1913. *Sappho und Simonides. Untersuchungen über griechische Lyriker*. Berlin.

Wilkins, J. 2000. Dialogue and Comedy: The Structure of the *Deipnosophistae*. In Braund and Wilkins 2000: 23–37, 539–541.

Wilkins, J. 2008. Athenaeus the Navigator. *JHS* 128: 132–152.

Yatromanolakis, D. 2007. *Sappho in the Making: The Early Reception*. Cambridge, MA.

Zellner, H. 2006. Sappho's Supra-Superlatives. *CQ* 56: 292–297.

Zellner, H. 2010. *The Poetic Style of the Greek Poet Sappho: A Study in Word Playfulness*. Lewiston.

Editions Cited

Austin, C. and Bastianini, G., eds. 2002. *Posidippi Pellaei quae supersunt omnia*. Milan.

Campbell, D.A., ed. 1982. *Greek Lyric. Vol. 1: Sappho and Alcaeus*. Cambridge, MA.

Canfora, L. and Jacob, C., eds. 2001. *Ateneo. I Deipnosofisti—i dotti a banchetto. Vol. I–III: Libri I–XV, Vol. IV: Testo greco*. Rome.

Cavallini, E., ed. 2001. *Ateneo di Naucrati. Il banchetto dei sapienti. Libro XIII—sulle donne*. 2nd edn. Bologna.

Diels, H. and Kranz, W., eds. 1951–1952. *Die Fragmente der Vorsokratiker. Griechisch und Deutsch. Vol. I–III*. 6th edn. Berlin.

Kaibel, G., ed. 1887–1890. *Athenaei Navcratitae Dipnosophistarum Libri XV. Vol. I–II* (1887), *Vol. III* (1890). Stuttgart.

Kassel, R. and Austin, C., eds. 1983–2001. *Poetae Comici Graeci. Vol. I–II, III.2, IV–V, VI.2, VII–VIII* [= *PCG*]. Berlin.

Lobel, E. and Page, D., eds. 1955. *Poetarum Lesbiorum Fragmenta*. Oxford.

Olson, S.D., ed. 2006–2012. *Athenaeus. The Learned Banqueters. Books 1–15. Vol. I–VIII*. Cambridge, MA.

Page, D., ed. 1962. *Poetae Melici Graeci* [= *PMG*]. Oxford.

Powell, J.U., ed. 1925. *Collectanea Alexandrina*. Oxford.

Snell, B. and Maehler, H., eds. 1975. *Pindarus. Pars II: Fragmenta. Indices*. 4th edn. Leipzig.

Voigt, E.-M., ed. 1971. *Sappho et Alcaeus. Fragmenta*. Amsterdam.

West, M.L., ed. 1989. *Iambi et Elegi Graeci. Ante Alexandrum Cantati. Vol. I: Archilochus, Hipponax, Theognidea. Editio altera*. Oxford.

CHAPTER 16

Solon and the Democratic Biographical Tradition

Jessica Romney

1 Introduction*

Solon—whether poet, politician, or sage—was a popular figure. He appears in works by philosophers, scholiasts, historians, and comedians; he is the subject of biography and table talk and an *exemplum* of virtue for orators and church fathers. He is a democrat (Diogenes Laertius 1.66–67), an oligarch (Diodorus 18.18.5), a sophist (Isocrates 15.232), and a wise advisor (Herodotus 1.33). As a man engaged in life and the act of living, he serves as a contrast to the detached philosophical life (Plutarch *Solon*). He is to be imitated, in word (Demosthenes 19.252–254) and deed (Aeschines 1.6). By his own account, he is everything and nothing to both sides of an argument—an Athenian Proteus just as difficult to pin down as the divine original. At the core, however, the various forms of "Solon" claim the same thing: they are fair, moderate, and patriotic, standing apart from the stasiotic population of sixth-century Athens and refusing to deviate from their moral code.[1] This stable core takes its form from the "Solon" glimpsed within the verses haranguing his countrymen and defending his *polis*. The subsequent use of the verses and the re-telling of Solon's story, aggrandized in the years following the Peloponnesian War, have reinforced this core "Solon" and have influenced our reception of the poet-politician and his verses.

Solon's poetry contributes to this story and its hero "Solon", a politically understated individual who will, nevertheless, enter the fray when called to do so by his *polis*. The extant verses highlight the poet-politician's foresight and political skill, his avoidance of personal gain, and his unwillingness to damage Athens' interests for anyone—himself included. His later readers and disciples

---

* I would like to thank those who asked questions and who took the time to speak with me about this chapter at the conference, as well as Robert Fowler, Reyes Bertolin Cebrian, Loriel Anderson, and Ilaria Andolfi, as well as the reviewers for the publisher and Bruno Currie, for their comments on earlier drafts. Between the writing and publication of this contribution, a special volume on the fifth- and fourth-century reception of Solon was published (Nagy and Noussia-Fantuzzi [2015]); the contributors focus on the early reception of Solon, which would then affect the reception of Solon in Aristotle and Plutarch, as discussed in this contribution.
1 Unless otherwise noted, all dates are BCE.

repeated these claims and quoted the poems for us, thereby creating a circle of self-reinforcement for the story of Solon of Athens.[2]

This chapter presents a review of Plutarch's *Solon*, the major extant source for Solon's life, and its influence on modern interpretations of Solon, his poetry, and his place in sixth-century Athens. In particular, it is interested in examining a set of underlying assumptions concerning Solon and his work that have persisted despite general scepticism towards Plutarch's account of Solon's life in order to destabilize Solon's biographical tradition and the poet's self-presentation as a selfless, beleaguered individual reformer.[3] By and large, and despite recent studies re-appraising Solon's place in archaic Athens,[4] the relationship between Solon and Athens that we see in his poetry and in Plutarch's account is accepted as presented: Solon acts alone, apart from his socio-economic peers, and mediates the *stasis* between two mutually exclusive economic groups out of a patriotic desire to protect his *polis*. Yet, if we question this story a little further, and look at material from other archaic *poleis*, we see that group politics was the norm, even for the personal rule of the tyrants, and that Solon's verses can suggest supporters; that *stasis* in the archaic period was driven by intra-elite conflict as much as, if not more than, by agitation from small farmers and *thētes*; and finally, that claims to defend the *polis* and/or *dēmos* were made by traditional "aristocratic" poets (Alcaeus, for one [fr. 129]) as well and may have been a common way of acquiring a broader base of support. The consequence of Plutarch's *Solon* and its influence upon our reception of Solon is the reluctance to question the "story of Solon", to apply the level of scepticism seen in analyses of Alcaeus' rhetoric, for example, to Solon's.

Plutarch's *Lives* have had a considerable influence on Western reception of Greco-Roman history and culture as the texts have enjoyed almost continuous popularity in one form or another since Plutarch's day, thereby shaping how we view the ancient world and its major players.[5] These texts, composed some 800 years after Solon's archonship in 594/3, present an important resource for us, albeit one with an accompanying cautionary note. Plutarch depended, as do

---

2 While the danger of circularity concerning the *Ath. Pol.* and the *Sol.* has been raised (notably Irwin [2005] 87n7), this is generally less recognized for other works. Irwin seems to suggest this problem is less acute with fr. 4, as it was quoted by Demosthenes (Irwin [2005] 87n7). As will be argued below, however, the citations by the Attic orators are no less problematic.

3 Irwin (2005) 87–88 on scepticism to Plut. *Sol.* and the *Ath. Pol.*; see Rhodes (2006) and Owens (2010) for *contra*. De Blois has recently argued that Plutarch's *Solon* contains 'good factual material' despite influence from the biographer's favourite stereotypes ([2006] 439); he seems to have a similarly positive view of the *Ath. Pol.*'s account of Solon.

4 See especially those in the Blok and Lardinois (2006) and Irwin (2005).

5 See Russell (1973) chs 9–10 and Lamberton (2001) ch. 4.

we, on mid-fifth and fourth-century sources for Solon's life, all of which date to a period of constitutional debates in Athens, which ultimately resulted in the declaration of Solon as the author of the πάτριος πολιτεία (*patrios politeia*, 'ancestral constitution') and the first προστάτης τοῦ δήμου ('champion of the *dēmos*'). Additionally, the fourth century saw the equation of the social terms *agathos/aristos* with the economic term *plousios* ('rich'),[6] and by accepting this conflation, we eclipse the tension that existed in the early archaic period as a result of disparities between wealth and political power amongst the economically well-off and the regional conflict amongst power blocks headed by a family of *agathoi* and supported by their dependents (*kakoi*).[7] An author's agenda in writing and invoking Solon is another issue. The Attic orators used Solon to convict their opponents; Aristotle and the author of the *Athēnaiōn Politeia*[8] to support their concept of good government; and Plutarch to reinforce the ethical character and pedagogical agenda of his *Lives*. These authors shape their quotations to suit their arguments, which are often based on oral traditions and their own understanding of what was "reasonable" concerning their subject.[9]

Solon's poetry speaks to many audiences and was designed to last beyond its performance.[10] Yet by accepting the democratic-influenced narrative and contextualizations offered by Plutarch and his predecessors,[11] we obscure the subtle rhetoric of Solon's verses and restrict the number of audiences to which the poems potentially spoke. The participants within the poems are vague and can be adopted by any audience, with the poetic enemies mapping onto the audience's. As in the stories of Solon's political manoeuvring, so too his poetry places him somewhere in the middle,[12] promising things to all players, but without hemming himself in. This chapter seeks to reopen the political and

---

6   Stanley (1999) 173.
7   That is, *horizontal* conflict within classes alongside the vertical conflict between classes. For power blocks in archaic Athens, see Forrest (1966), followed by Ellis and Stanton (1968) and Stanton (1990) 4–5. Compare Morris (1987) 91 and Sealey (1960) 168. On class conflict in the archaic period, Rose (2012).
8   On the disputed authorship of the *Ath. Pol.*, see the discussions in Hendrickson (2013) and Rhodes (1981), esp. 58–61, with bibliography.
9   Hendrickson (2013) discusses this process in biographical writing; cf. Lardinois (2006) 28–32.
10 On which, see also Irwin (2005) 133; Mülke (2002) 91; and Martin (2006) 169. Owens (2010) 58–59, however, argues that Solon had eyes only for the present.
11 As in, for example, Noussia-Fantuzzi (2010) 22; Anhalt (1993) 1; Ehrenberg (1996) 62–64; Podlecki (1969) 79. For a middle approach to the issue, see Moore (1983) 215.
12 On Solon's middle position as constructed by the similes in his poems, see Irwin (2006) and Martin (2006); cf. Lewis (2006) 63 and Noussia-Fantuzzi (2010) 70–73.

poetic space in which this poet-politician turned, to situate Solon and Athens within the context of intra-elite conflict accompanied by class conflict between the major landowners, small-holders, and *thētes*. To such an end, the first two sections review the fifth- and fourth-century reception of Solon and Plutarch's *Solon* respectively, noting in particular the ways Solon is used and the impact of this reception. The final section then turns to a re-evaluation of Solon and his poems, focusing on fragment 15.

2 The Reception of Solon before Plutarch

As one of the Seven Sages of archaic Greece and as *the* Athenian legislator, there were several traditions regarding Solon: poet and sage, lawgiver and politician, and philosopher. Our first extant source is Herodotus' *Histories*; after that are the remnants of the Atthidographers' accounts of archaic Athens, the speeches of the Athenian orators, Plato's dialogues, and Aristotle's political theorizing. As this brief overview will argue, "Solon", while possessing a stable core based on his reputed wisdom and moderation, was moulded to fit the specific needs of the authors invoking his presence.

For Herodotus, Solon was a lawgiver (1.29.1) and, more importantly, a "wise advisor" (1.29.2–33) whose advice to Croesus is a variant on his programmatic statement at the beginning of the *Histories*, that large nations become small and vice versa (1.5.4).[13] This parallel is strengthened by the fact that the travelling sage, querying the locals and seeking knowledge from foreign lands (2.177.2), resembles the travelling historian himself.[14] The account of "Solon the Lawgiver" becomes more pronounced in the fourth century with the Atthidographers and the Attic orators, both of whom name Solon the founder of Athenian democracy.[15] This shift reflects the constitutional debates that took place in Athens, as Solon was conscripted to support the *patrios politeia* of first the oligarchs in 411 and then the democrats in 403.[16] The Atthidographers established Solon's definitive place in Athenian political history, while the orators wielded him as the ultimate weapon, the trump card in their legal and political battles (e.g. Lysias 30.28; Aeschines 1.16–20; Demosthenes 29.102–104).

---

13   Shapiro (1996); also Flores (2013) 10.
14   Flores (2013) 10.
15   Jacoby (1949) 154. For Solon in the Atthidographers, see Jacoby (1949) 77 and Harding's commentary on Androtion F 34 and Philochorus F 21, 114 ([2008] 88–90).
16   Mossé (2004) and Osborne (1996) 217 discuss this process regarding the Attic orators.

Plato's dialogues incorporate various Solonian traditions.[17] "Solon the Lawgiver/Politician" begins the archon list (and thus democratic history) in the *Hippias Major* (285e4; cf. *Symposium* 209a7; *Phaedrus* 258c1; *Laws* 858c3).[18] The *Critias* and *Timaeus* with their tales of Atlantis co-opt Solon for philosophy,[19] and Flores argues that Solon appears in Plato's dialogues in general as 'a figure to advance the practice of philosophy, as Solon stands as a starting point for philosophy in Plato's *Protagoras*'.[20] For Aristotle, Solon established the 'mixed' democracy that Aristotle considers the best form of democracy and the Athenian ancestral constitution (*Politics* 1273b35) as he interprets Solon's actions through his conception of virtue as a mean between extremes.[21] Solon is of the best sort of lawgiver, as he is one of the *mesoi*, a status Aristotle claims can be told from his poetry (1296a19–20). Similarly, in the *Athēnaiōn Politeia*,[22] Solon, the first 'champion of the *dēmos*' (2.1), is 'by wealth and position' one of the *mesoi*, though one of the elite 'by birth' (5.3).[23] Both works seek to protect Solon from charges that he was a radical democrat (*Politics* 1274a1–5; *Athēnaiōn Politeia* 6.2–4) and therefore emphasize his political moderation, protecting the *dēmos* by giving it enough power to protect itself but not so much that it runs out of control.[24] At the same time, however, Solon supports the poor as 'he always attached the cause of the strife entirely to the rich' (*Athēnaiōn Politeia* 5.3).

Turning from the *Athēnaiōn Politeia* to Solon and his poetry, however, we see that the poet does not always blame "the rich", or even name them as such.[25] It is increasingly being acknowledged that Solon criticizes the *dēmos* and *astoi* (frr. 4.5; 5; 10; 37.1–3) alongside the elite groups (fr. 4.11; possibly fr. 4c), the 'leaders of the *dēmos*' (fr. 4.7), and 'men of unsound minds' (fr. 6.3–4).[26] Solon's poetry

---

17 On the use of Solon in Plato's dialogues, see Flores (2013).
18 Flores (2013) 19–20 discusses the implications of this. The connection between Solon and democracy in Plato, however, was generally weak; Sagsetter suggests an alternative aristocratic tradition regarding Solon may be the cause ([2013] ch. 3).
19 Flores (2013) 93.
20 Flores (2013) 18.
21 Gehrke (2006) 278.
22 Gehrke (2006) 278–279 notes the similarities between the accounts of Solon in the *Ath. Pol.* and the *Politics*.
23 On Solon in the *Ath. Pol.*, see Hendrickson (2013).
24 Gehrke (2006) 277, 280.
25 That the poems quoted by Aristotle and the *Ath. Pol.* do not support their arguments has been noted by Gehrke ([2006] 280n12); compare Klooster's contribution to this volume on Plutarch and Solon's poetry.
26 Fr. 11 may criticize the *dēmos* or a small aristocratic group (cf. Gottesman 2005). Fr. 4c is often taken as a criticism of the rich, following Aristotle's narrative frame, but see Lewis

and the traditions around him provided a variety of interpretations, facilitating the moulding of this poet-politician to the needs of those writing about him. Yet the binary categories of "rich" and "poor" continue, as does Solon's ideological and economic place between the two, and the fact that Aristotle used these categories has influenced our acceptance of these divisions in Plutarch's narrative.[27]

3   Plutarch's *Life of Solon*

Plutarch's *Parallel Lives* link notable Greeks and Romans to one another through the juxtaposed biographies, some of which have prologues and/or conclusions (*synkriseis*). Plutarch states that the *Lives* are to provide moral *exempla* of character, so that readers could reflect on the subjects' actions and thereby improve themselves (*Alexander* 1.2).[28] These character lessons generally occur in descriptive accounts where the subject's actions and the responses of onlookers reveal the judgement to be made by a critical reader.[29] The *Lives* thus provide practical exercises in judging character alongside theoretical lessons of character. Yet while there are strong indications that each pairing was to be read as a whole, for the past 50 years or so each *Life* has been read individually, without any accompanying prologue and/or *synkrisis*.[30]

As the most extensive extant source for Solon, the *Solon* is an important resource, and an influential one. The "Solon" within it possesses a strong moral compass from which he does not deviate, and this compass is guided by notions of moderation and political "fairness" that colour Solon's activities as both sage and lawgiver. Like the subject of the partnering *Life*, Publicola, Solon serves as an example of managing a *polis* under *stasis*, and of how to educate the populace so that they will restrain their tempers and desires for the benefit of the state. This aspect of the Solonian character strongly influences modern scholarship; Almeida, for example, argues that Solon 'became one of [the *polis*'s]

  (2006) 37 on alternative readings. On Solon's critique of the *dēmos*, see, e.g., Balot (2001) 93; Raaflaub (2006) 400; and Rose (2012) 329–330.

27 This is not often stated; see though de Blois (2006) 437–438 for a statement of accepting Plutarch's account because of the parallels with Aristotle.

28 Duff (1999) 68; cf. Duff (2011).

29 Pelling (2002) 239; Duff (2011) 61–75.

30 The Penguin editions of Plutarch's *Lives* are a good example of this (e.g., Scott-Kilvert [1973]). This splitting of the *Lives* is a twentieth-century CE trend (Lamberton [2001] 68). Duff (1999) argues convincingly for rehabilitating the *synkriseis*; see also Lamberton (2001) 91 and Russell (1973) 110–113.

greatest citizens and ultimately ... its champion in Athens at a time of critical change'.[31] This 'greatest citizen', however, was only so in hindsight and as used by later politicians and writers. In the immediate aftermath, Solon seems to have changed little: archons refused to give up office, and political *stasis* allowed Pisistratus three tries at the tyranny. In this setting, Solon's reforms were a stopgap measure that later became influential. Yet, because Plutarch, Aristotle, and others reinforce Solon's own declarations of a unique vision to save Athens, we too accept those claims on the part of this poet-*politician*. This section summarizes the major points of Plutarch's *Solon*, demonstrating how the biographer's interest in Solon's character, supported to varying degrees by his quotations of Solon, has impacted on the basic assumptions we bring regarding Solon's attitude towards Athens, his place in the conflict,[32] and his socio-economic status.

The *Solon* begins with a historical and genealogical link to Athenian democracy: Solon is the descendant of Codrus (1.1–2), the last Athenian king whose heroic sacrifice marked the end of the monarchy and which provides a model for Solon's actions. Despite this high social ranking, Solon possesses no great wealth (cf. *Athēnaiōn Politeia* 5.3), which translates to a political stance as he favours the poor over the wealthy (*Solon* 3.2, quoting fr. 15). Solon appears as both philosopher (3.3–5) and sage (4–7) before his political activities are introduced. "Solon the Sage" thus appears before "Solon the Legislator" or "Solon the Politician", and while the characters are chronologically inverted, "Solon the Sage" is important for how Plutarch presents and understands "Solon the Politician". The former is especially important for Plutarch's readers as Solon's political actions and motivations are to be interpreted in light of his actions as a sage. By introducing the sage first, Plutarch primes the reader to agree with his later disregard of the stories which seek to malign Solon: the greed and duplicity Solon is accused of are unthinkable for one of the Seven Sages.

From moderation to patriotism: Plutarch's narrative of Solon's political activities reinforce the poet-politician's love of Athens and desire to protect the *polis*

---

31   Almeida (2003) 125; cf. Balot (2001) 74–75; Anhalt (1993) 93–95; Podlecki (1969) 81; Owens (2010) 62; Irwin (2006) 71–72. On Solon's *persona*, see the discussions in Lardinois (2006) 27; Stehle (2006); and Romney (2015) 134–136; cf. Noussia-Fantuzzi (2010) 54–55.

32   Like the *Ath. Pol.*, Plutarch attributes the conflict to the rich versus the poor. The most recent and explicit arguments in favour of the rich/poor conflict are those by Wallace (1997) and Lavelle (2005) 73–76; cf. Owens (2010) and Anhalt (1993). On the interpretation of the pronouns and social groups in line with the rich/poor conflict, see e.g., Forsdyke (2006) 338, naming the "they" of 4.12–14 'the rich'; Owens (2010) naming 'the rich' (61; cf. 57–58) as the target of fr. 13 and 'the rich and powerful' as that for fr. 4 (157). See also Irwin (2005) 109n60; Anhalt (1993) 92n40.

and its poorer members. Always the *polis* comes before his personal and political well-being (e.g. 15.6, 16.1–2; 30.2–31.2). By mediating the *stasis* from the Cylonian affair (12.1–3), Solon establishes himself as a neutral party amongst the elite, and then as such for the whole population in his arbitration amongst the Hill Men, the Plains Men, the Coastal Men, and the *thētes* (13). According to Plutarch, the 'most sensible men' (οἱ φρονιμώτατοι) of Athens chose Solon because he was neither viciously greedy nor desperately poor (14.1)—this not only divides the population of Athens by a large, economic line, but it also sets Solon in the middle, separate from his fellow citizens economically and ideologically.[33] This solitary, heroic stance also appears in Solon's poetry, and it has virtually been uncontested.[34]

The moderation of the sage pokes through into the political as the account progresses. While archon, Solon left good laws alone, changing only those that needed to be in a political display of μηδὲν ἄγαν (nothing too much). This suggests a good deal of self-control on Solon's part, and it obscures the issue of who decided which laws needed to be fixed, why, and who (actually) benefited. Once appointed 'straightener of the constitution and lawgiver' (τῆς πολιτείας διορθωτὴς καὶ νομοθέτης [16.5]), Solon then set out to "fix" Athenian society, allegedly by curbing the excesses of the rich. The laws that Plutarch quotes as proof, however, say no such thing, with the possible exception of the dowry law. Yet the reading of Solon's reforms as benefiting the *dēmos* or poor more than the rich and/or aristocrats is the most resilient of the traditions. This is despite the organization of the *telē* on the basis of wealth requirements, which favoured those with property and possibly non-landed wealth.[35] Like-

---

[33] On Solon's separation from the Athenian population, see, for example, Harris (2006) 297–298; Raaflaub (2006) 414; Moore (1983) 215; Manville (1990) 125–126; Anhalt (1993); Irwin (2005) 207–210. See Noussia-Fantuzzi (2010) 5 *contra*. Stehle (2006) and Irwin (2006) attribute the separation to a fourth-century composition date and to engagement with rhetorical discourses respectively. As they also note, this disassociation on the poet's part is a rhetorical strategy. It therefore need not correlate to circumstances outside of the poetry.

[34] So, for example, Bowie (1986) 20 argues that fr. 4c is Solon's quotation of the two quarrelling sides, and not his own stance (cf. Plut. *Sol.* 14 and Stehle [2006] 88–89), and Bannert (2005) 8 states that '*Solon war niemals ein Parteimann*'. See n. 12 above on Solon's middling persona in his poems.

[35] The *telē* are generally understood to cover landed and non-landed income; for an argument *contra*, see Stanley (1999) 120 and van Wees (2006) 364. Traditionally, the *zeugitai* are considered to be 'non-elite' along with the *thētes*. Van Wees (2006), however, argues that the *zeugitai* were considered amongst the elite. Rhodes, commenting on the *telē*, states that 'it is embarrassing that the qualifications stated for *hippeis* and *zeugitai* would probably make the three highest classes a small, élite minority within the citizen body' ([2006]

wise, Solon's position as a mediator is always a concession of the rich to the poor, never vice versa.[36]

Plutarch includes in his discussion of the reforms (17–25.1) an aside on the moral impetus behind some of them:[37] the law against abstaining from factions, for example, derives from his desire that all citizens concern themselves with the *polis*, and thereby lead an active life (20.1). This aside, odd as it may seem, fits both the pedagogical agenda of the *Lives* and reinforces the importance of the sage character for the readers' understanding of the politician. "Solon the Sage" returns as Plutarch narrates Solon's travels (26–28), complete with the visit to Croesus, where an admonitory encounter with Aesop enhances the heroic tenor of Solon's advice to the Lydian king. The poet-politician then returns to Athens where, despite his best attempts, Pisistratus assumes the tyranny (29–30). Solon then retreats into private study, upon which the *Solon* ends with his death.

In addition to the *Solon*, the poet-politician appears in Plutarch's *Moralia*, but the "Solon" that emerges from the biography is the most influential. The other "Solons" are similar, but significantly different in certain respects. The staunch "anti-tyrant Solon" from the *Solon*, for example, is challenged by the "Solon" in the *Dinner of the Seven Sages*, who, despite relating all of the questions posed to him to democracy, maintains possession of the "democratic" wine cup which grants its holder the right to speak (ἀλλ' οὐδὲ τοῦτ' ... τὸ ποτήριον δημοτικόν ἐστι· Σόλωνι γὰρ ἔκπαλαι παράκειται μόνῳ [155f]). We might see, and remember, this as a questioning of Solon's reputed democratic conscience, or his even-handedness.[38]

If we follow the narrative suggested by the *Solon*, we have a Solon who acts alone, despite the relatively large body of comparative evidence that archaic politics revolved around aristocratic sociopolitical blocks commonly called *hetaireiai*.[39] Athens during the seventh and sixth centuries was not an atyp-

---

253). Rhodes' comment betrays the notion that Solon's reforms, regardless of his ambivalence to the non-governing members of Athens in his extant poems, must have aimed at increasing the number of politically efficacious citizens, as argued by Plutarch and the *Ath. Pol.* Such a view of the situation would make the *telē* 'embarrassing', but we need not take it this way.

36 Among other, Ellis and Stanton (1968) 99 (even though they question this logic); Anhalt (1993) 1; Rose (2012) 335.

37 Russell notes that legislation serves as evidence for the moral qualities of the lawgivers in Plutarch ([1973] 116).

38 Irwin (2005) 259 sees this as evidence of Solon's play with tyrannical discourses within his poetry; cf. Irwin (2005) 205–261; Irwin (2006) esp. 72–75; Sagsestter (2013).

39 Mytilene is probably the best example for the archaic period; Caciagli (2011) discusses

ical *polis*;⁴⁰ it seems to have followed similar patterns of intra-elite conflict amongst *hetaireiai* resolved by a tyranny which led, one way or another, to a wider political base. Classical Athens' uniqueness in relation to the rest of the mainland *poleis* has, however, been retrojected to the sixth century, which also impacts on the contextualization of Solon's poetry and politics. This is helped by Plutarch's narrative, the consequence of which is a continued insistence on Solon's visionary and individual actions, pulling him away from his fellow members of the elite and fellow elegists.⁴¹ As the other elegists of the early archaic period are being returned to their social contexts from the progressive narratives into which they had been schematically placed, Solon remains apart, and his poetry is still seen as addressed to a civic community in defence of the poor.⁴²

The *Solon* partners the *Publicola*, the biography of Publius Valerius, a Roman statesman whose fame and honorary name, Publicola (Caretaker of the People), come from his actions during and following the expulsion of the Tarquinii from Rome. Plutarch states that 'it was clear straightaway that, should Rome become a democracy, Publicola would be first' (δῆλος ἦν εὐθύς, εἰ γένοιτο δημοκρατία, πρωτεύσων [*Publicola* 1.2]). This teleological opening should put us on guard, for both lives; it invites reflection whether the Rome of Publicola and the Athens of Solon were democracies, and if so, how much so (compare the use of πρωτεύσων). Like Solon, Publicola in Plutarch's account always puts the interests of Rome before his own, even to the detriment of his own political advancement, and he too demonstrates an affinity for managing the strife between the "rich" and the "poor". His political acumen is matched by his moderation, like Solon's, and, as Plutarch notes in the *synkrisis*, Publicola's death at the height of his political career and popularity demonstrates the validity

---

Mytilenian *hetaireiai* alongside Sappho's and Alcaeus' poetry. Herodotus records aristocratic factional struggles around Cypselus' rise to power in Corinth which can likely be attributed to agitation amongst *hetaireiai* against the ruling Bacchiadai (Hdt 5.92β1-ε2), and the *stasis* amongst Pesistratus, Megacles, and Lycurgus in post-Solonian Athens also likely involved *hetaireiai*. It will be argued further below that Solon operated in this political context as well.

40   Hall (2007) 230–233.
41   For instance, Podlecki (1969) 79; Ehrenberg (1996) 1, 62–70; Almedia (2003) 238; Irwin (2006) 74; Anhalt (1993) 1–2. Concerning Solon's stance apart from his contemporary poets, see Irwin (2005, 2006) and Anhalt (1993).
42   For instance, Ellis and Stanton (1968) 99; Podlecki (1969) 81; Anhalt (1993); Noussia (1999) 71; Balot (2001) 74, 82; Almeida (2003); Irwin (2005) 87; Stehle (2006) 102 (though concerning the "real" Solon and not the fourth-century persona); Morris (1996, 2000); Kurke (1999). See Osborne (1996) 219 and Tedeschi (1991) *contra*.

of Solon's admonition to Croesus concerning happiness (*Comparatio Solonis et Publicolae* 1.1–3). Publicola is proof of Solon's famous advice, and between the two, young men have an example of how to acquire such happiness through service to the state.

The *Solon-Publicola* does not include a prologue, but it does have a *synkrisis*, which begins with the interesting supposition of: 'is there not something peculiar to this *synkrisis* and is it not somewhat out of step with any other of the *Lives* already written, that the one imitated the other and that the one was a witness (for the other)?' (ἆρ' οὖν ἴδιον τι περὶ ταύτην τὴν σύγκρισιν ὑπάρχει καὶ μὴ πάνυ συμβεβηκὸς ἕτερα τῶν ἀναγεγραμμένων, τὸν ἕτερον μιμητὴν γεγονέναι ἑτέρου, τὸν ἕτερον δὲ μάρτυν [*Comparatio Solonis et Publicolae* 1.1]). I have purposely repeated Plutarch's vague language here because I would like to note the rhetorical play: who imitates whom and who bears witness for whom? Chronologically, the answer is that Publicola imitated Solon and that Solon bore witness for Publicola, and Plutarch does explain his cryptic statement in these terms. Yet do we need to answer this question in this manner? For Plutarch's Roman, and possibly even non-Athenian, audience, the relationship may well have been the reverse. I would submit that Plutarch demonstrates an awareness of a problem inherent in comparison of ancient figures: his, and our, reception of them. How much of Plutarch's and the reader's understanding of Publicola derives from the comparison with Solon, and vice versa? The pairing of lives allows for comparisons and themes to resound over the geographical and temporal distances between the two men, but it also forces them. It is likely that the *Publicola* has not influenced our reading of the *Solon*, but did have some impact on the *writing* of the latter life, and this may be acknowledged in Plutarch's musing quoted above.

The *synkriseis* are Plutarch's opportunity to display his rhetorical and literary ingenuity through a seemingly straight-forward comparison of the paired lives. Their ethical character-focus reveals what is to be taken away from the paired biographies by the reader;[43] in this instance, the duty of a "leading man" to serve and benefit the state is stressed. Neither politician is actually "democratic" in Plutarch's narrative. Rather, they demonstrate how best to handle the entirety of the citizen population so as to benefit the state most by managing the non-elite population and its potential for disrupting the running of the state. Furthermore, they do not bend their values, regardless of any temptation concerning power and wealth. That is where their importance for Plutarch and his pedagogical programme lies.

---

43   Duff (1999) 256.

Plutarch's *Solon*, and the "Solons" before it, have constructed a tradition that ensconces the extant verses of Solon's poetry, presenting us with narrative frames that impact on our reception and interpretation of the fragments and their poet. This tradition constructs a poet-politician who heroically stands in-between two warring factions, trying to accommodate both while protecting the interests of Athens. Originally "Solon" was a (proto-)democrat, and while he is no longer viewed as such, the democratic tradition around him and his poetry still holds strong concerning his motivations and actions, as well as his visionary individualism in sixth-century Athens. The consequences of this are that we take Solon's words and intentions more or less at face value, while we are more than willing to question those of his contemporaries and of his political predecessors and descendants. For the remainder of the chapter, I will present a reading of Solon's poetry that seeks to destabilize this tradition, contextualizing the fragments in the setting of archaic politics as seen in the Greek *poleis* as a whole.

4   Re-reading Solon and His Poetry

Solon's poetry is vague concerning the players and political groups that appear within its lines.[44] The groups he names include the *astoi* (citizens), the *dēmos*, and the leaders of the *dēmos* (ἡγεμόνες τοῦ δήμου [fr. 4.3]), as well as the *agathoi*, *esthloi*, *kakoi*, and 'those notable in power and wealth' (οἳ δ' εἶχον δύναμιν καὶ χρήμασιν ἦσαν ἀγητοί [fr. 5.3]).[45] None of these groups have any further elaboration in the extant lines about who might be amongst their number. If we consider the narratives of early archaic Athens, however, we can determine some of the major players during the late-seventh and early-sixth centuries. Before Solon's archonship there would have been Cylon and his supporters, the Alcmaeonidae and their supporters, other opponents of Cylon, and then, following Cylon's

---

44   I accept a sixth-century date and Solon's authorship; see Stehle (2006) and Lardinois (2006) for alternatives.

45   Van Wees argues that Solon knew only two social groups: the *dēmos* and the 'leaders of the *dēmos*' ([2006] 351). Yet even within fr. 4 there are likely more than two groups; the *astoi* and *dēmos* may not be the same group (the former restricted to Athens perhaps, the latter encompassing all of Attica), and the 'enemies' who consume the *polis* in private gatherings may encompass a larger group than the 'leaders of the *dēmos*' but a smaller set than the *astoi*. That Solon only knew the two groups named by van Wees follows the narrative of Athenian society provided by Plutarch and the *Ath. Pol.*: two warring groups with Solon, independent and in the middle.

fall, the opponents of the Alcmaeonidae who succeeded in exiling them. Draco would have had supporters and opponents. Following Draco's appointment, these blocks would have included supporters of the Alcmaeonidae, since they were able to return to Athens in time for Pisistratus, Solon and his supporters, and Solon's opponents (cf. fr. 33), who may or may not have consisted of several blocks. Once Solon established his laws and left, there then were the three major power blocks which followed Pisistratus, Megacles, and Lycurgus. Additionally, there would have been varying amounts of class conflict amongst large-landowners, small-landowners, and *thētes*. Factional politics did not end with Solon, nor, I would argue, did he manage to establish himself well enough to be appointed as first archon and then as lawgiver without participating in them.[46]

Fragments 15 and 4c are often presented as evidence for Solon's middle economic and/or ideological status. For both fragments, this can be attributed to the narrative frames provided by Plutarch and the *Athēnaiōn Politeia* which surround the quotations.

πολλοὶ γὰρ πλουτοῦσι κακοί, ἀγαθοὶ δὲ πένονται·
ἀλλ' ἡμεῖς αὐτοῖς[47] οὐ διαμειψόμεθα
τῆς ἀρετῆς τὸν πλοῦτον· ἐπεὶ τὸ μὲν ἔμπεδόν ἐστιν,
χρήματα δ' ἀνθρώπων ἄλλοτε ἄλλος ἔχει.

For many *kakoi* are rich, while many *agathoi* are poor; but we will not exchange wealth for *aretē* with those men; the latter is secure, but one man, then another, holds property

SOLON, fr. 15

ὑμεῖς δ' ἡσυχάσαντες ἐνὶ φρεσὶ καρτερὸν ἦτορ,
οἳ πολλῶν ἀγαθῶν ἐς κόρον [ἠ]λάσατε,
ἐν μετρίοισι τίθεσθε μέγαν νόον· οὔτε γὰρ ἡμεῖς
πεισόμεθ', οὔθ' ὑμῖν ἄρτια τα[ῦ]τ' ἔσεται.

---

46   Cf. Stehle (2006) 102: 'Solon ... must have had allies.'
47   I maintain the αὐτοῖς in v. 2, as do Gentili and Prato fr. 6 [= fr. 15 West], where West has τούτοις (following Thgn. 315–318). West's emendation divides the four groups into two, where the *agathoi*/"we" opposes the *kakoi*/οὗτοι. The importance in this version is the refusal to betray *aretē* for money; we do not know if the "we" are poor, just that they are a part of the *agathoi* group; 'many' are poor, not all. Again, this refusal to trade *aretē* for money asserts a moral and possibly class superiority where social terms do not map onto economic statuses equally but rather rely on the respective valuation of *aretē*.

> You there, calm the strong heart in your breast, you who have reached the limit of good things, and set your great mind into moderation. For we will not suffer for it,[48] and these things will not be sufficient for you
> SOLON, fr. 4c

Plutarch introduces fragment 15 as evidence that Solon may have been fond of luxury, since he was a merchant, but still considered himself as one of the poor (*Solon* 3.2). For fragment 4c, the *Athēnaiōn Politeia* asserts that the lines bear evidence of the claim that Solon was 'by nature and reputation one of the leading men (τῶν πρώτων) but in terms of property and deeds one of the *mesoi* (τῶν μέσων)' (5.3). Fragment 4c, however, does not bear evidence of an economic middle for Solon,[49] though it does follow a discourse of moderation common in archaic lyric (ἐν μετρίοισι [4c.3]), and the lack of a referent for the opening ὑμεῖς makes it difficult to ascertain whether or not it is, as the *Athēnaiōn Politeia* claims, 'the rich' (οἱ πλούσιοι).[50] For Plutarch, the terms *agathos* and *kakos* are ethical terms, referring to a man's moral character with a small nod, if any, to economic status.[51] Solon's refusal to trade his *aretē*, despite apparent poverty, is one of the first examples in the *Solon* of the moderation and wisdom that will reappear throughout the life. He knows that *aretē* is more stable and more

---

48 πείσομαι can be the future middle of either πείθω (persuade; *med.* obey) or πάσχω (experience, have happen to one; suffer) and is mostly commonly translated as the future middle of πείθω: 'for we will not obey/ comply' (e.g., the translations in Gerber [1999] 119, Irwin [2005] 106, and Owens [2010] 161). There is nothing, however, to suggest forced compliance to the whims of the rich; for such a context, we must go to the familiar narrative of rich versus poor. If, however, we understand πεισόμεθ' in line 4 as belonging to πάσχω, then our range of interpretation broadens. It does not excise the possibility of an economic conflict between rich and poor (cf. Moore's translation in [1983] 160), but importantly it does not restrict us to such a reading. The ὑμεῖς can be a large group, such as "the rich" or the *dēmos*, a rival *hetaireia*, or a section of Solon's sympotic group or followers who have crossed the party line of moderation. Cf. Stehle's translation of the poem ([2006] 89).

49 See also Noussia (1999) 109.

50 And even then, are they "the rich" in general, or a select segment? Again, we do not know *whose* greed and arrogance Solon referred to as the cause of rebuke in the fragment. This leads to the larger issue of ascribing the 'unprincipled quest for wealth' (Forsdyke [2006] 337) solely at the feet of the rich. Neither Theognis nor Solon, the most cited authors on this issue, give economic or even specific group names; rather, they use general social terms, if at all, which can refer to a range of contested economic and social statuses. Ascribing such behaviour to "the rich" restricts us: why can the *dēmos* not be grasping, or the moderately well-off, as their more wealthy fellow citizens can be?

51 This can be seen in the translation of fr. 15.1 provided by the Loeb translation of the *Solon*: 'For often evil men are rich, and good men poor' (*Sol.* 3, translated by Perrin [1967]).

valuable, and so he does not squander what he has. Yet while *agathos* and *kakos* were ethical terms for Plutarch, they were social terms in the sixth century. Furthermore, just as fragment 4c does not establish Solon definitively as an economic *mesotēs*, so too fragment 15 does not put Solon in the group of poor *agathoi*: he merely comments on their existence.

The issue of mental capacity or a fit mind (*noos*, νόος) and the ability to moderate one's appetite(s) reappears throughout Solon's extant corpus, as well as those of other lyric poets (for instance, Theognis 28–38, 153–154; Alcaeus 129; cf. Xenophanes 1, 3). In fragment 6 the *dēmos* have an insufficient *noos* for handling *koros* (sufficiency; excess), while in fragment 4 it is the 'leaders of the *dēmos*' and possibly the *astoi*,[52] and in fragment 4c, as seen above, it is the unnamed ὑμεῖς. The actions of the greedy citizens in fragment 34 reveal their faulty *noos*, as they thought that Solon had a harsh one (τραχὺν ... νόον [34.3]). Likewise, the *persona loquens* of fragment 33, who is not Solon but one of his critics, shows his poor *noos* through his desire for power and his mockery of Solon's moderation. This consistency across Solon's extant poetry and the placement of *noos* and moderation within the context of the political situation in Athens suggests a sort of political platform for Solon: he and his supporters have the necessary *noos* and corresponding ability to restrain their consumption that will save Athens from the (alleged) greed of the current leaders.[53] This linking of one's *noos* with the ability to moderate appetite is not new, nor is the connection amongst *noos*, appetite, and political legitimacy (cf. the suitors in the *Odyssey* and Pittacus [Alcaeus 70, 129]); Solon's consistency in making these

---

52 Lines 5–8 in fr. 4 consist of a double subject of the *astoi* and the unjust mind of the leaders of the *dēmos* (αὐτοί ... ἀστοί ... δήμου θ' ἡγεμόνων ἄδικος νόος [5–7]) who pose a threat to the well-being of the *polis* in line 1. This is followed by another couplet stating that 'they do not know how to restrain *koros*' (οὐ γὰρ ἐπίστανται κατέχειν κόρον [9]) with an unstated third-person plural subject. This subject may just be the leaders of the *dēmos* or it may be the entirety of the double subject from the preceding clause; as there is a lacuna following lines 9–10 which may have clarified the subject, it is difficult to tell.

53 This is not to say that the power blocks governing Athens at the time, or fighting to do so, were not greedy, but rather to remind us that we only have Solon's word about what happened. How different would the picture of contemporary American politics be, for example, if all that future historians had of Barack Obama's presidency were his 2008 campaign speeches and later, favourable accounts of his presidency? Lacking the material from the McCain-Palin and Romney-Ryan campaigns and Obama's opponents amongst the lobbyists and private citizens, we may well end up with the story of a great politician who rose above the factionalism of American politics to effect a policy of change that responded to the needs of the greater American populace while still respecting the role of corporations and wealthy Americans, as the speeches of his first campaign promised.

connections, however, is striking, as is the number of times he raises the issue of noetic ability as it pertains to moderating one's appetite and political behaviour.

As I noted above, it is unlikely that Solon became archon and then 'straightener of the constitution' without political supporters, and due to his prominence in the historical record for the period, it is likely that he was the head of his *hetaireia*. Gottesman argues that it is to such an audience that fragment 11 was delivered.[54] Plutarch (*Solon* 30.8), Diodorus (9.20), and Diogenes Laertius (1.51) preserve the fragment and attribute it to Solon's rebuke of the *dēmos* after Pisistratus became tyrant. Gottesman, however, notes the incongruity of τούτους ('those men') in line 2 for this reading and argues that line 5 ('each one of you walks in the tracks of a fox' [ὑμέων δ' εἷς μὲν ἕκαστος ἀλώπεκος ἴχνεσι βαίνει]) refers not to Pisistratus, but to a gnomic formulation for losing one's bearings, 'to listen to words but to ignore deeds'.[55] Fragment 4 is also likely addressed to a group of *hetairoi* as seen in the opening of ἡμετέρη δὲ πόλις (*Our polis* [4.1]).[56] The difference between the model of a *hetaireia* as we see in Solon's poetry and the perhaps more familiar model as seen in Alcaeus' is that in the case of the latter, the "we" of the group is more important than the "I" of the speaker or individual, in spite of the fact that the "we" is continually being shaped by individuals. In Alcaeus' poetry, the individual political actor is dangerous, whether it is Pittacus (frr. 70, 129) or the unnamed fox of fragment 69 (compare fr. 72).[57] For Solon, however, the "we" of a *hetaireia* exists to support his "I". In fragment 4, the opening "we" in ἡμετέρη δὲ πόλις becomes the "I" of Solon (θυμὸς ... με κελεύει [v. 30]) as the audience becomes the medium through which Solon's lesson concerning Eunomia reaches the Athenians and the means of substantiating the validity of this message. The use of the first-person plural in fragments 4c and 15 directly includes the audience of the fragments in the ethical worldview of the speaker as the pronoun associates the audience with the speaker's "I".[58] While we remember Alcaeus of all his nameless *hetairoi*, his "I" is not asser-

---

54 Gottesman (2005) 415; cf. Bowie (1986) 20.
55 Gottesman (2005) 414. On the inconsistency and cunning of foxes, see the proscriptions against fox hunting in Xenophon (*Cyn.* 5.4, 6.3) and Semonides' complaints concerning the fox-woman (fr. 7.7–11).
56 Argued by Romney (2015) 139–161.
57 The related danger of being an exile without a group can be seen in fr. 130b. Groups are positive in Alcaeus' poetry, whether it be a group of political actors at home or in exile.
58 The first-person plural pronoun has 'associative semantics', which condenses the distance between speaker and addressee(s); on which, see Wechsler (2010) 333. Thus, even if the first-person plural in frr. 4, 4c, and 15 is a poetic plural (I/mine instead of we/our), this associative force would have been felt, particularly due to the close setting of the *sympo-*

ted at the expense of the group;[59] Solon, however, does assert his opinions and his "I", while maintaining the balance needed for the group to continue to operate effectively.

Returning to fragment 15, then, I would like to finish with a brief reappraisal, set within the performance context of the archaic *symposion* and the political context of *hetaireiai*.[60] 'Many *kakoi* are rich, and many *agathoi* are poor' (v. 1) could, as Plutarch has read it, be an ethical statement, so that, if we were to translate the terms *kakoi* and *agathoi*, it would read: 'many base men are rich, and many good men are poor'. In such a formulation, ethical character does not correlate directly to economic status, nor should such a correlation be sought, for that would mean exchanging *aretē*, the virtue at the heart of an individual's ethical *agathos* status, for wealth (cf. vv. 2–3). Plutarch's pedagogical agenda insists on this reading so that the young men who form the target audience of his *Lives* will not assume that wealth is the same as moral character nor value the latter over the former. For sixth-century audiences, however, these four lines operate within the fraught social concepts around the terms *agathos, kakos*, and *aretē*. In such a context, *agathos* referred to not just "good character" but, more importantly, "good birth", which had also been accompanied by a secure economic status. The problem in the sixth century, as Theognis complains, is that the formulation of *agathos* as nobly born, of good character, and wealthy no longer applied in all cases, especially when it came to money. Men of *kakos* social status were becoming wealthy, even wealthy enough to claim *agathos* status, and be accepted as such (cf. Thgn. 53–68, 183–192).[61] In this context, the opening line would read as 'Many non-aristocrats are rich, and many aristocrats are poor' as economic well-being no longer correlates directly to birth and social status in all cases.

---

    sion and to the speaking stance, which purports to address a third party. As the audience receive the poem, they notionally give the address with the poet.

59 On Alcaeus and his group, see Rösler (1980).

60 For Solon's sympotic performances, see Tedeschi (1991) for fr. 4 and Noussia-Fantuzzi (2010) 49 in general. Mülke (2002) 97–99 discusses both public and sympotic performance contexts, but remains agnostic as to which is more likely. For a general argument against public performance, Bowie (1986) 19–21.

61 Duplouy ([2006] esp. 23–24, 30) and Węcowski ([2014] 19–26) argue that elite status in the archaic period was performative; for an archaic elite to be accepted as such by his community (Duplouy) and his peers (Węcowski), he had to be seen as living as such. This allowed for permeable social boundaries as changing economic statuses allowed individuals to move up and down while stability at the top of the *agathos* group allowed them in turn to continue dictating what it meant to live as an *agathos*.

The first line of fragment 15 reads as a gnomic statement, as do the last line and a half. The emphasis, then, is on the assertion that 'we/I will not exchange wealth for *aretē* with those men' (vv. 2–3). The ἡμεῖς can either be read as a true plural, associating audience with speaker and subordinating them to his value scheme, or as a poetic plural referring to the speaker alone. If it is the latter, we have an assertion of individual moral steadfastness: Solon will not trade his *aretē* for wealth, whatever others are doing. This may be a critique of poor *agathoi* who decide to "settle" in order to recuperate lost fortunes, who would appear through the αὐτοῖς of line 2, which can refer to either group or both, as the pronoun does not connote distance. If the ἡμεῖς is a genuine plural, then Solon sets his group against the αὐτοῖς in a contest of morals that separates his we-group from both the rich *kakoi* and the poor *agathoi*, who together form the referent for αὐτοῖς. Solon's ἡμεῖς do not need to trade either money or *aretē* because they have both in sufficient quantities and feel no need to trade one to increase the other. The ἡμεῖς are set apart from the other groups, and this isolation of the speaker's group compares nicely with the isolation of the 'we' group in fragment 4. Looking beyond Solon's poetry, we see that Alcaeus also uses the strategy of portraying the speaker and audience as politically detached from society or other political groups (e.g., frr. 6, 70, 129). While traditionally such a stance has been ascribed to a dislike of an increasingly vocal *dēmos*, this detachment defines a political group in sharp relief against other groups and forces the *hetairoi* to look inwards, strengthening the cohesion of the group. In the case of Solon 4 and 15, this process occurs due to the disparity in size between the speaker's group (small, if we accept a sympotic performance and thus audience group) and those it is separated from—in fragment 4 it is the *astoi* and the leaders of the *dēmos*, while in fragment 15 it is 'many' of the *kakoi* and 'many' of the *agathoi* who together make up 'many' of the people of Athens. Fragment 4c may also use this strategy, though without knowing who the ὑμεῖς are, it is difficult to tell. While the ὑμεῖς are usually read as a group of wealthy individuals or "the rich" as a whole following the narrative frame provided by the *Athēnaiōn Politeia*,[62] there is, in fact, nothing to say that the ὑμεῖς does not refer to the *dēmos* (cf. fr. 37) or a rival political/sympotic group.

Fragment 15, then, does not, as Plutarch would have it, declare Solon's economic status and his unwillingness to gain wealth through morally dubious measures like trading one's *aretē*. Rather, it is yet another fragment supporting the platform of moderation that Solon crafts in his poetry. By stating that 'many' of the *kakoi* are rich and 'many' of the *agathoi* poor, he excludes himself

---

[62] E.g., Owens (2010) 161; Irwin (2005) 109n60.

and his audience from both of those groups: the majority of the population may have switched their economic status, but Solon and his supporters have not, and they feel no need to increase their fortunes. His/their preference for *aretē* demonstrates that they, unlike the ὑμεῖς in fragment 4c, know when they have reached the limit of *koros*. Fragment 15, along with fragments 4, 4c, 6, 33, and 34, can be thought of as a campaign ad, crafting the *persona* of Solon the moderate politician and arguing for his ability to govern Athens along with his supporters.

5   Conclusion

Solon's integral place in Athenian political history does not necessitate that we take his words at face value. Scholars attach to him a high level of patriotism, and this reading does follow what he himself says. But the poems are skilfully crafted political rhetoric,[63] and one must wonder what makes Solon's rhetoric more genuine than Alcaeus', for example. Alcaeus rails against tyranny and depicts it as harmful to the *dēmos* and *polis*; Solon does much the same, though without the Mytilenean poet's venom. Alcaeus swears to rescue the *dēmos* from its woes, namely Pittacus' tyranny; Solon claims that he protected the *dēmos* from the excesses of an unnamed sector of society and the potential tyranny of a less scrupulous man. Why then do Alcaeus' words 'suggest the hollowness of a quickly learned catchphrase',[64] but not Solon's?

The Solonian biographical tradition looms large not only in our reception of Solon but also in our interpretation of his verses. The fifth and fourth centuries, along with Plutarch's *Solon*, strongly influence our reading of this poet. This chapter has sought to destabilize that tradition by presenting some alternatives to its narrative of Solon, his poetry, and political actions. Plutarch's *Lives* provide information on ancient figures that we would not otherwise have, and they are an important source for us. Yet they are skilfully crafted exercises in rhetorical and moral education, designed to provide *exempla* and comparative material to the edification of Plutarch's young, elite audience. This underlying agenda should be taken into consideration when the *Lives* are used to contextualize Solon's poetry, and other figures as well. The same should be done for the different "Solons" that we saw in the survey at the beginning of the paper: Herodotus' wise advisor and travelling sage

---

[63] Yet, as Noussia notes, 'There is still no widespread recognition of the rhetorical dimension of Solon's poetry' ([2006] 134 with bibliography).

[64] Argued by Irwin (2005) 240n103 in her comparison of the two.

becomes Plato's philosopher and authority on Atlantis, the champion of the *dēmos* for Aristotle, and founder of the *patrios politeia* for both the oligarchs of 411 and the democrats of 403. Solon's rhetoric was vague and designed to include whomever was in the audience, whether his contemporary or years later, and this adaptability has facilitated the reception of his verses as democratic, especially after they were adopted by the restored democracy of 403. Solon is like the Theognidean octopus (213–218), changing colours to suit his surroundings and to persuade his audiences that he is one of them. To see beyond his colour changes, then, it is necessary to take him out of his familiar settings and narratives, set him in less familiar contexts, and watch what happens.

References

Almeida, J.A. 2003. *Justice as an Aspect of the Polis Idea in Solon's Political Poems: A Reading of the Fragments in Light of the Researches of New Classical Archaeology*. Leiden.

Anhalt, E.K. 1993. *Solon the Singer: Politics and Poetics*. Lanham.

Balot, R.K. 2001. *Greed and Injustice in Classical Athens*. Princeton.

Bannert, H. 2005. Strategien politischer Propaganda: Solons Dichtung als Wahlwerbung—ein Lektürevorschlag. *Wiener Humanistische Blätter* 47: 5–27.

Blok, J.H. and Lardinois, A.P.M.H., eds. 2006. *Solon of Athens: New Historical and Philological Approaches*. Leiden.

Bowie, E.L. 1986. Early Greek Elegy, Symposium and Public Festival. *JHS* 106: 12–35.

Caciagli, S. 2011. *Poeti e Società: Communicazione poetica e formazioni sociali nella lesbo del VII/VI secolo a.C*. Amsterdam.

de Blois, L. 2006. Plutarch's Solon: A Tissue of Commonplaces or a Historical Account? In Blok and Lardinois 2006: 429–440.

Duff, T.E. 1999. *Plutarch's Lives: Exploring Virtue and Vice*. Oxford.

Duff, T.E. 2011. Plutarch's *Lives* and the Critical Reader. In *Virtues for the People: Aspects of Plutarchean Ethics*, ed. G. Roskam and L. Van der Stockt, 59–82. Leuven.

Duplouy, A. 2006. *Le Prestige des Élites: Recherches sur les modes de reconnaissance sociale en Grèce entre les Xe et Ve siècles avant J.-C*. Paris.

Ehrenberg, V. 1996. *From Solon to Socrates: Greek History and Civilisation during the 6th and 5th Centuries BC*. London.

Ellis, J.R. and Stanton, G.R. 1968. Factional Conflict and Solon's Reforms. *Phoenix* 22: 95–110.

Flores, S. 2013. The Roles of Solon in Plato's Dialogues. PhD diss., Ohio State University.

Forrest, W.G. 1966. *The Emergence of Greek Democracy: The Character of Greek Politics, 800–400 BC*. London.

Forsdyke, S. 2006. Land, Labour, and Economy in Solonian Athens: Breaking the Impasse between Archaeology and History. In Blok and Lardinois 2006: 334–350.

Gehrke, H.-J. 2006. The Figure of Solon in the *Athênaiôn Politeia*. In Blok and Lardinois 2006: 276–289.

Gentili, B. and Prato, C. 1988. *Poetarum elegiacorum testimonia et fragmenta*. Leipzig.

Gerber, D.E. 1999. *Greek Elegiac Poetry: From the Seventh to the Fifth Centuries BC*. Cambridge, MA.

Gottesman, A. 2005. Two Notes on Solon Fr. 11W. *Mnemosyne* 58: 412–415.

Hall, J.M. 2007. *A History of the Archaic Greek World, ca. 1200–479 BCE*. Oxford.

Harding, P. 2008. *The Story of Athens: The Fragments of the Local Chronicles of Attika*. London.

Harris, E.M. 2006. Solon and the Spirit of the Laws in Archaic and Classical Greece. In Blok and Lardinois 2006: 290–318.

Hendrickson, T. 2013. Poetry and Biography in the *Athēnaiōn Politeia*: The Case of Solon. *CJ* 109: 1–19.

Irwin, E. 2005. *Solon and Early Greek Poetry: The Politics of Exhortation*. Cambridge.

Irwin, E. 2006. The Transgressive Elegy of Solon? In Blok and Lardinois 2006: 36–78.

Jacoby, F. 1949. *Atthis: The Local Chronicles of Ancient Athens*. Oxford.

Kurke, L. 1999. *Coins, Bodies, Games and Gold: The Politics of Meaning in Archaic Greece*. Princeton.

Lamberton, R. 2001. *Plutarch*. New Haven.

Lardinois, A.P.M.H. 2006. Have We Solon's Verses? In Blok and Lardinois 2006: 15–35.

Lavelle, B.M. 2005. *Fame, Money, and Power: The Rise of Peisistratos and "Democratic" Tyranny at Athens*. Ann Arbor.

Lewis, J.D. 2006. *Solon the Thinker: Political Thought in Archaic Athens*. London.

Manville, P.B. 1990. *The Origins of Citizenship in Ancient Athens*. Princeton.

Martin, R.P. 2006. Solon in No Man's Land. In Blok and Lardinois 2006: 157–172.

Moore, J.M. 1983. *Aristotle and Xenophon on Democracy and Oligarchy*. Berkeley.

Morris, I. 1987. *Burial and Ancient Society: The Rise of the Greek City-State*. Cambridge.

Morris, I. 1996. The Strong Principle of Equality and the Archaic Origins of Greek Democracy. In *Demokratia: A Conversation on Democracies, Ancient and Modern*, ed. J. Ober and C. Hedrick, 19–48. Princeton.

Mossé, C. 2004 [1979]. How a Political Myth Takes Shape: Solon, "Founding Father" of the Athenian Democracy. In *Athenian Democracy*, ed. P.J. Rhodes, 242–259. Edinburgh.

Mülke, C. 2002. *Solons politische Elegien und Iamben (Fr. 1–13; 32–37 West): Einleitung, Text, Übersetzung, Kommentar*. Munich.

Nagy, G. and Noussia-Fantuzzi, M., eds. 2015. *Solon in the Making: The Early Reception in the Fifth and Fourth Centuries*. Berlin.

Noussia, M. 1999. A Commentary on Solon's Poems. PhD diss., University College London.
Noussia-Fantuzzi, M. 2010. *Solon the Athenian, the Poetic Fragments*. Leiden.
Osborne, R. 1996. *Greece in the Making: 1200–479 BC*. London.
Owens, R. 2010. *Solon of Athens: Poet, Philosopher, Soldier, Statesman*. Brighton.
Pelling, C. 2002. *Plutarch and History*. London.
Perrin, B. 1967. *Plutarch's Lives*, vol. 1: Theseus and Romulus; Lycurgus and Numa; Solon and Publicola. Cambridge, MA.
Podlecki, A.J. 1969. Three Greek Soldier Poets: Archilochus, Alcaeus, Solon. *CW* 63: 73–81
Raaflaub, K.A. 2006. Athenian and Sparta *Eunomia*, or: What to do with Solon's Timocracy? In Blok and Lardinois 2006: 390–428.
Rhodes, P.J. 1981. *A Commentary on the Aristotelian* Athenaion Politeia. Oxford.
Rhodes, P.J. 2006. The Reforms and Laws of Solon: An Optimistic View. In Blok and Lardinois 2006: 248–260.
Romney, J.M. 2015. Group Identity, Rhetoric, and Discourse in Early Greek Poetry. PhD diss., University of Bristol.
Rose, P. 2012. *Class in Archaic Greece*. Cambridge.
Rösler, W. 1980. *Dichter und Gruppe: Eine Untersuchung zu den Bedingungen und zur historischen Funktion früher griechischer Lyrik am Beispiel Alkaios*. Munich.
Russell, D.A. 1973. *Plutarch*. London.
Sagsetter, K. 2013. Solon of Athens: The Man, the Myth, the Tyrant? PhD diss., University of Pennsylvania.
Scott-Kilvert, I. 1973. *Plutarch: The Rise and Fall of Athens: Nine Greek Lives*. London.
Sealey, R. 1960. Regionalism in Archaic Athens. *Historia* 9: 150–180.
Shapiro, S.O. 1996. Herodotus and Solon. *ClAnt* 15: 348–364.
Stanley, P.V. 1999. *The Economic Reforms of Solon*. St. Katharinen.
Stanton, G.R. 1990. *Athenian Politics c. 800–500 BC: A Sourcebook*. London.
Stehle, E. 2006. Solon's Self-Reflexive Political Persona and its Audience. In Blok and Lardinois 2006: 79–113.
Tedeschi, G. 1991. Solone e lo Spazio della Comunicazione elegiaca. In *OINHPA TEYXH: Studi Triestini di Poesia Conviviale*, ed. K. Fabian, E. Pellizer, and G. Tedeschi, 105–117. Alessandri.
van Wees, H. 2006. Mass and Elite in Solon's Athens: The Property Classes Revisited. In Blok and Lardinois 2006: 351–389.
Wallace, R.W. 1997. Solonian Democracy. In *Democracy 2500? Questions and Challenges*, ed. K.A. Raaflaub and I. Morris, 11–29. Dubuque.
Wechsler, S. 2010. What "You" and "I" Mean to Each Other: Person Indexicals, Self-Ascription, and Theory of Mind. *Language* 86: 332–365
Węcowski, M. 2014. *The Rise of the Greek Aristocratic Banquet*. Oxford.

CHAPTER 17

Strategies of Quoting Solon's Poetry in Plutarch's *Life of Solon*

Jacqueline Klooster

1   Introduction*

Plutarch's *Life of Solon* is one of our principal providers of bibliographical data for Solon but also the source of the majority of the fragments of his poetry.[1] This makes it an interesting showcase for the ways in which archaic lyric poetry such as that of Solon was transmitted. How, where, and for what reasons does Plutarch quote Solon's poetry in his biography? This is the main question I will be trying to answer in my contribution.

The *Solon* was written approximately seven to eight centuries after the time Solon lived. Plutarch refers to numerous historical sources for information on his life and it is also clear that he had access to texts of the Solonian laws and collections or anthologies of poetry attributed to him,[2] even if we cannot say with much confidence what these may have looked like. Out of all these sources Plutarch creates an image of Solon that is recognizably "Plutarchan": as de Blois has argued, Plutarch regards Solon as a sage, but perhaps not of the first order, as for instance Lycurgus.[3] It is particularly the way Plut-

---

* This chapter has benefited from the suggestions of the audience at the Reading Conference on the Reception of Archaic Lyric. In addition, I would like to thank the editors and the anonymous readers for their many useful suggestions, which made me rethink my argument. A version of this paper was presented to the members of the Amsterdam Hellenistenclub, whose comments also improved it. I would like to thank in particular Marietje Van Erp Taalman Kip and Bas van der Mije for their written remarks.
1 The other important sources for Solon's life are, chronologically, Herodotus, [Aristotle's] *Athenaion Politeia*, (on the authorship of this work, see Rhodes [1981]), Diodorus Siculus, and Diogenes Laertius. The other major source for Solon's poetry is Demosthenes 19. All testimonia concerning Solon can be found in Martina (1968).
2 Androtion, Aristotle, Daimachus of Plataea, Demetrius of Phalerum, Didymus Grammaticus, Aeschines, Heracleides Ponticus, Hereas of Megara, Hermippus, Phanias of Eresus, Plato, Polyzelus of Rhodes, Theophrastus, and finally the Delphian Archives. See Von der Mühl, (1942) 89–102 and Flacelière (1961) 5.
3 On the image of Solon in this biography, see especially de Blois (2006) 429–440.

arch uses Solon's poetry to argue for certain character traits of his biographical subject that interests me.[4] The observation that he reads the poetry in a biographical mode is of course not new; what I wish to establish, rather, is whether his strategies in selecting and interpreting the poetical fragments conform to a recognizable pattern. I will therefore confront Plutarch's treatment of Solon's poetry in the *Life* and in selected passages from the *Moralia* with his own remarks in his treatise usually known under the Latin title *Quomodo adolescens poetas audire debeat* (*How To Study Poetry*; *Moralia* 14–37).

The relation between Solon's poetic testimonials and the *political* side of his biography has received ample scholarly attention,[5] and I will not be going into this here in detail. Rather, I will concentrate on Solon's personal life as represented by Plutarch, in particular his financial circumstances and his love interests as far as these are reflected in his poetry.[6]

2   Plutarch's Selection of Poetic Fragments in the *Solon*

To begin with, what rationale lies behind Plutarch's selection method in the *Solon* is a relevant question: what did he include, what did he leave out, and why? Plutarch says little about it, and owing to the fragmentary status of Solon's works and the lack of information about their transmission up to Plutarch's time, we can only form an incomplete idea of the original collection(s) he may have been quoting from.[7] Nor do we know what collections or anthologies of Solon's poetry Plutarch's readers themselves would have been familiar enough with to notice his choices. A later example of the type of imprecise and somewhat garbled information we have on Solon's oeuvre, is provided by Diogenes Laertius 1.61:

---

4   I will henceforth use the shorthand "Solon's poetry" although I am of course aware of the debates about its authenticity. On this topic, see Massaracchia (1958); Stehle (2006) 108–110; Lardinois (2006) 16; Noussia-Fantuzzi (2010) 45–65. It is important for my argument that Plutarch in any case held that this poetry was authentically Solonian.
5   On the issue of Solon's poetry being mined for confirmation of his political actions, see Lefkowitz (1981) 40–48; Irwin (2006) 13–30; Hendrickson (2013) 1–19.
6   See Hertzoff (2008) 339–369 on how the presentation of these two issues is connected to the way Solon's political stance is represented by Plutarch.
7   See Russell (1973) 42–62 on Plutarch's knowledge of Greek literature and his use of anthologies. A compendium of Plutarch's quotations is provided in Helmbold and O'Neil (1959). On Plutarch's quotation of elegiac and iambic poetry, see Bowie (1997) 99–108.

Γέγραφε δὲ δῆλον μὲν ὅτι τοὺς νόμους, καὶ δημηγορίας καὶ εἰς ἑαυτὸν ὑποθήκας, ἐλεγεῖα, καὶ τὰ περὶ Σαλαμῖνος καὶ τῆς Ἀθηναίων πολιτείας ἔπη πεντακισχίλια, καὶ ἰάμβους καὶ ἐπῳδούς.

He is undoubtedly the author of the laws which bear his name; of public addresses and counsels addressed to himself in elegiac metre, and the writings, on Salamis and on the Athenian constitution, five thousand lines in all, not to mention poems in iambic metre and epodes.[8]

Some interesting observations about Plutarch's selection methods can nevertheless be made.[9] Depending on numbering, we have forty-six poetical fragments,[10] twenty-one of which are cited (sometimes exclusively) by Plutarch in his *Vita*. In other writings, Plutarch cites Solon another nine times (two citations do not overlap with the *Vita*).[11] If we classify all extant fragments of Solon according to topic, a large number directly refer to his political activities (17) while an almost equally large number refer to ethical issues ('wisdom poetry', c. 14). A third group appears to refer to biographical facts like journeys or family members (3), and some fragments defy classification.[12]

In the *Solon*, eleven of the twenty-one fragments cited concern Solon's political measures. Six further fragments concern wisdom poetry (one about erotic/symposiastic behaviour, the rest about wealth), and three pertain to biographical facts. It will not surprise anyone that the fragments classified here as "wisdom poetry" are interpreted by Plutarch as personal statements, for instance the so-called *Hymn to the Muses* (fr. 13, cited in *Solon* 2.3), from which he cites an attitude towards money. This type of biographical reading was common practice in antiquity, and is made easier in Solon's case by the fact that poetic statements concerning ethical insights are mainly phrased as first-person expressions; they may well represent the εἰς ἑαυτὸν ὑποθῆκαι Diogenes mentions.[13]

---

8   Translation Hicks, adapted. The *Suda* more or less concurs, although without furnishing information about numbers of lines.
9   Information based on West's 1992 edition.
10 West (1992) counts forty-six fragments, Noussia-Fantuzzi (who bases herself on Gentili and Prato) forty, but the total amount of lines remains the same.
11 Of the twenty-one fragments Plutarch cites, six also occur in Aristotle's *Ath. Pol.*, and *Ath. Pol.* also contains fragments that Plutarch does not cite.
12 Political: frr. 1–11, 31–34, 36, 37; wisdom: 12–18, 20, 21, 23–27; biographical: 19, 22, 28; 'defying categorization': 29, 30, 35, 38–46.
13 Cf. Lefkowitz (1981) 7–11.

To conclude, all these "biographical fragments" and a substantial part of Solon's "wisdom poetry" (interpreted as personal utterances) can be found in Plutarch's *Solon*; a fact that reveals Plutarch's strong interest in Solon's personality. This in turn chimes well with Plutarch's well-known statement at the opening of the *Parallel Lives of Alexander and Caesar* (1.1–1.3) to the effect that it is not necessarily in great deeds that the stamp of character is revealed, but rather in jests or characteristic sayings: he clearly took Solon's poetry at face value as personal expressions. As I shall discuss in detail below, it is also highly significant that Plutarch thrice refers to frivolous, erotic, or symposiastic verses that might conceivably shed a negative light on Solon's character and way of life, but does *not* quote them (*Solon* 1.3; 3.1; 3.3).

3 Plutarch's Moral Project

Plutarch's explicit project, in his biographies and his *Moralia*, is the moral improvement of his audience. In the *Pericles*-prologue (1.4) for instance, he states that virtue elicits imitation. If he describes virtuous men, it is with the aim of inviting such imitation from his audience.[14] This is also the reason why he abhors 'malicious' historians, such as Herodotus (compare *de malignitate Herodoti*), who report 'the worse version' of events when a more edifying one is also available.[15] Plutarch's interest in poetry too is concerned with its potential moral and educational dangers and benefits, especially for young readers. In this he is very much a Platonist, albeit a pragmatic one.[16] This philosophical inclination in matters of literature finds its expression in the treatise *Quomodo adolescens*. The essay is dedicated to Plutarch's friend Marcus Sedatus, who has a son the same age as Plutarch's own son—but the applicability of the advice is meant to be wider. The treatise is, as F.C. Babbitt aptly phrases it:

> concerned with poetry only as a means of training the young in preparation for the study of philosophy later. This training is to be imparted
> (1) *not by confining the reading to selected passages* (15a–e)
> (2) but by teaching the young to recognize and ignore *the false and the fabulous* in poetry (16a; 25a–c)

---

14   Cf. Duff (1999) 42: 'This will be achieved, [Plutarch] says, not only by imitating the virtuous deeds he reads about, but also by *historia*, that is by his [own] narrative, his research, and by the reader's diligent attention and thought.'
15   Cf. Russell (1973) 61; Duff (1999) 58.
16   See Van der Stockt (1992) on Plutarch's attitude toward poetry. On *Quomodo adolescens* ..., see in particular Hunter and Russell (2011).

(3) to choose always *the better interpretation* (17; 23)
(4) in immoral passages where art is employed for art's sake, *not to be deluded into approving vicious sentiments because of their artistic presentation* (27f)
(5) such passages may be *offset by other passages from the same author or from another author* (20c; 35f; 36d)
(6) as a last resort, one may try one's hand at *emending unsavoury lines* to make them conform to a higher ethical standard (33e).[17]

Modern reaction to this treatise has often been derisive; especially with regard to the desperate measure Plutarch proposes last, emendation of poetry to suit one's didactic interests. But what I wish to establish here is whether its underlying philosophical stance can shed any light on the way Plutarch quotes Solon's poetry in the *Solon*.

It seems attractive to assume that Plutarch's specific (moralistically tinged) ideas about poetry are reflected implicitly in his *Vitae Parallelae*, and thus provide us with some information on what Plutarch thinks about the place of poetry in the life of the wise man and the politician, in this case, of Solon. Of course, Solon is exceptional in that he unites sage, poet, and statesman in one figure, which makes him unique in the *Vitae*. In his essay on Plutarch's opinion on the role of poetry and music in the life of Plutarch's statesman, Ewen Bowie concludes: 'Poetry ... is an inevitable component of literary culture, but it must be approached circumspectly. On the other hand, the composition of poetry seems to cause Plutarch little discomfort' ([2004] 123). Although broadly agreeing with this finding, I will suggest that things may in fact be more nuanced with regard to the *composition* of poetry in the *Solon*, which is considered problematic in some cases.

4   Dangers and Strategies

In *Quomodo adolescens*, Plutarch worries foremost about the possible detrimental effects of mimetic (i.e. narrative or dramatic) poetry, in particular the convincing representation of the false and the fabulous. In 16a–b, he in fact quotes the maxim attributed to Solon elsewhere that poets tell many lying tales

---

[17] Babbitt, introduction to Loeb edition originally 1927; reprint (1986) 72–73, my emphasis, numbering, and addition of passage numbers from Loeb edition. Cf. Hunter and Russell (2011), introduction.

(fr. 29) to underscore this worry.[18] In accordance with the negative attitude this adage seems to express towards such poetry, Solon's own poetry, or at least what we have of it now, is not mimetic in the sense of narrative or drama, nor does it contain the false and the fabulous. Indeed, what we have is notable for its complete lack of this: Solon tells no mythical tales,[19] and hardly ever has recourse to imagery from this sphere, although he does use some striking metaphors.[20] He is of course not unique among archaic elegists in this sense, even if there is limited but documented use of elegy for mythical narration.[21] In any case, there could be no worries on this count regarding Solon's poetry, for Plutarch.

Nevertheless, in his *Quomodo adolescens* Plutarch also cites examples of harmful sentiments in non-mimetic passages, for instance from Pindar (*Quomodo* 21a 3–8). He demonstrates how these may be countered by more acceptable lines from the same poet, as follows:

καὶ τοῦ Πινδάρου σφόδρα πικρῶς καὶ παροξυντικῶς εἰρηκότος
   χρὴ δὲ πᾶν ἔρδοντ' ἀμαυρῶσαι τὸν ἐχθρόν,
ἀλλ' αὐτός γε σὺ λέγεις ὅτι
   τὸ πὰρ δίκαν
   γλυκὺ πικροτάτα μένει τελευτά ...

And when Pindar very harshly and provocatively has said 'Do what you will so you vanquish your foe' [*Isthmian* 4.48], we may reply, but you yourself say 'A most bitter end must surely await sweet joys that are gained by an unfair means' [*Isthm.* 7.47].[22]

Here the moral turpitude of the sentiment of the first Pindaric verses lies clearly in its callousness; it is contradicted by citing Pindar again, now stating that all bad actions must have bad endings. Something similar happens with a verse by

---

18   It must be noted however that Plutarch does not identify the statement as Solonian. The connection with Solon is furnished in the scholium to Ps-Plato περὶ δικαίου 374a. (p. 402 Greene), where it is claimed that Solon mentioned it in his elegies. It may therefore have been an originally anonymous adage that was used by Solon.
19   He is supposed to have started writing a poem on Atlantis, cf. Plato *Tim.* 21c ff.; Plut. *Vit. Sol.* 31.3 ff. but never finished it; this might have been mimetic, of course, but it is entirely hypothetical. Indeed, modern scholarship does not give much credence to the idea that Solon brought the story of Atlantis to Athens, cf. Gill (1977) 287–304.
20   Cf. Martin (2006) 163; Noussia-Fantuzzi (2010) 67–69.
21   Bowie (1986) 13–35.
22   All translations for *Quomodo adolescens* ... and the poetry there quoted are adaptations from Babbitt.

Theognis (*Quomodo* 22a 4–9), although in this case another author is brought in to contradict the wrong sentiment. Theognis' lines to the effect that the poor man, due to his social inferiority, is helpless and unable to express his thoughts, are quoted with the repartee of the Cynic philosopher Bion of Borysthenes, who says 'How is it then, that you, who are poor, can talk much nonsense, and weary us with this rubbish?' (πῶς οὖν σὺ πένης ὢν φλυαρεῖς τοσαῦτα καὶ καταδολεσχεῖς ἡμῶν;). Here Plutarch objects to Theognis' misleading notion that lack of wealth forms a bar to freedom of speech.[23] This undermining idea is wittily contradicted by turning it against Theognis himself.[24]

Such morally unsound notions are dangerous, then, even when found in non-narrative and non-dramatic poetry, including, we may suppose, that of Solon, if it should voice "bad" sentiments: it is the artistic presentation, and the authority of the poet that make them so (cf. 27f). The embedding in mimetic poetry only makes these sentiments more treacherous because of the psychological identification such poetry additionally invites, as Plato had already warned (*Republic* 596a).

Besides contradicting detrimental sentiments in poetry by quotation of an apt poetic refutation by the same author or another one, Plutarch also argues that some poetic passages may seem morally flawed, while in reality they only need "correct interpretation" (23a–f). The examples he furnishes all concern the representation of gods. The (Platonic) idea underlying this reasoning is clearly that the gods are inherently good, and hence that poetic passages suggesting they are evil cannot form the basis for a sound moral education of young pupils. What is needed, then, is the correct reading of the poet's *ennoia* (conception). To explain his point, Plutarch cites two passages from Archilochus naming Hephaestus. In the first instance, a prayer, *the god himself* is meant:

κλῦθ' ἄναξ Ἥφαιστε καί μοι σύμμαχος γουνουμένῳ
ἵλαος γενοῦ, χαρίζευ δ' οἷάπερ χαρίζεαι,

Hear my prayer, O Lord Hephaestus, and be my propitious supporter as I kneel to you, and bestow what your mercy bestows.
    fr. 108

---

23   Cf. Hunter and Russell (2011) 123.
24   It may be noted that a Solonian instance of this practice is in fact provided in the *comp. Sol. et Publ.* 1.5, where Solon contradicts Mimnermus about the age one should long to reach (possibly from the same poem as fr. 20).

In the second, where the poet speaks of the body of his dead brother-in-law, "Hephaestus" stands metonymically for "fire".

> εἰ κείνου κεφαλὴν καὶ χαρίεντα μέλεα
> Ἥφαιστος καθαροῖσιν ἐν εἵμασιν ἀμφεπονήθη

> If upon his head and his beautiful body, in garments clean, Hephaestus had done his office.
> fr. 9.10–11

Once this has been set out, Plutarch continues to explain that especially in the case of Zeus one should interpret carefully. "Zeus" sometimes metonymically denotes fate; one should however not mix up the Father of Gods and Men with destiny (*heimarmenē*) in all cases, since this would lead to the morally objectionable situation that the poet apparently thinks that "Zeus" causes evil for mankind (τὸν θεὸν ὁ ποιητὴς οἴεται κακὰ μηχανᾶσθαι τοῖς ἀνθρώποις). This is, for instance, what the opening of the *Iliad* suggests, when incorrectly understood.

> πολλὰς δ' ἰφθίμους ψυχὰς Ἄϊδι προΐαψεν
>   ἡρώων, αὐτοὺς δὲ ἑλώρια τεῦχε κύνεσσι
> οἰωνοῖσί τε δαῖτα, Διὸς δ' ἐτελείετο βουλή

> Many valiant souls it sent to the realm of Hades, heroes, and their bodies gave to the dogs as quarry and to birds a feast—the will of Zeus was accomplished.
> *Iliad* 1.3–5

In reality, so Plutarch argues, Homer here quite rightly demonstrates the workings of "necessity" underlying the events (τὴν τῶν πραγμάτων ἀνάγκην ὀρθῶς ὑποδείκνυσιν). He is not speaking about the divinity in his benign and just guise of Father of Gods and Men. Finally, as we saw, Plutarch proposes the simple, if to modern eyes rather drastic, solution of emending a verse by replacing the offending words in order to make the poetic phrase say something that is morally correct, and edifying (33d–e).[25] After citing some precedents of this practice, Plutarch asks:

---

25 We might note that Solon himself in fr. 20 explicitly "corrects" Mimnermus who had expressed in poetry the wish to die at sixty, as Diogenes Laertius 1.60 relates.

τί δὴ κωλύει καὶ ἡμᾶς ταῖς τοιαύταις ὑποφωνήσεσι τοὺς νέους παρακαλεῖν πρὸς τὸ βέλτιον, οὕτω πως χρωμένους τοῖς λεγομένοις;
    τόδ᾽ ἐστὶ τὸ ζηλωτὸν ἀνθρώποις, ὅτῳ
    τόξον μερίμνης εἰς ὃ βούλεται πέσῃ.
οὔκ, ἀλλ᾽
                                ὅτῳ
    τόξον μερίμνης εἰς ὃ συμφέρει πέσῃ.
τὸ γὰρ ἃ μὴ δεῖ βουλόμενον λαμβάνειν καὶ τυγχάνειν οἰκτρόν ἐστι καὶ ἄζηλον.

What, then, is to hinder us also from encouraging the young to take the better course by means of similar rejoinders, dealing with the citations like this:
    'most enviable is the lot of him the shaft of whose desire hits what he wishes for'. [*TrGF* Adesp. 354]
'No', we will say, 'but rather ...
    ... the shaft of whose desire hits what benefits him'.
For to gain and achieve one's wish, if what one wishes is not right, is pitiable and unenviable.

Here it is the simple replacement of a single verb that sanitizes the poetic phrase, restricting and qualifying its meaning in a morally uplifting way (based on the insight that what a person desires is not necessarily good for him).

5 Solon and Money

We have now briefly seen how Plutarch proposes to make the reading of poetry a viable, and indeed profitable, practice for young men, a propaedeutic to the study of philosophy. In the following I will look at some salient passages in the *Solon*, which, as I argue, surprisingly accurately illustrate these strategies in practice. We must keep in mind that Plutarch wishes to write a life from which a moral may be drawn. This, I would argue, explains his wish to contravene any negative ideas that might arise from Solon's poetry. So it is not in the first place to rehabilitate Solon, but perhaps rather to furnish the right moral example that he applies the strategies discussed above with regard to Solon's writings.

First I will look at some longer passages considering Solon's wealth. In chapter 2, Plutarch seems bothered by the economic status of Solon, and especially his activity as a merchant.[26] The unspoken premise seems to be that to

---

26 Russell (1973) 55 notes that Plutarch is always interested in the wealth of his heroes.

the educated gentleman of Plutarch's circle this is an inferior pursuit connoting both greed and an absence of hereditary lands. Besides, it might seem hard to reconcile with Solon's status of sage and statesman. Plutarch uses an array of arguments to explain this incongruence away. Or, perhaps it is better to say that, while he is not actually 'defending' Solon, it seems clear in any case that Plutarch wants his audience to understand that living the mercantile life is not among Solon's traits that should elicit admiration or indeed imitation.

In the first place, he refers to information taken from the biographer Hermippus (*FHG* III 38), to imply that Solon's motivation was a laudable pride: Solon's modestly wealthy but aristocratic father had given away a large part of his estate,[27] and not wishing to depend on charity himself, Solon chose to become a merchant. Not content to let it rest at this, Plutarch then adduces 'sources' (φασὶν ἔνιοι) and quotations from Solon's own poetry to vouch for Solon's philosophical nature, in order to prove that Solon simply took pleasure in travelling for the sake of knowledge and moreover understood that wealth was not a good in itself (2.1–2.6):

> καίτοι φασὶν ἔνιοι πολυπειρίας ἕνεκα μᾶλλον καὶ ἱστορίας ἢ χρηματισμοῦ πλανηθῆναι τὸν Σόλωνα. σοφίας μὲν γὰρ ἦν ὁμολογουμένως ἐραστής, ὅς γε καὶ πρεσβύτερος ὢν ἔλεγε (fr. 18) 'γηράσκειν αἰεὶ πολλὰ διδασκόμενος'· πλοῦτον δ' οὐκ ἐθαύμαζεν, ἀλλὰ καὶ φησιν ὁμοίως πλουτεῖν ᾧ τε (fr. 24.1–6)
>
>> πολὺς ἄργυρός ἐστι
>> καὶ χρυσὸς καὶ γῆς πυροφόρου πεδία
>> ἵπποι θ' ἡμίονοί τε, καὶ ᾧ μόνα ταῦτα πάρεστι
>> γαστρί τε καὶ πλευρῇ καὶ ποσὶν ἁβρὰ παθεῖν,
>> παιδός τ' ἠδὲ γυναικός, ἐπὴν καὶ ταῦτ' ἀφίκηται,
>> ἥβῃ, σὺν δ' ὥρῃ γίνεται ἁρμόδια.
>
> ἀλλ' ἑτέρωθι λέγει (fr. 13.7–8)
>
>> χρήματα δ' ἱμείρω μὲν ἔχειν, ἀδίκως δὲ πεπᾶσθαι
>> οὐκ ἐθέλω· πάντως ὕστερον ἦλθε δίκη.
>
> κωλύει δ' οὐδὲν τὸν ἀγαθὸν καὶ πολιτικὸν ἄνδρα, μήτε τῶν περιττῶν τὴν κτῆσιν ἐν σπουδῇ τινι τίθεσθαι, μήτε τῆς χρείας τῶν ἀναγκαίων καὶ ἱκανῶν καταφρονεῖν.

And yet some say that he travelled to get experience and learning rather than to make money. For he was indeed a lover of wisdom, since even when he was well on in years he would say that he 'grew old ever learn-

---

27   Execestides, descended from King Codrus, according to the majority, cf. *Vit. Sol.*1.

ing many things'; and he was no admirer of wealth, but actually says that two men are alike wealthy of whom one 'has much silver and gold and wide domains of wheat-bearing soil, horses and mules; while the other possesses only enough to give him the comfort of food, and clothes and shoes, the youthful age of a child and wife, and all fitting things in their season'.

However, in another place he says:
'Wealth I desire to have; but to obtain it wrongfully, I do not wish. Justice, even if slow, is sure'.

And there is no reason why a good statesman should either set his heart too much on the acquisition of superfluous wealth or despise unduly the use of what is necessary or convenient.[28]

In other words, Solon is argued to have had an ethically correct as well as common-sense approach to wealth. As regards the two poetic fragments concerned with money (fr. 24 and 13), they in reality probably both exemplify the attitude towards wealth to be encouraged in Athenian citizens, and they might even be linked with Solon's *seisachtheia*-reforms.[29] The sequence forms an example of how Plutarch attempts to contradict what he regards as morally damaging traditions about Solon by selecting quotations from the latter's own poetry.

A related technique is also used: immediately afterwards, Plutarch tries to make yet another point about Solon's mercantile activities by quoting *another author* completely out of context, namely Hesiod (2.6):

ἐν δὲ τοῖς τότε χρόνοις καθ' Ἡσίοδον 'ἔργον οὐδὲν ἦν ὄνειδος' οὐδὲ τέχνη διαβολὴν ἔφερεν, ἐμπορία δὲ καὶ δόξαν εἶχεν, οἰκειουμένη τὰ βαρβαρικὰ καὶ προξενοῦσα φιλίας βασιλέων καὶ πραγμάτων ἐμπείρους ποιοῦσα πολλῶν.

In those earlier times, in the words of Hesiod 'work was no disgrace' [*Erga* 311], nor did a trade bring with it social inferiority, and the calling of a merchant was actually held in honour, since it gave familiarity with foreign parts, friendships with foreign kings and a large experience in affairs.[30]

---

28   All translations of *Solon* are adapted from Bernadotte Perrin.
29   See e.g. Mülke (2002) ad loc.
30   Of course, this is a completely random quote from Hesiod's *Erga*. Lines 678–694 in fact express Hesiod's dislike of the seafaring merchant life. It is moreover worthy of note that the quote is garbled. The actual line reads: ἔργον δ' οὐδὲν ὄνειδος, ἀεργίη δέ τ' ὄνειδος.

There follows a list of philosophers and sages who likewise engaged in trade ventures, including Thales and Plato.

All of this is already somewhat reminiscent of Plutarch's strategy with regard to damaging sentiments in poetry in the *Quomodo adolescens* as set out above, with the difference of course that it is here *historical traditions* that are being contradicted, not, at least in the first instance, poetry. Nevertheless, as we shall presently see, there was also Solonian poetry that described Solon's attitude as a merchant; this was apparently considered dangerous by Plutarch. This poetry is discussed in the subsequent paragraph of the *Solon* (3.1–3.2), and so the excuses made in 2.1–8 seem to be meant to defuse the damage of that poetry in advance.

6 What Plutarch Does Not Quote

So what was this poetry by Solon that Plutarch refrained from citing? As suggested above, we find a first indication that some of it was related to Solon's mercantile attitude towards luxury (3.1–3.2):

> Τὸ δ' οὖν εὐδάπανον τῷ Σόλωνι καὶ ὑγρὸν πρὸς τὴν δίαιταν καὶ τὸ φορτικώτερον ἢ φιλοσοφώτερον ἐν τοῖς ποιήμασι διαλέγεσθαι περὶ τῶν ἡδονῶν τὸν ἐμπορικὸν οἴονται βίον προστετρίφθαι· πολλοὺς γὰρ ἔχοντα κινδύνους καὶ μεγάλους ἀνταπαιτεῖν πάλιν εὐπαθείας τινὰς καὶ ἀπολαύσεις. ὅτι δ' ἑαυτὸν ἐν τῇ τῶν πενήτων μερίδι μᾶλλον ἢ τῇ τῶν πλουσίων ἔταττε, δῆλόν ἐστιν ἐκ τούτων (fr. 15)·
> πολλοὶ γὰρ πλουτοῦσι κακοί, ἀγαθοὶ δὲ πένονται·
> ἀλλ' ἡμεῖς αὐτοῖς οὐ διαμειψόμεθα
> τῆς ἀρετῆς τὸν πλοῦτον· ἐπεὶ τὸ μὲν ἔμπεδόν ἐστιν,
> χρήματα δ' ἀνθρώπων ἄλλοτε ἄλλος ἔχει.

Accordingly, if Solon's way of living was expensive and profuse, and if, in his poems, he speaks of pleasure more in a vulgar than in a philosophical way, this is thought to be due to his mercantile life; he encountered many and great dangers, and sought his reward for them in all sorts of luxuries and enjoyments. But that he classed himself among the poor rather than the rich, is clear from these verses: 'For often evil men are rich and good men poor; but we will not exchange with them our virtue for their wealth, since one abides always, while riches change their owners every day'.

What Plutarch is here doing is again comparable to what he propounds in *Quomodo adolescens*, but we might say, even more thoroughly. Not only does he contradict "bad sentiments" to be allegedly found in Solon's poetry with more creditable ones, he even refrains from quoting the bad ones at all, presumably on the reasoning that the less quoted, the better. Simultaneously he gives a possible extenuating explanation for these sentiments, all in one go.

The above passage bleeds into yet another set of excuses for the nature of some of Solon's poetry, namely his youth. Plutarch states that Solon was not serious about poetry at first, and became so only later in life, when he started using his poetry as a medium to express his political thought and support his actions (3.3–4):

τῇ δὲ ποιήσει κατ' ἀρχὰς μὲν εἰς οὐδὲν ἄξιον σπουδῆς, ἀλλὰ παίζων ἔοικε προσχρήσασθαι καὶ τέρπων ἑαυτὸν ἐν τῷ σχολάζειν· ὕστερον δὲ καὶ γνώμας ἐνέτεινε φιλοσόφους, καὶ τῶν πολιτικῶν πολλὰ συγκατέπλεκε τοῖς ποιήμασιν, οὐχ ἱστορίας ἕνεκεν καὶ μνήμης, ἀλλ' ἀπολογισμοὺς τῶν πεπραγμένων ἔχοντα καὶ προτροπὰς ἐνιαχοῦ καὶ νουθεσίας καὶ ἐπιπλήξεις πρὸς τοὺς Ἀθηναίους.

> And [Solon] seems to have composed his poetry at first with no serious end in view, but as amusement and diversion in his hours of leisure. Then, later, he put philosophic maxims into verse, and interwove many political teachings in his poems, not for the sake of historical record or remembrance, but because they contained justifications of his acts and sometimes exhortations, admonitions, and rebukes for the Athenians.

Solon initially composes poetry for his own amusement (παίζων), as his unserious choice of subject matter must have betrayed (cf. above). But he later comes round to the important and correct insight that actual wisdom might, or indeed should, be incorporated into the poetry. Solon therefore versifies his judgements. An intriguing remark addressing Solon's motivation for the writing of this political and wisdom poetry is οὐχ ἱστορίας ἕνεκεν καὶ μνήμης ('not for the sake of historical record or remembrance'). This asseveration seems to have been inserted to prevent Plutarch's contemporaries from getting the wrong idea, presumably because (political) poetry was used in such different contexts in their own day and age. Solon did not write in order to glorify and preserve remembrance of his actions—even if his biographers do of course use his poetry for precisely that purpose. Rather, as Plutarch claims, Solon wished to benefit his fellow-citizens, and he thus furnished poetic explanations for his deeds, as well as exhortations, admonitions, and rebukes.

7 Solon in Love

There is yet another passage that implies that some of Solon's youthful poetry was excessively concerned with the pleasures of life. The instance occurs in connection with Solon's alleged love for beautiful young men, among whom, according to some informants, Pisistratus, the later tyrant, should also be reckoned (1.3):

> ὅτι δὲ πρὸς τοὺς καλοὺς οὐκ ἦν ἐχυρὸς ὁ Σόλων οὐδ' ἔρωτι θαρραλέος ἀνταναστῆναι 'πύκτης ὅπως ἐς χεῖρας' ἔκ τε τῶν ποιημάτων αὐτοῦ λαβεῖν ἔστι …

> That [Solon] could not control himself in the presence of beautiful young men and did not boldly oppose desire 'as a boxer in the fistfight' (Soph. *Trach*. 441) can be gathered from his poetry …

We may note once more the laudable sentiment expressed in the Sophoclean quote exemplifying, in passing, the right stance towards such temptations. The context in which this reference to erotic poetry is placed again elaborately attempts to contravene the potential wrong impressions such poetry might give readers of Solon by all sorts of means. Right before the passage quoted, mention is made of Solon's alleged passionate love affair with the young Pisistratus, which is interpreted as turning into a "Platonic" friendship that enabled the two, despite their political differences, to remain on good terms later on.[31] Directly afterwards, Plutarch relates that Solon passed a law that forbade slaves to anoint themselves in the gymnasia, or to have love affairs.[32] This was presumably meant to ensure that pederasty would remain an aristocratic privilege, and to prevent slaves from gaining access to privileged circles through erotic affairs. The implication may be that Solon's erotic desire for young men, which was apparently expressed in his poetry, did not negatively interfere with his political persona, but rather found a way of enhancing his political power. On the one hand, it enabled Solon to stay on good terms with Pisistratus; on the other, it made him realize the social dangers of giving homoerotic desires a loose hand, and hence made him draft fitting legislation on that score.[33]

---

31 *Sol*. 1.5–6 ἀλλὰ παρέμεινεν ἐκεῖνα τὰ δίκαια ταῖς ψυχαῖς καὶ παρεφύλαξε 'τυφόμενα Δίου πυρὸς ἔτι ζῶσαν φλόγα' (Eur. *Bacch*. 8), τὴν ἐρωτικὴν μνήμην καὶ χάριν. ('But their former mutual affection lingered in their spirits, and preserved there, "smoldering with a lingering flame of Zeus-sent fire" the grateful memory of their love.')
32 *Sol*. 1.6.4–1.7.1.
33 On Solon's balance between Eros and moderation as represented in the *Solon*, cf. Hertzoff (2008) 339–369.

8 The Right Explanation

Finally, there is a potentially disreputable Solonian distich concerning the pleasures of love and conviviality that Plutarch does cite, and in fact no less than three times, in the *Solon*, in the *Septem sapientium conuiuium*, and in the *Amatorius*, a philosophical dialogue about the nature of love. The three passages are held together by interesting connections. In all three passages the distich is explicitly linked to old age, and in both the *Conuiuium* and the *Vita* it is interpreted, in line with Plutarch's own ideas about the aims of the genteel symposium,[34] as describing the educated man's correct way of spending his leisure (31.3).

> ... ἐξέκαμεν, οὐ δι' ἀσχολίας, ὡς Πλάτων φησίν, ἀλλὰ μᾶλλον ὑπὸ γήρως, φοβηθεὶς τὸ μέγεθος τῆς γραφῆς. ἐπεὶ σχολῆς γε περιουσίαν αὐτοῦ μηνύουσιν αἱ τοιαῦται φωναί·
> γηράσκω δ' αἰεὶ πολλὰ διδασκόμενος (fr. 18),
> καὶ
> ἔργα δὲ Κυπρογενοῦς νῦν μοι φίλα καὶ Διονύσου
> καὶ Μουσέων, ἃ τίθησ' ἀνδράσιν εὐφροσύνας. (fr. 26)·

> ... He abandoned it [a poem about Atlantis], not for lack of leisure, as Plato says,[35] but rather because of his old age, fearing the magnitude of the task. For that he had abundant leisure, such verses as these testify: 'I grow old ever learning many things' and again,
> 'But now the works of the Cyprus-born goddess are dear to my soul, of Dionysus too, and the Muses, which impart delights to men.'[36]

The Plutarchan context here links the convivial distich (where love, wine and the pleasure of *mousikē* are aligned as symbols of the good life) with a lifelong striving for gaining knowledge. It is noteworthy that fragment 18 (about Solon's lifelong learning) was quoted by Plutarch in the beginning of the biography as well, in the context of Solon's occupation as a merchant. This suggests that Plutarch felt that Solon's love of learning, and his philosophical tendencies, as expressed in this line, could or should excuse and explain a lot of his activities that might otherwise seem blameworthy, and furnish a positive example for young readers.

---

34 Cf. *Qu. Conuiu.* proems and esp. 612d, 621c, 716f; Stadter (2014) 98–107; 108–115.
35 Plat. *Tim.* 21c.
36 =*Amatorius* 751e (156b) and *Septem sapientium convivium* 403a.

In the *Amatorius*, on the other hand, the distich fr. 26 is quoted to contrast with one of Solon's allegedly youthful and even more racy poems, in order to illustrate the right moments in the life of a man for pederasty (youth) and heterosexual love (advanced age).

> 'εὖ γε νὴ Δί,' ἔφη, 'τοῦ Σόλωνος ἐμνήσθης καὶ χρηστέον αὐτῷ γνώμονι τοῦ ἐρωτικοῦ ἀνδρός·
> "ἔσθ' ἥβης ἐρατοῖσιν ἐπ' ἄνθεσι παιδοφιλήσῃ
> μηρῶν (ἱμείρων) καὶ γλυκεροῦ στόματος" (fr. 25).
> Σόλων ἐκεῖνα μὲν ἔγραψε νέος ὢν ἔτι καὶ "σπέρματος πολλοῦ μεστός," ὥς ὁ Πλάτων φησί· ταυτὶ δὲ πρεσβύτης γενόμενος (fr. 26)·
> "ἔργα δὲ Κυπρογενοῦς νῦν μοι φίλα καὶ Διονύσου
> καὶ Μουσέων, ἃ τίθησ' ἀνδράσιν εὐφροσύνας",
> ὥσπερ ἐκ ζάλης καὶ χειμῶνος [καὶ] τῶν παιδικῶν ἐρώτων ἔν τινι γαλήνῃ τῇ περὶ γάμον καὶ φιλοσοφίαν θέμενος.' (751c–f)

'Thanks for citing Solon,' he said; 'he is also useful for his opinion on the lover:
> "until he has loved a lad in the flower of youth desiring thighs and a sweet mouth"

(…) those verses I quoted were written by Solon when he was still quite young and "teeming" as Plato says, "with seed". [*Laws* 8.839b] Here, however, is what he wrote when he had reached an advanced age:
> "But now the works of the Cyprus-born goddess are dear to my soul, of Dionysus too, and the Muses, which impart delights to men."

as though after the pelting storm of his love for boys he had chosen his harbour in the peaceful sea of marriage and philosophy.'[37]

In this case Plutarch (speaking in the voice of Daphnaeus) once again offsets a potentially harmful sentiment (unrestrained homoerotic desire) found in Solon's poetry with another one that is understood to be morally sound (the affections found in conjugal life), cf. *Quomodo adolescens* 20c; 35f; 36d. It is acceptable that young men should be interested in pederasty, or so the speaker implies, but older men should really outgrow this practice, get married and philosophize, or so the underlying advice seems to be.

This seems a somewhat surprising interpretation of the distich 26. First of all, we have no firm evidence that Aphrodite should always stand for hetero-

---

37 Translation Babbitt, adapted.

sexual desire, much less for the marital variant of such desires.[38] Also, it would be nice to know why Plutarch attributes these lines to Solon's old age so consistently. This may have been mere conjecture, influenced by the apparently current notion that pederasty belonged to a young man's pursuits rather than to those of the older, married man (and perhaps the combination δέ ... νῦν was some kind of trigger).[39] But there may also have been a now lost context that facilitated this interpretation. This seems to be suggested by the testimony of P. Hercul. 1384 fr. 1 (*Hercul. Vol. coll.* Alt. xi 52), which also cites the distich. Although it is of course possible that Plutarch and the author of this papyrus both independently drew the wrong conclusion, or that the author of this papyrus draws on Plutarch, or vice versa.

καὶ ἐλ[εγείας γε περὶ] τοῦ ἐρᾶν [συνέγραψεν] ἐν αἷς ἀπ[ένεμε τοῦτο] γήραι, λέγων· 'ἔργα δὲ Κυπρογενοῦς νῦν μοι φίλα καὶ Διονύσου καὶ Μουσῶν, ἃ τίθησιν ἀνδράσιν εὐφροσύνας', νῦν φάσκων τ........ σθαι καὶ ταυτ .... ἐπιτηδεύ [ματα.....] τὰ φιλόμου[σα ......]στον[[40]

For he also wrote elegies/elegiac verses about love in which he attributed this to old age, saying: 'But now the works of the Cyprus-born goddess are dear to my soul, of Dionysus too, and the Muses, which impart delights to men.' Saying 'now' ... and these ... tasks ... Muse-loving ...

In any case, the resemblance between the explanations is striking. Moreover, the unknown author of the papyrus seems to be claiming that Solon had produced erotic verses, in which he attributed the pleasures of the symposium described in fr. 26 to old age. It also seems to be the case, if I am interpreting the text correctly, that the unknown papyrus author at least interpreted the word νῦν as referring to Solon's advanced age. The last near-complete word φιλόμου[σα, finally, suggests the same connection with education and cultured leisure as Plutarch presupposes for this fragment by coupling it with fr. 18 (γηράσκω δ' αἰεὶ πολλὰ διδασκόμενος) in his *Solon*.

---

38   Cf. Noussia-Fantuzzi (2010) 391.
39   It seems likely that the νῦν in the original context brought the singer/performer back to the *hic et nunc* of the actual performance (the symposium). Of course old age and the overcoming of old age through drinking at the symposium is an important theme in sympotic poetry (cf. e.g. Campbell [1983] 215–220), and it could be that the I-person spoke about old age which he 'now' dispels through the works of Aphrodite, Dionysus, and the Muses.
40   West (1992) 135, ad fr. 26.

Similarly, it would be interesting to know in what context the other erotic fragment (25) originally belonged: did this too derive from some kind of description of a man's life and loves according to age (perhaps even from the same poem, the one referred to in P. Hercul. 1384?). Such a hypothetical poem could then be similar in conception to Solon fr. 27, but with an erotic outlook. What happens in the context of the *Amatorius*, at any rate, is similar to what we saw in *Solon* 3.1: the older and wiser Solon is positively offset against the younger, less controlled one. The older Solon's ideas are respectable, and indeed are even argued to belong to the kind of person who "philosophizes". It is clear that this offers a confirmation of the reading in the *Solon*, and should be interpreted as a positive example of how an initially less than wise individual may grow wise with age.

In the *Conuiuium*, finally, we get a beautiful example of "giving the right explanation" (cf. *Quomodo adolescens* 17; 23) to the otherwise conceivably objectionable poetic lines of fr. 26. As in the treatise, the explanatory strategy is here applied to a passage that could give the wrong ideas about the gods, or in this case, to be more precise, the works or tasks of a specific god (Aphrodite, Dionysus, and the Muses). This observation would in turn lend plausibility to the suggestion that the elaborate explanation here provided by Plutarch should also be understood to underlie the passages in the *Solon* and the *Amatorius* that discuss the same poetic fragment.[41] One Mnesiphilus here explains the distich on a principle similar to that of metonymy: the final result of each art and faculty is essential for its evaluation, not the means of its production.

> "Καὶ λέγω," ὁ Μνησίφιλος εἶπεν, "εἰδὼς ὅτι Σόλωνι δοκεῖ πάσης τέχνης καὶ δυνάμεως ἀνθρωπίνης τε καὶ θείας ἔργον εἶναι τὸ γιγνόμενον μᾶλλον ἢ δι' οὗ γίγνεται, καὶ τὸ τέλος ἢ τὰ πρὸς τὸ τέλος. αἱ δὲ Μοῦσαι καὶ παντάπασιν, εἰ νομίζοιμεν αὐτῶν ἔργον εἶναι κιθάραν καὶ αὐλούς, ἀλλὰ μὴ τὸ παιδεύειν τὰ ἤθη καὶ παρηγορεῖν τὰ πάθη τῶν χρωμένων μέλεσι καὶ ἁρμονίαις. οὐκοῦν οὐδὲ τῆς Ἀφροδίτης ἔργον ἐστὶ συνουσία καὶ μεῖξις, οὐδὲ τοῦ Διονύσου μέθη καὶ οἶνος, ἀλλ' ἣν ἐμποιοῦσι διὰ τούτων φιλοφροσύνην καὶ πόθον καὶ ὁμιλίαν ἡμῖν καὶ συνήθειαν πρὸς ἀλλήλους· ταῦτα γὰρ ἔργα θεῖα καλεῖ Σόλων, καὶ ταῦτά φησιν ἀγαπᾶν καὶ διώκειν μάλιστα πρεσβύτης γενόμενος."
>
> Moralia 405 = *Septem sapientium conuiuium* 156b–d

---

41 The words are spoken by Mnesiphilus, but they are so similar to Plutarch's ideas about the role of Dionysus and the Muses in the *Quaestiones Conuiuales* that we may confidently attribute them to him.

'I say this', Mnesiphilus said, 'in the knowledge that it is Solon's opinion that the task of every art and faculty, both human and divine, is the thing that is produced rather than the means employed in its production, and the end itself rather than the means that contribute to that end ... the Muses would most assuredly [feel aggrieved], if we should regard as their task a lyre or pipes, and not the development of the characters and the soothing of the emotions of those who make use of songs and melodies. And so again the task of Aphrodite is not carnal intercourse, nor is that of Dionysus strong drink and wine, but rather the friendly feeling, the longing, the association, and the intimacy, with one another, which they create in us through these agencies. These are what Solon calls "tasks divine", and these he says he loves and pursues above all else, now that he has become an old man.'[42]

So we are finally informed about the true meaning of Solon's distich, by receiving "the right interpretation": the lines refer not to *Wein, Weib und Gesang*, but to the fostering of education (the Muses) and friendly feeling among people (Dionysus and Aphrodite). Again, this explanation of the tasks of the various gods at the symposium is very close to what we find in the proems to Plutarch's *Quaestiones Conuiuales*. The Muses are to temper Dionysus, or in other words, clever and friendly conversation must prevail, not heavy drinking, in order to foster friendship (Aphrodite).[43] This means we can also fully appreciate why the activities alluded to here should form the respectable pleasures of the leisured Greek gentleman of a certain age.

What comes to light in these passages, again, is that Plutarch uses several strategies, most of them also to be found in his *Quomodo adolescens*, to ensure that Solon's erotic or conceivably frivolous poetry will not negatively influence our final judgement on Solon's probity as a sage and as a politician, or indeed cause youthful readers to draw the wrong example from his authority. This shows that poetry needed to answer to very clearly circumscribed parameters if it was to be acceptable for a prominent statesman of Solon's character and sagacity, at least in the eyes of this Platonically biased second-century biographer.

---

42   Translation Goodwin.
43   In particular, the proems; see Stadter (2014) 98–107.

9 Conclusion

I set out to answer the question whether the way in which Plutarch uses poetry in the *Solon* can be explained by looking at the strategies he propounds for studying poetry in his *Quomodo adolescens*. It is clear that, for the passages we have been looking at, this is indeed the case. Plutarch is especially prone to contrasting disreputable ideas about Solon, whether independently existing or arising from Solon's own poetry, with edifying quotations from this same poet, to contravene the potential damage that might ensue if young people were to consider the 'un-censured' Solon as their example. Another strategy he combines this with, is that of providing the "right interpretation", as we saw in the case of fr. 26. It is worthy of note that often he does not even cite the problematic Solonian poetry in question, but nevertheless feels it must be contradicted in this manner.

To continue this last point: another thing this investigation has highlighted is precisely the fact that there must have been some erotic poetry of Solon that Plutarch thought problematic and therefore did not quote in his biography of the sage and statesman. It was clearly sufficiently well known for Plutarch to feel obliged to excuse Solon for composing it, in order to prevent misunderstandings. Plutarch in fact refers to it repeatedly and, paradoxically, makes enough excuses for it to become especially intriguing for us, twenty-first century readers, who might otherwise not have dreamt of this kind of poetry coming from the Athenian sage and lawgiver. In Plutarch's *Amatorius* we can probably find one tantalizing sample of it, fr. 25W, and we can only imagine what else a less moralistically inclined biographer might have left us.

References

Blois, L. De. 2006. Plutarch's Solon: A Tissue of Commonplaces or a Historical Account? In Blok and Lardinois 2006: 429–440.

Blok, J. and Lardinois, A.P.M.H., eds. 2006. *Solon of Athens: New Historical Approaches*. Leiden.

Bowie, E.L. 1986. Early Greek Elegy, Symposium and Public Festival. *JHS* 106: 13–35.

Bowie, E.L. 1997. Plutarch's Citations of Early Elegiac and Iambic Poetry. In *Plutarco y la Historia*, ed. C. Schrader, V. Ramón, and J. Vela, 99–108. Zaragoza.

Bowie, E.L. 2004. Poetry and Music in the Life of Plutarch's Statesman. In *The Statesman in Plutarch's Works*. Vol. 1, ed. L. De Blois, J. Bons, T. Kessels, and D.M. Schenkeveld, 115–126. Leiden.

Campbell, D. 1983. *The Golden Lyre: The Themes of the Greek Lyric Poets*. London.
Duff, T.E. 1999. *Plutarch's Lives: Exploring Virtue and Vice*. Oxford.
Gill, C. 1977. The Genre of the Atlantis Story. *CPh* 72: 287–307.
Gill, C. 1979. Plato's Atlantis Story and the Birth of Fiction. *Ph&Lit* 3: 64–78.
Goodwin, W. 1878. *Plutarch's Morals*. Cambridge, MA.
Hendrickson, T. 2013. Poetry and Biography in the *ATHĒNAIŌN POLITEIA*: The Case of Solon. *The Classical Journal* 109(1): 1–19.
Helmbold, W.C. and O'Neil, E.N. 1959. *Plutarch's Quotations*. London.
Hertzoff, A. 2008. Eros and Moderation in Plutarch's Life of Solon. *The Review of Politics*, 70(3): 339–386.
Hunter, R. and Russell, D. 2011. *Plutarch: How to Study Poetry*. Cambridge.
Irwin, E. 2006. The Biographies of Poets: The Case of Solon. In *The Limits of Ancient Biography*, ed. B. McGing and J. Mossmann, 13–30. Swansea.
Lardinois, A. 2006. Have we Solon's Verses? In Blok and Lardinois 2006: 15–35.
Lefkowitz, M. 1981. *The Lives of the Greek Poets*. Baltimore.
Linforth, I. 1919. *Solon the Athenian*. Berkeley.
Martin, R. 2006. Solon in No-man's Land. In Blok and Lardinois 2006: 157–174.
Martina, R. 1968. *Solon*. Rome.
Massaracchia, A. 1958. *Solone*. Florence.
Mülke, C. 2002. *Solons politische Elegien und Iamben (Fr. 1–13; 32–27 West): Einleitung, Text, Übersetzung, Kommentar*. Munich.
Mühl, P. von der. 1942. Antiker Historismus in Plutarchs Biographie des Solon, *Klio* 35: 89–102.
Noussia-Fantuzzi, M. 2010. *Solon the Athenian, the Poetic Fragments*. Leiden.
Rhodes, P.J. 1981. *A Commentary on the Aristotelian* Athenaion Politeia. Oxford.
Russell, D.A. 1973. *Plutarch*. London.
Stadter, P.A. 2014. *Plutarch and his Roman Readers*. Oxford.
Stehle, E. 2006. Solon's Self-reflexive Political Persona and its Audience. In Blok and Lardinois 2006: 79–113.
Van der Stockt, L. 1992. *Twinkling and Twilight: Plutarch's Reflections on Literature*. Brussels.

Editions Cited

Babbitt, F.C., ed. 1927. *Plutarch's* Moralia, Vol. 1. Cambridge, MA.
Babbitt, F.C., 1928. *Plutarch's* Moralia. Vol. 2. Cambridge, MA.
Flacelière, R., ed. 1961. *Plutarque Vies, Tome II (Solon-Publicola-Themistocle-Camille) texte et traduction*. Paris.
Helmbold, W.C. 1961. *Amatorius*, in *Plutarch's* Moralia. Vol. 9. Cambridge, MA.
Hicks, R.D. 1925. *Diogenes Laertius, Lives of Eminent Philosophers, with an English Translation*. Cambridge, MA.

Hubert, C., ed. 1938. *Plutarchi moralia*. Vol. 4. Leipzig.
Oppermann, H., ed. 1928. *Aristotelis Ἀθηναίων Πολιτεία*. Leipzig.
Perrin, B. 1914. *Plutarch's* Lives. Vol. 1. Cambridge, MA.
West, M.L., ed. 1992. *Iambi et elegi Graeci ante Alexandrum cantata*. Vol. 2. Oxford.
Ziegler, K., ed. 1969. *Plutarchi vitae parallelae*. Vol. 1.1. 4th edn. Leipzig.

CHAPTER 18

Playing with Terpander & Co.: Lyric, Music, and Politics in Aelius Aristides' *To the Rhodians: Concerning Concord*

Francesca Modini

1   Introduction*

Over the past few decades the ground-breaking studies carried out by Ewen Bowie on the surviving traces of imperial Greek poetry have helped challenge the traditional, flawed assumption that Second Sophistic forced poetry into a 'servile existence' as the 'handmaiden' of prose.[1] This notwithstanding, imperial rhetoric has continued to be seen as the obvious successor to ancient poetry, in particular lyric. Given the praising and blaming functions fulfilled by ancient lyric genres, they naturally represented authoritative precedents for the exercises in both encomium and reproach on the part of sophists, who in turn recalled lyric poets, their biographies, and their texts.[2] In addition, the presence of lyric references in epideictic treatises like those ascribed to Menander Rhetor reinforces the sense of a substantial continuity between ancient lyric and sophistic rhetoric.[3]

It cannot be denied that with their oratorical displays sophists sometimes played roles similar to those that, in the imperial reception of archaic and classical lyric, were ascribed to ancient lyric authors. Aelius Aristides described the Spartan poet Alcman as 'the praiser and counsellor of the maidens' (ὁ τῶν παρ-

---

* I would like to thank Bruno Currie and Ian Rutherford for inviting me to contribute to this volume. I am also grateful to Pavlos Avlamis, Janet Downie, and Michael Trapp for their comments on a previous version of this chapter.

1   Bowie (1989) 207; see also Bowie (1990, 2006).

2   The idea of a 'succession' from ancient poets to imperial orators is suggested by Pernot (1993) 635–657; cf. Race (2007). On the affinity between epideictic and lyric as far as praise is concerned see Pernot (2015) 50, whereas Hawkins (2014) 186–215 offers a thorough analysis of the close relation between Dio Chrysostom and iambic poetry. On lyric quotations by imperial authors see Bowie (2000, 2008a, 2008b, 2009).

3   See Russell and Wilson (1981) xi–xv; xxxi–xxiv; cf. also the overview on the reception of lyric in the Roman period provided in the Introduction to this volume ('Stage 5'), pp. 11–12.

θένων ἐπαινέτης τε καὶ σύμβουλος);[4] but also his rhetoric was expected to both advise and celebrate his addressees.[5] On the other hand, sophists' quasi-lyrical performances took place in contexts that could not be remoter from the archaic and classical Greece in which lyric genres had developed. The major political, socioeconomic, and cultural changes characterizing the imperial period must have affected the way in which rhetoricians received and deployed their lyric models, which had to be adapted and reshaped to fit their new, Roman context.

How did contemporary imperial reality interact with the distant past reflected in the lives and works of the lyric poets? To what extent could lyric materials be of use to such later authors? Ultimately, what did it mean to recall and restage ancient lyric under the Empire? The present chapter attempts to address these issues by focussing on the case study represented by Aelius Aristides' *To the Rhodians: Concerning Concord* (*Or.* 24). As I shall demonstrate, this speech refers and, in some points, alludes to the traditions of political lyric represented by figures such as Terpander and Alcaeus. These archaic lyric traditions are then combined with a reference to choruses—this also, open, and indeed subjected by Aristides, to a detailed political interpretation, in line with the peculiar political content and aim of the oration. As a result, this study relates to the objectives of the present volume in two, interrelated, ways. On the one hand, it examines the broader impact of lyric on imperial Greek literature and culture by taking into account Aristides' own reception, not of lyric texts, but of lyric figures and performances such as Terpander, citharodia, and choruses. On the other hand, by suggesting that a passage of *Or.* 24 gestures towards Alcaeus' poetry on *stasis*, this chapter also takes into account the issue of the circulation and transmission of lyric texts in the imperial period.

2   A Greek *polis* under the Empire

Aristides' oration *To the Rhodians: Concerning Concord* (*Or.* 24) might well be regarded as a speech on the boundary between Greek past and Roman present because of the peculiar political status of its addressee. The island of Rhodes

---

4   Aristid. *Or.* 2.129. Aristides' translations are adapted from Behr (1981).
5   Cf. Aristid. *Or.* 27.42: 'And do not be surprised that, although I have nothing to censure, I think that I should offer some advice (παραινεῖν ἀξιῶ), and do not think that advice is the act of those who come to speak in criticism only; on the contrary, it also befits those who bestow praise (τοῖς ἐπαινοῦσι)'.

and its major city, bearing the same name,[6] seem to have enjoyed some freedom from direct Roman control even after the battle of Corinth and the resulting subjugation of Greece. On the basis of the sources at our disposal, it is difficult to define precisely which freedoms characterized *ciuitates liberae* such as Rhodes, in part because 'the meaning of all the different statuses enjoyed by cities under the Empire was subject to change over time, and to constant dialogue, dispute and redefinition'.[7] Generally, however, *ciuitates* of this type were allowed to maintain their own laws, were entitled to tax exemptions, and could avoid governors' supervision of their own affairs. For these reasons, Rhodes was frequently depicted as the closest one could get under the Empire to an ancient free Greek city, to a traditional *polis*: according to Dio Chrysostom, 'when the rest of Greece had been somehow extinguished' their valour made the Rhodians 'guard the national honour of the Greeks'.[8]

But things could be more complex than usually presented. As Aristides remarks, despite 'taking pride in being free' (σεμνύνεσθε ὡς ὄντες ἐλεύθεροι) and boasting about their allegedly democratic institutions to the extent that they would renounce immortality to keep their form of government, the Rhodians were still in danger of being deprived of their 'apparent liberty' (ἀποστερηθῆναι τῆς δοκούσης [...] ἐλευθερίας).[9] Playing on the ambiguity intrinsic to the verb δοκέω ('to seem'), this description of Rhodian freedom conveys vividly the not real but 'apparent' and precarious nature of Rhodian *libertas*.[10] As the result of the city's own identity construction and pride, Rhodian 'liberty' was indeed a function of appearance, the fiction of a free Greek *polis* performed by the Rhodians, just like actors or sophists, on the stage of the Empire.[11] Their per-

---

6   The city of Rhodes was founded in 408/7 BCE as the result of a synoecism between the leading cities of Camiros, Lindos and Ialysos; cf. Diod. Sic. 13.75.1.
7   Millar (1999) 112.
8   Dio Chrys. *Or*. 31.18.
9   *Or*. 24.22. On democracy in imperial Rhodes cf. Strab. 14.2.5: 'The Rhodians care for the people, even if they do not have a democratic rule; still, they wish to take care of their multitude of poor people. As a result, the people are supplied with provisions and the rich support the indigent, by a certain ancestral custom.'
10 The interpretation of δοκούσης as 'apparent' has been questioned by Bresson (1996) 228n30, who has proposed to read the participle as 'fameuse'; cf. Franco (2008) 245n123. Yet, despite the common use of δόξα with the sense of 'glory', δοκέω does not seem to have been used with the meaning of 'being famous' (with the ellipsis of εἶναί τι it could mean at most 'to be of some reputation', cf. Eur. *Hec*. 295). The idea of an 'apparent freedom', on the other hand, fits nicely the political situation of Rhodes as a Greek city under Rome; cf. Dio Chrys. *Or*. 44.12, addressed to the city of Prusa: 'what is called freedom (τὴν [...] λεγομένην ἐλευθερίαν)' is at the mercy of 'those who are strong and powerful'.
11 Cf. Whitmarsh (2001b) 303: 'to "Hellenise," to "be Greek", is to *seem* Greek: all identities

formance, though, was strictly supervised and judged by Roman rulers,[12] as confirmed by fairly recent events: first Claudius and then Vespasian revoked Rhodian autonomy, and even if in both cases Rhodes' status of *civitas libera* had been restored soon after, such precedents made clear how quick and effective imperial intervention could be.[13]

This was the political situation of Rhodes around the middle of the second century CE when civil strife broke out in the city with sufficient severity to induce Aristides, then stuck in Smyrna through ill health, to send to the Rhodian community his oration on concord, in the attempt to persuade the city to end its political unrest. Because of Rhodes' peculiar position within the Empire, there was far more at stake than internal civic harmony. As they typically identified their dominion with the establishment and preservation of universal order,[14] Roman rulers could hardly tolerate the spread of faction and turbulence in a city under their control, no matter how 'free' this might be, or depict itself to be. Aristides puts it bluntly: if the Rhodians do not want to ward off *stasis* from their own community, 'another will come to save' them 'by force' (ἄλλος ἀφίξεται ὅστις ὑμᾶς σώσει πρὸς βίαν), since 'as a rule, rulers neither ignore such things nor make light of them'.[15]

3   Public Calamities and Communal Music: Aristides' *prooimion*

In 142 CE, some years before Aristides' speech promoting civic concord, a massive earthquake had shaken Rhodes: the *Rhodian Oration* included in Aristides' corpus (*Or.* 25) gives an impressive account of this disaster,[16] describ-

---

are fictions narrated and performed in the present'. For δοκέω as epitomising the 'artificial, mimetic aspects' of identity negotiation in the imperial period, cf. [Dio Chrys.] *Or.* 37.25–27 (Favorinus), which discusses the relation between Ἕλληνι δοκεῖν and εἶναι; on this passage see also Whitmarsh (2001a) 119–120.

12   According to Plut. *Praec. ger. rei.* 813f, those who wanted to engage in Greek civic life under Roman rule should 'imitate the actors (μιμεῖσθαι τοὺς ὑποκριτάς), who, while putting into the performance their own passion, character, and reputation, yet listen to the prompter and do not go beyond the degree of liberty in rhythms and metres permitted by those who rule over them (μὴ παρεκβαίνοντας τοὺς ῥυθμοὺς καὶ τὰ μέτρα τῆς διδομένης ἐξουσίας ὑπὸ τῶν κρατούντων)'. For an analysis of Plutarch's passage in context, see Swain (1996) 165–168.

13   On these episodes see Magie (1950) 1.548; 569.

14   See e.g. Aristides' oration *To Rome* (*Or.* 26), which closes with a resounding celebration of the well-ordered Roman Empire as the reflection of divine *kosmos* on Earth.

15   *Or.* 24.22.

16   The Aristidean authorship of this text has frequently been called into question; on the

ing scenes of utter devastation within a city turned into a heap of ruins and corpses.[17] As he himself recalls, already at that time Aristides had come to the aid of the island, probably with a consolatory speech.[18] In his view, however, no material destruction could equal the catastrophic consequences of the *stasis* now raging in Rhodes:

ὃν μὲν οὖν τρόπον διετέθην ἐπὶ τῇ περὶ τὸν σεισμὸν συμφορᾷ καὶ ὁποῖόν τινα ἐμαυτὸν παρέσχον τοῖς πρεσβεύσασιν ὑμῶν εἰς Αἴγυπτον κατ' ἐκείνους τοὺς χρόνους, παρ' αὐτῶν κάλλιστ' ἂν πύθοισθε. ἀγγελλομένων δέ μοι πολλῷ δεινοτέρων, εἰ οἷόν τε εἰπεῖν, τῶν νῦν, ὅτι ἀπιστεῖτε ὑμῖν αὐτοῖς καὶ διῄρησθε καὶ ταραχὰς οὐ προσηκούσας ὑμῖν ταράττεσθε, οὔθ' ὅπως χρὴ πιστεύειν οὔθ' ὅπως ἀπιστεῖν εἶχον. οἵ τε γὰρ ἀγγέλλοντες ὑμέτεροι πολῖται καὶ τἆλλα τῶν ἀξιοπίστων καὶ καθ' ὑμῶν τὸ παραδέξασθαι ῥᾳδίως τοιαύτας αἰτίας οὐκ ἐνῆν. εἰ μὲν οὖν περιῆν Τέρπανδρος ὁ Λέσβιος, ἐκεῖνον ἂν ὑμῖν συνευξάμην ἐλθεῖν· ἐπεὶ δὲ λόγῳ ψιλῷ δεῖ πείσαντα καταστήσασθαι τὰ πράγματα, ἐμαυτοῦ τὸ ἀγώνισμα ποιοῦμαι.

You would best learn from your ambassadors how I reacted to the misfortune of the earthquake and behaved towards them when they came to Egypt in those times. But when the present situation, which is much more terrible, if it is possible to say so, was reported to me, that you distrust one another, have taken sides, and are involved in turbulences inappropriate for you, I did not know whether I should trust or disbelieve it. For the messengers were your fellow citizens and otherwise trustworthy men, and yet it was impossible to accept easily such accusations against you. Therefore, if Terpander of Lesbos were alive, I would have prayed that he come to you. But since you must be persuaded and your affairs settled in prose, I make the contest mine.[19]

Commenting upon this passage, Charles Behr suggested that Aristides mentioned the earthquake because it might have been at the origin of Rhodian civic turmoil: 'a class struggle ... broke out in Rhodes, perhaps in connection with public loans taken to repair the damages of the terrible earthquake'.[20]

---

issue see Franco (2008), who draws on Jones (1990) to argue for the authenticity of the oration.
17 See *Or.* 25.17–33.
18 See Behr (1968) 16.
19 *Or.* 24.3.
20 Behr (1981) 368n1.

Financial issues and tensions between lower and upper classes do feature in Aristides' discussion throughout the oration,[21] but to my mind there is no need to think that they were brought about by the recent disaster. Rather, by drawing a direct comparison between the past earthquake and current *stasis*, Aristides could better persuade his audience of the seriousness of their situation: it is no coincidence that he resorts to the same rhetorical move once again at the very end of the speech, when he pleads with the Rhodians to bring to an end the 'earthquake that surrounds' them 'everywhere' (παύσασθε τοῦ σεισμοῦ τούτου, ὃς ὑμῖν πανταχοῦ συμπεριέρχεται).[22]

On the other hand, such a view of *stasis* as a dreadful public calamity comparable to an earthquake matches perfectly Aristides' subsequent reference to the archaic poet Terpander as his precedent in assisting a struggling community. According to the treatise *On Music* traditionally ascribed to Plutarch and dated to the first or second centuries CE,

> ὅτι δὲ καὶ ταῖς εὐνομωτάταις τῶν πόλεων ἐπιμελὲς γεγένηται φροντίδα ποιεῖσθαι τῆς γενναίας μουσικῆς, πολλὰ μὲν καὶ ἄλλα μαρτύρια παραθέσθαι ἔστι, Τέρπανδρον δ' ἄν τις παραλάβοι τὸν τὴν γενομένην ποτὲ παρὰ Λακεδαιμονίοις στάσιν καταλύσαντα, καὶ Θαλήταν τὸν Κρῆτα, ὅν φασι κατά τι πυθόχρηστον Λακεδαιμονίοις παραγενόμενον διὰ μουσικῆς ἰάσασθαι ἀπαλλάξαι τε τοῦ κατασχόντος λοιμοῦ τὴν Σπάρτην, καθάπερ φησὶ Πρατίνας (= fr. 713 iii *PMG*).

> We could find many pieces of evidence to show that the cities with the best laws and customs have been careful to cultivate music of the noble kind. One might cite Terpander, who resolved the civil war that broke out at one time in Sparta, and Thaletas the Cretan, of whom it is said that he went to Sparta as the result of a pronouncement by the Delphic oracle, and cured the people there by means of music, releasing Sparta, as Pratinas says, from the grip of the plague.[23]

The same narrative, featuring civic disasters and the curative powers of music and poetry to avert them can be found in other sources of the Roman period. As reported by John Tzetzes, Diodorus Siculus told how, with his harmonious

---

21 See e.g. § 29: 'it is not necessary for you ... as proof of your good faith to join those who borrowed money disadvantageously for you in paying back however many talents it may be'; cf. also §§ 32–40, where rich and poor Rhodians are depicted as struggling.
22 *Or.* 24.59.
23 [Plut.] *De mus.* 1146b–c (trans. Barker [1984]). On the issue of authenticity and date of the treatise, see Cannatà Fera (2011) and D'Ippolito (2011).

kithara, Terpander managed to reconcile the Lacedaemonians, who 'hugged and kissed each other in tears'.[24] Spartan dependence upon external musical aids was taken by Aelian as a convincing proof of the city's ignorance of *mousikē*, which forced them to send for 'foreigners' like Terpander and Thaletas 'if ever they needed help from the Muses in plague or madness or any other such public calamity'.[25] This was the mainstream reception background against which Aristides' audience were expected to unpack his mention of the poet from Lesbos within his discourse on earthquakes and civic turmoil: Terpander's popularity, in the imperial period, as bearer of harmonizing music effective against *stasis* explains why Aristides chose him as ideal precedent for his intervention against the public misfortune represented by Rhodian discord.

But the Terpandrean model fitted Aristides' appeal to the Rhodians nicely for at least one other reason. As the archaic citharode brought his musico-political *sophia* from Aeolian Lesbos to Dorian Sparta, so Aristides' speech now comes from Smyrna to Rhodes, an ancient Dorian foundation, to try and bring to an end its political chaos. Imperial rhetoricians were always particularly mindful of ethnic origins and traditions, which imperial cities constantly deployed as powerful means to shape and promote their Greek identity.[26] By comparing Terpander's political intervention among the Lacedaemonians with his own attempt to persuade Rhodes into concord, then, Aristides was playing on a Dorian string to win the favour of his Dorian audience.

To this it should be added that the precise lyric genre brought into play by the figure of Terpander was in fact far from foreign to imperial listeners. Citharodia continued to be performed well into the imperial period,[27] and sophists were aware of its popularity. Addressing the Alexandrians, Dio complained about their excessive enthusiasm for the *kithara*; whereas in Cyzicus he was exempted from giving a speech by the arrival of a citharode, whose perform-

---

24　Diod. 8.28 *ap.* Tzetz. *Chil.* 1.385–392.
25　Ael. *VH* 12.50. On the political effect of Terpander's citharodia, see also Phld. *De mus.* 4, coll. 47.23–45 and 132.24–134.16 Delattre (= Diog. Bab. 3.232.10–233.2 Arnim).
26　Cf. Men. Rhet. 1.354.5–14 Spengel (trans. Russell and Wilson [1981]): 'they [Greeks] should belong to the races believed to be the noblest. The three races which are the primary ones and also the best known are those of the Dorians, Aeolians, and Ionians … A Hellenic city should therefore be shown to come from one of these stocks.' On the growing importance of local identities under the Empire see Whitmarsh (2010) 1–16. As underlined in Whitmarsh (2001a) 24, even 'cities that were not familiar Greek settlements … established their own right to be called Greek by means of clever genealogies', linking them to the Greek greatest 'stocks'.
27　See Power (2010) xi–xiii.

ance aroused 'tremendous interest' in the Cyzicans.[28] As suggested by Timothy Power, 'a certain degree of professional rivalry' must have existed between wandering sophists and citharodes,[29] which makes even more notable Aristides' parallel between himself and Terpander. This may reveal the sophist's self-positioning in relation to contemporary music culture: while citharodia was especially popular and probably competed with rhetoric for attracting imperial audience, Aristides' response was to model his role on one of the founders of Greek citharodia.

Unlike Terpander or any other singer, however, for his political mission in Rhodes Aristides could not count on poetry and music, having at his disposal a λόγος ψιλός, literally a 'bare', 'naked discourse'.[30] To be sure, for the author of the *Hymn to Sarapis* (*Or.* 45), where the traditional superiority of poetry over prose is emphatically rejected,[31] the prose nature of his address could not represent a serious obstacle to its persuasive function. And yet, I suggest, a few striking details indicate that it would be a mistake to take at face value Aristides' claim about the 'nakedness' of his speech in terms of music and poetry.

In fact, the expression used by Aristides to define the aim of the oration, καταστήσασθαι τὰ πράγματα, may bring us back to Terpandrean lyric. Again according to the *On Music*, citharodic *nomoi* 'were established in the time of Terpander' (κατεστάθησαν ἐπὶ Τερπάνδρου), who was also responsible for 'establishing' the first musical institutions in Sparta (ἡ μὲν οὖν πρώτη κατάστασις τῶν περὶ τὴν μουσικὴν ἐν τῇ Σπάρτῃ, Τερπάνδρου καταστήσαντος, γεγένηται).[32] Meaning 'to set (something) in order', the term καθίστημι could be applied to both a promoter of sociopolitical order and a founder of institutional music, as ancient musical theory seems to have done with Terpander and his citharodic activity in Sparta. When applying this verb to his speech, therefore, Aristides transfers to his own rhetoric the musico-political legacy of his lyric forerunner, enhancing his identification with him.

Aristides then claims to 'make the contest' his (ἐμαυτοῦ τὸ ἀγώνισμα ποιοῦμαι). Apart from conveying the difficulty of his task, the idea of the rhetorician entering a competition can undoubtedly be understood as a reference to the agonistic character of his role as a public speaker on the sophistic stage. Each

---

28 Dio Chrys. *Or.* 32.60–61; 19.1–5.
29 Power (2010) 326.
30 In Pl. *Menex.* 239c, quoted in Aristid. *Or.* 2.341, the same phrase is applied to Socrates' prose celebration of the battles of Marathon and Salamis.
31 On the relationship between poetry and prose in this text cf. Russell (1990); Vassilaki (2005); Whitmarsh (2006).
32 [Plut.] *De mus.* 1132d; 1134b.

oratorical performance represented a contest for success, and as just pointed out with regard to imperial citharodia, sophists had to compete with other kinds of public performers too.[33] Moreover, our passage may be read in the light of what Laurent Pernot has defined 'la rivalité entre l'encomiaste et le poète':[34] as his authoritative precedent, Terpander represents not just Aristides' model but also his competitor.

If we take into account the traditional features of the ancient rival chosen by Aristides, however, the mention of a 'contest' proves even more significant. Traditions about musical history had it that, playing his *kithara* in a highly competitive environment (in a sense, not differently from imperial sophists), Terpander usually took part in musical agones. According to the musical theorist Heraclides of Pontus, quoted by pseudo-Plutarch, the citharode 'set his own hexameter verses and those of Homer to music appropriate to each *nomos*, and sang them in competitions' (ἐν τοῖς ἀγῶσιν).[35] Among these there were probably the Pythian contests held in Delphi, where Terpander won four times in succession,[36] and the Spartan Carnea, which he won for the first time, almost certainly after founding them as part of his musical institutions for the city.[37] With the description of his attempt to avert *stasis* as an ἀγώνισμα, Aristides does something more than stressing his efforts to persuade the Rhodians and to measure up to his diverse rivals; rather, he dresses up as an archaic citharode competing in musical contests.

All the lyric elements analyzed so far, I suggest, contribute to transform the proem of *Or.* 24 into a sort of citharodic *prooimion*, a 'prelude' to the main musical performance that Terpander himself traditionally adopted.[38] Still, whereas citharodic *prooimia* could function as detached and autonomous pieces preceding the central song,[39] in the case of Aristides' Rhodian speech,

---

33 As explained by Whitmarsh (2005) 3, 'within the demanding environment of imperial aristocratic culture', through their oratorical displays, sophists competed for cultural and social prestige; on Second Sophistic displays as a prime form of elite competition, see also Gleason (1995); Schmitz (1997, 2017).

34 Pernot (1993) 2.646.

35 [Plut.] *De mus.* 1132c (trans. Barker [1984]).

36 [Plut.] *De mus.* 1132e.

37 Ath. 14.635e.

38 On the *prooimia* traditionally ascribed to Terpander, see West (1992) 18–19.

39 On the function of citharodic *prooimia*, see Power (2010) 187–200. For the relation between musical preludes and rhetorical proems, cf. Quint. *Inst.* 4.1.2: 'Now *oimē* means song, and the lyre-players (*citharoedi*) gave the name *prooimion* to the short pieces they perform to win favour before they begin the formal competition; it may be for this reason, therefore, that orators also chose this name to denote what they say with the object of winning over the minds of the judges before they start on the actual case'; Cic. *De or.* 2.80:

the proem/*prooimion* is well connected to the remainder of the oration: as we shall see presently, in *Or.* 24 music is by no means confined to its 'prelude'; on the contrary, elsewhere in the text the civic setting of Aristides' political address may be found to be reflected in a distinctively politicizing view of lyric.

4   Like a Chorus out of Harmony

The first section of the speech (§§ 4–31) repeatedly contrasts civil strife and concord in order to present them respectively as the greatest evil and the supreme good for cities. This point is argued through a series of references to ancient historical examples and famous literary sources, among which a lyric trace is found in the paraphrase of a few lines by Solon concerning class struggle.[40] Once he has discussed *stasis* and harmony in general, Aristides turns to consider the situation of Rhodes in more detail, providing pieces of advice to help his listeners restore a harmonious relationship between the 'superior' and the 'inferior' within the city (§§ 32–40). To give strength to his admonitions, the orator then proceeds to underline how inappropriate discord is to the island and its legendary origin: Rhodes emerged from the sea to be the special possession of the Sun, but the Rhodians are now behaving as if they lay in darkness.[41] As already pointed out by Theodoros Gkourogiannis, this passage clearly draws on another lyric source, Pindar's *Olympian* 7 and its famous narrative about the birth of Rhodes.[42] The picture of the passage's engagement with lyric tradition, however, is further complicated by what follows:

> ἀποβλέψατε δὴ καὶ πρὸς τοὺς τρίποδας τοὺς ἐν Διονύσου τουτουσί, πάντως δὲ χαίρετε αὐτοὺς προσορῶντες. ἆρ' οὖν ποτ' ἂν οὗτοι σταθῆναι δοκοῦσιν ὑμῖν, τῶν χορῶν ἐν αὐτοῖς μαχομένων; ἢ τοῦτό γε εὔδηλον ὅτι κἂν εἰ μὴ τἀναντία μηδ' ἄλλος ἄλλο τι, ταὐτὰ δὲ ῥήματα μὴ κατὰ ταὐτὸν ἅπαντες ᾖδον, φεύγειν λοιπὸν ἦν αὐτοῖς; καὶ μὴν οὐδεὶς χορὸς ἀσύμφωνος οὕτως ἄωρον θέαμα ὡς ὁ Ῥοδίων δῆμος μὴ ταὐτὸν φθεγγόμενος.

---

in an oration, 'the opening passage should be so closely connected with the speech that follows as to appear to be not an appendage, like the prelude to a piece of music, but an integral part of the whole structure'.

40   *Or.* 24.14; Solon fr. 5.1–3 West.² On Aristides' knowledge of Solon's poems, possibly first hand, see Bowie (2008a) 20–21.
41   *Or.* 24.50–51.
42   Gkourogiannis (1999) 268–269; cf. Pind. *Ol.* 7.55–71.

Look at these tripods in the Temple of Dionysus—and you take great delight in looking at them. Now, do you think that these would have ever been erected if the members of each chorus fought among themselves? Or is it quite clear that even if they did not sing in opposite ways or each member something different, but all sang the same text, yet not in time with each other, all that would be left for them would be to flee the stage? Indeed, no chorus out of harmony is so unfitting a sight as the people of Rhodes in disagreement.[43]

Choral metaphors were quite common in imperial rhetoric, and given the traditional role of choruses as representatives of the community,[44] they were often used by sophists to discuss the issue of civic harmony.[45] Urging to concord his fellow citizens in Prusa, for example, like Aristides Dio reminded them that 'it is a fine thing, just as it is with a well-trained chorus, for men to sing together one and the same tune'.[46] Analyzing these and other similar metaphors, Bowie has stressed how imperial writers were 'sensitive to the importance of *choroi* in the political life of Greek cities'.[47] The observation that such metaphors were highly charged in sociopolitical terms, however, makes necessary a closer look at the presence and function of choruses within the appeal to Rhodes.

To begin with, choruses found their ideal place in a speech addressed to a Dorian city: ancient Sparta, implicitly compared with Rhodes through the initial reference to Terpander,[48] could claim an outstanding choral tradition, still widely famous in imperial times.[49] More importantly, by pointing to actual dedications, Aristides links his choral metaphor to the concrete reality of choral performances in Rhodes. With regard to this last point, we might wonder whether the tripods were looked at with pleasure by the Rhodians as *old* monu-

---

43   *Or.* 24.52.
44   As stressed by Nagy (1990) 345, ancient choruses were 'by nature a microcosm of society'; cf. similarly Kowalzig (2007) 5 and (2013) 173. Precisely as a mass medium of civic consciousness choruses hold a prominent place in the education of the citizens of the ideal city envisioned in Plato's *Laws*: see e.g. Peponi (2013) 6; Prauscello (2014) 5, 106; Folch (2015) 97.
45   On the use of choral images by imperial rhetoricians in general, see Korenjak (2000) 210–214 and Bowie (2006).
46   Dio Chrys. *Or.* 48.7.
47   Bowie (2006) 92.
48   Cf. also § 24: 'Consider the city of the Lacedaemonians, who are your fellow tribesmen'.
49   See e.g. Ath. 678b–c, where it is recalled that during the Spartan festival of the Gymnopaediae choruses of boys and men danced naked while singing 'the songs of Thaletas, Alcman, and the paeans of Dionysodotus the Laconian'. Another well-known imperial account of Spartan choral activity is found in Plut. *Lyc.* 21.2.

ments of *past* choral activity, or if they celebrated choruses and choregic successes *still ongoing* in Rhodes. Such a question is by no means trivial; for, if choruses belonged to the musico-lyric horizon of Rhodes' imperial citizens, their first-hand choral experience could contribute significantly to the effectiveness of the metaphor, in turn adding to the persuasiveness of the speech as a whole.

Immediately after introducing the comparison between Rhodes and a (discordant) chorus through the mention of the choregic tripods, Aristides turns to the 'beaks and great triremes' which adorned the docks of Rhodes before the earthquake, and which Rhodian sailors had pillaged from pirates in ancient, pre-imperial times.[50] In this sense, if Rhodian choregic dedications are to be put on the same level of Rhodes' maritime trophies, we might think that Aristides' reference to tripods also related to antiques.

Such an interpretation, though, would be at odds with the fact that, as far as we can see, at least some choral performances were still taking place under the Empire. As late as the first half of the third century CE, for instance, a paean ascribed to Sophocles was sung in Athens by distinguished citizens; this performance was recorded on the base of a monument commemorating another, earlier chorus: the dithyrambic victory obtained by Sarapion, a friend of Plutarch's, towards the end of the first century CE.[51] Dithyrambic choruses themselves provide an outstanding example of choral practice in imperial Athens, where they have left a substantial series of choregic monuments and inscriptions. These have been recently reconsidered by Julia Shear, who has argued that 'they ... presented opportunities for linking the present with the city's historical past and for (re)negotiating what exactly it meant to be Athenian' under Rome.[52] As we have seen above, imperial Rhodes appears also to have been interested in shaping its identity as a Greek city within the Empire, and choruses might have helped.

In fact, according to Peter Wilson, choral practice on Rhodes lived on well into the Hellenistic and Roman periods, and the passage of *Or.* 24 should be read as 'much more than "pure" metaphor', as it indicates that on the island choruses continued to represent 'an effective social form'.[53] In support of this hypothesis, Wilson mentions an inscription preserved on a marble base for a

---

50   *Or.* 24.53.
51   On the paean, see Rutherford (2001) 39; on the monument see Oliver (1936, 1949). Further evidence of imperial choral songs like paeans and hymns is analyzed in Bowie (2006) 83–88.
52   Shear (2013) 390.
53   Wilson (2000) 292.

tripod probably coming from the Rhodian Dionysion. This monument honoured a certain Timostratus son of Lycon for its victory as *khoragos* of boys, and was dedicated between the second and the first century BCE.[54] But other epigraphic records, and more recent than that quoted by Wilson, may corroborate the idea of imperial choral performances in Rhodes. Another *khoragos* was celebrated in an inscription from Lindos, scarcely readable but usually dated to the Roman period since it names Rome.[55] We can be more precise in dating the inscription found on the base of a statue in honour of the priest Lysistratus son of Moiragenes, who was 'twice *khoragos* and winner in the Alexandreia and Dionysia'.[56] The same priest appears in an epigraph from Lindos dated with certainty to 82 BCE;[57] also Lysistratus' *khoragiai*, therefore, may be reasonably assigned to the first half of the first century BCE. From a later period comes an inscription honouring a certain Tiberius Claudius Antipater, he too 'twice *khoragos*'.[58] According to the editor Christian Blinkenberg, the epigraph may be subsequent to Trajan's adoption by Nerva, which took place at the end of 97 CE.[59] Its imperial date, however, is not the most fascinating feature of this inscription. What should attract our attention the most is rather the fact that Tiberius was celebrated also as a 'sophist', 'excelling in Greek *paideia*'.[60]

As a result of these observations, it is tempting to imagine that even in the age of the Second Sophistic choruses had not died out completely in Rhodes, and could represent, *mutatis mutandis*, a means of 'staging the cohesion and the identity' of the Rhodian community.[61] As if it was a proper choral song, also Aristides' discourse on choral songs was aimed at staging and so realizing communal harmony; in so doing, it might have been mimicking not just ancient but more recent choruses.

---

54 Wilson (2000) 390n127; *Clara Rhodos* 2.215.55.
55 *N. Suppl. Epigr. Rodio* 175.29; l. 11: 'Ρώ[μ]αν.
56 *Clara Rhodos* 2.201.33. On the Alexandreia and Dionysia see Wilson (2000) 290; Buraselis (2012) 254–255.
57 *I.Lindos* 2.197d.
58 *I.Lindos* 2.449.
59 Blinkenberg bases this hypothesis on the mention of 'emperors' in l. 6 (αὐτοκρατόρων), identifying them with Nerva and Trajan.
60 ll. 17–18: διενένκαντα δὲ κ[αὶ]|ἐν παιδείᾳ τῶν Ἑλλάνων, τὸν σοφιστ[άν].
61 I owe this formulation to an unpublished paper of G.B. D'Alessio: 'choral performances on behalf of the whole civic community seem to have been one of the most suitable media for staging the cohesion and the identity of the Greek (and, occasionally, of other) *poleis* at least until the first centuries of the Roman empire'.

5   *Stasis*, Ships, and Lesbos

As already mentioned, after the comparison with victorious choruses Aristides refers to the past maritime glories of the island, which offer him another opportunity to praise concord:

οἱ δὲ τοὺς λῃστὰς ἐκεῖνοι καταδιώξαντες καὶ τὰ νεώρια κοσμήσαντες τοῖς ἐμβόλοις καὶ ταῖς μεγάλαις ἐκείναις τριήρεσιν, ἃς ἡμεῖς εἴδομεν πρὸ τοῦ σεισμοῦ, πρὸς θεῶν εἰ μὴ Τυρρηνοῖς μηδὲ τοῖς πλοίοις τοῖς λῃστικοῖς, ἀλλ' αὐτοῖς κατὰ ναῦν ἐμάχοντο, ἆρ' ἄν ποτε τῆς θαλάττης ἦρξαν, ἢ τοὺς κόσμους τούτους εἰσήγαγον εἰς τὴν πόλιν, ἢ φιλοτιμεῖσθαι τοῖς ἐξ αὐτῶν ἐπὶ τοῖς ἔργοις τούτοις κατέλιπον; ἀλλ', οἶμαι, περὶ σωτηρίας ἂν αὐτοῖς πρότερον ἐγένετο. εἶτα ἐν νηὶ μὲν στάσις οὐχὶ σωτήριον, ἐν δὲ πόλει καὶ ταύτῃ περιρρύτῳ φθείρειν ἀλλήλους συνεζευγμένους σῶφρον [...];

Consider the men who ran down the pirates and adorned the docks with those beaks and great triremes which we saw before the earthquake. By the gods, if they had not fought against the Etruscans or the pirate vessels, but against themselves, ship against ship, would they ever have ruled the sea or have brought these adornments into the city or have left their descendants the right to be proud over their deeds? I think, their first concern would have been their survival. While faction is unsafe on a single ship, in a city, and at that sea-girt, is it an act of moderation for men closely united to slay one another?[62]

Like choral imagery, the political metaphor of the ship was quite common among imperial sophists, certainly because of its ancient, authoritative tradition.[63] A ship represented the civic community endangered by its own state of disorder in a section of the *Corpus Theognideum*, now generally ascribed to Euenus of Paros, a contemporary of Socrates.[64] Drawing on the same imagery Plato then devised the famous allegory of the Ship of State, troubled by its quarrelling and mutinous crew.[65] These texts provide the literary background of Aristides' maritime *stasis*; and yet another tradition of political metaphors seems to be brought into play by what Aristides adds just after introducing his ship:

---

62   *Or.* 24.53–54.
63   Cf. e.g. Dio Chrys. *Or.* 48.7; Philostr. *VA* 4.9.
64   Thgn. 667–682 = Euenus fr. 8b.
65   Pl. *Resp.* 487d–488e. Corrêa (2016) analyses the relationship between the Platonic and the Theognidean passages.

εἶτα ἐν νηῒ μὲν στάσις οὐχὶ σωτήριον, ἐν δὲ πόλει καὶ ταύτῃ περιρρύτῳ φθείρειν ἀλλήλους συνεζευγμένους σῶφρον, ἢ τὰ Λεσβίων καὶ τὰ Μυτιληναίων κακὰ μιμεῖσθαι Ῥοδίους ὄντας; ἀλλὰ πολλῷ βέλτιον ἦν ἐκείνους τῆς ὑμετέρας εὐνομίας ἐπιθυμήσαντας ὁρᾶσθαι ἢ τῆς ἐκείνων δυστυχίας ὑμᾶς ὑπομεῖναι μιμητὰς γενέσθαι. καίτοι πρέποντα μὲν ἄν τις ἔχοι καὶ πρὸς ἐκείνους εἰπεῖν καὶ ἱκνούμενα, ἄνδρες Λέσβιοι ποῖ προήχθητε; οἳ φατὲ μὲν τὴν νῆσον ἅπασαν ὑμῖν εἶναι μουσικὴν καὶ τούτου τὴν Ὀρφέως κεφαλὴν αἰτιᾶσθε, αὐτοὶ δ' οὐκ αἰσχύνεσθε οὕτως ἀμούσως διακείμενοι; καὶ κιθαρῳδοῖς μέν ποτε τοὺς Ἕλληνας ἐνικᾶτε, τῷ δ' ὑπὲρ ὑμῶν αὐτῶν μὴ δύνασθαι βουλεύσασθαι κινδυνεύετε ἡττᾶσθαι καὶ πάντων ἀνθρώπων; καὶ πρότερον μὲν παρ' ὑμῶν ἑτέρωσε βαδίζοντες ἔπαυον τὰς στάσεις, νῦν δὲ οὐδὲ παρ' ὑμῖν αὐτοῖς ὑμᾶς αὐτοὺς γνῶναι δύνασθε; ταῦτ' ἔμοιγε δοκεῖ τις ἂν ὀρθῶς καὶ ὑπὲρ αὐτῶν εἰπεῖν νουθετῶν. οὐ μὴν ἀλλ' ἐκείνοις μέν, ὡς ἔοικεν, ἐκ παλαιοῦ τὸ ἄλογον τοῦτο τῆς δυστυχίας συνείμαρται καὶ πολλάκις ἠλέγχθησαν οὐχ ὡς δεῖ διακείμενοι, ὑμῖν δὲ οὐδαμόθεν προσήκει τὸ νόσημα.

While faction is unsafe in a single ship, in a city, and at that sea-girt, is it an act of moderation for men closely united to slay one another, or being Rhodians to imitate the evils of the Lesbians and the Mytilenaeans? It was much better for them to appear desirous of your good order than for you to endure to become imitators of their misfortune. Yet one could say fittingly and properly even to them: 'O men of Lesbos, to what extremes have you been carried? You say that your whole island is musical and that Orpheus' head is the cause of this. But are you not ashamed to be so inharmoniously disposed? And once you surpassed the Greeks with your citharodes, but in your inability to take measures on your own behalf, you are in danger of being inferior to all mankind. And formerly men came from you to other places and put an end to faction, but now you are not even able in your own home to know yourselves.' I think that someone would be right in offering such admonitions on their behalf. However, as it seems, this senseless misfortune has been their fate from the time of antiquity, and they have often been shown to be disposed differently from the way they ought to be disposed. But this disease in no way befits you.[66]

Through the discourse on music and politics underpinning the oration, Aristides reintroduces the Lesbian connection established with the initial mention of Terpander. In contrast to the proem, though, here the focus moves from the citharode to the musico-lyric history in which he belonged. According to

---

66   Or. 24.54–56.

a story apparently well known in imperial times,[67] when the mythical singer Orpheus was ripped into shreds by the Thracian women his head came ashore on Lesbos, inaugurating the citharodic tradition which then flourished with Terpander. But the Lesbian musico-lyric *diadokhē* did not end with Terpander, nor with citharodia. In a *scholion recentius* on Aeschylus' *Persians* the legend about Orpheus' head is interpreted as the result of the presence on the island of prominent figures such as Arion, Pittacus, Sappho, and Alcaeus.[68] Aeolian poets themselves were probably acquainted with the great citharodic tradition that had preceded them: to praise 'an outstanding man' Sappho called him 'superior, as the Lesbian singer to those of other lands', a comparison that has been taken by Power as referring to Terpander and his successors in Sparta.[69]

The political situation in which Aeolian monodic lyric flourished, however, was the exact opposite of the state of civil concord brought about by Terpander's music, and rather corresponded to the 'inharmonious' era of post-Terpandrean politics described by Aristides. In particular, the Lesbian city singled out in the oration, Mytilene, became notorious for the unending civil strife in which the poet Alcaeus engaged fiercely. Strabo recalled that 'the so called *stasiotic* poems by Alcaeus' were all about Mytilenaean civil conflict and tyrannies.[70] Whether these στασιωτικά coincided with an editorial division of the poet's corpus or not,[71] Strabo's observation suggests that in Roman times the connection between *stasis* and Alcaeus was still clear and active. It is in light of this connection, I argue, that Aristides' ship image may be further unpacked.

In a famous Alcaean fragment, a vivid description of a ship repeatedly hit by violent waves precedes a mention of 'tyranny', whereas in another well-known poem the speaking *persona* expresses his confusion about the 'direction of the winds', τῶν ἀνέμων στάσιν, an expression that might subtly allude to Mytilene's faction, when read in political terms.[72] Precisely this appears to have been a way in which ancient and especially imperial readers interpreted Alcaeus' troubled ships.[73] In the *Homeric Problems* of the grammarian Heraclitus, usu-

---

67 Cf. e.g. Luc. *Ind.* 11; Philostr. *VA* 4.14; *Her.* 28.9.
68 Schol. rec. Aesch. *Pers.* 883.
69 Sappho fr. 106 Voigt; Power (2010) 378–385. In the *Suda*, the expression 'after the Lesbian singer' (μετὰ Λέσβιον ᾠδόν) is explained as 'a proverb for those that take second place, as the Lesbian citharodes were the first to be invited by the Lacedaemonians'. On the relationship of Alcaeus' and Sappho's lyric with other, more ancient Lesbian poetic traditions, including Terpander's citharodia, see also Budelmann (2018) 17–18.
70 Strab. 13.2.3.
71 A much-debated issue; see Liberman (1999) xlviii–lx with further bibliography.
72 Frr. 6 and 208a Voigt. On the 'hinting' nature of the term στάσις see Silk (1974) 122–123.
73 The interpretation of Alcaeus' maritime images as political metaphors, supported by Page

ally dated to the first century CE, both these fragments are quoted to show how the poet 'compares the upheavals caused by tyrants with stormy conditions at sea'.[74] As underlined by Antonietta Porro, Heraclitus' allegorical readings were deeply influenced by the literary approach of the School of Pergamon, and ultimately aimed at defending Homer's treatment of the gods, often regarded as blasphemous.[75] Other ancient scholarly traditions, however, seem to have read Alcaeus' maritime images allegorically. In a papyrus dated to the second century CE,[76] expressions such as ἀλ]ληγορῶν or ἐ]πὶ τῆς ἀλληγορία[ς feature in what must have been the detailed explanation of a complex nautical metaphor, involving 'a superannuated vessel which, after many blows in a long career, would now like to give up the struggle against the elements, to strike at last on a reef, and so end her days'.[77] More interestingly, in another second-century CE papyrus preserving the remains of a commentary to the poem on the ἀνέμων στάσιν, the almost certain mention of the tyrant Myrsilus suggests that this Alcaean ship was interpreted as a political metaphor.[78] The political reading also came to be applied to the Latin poet who made Alcaeus known in Rome: according to Quintilian, in his *Carm.* 1.14, closely modelled on Alcaeus, Horace 'represents the state as a ship, the civil wars as waves and storms, and peace and concord as the harbour'.[79]

The ship image deployed in the oration to Rhodes features no waves or storms. Yet, if we consider the imperial reception just outlined, as well as the Lesbian example he explicitly cites, Aristides' comparison between ship and state takes on a conspicuous Alcaean flavour. We know that Alcaeus was included among the authors 'adorned and explained' by Aristides' teacher Alexander of Cotiaeum.[80] Furthermore, the papyri cited above and others dating to the first centuries of the common era show that, even if not at an elementary level, Alcaeus was studied and read by advanced pupils and readers under the

---

(1955) and Gentili (1988), has recently been questioned by Uhlig (2018) 64. Whatever the original meaning of the Alcaean ships, as discussed here the imperial reception of such imagery included some markedly political readings. With the following discussion, compare Bowie's contribution to this volume, pp. 285–293.

74 *Alleg.* 5.5–9.
75 Porro (1994) 22–23.
76 P.Oxy. 21.2307 frr. 14, 16 = Alc. fr. 306i Voigt.
77 Page (1955) 194. The idea that the ancient commentator considered this particular Alcaean ship as a *political* metaphor has often been questioned. On the basis of the commentary, Page read it as the allegory of an old courtesan, a view rejected by Gentili (1988) 209–212, preferring a political interpretation. Porro (1994) 108–110 combines both these readings.
78 P.Oxy. 21.2306 col. 2 = Alc. fr. 305b Voigt; see Porro (1994) 55.
79 Quint. *Inst.* 8.6.44.
80 *Or.* 32.24.

Empire.[81] It was these learned readers that Aristides could expect to appreciate the lyric character of his discourse about *stasis*, ships, and Mytilene.

Obviously, Aristides hints at Alcaeus while distancing himself and the Rhodians from the poet's and his fellow citizens' *stasiotic* nature. Strikingly, both Dionysius of Halicarnassus and Quintilian recognized in Alcaeus' lyric the traces of the same political rhetoric (ῥητορείαν πολιτικήν; *plerumque oratori similis*) that Aristides wants to achieve with his address to Rhodes.[82] Alcaean 'rhetoric', however, was renowned for being abusive and violent, and for instigating *stasis* rather than quelling it.[83] Affected by a sociopolitical disorder that put its 'apparent liberty' at risk, imperial Rhodes did not need a follower of the harsh Alcaeus, but rather a new Terpander. So, Alcaeus and his political context lurk beneath the surface of Aristides' contrast between Lesbos/Mytilene and Rhodes, as the negative yardstick against which Rhodes' departure from civic *harmonia* is measured.

If my analysis is correct, Aristides' Ship of State reaches well back into archaic Greek lyric and politics, showing how the lyric past could combine with the imperial present that concerned the sophist directly. Curiously, though, the opposition between Rhodes and Lesbos/Mytilene might have functioned also within the Roman context in which it is recalled. Aristides says that the Lesbians 'have often been shown to be disposed differently from the way they ought to be disposed' (§ 56, quoted above). Now, during the First Mithridatic War, Lesbos sided with the king of Pontus against Rome, and Mytilene seems to have been a key promoter of such an anti-Roman policy. According to Livy, Mytilene was the 'only city still in arms after the defeat' of the king,[84] and Velleius Paterculus contrasted the 'perfidy' of its people with the 'loyalty to the Romans' shown specifically by the *Rhodians*.[85] Even if this episode does not seem to have had stasiotic implications, its memory, I suggest, could be triggered by Aristides' insistent comparison between Rhodes and Lesbos, reminding his audience of the right way of dealing with the Romans, now that Rhodes was 'free' under their Empire.

---

81   See McNamee (2007) 99. On Alcaeus' imperial readership cf. also Liberman (1999) lxi–lxvi.
82   Dion. Hal. *De imit.* 2.8; Quint. *Inst.* 10.1.63.
83   Strab. 13.2.3 reports that the poet 'abused (ἐλοιδορεῖτο) Pittacus and all the other tyrants' even if he himself was implied in some of their 'revolutionary attemps'. Alcaeus' λοιδορία makes Julian. *Or.* 12.1 pair him with Archilochus, and Horace's description of the lyricist's *Camenae* as 'threatening' (*Carm.* 4.9.7: *minaces*) was explained by Porphyrio (p. 152 Holder) as a reference to the 'harshness' (*austeritas*) of his poetry, which 'drove many people from the state'.
84   Livy, *Per.* 89.
85   Vell. Pat. 2.18.3.

6 Conclusion

The analysis of Aelius Aristides' *Or.* 24 proposed in this chapter has aimed at contributing to the study of lyric reception in a Second Sophistic context. In particular, Aristides' use of lyric poets, performances, and, possibly, of a specific textual allusion in his appeal for Rhodian concord has been treated as a useful case study to illuminate how some specific strains of ancient lyric, concerning civic harmony as well as *stasis*, could be deployed by an imperial orator to address a contemporary political crisis. At the same time, the discussion regarding Aristides' take on the metaphor of the Ship of State has allowed us to consider also the transmission and circulation of Alcaean political lyric under the Empire.

Instead of representing the prose version of Terpander's harmonious poetry, Aristides' 'naked discourse' has thus been shown to play its own 'music', resorting to a complex web of lyric traditions: mythical and famous singers; citharodia, monody, and choruses. All these elements appear to have been carefully chosen and adapted to blend with the political context of a Greek city under Rome. As underlined, contemporary music and performances too might have influenced Aristides' reception and use of lyric in the speech. Despite its imperial distinctiveness, though, the sophist's peculiar performance aimed at the same political effectiveness of ancient music, and found its perfect audience in Rhodes: just as it played the part of the Greek-style free city, Aristides wore the clothes of ancient poets, matching the Rhodians' fiction of politics with his manifold fiction of lyric.

References

Barker, A. 1984. *Greek Musical Writings* I: *The Musician and his Art*. Cambridge.
Behr, C.A. 1968. *Aelius Aristides and the* Sacred Tales. Amsterdam.
Behr, C.A. 1981. *P. Aelius Aristides: The Complete Works*, vol. 2. Leiden.
Bowie, E.L. 1989. Greek Sophists and Greek Poetry in the Second Sophistic. *ANRW* 2.33.1: 209–258.
Bowie, E.L. 1990. Greek Poetry of the Antonine Age. In *Antonine Literature*, ed. D.A. Russell, 53–90. Oxford.
Bowie, E.L. 2000. Athenaeus' Knowledge of Early Greek Elegiac and Iambic Poetry. In *Athenaeus and his World: Reading Greek Culture in the Roman Empire*, ed. D. Braund and J. Wilkins, 124–135. Exeter.
Bowie, E.L. 2006. Choral Performances. In *Greeks on Greekness: Viewing the Greek Past under the Roman Empire*, ed. D. Konstan and S. Said, 61–92. Cambridge.

Bowie, E.L. 2008a. Aristides and Early Greek Lyric, Elegiac and Iambic Poetry. In *Aelius Aristides between Greece, Rome, and the Gods*, ed. W.V. Harris and B. Holmes, 9–29. Leiden.

Bowie, E.L. 2008b. Plutarch's Habits of Citation: Aspects of Difference. In *The Unity of Plutarch's Work*: Moralia Themes in the Lives, Features of the Lives in the Moralia, ed. A.G. Nikolaidis, 145–157. Berlin.

Bowie, E.L. 2009. Quotation of Earlier Texts in τὰ ἐς τὸν Τυανέα Ἀπολλώνιον. In *Theios Sophistes: Essays on Flavius Philostratus' Vita Apollonii*, ed. K. Demoen and D. Pratt, 57–73. Leiden.

Bresson, A. 1996. L'onomastique romaine à Rhodes. In *Roman Onomastics in the Greek East: Social and Political Aspects: Proceedings of the International Colloquium, Athens 7–9 September 1993*, ed. A. Rizakis, 225–238. Athens.

Budelmann, F. 2018. *Greek Lyric: A Selection*. Cambridge.

Buraselis, K. 2012. Appended Festivals: The Coordination and Combination of Traditional Civic and Ruler Cult Festivals in the Hellenistic and Roman East. In *Greek and Roman Festivals: Content, Meaning, Practice*, ed. J.R. Brandt and J.W. Iddeng, 247–265. Oxford.

Cannatà Fera, M. 2011. Plutarco nel *De Musica*. QUCC 99: 191–206.

Corrêa, P. Da C. 2016. The 'Ship of Fools' in Euenus 8b and Plato's *Republic* 488a–489a. In *Iambus and Elegy: New Approaches*, ed. L. Swift and C. Carey, 291–309. Oxford.

D'Ippolito, G. 2011. Il *De Musica* nel *corpus* Plutarcheo: una paternità recuperabile. QUCC 99: 207–226.

Folch, M. 2015. *The City and the Stage: Performance, Genre, and Gender in Plato's Laws*. Oxford.

Franco, C. 2008. Aelius Aristides and Rhodes: Concord and Consolation. In *Aelius Aristides between Greece, Rome, and the Gods*, ed. W.V. Harris and B. Holmes, 217–252. Leiden.

Gentili, B. 1988. *Poetry and Its Public in Ancient Greece*. Baltimore.

Gkourogiannis, T.K. 1999. Pindar in Aelius Aristides. PhD diss., University College London.

Gleason, M.W. 1995. *Making Men: Sophists and Self-presentation in Ancient Rome*. Princeton.

Hawkins, T. 2014. *Iambic Poetics in the Roman Empire*. Cambridge.

Jones, C.P. 1990, The *Rhodian Oration* Ascribed to Aelius Aristides. CQ 40: 514–522.

Korenjak, M. 2000. *Publikum und Redner: Ihre Interaktion in der sophistischen Rhetorik der Kaiserzeit*. Munich.

Kowalzig, B. 2007. *Singing for the Gods: Performances of Myth and Ritual in Archaic and Classical Greece*. Oxford.

Kowalzig, B. 2013. Broken Rhythms in Plato's *Laws*: Materialising Social Time in the Chorus. In *Performance and Culture in Plato's Laws*, ed. A.-E. Peponi, 171–211. Cambridge.

Liberman, G. 1999. *Alcée: Fragments*. Paris.

Magie, D. 1950. *Roman Rule in Asia Minor* I–II. Princeton.

McNamee, K. 2007. *Annotations in Greek and Latin Texts from Egypt*. Oxford.

Millar, F. 1999. *Ciuitates liberae, Coloniae* and Provincial Governors under the Empire. *Mediterraneo Antico* 2: 95–113.

Nagy, G. 1990. *Pindar's Homer: The Lyric Possession of an Epic Past*. Baltimore.

Oliver, J.H. 1936. The Sarapion Monument and the Paean of Sophocles. *Hesperia* 5: 91–122.

Oliver, J.H. 1949. Two Athenian Poets. *Hesperia Suppl.* 8: 243–258.

Page, D. 1955. *Sappho and Alcaeus: An Introduction to the Study of Ancient Lesbian Poetry*. Oxford.

Peponi, A.-E. 2013. Introduction. In *Performance and Culture in Plato's Laws*, ed. A.-E. Peponi, 1–12. Cambridge.

Pernot, L. 1993. *La Rhétorique de l'Éloge dans le Monde Gréco-Romain* I–II. Paris.

Pernot, L. 2015. *Epideictic Rhetoric*. Austin.

Porro, A. 1994. *Vetera Alcaica: L'esegesi di Alceo dagli Alessandrini all'età imperiale*. Milan.

Power, T. 2010. *The Culture of Kitharôidia*. Washington, DC.

Prauscello, L. 2014. *Performing Citizenship in Plato's Laws*. Cambridge.

Race, W. 2007. Rhetoric and Lyric Poetry. In *A Companion to Greek Rhetoric*, ed. I. Worthington, 509–525. Oxford.

Russell, D.A. 1990. Aelius Aristides and the Prose Hymn. In *Antonine Literature*, ed. D.A. Russell, 199–219. Oxford.

Russell, D.A. and Wilson, N.G. 1981. *Menander Rhetor*. Oxford.

Rutherford, I. 2001. *Pindar's Paeans: A Reading of the Fragments with a Survey of the Genre*. Oxford.

Schmitz, T.A. 1997. *Bildung und Macht: Zur sozialen und politischen Funktion der zweiten Sophistik in der griechischen Welt der Kaiserzeit*. Munich.

Schmitz, T.A. 2017. Professionals of Paideia: The Sophists as Performers. In *The Oxford Handbook of the Second Sophistic*, ed. W.A. Johnson and D.S. Richter, 169–180. Oxford.

Shear, J.L. 2013. Choruses and Tripods: The Politics of the Choregia in Roman Athens. In *Dithyramb in Context*, ed. B. Kowalzig and P. Wilson, 389–408. Oxford.

Silk, M. 1974. *Interaction in Poetic Imagery*. Cambridge.

Swain, S. 1996. *Hellenism and Empire: Language, Classicism, and Power in the Greek World, AD 50–250*. Oxford.

Uhlig, A. 2018. Sailing and Singing: Alcaeus at Sea. In *Textual Events: Performance and the Lyric in Early Greece*, ed. F. Budelmann and T. Phillips, 63–91. Oxford.

Vassilaki, E. 2005. Réminiscences de Pindare dans l'*Hymne à Sarapis* d'Aelius Aristide (*Or.* XLV). *Euphrosyne* 33: 325–339.

West, M.L. 1992. *Ancient Greek Music*. Oxford.

Whitmarsh, T. 2001a. *Greek Literature and the Roman Empire: The Politics of Imitation*. Oxford.

Whitmarsh, T. 2001b. 'Greece is the World': Exile and Identity in the Second Sophistic. In *Being Greek Under Rome: Cultural Identity, the Second Sophistic and the Development of the Empire*, ed. S. Goldhill, 269–305. Cambridge.

Whitmarsh, T. 2005. *The Second Sophistic*. Oxford.

Whitmarsh, T. 2006. Quickening the Classics: The Politics of Prose in Roman Greece. In *Classical Pasts: The Classical Traditions of Greece and Rome*, ed. J.I. Porter, 353–376. Princeton.

Whitmarsh, T. 2010. Thinking Local. In *Local Knowledge and Microidentities in the Imperial Greek World: Greek Culture in the Roman World*, ed. T. Whitmarsh, 1–16. Cambridge.

Wilson, P. 2000. *The Athenian Institution of the 'Khoregia': The Chorus, the City and the Stage*. Cambridge.

PART 7

Scholarship

∴

CHAPTER 19

Historiography and Ancient Pindaric Scholarship

Tom Phillips

1 Introduction*

The critical manoeuvre of setting Pindar's epinicians against an historical backdrop, impelled chiefly by the texts' occasionality, dates from the earliest extensive interpretation of Pindar, and remains a contested issue today. This chapter explores two aspects of this impulse in antiquity. I focus first on the interrelation of historical and formal approaches to Pindar in the second century BCE, arguing that attempts to contextualize the poems historically played an important part in the development of the critical methods that came to dominate approaches to the texts. The second part of my argument looks at the role of historiographical citations in ancient Pindaric commentaries, and their possible effects on reading practices. Like their modern counterparts, ancient commentaries served as repositories of historical and mythographical information, and while this information is in some cases marshalled in the service of precise historicizing readings, there are also cases where the relationship between the primary texts and the metatextual information is more indirect and open-ended. As well as constituting valuable evidence for how processes of cultural memory operated in the intellectual culture of the Hellenistic period, this aspect of commentaries will be seen to differ significantly in both form and function from the majority of scholia in which paraphrastic and rhetorical analyses predominate.

2 Historical Interpretation and Early Pindaric Scholarship

Consideration of Aristarchus is central to any discussion of early Pindaric scholarship, and is especially important for an understanding of the methodology and influence of historicizing readings. Ekaterini Vassilaki has recently shown that the traditional view of him as an "ahistorical" critic is problematic,

---

* I am grateful to the audience at the Reading conference for discussion and to the editors for their helpful comments and suggestions.

citing several passages where Aristarchus engages in interpretations based on historical materials.[1] One such is Σ *Olympian* 3.1a, which deals with the invocation of the Dioscuri at the beginning of *Olympian* 3 (Τυνδαρίδαις τε φιλοξείνοις ἁδεῖν καλλιπλοκάμῳ θ' Ἑλένᾳ / κλεινὰν Ἀκράγαντα γεραίρων εὔχομαι).[2] We are told that 'Aristarchus solves the difficulty by saying that these gods were paid great honour in Acragas' (Ἀρίσταρχος μὲν οὖν τὴν ἀπορίαν διαλύων τοὺς θεοὺς τούτους σφόδρα ἐν Ἀκράγαντί φησι τιμᾶσθαι); he also noted that 'the Acragantines still use ancestral custom' (πατρίῳ ἔθει, Σ *Olympian* 3.1d) with regard to the Dioscuri. To Vassilaki's arguments I add simply that Aristarchus' conception of the general historical relevance of the Dioscuri both presupposes a more complex literary function for the passage than the interpretation he was concerned to rebut, that Heracles should have been the subject of the opening invocation because he was associated with Olympia (Σ *Olympian* 3.1a). This complexity is manifest in the resonance lent to the phrase Τυνδαρίδαις τε φιλοξείνοις by the different interpretations. For a reading such as that of Σ *Olympian* 3.1c that sees the invocation as alluding to Theron being told about his victory while sacrificing at the θεοξένια,[3] φιλοξείνοις appears to act as a verbal allusion to that festival, although this is not made explicit. Aristarchus' reading allows the adjective to be understood as a metonymic reference to Acragas as a whole, based on the special bond his reading brings out between the Dioscuri and the city, underscoring the relationship of ξενία between poet, *laudandus*, and audience. Whereas the other historicizing readings posit a more determinative role for context and see the language of the text in a straightforwardly referential fashion, Aristarchus' positing of a looser relationship between the poem and its historical circumstances entails attributing to Τυνδαρίδαις ... φιλοξείνοις more complex poetic workings.

The relationship between historical contextualization and literary functionality can also be seen in the debate over the function of Heracles' myth in *Nemean* 1 recorded by Σ *Nemean* 1.49c:[4]

---

1 Vassilaki (2009), arguing against e.g. Irigoin (1952) 56. While Vassilaki is right to argue for Aristarchus' use of historical materials, her contention that '*son interprétation peut aller dans le même sens que le témoignage d'historiens comme Timée, et encore dans le même sens que l'explication pindarique de Didyme*' (124) may be too strong: see p. 601. For an account of the uses of ἱστορία and its cognates in the scholia, see Calvani (2006), and for remarks about interpretative use of historical material Braswell (2012) 13–18.
2 Cf. Vassilaki (2009) 135–139. The poem was composed for Theron of Acragas in 476 BCE.
3 An event for which there is no historical evidence.
4 I use the translation of Braswell (2013) 202, with some modifications.

ἄλλως· ἐγὼ δ' Ἡρακλέος· διαπορεῖται τίνι ἀφορμῇ εἰς τοὺς περὶ Ἡρακλέους λόγους παρῆλθε· μηδεμίαν γὰρ ἔχειν εἰς τὰ παρόντα Ἡρακλέα οἰκείωσιν· ὁ μὲν οὖν Ἀρίσταρχός φησιν, ὅτι οἴονταί τινες, ὅτι ὑπόθεσις αὐτῷ ἐδέδοτο τοιαύτη ὥστε μνησθῆναι τοῦ θεοῦ, ὅπερ ἐστίν, ὡς καὶ αὐτός φησιν Ἀρίσταρχος, ἀπίθανον. μήποτε δὲ, ὅτι ἀεὶ ὁ Πίνδαρος ἐπαινεῖ τοὺς φύσει μᾶλλον τῶν ἐκ διδαχῆς περιγινομένων, ὁ δὲ Ἡρακλῆς τοιοῦτος. τοῦτο δὲ ἀπίθανον. τί γάρ, ὅτι τὴν πρώτην περὶ Ἡρακλέους γενομένην συμφορὰν ἰδίως ἐξύμνησεν, εἰς ἔνδειξιν τῶν φυσικῶν ἀγαθῶν; Ἡρακλῆς γὰρ μέχρι παντὸς ἐκ φύσεως ἀγαθὸς ὢν ἀνεφάνη, ὥστε οὐκ ἂν ὡμοίωσε τὸν ἔπαινον, ἓν μόνον τὸ περὶ τοὺς δράκοντας αὐτῷ διαπραχθὲν εἰπών· ἀλλ' εἴπερ ἄρα, ἀπὸ τῶν ἐπιφανεστέρων ἂν ἐπῄνει τὸν Ἡρακλέα. ὁ δὲ Χαῖρίς φησιν, ὅτι ὁ Χρόμιος πολλὰ συμπονήσας τῷ Ἱέρωνι κατὰ τὴν ἀρχὴν ἀμοιβῆς ἔτυχεν ἐξ αὐτοῦ, ὥστε ἐκ περιουσίας καὶ ἱπποτροφῆσαι· ὡς οὖν οὗτος ἔπαθλον πόνων ἔλαβε τὴν ἐπιφάνειαν, οὕτω καὶ Ἡρακλῆς πολλὰ ταλαιπωρήσας ἔπαθλον ἔσχε τὴν ἀθανασίαν καὶ τὸν γάμον τῆς Ἥβης.

Alternatively: I [keep to] Heracles: it is disputed on what pretext he Pindar made the transition to stories about Heracles. For Heracles is not germane to the present circumstances. Aristarchus says that some think that the subject had been assigned to him in such a way that he should mention the god: that is, as Aristarchus himself says, unconvincing. Perhaps it is because Pindar always praises those who prevail by virtue of their nature rather than those who do so by teaching, and that Heracles was of this type. This is unconvincing. For why is it that he specifically celebrates the first misfortune that befell Heracles to serve as an illustration of those who are excellent by nature? For Heracles proved consistently to be excellent from his nature, so that Pindar would not make the praise correspond when he related the deed with the serpents as the only one, but rather if he praised Heracles for his more illustrious deeds. **Chaeris however says that Chromius shared many labours with Hiero from the beginning and was requited by him for it, so that from his wealth he also raised horses. As he achieved distinction as a reward for his toils, so too did Heracles, who had endured much hardship, have as his reward immortality and marriage to Hebe.**

Here a literary critical issue, namely how the narrative of Heracles and the snakes is to be interpreted in relation to the rest of the poem, is set against a variety of historical frames by different interpreters. For the compiler of the extant passage at least, this problem is conceived in terms of the apparent lack of 'germaneness' (οἰκείωσις) between Heracles and the formal demands of the poem (εἰς τὰ παρόντα).[5] As in the above examples, we cannot be sure whether this phrasing represents how Aristarchus or another early critic posed the problem in his commentary.[6]

For the present argument, however, the crucial point is the nature of the relation between the poem and its historical situation that Chaeris outlines.[7] As in Aristarchus' reading of the Dioscuri, we can see a development from an earlier view to a more sophisticated treatment. Unlike the view reported by Aristarchus that the poem originated in a 'proposal' to the poet, Chaeris proposes seeing the mythical narrative as a kind of metaphorical history that partially maps onto the *laudandus*' circumstances. A later part of the scholium tells us that Didymus saw a connection between Tiresias prophesying further victories for Heracles and Pindar anticipating further athletic successes for Chromius (καὶ ὥσπερ τούτου περὶ τὸν Ἡρακλέα γεγενημένου ὁ Ἀμφιτρύων Θηβαῖον ὄντα τὸν Τειρεσίαν προανέκρινε περὶ τοῦ παιδός, ὁ δὲ προεμαντεύσατο τοὺς ἐσομένους αὐτῷ ἄθλους, οὕτως αὐτὸς ὁ Πίνδαρος ἀπὸ τῆς πρώτης τοῦ Χρομίου νίκης προμαντεύεται, ὅτι καὶ τῶν λοιπῶν στεφάνων τεύξεται, Σ *Nemean* 1.49c: 'and just as when this happened in Heracles' case Amphitryon consulted in advance Tiresias the Theban about the child, and he foretold the ordeals that he would undergo [sc. Heracles], so Pindar from Chromius' first victory foretells that he will achieve the rest of the crowns'). This reading was clearly meant to strengthen Chaeris'

---

5 This phrase is somewhat unclear (reflected in Braswell's 'the present circumstances'), but after διαπορεῖται τίνι ἀφορμῇ εἰς τοὺς περὶ Ἡρακλέους λόγους παρῆλθε, the referent of τὰ παρόντα is best taken as the formal demands of the text, specifically the perceived requirement for a congruence between Heracles and the circumstances of the *laudandus*. This scholium is formulating the same problem as Σ *Nem*. 1.49b: 'someone might question why he [sc. Pindar] mentions Heracles; for the recollection of Heracles does not seem apposite at this point' (ἐπαπορήσειεν ἄν τι, διατί τοῦ Ἡρακλέους μνημονεύει· οὐ γὰρ εὔκαιρος δοκεῖ ἡ μνήμη νῦν Ἡρακλέους); for a similar use of εὔκαιρος cf. Σ *Ol*. 2.161b. οἰκείωσις occurs only here in the Pindaric scholia, and is only used in other scholiastic corpora of attitudes or behaviour (e.g. glossing προσφίλεια at Σ Aesch. *Th*. 515f–h; cf. also Σ Thuc. 1.53.4). Its use here derives from the concept of τὸ οἰκεῖον in rhetorical criticism: see e.g. Arist. *Poet*. 1449a.23–24, where satyr drama adopts the metre 'appropriate' to the spoken element (λέξεως δὲ γενομένης αὐτὴ ἡ φύσις τὸ οἰκεῖον μέτρον εὗρε); Ar. *Rhet*. 3.1414a.12–13, of the 'apposite' and 'inapposite' aspects of a speech (εὐσύνοπτον γὰρ μᾶλλον τὸ οἰκεῖον τοῦ πράγματος καὶ τὸ ἀλλότριον); cf. also the use of the verb at Isoc. 15.11 of fitting related parts of a speech together (τὰς ἐπιφερομένας οἰκειῶσαι ταῖς προειρημέναις).
6 διαπορεῖται is used at Σ *Pyth*. 2.26b and Σ *Isthm*. 1.11c to introduce interpretative disputes, but in neither case is its use connected with a named critic, so we have no grounds for associating it with e.g. Aristarchus or Didymus here. The terminology of ἀφορμή is likewise not obviously associated with a named scholar: cf. Σ *Ol*. 6.37e, Σ *O*.8. inscr.b, Σ *Nem*. 6.75, Σ *Isthm*. 2.47, Σ *Isthm*. 4.1b. On Aristarchus' explanation see the comments of Meijering (1987) 258.
7 For modern responses to Chaeris' view cf. Braswell (1992) 56 with further references, and cf. Bitto (2012) 104–105.

analogy between Chromius and Heracles by the addition of further details. The citation of Didymus, together with the quotation of Chaeris himself, makes it clear that Chaeris' interpretation posits an analogical relation between frame and myth without seeing the myth as a totalizing allegory in which every element of the narrative needed to correspond to an historical comparandum.

This reading can be contrasted with, for instance, the rather less subtle interpretation of the mythical narrative in *Pythian* 11. At Σ *Pythian* 11.58a, we find a reading that takes at face value the narrator's criticism of himself at *Pythian* 11.38–40 (ἦρ', ὦ φίλοι, κατ' ἀμευσίπορον τρίοδον ἐδινάθην, / ὀρθὰν κέλευθον ἰὼν τὸ πρίν· ἤ μέ τις ἄνεμος ἔξω πλόου / ἔβαλεν, ὡς ὅτ' ἄκατον ἐνναλίαν; 'Was I indeed whirled away where the path divided, having travelled a straight road previously, or did some wind cast me from my course, like a small boat at sea'?). The scholium comments that the narrator has 'us[ed] an inopportune digression' (ἀκαίρῳ παρεκβάσει κεχρημένος), and gives no consideration to how the myth might function as part of the poem as a whole. Such an approach to 'digressions' is common in the scholia, and seems to have been the norm in Pindaric scholarship of the later Hellenistic period.[8] By contrast, we can see that Chaeris' interpretation of *Nemean* 1 conceives the mythical narrative not as a departure from an *a priori* compositional norm but as creating what a modern critic might call a dynamic relationship between narrative and historical events, a relationship that demands considerable interpretative subtlety of readers.

This reading may also be connected to a wider debate about the function of Pindaric myths in the second century BCE, traces of which are evident in the scholia. At Σ *Nemean* 4.53a, which glosses τὰ μακρὰ δ' ἐξενέπειν ἐρύκει με τεθμός ('a law prevents me from speaking at length', *Nemean* 4.33), we are told that Aristarchus interpreted the phrase as follows:

Ἀρίσταρχος· εἰς νουμηνίαν ἐπιοῦσαν ὑποκείμενόν ἐστιν αὐτῷ ἀποδοῦναι τὸν ἐπίνικον. πάντα γάρ, φησί, τὰ περὶ τὸν Ἡρακλέα καὶ Ἀλκυονέα μακρῶς διελθεῖν κωλύομαι ⟨...⟩ ἐξειπεῖν ἐρύκει με καὶ κωλύει με ὁ τεθμός· ποῖος δὲ τεθμός; ὁ νόμος τοῦ ἐγκωμίου. ὁ νόμος οὖν τοῦ ἐγκωμίου, φησί, κωλύει με μακραῖς παρεκβάσεσι χρῆσθαι.

Aristarchus: it has been pledged by him [sc. Pindar] to deliver the epinician at the coming new-moon [cf. *Nemean* 4.35]. For I am prevented, he says, from going through at length everything pertaining to Heracles and Alcyoneus ⟨...⟩ the law prevents and holds me back from speaking

---

8 Cf. Wilson (1980) 108; Lefkowitz (1985); Bitto (2012) 188–189.

out. What sort of law? The law of the encomium. The law of the encomium, he says, prevents me from employing long digressions.

Unfortunately it is not clear whether the second half of the scholium, beginning with ἐξειπεῖν, is to be attributed to Aristarchus. It is difficult to see how this could be the case, however, as Aristarchus seems to be interpreting τεθμός as a local injunction (ὑποκείμενόν ἐστιν αὐτῷ) that prevented Pindar spending a long time on the composition.[9] This position has the correlative that lengthy mythical narratives of oblique relevance to a central encomiastic aim were theoretically permissible, although of course Aristarchus does not spell out this position. It seems likely that the reading of Pindar's phrasing as referring to a general rule of poetic practice may have developed as a counter to Aristarchus' local interpretation. To whom the generalizing reading should be attributed and when it developed are unclear.[10] But given the parallelism between this scholium's picture of Aristarchus offering an historically localized interpretation that is opposed by a more general reading, and the similar dynamic at work in Σ *Nemean* 1.49c, it is possible to see both as testifying, however exiguously, to a process of debate about the function of myths in which relations between poems and the circumstances of their composition and performance were of central importance.[11] Views about the type of poet Pindar was understood to be, and the type of epinician he was thought to have composed, are thoroughly bound up with historical issues.

The above argument should not be taken to imply that interpretative approaches became fixed in the middle of the second century and were not subject to further negotiation, still less that the deployment of historical material in commentaries was of less importance after this point. Didymus proves the incorrectness of the latter notion, and as we shall see below there is a considerable amount of historiographical citation that seems to have entered the tradition after the mid-second century. We may posit a rough model as follows: interpretative approaches were fairly fluid in the second century, a period in which scholarly methodologies and aims were subject to debate.[12] Formal

---

[9] Although Vassilaki (2009) does not discuss this scholium, it offers further support to her position that Aristarchus was not averse to drawing on historical data.

[10] The scholium also records that Ammonius defended and elaborated Aristarchus' position. This suggests that the opposing, more general interpretation of ὁ νόμος τοῦ ἐγκωμίου, was already part of the critical debate by the time he wrote.

[11] In the light of Aristarchus' dissatisfaction with his suggested solution, it may be better to conceive both the initial question and the response to it as remnants of a process of thinking about the issues rather than as definitive interpretations.

[12] Cf. Porro (2009) 186–188.

interpretative models tended towards ossification over time, doubtless due in large part to the influence of rhetorical theory, and the use of Pindar as part of rhetorical teaching in schools.[13] We should not, however, press this too far; figures such as Theon and Didymus show that creative commentaries making extensive use of historical material were being written into the Augustan era, and, as ever, the nature of the evidence compels caution.

We might also wonder about the relationship between modes of historical thought and types of literary analysis, and ask whether the kind of historical readings elaborated above affected how later authors thought about Pindar. Didymus frequently attempted to interpret details of Pindar's poems in the light of historical information, but it is hard to gauge the extent to which other scholars employed historicizing approaches. Many of the rhetorical readings in the scholia, on the other hand, show little or no signs of engagement with history. Part of the reason for this is doubtless the formalizing nature of much rhetorical analysis, but a negative cause should also be considered. While we have seen that loose cause-and-effect schemata were at work in how scholars conceptualized how Pindar and his poems interacted with his historical environment, a systematic and conceptually elaborated thinking of the relationship between historical events and literary texts does not seem to have emerged; whereas rhetorical categories were well defined, modes of historicity were less so. This obviated the development of systematic historicizing scholarship, and had implications for readers to which I shall return in my conclusions, but it also allowed for the development of broadly 'archival' sections of commentaries that gathered information of oblique relevance to the texts. It is this mode of commentary to which I now turn.

3 Commentaries and Historical Citations

Before tackling these parts of commentaries directly we need to address the question of when citations of historians first began to be deployed in Pindaric ὑπομνήματα. It has long been established that Didymus drew extensively on historical material in his commentary, and numerous scholia report that he cited historians to reinforce his views.[14] When we attempt to form a picture

---

13 Cf. Bitto (2012) 36–39.
14 See e.g. Σ *Ol.* 6.55a, in which Didymus is reported as citing the historian Istrus on the location of the city of Phaenasa, and Σ *Ol.* 6.158c, where he cites Philistus and Timaeus for Hiero's status as hierophant of Demeter and Persephone. Didymus is also recorded as

of the situation in earlier scholarship, things become more difficult. There are no secure attestations of pre-Didyman scholars citing historians by name, as opposed to drawing on historical material.[15]

Aristarchus is by some distance our best attested scholar of this period, but although there are numerous places where he makes use of historical information as part of an interpretation, and several instances where he cites Homer and other poets, no scholium records him citing a named historian.[16] The distinction is important as it implies the use of a separate authority, and a specifically authorized narrative. It may, however, be the case that such explicit citations have dropped out of the scholia as a result of redaction, and the influence of Didymus on subsequent commentaries may also have played a significant part: if Didymus' practice was to surmise an Aristarchan argument without citing his opponent's sources before going on to give his own judgement,[17] this may have had a considerable influence on the form of subsequent scholia. In the case of other early Pindarists, the evidential problem is even more acute: we do not know what form the critical interventions of figures such as Chaeris, Apollodorus of Athens, and Asclepiades of Myrlea took, whether they were part of fully formed commentaries (ὑπομνήματα) or circulated as marginalia to works such as that of Aristarchus. The case of Artemon, a Pergamene grammarian of uncertain date, is similarly difficult. He is cited several times in the Pindar scholia, and may have written a commentary on the Sicilian odes.[18] Given that his comments are frequently related to historical matters it is

---

citing Timaeus at Σ Ol. 13.29b and Σ Nem. 9.95a. See Braswell (2011) for an overview and further references.

15   A possible exception may be Σ Ol. 9.62b, where Apollodorus of Athens may have cited Hellanicus for information about Deucalion, but the phrasing of ἱστορεῖ δὲ ταῦτα καὶ Ἑλλάνικος strongly suggests that a compiler is comparing Hellanicus' statement with that of Apollodorus. Cf. also Σ Pyth. 3.137b.

16   Cf. e.g. Σ Nem. 3.16b for an apparent citation of or reference to Mimnermus and Alcman. For possible points at which he may have cited historians directly, cf. e.g. Σ Ol. 2.16a, Σ Ol. 5.20e, Σ P.5.76b.

17   This need not have been bad practice on his part, as he may have assumed that interested readers would then have consulted Aristarchus' commentary.

18   Cf. Σ Ol. 2.16b, Σ Ol. 5.1b, Σ Pyth. 1. inscr.a, Σ Pyth. 1.31c, Σ Pyth. 3.52b, and Σ Isthm. 2 inscr.a, with Irigoin (1952) 62; Phillips (2013) 159–160. Σ Isthm. 2.inscr.a mentions that 'he enquired diligently into the affairs of the Siciliots' (ὁ δὲ Ἀρτέμων σφόδρα τὰ περὶ τοὺς Σικελιώτας πεπολυπραγμονηκώς), although whether this implies a history of Sicily from which his Pindaric comments have been drawn or a digression in a Pindaric commentary is hard to tell. For further comments on Artemon's work cf. FGrH 569 (= BNJ 569); Broggiato (2011). Jacoby assigns him to the middle of the second century BCE. This is plausible, but we have no strong evidence for the date.

plausible to think that if he did write on Pindar he would have cited sources for his views, but our knowledge of his work does not permit a strong hypothesis.

Our evidence, though limited, suggests that citation of historians was not especially common before Didymus. Another fact to note in this respect is that the scholia occasionally comment on Didymus' views being grounded in greater historical elaboration than those of his predecessors.[19] This is doubtless due in part to Didymus' own self-presentation and the influence his commentary seems to have exerted over later redactions,[20] but when combined with the absence of historical citations in the fragments of earlier scholars, it is at least suggestive of a shift towards more explicit historicization in Didymus' work. Although the state of the evidence renders our conclusions about such developments frustratingly imprecise, it does allow us to draw attention to a bifurcation in scholarly writing on Pindar. As mentioned above, much of the scholiastic corpus consists of paraphrastic exegesis and analysis of the texts' rhetorical structures, yet there is also a large amount of material in the scholia that derives from those parts of commentaries that acted more as repositories of information than textual exegeses. Such comments include historical data,

---

19 See e.g. Σ *Ol.* 3.1d, where Didymus' explanation of the invocation of the Dioscuri (that Theron is an Argive by descent and the Dioscuri are worshipped in Argos) is said to be ἱστορικώτερον than that of Aristarchus (for which see above p. 442). The meaning of ἱστορικώτερον is somewhat uncertain; Calvani (2006) 168 comments that the adverb 'o sottolinea la concretezza degli argomenti utilizzati oppure ne indica il rapporto con la storia', but it seems likely to refer to the additional detail that Didymus has added to Aristarchus' explanation: see Braswell (2013) 142. The domains of 'myth' and 'history' are not rigorously distinguished in the scholia, as is demonstrated by the only other use of ἱστορικώτερον in the Pindaric scholia at Σ *Nem.* 1.3, where it is used of a mythographical account of Ortygia and Arethusa, and refers to the level of detail involved in the explanation rather than the 'factual' status of the details discussed: see also Meijering (1987) 76–78, Calvani (2006) 167, and *Scholies* pp. 117–118 on Σ *Ol.* 1.40a. Nevertheless, considerations of accuracy do emerge in assessments of arguments based on historical evidence, as at Σ *Ol.* 2.29d, where Didymus cites Timaeus as background for Theron's historical situation, and is said to give a 'more accurate' account than that of Aristarchus (ὁ δὲ Δίδυμος τὸ ἀκριβέστερον τῆς ἱστορίας ἐκτίθεται, μάρτυρα Τίμαιον).

20 Suggestive in this respect is Σ *Pyth.* 5.34, which records that Didymus substantiated his view that Carrhotus was not only Arcesilaus' charioteer but also recruited an army for him in Greece, by citing a passage from the historian Theotimus' *On Aegina*. The scholium prefaces the citation with the phrase 'he [sc. Didymus] proves these things by citing' (ταῦτα δὲ πιστοῦται παρατιθέμενος). Even if the phrasing of ταῦτα δὲ πιστοῦται does not derive from Didymus' presentation of the evidence, it reflects a concern on the part of the scholiast with the verificatory function of such citations. The language of 'proof' is relatively rare in the Pindaric scholia: the verb reoccurs in a comparable sense only at Σ *Nem.* 7.1a where it is used of the scholar Aristodemus citing Simonides to support an interpretation (ἐπιστοῦτο δὲ τοῦτο ἐξ ἐπιγράμματος Σιμωνίδου).

citations of other poets, rationalizations of myths, etymologies, and various other types of antiquarian information. This material is often quoted anonymously; some may derive from Didymus, attribution to him having dropped out as a result of the material's lack of pertinence to his engagement with earlier scholars, but we should not rule out the possibility of other sources.[21]

We face considerable interpretative problems both in attempting to give an account of how this aspect of Pindaric commentary developed, and in attempting to reconstruct the interpretative horizons that this material would have created for ancient readers.[22] Scholars have pointed out that, in the ancient world as well as today, the process of commentary shifts the grounds upon which texts are read, increasing readers' competence by prompting consideration of exegetical methodologies, drawing attention to interpretative problems, and facilitating comparisons between the text being glossed and other texts or cultural data.[23] In what follows, I shall consider the question how historiographical citation contributes to the processes of cultural memory at work in Hellenistic scholarship, and how these processes affect understanding of Pindar's texts. Pindar is often cited in other scholiastic corpora as a source of mythographical information, and this construction of Pindar as an authority is also occasionally evident in the Pindaric commentaries. The scholia gloss φαντὶ δ' ἀνθρώπων παλαιαὶ ῥήσιες (*Olympian* 7.54) by saying that in the days before historiography developed, poets gleaned information about local traditions from learned and experienced men (τῶν ἐν ταῖς πόλεσι λογίων καὶ γεγηρακότων, Σ *Olympian* 7.100a, and cf. also Σ 101 which specifies that these 'learned men' were sources for τὰ ἐπιχώρια). The second scholium adds that 'before Pindar, this ⟨story⟩ was not recorded' (πρὸ Πινδάρου δὲ τοῦτο οὐχ ἱστόρητο), a comment that assimilates Pindar to a wider mode of writing the primary functional purpose of which is to convey information.[24] This assimilation is also reflected in

---

21   The Augustan grammarian Theon wrote an extensive commentary that may well have contained much historical material. Moreover, these modes of commentary are not mutually exclusive in the sense that they were doubtless often combined or juxtaposed.
22   The anonymity of many of the scholia means that the former problem does not admit of straightforward solution. Didymus' commentary clearly exerted an influence, and from a synchronic perspective the more archival sections of commentaries clearly catered for the demands of older and more advanced readers.
23   See the general comments of Most (2000) x–xi; for Pindaric scholarship as expanding readers' interpretative horizons see *Scholies* pp. 18–20.
24   Cf. Calvani (2006) 170n36. This function is dependent on the use made of texts by readers and scholars. Historiographical and mythographical texts are of course frequently used in this way, but poetry is also frequently treated as a source of cultural data: see e.g. Σ Ap. Rh. 2.498–527a for Pindar being cited alongside various mythographers as a source for the foundation of Cyrene.

how commentaries assemble historical and mythographical details, and it is this process on which I shall focus for the remainder of this paper. In order to sketch out some of the issues involved I shall address two sets of scholia. The first displays a fairly close integration of historical and exegetical material, while in the latter the citations have a less clearly defined role.

My first group of passages is taken from *Olympian* 13, an epinician composed for Xenophanes of Corinth in 464 BCE. Historical explanation is at work in the scholia's gloss on *Olympian* 13.23 (ἐν δ' Ἄρης ἀνθεῖ νέων οὐλίαις αἰχμαῖσιν ἀνδρῶν, 'there Ares blooms in the deadly spears of young men'). Σ *Olympian* 13.32b interprets ἐν δ' Ἄρης ἀνθεῖ as a reference to events of the Persian war, citing Theopompus (*FGrH* 115 F 285b) for the story that the women of Corinth prayed to Aphrodite to inspire their men with martial lust against the Persians:

> τὸν Ἄρην φησὶν ἐν Κορίνθῳ λάμπειν τείνων εἰς τὰ περὶ Περσίδα, ἐν οἷς ὑπὲρ τῆς τῶν Ἑλλήνων σωτηρίας ἠνδραγάθησαν οἱ Κορίνθιοι. Θεόπομπος δέ φησι καὶ τὰς γυναῖκας αὐτῶν εὔξασθαι τῇ Ἀφροδίτῃ ἔρωτα ἐμπεσεῖν τοῖς ἀνδράσιν αὐτῶν μάχεσθαι ὑπὲρ τῆς Ἑλλάδος τοῖς Μήδοις, εἰσελθούσας εἰς τὸ ἱερὸν τῆς Ἀφροδίτης, ὅπερ ἱδρύσασθαι τὴν Μήδειαν λέγουσιν Ἥρας προσταξάσης.

> He says that Ares shines in Corinth alluding to the events of the Persian wars, in which the Corinthians displayed bravery on behalf of the Greeks' freedom. Theopompus says that their women, going to the temple of Aphrodite which they say Medea founded at Hera's behest, prayed to Aphrodite that a desire might fall upon the men to do battle with the Medes on behalf of Greece.

The scholia then cite an epigram of Simonides that was written on the temple to commemorate the event, and which begins with a reference to 'these women [who] stood and prayed to the Cyprian goddess on behalf of the Greeks' (αἵδ' ὑπὲρ Ἑλλάνων ... / ἔστασαν εὐχόμεναι Κύπριδι δαιμονίᾳ, *EG* 14.1–2). This kind of historicizing interpretation has been rightly criticized in modern scholarship for taking no account of the 'grammar' of epinician composition.[25]

Such scholia do, however, shed important light on the influences to which ancient reading practices were subject. In citing a text contemporary with the poem's initial performance(s) and a story presumably well known to Pindar's first audiences, the scholium creates a potential connection between the reader

---

25   Cf. e.g. Young (1971) 29–30n99; Lefkowitz (1975) 174–177.

and the interpretative horizons of those audiences. Implicit in this connection is an invitation to engage in interpretative self-definition, in which a reader might confront the historical sitedness of his own relation to the text, and attempt to see the poem through the lens of an imagined Corinthian audience. Of course we cannot know whether any ancient reader responded in this way, and it is possible to envision a reader responding sceptically to the claim for a specific allusion (τείνων εἰς τὰ περὶ Περσίδα) and the citation that supports it, and instead seeing Pindar's ἐν δ' Ἄρης ἀνθεῖ νέων οὐλίαις αἰχμαῖσιν ἀνδρῶν as a general reference to Corinthian bravery. Nevertheless, the important point for my argument is that the scholium opens up the possibility of such readings, and confronts readers with the question of whether the text should be interpreted in historicizing terms.[26]

The reference to the women's supplication is a shorter version of an account also found in a fragment of Chamaeleon of Heraclea's *On Pindar* (= Athenaeus 13.573e, fr. 31 Wehrli), which mentions that whenever Corinth was faced with severe difficulties, the temple prostitutes would pray to Aphrodite.[27] The phrasing of the scholium is similar to that of Plutarch, where he says that 'the women of Corinth alone of the women of Greece made that fine and wondrous prayer, that the goddess should make a lust for battle against the barbarians fall on the men' (καὶ μὴν ὅτι μόναι τῶν Ἑλληνίδων αἱ Κορίνθιαι γυναῖκες εὔξαντο τὴν καλὴν ἐκείνην καὶ δαιμόνιον εὐχήν, ἔρωτα τοῖς ἀνδράσι τῆς πρὸς τοὺς βαρβάρους μάχης ἐμβαλεῖν τὴν θεόν, *De Herodoti malignitate* 871a). This similarity suggests that Plutarch drew (at least in part) on Theopompus' account, and that the latter's narrative cast the Corinthian action in a similar light.[28] The scholium functions in part to bridge cultural and geographical divides. Making a connection between the poem and the Persian wars sets the poem against a Panhellenic background: by interpreting Pindar's generalizing reference in the light of this celebrated event, the scholium may in part be aimed at making the poem's rhetoric more accessible to readers, especially those from outside mainland Greece. Moreover, the citation of Theopompus participates in and reinforces the text's encomiastic strategy by highlighting an important episode in Corinthian history, while Pindar's praise is reframed as a generality exemplified by the historical events mentioned. The reference to Medea founding the temple

---

26 Cf. the remarks of Goldhill (2000) 397 on the questions opened up by citation.
27 Cf. Kurke (1996) 64–65n38 for the argument that the citation in the Pindar scholia airbrushes the prostitutes out of the story in order to simplify it.
28 Given Plutarch's concern to praise Corinthian conduct, he would surely have rebutted any criticisms of Corinth in Theopompus had he found them (cf. *Mor.* 855a). On Theopompus' high esteem for traditional religious practices cf. Flower (1994) 70–71.

of Aphrodite operates in a similar fashion.[29] This detail connects Medea with the women's supplication at that temple during the Persian wars, and suggests a parallel between the actions of the Corinthian women and those of Medea in saving the Argonauts at *Olympian* 13.53–54. Their use of Aphrodite to engender martial lust in the men of Corinth, shifting the goddess' normal function into the realm of warfare (marked by the lexis of ἔρωτα ἐμπεσεῖν τοῖς ἀνδράσιν), parallels Medea's communally beneficial transgression of gender roles. By raising the possibility of reading an historical episode, and Theopompus' narrative of it, as illuminated by the poem, the scholium also instantiates the text's exemplifying strategies, further elaborating Medea's status as a Corinthian 'hero'. The combination of gloss and primary text thus instantiates how scholarly commentary and the dislocations of literary history can add new meanings to a text, and how the rhetoric of a text can take on new resonances in the light of subsequent interpretations.

The second group of texts I want to think about likewise demonstrate the recontexualizing force of scholarly practice. In his epinician for Aristocleides of Aegina, Pindar makes glancing reference to the fact that the Myrmidons had previously lived on the island: Μυρμιδόνες ἵνα πρότεροι / ᾤκησαν ὧν παλαίφατον ἀγοράν / οὐκ ἐλεγχέεσσιν Ἀριστοκλείδας τεάν / ἐμίανε ... ('where the Myrmidons previously lived, whose meeting place, famed long ago, Aristocleides did not stain with dishonour' [*Nemean* 3.13–14]). The passage is glossed as follows (Σ *Nemean* 3.21):

περὶ τῶν Μυρμιδόνων Ἡσίοδος μὲν οὕτω φησίν (fr. 205 Merkelbach and West)·

ἡ δ' ὑποκυσαμένη τέκεν Αἰακὸν ἱππιοχάρμην.
αὐτὰρ ἐπεί ῥ' ἥβης πολυηράτου ἵκετο μέτρον,
μοῦνος ἐὼν ἤσχαλλε. πατὴρ δ' ἀνδρῶν τε θεῶν τε,
ὅσσοι ἔσαν μύρμηκες ἐπηράτου ἔνδοθι νήσου,
τοὺς ἄνδρας ποίησε βαθυζώνους τε γυναῖκας.
οἳ δή τοι πρῶτον ζεῦξαν νέας ἀμφιελίσσας.

Θεογένης δὲ ἐν τῷ περὶ Αἰγίνης οὕτω γράφει (*FGrH* 300 F 1a)· ἄλλοι δέ τινες πιθανώτερον ἐξηγοῦνται περὶ τούτων. ὀλιγανθρωπούσης γὰρ τῆς νήσου φασὶ

---

29   This detail may reflect an attempt on the part of early commentators to link the mythical past with historical events in connection with the details of Medea's role in Corinthian cult in Σ *Ol.* 13.74d and f, and Medea's connection with the Medes (for which cf. Hdt. 7.62.1) may also have been relevant in prompting the Corinthians' supplication. We might also compare Σ *Isthm.* 5.63a, which cites Ephorus and Herodotus for the information that the Aeginetans displayed the most conspicuous bravery amongst the Greeks at Salamis.

τοὺς ἐνοικοῦντας αὐτὴν ἐν σπηλαίοις καταγείοις διαιτᾶσθαι, αὐτοὺς παντελῶς ἀκατασκεύους ὄντας, καὶ τοὺς μὲν γινομένους καρποὺς εἰς ταῦτα καταφέρειν, τὴν δὲ ἐκ τούτων ὀρυττομένην γῆν ἐπὶ τὰ γεώργια ἀναφέρειν, οὔσης ἐπιεικῶς ὑπάντρου τε καὶ ὑποπέτρου τῆς νήσου, μάλιστα δὲ τῶν πεδινῶν τόπων αὐτῆς. διόπερ ἀφομοιούντων αὐτούς, ὡς εἶδον ταῦτα πράττοντας, τῶν ἔξωθεν ἐρχομένων μύρμηξι, Μυρμιδόνας κληθῆναι. μεθ' ὧν συνοικίσαντα τὸν Αἰακὸν τοὺς ἐκ Πελοποννήσου μεθ' ἑαυτοῦ παραγενομένους, ἐξημερῶσαί τε καὶ νόμους δοῦναι καὶ σύνταξιν πολιτικήν, ᾗ χρησαμένους αὐτοὺς παντελῶς δοκεῖν ἐκ μυρμήκων γενέσθαι ἀνθρώπους.

The Myrmidons lived there previously. Concerning the Myrmidons Hesiod speaks as follows:

> She [sc. Aegina] became pregnant and bore Aeacus who delighted in horses. Yet when he came to the desirable age of youthfulness, he was alone and felt disheartened. The father of gods and men made all the ants, all of those that lived there in the lovely island, into men and deep-girdled women. They were the ones who first constructed ships with curving prows.

> But Theogenes in his *On Aegina* writes as follows: some others have explained these matters in a more plausible way. They say that when the island was only sparsely populated, the inhabitants spent their time in caves under the earth, and were completely uncivilized [lacking equipment?]. They brought the fruit that grew there down to these places, and brought up the earth that they dug up from there to the fields, the island being fairly rocky and with numerous caves, especially in its flat areas. And so the people who came from outside, when they saw them acting in this way, likened them to ants, and called them 'Myrmidons'. After which Aeacus, having joined them together in a state with those who had come with him from the Peloponnese, civilized them and gave them laws and a political constitution, and it seemed that they, enjoying this constitution, had in every way become men from ants.[30]

It is notable that the above gloss as we have it does not aim at explicating Pindar, and thus contrasts with Σ *Nemean* 3.23:

---

30   Both Theo/agenes name and date are uncertain. His narrative of Aeginetan history is also cited three times with minor variations by Tzetzes *Commentary on Lycophron* 176, *Chiliades* 7.302–317, and *Exegesis in Homeri Iliadem* 1.97–609, ad 180, scholium 72. There is an emphasis on military prowess in these sources absent from the citation at Σ *Nem.* 3.21.

ὧν παλαίφατον ἀγοράν: ὧν, τῶν Μυρμιδόνων, τὴν πάλαι πεφατισμένην, τουτέ-
στιν ὑμνουμένην ἀγορὰν καὶ σύνοδον οὐδαμῶς ὕβρισε καὶ ὀνειδισμοῖς ἐμίανεν ὁ
Ἀριστοκλείδης, ἀλλὰ τοὐναντίον καὶ προσηύξησεν· ὡς καὶ Ὅμηρος (*Iliad* 15.11)·
ἐπεὶ οὔ μιν ἀφαυρότατος βάλ᾽ Ἀχαιῶν· ἀλλὰ ἰσχυρότατος δηλονότι.

'Whose meeting place, famed long ago': whose (that is to say, the Myrmidons') marketplace, i.e. place of assembly, that is spoken of of old, i.e. celebrated, Aristocleides has in no way dishonoured or defamed with reproaches, but on the contrary he has even increased its renown. Similarly Homer: 'since not the weakest of the Achaeans had struck him':—but, plainly, the mightiest.

These scholia exemplify the different modes of commentary mentioned above. The latter develops a paraphrastic exegesis designed to assist the reader in understanding the passage's meaning: in doing so, the scholium draws out the function of the litotes (ἀλλὰ τοὐναντίον καὶ προσηύξησεν), and compares Pindar's rhetoric to an Homeric precursor. The former is not strictly exegetical, but rather gathers material relevant to the Myrmidons that bears only an oblique relationship to the encomiastic thrust of the passage.

One obvious feature of the gloss is the contrasting modes of the two 'histories' given; Hesiod's mythological narrative is opposed by the 'more plausible' (πιθανώτερον) rationalizing account cited from Theogenes.[31] Both narratives in

---

31 Although the form of the scholium as we have it makes ἄλλοι δέ τινες πιθανώτερον ἐξηγοῦνται περὶ τούτων part of the quotation from Theogenes, it is possible that this phrase is a duplication of Θεογένης δὲ ἐν τῷ περὶ Αἰγίνης οὕτω γράφει, which having been written as a gloss or alternative to that phrase, then intruded into the quotation. Equally, it is possible that the two phrases are the result of an inaccurate redaction of two or more separate sources. These interpretations are supported by the fact that πιθανός and its cognates are fairly common in the scholia, and are used both of scholiasts' verdicts on Pindar himself and of scholarly interpretations: see e.g. Σ *Ol.* 7.118a for πιθανῶς used of Pindar's choice of Lachesis: cf. also Σ *Nem.* 1.44 and Σ *Nem.* 8.6; at Σ *Pyth.* 4.14 πιθανῶς is used to commend a reading by Aristarchus. More relevant to the present case is Σ *Pyth.* 1.31c, where πιθανώτερον used in the scholium of Artemon's account of the etymology of Typhos (although it is unclear whether the following remark ἔστι δὲ τὸ πιθανὸν ἐξ αὐτῆς τῆς τοῦ ὀνόματος ἱστορίας derives from Artemon or from the scholia: it is possible that the scholium's phrasing may reflect Artemon's use of πιθανός lexis, but this seems less likely). However, at Σ *Pyth.* 4.10 (ὁ γοῦν Μενεκλῆς πιθανωτέραν δοκεῖν φησι τῆς στάσεως τὴν αἰτίαν, μυθικωτέραν δὲ τὴν περὶ τῆς φωνῆς) it is unclear whether the πιθανωτέραν ... μυθικωτέραν opposition reflects the wording of Menecles' text or the scholiast's interpretation of it. Nevertheless, the example of Σ *Pyth.* 1.31c shows that ἄλλοι δέ τινες πιθανώτερον ἐξηγοῦνται could well derive from the scholia rather than Theogenes.

turn differ from the kind of 'history' Pindar constructs.[32] Whereas Pindar gives us snapshots of Aegina's great heroes (e.g. *Nemean* 3.36–39, 43–52) in order to relate Aristocleides' achievement to the island's glorious past, Hesiod's narrative documents the beginnings of Aeginetan history, and the mention of ships in the final lines marks the transition to civilized, political life on which Theogenes' account expands. The latter seeks systematically to uncover the historical events that underlie the distortions of mythical accounts. Theogenes also gives us a picture of Aeacus as performing a synoecism and organizing political institutions that is different from anything in Pindar or Hesiod. Taken together, the text and commentary form a confluence of narrative styles and intellectual approaches and have the potential to complicate the interpretative situation that would have confronted ancient readers to whom commentaries were available. At one level, the glosses sketch out a condensed literary history: the Hesiodic quotation acts as an example of archaic storytelling in contrast to a later model. Deriving from a Panhellenic text of considerable cultural authority, the citation also connects the individual reader to a wider reading community to which the Hesiodic text would have been familiar, including (presumably) Pindar's original Aeginetan audiences.[33]

The citation of Theogenes, on the other hand, brings to the reader's attention the very different intellectual tradition of rationalizing analysis of mythical narratives.[34] We cannot be sure who the ἄλλοι δέ τινες were,[35] but the phrase, together with the commendation of the account being 'more plausible' (πιθανώτερον), encourages the reader to site himself in relation to this intellectual tradition. Pindar, however, does not explicitly mention the myth of the ants, and so Theogenes' rationalization cannot simply be seen as a critique of *Nemean* 3. Yet by mentioning 'plausibility', the scholium implicitly raises the

---

32 Cf. the comments of Most (2000) x on commentaries' potential for subversiveness, which derives from the fact that they 'explicitly relate the discourse of authority [sc., that at work in the primary text] to other discourses available within the society'.

33 There may also be an educational dimension at work here, glossing Pindar's slightly obscure reference with a well-known text. Cf. Carnes (1990) for the argument that παλαίφατον ἀγοράν refers to the creation from ants myth, that Pindar and his audience would have known the story, and that Pindar implies that the Myrmidons took on the qualities of the ants from which they were created, a common feature of this story-type.

34 For this tradition cf. e.g. Winiarczyk (2013) 46–47 with further references. For other rationalizing accounts in the scholia cf. e.g. Σ *Pyth.* 3.177b (accounts of the origins, names, and etymologies of Semele and Thyone) and Σ *Pyth.* 4.10a (Menecles cited for a rationalizing account of Battus' journey to Delos; see above n. 31).

35 The ἄλλοι δέ τινες may be accounts referenced by Theogenes, but the phrase could well be a garbled reference to Theogenes himself by a scholiast; see above n. 31.

question of how this might be applied to Pindar's mythopoeia,[36] perhaps especially with regard to the narrative of Achilles' great deeds as a child at *Nemean* 3.43–52, a passage introduced by an oxymoronic phrase, παῖς ἐὼν ἄθυρε μεγάλα ἔργα, that registers the qualities by which Achilles is radically differentiated from other men.[37] There are, however, no signs in the scholia that this narrative was felt to be 'implausible': Σ *Nemean* 3.75 interprets the myth as showing that Pindar 'always prefers those successes that proceed from nature to things achieved by training' (διαπαντὸς δὲ ὁ Πίνδαρος μᾶλλον τὰ ἐκ φύσεως ἀγαθὰ τῶν ἐκ διδασκαλίας παραγινομένων προκρίνει). It is tempting therefore to see the two citations as forming a spectrum in which Pindar is a middle term, located somewhere between Hesiod's archaism and Theogenes' modernity; unlike the latter, he is engaged in the dissemination of traditional myth, but unlike the former his narratives are not open to straightforward empirical critique.

However the relationships between the different texts are conceptualized, it is perhaps the fact of readers being made to negotiate them that is the most telling point. The extant scholium does not formulate how text and metatexts should be related,[38] opening up a space for individual readers' interpretative decisions. Whether the citation of Theogenes is read as creating a sharper, contrastive appreciation of Pindar's techniques and mode of thought, or whether it is understood as highlighting the cultural and historical gap between Pindar and his modern readers, and thus perhaps feeding into a cultural narrative of Pindar as a sublime, distanced figure,[39] is less important for my argument than that the citations open up a space of interpretative possibility in which such alternatives can emerge. The primary text is thus incorporated into a scholarly construction of the past in a move that shifts the grounds and focus of the reading experience. Multiple authorities are now in play; the persona of the Pindaric narrator, enunciating the generic aim of 'bringing the Muse to Aegina' (*Nemean* 3.28) and 'praising the good man' (ἕπεται δὲ λόγῳ δίκας

---

36 Hellenistic interest in plausibility as an evaluative criterion is also manifest at Σ *Pyth.* 3.52a, which records that Artemon 'praised' Pindar for making Apollo find out about Coronis' adultery himself, rather than relying on the crow as in Hesiod's version (fr. 60 M-W = 239 Most), a story Artemon judged παράλογον.

37 A feature highlighted by the gods' role as spectators at *Nem.* 3.50.

38 On this issue cf. Phillips (2013) 155–161. Cf. Goldhill (2000) 411 for the argument that in modern commentaries 'the citation of parallels, for all that it may appear to open the possibilities of understanding by bringing to bear new knowledge … all too often serves to reinstate the commonplace as the limit of discussion—and thus to close down meaning'. I would suggest that, at least as regards historical citations, the situation in Hellenistic commentaries is rather more open-ended.

39 Cf. e.g. Antipater of Sidon 18 GP (= *AP* 7.34); *AP* 9.184.

ἄωτος, 'ἐσλὸν αἰνεῖν'), is juxtaposed with the anonymous (in this case) voice of the commentator mapping out different explanatory narratives, and the voices of the cited authors. Scholarly recontextualization sets such phrases in a new light, emphasizing how the poems have transmitted their subjects' fame and achievements across the centuries. As a result of its recontextualization, ἐσλὸν αἰνεῖν subsumes the diachronic aspect of Pindar's text, its status as a classic receptacle of values and a canonical representation of ethical and poetic authority. By juxtaposing Pindar's text with others, the process of commentary sensitizes readers to these shifts in the historicity of the text.

4 Conclusions

Implicit in the project of subjecting canonical poetry to interpretation is the emergence, as the above examples demonstrate, of a composite mode of semantic authorization: canonical author, modern commentator, and reader all contribute to the construction of meaning, in a process that reflects the larger cultural appropriations at work in the Hellenistic period.[40] Common to all the examples I have discussed is a dynamic of historical continuity and dislocation; in each case, the glosses assimilate Pindar to subsequent conceptions of literature and history, while also creating a situation in which an awareness of his distinctive narrativity and mode of constructing history is sharpened by their differences from other texts cited in commentaries. We have seen that interpretative glosses can reinforce or expand strategies at work in the primary texts, as in the story about the Corinthian women at Σ *Olympian* 13.32b, but there is also a potential discontinuity between the mode of poetic authority that emerges from Pindar's self-assertion and the relational processes into which his text is inserted by scholarly commentary.

Readers' cultural agency is likewise implicated. In addition to the dynamic of otherness and cultural continuity at work in readers' encounters with Pindar's poetry itself, commentaries provided means for readers to assimilate themselves to other interpretative communities, as in the case of *Olympian* 13 and the scholia's citation of Corinthian material, and to engage with different interpretative traditions, but glosses can also affirm the distance between Pindar and the reader by drawing attention to the former's cultural otherness. Commentaries enable readers to exert an individual authority over the cultural past by becoming πεπαιδευμένοι, defining and exploring meanings, understanding

---

40   Cf. Phillips (2013) 175–176.

contexts, and weighing different scholarly views. Yet as sites where meanings are multiplied, contested, and destabilized, as well as fixed and affirmed, commentaries also challenge the notion that an individual reader can ever exert a mastery over their contents. This dynamic is common to modern as well as ancient use of commentaries, but was in the Hellenistic period informed by a deeper tension specific to that interpretative environment: notwithstanding the importance of rhetorical modes of criticism, no clear model emerges from the extant scholia of what it means to be an authoritative, πεπαιδευμένος, reader of Pindar, in relation to the interpretative use of historical and other materials that do not fall within the remit of a rhetorical response. The absence of theoretical elaboration from early historicizing readings allows for the kind of 'archival' developments noted above, and both contribute to a critical environment that, at least in respect of its understanding of history, was markedly uncircumscribed: reading commentaries seems to have been an archivally rich experience, allowing for contact with a multiplicity of texts and authorities, and yet one that imposed few parameters on the ends at which this particular form readerly activity was to be directed.[41] It was perhaps negotiating this dynamic of informational abundance and interpretative openness that created the greatest interpretative challenges and opportunities for Pindar's ancient readers.

References

Bitto, G. 2012. *Lyrik als Philologie: zur Rezeption hellenistischer Pindarkommentierung in den Oden des Horaz*. Rahden.

Braswell, B.K. 1992. *A Commentary on Pindar* Nemean *One*. Fribourg.

Braswell, B.K. 2011. Didymus on Pindar. In *Ancient Scholarship and Grammar: Archetypes, Concepts and Contexts*, ed. S. Matthaios, F. Montanari, and A. Rengakos, 185–201. Berlin.

---

41 It is instructive to compare the situation of a contemporary reader approaching historical citations and information in modern Pindaric commentaries. Although such information is not always accompanied by extensive methodological or theoretical reflection, especially in older commentaries such as those of Gildersleeve and Farnell, a reasonably well-informed Pindaric reader is likely to be familiar with a range of highly developed and theoretically grounded approaches to the historical dimension of Pindar's poetry, such as the biographical criticism prevalent in the first half of the twentieth century, the functionality that underpins Bundyan formalism, and more recent cultural critical methods (to name only some of the more obvious trends), and to be able to draw on these methodologies for different ways of thinking about the significance of a given historical datum for the primary text.

Braswell, B.K. 2013. *Didymos of Alexandria: Commentary on Pindar*. Basle.
Broggiato, M. 2011. Artemon of Pergamon (FGrH 569): A Historian in Context. CQ 61: 545–552.
Calvani, G. 1996. Modi e fini delle parafrasi negli *scholia vetera* a Pindaro. SCO 46: 269–329.
Calvani, G. 2006. Ἱστορία negli *Scholia Vetera* a Pindaro. In *Ricerche di filologia classica v: esegesi letteraria e riflessione sulla lingua nella cultura greca*, ed. G. Arrighetti and M. Tulli, 159–172. Pisa.
Carnes, J.S. 1990. The Aeginetan Genesis of the Myrmidons. CW 84(1): 41–44.
Cribbiore, R. 2001. *Gymnastics of the Mind: Greek Education in Hellenistic and Roman Egypt*. Princeton.
Daude, C. 2009. Problèmes de traduction liés à la reformulation du texte pindarique par les scholiastes. In *Traduire les scholies de Pindare I: De la traduction au commentaire: problèmes de méthode*, ed. S. David, C. Daude, E. Geny, and C. Muckensturm-Poulle, 19–57. Besançon.
Flower, M.A. 1994. *Theopompus of Chios*. Oxford.
Goldhill, S. 2000. Wipe Your Glosses. In *Commentaries*, ed. G. Most. 380–425. Göttingen.
Irigoin, J. 1952. *Histoire du texte de Pindare*. Paris.
Kurke, L. 1996. Pindar and the Prostitutes, or Reading Ancient "Pornography". *Arion* 4.2: 49–75.
Lefkowitz, M. 1975. The Influential Fictions in the Scholia to Pindar's Pythian 8. CP 70(3): 173–185.
Lefkowitz, M. 1985. The Pindar Scholia. AJP 106: 269–282.
Meijering, R. 1987. *Literary and Rhetorical Theories in Greek Scholia*. Groningen.
Most, G. 2000. Preface. In *Commentaries. Kommentare*, ed. G. Most, vii–xv. Göttingen.
Phillips, T. 2013. Callimachus in the Pindar Scholia. CCJ 59: 152–177.
Porro, J. 2009. Forms and Genres of Alexandrian Exegesis on Lyric Poets. *Trends in Classics* 1: 183–202.
Scholies = 2013. *Scholies à Pindare*: Volume I Vies de Pindare et scholies à la première Olympique. 'Un chemin de paroles' (O.1.110), ed. C. Daude, S. David, M. Fartzoff, and C. Muckensturm-Poulle. Besançon.
Vassilaki, E. 2009. Aristarque interprète des odes siciliennes de Pindare: explication interne et explication externe. In *Traduire les scholies de Pindare I: De la traduction au commentaire: problèmes de méthode*, ed. C. Daude, S. David, E. Geny, and C. Muckensturm-Poulle. 121–145. Besançon.
Wilson, P. 1980. Pindar and His Reputation in Antiquity. PCPS 26: 97–114.
Winiarczyk, M. 2013. *The* Sacred History *of Euhemerus of Messene*. Berlin.
Young, D.C. 1971. *Pindar, Isthmian 7, Myth and Exempla*. Leiden.

CHAPTER 20

Poem-Titles in Simonides, Pindar, and Bacchylides

Enrico Emanuele Prodi

1   Introduction*

A volume devoted to, among other things, the lyric paratext invites a discussion of one of its key elements: the titles that accompany the beginning of individual poems in the text of Simonides, Pindar, and Bacchylides. (I refer to the text rather than to the individual manuscripts for reasons that will become apparent in the next section.) Of the various thresholds to the text anatomized by Gérard Genette, the title is perhaps the most obvious as well as, at least in our day, one of the most pervasive.[1] Egon von Komorzynski was somewhat over-optimistic when he suggested that 'a comprehensive and thorough history of the book-title could be at the same time a reliable and useful history of intellectual life';[2] nonetheless, the study of titles can tell us much about how their creators—be they the authors or the editors of the respective texts—represent such texts to their readership.

Unlike the titles of other kinds of compositions, such as tragedies and comedies, which have been investigated several times since the nineteenth century,[3] the titles of Greek lyric poems have been treated mostly piecemeal: genre by genre, book by book, individual example by individual example.[4] The main

---

* I am grateful to the editors of the volume, the anonymous reviewer, and David Sider for their thoughtful and valuable comments. They have much improved this chapter and bear no responsibility for any remaining mistakes. All translations are mine.
1 For modern works of *titrologie*—a term coined by Duchet (1973)—see for instance Levin (1977), the impressive monograph of Hoek (1981), and Genette (1987) 54–97 and (1988); references to further literature in Genette (1987) 54n1, Hoek (1981) 339–349. Titles of poetry are investigated by Levenston (1978) and Ferry (1996).
2 Komorzynski (1903–1904) 284.
3 On drama see among others Hippenstiel (1887); Bender (1904); Breitenbach (1908); and most recently Sommerstein (2002). More general treatments of Greek titles are Lohan (1890); Nachmanson (1969); Schmalzriedt (1970); see also many of the papers in Fredouille et al. (1997), concerned with Latin as well as with Greek. Swedish-speaking readers may profit from Zilliacus (1938).
4 See for instance Schmalzriedt (1970) 26–27n10; Braswell (1988) 55–56; Rutherford (1988) 65n3, (1990) 172, (2001a) 150–152. Beside B.-J. Schröder (1999) 164–168, the only attempt known to

exception is Bianca-Jeanette Schröder's volume on poem-titles in Latin poetry, which contains a brief overview of the titles of late archaic Greek lyric, their typology, and their treatment in the manuscripts.[5] Schröder's discussion gathers a great deal of data and provides many valuable interpretative insights, but a comprehensive analysis of the evidence remains to be attempted. This is therefore the purpose of the present chapter.

A catalogue of all surviving titles from the poetry of Simonides, Pindar, and Bacchylides is provided at pp. 470–478. It will be referred to with bold Arabic figures. Throughout the chapter the term 'title' will refer to poem-titles; book-titles will be called such. Admittedly, a more neutral term such as 'heading' or indeed 'rubric' would have been more appropriate: we twenty-first-century readers think of titles as the *names* of certain pieces of literature (*Les misérables* is called *Les misérables* much as Victor Hugo is called Victor Hugo), which is not true of most of the titles we shall examine. However, 'title' is the word most commonly used in English-language scholarship to designate them, like the equivalent terms in other languages (*titre, titolo, Titel*, etc.). Consequently, when a distinction is needed, we shall resort to calling 'titles proper' those that constitute the name of the poem they introduce, that is (for our purposes) titles of dithyrambs such as Ἴδας or Λευκιππίδες (100, 102). Finally, since our titles were probably systematized (if not devised altogether) in the "standard" Alexandrian editions of the respective poets,[6] the term 'genuine' in this paper will be used with reference to such editions, not to the earlier time when a poem was composed and first performed.

---

me of a general (if cursory) survey of lyric titles is Lohan (1890) 12–19, who, however, neglected those found in the medieval manuscripts of Pindar and (naturally) could not take into account the numerous papyri that were published from the last decade of the nineteenth century onward. Similar titles in Latin poetry are treated extensively by B.-J. Schröder (1999).

5 B.-J. Schröder (1999) 164–168.
6 See B.-J. Schröder (1999) 168. The "standard" Pindar is traditionally associated with Aristophanes of Byzantium (P.Oxy. 2438 col. ii.35–36 = fr. 381 Slater, *Vita Vaticana* [also known as *Thomana*] ΕΚΘ I 7 Drachmann); this has been disputed by Slater ad loc., but see D'Alessio (1997) 51–55 and Negri (2004) 16–27 in favour of the traditional attribution. There is no such explicit evidence for Bacchylides, but an argument can be made that the person responsible was Aristarchus, see D'Alessio (1997) 53–54. Likewise no evidence is available for Simonides, but Aristophanes' quotation of the title of one of his poems (12, in fr. 124 Slater) may suggest that he edited his works; similarly Poltera (2008) 12. For our present purposes, what name one attaches to each of these editions matters little, as long as the principle stands of one "standard" edition for each poet, or at least book.

2   Transmission

Titles seem to have been a constant feature of the manuscripts of our three lyricists at least from their "standard" Alexandrian editions onward.[7] Of the twenty-five published papyri of Simonides *lyricus*, Pindar, and Bacchylides in which the division between one poem and the next can be recognized, at least nineteen verifiably have titles,[8] none verifiably has not. In terms of layout, titles come in one of two formats: either inset in the column of writing, variously indented and sometimes spaced away from the verses above or below them (ten to eleven papyri); or written in the margin to the left of the column, with varying degrees of formality, beside or below the marginal signs that marked the end of the previous poem (nine to fourteen).[9] Although the dataset is too small to allow reliable statistics, the evidence suggests that insetting titles in the column is a later fashion, emerging between the first and the second century CE and becoming prevalent only with the 'severe style' that straddles the second and the third; until some time into the second century, a majority of titles are written in the margins. Marginal titles are sometimes written by the same hand as the text (at least three papyri), sometimes by one or more others (at least four).[10] Normally these further hands are roughly contemporary to that of the main scribe, but there is one important exception: Bacchylides' P, where the title of fr. *20C Maehler (106) seems to have been added a long time after the text was written.[11]

These data do not necessarily indicate that intitulation is a later practice that crept into the manuscripts, first added in the margins by readers' hands, then slowly incorporated into the text. Among our three authors there is not one certain instance of a papyrus that lacked titles altogether; even P was furnished with titles eventually. Of course, given that P had no titles originally

---

[7]   The bibliological aspect of titles in the papyri of our three authors is treated in greater detail in Prodi (2016); this paragraph and the next largely summarize some of its conclusions.

[8]   A possible twentieth is Π[10], where the argument for the presence of the title of fr. 94b Snell-Maehler (*76) relies on a single trace on the edge of a lacuna and is therefore doubtful: see Prodi (2016) 1144–1145.

[9]   For a table of the evidence for the different formats and hands see Prodi (2016) 1176; for their distribution over time, 1179.

[10]   The inset titles are all written by the same hand as the text, as one would expect.

[11]   The text dates from the late first century BCE or early first CE, as shown by Cavallo (1974) 36n20; the hand of the title belongs in the second or even third century CE, see Prodi (2016) 1146.

and that our papyrus evidence is heavily concentrated in the second and third centuries CE, it cannot be excluded that (some) early manuscripts of the Alexandrian vulgate of our authors may have had no titles by design. The Hellenistic period was one of experimentation and variety in matters bibliological no less than in others, and not all paratextual features need to have been as standard then as they would go on to be. Two important early manuscripts of 'choral' lyric—P itself and P.Oxy. 1790 (Ibycus' 'Ode to Polykrates', *PMGF* S151)—lack the marginal markers of metrical articulation that almost all our other papyri have. Even such a (later) regular feature of the literary book-roll as the end-title only becomes generalized at the turn from the Hellenistic to the Roman period, at least in Egypt.[12] Nevertheless, titles in at least one book certainly had an early origin: Bacchylides' *Dithyrambs* were arranged alphabetically by title, indicating that their titles go back to (at least) the Alexandrian edition itself, in which that order of the poems was established.[13] Likewise, if Simonides' *Europa* was one of his *Dithyrambs* (see 12 with *n*.), the citation of its title by Aristophanes of Byzantium suggests that it goes back at least as far as his (?) edition of that book.[14] While it is possible that dithyrambic titles, being the only titles 'proper' in our dataset, had a special status and therefore were canonized earlier than the rest,[15] nothing in our evidence requires this conclusion. The question why it was relatively common for titles to be written by further hands remains open. One may imagine a fashion of sorts—even though not one associated with a

---

12 See Schironi (2010) 25–28, (2016) 85. In Herculaneum some 90 per cent of the rolls whose final portion is preserved (mostly dating to the first century BCE) have end-titles: Del Mastro (2014) 7.

13 B.-J. Schröder (1999) 164–165, Rutherford (2001a) 150. The same will apply to any other books that were similarly organized, even though it is unclear how many were. Such an arrangement has been suggested for Simonides' *Epinicians for equestrian victors* (or a section thereof: D'Alessio [1997] 53n175) and *Paeans* (Poltera [2008] 169–170) as well as Pindar's *Prosodia* (D'Alessio [2004] 114) and a section of his *Paeans* (Rutherford [1995] 49n24; D'Alessio [1997] 31n45 and [2001] 84). I have expressed some doubts regarding Pindar's *Prosodia* in Prodi (2013) 56–58; as regards Simonides, the apparently identical format of 2 and 4—which shows that *PMG* 511 = fr. 7 Poltera was not necessarily the first poem in a subsection—weakens the argument on the *Epinicians for equestrian victors* somewhat, but does not disprove its conclusions. I do not know on what evidence Poltera (2008) 12 claims that Simonides' *Dithyrambs* were also alphabetically arranged. Unable to resist the temptation to add some speculation of my own, I have suggested that also Pindar's *Partheneia*, or a section thereof, may have been arranged alphabetically; Prodi (2014) 104–105.

14 See n. 6 above.

15 On the possibility that some of them may predate their Alexandrian canonisation, see pp. 502–507 below.

particular script or layout—or a belief that only the poet's words were the main scribe's province, while paratextual material such as titles ought to be left to the *diorthotes*.

At all events, titles were normally transmitted together with the poems they accompanied. In at least two of the four papyri where titles are written by a second hand, these are in the corrector's hand, not in that of a subsequent annotator.[16] The Pindaric scholia—later in form but largely Hellenistic and early Imperial in content—begin their exposition of each ode with a headnote (*inscriptio* in Drachmann's Latin) which is, for all intents and purposes, a scholion to its title. Occasionally a headnote actually comments on the title as if it were part of the text: for instance those of *Olympians* 3 and 11, *Pythian* 10, and *Isthmian* 3.[17] Similarly, the odd position of a scholion to Pindar's *Paean* 6(b) in Π[4], written beside the second line of the piece rather than the first,[18] is best understood as aligned with the word προc[ό]δι[ο]ν in the title on the other side of the column (65), which is the target of the explanation. Although Pindar's *Nemeans* from the eighth onward and all of the *Isthmians* have no titles in the surviving medieval manuscripts, some of their titles are preserved elsewhere. Those of *Nemean* 10 and *Isthmian* 4 partly survive on papyrus (47, 51).[19] That of *Ishmian* 3 is referred to by the scholia, as we have just seen (*50); so is that of *Isthmian* 1 (*48).[20] The title of *Isthmian* 5 is implied by two of its *inscriptiones* or headnotes (*52 with *n.*), and the same is probably true of that of *Nemean* 8 (*46 with *n.*).[21] So, whenever independent evidence is available, the absence of

---

16 Π[4] of Pindar and **A** of Bacchylides; a third, doubtful case is Π[9], where however Houston (2014) 169 suggests ascribing the title to the annotator. **A** is a particularly obvious case, in that except for the corrections it was not annotated at all (more on which at pp. 467–468 below). Another papyrus that may have had titles but apparently no annotations is Π[10], on which see n. 8 above.

17 *Inscrr.* **A** *Ol.* 3, I 105 Drachmann; **BCDEQ** *Ol.* 11, I 342 Drachmann; **BDEGQ** *Pyth.* 10, II 241–242 Drachmann; **BD** *Isthm.* 3, III 223 Drachmann. See B.-J. Schröder (1999) 167.

18 Schol. 124, 304 Rutherford. This is not the place to discuss in detail the status of the "third triad" of *Pae.* 6 = *Pae.* 6(b) following the discovery of its title and the correct supplementation of schol. 124 by Rutherford and D'Alessio *ap.* Rutherford (1997a) 3–8. Secure data are that the piece—I use this term so as not to prejudge the complex question of whether it was ever an independent poem—appeared both in the *Paeans* and in the *Prosodia*, and that it was accompanied by a title of its own in the former book too (65); the evidence further suggests that at least it was *treated as* an independent poem in the Alexandrian edition of Pindar, not only in the *Prosodia* but also in the *Paeans*. My discussion in this chapter assumes this conclusion, as well as the corollary that the "first two triads" of *Pae.* 6 = *Pae.* 6(a) were also treated as a self-standing composition.

19 P.Oxy. 5043 fr. 15 (*Nem.* 10), Π[25] **A** fr. 2(a) (*Isthm.* 4).

20 *Inscr.* a **BD**, III 196 Drachmann.

21 *Inscrr.* b **BD**, c **B** *Isthm.* 5, III 241 Drachmann; **BD** *Nem.* 8, III 140 Drachmann.

a title from the medieval manuscripts of Pindar can be shown to be a later loss. The other odes whose titles are not preserved probably lost them in transmission, too.

To summarize, the evidence at our disposal supports two related conclusions, at least on a general level. First, in most manuscripts of Pindar, Bacchylides, and Simonides individual poems were furnished with titles as a matter of routine. Second, in the respective "canonical" editions every ode had a title, which it tended to retain from copy to copy, at least in antiquity, unless error or negligence intervened.[22] And it is to antiquity that this discussion will be confined; the Byzantine manuscripts will only be used as sources for their Hellenistic and Roman ancestors.

Despite the variation that the medieval manuscripts sometimes display in matters of detail, titles appear to have been transmitted fairly consistently. Even the medieval manuscripts tend to agree with one another in the essentials. Overlap between papyri and medieval manuscripts is scarce (but see nonetheless 14 and 37), and overlap between different papyri is practically non-existent, but the overall coherence in terms of pattern—which we shall examine shortly—does not suggest that titles were in a state of generalized chaos. A scholiast remarks that the title of *Pythian* 10 (36) appears to be wrong to use an Atticised form of the laudandus' name: δοκεῖ δὲ μὴ ὑγιῶς ἐπιγεγράφθαι ἡ ᾠδὴ Ἱπποκλεῖ· δέον γὰρ Ἱπποκλέαι· τὸ γὰρ ὄνομα ἦν Ἱπποκλέας, ὡς καὶ αὐτὸς ὁ Πίνδαρος δηλοῖ.[23] Pedantic, perhaps, but correct; yet nobody amended the title accordingly. Apparent exceptions are not entirely such. The title of *Pythian* 11 in P.Oxy. 5042 (37) is likely to have been incomplete; the same may be true of that of *Partheneion* 2 in Π[10] (*76), if it was present at all.[24] But partial omission is not equivalent to outright invention or wilful alteration. As far as one can judge, the process that took place across the Hellenistic and Roman period after the "standard" editions of our three poets were established is largely one

---

22 Irigoin (1952) lists the titles that, by stemmatic inference from the Byzantine manuscripts, go back at least to the commented edition of Pindar's *Epinicians* that was probably compiled in the second century CE (101), to the archetype of the Vatican recension in the early fifth century (108–109), and to the nearest common ancestor of the shortened Vatican recension in the late tenth century (132). Nothing in his inquiry contradicts the present argument that the titles are all in fact earlier, ultimately going back to Alexandria.

23 'It seems that the ode is not titled "to Hippokles" properly: it should have been "to Hippokleas", for the name is Hippokleas, as Pindar himself makes clear' (*inscr.* BDEGQ, II 241–242 Drachmann). On the (partial) Atticisation of personal names in our titles, see pp. 469 below.

24 See also the discussion of the titles in Bacchylides' A, pp. 467–468 below.

of direct transmission, not of active recreation at each copyist's or reader's whim. Although titles were not always complete in every manuscript (but they were far more frequently than not), it is plausible that what *was* written was indeed, usually, genuine.[25]

One possible problem is the London Bacchylides, **A**.[26] Its text was corrected four times: by the main scribe (**A¹**) and by three correctors, conventionally known as **A²**, **A³**, **A⁴**.[27] The main scribe wrote no titles, at least in the surviving portions of the manuscript. **A²** supplied those of odes 2, 19, 20, and perhaps, mistakenly, 7;[28] **A³** took care of odes 3, 4, 6–15, 17, and 18 (see 87–95, 97–101). Ode 5 was left untitled, probably by mistake. There is no obvious explanation for why it took two people to fill in the titles (perhaps like Π⁴ of Pindar's *Paeans*),[29] and as the question has no obvious impact on our discussion, it will be left aside. But a more important issue is the two correctors' sources. **A³** certainly corrected by collation, whether of the exemplar from which **A** was copied or of a second manuscript,[30] but this may not be true of **A²**. The latter's corrections

---

25 Once again, 'genuine' from a purely text-critical and text-historical perspective—for our purposes, 'faithfully representing the respective Alexandrian original'—with no implication of veracity. On the reliability or otherwise of the information provided by titles, see section 6, pp. 490–507 below.

26 With reference to **A**, I use the singular 'papyrus' or 'manuscript' for the sake of convenience, without prejudice to the question whether it was one book-roll or two: see Prodi (2016) 1159n73.

27 See Kenyon (1897) xix–xx, liii; Jebb (1905) 132–135.

28 According to Kenyon (1897) 65, the title of 7 (90) added by **A³** is 'written over three washed-out lines, perhaps a repetition of the full title as given at the beginning of the previous poem'; he did not speculate that the earlier writing was by **A²**, as Snell (1934) 11* went on to suggest. Snell's reconstruction of the deletion and replacement of the title of 7, if correct, is the only evidence that **A³** corrected the manuscript after **A²**: if Snell is mistaken—for instance, if **A³** himself had miswritten the title that he then deleted and corrected—the reverse order is equally possible. It is unclear what importance a reversal of the two correctors may have for our discussion, but the more limited role played by **A²** would be easily explained if most of the corrections had already been made by **A³**.

29 According to Grenfell and Hunt (1908) 15, the two titles found on that manuscript (64, 65) are in the same hand; according to Rutherford (1997a) 4, 20, they are not. Given how little text survives, the question is hard to settle.

30 Supplementation by **A³** of lines omitted by **A** proves that he had access to a manuscript other than **A** itself, as Kenyon (1897) xviii remarks; the false corrections he made to several authentic readings of **A** suggest that his exemplar was different from that of **A**, but other hypotheses have been entertained, see Prodi (2016) 1182. As we saw, the mere fact that the main scribe did not copy titles is no evidence that there were none in his antigraph.

to the poetic text are all simple enough to have been conjectural, even though there is no proof that they were. The implications for the titles are obvious: if A^2 relied on nothing but A and his own ingenuity, it follows necessarily that the titles he wrote are conjectural too. Bruno Snell argues precisely this, on the grounds that A^2 could easily have extracted the necessary information from the text of the poems.[31]

This is of particular import for the *Dithyrambs*. The two whose title was supplied by A^2, 19 and 20, are the only ones where the title 'proper' is followed by the indication of the community for whom the poem was composed (100, 101), which is not found in those written by A^3. What are we to make of this? It seems uneconomical to suggest that A^2 and A^3 used the same manuscript, whether the exemplar of A or another copy, but A^2 transcribed the titles faithfully while A^3 ignored the second component of each (and yet preserved the double titles of 97 and 98).[32] To suppose that A^2 and A^3 availed themselves of different exemplars, one with longer and one with shorter titles, merely pushes the conundrum up the stemma. Moreover, if *PSI* 1811 does represent Bacchylides' *Dithyrambs*,[33] there is another, independent example of a title without an indication of the commissioning community (102). If this was a mere omission, it was suspiciously widespread. On the other hand, it would also be strange—albeit certainly not impossible—for A^2 to have conjectured titles beyond the attested format. The Alexandrian Pindar may have contributed to the error by providing misleading parallels (75), but titling patterns in the two authors do tend to correspond, as we shall see. At least the titles 'proper' of 100 and 101 must be correct, in that they respect the alphabetic arrangement. Furthermore, a title may be more memorable than other elements of the text: if A^2 knew his Bacchylides, he might have remembered, rather than conjectured, the few titles he filled in even if he did not have a copy to hand against which to collate the text on a large scale. But it is also possible that A genuinely reflects the condition of titles in Bacchylides' *Dithyrambs*—some with datives, some without—and that the coincidence between typologies and hands is only that—a coincidence.

---

31 Snell (1934) 10*.
32 A^3 also omitted the specification παιδί in 90 (see *n.*), but copied it correctly in 93. It is hard, though possible, to argue that he was prone to omitting seemingly less relevant details generally.
33 First attributed to Bacchylides by Vogliano (1932) 172; this ascription is generally accepted, despite the attempt by Davison (1934) to suggest Simonides instead. See most recently Hadjimichael (2014) 81–85.

We have seen how our titles probably go back to the "standard" Alexandrian editions of our three poets. In the last section we shall examine some cases in which a title (or part of one) may be earlier than those editions. It is also likely that, in the two-and-a-half centuries before the activity of the Alexandrian philologists, odes were at least occasionally referred to with something resembling our titles (we have a few examples thanks to Athenaeus),[34] whether or not these accompanied them in their written form too. However, titles as we have them seem to be largely an Alexandrian creation, or at least systematization. The consistency of their format within books and genres as well as across the three authors betrays the hand of the editor, if not of the librarian; that they may have arisen independently in all of the (presumably) many streams of tradition that brought the poetry of Simonides, Pindar, and Bacchylides from all over the Greek-speaking world to Alexandria defies belief. Their peculiar semi-Attic veneer, with its distinctive combination of inconsistently Atticised endings and retained non-Attic vowels in the stem (see 18, 22, 30, 36, 41, 42, *52, *53), also tells against direct provenance from the poet's own estate or from the different localities (most of them outside the Attic-speaking sphere) for which the poems had been composed. Given the important role that Athenian audiences, and indeed readerships, probably played in the transmission of Pindar's poetry between the fifth and the third century,[35] it is tempting to wonder whether the Alexandrian system of titles may have been built upon an Attic antecedent, or at least upon Attic examples. But the scarce evidence for pre-Alexandrian titles complicates any attempt to assess of this question, which is best left aside now.

---

34 Aristox. fr. III 3 110 Kaiser = 99 Wehrli διόπερ καὶ Πίνδαρον εἰρηκέναι ἐν τῶι πρὸς Ἱέρωνα ϲκολίωι 'and Pindar said in the *skolion* to Hieron'; Heraclid. Pont. fr. 39 Schütrumpf = 55 Wehrli Πίνδαρος παραινῶν Ἱέρωνι Ϲυρακοϲίων ἄρχοντι 'Pindar while advising Hieron the lord of Syracuse'; Chamael. fr. 35 Martano = 31 Wehrli Πίνδαρός τε τὸ μὲν πρῶτον ἔγραψεν εἰς αὐτὸν ἐγκώμιον οὗ ἡ ἀρχή Τριϲολυμπιονίκαν ἐπαινέων οἶκον, ὕϲτερον δὲ καὶ ϲκόλιον τὸ παρὰ τὴν θυϲίαν ἀιϲθέν 'and first Pindar wrote in [Xenophon of Corinth's] honour the *enkomion* that begins "In praising a house with three Olympic victories" [*Ol.* 13], and later also the *skolion* sung at the sacrifice'. Cf. already Pl. *Prot.* 339a λέγει γάρ που Ϲιμωνίδης πρὸς Ϲκόπαν τὸν Κρέοντος υἱὸν τοῦ Θετταλοῦ 'for Simonides says to Scopas the son of Creon the Thessalian'. For another possible hint, see n. 45 below.

35 See Hadjimichael's contribution to this volume. Compare the argument in D'Alessio (2016) 80–84 for an Athenian tradition of sympotic performances of Bacchylides' *skolia*.

3   Catalogue

The Catalogue aims to include all attested poem-titles in the poetry of Simonides, Pindar, and Bacchylides, both those preserved directly by papyri or (in Pindar's case) medieval manuscripts of the poetry itself, and those quoted by other sources with varying degrees of fidelity. When there is a reasonable possibility that a title is not quoted verbatim or in its entirety, the relevant entry is marked with an asterisk. In several cases one may doubt whether the source was actually referring to the title or rather giving an unrelated piece of information on the poem, but I have chosen to err on the side of inclusiveness; likewise with the information given by the headnotes in the Pindaric scholia, whose derivation from the respective titles is not beyond doubt. As a rule, I have not tampered with transmitted material so as to produce a neater picture. Nonetheless, some patently tralaticious information that leaked into the titles from the scholia in some Byzantine manuscripts of Pindar's *Epinicians* is relegated to the apparatus for the sake of clarity.[36] Manuscript readings for the titles of Pindar's *Epinicians* are taken from Turyn (1944, 1948), retaining his *sigla* but neglecting orthographical minutiae (Cυρακουcίωι, κέλητι, and the like). For a more complete overview of the manuscript evidence, readers should refer, as always, to Mommsen (1864). I have examined all the papyri either personally or on good photographs; reference to them is made with Snell and Maehler's *sigla* when available, otherwise with the respective publication numbers. Readings and supplements are due to the respective *editores principes* unless otherwise stated.

Simonides
Epinicia
*1   *PMG* 507 = fr. 16 Poltera : εἰc Κρίον τὸν Αἰγινήτην
    schol. RVE Ar. *Nub.* 1356aβ Holwerda ἀρχὴ ὠιδῆc εἰc Κρίον τὸν Αἰγινήτην
2   *PMG* 511 fr. 1 = fr. 7 Poltera : κέλητι τοῖc Αἰατίου παιcίν
    P.Oxy. 2431 fr. 1
*3   *PMG* 514 = fr. 3 Poltera : εἰc Ὀριλλαν
    Diogenian. *CPG* I 79 καὶ Cιμωνίδηc δ' αὐτοῦ μνημονεύει ἐν τῶι εἰc Ὀριλλαν ἐπινικίωι

---

36   See Irigoin (1952) 108–109.

4   *PMG* 519 fr. 120(b) = fr. 8 Poltera : κέλη]τι Ἀθηναίωι Λ[
    P.Oxy. 2430 fr. 120(b) || Λ[ακεδαιμονίωι vel Λ[άκωνι Poltera (2008) 292 duce Lobel (1959a) 81

Paeanes
5   *PMG* 519 fr. 35(b) = fr. 101 Poltera : Ἀνδρίοις εἰς Πυθώ
    P.Oxy. 2430 fr. 35

Hymni
6   *PMG* 550 = fr. 242 Poltera : εἰς Ποσειδῶνα
    schol. B Eur. *Med.* 5, II 142 Schwartz καὶ Cιμωνίδης ἐν τῶι εἰς Ποσειδῶνα ὕμνωι

Threni
*7 *PMG* 530 = fr. 248 Poltera : εἰς Λυcίμαχον Ἐρετριέα
    Harp. τ 3 Keaney Cιμωνίδης ἐν τῶι εἰς Λυcίμαχον τὸν Ἐρετριέα θρήνωι

Dithyrambi
8   *PMG* 539 = fr. °°351 Poltera : Μέμνων
    Strabo 15.3.1 ὡς εἴρηκε Cιμωνίδης ἐν Μέμνωνι διθυράμβωι τῶν Δηλιακῶν | Cιμωνίδης ἐν Μέμνωνι διθυράμβωι ⟨καὶ Cῆμος ὁ Δήλιος ἐν …⟩ τῶν Δηλιακῶν Schneidewin (1846) 40 : Cῆμος ἐν δ' Δηλιακῶν Poltera (2005) 185 : Cῆμος ὁ Ἠλεῖος Casaubon (1587a) 500, (1587b) 208

Incerta
*9 *PMG* 532–535 = frr. 249–251 Poltera : ἡ ἐπ' Ἀρτεμισίωι ναυμαχία
    Prisc. *gramm.* III 428 Keil *Simonides in Epartemisio Naumachia* | cf. *Sud.* c 439 Adler καὶ ἡ ἐπ' Ἀρτεμισίωι ναυμαχία δι' ἐλεγείοις, ἡ δ' ἐν Cαλαμῖνι μελικῶς, schol. L A.R. 1.211–5c p. 26 Wendel
*10 *PMG* 536 = fr. 252 Poltera : ἡ ἐν Cαλαμῖνι ⟨ναυμαχία⟩
    Sud. c 439 Adler cit. ad *9
11 *PMG* 537–538 = fr. 301 Poltera : κατευχαί
    schol. HP¹ *Od.* 6.164d, III 187 Pontani ἡ δὲ ἱστορία καὶ παρὰ Cιμωνίδηι ἐν ταῖς κατευχαῖς | schol. Plut. *Mor.* 91e ap. Paton (1912) Cιμωνίδης ἐν κατευχαῖς
12 *PMG* 562 = fr. 253 Poltera : Εὐρώπη
    Ar. Byz. 124 Slater Cιμωνίδης δὲ ἐν τῆι Εὐρώπηι

Pindarus
Epinicia
13 *Ol.* 1 : Ἱέρωνι Cυρακοcίωι κέλητι
    LEHUCN

14 *Ol.* 2 : Θήρωνι Ἀκραγαντίνωι ἅρματι
    ABLEGHCN Π¹ || Θήρωνι ακρα[Π¹
15 *Ol.* 3 : τῶι αὐτῶι εἰς θεοξένια
    ABLEGHCN || Θήρωνι add. L | ἅρματι add. ANC | εἰς om. AC, fort. recte
16 *Ol.* 4 : Ψαύμιδι Καμαριναίωι ἅρματι
    ABLEGHCN || ἵπποις BLEGHCN | νικήσαντι τὴν πβ' Ὀλυμπιάδα τεθρίππωι παιδὶ Ἄκρωνος add. BE | τοῦ αὐτοῦ εἰς Ψαύμιον Ø
17 *Ol.* 5 : τῶι αὐτῶι ἀπήνηι καὶ κέλητι καὶ τεθρίππωι
    ABLEGHCN || ἀπήνηι κέλητι E | καὶ τεθρίππωι om. BLEGHN
18 *Ol.* 6 : Ἁγησίαι Συρακοσίωι ἀπήνηι
    ABLEGHCN || υἱῶι Σωστράτου add. BLEGH
19 *Ol.* 7 : Διαγόραι Ῥοδίωι πύκτηι
    ABDLEGHCNOΦ || υἱῶι Δαμαγήτου add. A : νικήσαντι τὴν (om. BGH) οθ' (ξθ' N : οζ' ODΦ) Ὀλυμπιάδα add. BDLGHNOΦ
20 *Ol.* 8 : Ἀλκιμέδοντι παιδὶ παλαιστῆι καὶ Τιμοσθένει παλαιστῆι Νεμέα καὶ Μελησίαι ἀλείπτηι Αἰγινήταις
    ABLEGHCO || Ἀλκ. παλ. καὶ Τιμ. παλ. καὶ Μελ. παγκρατιαστῆι Νεμ. Αἰγ. A : Ἀλκ. παλ. καὶ Τιμ. παλ. Νεμ. καὶ Μελ. ἀλ. BLEG : Ἀλκ. παλ. Τιμ. παλ. Νεμ. καὶ Μελ. ἀλ. H : Ἀλκ. παι. παλ. καὶ Τιμ. καὶ Μελ. παγκρατιαστῆι C : Ἀλκ. παι. παλ. καὶ Τιμ. παλ. Νεμ. καὶ Μελ. ἀλ. παγκρατιαστῆι Νεμ. Αἰγ. O | cf. inscrr. a, b BCDEQ, I 237 Drachmann.
21 *Ol.* 9 : Ἐφαρμόστωι Ὀπουντίωι παλαιστῆι
    ABEFGHC || νικήσαντι τὴν πα' Ὀλυμπιάδα add. in marg. F²
22 *Ol.* 10 : Ἁγησιδάμωι Λοκρῶι Ἐπιζεφυρίωι παιδὶ πύκτηι
    ABEFGCNO || πύκτηι παιδὶ CNO : πύκτηι A : om. EF | Ἀρχεστράτω κέλητι νικήσαντι τὴν πβ' Ὀλυμπιάδα add. F²
23 *Ol.* 11 : τῶι αὐτῶι τόκος
    ABEF²GCNO || Πινδάρου τόκος F²
24 *Ol.* 12 : Ἐργοτέλει Ἱμεραίωι δολιχεῖ καὶ Ἴσθμια καὶ Πύθια
    ABEFGCNO || δολιχοδρόμωι Πύθια καὶ Ἴσθμια νικήσαντι τὴν (om. BG) οζ' (.α F²) Ὀλυμπιάδα BEFG : δολιχεῖ CNO
25 *Ol.* 13 : Ξενοφῶντι Κορινθίωι σταδιοδρόμωι καὶ πεντάθλωι
    EFGUCNO || σταδιοδρόμωι καὶ om. CNOᵃᶜ (σταδιοδρόμωι add. Oᵖᶜ) | νικήσαντι τὴν (om. EG) οθ' (πθ' F²) Ὀλυμπιάδα add. EFGU
26 *Ol.* 14 : Ἀσωπίχωι Ὀρχομενίωι σταδιεῖ παιδὶ
    ΦEGHCN || Κλεοδάμου add. CN : Κλεοδάμου νικῶντι (νικήσαντι E) τὴν ος' (οθ' Φ) Ὀλυμπιάδα add. ΦEGH
27 *Pyth.* 1 : Ἱέρωνι Αἰτναίωι ἢ Συρακοσίωι ἅρματι
    EGHC || Πύθια add. codd.

28 *Pyth.* 2 : τῶι αὐτῶι
    ΦEGHV ‖ Ἱέρωνι τῶι αὐτῶι ἅρματι C
29 *Pyth.* 3 : τῶι αὐτῶι κέλητι
    ΦEGC ‖ κέλητι om. ΦC | Ἱέρωνι V
30 *Pyth.* 4 : Ἀρκεcιλάωι Κυρηναίωι ἅρματι
    ΦEGHCV ‖ Ἀρκεcίλαι C
31 *Pyth.* 5 : τῶι αὐτῶι
    EGHCV ‖ Ἀρκεcιλάωι add. EGH
32 *Pyth.* 6 : Ξενοκράτει Ἀκραγαντίνωι ἅρματι
    EGHV²
33 *Pyth.* 7 : Μεγακλεῖ Ἀθηναίωι ἵπποις Ὀλύμπια Ἴcθμια Πύθια
    EGHV ‖ Πύθια om. E, del. Drachmann II 200
34 *Pyth.* 8 : Ἀριcτομένει Αἰγινήτηι παλαιcτῆι
    EGHV² ‖ νικήcαντι λε' Πυθιάδα add. GHV² : νικήcαντι Πύθια add. E
35 *Pyth.* 9 : Τελεcικράτει Κυρηναίωι ὁπλιτοδρόμωι
    EGHV²
36 *Pyth.* 10 : Ἱπποκλεῖ Θεccαλῶι παιδὶ διαυλοδρόμωι
    EFGHV² ‖ bis H
37 *Pyth.* 11 : Θραcυδαίωι Θηβαίωι παιδὶ cταδιεῖ
    EFGHV P.Oxy. 5042 ‖ cταδιοδρόμωι G : om. F^pc | solum Θρ[α]cυδ[αίωι fort. habebat P.Oxy. 5042
38 *Pyth.* 12 : Μίδαι αὐλητῆι Ἀκραγαντίνωι
    EFGHV²
39 *Nem.* 1 : Χρομίωι Αἰτναίωι ἵπποις
    UV²
40 *Nem.* 2 : Τιμοδήμωι Ἀθηναίωι Ἀχαρνεῖ παγκρατιαcτῆι
    DTU ‖ παγκρατιαcτῆι Moschopulus : παγκρατεῖ D : παγκράτιον TU
41 *Nem.* 3 : Ἀριcτοκλείδηι Αἰγινήτηι παγκρατιαcτῆι
    D
42 *Nem.* 4 : Τιμαcάρχωι Αἰγινήτηι παλαιcτῆι
    D
43 *Nem.* 5 : Πυθέαι παγκρατιαcτῆι
    D ‖ Πυθέαι υἱῶι Λάμπωνος παγκρατιαcτῆι D
44 *Nem.* 6 : Ἀλκιμίδ(ηι) Αἰγιν(ή)τ(ηι) παιδὶ παλαιcτῆι
    D
45 *Nem.* 7 : Cωγένει Αἰγινήτηι πεντάθλωι παιδί
    D
*46 *Nem.* 8 : Δεινίαι διαυλοδρόμωι
    schol. BD, III 140 Drachmann ἔνιοί φαcι cταδιεῖς αὐτόν τε τὸν Δεινίαν καὶ τὸν πατέρα

47   *Nem.* 10 : Θε(ι)αίωι Ἀργείωι π]αλαιστῆ[ι
     P.Oxy. 5043 fr. 15
*48 *Isthm.* 1 : Ἡροδότωι Θηβαίωι ἵπποις
     inscr. a BD, III 196 Drachmann γέγραφε τὴν ὠιδὴν Ἡροδότωι τῶι Θηβαίωι, τινὲς δὲ Ὀρχομενίωι· βέλτιον δὲ Θηβαίωι ἐπιγεγράφθαι | Π²⁵ A fr. 1(a) col. i τὴν ὠιδὴν ταύ]την ἔ[γ]ραψεν Ἡροδό(τωι) [– – – ἵπ]ποις ἔγραψεν
*49 *Isthm.* 2 : Ξενοκράτει Ἀκραγαντίνωι
     inscr. a BD, III 212 Drachmann οὗτος ὁ ἐπίνικος γέγραπται μὲν εἰς Ξενοκράτην Ἀκραγαντῖνον
*50 *Isthm.* 3 : Μελίσσωι Θηβαίωι ἵπποις Ἴσθμια καὶ Νεμέα
     inscr. BD, III 223 Drachmann γέγραπται Μελίσσωι Θηβαίωι· οὗτος ἐνίκησεν Ἴσθμια καὶ Νέμεα. πρόσκειται δὲ τῆι ὠιδῆι ἵπποις διὰ τὸ μὴ δηλοῦν τὸν Πίνδαρον τὸ τοῦ ἀγωνίσματος εἶδος, πότερον κέλητι ἢ τεθρίππωι· μόνον δὲ ἱπποδρομίαι λέγει ἐστεφανῶσθαι.
51   *Isthm.* 4 : τ]ῶι αὐτ[ῶι
     Π²⁵ A fr. 2(a)
*52 *Isthm.* 5 : Φυλακίδαι καὶ Πυθέαι
     inscr. b BD, III 241 Drachmann προκατασκευάζοντες ἔνιοί ὅτι Φυλακίδαι μόνωι γέγραπται | inscr. c B ibid. Καλλίστρατος Φυλακίδαι μόνωι γεγράφθαι φησί
*53 *Isthm.* 6 : Φυλακίδαι καὶ Πυθέαι καὶ Εὐθυμένει παγκρατιασταῖς καὶ Νεμέα
     inscr. BD, III 251 Drachmann πεποίηται ὁ ἐπίνικος οὗτος Φυλακίδαι καὶ Πυθέαι καὶ Εὐθυμένει παγκρατιασταῖς καὶ Νεμέα : 〈Ἴσθμια〉 καὶ Νεμέα Boeckh (1811–1821) II/1 545
*54 *Isthm.* 8 : Κλ[εάνδρωι - - -] Νικ[οκλεῖ
     Π²⁵ A fr. 4(a)
55   ].εν.[
     Π²⁵ B fr. 4 ||]γενε[D'Alessio (2012) 56, nomen victoris -]γένε[ι pot. qu. ἀ]γενε[ίωι hoc esse ratus
*56 frr. 2–3 Snell-Maehler : εἰς Κασμύλον Ῥόδιον πύκτην
     schol. R Lucian. *Dial. mort.* 10, 255 Rabe Πίνδαρος ἐν τῆι ὠιδῆι τῶν Ἰσθμιονικῶν τῆι εἰς Κασμύλον Ῥόδιον πύκτην
*57 fr. 4 Snell-Maehler : Μειδίαι
     inscr. b BD *Isthm.* 5, III 241 Drachmann ἐν γὰρ τῆι γεγραμμένηι ὠιδῆι Μίδαι (Μιᵟ ὠιδῆι B) || corr. Wilamowitz (1922) 169 adn. 2 : 〈Ἀλκι〉μίδαι dub. Maehler (1989⁸) 3
58   fr. 6a Snell-Maehler :]ωι Μεγαρεῖ σταδιεῖ
     Π²⁵ B fr. 14
59   fr. 6a(i)–(l) Snell-Maehler :] παγκρατιασταῖς Ἑλλώτια
     Π²⁵ B fr. 14 || ελωνιο( ) Π²⁵ : Ἑλλώτια vel Ἑλλωτιονίκαις D'Alessio (2012) 52, 57
60   fr. 6c Snell-Maehler : Ἀθ]ηναίωι ὠσχοφ[ορικόν
     Π²⁵ B fr. 17 || ὠσχοφ[όρια vel ὠσχοφ[όρωι possis

Hymni
*61 fr. 36 Snell-Maehler : Ἀμμωνίοις Ἄμμωνι
Paus. 9.16.1 ἀπέπεμψε δὲ ὁ Πίνδαρος καὶ Λιβύης ἐς Ἀμμωνίους τῶι Ἄμμωνι ὕμνον

*62 fr. 37 Snell-Maehler : εἰς Δήμητρα
Vita Ambrosiana I 2 Drachmann ὁ δὲ εἰς αὐτὴν (sc. Demetram) ἐποίησε ποίημα | Eust. *Prooem. ad Pind.* 27 Kambylis = III 299 Drachmann ὁ δὲ καὶ εἰς αὐτὴν ἐποίησεν | Paus. 9.23.4 Πίνδαρος ... ὕμνον ᾖςεν εἰς Περσεφόνην

Paeanes
*63 *Pae.* 4 = D4 Rutherford (?) : Κείοις εἰς Δῆλον προσοδιακός
inscr. b BD *Isthm.* 1, III 196 sq. Drachmann οἱ Κεῖοι Δηλιακὸν παιᾶνα ἠξίουν τὸν ποιητὴν γράψαι | ibid. μέλλοντος γὰρ Κείοις γράφειν προσοδιακὸν παιᾶνα | ibid. τὸ εἰς Δῆλον ποίημα | schol. BD *Isthm.* 1.3, III 197 Drachmann δῆλον ὅτι εἰς Δῆλον ἔγραφε Κείοις

64 *Pae.* 6(a) = D6.1–122 Rutherford : Δελφοῖς εἰς Πυθώ
Π⁴ col. xxii

65 *Pae.* 6(b) = D6.123–183 Rutherford : Αἰγ[ινήτα]ις [εἰ]ς Αἰα[κὸ]ν προς[ό]δι[ο]ν
Π⁴ col. xxx || suppl. Rutherford (1997a) 3–6

66 *Pae.* 7 = D7 Rutherford : Θηβαίοις ἐ[ὶς - - -] προςῳδι[ακός
Π⁵ fr. vᵛ || προςῳδι[ακός D'Alessio ap. D'Alessio and Ferrari (1988) 169 adn. 29 : προςῳδι[ον Rutherford (1997a) 5 adn. 17

67 *Pae.* 7b = C2 Rutherford : Π[- - -] .. [...]αις εἰς Δῆλο[ν
Π²⁸ fr. 1, Π²⁶ fr. 14 || Π[αλλ]ηνί[τ]αις Snell (1964³) 105, obl. Prodi (2016) 1166 adn. 95 : π[αιὰν προσοδιακὸς Δηλι]ας[τ]αῖς Rutherford (2001a) 245, 'or perhaps the two papyri have different titles'

68 *Pae.* 8 = B2 Rutherford : Δελ]φοῖς [εἰς Πυθώ
Π⁴⁵ fr. 5

69 *Pae.* 8b(a) = G7 Rutherford : παιὰν εἰς [
Π⁴⁵ fr. 1

70 *Pae.* *19 = G8.1 f. Rutherford : Π]αρίοις [
Π²⁶ fr. 16 || suppl. Maehler (1989⁸) 62

Prosodia
71 'Pae.' *15 = S4 Rutherford : Α[ἰ]γινήταις εἰ[ς] Αἰακόν
Π²⁹ fr. 1

72 'Pae.' 18 = S7 Rutherford : Ἀ]ργείοις ε̣ἰ[ς τοὺ]ς Ἠλεκτρύω[νος παῖδας
Π²⁶ fr. 7 || Ἀ]ργείους Π²⁶ ᵃ·ᶜ· | ε̣ἰ[ς τοὺ]ς Ἠλεκτρύω[νος παῖδας vel Ἠλεκτρυω[νίδας D'Alessio (1997) 41

73 'Pae.' 22(h) = Z24 Rutherford : Αἰγινή[ταις
Π²⁶ fr. 86 || idem ac **64** sec. D'Alessio (1997) 37 adn. 92

74   Z28 Rutherford : τοῖc αὐτοῖc
     Π²⁹ fr. 3

Dithyrambi
75   *Dith.* 2 : Ἡρακλῆc ἢ Κέρβεροc Θηβαίοιc
     Π⁹ fr. 1

Parthenia
*76 fr. 94b Snell-Maehler : Ἀ[γαcικλεῖ
     Π¹⁰ col. ii ‖ Prodi (2014) 104 n. 25 duce Lehnus (1984) 78
*77 fr. 94c Snell-Maehler : Δαϊφάντωι δαφνηφορικόν
     Vita Ambrosiana I 3 Drachmann ἔcχεν υἱὸν Δαΐφαντον, ὧι καὶ δαφνηφορικόν ᾆcμα ἔγραψεν

Separata a Partheniis
*78 frr. 95-*100 Snell-Maehler : εἰc Πάνα
     Vita Ambrosiana I 2 Drachmann διὸ καὶ ᾆcμα ἐποίηcεν εἰc τὸν θεόν (sc. Panem)

Hyporchemata
*79 fr. 105 Sn.-M.: Ἱέρωνι
     schol. BEFGQ *Pyth.* 2.127, II 52 Drachmann ὁ Πίνδαροc ἐκ περιττοῦ cυνέπεμψεν αὐτῶι (sc. Hieroni) προῖκα ὑπόρχημα
*80 fr. 109–110 Sn.-M.: Θηβαῖοιc
     Polyb. 4.31.6 Πίνδαρον τὸν cυναποφηνάμενον αὐτοῖc (sc. Thebanis) ἄγειν τὴν ἡcυχίαν διὰ τῶνδε τῶν ποιημάτων

Encomia
*81 fr. *120–121 Sn.-M.: εἰc Ἀλέξανδρον Μακεδόνα
     Dion. Hal. *Dem.* 26 Πίνδαροc τοῦτο πεποίηκεν εἰc Ἀλέξανδρον τὸν Μακεδόνα | cf. Dio Chrys. *Or.* 2.33

Threni
82   fr. 128c Snell-Maehler = 56 Cannatà Fera :]γ
     Π³² fr. 4(b)
*83 fr. *137 Snell-Maehler : εἰc Ἱπποκράτη
     schol. BDEGQ *Pyth.* 7.18a, II 204 Drachmann εἰc ὃν (sc. Hippocratem) καὶ θρῆνον γράφει ὁ Πίνδαροc

Incerta
*84 fr. 89b Snell-Maehler : Αἰγινήταις εἰς Ἀφαίαν
     Paus. 2.30.3 Ἀφαίας ἱερόν, εἰς ἣν καὶ Πίνδαρος ἆισμα Αἰγινήταις ἐποίησε
85   fr. 140b Snell-Maehler = G9 Rutherford :].α.ο.ις [- - -]. .[- - -]. .[- - - Ἀπό]λλ(ωνα)
     Π[11] fr. b ‖ initium dispexit D'Alessio ap. Rutherford (2001a) 382 : Θη]βαίοις, Ἀθη]γαίοις nol. Prodi (2016) 1150 adn. 38 | Ἀπό]λλ(ωνα) Rutherford (2001a) 382 : Ἀπό]λλ(ωνι) Grenfell and Hunt (1903) 17
86   Z27 Rutherford : Λε[
     Π[26] fr. 94 ‖ Λε[οντίνοις dub. Prodi (2016) 1167

Bacchylides
Epinicia
87   2 : τῶι αὐτῶι
     A[2]
88   3 : Ἱέρωνι Συρακοσίωι ἵπποις [Ὀλύ]μπια
     A[3]
89   4 : τῶι αὐτῶι Πύθια
     A[3]
90   6 : Λάχωνι Κείωι σταδιεῖ Ὀλύμπ(ια)
     A[3]
91   7 : τῶι αὐτῶι
     A[3] in rasura ‖ Λάχωνι Κείωι σταδιεῖ Ὀλύμπια (cf. 89) scriptum erat sec. Kenyon (1897) 65
92   9 : Αὐτομήδει Φλειασίωι πεντάθλωι Νεμέα
     A[3]
93   11 : Ἀλεξιδάμωι Μεταποντίνωι παιδὶ παλαιστῆι Πύθια
     A[3]
94   12 : Τεισίαι Αἰγινήτηι παλαιστῆι Νεμέα
     A[3]
95   14 : Κλεοπτολέμ[ωι] Θεσσαλῶι ἵπποις Πετραῖ[α
     A[3]
96   14B :]α [- - -]πα
     L ‖ Ἀριστοτέληι Λ]α[ρισαίωι ἱπ]πά(ρχηι) Maehler (1982) I 136 : Ἀριστοτέλει Λ]α[ρισαίωι] πα[λαιστῆι Πύθια Carey (1983) 165, obl. Fearn (2009) 24–26

Dithyrambi
97   15 : Ἀντηνορίδαι ἢ Ἑλένης ἀπαίτησις
     A[3]O[ac]

98   17 : Ἠΐθεοι [ἢ] Θηcεύc
     A³ || [ἢ] Blass (1898) 121 : [καὶ] Kenyon (1897) 153
99   18 : Θηcεύc
     A³
100 19 : Ἰὼ Ἀθηναίοιc
     A²
101 20 : "Ιδαc Λακεδαιμονίοιc
     A²
102 **23 (= fr. dub. 60 Maehler?) : Κάcc]ανδρα
     B || v. infra, pp. 505–507
103 fr. dub. 61 Maehler : Λευκιππίδεc
     PSI 1181

Hymni ?
104 fr. 1B Maehler : εἰ[c Ἑκάτην
     H || Ἑκάτην Lobel ap. Snell (1958) 82

'Encomia'
105 fr. *20B Maehler :]ν [- - -]α [- - -].
     P² || Ἀλεξά]ν[δρωι Ἀμύντ]α Grenfell and Hunt (1915) 69, obl. D'Alessio : incertum utrum titulus sit necne
106 fr. *20C Maehler : Ἱ]έρωνι C[υ]ρακοcίωι
     P²

Notes

4   Fr. 115 of the same papyrus (*PMG* 519 fr. 115 = fr. 30 Poltera)] Cικυωνι[may also preserve a portion of a title, but the supplement is not certain and nothing clearly marks the writing as that of a title. See Poltera (2008) 345.

8   Poltera's radical intervention presupposes (i) a confusion of names (which in and of itself is easy enough with an unfamiliar name like Semos), (ii) the misplacement of Μέμνωνι, *and* (iii) that a hapless scribe managed to extract διθυράμβωι from a mere δ. If we are adamant that Simonides' *Dithyrambs* did not have a subsection of *Deliaka* (the likes of 97?) and that the transmitted text is accordingly corrupt, Schneidewin's emendation is more economical. On subsections in Simonides' *Epinicians*, see n. 13 above.

*9–*10   The *Suda* lists a *Battle at the Artemision* in elegiacs and a *Battle at Salamis* in lyric metre, but Priscian's quotation of *PMG* 533a–b shows

	that the (or at least 'a') *Battle at the Artemision* was in lyric metre. Bergk (1866–1867) III 1145 argued that the *Suda* had simply inverted the correct metres, but if Parsons (1992) 6, 41 is correct in recognizing a description of the battle in P.Oxy. 3965 fr. 20, 'the busy poet celebrated (or mentioned) the same victory twice' (6). For a fuller discussion see Kowerski (2005) 4–16 with bibliography. What the metre of the 'battle at Salamis' was remains uncertain: see Rutherford (2001b) 37–38, Obbink (2001) 82.
11	It is unclear whether these *Prayers* were a poem (and of what sort) or a book. Pontani (2012) suggests that they were a poem, one of the *Dithyrambs*; Rutherford (forthcoming) inclines towards a separate book.
12	Given the title, one would suppose that the *Europa* was a dithyramb: so already Bergk (1878–1882) III 399.
*46	The scholiast's remark that 'some say that both Deinias himself and his father were *stadion*-runners' suggests that the title had chosen the other possibility, viz. that they won in the *diaulos*. αὐτόν may suggest that only Deinias was named in the title, but it cannot be excluded that also his father Megas was.
47	It is likely that the brief description of the Hekatombaia in the headnote (**BD**, III 165 Drachmann) stemmed from a (now lost) reference to that *agon* in the title, just as 58 and 59 probably occasioned the headnotes on Π²⁵ B frr. 14.i.28, 17.11–18; cf. 15 with *inscr.* A *Ol.* 3, I 105 Drachmann. The same could be suggested of *Nem.* 9, cf. *inscr.* **BD**, III 149 Drachmann. See further p. 465 above.
*52	If the title had said that the ode was addressed to Pytheas alone, Kallistratos would not have needed to specify as much. His remark, and the scholiast's decision to quote it, suggest that the title referred to both Pytheas and Phylakidas. For a contrary view see Negri (2004) 197–198. For titles referring to multiple dedicatees cf. 2, 20, *53, 58, and perhaps *54.
*62	Despite mentioning different deities as dedicatees of the hymn, the *Vita Ambrosiana* (followed by Eustathius) and Pausanias must refer to the same composition, as is suggested by their respective quotations from the text. Lehnus (1973b) 5–11 argues persuasively that the *Vita* is correct and suggests an explanation for Pausanias' mistake; see also Daude et al. (2013) 89n62.
75	The traces above these words in the papyrus are not a further line of the title, as thought by several editors, but the bottom of an *asteriskos* marking the end of the previous poem: Prodi (2016) 1164.
82	It seems that (only) this letter, and not (also) the note written in a

tiny script between the *koronis* and the column, belongs to the title: Prodi (2016) 1163. Two alternatives can be conceived—that]ν is the final letter of an extraordinarily long line of the previous column, or an unmarked stichometric letter marking line 1,300 of the book—but neither carries overwhelming conviction.

86 Given the small size of the fragment and the crowd of annotations around the text, it is difficult to determine with certainty that λε[is the beginning of a title, but this seems the most satisfactory explanation of the data: Prodi (2016) 1166–1167. How to supplement it remains an open question.

4 Typology

As can be seen at a glance from the Catalogue, titles come in more or less fixed patterns book by book, that is (at least notionally) genre by genre. This is confirmed by how these patterns tend to be the same in all three authors, unless the different secondary arrangement of one genre into multiple books required otherwise. An example of the latter are the victory odes. Pindar's were divided by games, with few exceptions.[37] Simonides' were arranged by discipline, although the details are not entirely clear.[38] Bacchylides had just enough to fill one book, so the problem did not pose itself.[39] The information offered by their titles differs accordingly. The identification of the victor with name and (usually) ethnic in the dative, as well as the indication παιδί when applicable, is common to all three poets.[40] Simonides' titles also specified the discipline, again in the dative, when a book included several (2, 4).[41] Pindar's did the same, because his book-titles were silent on the subject (13–60); for athletic

---

37 The last three *Nemeans* are not actually Nemean odes (*inscr.* BD *Nem.* 9, III 150 Drachmann), and we know from Π[25] that at least two poems at (or near) the end of the *Isthmians* are not actually Isthmian odes (59, 60). The ancient debate about the proper classification of *Pyth.* 2 (*inscr.* DEFGQ, II 31 Drachmann) is of a different order, in that the ode was classed among the *Pythians* because arguably (if controversially) connected to the Pythian games.
38 See Lobel (1959b) 89, Obbink (2001) 75–77, Poltera (2008) 12–14.
39 First noted by Blass (1898) iv.
40 The specification παιδί is not actually attested for Simonides; παιςίν in 2 is a different matter.
41 See Lobel (1959b) 89. I do not take into account P.Stras. inv. 1406–1409, attributed to Simonides' *Epinicians for Runners* by Snell (1937) 98 and mentioned in this connection by B.-J. Schröder (1999) 165: as Ucciardello (2016) demonstrates, the text it preserves is not Simonides but the sayings of Secundus the Silent Philosopher.

and musical disciplines the dative is an apposition to the victor's name, while for equestrian disciplines it is instrumental.[42] Bacchylides' indicated both the discipline and the games, the latter in an accusative that may have been envisaged as depending on an implied νικήcαντι or νενικηκότι (87–95).[43] Thus, with one important exception, the conspicuous absence of any reference to games in Simonides' surviving titles,[44] the information given by book-titles and poem-titles combined is much the same in all three authors. It is the difference in the former that necessitates a complementary difference in the latter.

In the case of other books, the picture is one of greater cross-author consistency, scarcer though the evidence is. The titles of both Pindar's and Simonides's *Paeans* indicated the community that was thought to have commissioned and presumably performed the ode, in the dative, and the sanctuary to which the song was said to be destined, with εἰc and the accusative (5, *63–64, 66–69).[45] The reason why the deity was not indicated is probably that paeans were taken to be dedicated to Apollo by default. 65 follows the titling pattern of the

---

42   B.-J. Schröder (1999) 165.
43   A similar formula, with νενικηκότι (and a form of γράφω governing the sentence) made explicit, opens the headnotes to several of Pindar's odes, see p. 489 below.
44   The only title of a Simonidean victory ode where the games were certainly not indicated is 2 (*PMG* 511 = fr. 7 Poltera). Line 5 of the poem clearly intimates a Pythian victory, but given the state of the text there is a possibility—though I should not say a likelihood—that the ἱπποδρ[οµ]ίᾳ[ι (?) of the following line refer to a different set of games rather than specify the victory won in the Pythic contest. If the former, then the slot (as it were) for the indication of the games may have been left empty out of uncertainty. But this hypothesis has little to recommend it, unless the mention of Zeus at the very beginning of the ode is taken as 'an oblique reference to an Olympian or Nemean victory' (Lobel [1959b] 89), which it might but need not be. Also, if the peculiar format for the indication of the victors is taken from a victory catalogue (a likelihood on which see pp. 491–496 below), the catalogue would necessarily have clarified the matter—unless, of course, the same owners had won several games with the κέληc. Obbink (2001) 75n40 sees in Simonidean titles a general lack of information about the games and explains it by suggesting that 'Simonides did not regularly mention in his epinicia (as Pindar and Bacchylides did) the site of the competition, and thus his epinicians were, as far as this differentia was concerned, transparent to Hellenistic editors'.
45   Given the parallel of Callimachus' *Hymn to Delos*, where the island is clearly construed as the honorand in the very text of the poem, one may wonder whether εἰc + accusative in our titles was perhaps meant in the usual sense: a paean in honour of Delphi, Delos, etc. But there is no evidence that *Paeans* so titled were really taken to be dedicated more to the place than to the god. One may rather suppose that Callimachus riffed on an existing bibliographical practice—which would then have predated him and, consequently, the "standard" Alexandrian Pindar—and composed a poem that turned the topographical εἰc Δῆλον of (especially) 67 into the more common hymnic sense of that construction, with a very Callimachus-like twist.

Prosodia even among the *Paeans*, where indeed it is labelled a προc[ό]δι[ο]ν.[46] *Dithyrambs* had a title 'proper'—or two—that designated the poem with the name of a central character or (less frequently) event, in the nominative; at least in some cases it was followed by an indication of the commissioning community, in the dative.[47] *Hymns* must have been titled with εἰc and the accusative of the relevant deity, like the *Homeric Hymns* and those of Callimachus (and many others). It appears from Pausanias' citation of *61 (Pindar) that at least some titles of *Hymns* included the usual dative for the community as well, although 103 (Bacchylides) may be an example of the contrary.[48] Titles of *Threnoi* must have indicated the deceased whom the poem mourned, as all three of our sources suggest (7, 82, *83). The Pindaric scholiast who cites *83 would have had no syntactical reason to turn a dative into the form with εἰc and the accusative; the latter form is also supported by 82, if the one letter in question is rightly understood as the end of a title (see *n*.).

The evidence for other books is much thinner and limited to Pindar. Titles of *Partheneia*—or at least of the Theban δαφνηφορικά—probably indicated the *daphnephoros*, the boy who played a leading role in the ceremony and was therefore construed as the dedicatee of the ode (*76-*77). The one title that is known (indirectly) from the κεχωριcμένα τῶν παρθενείων (*78) follows the same format as the *Hymns*, but too little is known about this strangely titled book to assume consistency of titles, or indeed of generic identification, within it. Titles of *Hyporchemes* may have referred to the individual or community that commissioned the ode (*79, *80), although it is not certain that the two sources derive the respective information from the titles. In both passages the dative is required by the syntax and thus cannot be assumed to be a literal quotation. On the other hand, one wonders what other form that indication could have taken: one does not normally find a community introduced by εἰc in such context. There is a fair amount of first-hand evidence for titles of *Prosodia*, which are now one of the best-attested parts of Pindar's *œuvre* at least in terms of the

---

46   See just below, and also p. 488.

47   For Bacchylides see p. 468 above. Simonides' case is hard to judge: both the relevant titles (8, 11) are attested only indirectly, so the absence of a dative indicating the community in the sources could be due to omission on the part of the source. Moreover, neither is above doubt: the passage that preserves 8 is probably corrupt, although to an uncertain extent, and Aristophanes of Byzantium's citation of 11 does not explicitly state that the *Europe* was one of the *Dithyrambs* (but see the respective *nn*.).

48   Note, however, that the attribution of H to the *Hymns* is conjectural: Lobel (1956a) 40. All that is preserved of the title is εἰ[, but the scarcity of city names beginning with that combination of letters supports Lobel's supplement εἰ[c.

number of manuscripts.[49] The indication of the commissioning community in the dative is followed by that of the deity or hero to whom the song is dedicated (65, 71–73), the same format as the *Hymns* may have had. The *incerta* *84 and 85, which also follow that format, may therefore have been part of either book.[50]

One case remains to be discussed: the books of Pindar and Bacchylides commonly known as *Enkomia*. That this was the title in Pindar's case is guaranteed by the *Vita Ambrosiana* (I 3 Drachmann) and by the anonymous biography preserved by P.Oxy. 2438 (col. ii.38). The latter goes on to suggest that the book contained a sub-group of poems with a distinct identity, perhaps cκόλια (Gallo), παροίνια, or ἐρωτικά (D'Alessio)—the papyrus is lacunose.[51] No source cites the title of Bacchylides' equivalent, fragments of which are preserved by **P** and **Q+U**.[52] Athenaeus 15.667c quotes fr. 17 Maehler as ἐν ἐρωτικοῖc, but it does not follow that this was the book's title. Modern editors generally call it *Enkomia*, like Pindar's book, but Giambattista D'Alessio argues that *Skolia* or *Paroinia* is a likelier alternative.[53] Another possibility, suggested by David Fearn on the basis of the Pindaric parallel, is that *Skolia* or *Paroinia* was the title of a subsection within a book of *Enkomia*.[54] Whatever the case, we know from 106 that (some) titles in the book indicated the person for whom the poem had been composed, in the dative.[55] Perhaps because of the envisaged similarity with the better-known *Epinicians*, datives of the same sort had long been conjectured as the titles of Pindar's *Enkomia*, none of which is directly attested. However, our source for *81 presents the honorand's name not in the dative but in the accusative with εἰc, despite having no obvious syntactic obligation to

---

49   On identifying papyri of the *Prosodia* (Π7, Π8, Π29, and parts of Π26) see the seminal article by D'Alessio (1997). I ventured some additional speculation on Π34 in Prodi (2013) 53–55. The *Prosodia* are also one of three plausible candidates for the attribution of Π11.

50   On 85 see also Prodi (2016) 1149–1150.

51   Gallo (1968) 30; D'Alessio (2000), (2016) 83n77.

52   On **Q** and **U** as fragments of one manuscript see Irigoin, Duchemin, and Bardollet (1993) xxxvii; D'Alessio (2016) 79.

53   D'Alessio (2016) 82–83.

54   Fearn (2007) 27–28n2.

55   One important assumption must be flagged here: namely, that titles on **P**, although written long after the text was copied (see p. 463 above), were nevertheless copied from an exemplar rather than conjectured on the basis of the text itself. If instead the latter was the case, then they no longer testify reliably to the format that was used in the Alexandrian Bacchylides (although the person responsible may have been aware of the format even if he was not copying them directly). The absence of clear comparanda for such delayed suppletion of titles makes the case hard to adjudicate. For a partly similar case involving Bacchylides' **A** (but without the large time lag) see pp. 467–468 above.

do so. The presence of datives in the titles of Pindar's *Enkomia* is thus open to question. If there was indeed a sub-group of *Skolia* (or *Paroinia*) within Pindar's book of *Enkomia*, and if Bacchylides' corresponding book was titled *Skolia* (or *Paroinia*) or included a distinct subsection of such poems, it is also possible that both forms—the plain dative and εἰς with the accusative—were in use: poems regarded as *skolia* may have been titled with a dative indicating the person for whose drinking-party and at whose behest the song had been composed, while for poems regarded as *enkomia* proper—poems concerned more directly with praise of the individual in question—the phrase with εἰς and the accusative was felt to be more appropriate. This, however, would create a strange disparity with the *Epinicians*, which are surely no less encomiastic in nature.

5 Functions and Implications

Generally speaking, titles can serve two broad kinds of purposes, one largely text-internal and one largely text-external: orientation, whereby the title guides the reader's expectations about, and understanding of, the text; and reference, whereby the text can intelligibly be cited outside, and to some extent independently of, itself by means of its title.[56] In our case, the referential function is less prominent than we might expect from our experience as twenty-first-century readers of mostly recent (or recently processed) material, or even from our knowledge of other areas of the classics. Ancient authors cited lyric far more frequently by book than they did by any smaller unit. Even when they did refer to a specific composition within a book, its title was not the default mode of reference. Another was the *incipit*. The use of the latter was inevitable when the text in question had no individual identifier outside of itself (or when it was necessary to link securely such an identifier to the text itself), but it could be used even when the poem had a title of its own.[57] Our now preferred mode of

---

56 Levenston (1978) makes much the same distinction, using the terms 'contextualization' and 'reference'. '"Contextualising a poem" means establishing the participants, the immediate situation, the wider situation, the thesis and other components of the context of situation that determine the instantial meaning of the poem, considered as utterance. And one or more of these components, in greater or lesser detail, can be named and described in the title' (63). Following B.-J. Schröder (1999) 164, I prefer the term 'orientation' so as better to bring out the implicitly authoritative status of titles vis-à-vis the reader, on which see Hoek (1981) 2 and especially Ferry (1996) 2. Cf. also Genette (1987) 76–78 on the separation between the referential use of a title ('strict designation, or identification', 77) and the motivation for the choice of that title.

57 See Nachmanson (1969) 37–45; Holtz (1997) 474–477; Borgo (2007). For Pindaric examples

citation, the serial number of the poem within the book, was used exceedingly rarely. To my knowledge, its only sustained use in Greek-speaking antiquity is in the metrical scholia to Pindar, and perhaps in one fragmentary work of scholarship on Alcaeus (P.Oxy. 2734 = *CLGP* I.1.1 Alcaeus 15).[58] Otherwise it is almost entirely restricted to the first ode in a book, perhaps on account of its special position or its particular importance within the book or the author's work.[59] This should come as no surprise: in none of our authors' surviving papyri are the individual odes numbered.

It would be idle to speculate on the reasons for the simultaneous presence of these competing uses, for the failure of any of them to prevail, or indeed for the enduring preference for citation by book over citation by individual poem. However, this situation highlights one related fact: namely, that titles were not meant to be unique identifiers of the respective poems. Even in the titles of *Dithyrambs*—those titles that, as we have seen, approximate our modern usage the most—duplication can be found, and at very close quarters too. Θηϲεύϲ is the title of two consecutive *Dithyrambs* of Bacchylides, 17 and 18 (98–99). In the second of these it is even an alternative title introduced by ἤ: a far cry from any disambiguating function.[60] Other books fare no differently. Far from attempting to distinguish accurately between poems by means of their titles, the editor habitually flagged the notional reoccurrence of a title with substitutory phrases such as τῶι αὐτῶι, τοῖϲ αὐτοῖϲ, and the like (15, 17, 23, 28, 29, 31, 51, 74, 87, 89, 91):[61] a way of highlighting the repetition while ostensibly avoiding it, essentially reducing the title to a mere cross-reference.

---

cf. e.g. *Ol.* 6 in P.Oxy. 2438 col. ii.17–18; fr. 29 Snell-Maehler in schol. **BD** *Nem.* 10.1a, III 165 Drachmann; *Isthm.* 5, 6 and *Nem.* 5 in *inscrr.* a-b **BD** *Isthm.* 5, III 241 Drachmann.

58 Cf. fr. 1.20 ἡ δὲ τρίτη introducing fr. 343 Voigt after a citation of frr. 307a and 308 Voigt, which are otherwise known to have been the first and second poems in Alcaeus' first book. The exact nature of P.Oxy. 2734 is disputed: see Lobel (1968) 2 ('a set of summaries of the contents of each poem'); Porro (1994) 131–148 and in *CLGP* ad loc.

59 The only certain example in our three poets is Pind. fr. 29 Snell-Maehler, cited by Lucian. 58.19 and identified by schol. φU, 225 Rabe as ἀρχαὶ … τῶν Πινδάρου τοῦ μελοποιοῦ ὕμνων 'the beginnings of the *Hymns* of the melic poet Pindar'. Lehnus (1973a) 398 and Lavecchia (2000) 274–276 suggest that ἐν δὲ τῶι πρώτωι τῶν διθυράμβων 'in the first of the *Dithyrambs*' in schol. BCEQ *Ol.* 13.25c, I 361 Drachmann, διθυράμβων πρώτωι in *Etym. Magn.* 1317 Gaisford, and ἐν τῶι πρώτωι τῶν παρθενείων 'in the first of the *Partheneia*' in schol. REΓLh Ar. *Ach.* 720 Wilson (Pind. frr. 71, 72, and 94d Snell-Maehler respectively) indicate the first poem of the book, not the first book of the work, but this hypothesis runs against the established meaning of such phrases; see Filoni (2007) 75–76 and already Turyn (1948) 290.

60 On alternative titles see also pp. 504–507 below.

61 See B.-J. Schröder (1999) 165; Prodi (2013) 57.

A more important and complex role that a title fulfils is to orient the reader's understanding of the piece in question. Much as labels in a museum tell the viewer what type of object they are seeing, its function, its provenance, a rough or exact date, and perhaps its individual name, the titles of our poems filled in the information that the reader was thought to need or have use for. This applied especially to context, loosely intended, which otherwise for the reader was altogether lost. This dithyramb was written for the Athenians; this epinician, for Hieron of Syracuse; this hymn, to Poseidon. This information may well have been extracted from the text itself by whoever established the title, but in the original production of the song it would have been independent of it and situated in the reality outside it. The details of this *Orientierungshilfe* (Schröder's term) with regard to the editor's purposes and his readers' responses are beyond recovery,[62] but one can fruitfully speculate on the effects that titles *may* have had and the assumptions that *arguably* underlay them.

The way in which a title presents extra-textual information upfront, before and outside the poem, contributes to detaching the text from its mere textuality by enriching it with contextual, or purportedly contextual, elements. It conjures up an extra-textual "broader picture" to which the text can be anchored, effectively fictionalizing the text at the same time as ostensibly framing it in reality. Thus titles fulfil a performative function of sorts: by asserting that a certain poem was composed for the Aeginetans or dedicated to Pan, in the eyes of the obedient reader the title *makes* it—in a way—composed for the Aeginetans or dedicated to Pan. Similarly, if datives such as Ἀργείοις (72), Δελφοῖς (5, 64, 68), or Λακεδαιμονίοις (101) could be understood as indicating the community that performed, as well as commissioned, the poems in question (and indications such as εἰς Πυθώ and εἰς Δῆλον do imply a modicum of interest in the performance of the odes), then these portions of the relevant titles may have played a quasi-dramatic part, functioning as a sort of speakers' tags for the text itself. From the opposite viewpoint, titles also belie these extra-textual endeavours through their very textuality: by inscribing originally non-written, non-textual elements in written form they seal the textualization that these compositions had undergone before reaching their resting place in the Library.

The role of titles in the librification of our authors—in the process of integrating their poems into books, that is, of turning poems from self-standing pieces into parts of a larger entity—invites further comment. There is no hard evidence that these two processes, the coalescence of poems into books and the definitive attribution of titles to them, were simultaneous or interrelated.

---

62   B.-J. Schröder (1999) 164.

All we know is that both were probably finalized in the "standard" editions of the respective authors, and that both probably had an indeterminable number of precedents about which, in turn, very little is known. Nevertheless, titles have an important role in playing out the poems' belonging in the book in which they are situated. With their standardized patterns, titles highlight each poem's pertinence to the book by subsuming the difference that each title enunciates into the larger unity that their uniformity underscores.

This is all the more significant in view of the outwardly close association between books and genres in our authors. For all the complications, theoretical and practical, of ancient conceptualizations of the various genres of lyric poetry, nevertheless the book-titles of Simonides, Pindar, and Bacchylides simply advertise the respective books as a plurality of entities identifiable as poems of a specific kind:[63] the *Paeans* are a collection of paeans, the *Hymns* one of hymns, and so forth. Indeed, one effect of such ostensibly transparent book-titles is to conceal the book—and its fundamental constructedness as such—behind the poems it brings together, grouped and labelled according to the genre to which they are said to belong. From the generic perspective, as a result, poem-titles simultaneously individualize each poem through the specific indications that they offer, and contribute to characterising the genre through the elements that they consistently put forward for that purpose. This format also enables the editor to flag pieces regarded as extravagant by means of a simple deviation from the general pattern, such as the generic subtitles appended to 59, 62, 64, and 65. It is a pity that the titles of *Nemeans* 9 and 11 and the relevant portion of 47 are lost (but see *n.*), because they might have provided an interesting term of comparison; see also 95.

The titles of individual poems are necessarily in a dialogue with the title of the book.[64] The reader is required to combine the information provided on both levels in order to read a dithyramb for the Thebans called *Heracles* or *Cerberus* or an epinician for Hagesias of Syracuse who won the Olympics with the mule cart (74, 18). The addition of a generic subtitle complicates this dialogue. While in *63, as the citations make clear, προσοδιακός complements and specifies the generic indication provided by the book-title, Ἑλώτια in 59 and ὠςχοφ[ορικόν in 60 (if correctly restored) appear rather to overrule it: a 'prosodiac paean' is still a paean, but an oschophoric is not an Isthmian ode.[65]

---

63 Cf. B.-J. Schröder (1999) 63–64.
64 Compare the remarks on the cooperation of book-titles and poem-titles in Levenston (1978) 69–70.
65 The effect is slightly different if the subtitle is reconstructed as ὠςχοφ[όρια not ὠςχοφ[ορι-

Conversely, the indication of further games attached to 24, 33, and perhaps *50 and *53 (if genuine) clearly constitute additions to, not a denial of, the information offered by the book-title. Given the particularly complex status of 'Paean' 6(b),[66] the only piece by Pindar that is known to have appeared in two different places in his Alexandrian corpus, one does not quite know what to make of the subtitle προcόδιον (65). Does it imply that (genre-wise) the piece, being a prosodion, is not a paean? Or does it simply state that (book-wise) the poem was a *Prosodion* as well as a *Paean*? The former is suggested by the twin considerations that the format of the title is the one found in the *Prosodia*, not the *Paeans*, and that the editor opted for προcόδιον over the attested alternative προcοδιακόc (even though it is unclear what exactly the latter signified). Moreover, whoever glossed the subtitle with ἐν τῶι ᾱͅ [τ]ῶν προcοδί[ω]ν φέρεται clearly did not think that the subtitle itself was a sufficiently explicit indication that the piece also belonged to the book of the *Prosodia*.[67] However, the piece *was* included in both books—unlike frr. 6a.(i)–(l) and 6c Snell-Maehler, which had no other book where they should rightfully be—and it presents itself quite openly as a paean (127, cf. 182). Like many other aspects of that piece, the subtitle remains mysterious.

The editorial choices that shape the format of titles in each book inconspicuously orient the reader's expectation (*ex ante*) and understanding (*ex post*) of what kind of thing the poems—and, by extension, the genre—are. Naturally, a *Hymn* or a *Prosodion* are composed in honour of a certain divine or heroic being; but at least a *Prosodion* (the state of things with the *Hymns* is less clear, as we saw) is also the expression of a certain community, for whose worship it was composed. Consistently with some ancient conceptualizations of the genre, a *Dithyramb* is, first and foremost, a story;[68] whether the poem is named after an individual, or a group, or a specific episode, the title directs the reader's expectations towards a narrative or, more broadly, a presentation of events. (The similarity of dithyrambic titles 'proper' to the titles of other literary forms concerned with the narrative or non-narrative representation of events, such as tragedies or citharodic *nomoi*, is hardly coincidental.) While a *Prosodion* and, at least in some cases, a *Dithyramb* are composed for an entire community,

---

κόν, in that the correction would be phrased indirectly in terms of the contest won, not directly in terms of genre.

66 See n. 18 above.
67 'It is transmitted in the first (book) of the *Prosodia*' (schol. *Pae.* 6.124, 604 Rutherford).
68 Pl. *Resp.* 3.394b–c, [Plut.] *De mus.* 1134e (going back to Glaukos of Rhegion?), and by implication the commentary to Bacchyl. **23 (B) quoted below, p. 505. See Ieranò (1997) 322–325; S. Schröder (1999) 121; D'Alessio (2008), (2013) 119–121.

an *Epinician* or an *Enkomion* is composed for a single individual. Any factors that might—and in all likelihood did—concretely complicate this neat outline are overlooked or excised. Any public relevance of a privately commissioned victory ode for a tyrant or prominent citizen, or any less-than-communal concern of a public but privately sponsored composition such as a dithyramb (but the phenomenon must have been much more widespread[69])—all are carefully wrapped away from view, and so inconspicuously that we still find ourselves struggling with their implications for our understanding of the poetry's historical reality.

Another effect worth highlighting is how the datives employed in this connection foreground, however obliquely, the act of composition. A prosodion for the Argives or a Pythian ode for Telesikrates of Cyrene are a prosodion *composed* for the Argives and a Pythian ode *composed* for Telesikrates of Cyrene. In Greek even more than in English, this need for tacit and perhaps unconscious supplementation is almost intrinsic in the syntax. In fact, the scholia routinely make the verbal element explicit: the headnotes to most of Pindar's *Epinicians* open with statements such as γέγραπται μὲν ὁ ἐπινίκιος Ἱέρωνι τῶι Γέλωνος ἀδελφῶι νικήcαντι ἵππωι κέλητι τὴν ος' Ὀλυμπιάδα,[70] γέγραπται Θήρωνι Ἀκραγαντίνωι ἅρματι νικήcαντι τὴν οζ' Ὀλυμπιάδα,[71] and so forth, where the choice of γράφω as the default verb and of the perfect as the default tense filters the past of the occasion through the permanent present of the written text. As a result, the author and the circumstances of the poem's composition are implicitly brought to the fore. Indeed, titles such as Κείοιc εἰc Δῆλον (*63) or Ἀ]ργείοιc εἰ[c τοὺ]c Ἠλεκτρύω[νοc παῖδαc (72) can be taken as giving the essentials of the commission that originated the ode. As they entice the reader to look back in time to that foundational creative moment, these titles not only contextualize the poem, but tell how it came into being.

---

69 See for instance Kurke (2007) on aristocratic display at the Theban Daphnephoria and Fearn (2011a) on possible oligarchic patronage over Aeginetan cult song.

70 'The victory ode is written for Hieron, the brother of Gelon, who won the seventy-sixth Olympiad [476 BCE] with the single horse' (*inscr.* a **ADEFHKQ** *Ol.* 1, I 15 Drachmann).

71 'It is written for Theron of Akragas, who won the seventy-seventh Olympiad [actually the seventy-sixth in 476 BCE, cf. P.Oxy. 222 col. i.18] with the chariot' (*inscr.* **ABCD**ab**EHQ** *Ol.* 2, I 58 Drachmann).

6 Evidence

The factual-sounding snippets of information offered by a title can play a key role in our understanding of the context or destination of a given poem, especially—as is the case for a large part of our sample—when the poem is fragmentary. Therefore, the veracity or otherwise of that information can be a crucial factor for the correctness or otherwise of our reading and interpretation of that poem. Knowing as we do that titles were given their definitive form sometime between the late third and the early second century, to accept unquestioningly whatever a title claims is surely a risky business; but equally unwise it would be to ignore titles altogether out of a vague suspicion of spuriousness without further investigation.

In concrete terms, assessing the veracity of the information provided by titles means examining the material on which the respective editors based their titulatory choices. Such material can be divided into three broad categories: (i) the text itself, (ii) material external to the text but transmitted together with it, and (iii) material independent of the text. The first is the most obvious. Occasional praise poetry such as victory odes naturally gives ample information on the addressee of such praise and on the occasion for it. Cult songs will typically make it clear which divinity or hero is being worshipped. Often the setting of such a piece of poetry will also be easy to infer from its text. Examples could be multiplied. The second category, on the other hand, is much shadier. There is no undisputable evidence for its existence, only a reasonable doubt that a few hundred poems can all have reached Alexandria as bare texts with no further information attached to them whatsoever. Simply put, we know nothing precise about how Greek lyric ended up with the scholars of the Museum: we do know of some who read it and used it, so that we can profitably investigate (say) Aristophanes' Simonides or the lyricists in the Peripatos,[72] but the concrete details of its presumably multifarious transmission—how exactly each piece got into the Library, from where, through whose hands, and in what state—are obscure. Finally, the third category represents a variety of potential pieces of evidence, ranging from occasional references by other authors (such as Chamaeleon's account of the commission and performance of fr. *122 Snell-Maehler) to material that does not

---

72 References are to Rawles (2013) and to Hadjimichael's contribution to this volume. Hadjimichael rightly stresses the importance of textuality and of its practicalities, such as the availability of written texts and the uncertainties of their supply from abroad, in fourth-century receptions of the lyricists.

refer directly to the texts, such as victory records.[73] Given the considerable uncertainty that surrounds the details, and sometimes the very existence, of extra-textual evidence, it is hard to assess how much in a title derives from the text itself. On the one hand, our defective knowledge of subsidiary materials often makes it impossible to ascertain whether a certain datum in a title, which may seem to have been derived from the text, was in fact supported by external evidence too, and of what kind. On the other hand, the fragmentary state of so many poems often does not even allow one to see whether the information found in a title could have been inferred from the text in the first place. These difficulties, and the conjectural nature that much of the discussion is therefore bound to have, should be kept in mind throughout this final section.

Epinicians

Convenient starting points, given the uncommonly firm evidence at our disposal, are the Olympic and Pythic victor-lists. The only register of Pythic victors known to us was compiled by Aristotle with his nephew Callisthenes, as we know from a contemporary honorific decree (*FD* III/1 400 = *CID* IV 10).[74] Some fragments are preserved by later sources, which ascribe the work to Aristotle alone (frr. 615–617 Rose, tit. 131 Gigon) if they mention an author at all.[75] Authoritative victor-lists for the Olympics, apparently associated with a précis of the origins and history of the games, went under the names of Hippias (*BNJ* 6 F 2) and, once again, Aristotle (tit. 130 Gigon, not in Rose).[76] Parts of one such list are preserved by P.Oxy. 222 + 2381 (*BNJ* 415).[77] Other victor-lists included accounts of notable events that occurred in each Olympiad, such as Phlegon of Tralles' Ὀλυμπιάδες (*BNJ* 257 F 1–33) and the anonymous work preserved by P.Oxy. 2082 (*BNJ* 257a).[78] It is unclear if the Ὀλυμπιονῖκαι compiled by Eratosthenes

---

73 Fr. 35 Martano = 31 Wehrli *ap.* Ath. 13.573e–f. What Chamaeleon provides is probably for the most part his own reconstruction based on elements he extracted more or less imaginatively from the text itself, see Budin (2008) 150–152: a reminder that information provided by third parties is not necessarily independent, let alone reliable. See also Hadjimichael's contribution to this volume.

74 See Bourguet in *FD* ad loc. and Christesen (2007) 181–186.

75 See the discussion in Rose (1863) 545–550. On the Pythic victor-list see also Spoerri (1988) and Christesen (2007) 179–202, 374–381, with the respective bibliographies.

76 On Hippias' ἀναγραφὴ Ὀλυμπιονικῶν see Christesen (2007) 22–24, 45–160, 368 and Węcowski in *BNJ* ad loc., with the respective bibliographies.

77 Published by Grenfell and Hunt (1899), see also Christesen (2007) 202–206, 382–384, 519–523 and Anderson in *BNJ* ad loc.

78 On Phlegon see Christesen (2007) 32–33, 326–334, 437–444; on P.Oxy. 2082 see Hunt (1927);

(*BNJ* 241 F 4–8 and probably 11a–b, 14–15b, 44) included a wider spectrum of historical information beyond the history of the games and of athletics more generally;[79] if they did, P.Oxy. 2802 may plausibly represent a copy of that work.[80] The scholia to Pindar certainly made use of both Olympic and Pythic victor-lists, which allowed them to date the victory to which each *Olympian* and *Pythian* referred and to provide information on any other victories of the respective honorands.[81]

There is good evidence that titles did the same. At least seven of Pindar's odes are denoted by their title as having been composed for a boy victor, παιδί (20, 22, 26, 36, 37, 44, 45). While often the text itself makes clear that the honorand won in the boys' class, in at least two cases it does not: there is no reference to the victor's age in either *Olympian* 14 or *Pythian* 11. The information must come from elsewhere. A victor-list, which necessarily reported such information, is the most intuitive solution.[82] More strikingly, *Olympian* 14 makes no mention of the contest won,[83] which, however, is duly noted in the title (26). Similarly, in *Olympian* 12 Pindar praises Ergoteles' prowess in running (15 τιμά ... ποδῶν) but does not indicate the exact discipline, which the title specifies as the *dolichos* (24).[84] The same argument can be made for *Olympian* 4, where the contest is never named explicitly (the only reference is 11 ὀχέων, which can plausibly refer to the *apene* as well as the four-horse chariot) but the title non-

---

Christesen (2007) 335–336, 445–447; Rzepk in *BNJ* ad loc. Hunt (1927) 82–84 suggested identifying the papyrus with Phlegon's work despite recognizing that the level of detail in the narrative was scarcely compatible with how Phlegon must have compressed the relevant period; his suggestion was refuted by De Sanctis (1928) 70–74.

79   On Eratosthenes' Olympic victor-list see Geus (2002) 323–332 and Christesen (2007) 173–179, 371–373.
80   De Sanctis (1928) 68–77.
81   The Pythic victor-list used by the Pindar scholia is the Aristotelian work: Christesen (2007) 191, 197–198. Which Olympic list was used is more doubtful. Hippias', Aristotle's, and Eratosthenes' are all plausible candidates. Either of the first two may have been more authoritative on account of its age; the third may have been favoured as a recent, Alexandrian product. Also, like the Pindar scholia themselves, Eratosthenes' Ὀλυμπιονῖκαι provided additional information on victors' other victories (cf. *BNJ* 241 F 8, 15a, and P.Oxy. 2082 fr. 4). Of course there is no need to assume that only one list was used, or that Eratosthenes' list was independent of Aristotle's for the period that was covered by both (cf. *BNJ* 241 F 7).
82   Finglass (2007) 10 remarks that the scholiast to *Pyth.* 11 must have referred to the victor-list in order to identify the relevant victory. The point equally applies to whoever established the title.
83   Race (1997) I 203.
84   Confirmed by P.Oxy. 222 col. i.22, cf. Paus. 6.4.11.

etheless identifies it as the chariot race (16), albeit perhaps mistakenly.[85] The most economical explanation for the presence of all this extra-textual information is that it comes from the victor-lists.

This is not to say that they were always followed uncritically. If we can trust a puzzling piece of information given by the headnote to *Pythian* 10 (**BDEGQ**, II 242 Drachmann), Hippokleas won in the same day both the *diaulos* and the *stadion*, but the title follows Pindar's own indication and attributes to the boy only the victory in the *diaulos* (36, cf. 9 διαυλοδρομᾶν ὕπατον παίδων).[86] The examples of *Olympian* 4 and, on a different level, *Pythian* 3 also caution us from assuming that evidence from the victor-lists was always used correctly. Nonetheless, there is compelling evidence that the Olympic and Pythic victor-lists were consulted as the titles of Pindar's *Olympians* and *Pythians* were being established.

There is no such smoking gun for either Bacchylides or Simonides. The title of Bacchylides 6 (90) does not include the specification παιδί, which is not obvious from the text but is guaranteed by P.Oxy. 222 col. ii.18. This may suggest that the Olympic victor-list was not consulted, but an accidental omission in transmission is also a possible explanation. (The presence of παιδί in 93 is indecisive, as it could have been inferred from the text.) And what was the deal with Simonides' epinician 'for the sons of Aiatios' (2)? Pausanias testifies that a victorious mare could be designated with the name of the father of the present owners in the Olympic victor-list he consulted (6.13.10, the sons of Pheidolas).[87]

---

85   That Psaumis of Camarina won the Olympic chariot race is confirmed by P.Oxy. 222 col. ii.22 (misspelt Cάμιος). Based on Pindar's use of ὀχέων to describe the victory (11), Barrett (2007) 41–43 argues that really the ode was composed not for that chariot victory but for the one with the mule cart (ἀπήνη) which *Ol.* 5 also, and more explicitly, celebrates. If this is true, the editor's reliance on the victor-list is thrown into even sharper relief by the mistake that resulted. Victories with the ἀπήνη were not normally included in the Olympic victor-lists, as can be inferred from *inscr.* a A *Ol.* 6, I 153 Drachmann and verified on P.Oxy. 222; consequently, any reliance of 17 or 18 on a victor-list can safely be excluded.

86   That Pindar may have elided entirely a second victory gained in the same games defies belief; the scholiast's conjecture that he had only been paid to celebrate one victory clearly will not do. Bernardini (2012) 263 denies plausibility to the notice of the victory in the *stadion* altogether, but information such as this does not sound like something one would simply make up. If Hippokleas did only win in the *diaulos*, then the error may have been Aristotle's or, perhaps more probably, an accidental duplication that intervened at some point of the transmission of the Πυθιονῖκαι before the scholiast made use of them.

87   See already Lobel (1959b) 89. For a victor-list allegedly registering the joint ownership of a team see also schol. **BDEQ** *Ol.* 2.87b, I 82 Drachmann, although in that case the two owners

So any victor-list for the competition that our anonymous siblings won may have presented this information in a similar way, (τῶν) Αἰατίου παίδων κέλης or the like. The same information might perhaps have been extracted from the text itself, but this would require the assumption that either the poem did not name the παῖδες, or that whoever assigned titles to Simonides' epinicians thought it fit to label them in this way nonetheless.

Things are even more nebulous when we come to Isthmian and Nemean victories. With one exception, which we shall discuss shortly, the scholia to Pindar's *Nemeans* and *Isthmians* give no dates for the respective odes. This creates a presupposition that numbered victor-lists (the adjective is important here) were not consistently available.[88] However, Pausanias states that, at the time of the boxer Teisandros of Naxos, Κορινθίοις ... οὐκ ἦν πω τηνικαῦτα οὐδὲ Ἀργείοις ἐς ἅπαντας ὑπομνήματα τοὺς Νεμεάτας.[89] The last word is dubious, but the clear implication of the sentence is that at some unspecified later time both cities started keeping precisely such complete records, and that more piecemeal records existed earlier too.[90] The headnote to *Nemean* 8 also suggests that Nemean records existed and survived for consultation but were not complete, at least with regard to the fifth century:[91] neither Deinias nor his father Megas ἐν ταῖς Νεμεακαῖς νίκαις ἀναγεγράφθαι,[92] says Didymus (fr. 58 Braswell), whence the *aporia* on whether they won in the *stadion* or in the *diaulos*, since the text is indecisive. (The scholia seem to imply that the title went for the *diaulos*, see *46 with n.) On the other hand, the headnote to *Nemean* 7 gives precise Nemead dates for Sogenes' victory and for the introduction of the *pentathlon*

(Theron and Xenokrates of Akragas) seem to have been mentioned individually. However, the notice itself is open to doubt in view of schol. EQ *Ol.* 2.87e, I 82–83 Drachmann (citing the Πυθιονῖκαι, Arist. fr. 617 Rose = 410 Gigon) as corrected by Rose (1863) 549 and Grassi (1961) 137 (ignored by Gigon).

88 On the Isthmic and Nemean victor-lists see Christesen (2007) 108–111, arguing that the lists were incomplete and, at least in the case of the Isthmians, successive editions of the games were unnumbered. On the Isthmic records see also Gebhard (2002) 224.

89 'At that time neither the Corinthians nor the Argives had records concerning all the Nemean victors' (6.13.8).

90 One would expect a reference to both Isthmian and Nemean winners, not only to the latter, whence a series of similar conjectures: Νεμεάτας καὶ Ἰσθμιάτας Siebelis (1822–1827) III 50 after Amasaeus (1551) 232, Νεμέαι καὶ Ἰσθμῶι νικήσαντας Schubart (1847) 296, Νέμεια καὶ Ἴσθμια νενικηκότας Schmitt (1856) 479, νενικηκότας Kayser (1848) 1097.

91 *Inscr.* BD, III 140 Drachmann.

92 So BD; Drachmann prints ἐν τοῖς Νεμεονίκαις, as corrected by Boeckh (1811–1821) II/1 486. Boeckh's emendation is attractive, but perhaps not necessary, cf. the νῖκαι Διονυσιακαί attributed to Aristotle (tit. 135 Gigon). In any case, a catalogue of Nemean victors is what the phrase must mean, see Christesen (2007) 108n141.

in the Nemean games.[93] This is likely to come from a victor-list of some kind, or at any rate from a work concerned specifically with the Nemean games: the date by Nemeads—of which this is the only known example—is inexplicable otherwise.

An Ἰσθμιακὴ ἀναγραφή, evidently reaching back at least to Pindar's time, is mentioned by the scholia to *Isthmian* 1, but the headnote to *Olympian* 12, at least in its surviving form, shows no awareness of a numbering of the Isthmiads.[94] The headnote to *Isthmian* 3 deserves attention. It claims that πρόςκειται ... τῆι ὠιδῆι ἵπποις διὰ τὸ μὴ δηλοῦν τὸν Πίνδαρον τὸ τοῦ ἀγωνίςματος εἶδος, πότερον κέλητι ἢ τεθρίππωι, μόνον δὲ ἱπποδρομίαι λέγει ἐςτεφανῶςθαι.[95] In other words, the term ἵπποις that originally stood in the title (see *50 with *n.*) is alleged to be due to Pindar's own failure to specify which of the equestrian contests Melissos had won. The scholiast thus seems to have had no access to a victor-list that could provide the required clarification independently.[96] But was he right to assume the same of whoever gave the ode its title? The word ἵπποις is found in three other Pindaric titles (33, 39, *48), and in all three cases it refers to the chariot race.[97] While the reason for alternating ἅρματι and ἵπποις is unclear, the two words must refer to one and the same contest. If so, the fact that the title of *Isthmian* 3 specified the chariot race despite Pindar's ambiguity may suggest that a victor-list was consulted.

---

93   *Inscr.* BD, III 116 Drachmann.
94   Schol. BD *Isthm.* 1.11c, III 199 Drachmann, *inscr.* a A *Ol.* 12, I 349 Drachmann; see Christesen (2007) 110. Plut. *Ages.* 21.5 is able to associate a specific list of victors with the Isthmian games of 390, which were celebrated twice, but this very peculiarity may have made this Isthmiad identifiable in a way others perhaps were not. On the Plutarchean passage and its implications see Christesen (2007) 111–112n152.
95   'The ode is introduced by "with horses" because Pindar does not clarify the kind of contest, whether (it was) with the single horse or with the four-horse chariot, but simply says that [Melissos] was crowned "in horse-racing"' (*inscr.* BD *Isthm.* 3, III 223 Drachmann, where we may wish to read λέγειν for the mss' λέγει).
96   A few other scholiastic comments implicitly suggest that a complete Isthmic victor-list was not available, by treating as ambiguous a matter that would not have been so otherwise: e.g. *inscrr.* a BD *Nem.* 11, b BD *Isthm.* 5, III 185, 241 Drachmann.
97   In *Pyth.* 7 this will have been made clear by the Pythic victor-list, whereas in the other two poems it is explicitly stated in the text (*Nem.* 1.7, *Isthm.* 1.14). There may also be a fourth case, if the true reading in 16 is ἵπποις not ἅρματι. There too it is clear that the chariot race was meant, since a victory in the mule cart race (the only alternative allowed by the text, see n. 85) could hardly be labelled ἵπποις. The variation between different forms with the same meaning had already been noted by Robert (1900) 145–146. Bacchylides has ἵπποις twice (88, 95; never ἅρματι), and at least in 88 the word certainly refer to the chariot race (cf. 3.3–8).

Nonetheless, given the paucity of the evidence, two further (and equally speculative) alternatives should be kept in mind. One is that the information may have come not from more or less complete festival records but from a more limited, local compilation of some sort.[98] We have an example in *IG* XII/5(1) 608, a list of victorious athletes from Ceos probably dating from between 350 and 330,[99] which need not have been one of a kind. Otherwise, in *Isthmian* 3 as much as in *Nemean* 8, the lack of clarity on Pindar's part and of external guidance from a victor-list may have resulted in the editor making an arbitrary choice. The format of epinician titles required that the contest be specified, and writing e.g. Μελίccωι Θηβαίωι ἵπποιc ἢ κέλητι may not have been regarded as an acceptable solution.

Dithyrambs

A second group of poems for which external evidence may be suggested is dithyrambs, which accounted for two volumes in the Alexandrian edition of Pindar and one in Bacchylides.[100] Given the considerable diversity of original performance contexts and (presumably) of provenances in the corpus, one

---

[98] *Pace* Fearn (2011b) 220–221, an existing record of Cean victors is a good explanation for Bacchylides' claim in 2.10–11 that Argeios' victory was the seventieth Isthmian 'garland' gained by Ceos: see Gelzer (1985) 99 (although we need not postulate an 'offizielle Siegerliste', as he does; any reckoning, official or otherwise, would do). The alternative—that immediately after the victory somebody went through the official records at the Isthmus, counted all the Cean victories, and found out that together with the new one they made a usefully round figure—does not sound quite as plausible. In the Panhellenic games Cean victors were proclaimed as Ceans, not as citizens of the individual Cean *poleis*, and ode 2—which was probably performed at the Isthmus—makes no exception, as Fearn notes following Lewis (1962) 2. For all the complexities of Cean identity in the fifth century, it would be strange if the 'sentimental unity' (Lewis, ibid.) of the island was exclusively limited to the Panhellenic stage, without as much as basic record-keeping at home. Furthermore, the supposed absence of such local records would require the fourth-century list of Cean victories in *IG* XII/5(1) 608 (see above) to have been compiled directly from the Isthmian and Nemean victor-lists, which in turn requires such lists to have been complete, contrary to what we have just seen.

[99] See Schmidt (1999); Fearn (2011b) 227–228; on the date, Schmidt (1999) 72–74.

[100] Pindar: *Vita Ambrosiana* I 3 Drachmann, P.Oxy. 2438 col. ii.36, cf. schol. **BCEQ** *Ol.* 13.25c, I 361 Drachmann with n. 59 above. Bacchylides: see Blass (1898) v–vi. According to the apparent practice of the ancient classifiers of late archaic lyric, or at any rate of Bacchylides' poems, I use the term 'dithyramb' as an equivalent of 'song performed by a circular chorus', with no strict Dionysiac implications. On the ancient terminology, see Fearn (2007) 163–180; Wilson (2007) 164–169; further problematised by D'Alessio (2008), (2013); Ceccarelli (2013).

cannot expect all their titles to depend on similar material. Nonetheless, the possibility that *some* titles may have been based on material other than the bare texts is worth exploring.

First, just as for athletic competitions, there were probably records of victories also at the competitions of the *kyklioi khoroi* at least in some parts of Greece; Athens springs to mind. Each year at the City Dionysia the ten tribes competed against one another with a chorus of men and one of boys.[101] Competitions of 'circular choruses' took place at other Athenian festivals too.[102] As concerned the dramatic competitions, the key facts of the Dionysia—poets, *khorēgoi*, plays, results, and the like—were duly recorded by the archon, and Aristotle published them in the form of a catalogue known as *Didaskaliai*, 'Productions' (frr. 618–630 Rose, tit. 137 Gigon).[103] The archon's records, whether mediated by Aristotle or not, also formed the basis of several inscriptions that were set up for display in Athens and elsewhere in the centuries that followed.[104] Much like the Olympic and Pythic victor-lists in the study of epinician lyric, the *Didaskaliai*—'a complete chronicle of performances of plays at the Dionysia and Lenaea'—were sedulously used by students of Attic drama, as the scholia to both tragedy and comedy testify.[105] They could be used to date plays, to relate them to other plays produced on the same occasion, to assess their popularity with the judges, to trace and contextualize dramatists' careers, and (indirectly) to justify points of interpretation and literary history. But did they also include dithyrambs?

---

101   On the dithyrambic contest at the City Dionysia, see Pickard-Cambridge (1988) 74–78 (revision by Gould and Lewis); Ieranò (1997) 243–247.
102   Anthesteria: Friis Johansen (1959), based on Copenhagen NM 13817 (*ARV*² IX.57.35, 1145) and Pind. fr. 75 Snell-Maehler (but the latter can equally be related to the Dionysia, cf. Xen. *Eq. mag.* 3.2 with Deubner [1932] 140n7, *pace* Friis-Johansen [1959] 41n101); see also Pickard-Cambridge (1988) 16–17 (revision by Gould and Lewis). Thargelia: Pickard-Cambridge (1988) 75n2, 76nn1, 3; Ieranò (1997) 247–249; Wilson (2000) 33–34, (2007) esp. 54–64; Fearn (2007) 235–238. Panathenaea: Ieranò (1997) 249–250; Wilson (2000) 39–40; Fearn (2007) 238–240. On Athenian dithyrambic performances see also Kowalzig and Wilson (2013) 13–18.
103   On the *Didaskaliai* see Rose (1863) 550–561; Jachmann (1909); Blum (1977) 50–92.
104   *IG* II² 2318 (commonly known as *Fasti*), *IG* II² 2319–2323a + *SEG* XXVI 203 (Διδασκαλίαι), *IG* II² 2325A–H (*Victor-lists*), and *IGUR* 215–216, 218. On the three Athenian inscriptions see now Millis and Olson (2012); on the Roman fragments—perhaps representing Callimachus' revision of Aristotle's *Didaskaliai*, see p. 498 and n. 109 below—see Dittmer (1923).
105   Quotation from Blum (1977) 69, in its English translation (Blum [1991] 33). For a more sceptical take see Scullion (2002) 81–90; his argument, however, does not affect the use of didascalic records by more scholarly (or at least less credulous) sources than the playwrights' *Lives*, the *Suda*, and the like.

Rudolf Blum has denied this.[106] As he notes, dithyrambs are not included in the inscribed Διδαcκαλίαι and *Victor-lists*, which appear to have been extracts from Aristotle's *Didaskaliai*; dithyrambic victories are listed in the *Fasti*, which probably do not go back to Aristotle's work,[107] but only the victorious tribe and its *khorēgos* are named, not the author or title of the winning dithyramb. Moreover, neither of the testimonies that are usually thought to imply the presence of dithyrambic poets in the *Didaskaliai*—Harpocration and a scholion to Aristophanes' *Birds*—states explicitly that the respective poet, Pantacles and Cinesias, was recorded there as a dithyrambographer.[108] Finally, Callimachus' Πίναξ τῶν διδαcκάλων—which, in Blum's view, was a mere reorganization of Aristotle's *Didaskaliai*—is said by Choeroboscus to have contained αἱ ἀναγραφαί ... τῶν δραμάτων 'the records of plays', with no mention of dithyrambs.[109] But all these objections are open to doubt. First, Harpocration and the scholiast state that Pantacles and Cinesias were referred to in the *Didaskaliai*: since neither dithyrambographer is also known to have been active as a tragic or comic poet,[110] the natural implication is indeed that Aristotle included the dithyrambic contests in his records. Second, Choeroboscus—assuming that the Byzantine etymologist is reporting him accurately—said that Callimachus' didascalic register *contained* (ἐν οἷc ... ἦcαν) a register of dramatic victors, not that it exclusively consisted of one; and even if it did, Callimachus may well have chosen to excerpt from Aristotle only the data relating to the dramatic compositions.

More importantly, if we look beyond Aristotle's name, there is further and more solid evidence that records of dithyrambic victories by named poets were

---

106 Blum (1977) 52, 70–71.
107 Koerte (1906) 392–393; see also Blum (1977) 68–69.
108 Harp. δ 54 Keaney, schol. VEΓ Ar. *Av.* 1379b Holwerda (Arist. frr. 624, 629 Rose = 460, 445 Gigon); see Blum (1977) 70 with e.g. Jachmann (1909) 5–6, Pickard-Cambridge (1988) 71.
109 Callim. fr. 456 Pfeiffer *ap. Etym. Magn.* 1899 Gaisford; Blum (1977) 70.
110 Blum (1977) 70 suggests that Cinesias and Pantacles may have also composed tragedies, but there is no solid evidence to support this view. Schol. VMΘ Ar. *Ran.* 366c Chantry does make the extraordinary claim that Cinesias εἰcήνεγκεν ἐν δράματι τὴν Ἑκάτην καὶ κατετίληcεν αὐτῆc 'introduced Hecate in a play and defecated all over her', but the text is unlikely to be genuine: the corresponding scholion in R (366b Chantry) has the already part-corrupt οὗτοc γὰρ ᾄδων κατετίληcε τῆc Ἑκάτηc 'for while singing he defecated all over Hecate' (Aristophanes' text more plausibly mentions Ἑκαταῖα, whatever they were), of which 366c seems to be a misguided rationalisation. Cinesias is always referred to as a dithyrambographer, including in this very scholion, and the relevant line in *Frogs* explicitly locates the unfortunate episode within a dithyrambic performance (κυκλίοιcι χοροῖcιν ὑπᾴδων). Likewise, Pantacles is known as a dithyrambic poet also from several inscriptions (*IG* I³/2 958, 959, 967); see further Wilson (2007) 161.

available to later readers. The *Marmor Parium* (*BNJ* 239 A 47, 49, 54, 65) mentions and dates the victories 'in Athens' of four poets: in 494/3 Melanippides of Melos (the grandfather of the New Musician of the same name),[111] in 489/8 a certain Simonides (allegedly, but improbably, the grandfather of the more famous Simonides of Ceos),[112] Simonides of Ceos himself in 477/6, Telestes of Selinus in 402/1, and Polyidus of Selymbria sometime between 398/7 and 381/0.[113] One cannot exclude derivation from a work on the history of music, or of poetry, or of Athenian theatrical competitions (but how far could a work of that kind have been itself independent of a victor-list?); but precisely such a victor-list is a plausible alternative.[114] If the 'Simonidean' epigram 28 Page (*FGE* 796–801) is truly a post-classical product,[115] the source of the punctiliously detailed information it contains—archon (l. 1), tribe (2), *khorēgos* (3), division (4) and poet (5–6)—seems likely to have been a didascalic register. Finally, the author of the *Life of Pindar* preserved by P.Oxy. 2438 col. ii knows the date of one of Pindar's Athenian dithyrambs, which carried the prize in the archonship of Archias (497/6). While alternative explanations can no doubt be found, that of a list of dithyrambic victories seems the simplest. Aristotle's name may be the one most easily attached to such a list, but the identity of the compiler ultimately matters little.

A different question is whether such a list would have only included every year's winning dithyramb, as was the case for athletic victor-lists, or all those who competed. On the one hand, for tragedy and comedy the *Didaskaliai* did not limit themselves to victors, so if the dithyrambic records were also included

---

111 See *Suda* μ 454–455 Adler.
112 Wilamowitz (1913) 139n2 remarks on the chronological unlikelihood of this relationship between the two Simonidai and suggests that πάππος may be a mistake for 'uncle'.
113 On agonistic victories in the *Marmor Parium* and their Athenian slant see Rotstein (2016) 122–126.
114 Rotstein (2016) 123, 125–126 distinguishes between information on early figures such as Thespis and Susarion, which she argues derive from narrative sources perhaps concerned with πρῶτοι εὑρηταί, and more recent ones such as those mentioned above, which derive rather from didascalic records, 'perhaps ... used indirectly'.
115 Simonidean authorship was first challenged by Stella (1946) 5–10, whose conclusions are accepted by Page in *FGE* ad loc. (arguing for a late Hellenistic date, pp. 242–243). Stella's objection that τις could not possibly be appended to the *khorēgos*' name (3) in an actual choregic monument is particularly hard to overrule; the rebuttal attempted by Wilson (2000) 369n70 does not carry conviction, as David Sider points out (I am grateful to him for sharing with me the relevant chapter of his forthcoming commentary to the Simonidean epigrams). Sider inclines towards Simonidean authorship but takes the piece as a fragment of a sympotic elegy rather than as a self-standing public epigram, which may be a way to sidestep Stella's objection.

in them, one would naturally expect a full list of contestants for those too. On the other hand, contrary to drama, much of the preparation for dithyrambic performances took place at tribe level, not at *polis* level.[116] Although Blum's contention that the names of victorious poets were not recorded at all cannot be accepted, nevertheless it stands to reason that the authorities may only have recorded the only *polis*-wide datum, the victory. Furthermore, the number of dithyrambs that were performed every year greatly exceeded those of tragedies and comedies, and recording nine losers for every winner at the Dionysia alone may have been regarded as uneconomical. Like the other evidence examined at the end of the previous paragraph, P.Oxy. 2438 col. ii.8–10 cites a victory, not merely an entry. Since the anonymous biographer was evidently looking for the earliest date he could find in Pindar's career, the assumption that he (or his source) could consult a full list of contestants would require the inference that Pindar was victorious at his first attempt.[117] We have two references to dithyrambic placements other than the first, in Isaeus (6.36) and Neanthes of Cyzicus the elder (*BNJ* 84 F 10), and neither of them seems to derive from a didascalic record.

But another question is more relevant to this chapter: whether and how far items in a dithyrambic didascalic list could be univocally related to existing poems. This means, for our purposes, whether such a list included the title—or *a* title—for each dithyramb, whereby individual texts could be traced back to an individual festival and date. The parallel with the dramatic genres would suggest that titles were recorded, but the evidence fails to substantiate this suggestion. On the contrary, whereas at *P.Oxy.* 2438 col. ii.15–18 the biographer identifies what is apparently the latest Pindaric poem he could date (*Olympian* 4) by quoting its *incipit*, he offers no such identification for the Athenian dithyramb of 497/6.[118] Being an argument from silence, this consideration has limit-

---

116   Blum (1977) 71–72. Note, however, that poets seem to have been allocated to *khorēgoi* by lot, that is, centrally (Antiph. 6.11). Even if we take Antiphon's words to signify that *khorēgoi* 'drew lots for the order of choice between the available poets', as perhaps suggested by Ar. *Av.* 1404 and later testified by Dem. *Meid.* 13 for the choice of the *aulos*-player (Pickard-Cambridge [1988] 75–56 [revision by Gould and Lewis]), the shortlist of poets to be picked must still have been compiled centrally: the procedure would have made little sense otherwise.

117   Admittedly, nothing in the available evidence disproves this hypothesis, which may lie behind the anecdote reported by the *Vita Ambrosiana*, I 1 Drachmann: see Negri (2001) 1040. Alternatively, the biographer may only have been able to consult a shorter work that only listed winners, such as Aristotle's Νῖκαι Διονυσιακαί (if these too included dithyrambic as well as dramatic contests).

118   Noted by Arrighetti (1967) 132n20.

ed validity: the author's failure to identify the dithyramb explicitly need not mean that he could not have done so had he wished. It is also possible that the dithyramb in question had not survived to the biographer's day, or had an ambiguous title (cf. 98, 99) that did not allow it to be identified with certainty. Nonetheless, based on the present state of our knowledge there is no proof that the dithyrambic victor-list allowed specific poems to be identified, and the one available piece of evidence seems rather to suggest otherwise.

Therefore, there is also no proof that the indication of the commissioning community found in some titles derives from external evidence. If we could be certain that A faithfully represents the titles of the Alexandrian edition of Bacchylides' *Dithyrambs*,[119] the absence of such indications from most titles would at least tell against the supposition that they were routinely fabricated. To relate ode 18 to Athens would have required no great effort of the imagination, and the conclusion that ode 17 was composed for the Ceans is all but demanded by its text (130–132); yet the relevant datives are not found in the manuscript (99, 98). This would suggest that whenever the editor had no external documentation, he did not guess, but left a respectful blank. Tellingly, the only two titles where the commissioning community is indicated come from localities that we know had at least some victory records (100 from Athens, 101 from Sparta).[120] However, seeing a definite correlation between the availability or otherwise of records and the indication or otherwise of the commissioning community in a title requires the supposition that ode 19 was performed at the Dionysia, odes 15 and 18 (probably also Athenian, but with no such indication in the title) at a festival other than the Dionysia,[121] and ode 20 presumably at the Karneia. None of these hypotheses is new,[122] but all are speculative, and defending the lot of

---

119 On the problems raised by the two titling hands in A see pp. 467–468 above.

120 The only relevant Spartan victory records we know of are those of the Karneia compiled by Hellanicus of Lesbos (*BNJ* 4 F 85a–86); on that work see Franklin (2010–2011) and Pownall in *BNJ* ad loc. However, it is unclear whether dithyrambs were performed at the Karneia; see n. 122.

121 An alternative, if the *Didaskaliai* only recorded victories, is that they were performed at the Dionysia but were not victorious.

122 Ode 19 performed at the Dionysia: Fearn (2007) 181, 314n174. Ode 15 performed at the Panathenaia: Zimmermann (1992) 69; Maehler (2004) 157–158; Fearn (2007) 240–241, 257–337. Ode 18 performed at the Thargelia: Jebb (1905) 235; Wilson (2007) 172–175. At the Theseia: Merkelbach (1973) 57. At the Hephaistia: Gelzer *ap.* Zimmermann (1992) 99 with n. 24. At the Panathenaia: Zimmermann (1992) 100. Ode 20 performed at the Karneia: Fearn (2007) 230 and n. 9, noting however that performances by *kyklioi khoroi* in that context are not documented with certainty; see now D'Alessio (2013) 123–124. At the festival of Artemis in Karyai: Zimmermann (1992) 105, see also Gołąb (2012). Another good candidate for the Panathenaia is ode **23: Calame (2013) 82.

them together would be a formidable task. At all events, too much uncertainty surrounds A's titles for any such argument to have much traction.

Whether any of the titles 'proper' go back to the respective authors, or at least to their time, is also difficult to answer without support from the *Didaskaliai*.[123] Titles of dramatic pieces seemed to have been common currency relatively early, although not verifiably as early as the beginning of Pindar's career, even less of Simonides'. Alan Sommerstein argues

> that from the 470s at any rate, dramatic compositions were given titles by their authors which were recorded in the state archives; that from 446 or thereabouts, these titles were known to the public in advance of performance; that the titles by which plays were known in later antiquity and today are authentic in the overwhelming majority of cases; and that once the advance publication of titles began, dramatists started using them to mystify, tantalize and sometimes mislead their audiences as to what their play was going to be about.[124]

It is tempting to imagine that the same went for dithyrambs, which later authors cited by title as a matter of course. However, no secure attestation of a dithyrambic title predates Aristotle, who mentions Timotheus' *Scylla* in the *Poetics*, Philoxenus' *Banquet* in a fragment of the lost Περὶ δικαιοcύνηc, and probably Philoxenus' *Mysians* in the *Politics*.[125] Not long afterward the choregic inscription *IG* II² 3055 (dated to 320/19) records a reperformance of Timotheus' *Elpenor*. The latter piece must have been something of a classic by then; this may be the reason why the title was specified in the inscription, a unique occurrence among dithyrambic choregic dedications.[126] Going further back in time than the mid-fourth century involves treading on very thin ice. A statement in Herodotus can be taken to say that the sixth-century citharode Arion of Methymna was the first to give a dithyramb a title, but an alternative interpretation is that he gave 'the' dithyramb its name, and no consensus has been reached.[127] Nonetheless, the internal evidence provided by Bacchylides—since

---

123 A suggestion to this effect had been made by Lohan (1890) 19 after Bergk (1883) 535n32; see also Ucciardello (1996–1997) 72 with further bibliography at n. 25.
124 Sommerstein (2002) 1; see also Kaimio (2000) 54–55 and already Lohan (1890) 19.
125 *Poet.* 15, 1454a; fr. 83 Rose = 793 Gigon; and *Pol.* 8, 1342b, where the mss. have ποιῆcαι διθύραμβον τοὺc μύθουc but Μυcούc proposed by Schneider (1809) I 577, II 467 is very attractive.
126 Choregic inscriptions for dithyrambic victories are conveniently collected in Ieranò (1997) 331–361.
127 Hdt. 1.23, cf. *Suda* α 3886 Adler. See most recently D'Alessio (2013) 114, arguing for the second interpretation. The relevant section of the Herodotean passage runs διθύραμβον

the *Dithyrambs* of Simonides and Pindar, like their titles, are too fragmentary to provide much guidance—bears exploring.

The sons of Antenor do not seem to play a major part in Bacchylides' ode 15, titled Ἀντηνορίδαι ἢ Ἑλένης ἀπαίτησις (97). One can blame the lacuna that almost entirely obliterated lines 15–36—a good third of the ode—for depriving us of a fulsome account of the gallantry they displayed in introducing Odysseus and Menelaus to the Trojan assembly; at least their number was probably mentioned, on the testimony of a scholion to the *Iliad*.[128] But one is left with the feeling that titling the poem after the sons of Antenor would have been an odd choice for a later editor, who could have been content with the clearer and more informative *The Demand for Helen's Return*. Moreover, as Sir Richard Jebb realized, Antenor's fifty sons probably mirror the fifty choreutes of Athenian circular choruses, who will thus have visibly stood for them in performance.[129] It is tempting to think that this is the reason behind the choice of Ἀντηνορίδαι as the dithyramb's first title. (The comparison with the many tragedies and comedies named after their respective choruses springs to mind.) If so, this choice seems likelier to have been made in the fifth century, either by Bacchylides himself or by someone in his extended audience, than several centuries later by someone wholly unconnected with the performance.[130]

Similar considerations can be made about the first title of ode 17 (98). The 'twice seven' are hardly the central figures of the story, although their mention perhaps specifies the episode in question better than the simple Θησεύς would have done. Used three times in the ode itself (43, 93, 128), the word ἠΐθεοι

πρῶτον ἀνθρώπων τῶν ἡμεῖς ἴδμεν ποιήσαντά τε καὶ ὀνομάσαντα καὶ διδάξαντα ἐν Κορίνθωι. Although D'Alessio presents several parallels for ὀνομάζω applied to the naming of literary forms, two elements may also be taken to invite the interpretation of the verb as 'to title': the fact that in this passage both ποιήσαντα and διδάξαντα are certainly particular (referring to the composition and production of a specific dithyramb, not of 'the dithyramb' as a genre), thus suggesting that ὀνομάσαντα may be particular as well; and the position of ὀνομάσαντα in the sequence, which arguably suits a reference to titling ('he composed a dithyramb, gave it a title, and produced it') more smoothly than to devising a name for the genre. But the matter is highly uncertain. If ὀνομάσαντα is indeed particular, it does not prove that dithyrambs truly had titles in Arion's time, but suggests that they did in Herodotus'.

128 Schol. T *Il.* 24.496b Erbse.
129 Jebb (1905) 221, expanded by Zimmermann (1992) 68–69.
130 Despite the differences, one may compare tragic titles like Αἴας μαστιγοφόρος, Ἱππόλυτος καλυπτόμενος, Ἱππόλυτος στεφανηφόρος, where the reference to an element of the staging may suggest a fifth-century title. 'Such names will not have originated with scholars who knew the plays mainly from reading but with people who knew them as spectacles': West (1979) 131.

was almost a technical term for the fourteen Athenian youths sent to their death in Crete at Minos' behest. Interestingly, the Aristotelian *Constitution of the Athenians* applies the same term to the Athenian *theōroi* who were periodically sent to Delos to commemorate that mythical event (56.3). If scholars are right that the ode was performed by a Cean chorus on a mission to Delos, a hint of self-identification with the archetypal *theōroi* of the myth can be detected in the title as much as in the choice of theme and in the aetiological nod represented by the paean-singing at lines 128–129.[131] If this is true, one feels once again that the title *Youths* is somewhat likelier to date from fifth-century Ceos (or Delos) than from second-century Alexandria. But proof remains to be found.

The issue of alternative titles also requires investigation. Several Athenian dramas were known in antiquity with two titles joined by ἤ, although with an interestingly different distribution between tragedy and comedy.[132] The same is true of at least three lyric compositions regarded as dithyrambs by their ancient editors: the two of Bacchylides that we have just seen, and one by Pindar (75), close to half of the dithyrambic titles known from these two authors (seven in total, plus the uncertain case of 101 to be discussed presently). What are the implication of this practice for the history of our texts? Sommerstein argues that double titles of Attic drama are not authorial and probably originated in the book trade.[133] This may be true of dithyrambs too. Different manuscripts containing the same ode may have given it different titles.[134] Perhaps, if titles were included in the dithyrambic victor-lists after all, the didascalic title and the title given by one or more manuscripts may occasionally have been at variance.[135] But a further possibility is that some alternative titles may result from the scholarly systematization that we know the poetry (and titles) of our three authors underwent.[136]

---

131   Similarly Ucciardello (1996–1997) 73n26. On the overlap between the chorus and the mythical ἤίθεοι, see Fränkel (1962) 515; Zimmermann (1992) 85; the aetiological implications of the paean-singing are highlighted by Calame (2009) 175, see already Rutherford (1997b) 48.

132   Discussed in Sommerstein (2002) 5–8, with a convenient list at 14–16. See also Hunter (1983) 146–148.

133   Sommerstein (2002) 5–6; see also Hunter (1983) 146, emphasizing the role played by scholarly standardization. Bender (1904) proposes a much later (and much less likely) date.

134   Similarly Ucciardello (1996–1997) 72n25.

135   Note, however, that none of the titles in question can be linked compellingly to a performance occasion in which the existence of didascalic records can be proved. Ode 15 is probably Athenian, but need not have been performed at the Dionysia: see p. 501 and n. 122 above.

136   See again Ucciardello (1996–1997) 72n25.

Unfortunately, the only piece of direct evidence on the subject—a passage from an anonymous commentary on (probably) Bacchylides' *Dithyrambs*—is lacunose and can only be restored conjecturally:

ταύτην τ]ὴν ὠιδὴν Ἀρίσταρχ(ος)
10 .....διθ]υραμβικὴν εἶ-
ναί φηcι]ν διὰ τὸ παρειλῆ-
φθαι ἐν α]ὐτῆι τὰ περὶ Καc-
cάνδραc,] ἐπιγράφει δ' αὐτὴν
... Καcc]άνδραν
    CLGP I.1.4 BACCHYLIDES 4 = B col. i.9–14

14 τὴν nol. Lobel (1956b) 54 : οὕ(τω) Gallavotti (1957) 420 : καί Luppe (1987) 10 : Ἴλιον ἢ Luppe (1989) 29 : διό D'Alessio (1997) 37 n. 90 : οὖν Ucciardello (1996–1997) 76 ‖ cetera Lobel (1956b) 52

Aristarchus [says] that [this] ode is dithyrambic because the events concerning Cassandra are taken up [in] it, and [...] titles it *Cassandra*.

So Aristarchus was said to have given Bacchylides **23 a title, *Cassandra* (102). What is not obvious is whether this was an additional title of the kind we have just seen (supplying καί with Luppe at line 14) or the ode's only one.[137] The difficulty is compounded by uncertainty over whether Aristarchus was also the editor of the Alexandrian Bacchylides or only wrote a *hypomnema* like the ones he wrote on Pindar. ἐπιγράφει may suggest the former,[138] since commentaries would not seem to have normally been a place in which to propose titles (even though some did report them). If so, what to supply at the beginning of line 14 is crucial for our understanding of titling practices. Aristarchus simply titling the ode *Cassandra* would be evidence that dithyrambic titles 'proper' could on occasion be entirely devised by editors, whether to supplant an earlier title or because the ode lacked one altogether. If instead he titled it 'also' *Cassandra*, the fact that the other title is not mentioned at all suggests that Aristarchus' was an addition to a pre-existing title—and that the reader, faced with this comment and with the double title itself (which will have been in the book-

---

[137] It seems implausible that καί in this context and position can be asseverative, as suggested by Käppel and Kannicht (1988) 21. If it is the correct supplement it must mean 'also'.
[138] So D'Alessio (1997) 53–54.

roll where the text of the poem was), could be expected to infer this essential piece of information without being told it explicitly.[139]

On the one hand, the hypothesis that *Cassandra* was the poem's only title sits well with the alphabetical order of Bacchylides' *Dithyrambs*. The first letter of the title cannot have been earlier than ι, since the poem must have followed ode 20 (101). If Carlo Gallavotti was right to identify ode **23 with fr. dub. 60 Maehler,[140] it also cannot have been later than λ, given the title of fr. dub. 61 Maehler (103) which follows it. On the other hand, none of the other supplements that have been proposed for the beginning of line 14 compares favourably to καί. A whole further title is unlikely: Luppe's afterthought Ἴλιον ἢ Κασσ]άνδραν is too long for the space (his contention that it was in *ekthesis* has little to recommend it),[141] and a suitable two-letter title to precede ἤ is not easily found. A dislocated οὖν (Ucciardello) is possible,[142] but the unusual word-order tells against it somewhat. Other solutions are distinctly less attractive. On the whole, the less improbable reading seems to be καί: 'he called the song also Κασσάνδρα, i.e. gave it the alternative title ἢ Κασσάνδρα'.[143]

If this is true, then Aristarchus gave the poem an alternative title that was closely aligned to its subject matter. While we are ignorant of what the first title was, the pattern is not unfamiliar. In ode 15, as we saw, a meaningful but somewhat unperspicuous first title was clarified by the second (97). Perhaps a similar argument can be made with reference to ode 17 (98). We do not know a great deal about Pindar's second *Dithyramb*,[144] but the addition of Κέρβερος clarifies the subject-matter of the narrative—Heracles' descent to Hades—better than the plain Ἡρακλῆς (75). This raises the interesting possibility that at least some narrative lyric poems were already furnished with a title—perhaps, though not necessarily, going back as far as the fifth century—when they reached their editor, whereupon some of them received an additional one for clarification or completeness. But it is also possible that some poems reached Alexandria from two different sources and with two differ-

---

139 For a contrary view see Hadjimichael (2014) 90n36.
140 Gallavotti (1950) 267; see now Hadjimichael (2014) 95–100.
141 See in greater detail Ucciardello (1996–1997) 71. It is possible, of course, that Ἴλιον (or perhaps Ἰλιάδες, which would suit fr. dub. 60 Maehler well) was the first title of the poem even though it was not mentioned at this point in the commentary.
142 Parallels at Ucciardello (1996–1997) 76.
143 Luppe (1987) 10–11.
144 Note, however, the substantial improvement on earlier texts achieved by Lavecchia (1996) and (2000) 30–31, 106–109, who makes a strong case for also recognizing fr. 346a–c Snell-Maehler as a part of *Dithyramb* 2.

ent titles, or that an editor could not make up his mind which of two titles of his own invention was more appropriate for a given poem. Moreover, the editors of the respective poets were not the only scholars who could assign titles. Callimachus' monumental *Pinakes* were a work to be reckoned with, as demonstrated by Aristarchus' refutation of his classification of Bacchylides **23 in B. Other scholars too could refer to texts in non-canonical ways.[145] More importantly, when a poem only has one title in the relevant "standard" edition, it is impossible to assess whether it was an existing title with which the editor was satisfied, or the poem had reached the Library without a title and the editor then supplied one.

Conclusions

As is all too frequently the case, it is impossible to reconstruct with exactitude how the evidence we have came into being. The section dedicated to Pindar's *Epinicians* has shown that independent evidence was consistently used when available. Our examination of Bacchylides' *Dithyrambs* has tentatively suggested that at least in certain cases pre-existing data could be retained, although not necessarily unmodified. (The only datum we know with a good degree of plausibility is that the title *Cassandra* in 101 is a scholar's invention.) What we can glimpse is a picture of reasonable accuracy within the limits of Hellenistic scholarly practice and of the evidence that Aristophanes of Byzantium and his colleagues had at their disposal. Sources of relevant material were mined and put to use. Although occasionally guesswork will have been inevitable, it could also be eschewed in favour of an (implicit) admission of ignorance: contrary to the standard format for titles of *Paeans*, the dative indicating the commissioning community was not included in 69.[146]

This raises the possibility that material other than the bare texts of the poems could be resorted to even when we no longer have evidence for its use. Such a possibility cannot be demonstrated, much less determined or quantified. Nevertheless, it can be usefully taken into consideration on a general level. Possible examples (if we accept the possibility that the disunity of *Paean* 6 predates in some form the "standard" Pindar) are 64 and 65 (= 73?): the notion of a Delphic commission is not obviously supported by the substantial extant

---

145 See the passages collected by Hadjimichael (2014) 93n48, esp. Ath. 11.496e–f.
146 The presence of the word παιάν in its stead guarantees that its absence is not a case of scribal omission. Nor can it be ascribed to scribal idiosyncrasy, given that 67 on the same manuscript has the usual format.

remains of *Paean* 6(a),[147] and nothing in the opening or closing section of *Paean* 6(b) suggests a specific link to a cult of Aeacus. But other explanations for these indications can be hypothesized. The claim made in **64** may simply result from the lack of specific reference to a non-Delphic origin of the chorus in what is an ostentatiously Delphic milieu; that made in **65** may depend on the editor's awareness of the *Aiakeia* in Aegina more than of a specific connexion between that festival and *Paean* 6(b). Pindar's dictum seems once again most appropriate:

τὸ πόρϲω δ' ἐcτὶ cοφοῖc ἄβατον
κἀcόφοιc. οὔ νιν διώξω· κεινὸc εἴη.[148]

References

Amasaeus, R. 1551. *Pausaniae veteris Graeciae descriptio*. Florence.
Arrighetti, G. 1967. La biografia di Pindaro del papiro di Ossirinco XXVI 2438. *SCO* 16: 129–148.
Barrett, W.S. 2007. Pindar and Psaumis: *Olympians* 4 and 5. In *Greek Lyric, Tragedy, and Textual Criticism: Collected Papers*, ed. M.L. West, 38–53. Oxford.
Bender, G. 1904. *De Graecae comoediae titulis duplicibus*. Marburg.
Bergk, T. 1866–1867. *Poetae lyrici Graeci*. Vols 1–3. 3rd edn. Leipzig.
Bergk, T. 1878–1882. *Poetae lyrici Graeci*. Vols 1–3. 4th edn. Leipzig.
Bergk, T. 1883. *Griechische Literaturgeschichte*. Vol. 2, ed. G. Hinrichs. Berlin.
Bernardini, P.A. 2012. 'Pitica X'. In *Pindaro: Le Pitiche*, ed. B. Gentili, E. Cingano, P. Giannini, P.A. Bernardini. 5th edn, 263–269, 621–646. Milan.
Blass, F. 1898. *Bacchylidis carmina cum fragmentis*. Leipzig.
Blum, R. 1977. *Kallimachos und die Literaturverzeichnung bei den Griechen. Untersuchungen zur Geschichte der Biobibliographie*. Frankfurt am Main (Translated into English by H.H. Wellisch as: *Kallimachos. The Alexandrian Library and the Origins of Bibliography*, Madison, 1991.).
Boeckh, A. 1811–1821. Πινδάρου τὰ cωζόμενα. *Pindari opera quae supersunt*. Vols I–II/2. Leipzig.

---

[147] Indeed, that the performers of the united *Paean* 6 were Delphian has been doubted by several scholars in modern times, starting with Wilamowitz (1908) 350 almost immediately upon the publication of Π⁴; for further bibliography see Currie (2005) 323n143. Of course the lacuna that obliterated half of the first triad may well be to blame for the loss of any further information on the commission of the poem.

[148] 'What lies beyond neither wise men nor fools can tread. I will not pursue it; it would be foolish' (Pind. *Ol.* 3.44–45).

Borgo, A. 2007. Quando il libro si presenta da sé: *Arma virumque* e i titoli delle opere antiche. *Aevum* 81: 133–147.

Braswell, B.K. 1988. *A Commentary on the Fourth Pythian Ode of Pindar*. Berlin.

Breitenbach, H. 1908. *De genere quodam titulorum comoediae Atticae*. Basle.

Budin, S.L. 2008. *The Myth of Sacred Prostitution in Antiquity*. Cambridge.

Calame, C. 2009. Apollo in Delphi and in Delos: Poetic Performances between Paean and Dithyramb. In *Apolline Politics and Poetics*, ed. L. Athanassaki, R.P. Martin, and J.F. Miller, 169–197. Athens.

Calame, C. 2013. "Rien pour Dionysos?" Le dithyrambe comme forme poétique entre Apollon et Dionysos. In *Redefining Dionysos*, ed. A. Bernabé, M. Herrero de Jáuregui, A.I. Jiménez San Cristóbal, and R. Martín Hernández, 82–99. Berlin.

Carey, C. 1983. Review of Maehler (1982). *JHS* 103: 165–166.

Casaubon, I. 1587a. Στράβωνος Γεωγραφικῶν βίβλοι ιζ'. *Strabonis rerum geographicarum libri XVII*. [Geneva].

Casaubon, I. 1587b. *Commentarius et castigationes ad lib. Strabonis geograph. XVII*. [Geneva].

Cavallo, G. 1974. Lo stile di scrittura 'epsilon-theta' nei papiri letterari. *CErc* 4: 33–36. Reprinted in *Il calamo e il papiro. La scrittura greca dall'età ellenistica ai primi secoli di Bisanzio*, 123–128. Florence 2005.

Ceccarelli, P. 2013. Circular Choruses and the Dithyramb in the Classical and Hellenistic Period: A Problem of Definition. In *Dithyramb in Context*, ed. B. Kowalzig and P. Wilson, 153–170. Oxford.

Christesen, P. 2007. *Olympic Victor Lists and Ancient Greek History*. Cambridge.

Currie, B.G.F. 2005. *Pindar and the Cult of Heroes*. Oxford.

D'Alessio, G.B. 1997. Pindar's *Prosodia* and the Classification of Pindaric Papyrus Fragments. *ZPE* 118: 23–60.

D'Alessio, G.B. 2000. Review of S. Schröder (1999). *BMCR* 2000.01.24.

D'Alessio, G.B. 2001. Sulla struttura del libro dei *Peani* di Pindaro. In *I lirici greci. Forme della comunicazione e storia del testo*, ed. M. Cannatà Fera and G.B. D'Alessio, 69–86. Messina.

D'Alessio, G.B. 2004. Argo e l'Argolide nei canti cultuali di Pindaro. In *La città di Argo. Mito, storia, tradizioni poetiche*. Atti del convegno internazionale (Urbino, 13–15 giugno 2002), ed. P. Angeli Bernardini, 107–125. Rome.

D'Alessio, G.B. 2008. Review of Fearn (2007). *BMCR* 2008.11.14.

D'Alessio, G.B. 2012. The Lost *Isthmian* Odes of Pindar. In *Reading the Victory Ode*, ed. P. Agócs, C. Carey, and R. Rawles, 28–57. Cambridge.

D'Alessio, G.B. 2013. "The Name of the Dithyramb". Diachronic and Diatopic Variations. In *Dithyramb in Context*, ed. B. Kowalzig and P. Wilson, 115–132. Oxford.

D'Alessio, G.B. 2016. Bacchylides' Banquet Songs. In *The Cup of Song. Studies on Poetry and the Symposion*, ed. V. Cazzato, D. Obbink, and E.E. Prodi, 63–84. Oxford.

D'Alessio, G.B. and Ferrari, F. 1988. Pindaro, Peana 6, 175–183: una ricostruzione. *SCO* 28: 159–180.
Daude, C., David, S., Fartzoff, M., and Muckensturm-Poulle, C. 2013. *Scholies à Pindare*, I: Vies *de Pindare et scholies à la première* Olympique. Besançon.
Davison, J. 1934. The Authorship of the 'Leucippides' Papyrus. *CR* 48: 205–207.
Del Mastro, G. 2014. *Titoli e annotazioni bibliologiche nei papiri greci di Ercolano*. Naples.
De Sanctis, G. 1928. Lacare. *RFIC* NS 6: 53–77. Reprinted in *Scritti minori*. Vol. 1, 349–369, Rome 1966.
Deubner, L. 1932. *Attische Feste*. Berlin.
Dittmer, W.A. 1923. *The Fragments of the Athenian Comic Didascaliae Found in Rome (IG XIV 1097, 1098, 1098a)*. Leiden.
Duchet, C. 1973. "La fille abandonee" et "La bête humaine". Éléments de titrologie romanesque. *Littérature* 12: 49–73.
Fearn, D. 2007. *Bacchylides: Politics, Performance, Poetic Tradition*. Oxford.
Fearn, D. 2009. Oligarchic Hestia: Bacchylides 14B and Pindar, *Nemean* 11. *JHS* 129: 23–38.
Fearn, D. 2011a. Aeginetan Epinician Culture: Naming, Ritual, and Politics. In *Aegina: Contexts for Choral Lyric Poetry. Myth, History, and Identity in the Fifth Century BC*, ed. D. Fearn, 175–226. Oxford.
Fearn, D. 2011b. The Ceians and their Choral Lyric: Athenian, Epichoric and Pan-Hellenic Perspectives. In *Archaic and Classical Choral Song: Performance, Politics and Dissemination*, ed. L. Athanassaki and E.L. Bowie, 207–234. Berlin.
Ferry, A. 1996. *The Title to the Poem*. Stanford.
Filoni, A. 2007. *Il peana di Pindaro per Dodona (frr 57–60 M.)*. Milan.
Finglass, P.J. 2007. *Pindar*. Pythian *Eleven*. Cambridge.
Fränkel, H. 1962. *Dichtung und Philosophie des frühen Griechentums. Eine Geschichte der griechischen Epik, Lyrik und Prosa bis zur Mitte des fünften Jahrhunderts*. 2nd edn. Munich. (Translated into English by M. Hadas and J. Willis as: *Early Greek Poetry and Philosophy. A History of Greek Epic, Lyric, and Prose to the Middle of the Fifth Century*, Oxford, 1975.)
Franklin, J.C. 2010–2011. The Lesbian Singers: Towards a Reconstruction of Hellanicus' Karneian Victors. *Rudiae* 22–23: II 719–763.
Fredouille, J.-C., Goulet-Cazé, M.-O., Hoffmann, P., Petitmengin, P., Deléani, S. 1997. *Titres et articulations du texte dans les œuvres antiques*. Actes du Colloque International de Chantilly 13–15 décembre 1994, ed. J.C. Fredouille, M.-O. Goulet-Cazé, Ph. Hoffmann, and P. Petitmengin. Paris.
Friis Johansen, K. 1959. *Eine Dithyrambos-Aufführung*. Copenhagen.
Gallavotti, C. 1950. Review of *Bacchylidis carmina cum fragmentis*, ed. B. Snell, 6th edn. Leipzig 1949. *RFIC* NS 28: 265–267.
Gallavotti, C. 1957. Review of *The Oxyrhynchus Papyri* 23 (1956). *Gnomon* 29: 419–425.

Gallo, I. 1968. *Una nuova biografia di Pindaro (POxy. 2438). Introduzione, testo critico e commentario*. Salerno.

Gebhard, E.R. 2002. The Beginnings of Panhellenic Games at the Isthmus. In *Olympia 1875–2000: 125 Jahre deutsche Ausgrabungen. Internationales Symposion, Berlin 9–11 November 2000*, ed. H. Kyrieleis, 221–237. Mainz am Rhein.

Gelzer, T. 1985. Μοῦcα αὐθιγενής. Bemerkungen zu einem Typ Pindarischer und Bacchylideischer Epinikien. *MH* 42: 95–120.

Genette, G. 1987. *Seuils*. Paris. (Translated into English by J.E. Lewin as: *Paratexts. Thresholds of Interpretation*, Cambridge, 1997.)

Genette, G. 1988. Structure and Function of the Title in Literature. *Critical Inquiry* 14: 692–720.

Geus, K. 2002. *Eratosthenes von Kyrene. Studien zur hellenistischen Kultur- und Wissenschaftsgeschichte = Münchener Beiträge zur Papyrusforschung und antiken Rechtsgeschichte 92*. Munich.

Gołąb, H. 2012. Bacchylides' Spartan Dithyramb in the Light of Choral Projection. *Eos* 99: 15–22.

Grassi, E. 1961. Inediti di Eugenio Grassi. *A&R* NS 6: 129–165.

Grenfell, B.P. and Hunt, A.S. 1899. CCXXII List of Olympian victors. *The Oxyrhynchus Papyri* 2: 85–95.

Grenfell, B.P. and Hunt, A.S. 1903. 408 Odes of Pindar. *The Oxyrhynchus Papyri* 3: 13–17.

Grenfell, B.P. and Hunt, A.S. 1908. 841 Pindar, *Paeans*. *The Oxyrhynchus Papyri* 5: 11–110.

Grenfell, B.P. and Hunt, A.S. 1915. 1361 Bacchylides, *Scolia*. *The Oxyrhynchus Papyri* 11: 65–83.

Hadjimichael, T. 2014. Fr. 60 M. of Bacchylides and the *Kassandra*. *BASP* 51: 77–100.

Hippenstiel, G. 1887. *De Graecorum tragicorum principum fabularum nominibus*. Marburg.

Hoek, L.H. 1981. *La marque du titre. Dispositifs sémiotiques d'une pratique textuelle*. The Hague.

Holtz, L. Titre et incipit. In Fredouille et al. 1997: 469–489.

Houston, G.W. 2014. *Inside Roman Libraries: Book Collections and their Management in Antiquity*. Chapel Hill.

Hunt, A.S. 1927. 2082 Phlegon, *Chronica* (?). *The Oxyrhynchus Papyri* 17: 82–99.

Hunter, R.L. 1983. *Eubulus: The Fragments*. Cambridge.

Ieranò, G. 1997. *Il ditirambo di Dioniso. Le testimonianze antiche*. Pisa.

Irigoin, J. 1952. *Histoire du texte de Pindare*. Paris.

Irigoin, J., Duchemin, J. and Bardollet, L. 1993. *Bacchylide. Dithyrambes—Épinicies—Fragments*. Paris.

Jachmann, G. 1909. *De Aristotelis didascaliis*. Göttingen.

Jebb, R.C. 1905. *Bacchylides: The Poems and Fragments*. Cambridge.

Kaimio, M. 2000. Tragic Titles in Comic Disguises. In *Studies in Ancient Literary Theory and Criticism*, ed. J. Styka, 53–69. Kraków.

Käppel, L. and Kannicht, R. 1988. Noch einmal zur Frage 'Dithyrambos oder Paian?' im Bakchylideskommentar P.Oxy. 23.2368. *ZPE* 73: 19–24.

Kayser, K.L. 1848. Zur Kritik des Pausanias. *JfA* 6: 495–511, 997–1007, 1079–1101.

Kenyon, F.G. 1897. *The Poems of Bacchylides from a Papyrus in the British Museum.* Oxford.

Koerte, A. 1906. Aristoteles' Νῖκαι Διονυσιακαί. *CPh* 1: 391–398.

Komorzynski, E. von. 1903–1904. Zur Geschichte der Blume im deutschen Buchtitel. *Zeitschrift für Bücherfreunde* 7: 284–287.

Kowalzig, B. and Wilson, P. 2013. Introduction: The World of Dithyramb. In *Dithyramb in Context*, ed. B. Kowalzig and P. Wilson, 1–27. Oxford.

Kowerski, L.M. 2005. *Simonides on the Persian Wars: A Study of the Elegiac Verses of the 'New Simonides'*. New York.

Kurke, L. 2007. Visualizing the Choral: Epichoric Poetry, Ritual, and Elite Negotiation in Fifth-Century Thebes. In *Visualizing the Tragic. Drama, Myth, and Ritual in Greek Art and Literature: Essays in Honour of Froma Zeitlin*, ed. C. Kraus, S. Goldhill, H.P. Foley, and J. Elsner, 63–102. Oxford.

Lavecchia, S. 1996. P. Oxy. 2622 e il 'Secondo Ditirambo' di Pindaro. *ZPE* 110: 1–26.

Lavecchia, S. 2000. *Pindari dithyramborum fragmenta*. Rome.

Lehnus, L. 1973a. Una glossa pindarica in Corinna di Tanagra. *RIL* 107: 393–422.

Lehnus, L. 1973b. Contributo a due frammenti pindarici (frr. 37 e 168 Snell[3]). *SCO* 22: 5–18.

Lehnus, L. 1984. Pindaro: il *dafneforico per Agasicle* (Fr. 94b Sn.-M.). *BICS* 31: 61–92.

Levenston, E.A. 1978. The Significance of the Title in Lyric Poetry. *The Hebrew University Studies in Literature* 6: 63–87.

Levin, H. 1977. The Title as a Literary Genre. *The Modern Language Review* 72: xxiii–xxxvi.

Lewis, D.M. 1962. The Federal Constitution of Keos. *ABSA* 57: 1–4.

Lobel, E. 1956a. 2366 Bacchylides, Ὕμνοι? *The Oxyrhynchus Papyri* 23: 40–41.

Lobel, E. 1956b. 2368 Commentary on Bacchylides?, *Dithyrambs or Paeans*. *The Oxyrhynchus Papyri* 23: 51–54.

Lobel, E. 1959a. 2430 Choral lyric in the Doric dialect (?Simonides). *The Oxyrhynchus Papyri* 25: 45–87.

Lobel, E. 1959b. 2431 Simonides, *Epinicians? The Oxyrhynchus Papyri* 25: 87–94.

Lobel, E. 1968. 2734 On Alcaeus. *The Oxyrhynchus Papyri* 35: 2–8.

Lohan, E. 1890. *De librorum titulis apud classicos scriptores Graecos nobis occurrentibus*. Marburg.

Luppe, W. 1987. Dithyrambos oder Paian?—Zu Bacchylides Carm. 23 Sn./M. *ZPE* 69: 9–12.

Luppe, W. 1989. Nochmals zu Kallimachos' Gattungszuordnung bakchylideischer Lieder. *APapyrol* 1: 23–29.
Maehler, H., 1982. *Die Lieder des Bakchylides*. Vol. 1. *Die Siegeslieder*. Leiden.
Maehler, H. 1989. *Pindari carmina cum fragmentis*. Vol. 2: *Fragmenta, indices*. 8th edn. Leipzig.
Maehler, H. 2004. *Bacchylides: A Selection*. Cambridge.
Merkelbach, R. 1973. Der Theseus des Bakchylides (Gedicht für ein attisches Ephebenfest). *ZPE* 12: 56–62.
Millis, B.W. and Olson, S.D. 2012. *Inscriptional Records for the Dramatic Festival in Athens*. IG II^2 2318–2325 and Related Texts. Leiden.
Mommsen, C.I.T. 1864. *Pindari carmina*. Berlin.
Nachmanson, E. 1969. *Der griechische Buchtitel. Einige Beobachtungen*. Darmstadt.
Negri, M. 2001. La trattazione della cronologia pindarica nel POxy XXVI 2438. In *Atti del XXII Congresso Internazionale di Papirologia. Firenze, 23–29 agosto 1998*, ed. I. Andorlini, G. Bastianini, M. Manfredi, and G. Menci, vol. 2: 1033–1043. Florence.
Negri, M. 2004. *Pindaro ad Alessandria. Le edizioni e gli editori*. Brescia.
Obbink, D. 2001. The Genre of *Plataea*. Generic Unity in the New Simonides. In *The New Simonides. Contexts of Praise and Desire*, ed. D. Boedeker and D. Sider, 65–85. New York.
Parsons, P. 1992. 3965 Simonides, *Elegies*. *The Oxyrhynchus Papyri* 59: 4–50.
Paton, W.R. 1912. Simonides, fr. 68, and a fragment of Lupercus. *CR* 26: 9.
Pickard-Cambridge, A. 1988. *The Dramatic Festivals of Athens*. Second edition revised by J. Gould and D.M. Lewis, reissued with supplement and corrections. Oxford.
Poltera, O. 2005. *Deliaka* (Simon. PMG 539): zu einer vermeintlichen Gedichtsammlung. *SIFC* s. IV 3: 183–187.
Poltera, O. 2008. *Simonides Lyricus. Testimonia und Fragmente*. Basle.
Pontani, F. 2012. Le κατευχαί di Simonide (*PMG* 537–538). *QUCC* n.s. 102: 11–28.
Porro, A. 1994. *Vetera Alcaica. L'esegesi di Alceo dagli Alessandrini all'età imperiale*. Milan.
Prodi, E.E. 2013. *P.Oxy*. 2448 (Pi. fr. 215 Sn.-M.) and Pindar's *Prosodia*. *ZPE* 185: 53–59.
Prodi, E.E. 2014. A Bibliological Note on *P.Oxy*. 659 (Pindar, *Partheneia*). *APapyrol* 26: 99–105.
Prodi, E.E. 2016. Titles and Markers of Poem-end in the Papyri of Greek Choral Lyric. In *Proceedings of the XXVII International Congress of Papyrology*, ed. T. Derda, A. Łajtar, and J. Urbanik, vol. 2: 1137–1184. Warsaw.
Race, W.H. 1997. *Pindar*. Vols 1–2. Cambridge, MA.
Rawles, R. 2013. Aristophanes' Simonides: Lyric Models for Praise and Blame. In *Greek Comedy and the Discourse of Genres*, ed. E. Bakola, L. Prauscello, and M. Telò, 175–201. Cambridge.

Robert, C. 1900. Die Ordnung der olympischen Spiele und die Sieger der 75.–83. Olympiade. *Hermes* 35: 141–195.
Rose, V. 1863. *Aristoteles pseudepigraphus*. Leipzig.
Rose, V. 1886. *Aristotelis qui ferebantur librorum fragmenta*. Leipzig.
Rotstein, A. 2016. *Literary History in the Parian Marble*. Washington, DC.
Rutherford, I.C. 1988. Pindar on the Birth of Apollo. *CQ* n.s. 38: 65–75.
Rutherford, I.C. 1990. Paeans by Simonides. *HSCPh* 93: 169–209.
Rutherford, I.C. 1995. Et hominum et deorum … laudes (?): A Hypothesis about the Organisation of Pindar's *Paean*-book. *ZPE* 107: 44–52.
Rutherford, I.C. 1997a. For the Aeginetans to Aeacus a prosodion: An Unnoticed Title at Pindar, Paean 6, 123, and its significance for the poem. *ZPE* 118: 1–21.
Rutherford, I.C. 1997b. Odes and Ends: Closure in Greek Lyric. In *Classical Closure: Reading the End in Greek and Latin Literature*, ed. D.H. Roberts, F.M. Dunn, and D. Fowler, 43–61. Princeton.
Rutherford, I.C. 2001a. *Pindar's Paeans. A Reading of the Fragments with a Survey of the Genre*. Oxford.
Rutherford, I.C. 2001b. The New Simonides. Toward a Commentary. In *The New Simonides. Contexts of Praise and Desire*, ed. D. Boedeker and D. Sider, 33–54. New York.
Rutherford, I.C. forthcoming. Simonides, Anius and Athens. A note on *PMG* 537 (*Kateukhai*). In *Simonides lyricus*, ed. P. Agócs and L. Prauscello. Cambridge.
Schironi, F. 2010. Τὸ μέγα βιβλίον. *Book-ends, End-titles, and Coronides in Papyri with Hexametric Poetry*. Durham, NC.
Schironi, F. 2016. 5277 Oppian, *Halieutica* 4.683–693. *The Oxyrhynchus Papyri* 81: 85–87.
Schmalzriedt, E. 1970. Περὶ φύσεως. *Zur Frühgeschichte der Buchtitel*. Munich.
Schmidt, D. 1999. An Unusual Victory List from Keos: *IG* XII, 5, 608 and the Dating of Bakchylides. *JHS* 119: 67–85.
Schmitt, J.C. 1856. Beiträge zur Kritik des Pausanias. *Philologus* 11: 468–479.
Schneider, I.G. 1809. *Aristotelis Politicorum libri octo superstites*. Vols. 1–2. Frankfurt a.d. Oder.
Schneidewin, F.W. 1846. De Peplo Aristotelis Stagiritae. Accedunt Pepli reliquiae. *Philologus* 1: 1–45.
Schröder, B.-J. 1999. *Titel und Text. Zur Entwicklung lateinischer Gedichtsüberschriften. Mit Untersuchungen zu lateinischen Buchtiteln, Inhaltsverzeichnissen und anderen Gliederungsmitteln*. Berlin.
Schröder, S. 1999. *Geschichte und Theorie der Gattung Paian. Eine kritische Untersuchung mit einem Ausblick auf Behandlung und Auffassung der lyrischen Gattungen bei den alexandrinischen Philologen*. Stuttgart.
Schubart, J.H.C. 1847. Beiträge zur Kritik des Pausanias. *JfA* 5: 217–223, 225–230, 289–300.
Scullion, S. 2002. Tragic dates. *CQ* n.s. 52: 81–101.

Siebelis, C.G. 1822–1827. Παυcανίου τῆc Ἑλλάδοc περιήγηcιc. *Pausaniae Graeciae descriptio*. Vols 1–4. Leipzig.

Snell, B. 1934. *Bacchylidis carmina cum fragmentis*. 5th edn. Leipzig.

Snell, B. 1937. *Euripides Alexandros und andere strassburger Papyri mit Fragmente griechischer Dichter*. Berlin.

Snell, B. 1958. *Bacchylidis carmina cum fragmentis*. 7th edn. Leipzig.

Snell, B., 1964. *Pindari carmina cum fragmentis*. Vol. 2: *Fragmenta, indices*. 3rd edn. Leipzig.

Snell, B., 1965. *Dichtung und Gesellschaft. Studien zum Einfluß der Dichter auf das soziale Denken und Verhalten im alten Griechenland*. Hamburg

Sommerstein, A.H. 2002. The Titles of Greek Dramas. *SemRom* 5: 1–16. Reprinted with addenda in *The Tangled Ways of Zeus and Other Studies in and around Greek Tragedy*, 11–29. Oxford, 2002.

Spoerri, W. 1988. Epigraphie et littérature: à propos de la liste des Pythioniques à Delphes. In *Comptes et inventaires dans la cite grecque. Actes du colloque international d'épigraphie tenu à Neuchâtel du 23 au 26 septembre 1986 en l'honneur de Jacques Tréheux*, ed. D. Knoepfler, 111–140. Neuchâtel and Geneva.

Stella, L.A. 1946. Studi simonidei. *RFIC* NS 24: 1–24.

Turyn, A. 1944. *Pindari epinicia*. New York.

Turyn, A. 1948. *Pindari carmina cum fragmentis*. Kraków.

Ucciardello, G. 1996–1997. Riesame di *P. Oxy.* 2368: alcuni problemi di lettura e di interpretazione. *APapyrol* 8–9: 61–88.

Ucciardello, G. 2016. New Light on *P.Strasb. gr.* 1406–1409: An Early Witness of Secundus' *Sentences*. In *Proceedings of the XXVII International Congress of Papyrology*, ed. T. Derda and J. Urbanik, vol. 1: 251–257. Warsaw.

Vogliano, A. 1932. Frammenti di poemetti lirici. *Papiri greci e latini* 10: 169–179.

West, M.L. 1979. The Prometheus Trilogy. *JHS* 99: 130–148. Reprinted in *Hellenica. Selected Papers on Greek Literature and Thought*. Vol. 2, 250–286. Oxford 2013.

Wilamowitz-Moellendorff, U. von. 1908. Pindars siebentes nemeisches Gedicht. *SPAW* 1908: 328–352. Reprinted in *Kleine Schriften*. Vol. 6, 286–313. Berlin 1972.

Wilamowitz-Moellendorff, U. von. 1913. *Sappho und Simonides. Untersuchungen über griechische Lyriker*. Berlin.

Wilamowitz-Moellendorff, U. von. 1922. *Pindaros*. Berlin.

Wilson, P. 2000. *The Athenian Institution of Khoregia. The Chorus, the City and the Stage*. Cambridge.

Wilson, P. 2007. Performance in the *Python*: the Athenian Thargelia. In *The Greek Theatre and Festivals. Documentary Studies*, ed. P. Wilson, 150–182. Oxford.

Zilliacus, H. 1938. Boktiteln i antik litteratur. *Eranos* 36: 1–41.

Zimmermann, B. 1992. *Dithyrambos. Geschichte einer Gattung*. Göttingen.

CHAPTER 21

Ita dictum accipe: Pomponius Porphyrio on Early Greek Lyric Poetry in Horace

Johannes Breuer

1   Introduction

It is well known that early Greek lyric poetry has had a significant influence on the Augustan poet Horace. We frequently encounter passages throughout his œuvre in which he explicitly refers to, for example, Alcaeus, Sappho, Archilochus, or Pindar in order to characterize his own poetry. But there are even more poems in which he alludes to Greek lyric intertexts in an implicit manner.[1]

Both of these features also attracted the attention of the ancient commentators. Recent studies have brought renewed attention to the transmission of these commentaries, to the terminology they use and to their contextualization within the system of Roman education in late antiquity.[2] There is, however, a lack of research that systematically examines their way of commenting on Horace's poetic interplay with his Greek predecessors.[3]

Therefore, I would like to analyse the information provided on this score by the ancient *grammatici*. In which ways do they comment on Horace's explicit statements,[4] and how do they deal with his tacit adaptations? What kinds of differences can be found between their explanations of Horatian references to early Greek poets and, for example, those to Hellenistic or Roman ones? Where do their explanations evidently differ from the modern *communis opinio*?

As the ancient commentaries on Horace by Claranus, Modestus, Quintus Terentius Scaurus, and Helenius Acro have not been preserved,[5] I will focus on the *Commentum in Horatium Flaccum* by Pomponius Porphyrio, usually dated

---

1 On Horace's references to early Greek poets and genres, see e.g. Degani (1993); Feeney (1993); Paschalis (2002); Woodman (2002); Hutchinson (2007); Barchiesi (2009); Strauss Clay (2010); and Günther (2013). On his reception of Sappho's 'Brothers Poem', see Morgan (2016) 296–299.
2 Diederich (1999); Kalinina (2007).
3 Diederich (1999) 314, however, lists some of the passages that will be discussed in this chapter.
4 I will focus in the first section on the most prominent models, namely Alcaeus, Sappho, and Archilochus.
5 See Kalinina (2007) 13.

to the first half of the third century CE.[6] This restriction appears to be all the more justified, as the so-called pseudo-Acronian scholia seem to consist of at least two different commentaries that have been strongly influenced by Porphyrio's explanations,[7] a fact that makes it difficult to determine their authentic way of commenting.[8] Furthermore, I will take into consideration the *vita ⟨H⟩oratii* by Porphyrio.[9]

2 Porphyrio's Comments on Horace's Explicit References to Early Greek Lyric Poets

In this section, an overview of Horace's references to early Greek lyric poetry will be given; on this basis, I will take a closer look at Porphyrio's comments on the respective passages. When Horace published his collection of *Odes* I–III in 23 BCE, it did not take his readers long to recognize the impact Greek lyric poetry had had on it: at the end of the first poem, which—being the overture of the collection—conveys crucial poetological statements, Horace declares that his poetic efforts will succeed, 'provided … Polyhymnia does not refuse to tune the Lesbian lyre'.[10] Horace thus clearly characterizes these poems as Lesbian lyric poetry, that is, as poetry in the manner of Alcaeus and Sappho. The scholiast Porphyrio explains this paraphrase by naming precisely these two poets, but he classifies this piece of information as well known, using the expression *manifestum*.[11]

---

6   For the ancient and medieval testimonies on him, see Schmidt (1997) 259; Diederich (1999) 3; Kalinina (2007) 15–16. However, his text is very likely to have been modified by later redactors in the fifth century, cf. Diederich (1999) 3. Much more pessimistic is the assumption made by Schmidt (1997) 259: *'Der heutige Zustand gibt … nur einen blassen Abglanz der ursprünglichen Fassung.'*

7   Cf. Diederich (1999) 8–9; Kalinina (2007) 14.

8   The early medieval scholia λ φ ψ as well as π u r z, that are closely intertwined with the Porphyrionic tradition and with the pseudo-Acronian scholia, cannot be considered in this chapter; the same applies to the scholia of the so-called *Commentator Cruquianus* ('a set of notes printed in a sixteenth century edition of Horace based on a lost manuscript, but containing unique and unquestionably ancient material', as Zetzel [2009] puts it poignantly).

9   The *vita Horati* by the Roman biographer Suetonius contains no information about Horace's literary models or techniques (a fact that might, however, be due to problems of textual transmission).

10 *Carm.* 1.1.32–34. All translations from the *Carmina* and *Epodes* are quoted according to the Loeb edition by Rudd (2004). The texts of Horace are cited from the edition of Shackleton Bailey (2001).

11 Porph. ad Hor. *Carm.* 1.1.34. Porphyrio is quoted according to the edition of Holder (1967).

The last poem of this collection of *Odes*, which has been composed in the same metrical form as the first one, is dominated by a reference to its poetological pedigree as well: in the typical manner of a *sphragis* poem, the poet provides information about his biography and his literary intentions. In Horace's case, this *topos* creates an interesting contrast between the Roman terms *Capitolium, Aufidus,* and *Daunus* in stanzas 2 and 3 and the Greek terms *Delphica* and *Melpomene* in stanza 4. Right in the middle of this antithesis, however, we find the expression *princeps Aeolium carmen ad Italos / deduxisse modos*.[12] Horace hence does not only corroborate his claim to have written Aeolian, that is, Lesbian poetry, but he also adds two new points: by using the word *princeps*, he depicts himself as some kind of *prôtos heuretês*. Thereby, he ascribes the glory of this literary achievement to himself, although the neoteric poet Catullus—at least to a certain extent—could have laid claim to this title as well. Furthermore, the verb *deducere* evokes associations of bringing settlers to their new homes; that is, Horace claims to have provided a new home for Greek Lesbian poetry or to have incorporated it into Roman literature.

This time, Porphyrio omits Sappho and only points to Alcaeus, explaining that this poet wrote in Aeolian dialect. In addition, he paraphrases the claim uttered by Horace, but does not deal with any problems involved: he neither discusses the role of the earlier Roman lyric poet Catullus, although he is mentioned elsewhere in the commentary,[13] nor explains the specific meaning of *deducere* in this context, even though it could, for example, also be understood as a plain synonym for *scribere* or *componere*.[14] The same applies to his *vita ⟨H⟩oratii*, where he cites the same two verses from *Odes* 3.30 and connects them only to Horace's proud imitation of Alcaeus, omitting Sappho again.[15] Apart from Lucilius, this is the only literary model that this *vita* mentions at all.

Horace's idea of writing in the tradition of Sappho and Alcaeus is manifest not only with regard to the framework in which he places the collection. It also becomes evident when we look at the frequent use of the metrical form of Sapphic or Alcaic stanzas (in 55 of a total of 88 poems); and the great predecessors and their style are mentioned consistently: in 1.26.10 ff., Horace immortalizes his friend Lamia in a performative way by reminding the Muses to 'sanctify' this man 'with new strings and the quill of Lesbos' (*fidibus novis / … Lesbio*

---

12   Hor. *Carm.* 3.30.13–14.
13   Ad Hor. *Carm.* 1.16.22–24; *Sat.* 1.10.18; *Sat.* 2.3.299.
14   It is used in this sense in Hor. *Sat.* 2.1.4 and *Epist.* 2.1.225.
15   Porph. *vita ⟨H⟩oratii* p. 2, 1–4 Holder.

sacrare plectro). Again, Porphyrio explains the adjective *Lesbio* by naming the two archaic lyricists.[16] But this time (unlike when commenting on *Lesboum* in *Odes* 1.1.34) he does not connect them explicitly with the island of Lesbos (maybe because he assumes that his readers remember that piece of information from what he wrote on the first poem). If that consideration is true, it might indicate that Porphyrio expected his commentary to be read in the order of the Horatian poems and not to be checked selectively.[17] Nevertheless, in general information on Greek poets is repeated several times throughout the work.

In 1.32.3 ff., we hear the poet addressing his musical instrument and delivering an insight into its history: the *barbitos*, with which he wants to 'sing' a Latin song, was played for the first time by a Lesbian citizen, that is by Alcaeus. This man, whose ordeals in the civil war of Lesbos and at sea are alluded to, sang (as Horace says) about wine, the Muses, love, and a handsome boy named Lycus. In doing so, he already prefigured a good portion of Horatian themes. This time, Porphyrio does not content himself with identifying again the Lesbian citizen as Alcaeus, but he adds the information that Alcaeus even fought against tyrants. Although the commentator connects the two sentences only by *autem*, not by *enim*, he seems to explain Horace's wording *ciuis* by the second sentence. So according to Porphyrio, Horace thinks of Alcaeus as a tyrant-fighter.[18] This explanation is quite appropriate, since Horace himself calls Alcaeus in the same poem 'a valiant warrior' and specifies in *Odes* 2.13.31 'banished tyrants' as one of his topics. Surprisingly, Porphyrio even paraphrases the two Horatian lines about Alcaeus' toils at sea, yet without any reference to Alcaeus' famous poems about ships in distress at sea.[19] Nor does he mention these Greek poems, which were already in antiquity commonly regarded as allegories on the state, when he discusses *Odes* 1.14, for which they were obviously central intertexts. So it seems quite safe to assume that the commentator did not know these poems.

Finally, I would like to discuss *Odes* 2.13.21 ff. At the beginning of this poem, the speaker reports a dangerous episode from his life: one day, he was almost killed by a falling tree. Starting from this point, the speaker reflects that he was on the verge of entering the underworld and of meeting his great predecessors

---

16   Porph. ad Hor. *Carm.* 1.26.11–12.
17   A strong argument that points in the same direction are "cross references", as we find them for example with regard to a certain Cathillus, whose brother is said to have founded Tibur: this information is given three times throughout the commentary (ad *Carm.* 1.7.13; 1.18.2; 2.6.5), and in the last two passages Porphyrio uses the expression *supra ostendimus*. But such cross references are never used in the context of Greek lyric poetry.
18   Quintilian thinks similarly about Alcaeus (cf. *Inst.* 10.1.63).
19   On these, see e.g., Page (1955) 179–197, and Bowie's contribution to this volume, pp. 286–293.

there. Thus, after naming what he considers to be the central subjects of their writings (for Sappho: sad love poetry; for Alcaeus, with a shift of the focus in comparison to 1.32: the suffering experienced at sea, in exile, and at war), Horace illustrates the effects of their songs on the dwellers of the underworld: not only do the shades admire both of them, although Alcaeus' themes are even more fascinating, but even the monsters and the sinners of the underworld pause enthralled. So Alcaeus and Sappho (that is, actual historical persons) have the same effect on their imaginary audience in this scene as Orpheus had in mythology.[20] And as it is precisely these Lesbian poets whom Horace emulates in his *Odes*, he clearly conveys a self-referential statement about the power of song and poetry through these verses. Porphyrio, however, does not deal with any of these aspects; he does not discuss Horace's intentions in this poem at all. One might object that such a comment would have been too trivial, as the author's intention in this passage seems quite obvious. This, however, does not pose a real counter-argument, as Porphyrio is elsewhere not reluctant to explain matters that are just as obvious. For example, with regard to *Odes* 3.30.1, he points out that this poem was written to praise its own author—a function that is typical for a *sphragis* poem.

Instead, Porphyrio tries to provide some background information about the two poets: his explanation of the adjective *Aeoliis* runs as we have seen it already in 3.30 (poetry named after its dialect, which is this time connected with Sappho). But we also learn from him that Sappho complains about other girls, 'her fellow citizens', because they are in love with Phaon, Sappho's own object of desire, whose name is given in Greek characters.[21] This explanation is quite astonishing, for at least two reasons: (1) Horace himself never mentions Phaon, so Porphyrio cannot have received this idea from another passage of the Horatian œuvre; and (2) although Porphyrio reports elsewhere that Sappho was defamed as homosexual,[22] this rumour does not prevent him from depicting her here as someone who is in immoderate love with a man.[23] But

---

20   The passage in Horace also seems to allude to a specific poem of Sappho, discovered in 2002 and published in 2004: in this poem (P. Köln 21351.1–8), Sappho seems to express the wish that the dwellers of the underworld wonder at her after her death. Cf. Hardie (2005) 22–27.

21   Porph. ad Hor. *Carm.* 2.13.23–25: *Aeoliis fidibus inquit, quia Sappho Aeolid[a]e dialecto in carminibus suis usa est. queritur autem Sappho a puellis ciuibus suis, quod Φάων⟨α⟩ ament, quem ipsa diligebat amens.*

22   Porph. ad Hor. *Epist.* 1.19.28 and ad *Epod.* 5.41–42. See also Schlesier's contribution to this volume, p. 365.

23   This is, however, not a contradiction in the Greco-Roman understanding of sexuality. Ovid, for example, ascribes both inclinations to Sappho in *Her.* 15 as well (on the discussion

the Phaon-thesis, to my knowledge, is not popular in modern commentaries. But as Nisbet and Hubbard have pointed out,[24] sadness is a common feature of ancient love-poems and the verb *queri* particularly suits some of Sappho's remarks; so *queri* might just describe a general feature of Sappho's poetry, thus lacking a specific motivation in this poem.

With regard to Alcaeus, the choice of the adverb *plenius*, which Horace uses to characterize his way of singing, is, according to Porphyrio, due to the fact that his topics are more serious than Sappho's; it thus relates to content, not to style.[25] Modern commentators, however, tend to regard it as a statement on Alcaeus's way of reciting or his general style.[26]

But it is not only in *Odes* I–III that Horace talks about Lesbian poetry. In the first book of his *Epistles*, published about four years after this collection of the *Odes*, he defends himself (in *Epistula* 19, while discussing the characteristics that make a real poet) against his detractors who seem to have criticized him for a lack of originality. He claims to have been the first one to show Parian iambs to Rome, following the metre and the general mood of Archilochus, but without retaining his aggressive tone and subject matter. Subsequently, he justifies this way of adapting an already existing literary model for one's own purposes by pointing to Sappho and Alcaeus: these poets took on Archilochus' metres as well, but they changed the themes. In this context, Horace does not miss the opportunity to affirm once again that it was he who, as a *Latinus fidicen*, has made Alcaeus known to the Romans.[27]

When one takes a look at Porphyrio's annotations on these verses, they start conventionally: he explains that the adjective *Parius* refers to Archilochus from Paros, the first writer of iambics.[28] But then he creates a surprise, providing an interpretation of the passage that differs widely from the modern *communis opinio*. In his view, these lines do not constitute a historical justification of Horace's own approach; the commentator rather seems to understand the nouns *Sappho* and *Alcaeus* as metonymy for their respective writings. Hence, he para-

---

about its authorship, see e.g., Morgan [2016] 295). See again Schlesier's contribution to this volume, on same-sex and different-sex relationships in Sappho.

24 Nisbet and Hubbard (1978) 216 (ad *Carm.* 2.13.24).
25 Porph. ad Hor. *Carm.* 2.13.26–27: *plenius inquit sonantem, quia Alcaeus robustior est, id est bellicas res scripsit, et nauigationem suam, cum a tyrannis Mitulenensibus pulsus est. aureo autem plect⟨r⟩o propter dignitatem carminis dixit.*
26 E.g. Nisbet and Hubbard (1978) 217 (ad *Carm.* 2.13.26: 'with more resonance'), who cite also Quintilian *Inst.* 11.3.15, where the different kinds of voices are discussed (*qualitas* [sc. *vocis*] *magis varia. nam est ... et plena et exilis*).
27 Hor. *Epist.* 1.19.23 ff.
28 Porph. ad Hor. *Epist.* 1.19.23.

phrases: 'I use verses by Archilochus as well as by Sappho, and I even blend in Alcaeus' metre'.[29] His remark on verse 32 that the pronoun *hunc*, generally taken by modern interpreters to be referring to Alcaeus, naturally (*scilicet*) refers to Archilochus,[30] provides another instance where a surprising detail is presented by the scholiast. In both cases, therefore, Porphyrio's explanations do not really elucidate the Horatian text.

Moreover, Porphyrio offers two different explanations for the adjective *mascula*: Sappho is called 'manly' either because of her poetic ambitions, which are more typical for men, or because of her supposed homosexuality.[31] Finally, he reveals the story behind the allusion *nec socerum quaerit* by identifying the father-in-law as Lycambes and the fiancée as Neoboule, whose name is given in Greek characters. Subsequently, he reports the notorious legend of Archilochus driving his father-in-law and his fiancée into suicide by offensive verses,[32] but he does not name a specific Archilochean poem nor cite any Greek text.

There are three more passages that need to be briefly mentioned and that are in line with what we have seen so far: Horace's poetic fame is again closely connected with Aeolian song in *Odes* 4.3. Porphyrio comments on this score that 'Aeolian' is a synonym for 'lyric', because some lyricists, as for example Alcaeus,

---

29 Porph. ad Hor. *Epist.* 1.19.28: *et Archilochi, inquit, utimur et Safficis uersibus*. Ad 29: *miscemus, inquit, et Alcaei metrum, sed ⟨neque isdem rebus⟩ neque eodem ordine utimur uersuum.*

30 Porph. ad Hor. *Epist.* 1.19.32: *Archilochum scilicet*. There is, however, also a problem in the textual transmission: the codices give for Horace: *hunc ego*, and the text printed by Shackleton Bailey (*hunc quoque*), that almost excludes a reference to Archilochus, is only a conjecture by Lucian Müller. On the other hand, the lemma in Porphyrio is (the unmetrical wording) *hunc e[r]go*. If Porphyrio really read *ergo*, he could have understood the verses 26–31 as an excursus, at whose end Horace really would have returned to Archilochus.

31 Porph. ad Hor. *Epist.* 1.19.28. Cf. Porph. ad Hor. *Epod.* 5.41–42 [*non defuisse masculae libidinis / Ariminensem Foliam*]: *quod ait autem masculae libidinis, ad id pertinet, quod dicantur quaedam mulieres habere ⟨e⟩ natura[m] monstrosae libidinis concubitum ⟨cum⟩ feminis. Quo crimine etiam Sappho male audiit* ('And that he says "with her masculine lusts" refers to the fact that some women are said to have intercourse with women—according to the nature of their monstrous lust. Even Sappho had a bad reputation in this respect'). I have pointed out above that her love for Phaon is in Greco-Roman eyes compatible with her love for women. *Mascula* in Horace may point to her actively pursuing men (and women), as women were not supposed to do.

32 Porph. ad Hor. *Epist.* 1.19.30: *socerum Lycambam, ⟨s⟩ponsam* Νεοβούλην *dicit. hos enim ad laqueum dicitur Archilochus conpulisse infami carmine*. Ad 34, on *ingenuis*: *hoc uel ad Archilochum refertur multa obscena dicentem uel ad Lucil[l]ium, qui aeque multa [p]unice spurc[e]a conposuit*. Some verses before (ad 25), Porphyrio had already explained that Archilochus hounded Lycambes, because he had been rejected as son-in-law. Bagordo (2011) 139n8 gives an overview of the discussion on the historicity of this legend.

used the Aeolian dialect.[33] It seems that in Porphyrio's opinion not Sappho, but Alcaeus was the most prominent Aeolian poet. This hypothesis might be corroborated by the commentator's remarks on *Odes* 4.6.35–36: the speaker asks the chorus to 'observe the Lesbian beat' in this poem, which is a poetic paratext to the *Carmen saeculare*. But even though the poem consists of Sapphic stanzas, Porphyrio refers the adjective *Lesbium* only to Alcaeus, not to Sappho.

And finally, in *Odes* 4.9, Alcaeus and Sappho (among others) are used as examples in order to demonstrate that considerable fame can also be obtained by lyric poetry, even though the first place belongs to epic poetry. Horace here characterizes Alcaeus' poems as 'aggressive' (*minaces*, 8) and the ones by Sappho as 'passion ... which the Aeolian girl confided to the strings of her lyre' (11–12). Porphyrio's explanation for *Aeoliae puellae* consists in pointing to Sappho's dialect, but his comment on *minaces* is quite remarkable: 'and Alcaeus' Muses are called "aggressive", since he was so bitter that he expelled many people from the state by the bitterness of his song'. Horace does mention expelled tyrants as one of Alcaeus' topics in *Odes* 2.13.31, but it seems somewhat exaggerated to speak of many whom he expelled. Moreover, he expelled them by fighting, not by singing. Maybe Porphyrio wants to say in a quite dense way that Alcaeus' battle songs inspired his comrades to expel the tyrants. Or does he want to say that the Lesbian poet also wrote offensive poems (as Archilochus did) that drove some of his fellow citizens off? Anyway, this annotation to Alcaeus remains somewhat opaque.

At this point, I have to briefly mention another passage to complete the picture: in *Epistles* 2.2.99 ff. (19 or perhaps 12 BCE), Horace mocks the contemporary literary scene: as every poet wants to recite his writings to his colleagues and wants to be complimented by them, they all bore each other to tears and bestow exaggerated titles upon each other. At events like this, Horace declares one of his colleagues to be the new Callimachus or even Mimnermus, and he himself is declared to be a new Alcaeus. Thus, some years after the publication of *Odes* I–III, Horace looks back to his former literary ambitions with a touch of humour. Yet, Porphyrio only paraphrases the Horatian verses without explicitly hinting at their humorous dimension.[34] Moreover, it is interesting that—provided that

---

33 Hor. *Carm.* 4.3.10 ff.: *sed quae Tibur aquae fertile praefluunt / et spissae nemorum comae / fingent Aeolio carmine nobilem*; Porph. ad loc.: *autem ita dictum accipe, ut si diceret 'lyrico carmine', quia quidam lyrici, ut Alcaeus, Aeolid[a]e magis dialecto usi sunt.*

34 Porph. ad Hor. *Epist.* 2.2.99 ff.: *iudicio illius, inquit, Alcaeo lyrico comparor, et fio alter Alcaeus ... ⟨illum Callimachum⟩ uoco, ut me ille Alcaeum nominat ... et hic ostendit non pro merito poetas, sed pro uoluntate laudari ... Alcaeus autem lyrici carminis, Callimachus elegiaci auctor est.*

Meyer's conjecture *illum Callimachum* is correct—Porphyrio does not suggest any identification for this other Augustan poet, whom modern commentators identify as Propertius. We have, however, his comment ad 101 where he calls Callimachus 'a writer of elegies'—an explanation that can help to identify the anonymous Roman author as the elegiac poet Propertius. Besides, it is a conspicuous restriction to call Callimachus only a writer of elegies, as he published works of many other genres.[35] Especially when writing on Horace, one should also bear in mind that Callimachus wrote *iambi*, which became an important model for Horace's collection of the *Epodes* (he even wrote the same number of *iambi* as the Hellenistic poet, namely seventeen). But on the one hand, Porphyrio never mentions Callimachus with regard to the *Epodes*, so he probably did not know this work or did not consider it an important intertext. On the other hand, alluding also to Callimachus's iambs could have caused some confusion in this particular context, since indeed only his elegies are relevant for Horace's joke and for the identification of the other author here.

When we turn to the other lyric genre in which Horace has published, that is to the *Epodes* or *Iambi*, we find—besides the already mentioned retrospective text in *Epistles* 1.19—only one explicit link of Horace's own way of writing to his prominent predecessor Archilochus: in *Epode* 6, the lyric *persona* threatens an opponent by comparing his own aggressiveness to that of the Parian poet, who appears as the rejected son-in-law of 'treacherous' Lycambes, which evokes the story mentioned above. The commentator narrates the respective story again, but this time without naming the fiancée. Thus, as far as the *Epodes*, published about 30 BCE, are concerned, it seems to be less important for Horace explicitly to stress the connection with his archaic Greek model. There are two more passages throughout his works where Horace mentions Archilochus, yet without explicitly expressing any literary relationship to the Parian writer: the first one is *Sat.* 2.3.11–12, where the speaker is mocked by a slave for carrying, amongst other things, the works of Archilochus with him—a statement on which Porphyrio does not comment. In the second one (*Ars Poetica* 79), Archilochus is mentioned as a prominent figure in the evolution of Greek literature—on which occasion Porphyrio again gives a short version of the legend, calling Archilochus the first writer of iambs. But except for this 'absolute' attribute, he does not attempt to establish any chronological overview about the authors mentioned by Horace in this passage.

---

35   Yet for the prominence of his elegies cf. Quintilian *Inst.* 10.1.58, where Callimachus is called 'leader' of elegy (*elegiam ... cuius princeps habetur Callimachus*).

I would like to give a first summary of Porphyrio's method of commenting on Horace's explicit references to Lesbian and Parian poetry: the lion's share of his explanations consists in connecting geographical adjectives that Horace had used metonymically in order to utter poetological statements, to the respective poets to whom Horace alludes. Moreover, he adds pieces of information concerning the real or pseudo-biographies of the poets in order to facilitate the understanding of the Horatian allusions. But never does he refer to specific poems or display any interest in the chronology of the Greek poets mentioned.[36] In order to establish a contrast, I would like to single out one passage from the pseudo-Acronian scholia that shows much more creativity. With regard to the adjective *Lesboum* in *Odes* 1.1.34, those scholia offer three different explanations: apart from the predictable reference to Alcaeus and Sappho, they call to mind that the first lyric writer was from Lesbos without mentioning his name—Terpander. And there is even a mythological approach: the adjective could be derived from the Lesbian king Periander to whom the god Mercury gave the lyre as a present.[37] So the first explanation is quite similar to the one given by Porphyrio (the wordings of the relative clauses are almost identical), maybe it even *is* Porphyrio's (slightly modified) explanation, as these scholia have been strongly influenced by Porphyrio's commentary. The *communis opinio* that the scholia consist of at least two different layers, seems to be corroborated by the two other, quite divergent explanations.[38] These two suggestions are quite learned, which might even be appropriate, as *Lesboum* is a *hapax legomenon* in classical Latin.[39] Nevertheless, in my opinion, Porphyrio's explanation seems to be the most plausible one, even though it is of course conceivable that Horace himself did not want to confine this adjective to only one meaning.

To complete this overview: other archaic lyric Greek poets whom Horace mentions in order to characterize his own poetry are Stesichorus, Anacreon, Simonides, and—most prominently—Pindar. Interestingly, we find all four poets assembled in *Odes* 4.9.5 ff., where Horace, by using them, amongst others,

---

36 This lack of interest in chronology is not restricted to Greek authors, though. Cf. Diederich (1999) 345: '*Die Zeit der* veteres *wird en bloc betrachtet, mit wenig Neigung zur Chronologie.*'

37 Ps.-Acro ad Hor. *Carm.* 1.1.34: *Lesboum propter Alcaeum et Sappho, quos in Lesbo insula natos esse constat, aut ab eo Lesbio, qui primus fuit lyricus scriptor, aut a Periandro rege Lesbi, cui primum Mercurius lyram ostendit*. The Latin text is quoted according to Keller (1902–1904).

38 Yet this argument might still be problematic, as Porphyrio sometimes presents two different explanations for one verse, too (e.g. ad *Epist.* 1.19.28).

39 E.g. Mayer (2013) 60 comments on the adjective by pointing to Terpander, too (as well as to Sappho and Alcaeus).

as examples, wants to show the immortality of topics that have been treated by lyric poets. With regard to these authors, Porphyrio uses throughout his commentary basically the same principles of annotation we have already seen him applying to Sappho, Alcaeus, and Archilochus: most of his explanations consist in connecting geographical adjectives to the respective poets to whom Horace had alluded. But I should mention one single exception to that method: in commenting on the expression *Ceae ... munera neniae* in *Odes* 2.1.37–38, he traces the adjective *Ceae* back to Simonides, whose poems are subsequently designated with the Greek term θρήνους, given in Greek characters. Moreover, Porphyrio judges their literary quality by remarking that Simonides composed them very well (*optime*). This is a striking exception to his regular way of commenting on early Greek lyric poets: nowhere else does he formulate aesthetical statements on the literary quality of a specific Greek lyricist. It is the only passage of the whole commentary where Porphyrio uses this adverb with regard to an individual author.[40] He does not repeat this praise in the only other passage where Simonides is mentioned (ad *Odes* 4.9.7). His annotation to *Odes* 2.1.37–38 thus remains somewhat puzzling, since we do not learn what aspect of Simonides's work Porphyrio relates his approval to (to style? metrical form? content?) and it is quite difficult to tell why Simonides of all poets received this special appraisal.

3   Porphyrio's Comments on Horace's Tacit References to Greek Lyric Poetry

But this is not the whole picture: although Porphyrio's comments on explicit Horatian references to Greek lyric poetry are rather superficial, there are occasions where he provides deeper insights into Horace's use of archaic Greek lyric models: with regard to *Odes* 1.10, a hymn to Mercury, he remarks in a very unspecific way that it is 'from the lyric poet Alcaeus' (*ab Alcaeo lyrico poeta*), initially without indicating whether he wishes to convey that the Horatian poem is a translation of the Greek model or that it has just been inspired by it. Later on, however, he comments on verse 9 of the same poem stating that its theme (the new-born Mercury stealing Apollo's cattle) has been invented by Alcaeus.[41]

---

40   There is only one more instance for *optime* in his work (besides Fabricius's conjecture for ad *Carm.* 1.3.2); but in this other passage (ad *Epist.* 2.1.28), Porphyrio speaks in general about the oldest Greek authors who wrote 'in the best manner', without singling out one specific poet.
41   In fact, Horace probably alludes to what we know as Alcaeus, fr. 308b.

Much more specific is his comment on *Odes* 1.27: its basic concept, he says, has been taken from the third book of Anacreon.[42] What he might mean by 'taken' (*sumptus*) becomes evident when this verb occurs elsewhere: at the beginning of his commentary on *Odes* 1.12, Porphyrio informs us: 'He took this from Pindar' (*hoc a Pindaro sumpsit*). In this case, the verb *sumpsit* appears to mean 'render with modifications', as Horace's opening verses *quem virum aut heroa lyra vel acri / tibia sumis celebrare, Clio* in some points clearly evoke the beginning of Pindar's *Second Olympian*.[43]

Another way of describing Horace's attitude towards one of his supposed models has been chosen for *Odes* 1.15: Porphyrio characterizes Horace's poetic technique in this poem as an imitation of Bacchylides, because the Roman poet presents a mythological figure who utters a prophecy about the Trojan war—which is, according to Porphyrio, exactly what the Greek lyric poet did.[44] But there are several problems involved in this statement: first of all, Porphyrio speaks about Proteus foretelling the future, whereas the original wording in Horace seems to be *Nereus*.[45] In addition, it is not clear what the expression *imitatur* means in this specific case, as the scholiast uses it in different senses when talking about literature.[46] But the biggest problem is that we do not know much about Bacchylides' *Cassandra*. It is usually identified with what Maehler printed in his edition of Bacchylides as poem 23, yet this text is only a mutilated fragment from which we can study neither the structure nor any special features of the poem. Ian Rutherford, however, pointed out that even the attribution of this fragment to Bacchylides is only a hypothesis, and he considered it (remotely) possible that Porphyrio either refers to another Bacchylidean text or even confuses Bacchylides with Pindar, so that he might mean that Horace's model for *Odes* 1.15 actually was Pindar's *"Paean"* VIIIa.[47] Although it is quite

---

42   Cf. fr. 356.
43   Pind. *Ol.* 2.1–2: Ἀναξιφόρμιγγες ὕμνοι, / τίνα θεόν, τίν' ἥρωα, τίνα δ' ἄνδρα κελαδήσομεν;
44   Porph. ad Hor. *Carm.* 1.15.1: *hac ode Bacchylidem imitatur. nam ut ille Casandram* [sic!] *facit uaticinari futura belli Troiani, ita hic Proteum*.
45   Cf. on this, e.g., Rutherford (1991) 8n14 and Breuer (2008) 350n5.
46   In ad *Sat.* 1.2.68–69 *imitatus* means that Horace uses the word *mutto* in the same obscene sense as Lucilius did. In ad *Epist.* 1.1.45 Porphyrio expresses with the same verb that one Horatian verse displays a similar idea as a distich by Theognis (cf. n. 49). Moreover, in ad *Epist.* 2.1.57 the Latin author Afranius is said to have imitated the style of the Greek dramatist Menander. Finally, in ad *Epist.* 2.1.162 (*temptauit*) *imitari* appears to mean that according to Porphyrio the Romans tried to imitate the Greek culture or, more specifically, the Greek tragedy (the expression is somewhat vague).
47   Rutherford (1991) 11.

likely that the imitation Porphyrio speaks about refers to the structure of the two poems, we cannot verify or evaluate his statement.[48]

When we review Porphyrio's commentary for quotations from Greek authors as Horatian models, the vast majority consists of Homeric passages. Besides, he proposes a slightly modified elegiac couplet by Theognis as a model for a verse from *Epistles* 1.1.[49] Apart from that, Callimachus plays a certain role which remains, however, somewhat obscure: regarding an expression from the *Ars Poetica*, Porphyrio remarks that Horace took it from Callimachus. Subsequently, the commentator introduces the quotation with the relative clause *qui dixit*, but unfortunately then the text has a lacuna (it might have exhibited what we know today as fragment 215 Pfeiffer).[50] The situation is reversed for a passage from *Sermones* 2.3: Porphyrio cites one and a half Greek verses here without naming their author, but Holder, the editor of the commentary, identifies them as Callimachus, fragment 587 Pfeiffer.[51]

No other discernible quotations from Greek lyric poems appear elsewhere in the transmitted text of Porphyrio's commentary.[52] Thus, since modern scholarship has found a vast amount of passages from Greek poetry which shed light on Horace's way of creative adaptation, but which are not mentioned by Porphyrio, he is by no means an exhaustive and reliable source for Horatian intertexts, neither in general nor with regard to a specific author.[53]

---

48   Cf. on this Rutherford (1991) 9 and the overview in Breuer (2008) 362n38.

49   Porph. ad *Epist.* 1.1.45 [*impiger extremos curris mercator ad Indos*]: *hoc loco Theognidis uersus imitatus est* [for Porphyrio's use of the verb *imitari* cf. n. 46], *qui ait:* Χρὴ πενίην φεύγοντα[ς] καὶ ἐς βαθυκήτεα πόντον / Φεύγειν καὶ πετρῶν, Κύρ[η]ν[ι]ε κατ' ἠλι(β)άτων. Cf. Thgn. 175–176: ἦν δὴ χρὴ (χρὴ πενίην/-αν testes omnes) φεύγοντα καὶ ἐς μεγακήτεα (βαθυκήτεα A Plut. 1039f Luc. [ter] Porph. Clem. Stob.^A) πόντον / ῥιπτεῖν καὶ πετρέων (πετρῶν o Plut. [bis] Porph. Hermog. Apthon. Stob.^S sch. Thuc. Elias) Κύρνε κατ' ἠλιβάτων.

50   Porph. ad Hor. *Ars P.* 97 [*proicit ampullas et sesquipedalia uerba*]: *hoc a Callimacho sustulit, qui dixit* ⟨***⟩. Cf. Callim. fr. 215 Pfeiffer: ἥτις τραγῳδὸς μοῦσα ληκυθίζουσα.

51   Porph. ad Hor. *Sat.* 2.3.296 [*sapientum octavus, amico*]: *quia Graeci septem sapientes dicunt, quibus hunc addit:* ἑπτὰ σοφοὶ χαίροιτε, τὸν ὄγδοον ὥστε Κόρυβον / οὐ συναριθμέομεν (= Callim. fr. 587 Pfeiffer), where, however, the name is spelled Κόροιβον.

52   Porphyrio, however, comments on Hor. *Sat.* 2.1.43 [*ut pereat*]: *tractum ex Graeco* [*hoc:*] ὡ⟨ς⟩ ἀπόλ[λ]οιτο. Even though we find this wording in Callim. fr. 110.48 Pfeiffer, it is rather unspecific, and Porphyrio seems to identify it only as a Grecism, not as a quotation.

53   To give just two examples: Hor. *Carm.* 1.18.1 [*nullam, Vare, sacra vite prius severis arborem*] is clearly an adaptation of Alcaeus, fr. 342 (μηδὲν ἄλλο φυτεύσῃς πρότερον δένδριον ἀμπέλω). But Porphyrio does not point to any model for this ode, nor does he name a source for Hor. *Carm.* 1.9 (*uides ut alta stet nive candidum / Soracte* etc.), which is generally believed to be inspired by Alcaeus, fr. 338 (ὔει μὲν ὁ Ζεῦς, ἐκ δ' ὀράνω μέγας / χείμων κτλ.).

In contrast to that, we come across numerous quotations from Latin authors throughout the whole commentary, above all from Lucilius and Virgil, by which Porphyrio wants to illustrate either thematic and motival or linguistic parallels to the Horatian text. Therefore, provided that the text that has been transmitted to us does not differ fundamentally from what Porphyrio himself has written, we have to state that his interest in or ability to integrate Greek inter- and paratexts into his explanations of the respective Horatian poems substantially differs from his attitude towards comparable Latin inter- and paratexts. If we assume that his explanations were primarily intended for school use,[54] one might argue that this difference could be due to some kind of "pedagogical reduction". But this would not be very convincing, since we find citations not only from Homer, but, as we have seen, also from Theognis and from Callimachus. So it appears reasonable to assume that Porphyrio presented all the Greek texts that he knew and considered relevant for the understanding of the Horatian text—which leads to the conclusion that his knowledge on this score was rather limited, whereas he was aware of at least some (pseudo-)biographical details about the early Greek lyricists.

4   Conclusions

The primary aim of this chapter was to examine how Pomponius Porphyrio, the third-century commentator and author of a *vita ⟨H⟩oratii*, comments on Horace's explicit and implicit poetic interplay with his Greek predecessors, especially Alcaeus, Sappho, and Archilochus. The results of this investigation demonstrate that Greek lyric poetry and its authors are an interesting feature of the Horatian texts for Porphyrio. He integrates them into his explanations, which might have been primarily intended for school use, as he is aware of their general importance for Horatian poetry, although he grossly misunderstands a central poetological passage in the *Epistles*.

The bulk of his annotations on this score consists of explanations of names and geographical adjectives used by Horace and their poetological as well as (sometimes pseudo-)biographical implications. Even though we find cross references in his commentary like *supra ostendimus* with regard to other topics, information on early Greek lyric poets is repeated several times. When Porphyrio explains expressions that refer to Lesbian lyric, Alcaeus is referred to more often than Sappho, so that he seems to consider him the more promin-

---

54   Cf. Schmidt (1997) 259.

ent or important author. The geographical explanations are appropriate, and some of his biographical annotations are correct or at least mirror what Horace is likely to have learned from the legendary tradition or from the poems of the respective authors themselves (for instance, Alcaeus as a tyrant-fighter, Archilochus attacking his former father-in-law with iambs). Yet, sometimes he presents explanations that do not seem to do justice to the Horatian texts (for instance, the motivation for Sappho's complaining in the underworld).

Every now and then, Porphyrio draws the attention of his readers to a Greek model, either a whole poem or just single motives or verses, describing Horace's methods of adaptation by verbs such as *sumere*, *imitari*, or *tollere*. But never does he evaluate Horace's efforts in adapting his Greek models in terms like *bene*, *eleganter*, *suauiter*, or even *melius*, although he often expresses such aesthetical judgements with regard to other aspects of Horace's poetry.[55] He does not provide any information on the reactions of Horace's Roman readers, either—in contrast, for example, to what Aelius Donatus, the fourth-century *grammaticus*, did (based on Suetonius) in his *Life of Virgil* for Virgil: we learn from him amongst other things that a certain Perellius Faustus made lists of passages that, in his opinion, Virgil had "stolen" from other authors (*furta*). Moreover, Donatus points to a work by a certain Quintus Octavius Avitus in eight volumes, called Ὁμοιοτήτων, that 'contain the verses which he borrowed, with their sources'.[56] In Porphyrio, however, we do not find anything like that, although Horace is likely to have encountered similar criticism.[57] The scholiast's approach of naming sources is by no means comprehensive, not even for a single Greek lyric author, as many important intertexts are omitted; and he does not display any interest in a chronology of the mentioned Greek authors or in an overview of them,[58] even though Horace himself presents a history of Greek literature *in nuce* in his *Ars Poetica* (73 ff.).

On the whole, Porphyrio seems to be eager to display his knowledge of Horatian models. But while he includes numerous citations from Latin literature, the information provided on ancient Greek lyric poetry is rather vague: apart from a modified elegiac couplet by Theognis and two problematic passages containing wordings by Callimachus, he never cites Greek lyric poetry—a fact that is, in my opinion, not due to some kind of pedagogical reduction, but to his limited knowledge of the actual poems. From where he received the respective pieces of information that he did integrate in his work, can only be left to

---

55 On these aesthetical judgements, see Diederich (1999) 241–306.
56 Donat. *Vit. Verg.* 44–45.
57 He (or at least his *persona*) speaks of his detractors in *Epist.* 1.19.
58 Except for attributes like 'first writer of iambs' (ad *Ars P.* 79).

speculation. Thus—always provided that Porphyrio's text has been transmitted to us in a version that does not differ fundamentally from the original edition— if we are to judge from Porphyrio's commentary, we have to assume that in the third century CE even learned men of the Latin-speaking world were not very familiar with the texts of Greek lyric poetry and especially those of early Greek lyric poetry—which appears to be in line with the general tendencies in the reception of these texts during the Roman imperial period.[59]

References

Bagordo, A. 2011. Archilochos. In *Die Literatur der archaischen und klassischen Zeit*, ed. B. Zimmermann (Handbuch der griechischen Literatur der Antike, Vol. 1), 138–148. Munich.

Barchiesi, A. 2009. Lyric in Rome. In *The Cambridge Companion to Greek Lyric*, ed. F. Budelmann, 319–335. Cambridge.

Breuer, J. 2008. *Der Mythos in den Oden des Horaz. Praetexte, Formen, Funktionen* (Hypomnemata 178). Göttingen.

Degani, E. 1993. Orazio e la tradizione giambica greca. In *Letture oraziane*, ed. G. Bruno, 83–89. Venosa.

Diederich, S. 1999. *Der Horazkommentar des Porphyrio im Rahmen der kaiserzeitlichen Schul- und Bildungstradition* (Untersuchungen zur antiken Literatur und Geschichte 55). Berlin.

Feeney, D.C. 1993. Horace and the Greek Lyric Poets. In *Horace 2000: A Celebration. Essays for the Bimillennium*, ed. N. Rudd, 41–63. Ann Arbor.

Günther, H.-C., ed. 2013. *Brill's Companion to Horace*. Leiden.

Hardie, A. 2005. Sappho, the Muses, and Life After Death. *ZPE* 154: 13–32.

Holder, A., ed. 1967. *Pomponi Porfyrionis commentum in Horatium Flaccum*. Hildesheim (reprint of the edition Ad Aeni Pontem, 1894).

---

59 In Quintilian (first century CE) we find the recommendation not only to choose single lyric authors for reading, but also single passages of their works—due to moral concerns (*Inst.* 1.8.6 *alunt et lyrici, si tamen in iis non auctores modo sed etiam partes operis elegeris: nam et Graeci licenter multa et Horatium nolim in quibusdam interpretari*). Aulus Gellius (second century CE) sometimes refers to Greek lyric poets (e.g. *NA* 17.11.1 [Alcaeus]; 17.21.8 [Archilochus]; 20.7.2 [Sappho, Bacchylides, and Pindar]) and even reports an episode from a banquet where odes of Anacreon (or his imitators) and Sappho were sung; but it appears that this was rather an exceptional event (*NA* 19.9.4: *ac posteaquam introducti pueri puellaeque sunt, iucundum in modum* Ἀνακρεόντεια *pleraque et Sapphica et poetarum quoque recentium* ἐλεγεῖα *quaedam erotica dulcia et venusta cecinerunt*).

Hutchinson, G. 2007. Horace and Archaic Greek poetry. In *The Cambridge Companion to Horace*, ed. S. Harrison, 36–49. Cambridge.

Kalinina, A. 2007. *Der Horazkommentar des Pomponius Porphyrio. Untersuchungen zu seiner Terminologie und Textgeschichte* (Palingenesia 91). Stuttgart.

Käppel, L. 2000. 'Phaon [1]'. In *Der Neue Pauly*, Vol. 9. 736–737. Stuttgart.

Keller, O., ed. 1902–1904. *Pseudacronis scholia in Horatium vetustiora*. Leipzig.

Mayer, R. 2013. *Horace, Odes. Book I*. 3rd printing. Cambridge.

Morgan, L. 2016. The Reception of Sappho's Brothers Poem in Rome. In *The Newest Sappho: P. Sapph. Obbink and P. GC inv. 105, frs. 1–4*, ed. A. Bierl and A. Lardinois (Studies in Archaic and Classical Greek Song 2/Mnemosyne Supplements 392), 293–301. Leiden.

Nisbet, R.G.M. and Hubbard, M. 1978. *A Commentary on Horace: Odes Book II*. Oxford.

Page, D. 1955. *Sappho and Alcaeus: An Introduction to the Study of Ancient Lesbian Poetry*. Oxford.

Paschalis, M., ed. 2002. *Horace and Greek Lyric Poetry*. Rethymnon.

Rudd, N., ed. and trans. 2004. *Horace:* Odes *and* Epodes. Cambridge, MA.

Rutherford, I. 1991. Pindar "Paean" VIIIa, the "Cassandra" of Bacchylides and the Anonymous "Cassandra" in P. Oxy. 2368: An Exploration in Lyric Structure. *Eos* 79: 5–12.

Schmidt, P.L. 1997. Pomponius Porphyrion, Commentum in Horatium. In *Die Literatur des Umbruchs: von der römischen zur christlichen Literatur; 117 bis 284 n. Chr.*, ed. K. Sallmann (Handbuch der lateinischen Literatur der Antike, Vol. 4), 259–261. Munich.

Shackleton Bailey, D.R., ed. 2001. *Q. Horatius Flaccus: Opera*. 4th edn. Munich.

Strauss Clay, J.S. 2010. Horace and Lesbian Lyric. In *A Companion to Horace*, ed. G. Davis, 128–146. Chichester.

Woodman, T. 2002. *Biformis vates*: The *Odes*, Catullus and Greek lyric. In *Traditions and Contexts in the Poetry of Horace*, ed. T. Woodman and D. Feeney, 53–64. Cambridge.

Zetzel, J. 2009. Review of A. Kalinina, *Der Horazkommentar des Pomponius Porphyrio, Stuttgart 2007*, BMCR 2009.02.06 (http://bmcr.brynmawr.edu/2009/2009-02-06.html).

CHAPTER 22

Pindar and His Commentator Eustathius of Thessalonica

Arlette Neumann-Hartmann

1   Introduction

Pindar's poems were studied from the fifth century BCE onwards up to the Byzantine age and were read by countless pupils at school and commented on by many scholars. Among the commentators on his works, the Alexandrian scholars Aristarchus and Didymus are the best known, but none of the ancient commentaries on Pindar has come down to us.[1] In the second century CE a new edition of selected works of Greek poets began to circulate. This edition included from Pindar's poetry only the victory odes, which were chosen probably because of their topics and the persistence of the Panhellenic games. This edition was accompanied by a commentary lost today, but forming the basis of the ancient scholia on Pindar's victory odes.[2] The first preserved treatise on Pindar's poetry, dating from the twelfth century CE, is the *Introduction* to the commentary on Pindar written by the Byzantine bishop and scholar Eustathius of Thessalonica and preserved in only one manuscript that is now at the University of Basel's library. Eustathius' commentary on Pindar itself has been lost, probably not long after its completion.

Eustathius' *Introduction* has recently been studied in detail by Athanasios Kambylis and Monica Negri. In 1991, the Byzantinist Kambylis provided a new critical edition of the text and also the monograph *Eustathios über Pindars Epinikiendichtung* in which he offered an analysis of Eustathius' attitude towards Pindar's poetry, especially his victory odes.[3] He looked at Eustathius' remarks on Pindar's language and formal technique and set these in the context of earlier Pindaric scholarship. He concluded that Eustathius might be called '*ein Vorläufer der neuzeitlichen Pindarphilologie*'.[4] In 2000, the Italian scholar Monica Negri published the first translation of Eustathius' *Introduction* into a mod-

---

1 See Irigoin (1952) 31–75; Braswell (2013) 9–10, 105–106; Neumann-Hartmann (2019).
2 See Irigoin (1952) 93–100; Neumann-Hartmann (2019).
3 Kambylis (1991a, 1991b).
4 Kambylis (1991b) 113. See also Adorjáni (2011) 81–82.

ern language, with a discussion of textual problems and with comments on the exegetical and biographical parts of the treatise.[5]

Neither Kambylis nor Negri considered the many references to Pindar's poetry in Eustathius' other works that also provide insight into his handling of Pindar.[6] These references will be the subject of my chapter, which has two parts. In the first part, to get a general picture of Eustathius' approach to Pindar, I shall consider his *Introduction* to Pindar, drawing on the work of Kambylis and Negri. In the second part I shall focus on references to Pindar in Eustathius' other works, including references to his own commentary on Pindar.

2 The *Introduction* to Eustathius' Commentary on Pindar

The precise date of Eustathius' commentary on Pindar is not known, but it seems to be one of his earlier works, for, according to the title of the *Introduction*, he wrote it when he was still deacon at the Hagia Sophia, thus before becoming archbishop of Thessalonica (c. 1175). Furthermore, in the treatise itself, he refers only to his commentary on Aristophanes (now lost), with no mention of his commentaries on Homer and Dionysius Periegetes.[7]

The *Introduction* to Pindar is divided into two main parts: after a short introduction on lyric poetry in chapters 1 and 2, Eustathius summarizes observations on Pindar's poetry in chapters 3 to 24; the second part, chapters 25 to 34, deals with Pindar's life and, very briefly, with his works. The treatise concludes with some comments on the Olympic games in chapters 35 to 37 and with a short treatment of the metrical shape of the victory ode in chapter 38 leading to the commentary itself. I shall now consider the following three aspects of the treatise: the corpus of Pindar's works used by Eustathius, the features of Pindar's poetry discussed by him, and the content of his commentary on Pindar.

---

5   Negri (2000). Before publishing her edition, she had written several papers on selected passages of Eustathius' *Introduction* to Pindar: Negri (1994a, 1996, 1997, 1998, 1999).
6   These were mentioned briefly by van der Valk (1971–1987) vol. 1, p. xc (§ 94) who observes that Pindar is not among the most quoted poets in this commentary, adding that Eustathius sometimes refers to the scholia on Pindar and even to his own commentary on Pindar.
7   Eust. *Prooem. ad Pind.* 38.1: ..., καθὰ καὶ ἐν τοῖς τοῦ Κωμικοῦ δηλοῦται, and see Gallo (1977) 45; on the formulation pointing to a commentary written by Eustathius, see also below, p. 547. See also Negri (2000) 61n1 who, however, questions Eustathius' authorship of that commentary. On the chronological order of Eustathius' commentaries see Kambylis (1991b) 6–8 with reference to the detailed discussion by van der Valk (1971–1987; cf. vol. 1, pp. cxxxvii–cxxxix [§ 125] and vol. 2, pp. xci–xciii [§ 172]) and to previous studies.

2.1 The Corpus of Pindar's Works Used by Eustathius in His Introduction to Pindar

In his *Introduction*, Eustathius states that Pindar wrote 'many poems of which no few are in circulation' (34.1);[8] he mentions paeans, dithyrambs, prosodia, parthenia, hyporchemata, enkomia, threnoi, and the victory odes; apart from the hymns and the number of books, both of which he omits, the list is identical to that of the *Vita Ambrosiana*, transmitted with Pindar's victory odes, which was one of his main sources for the biographical section of his *Introduction*.[9] However, when he deals with aspects of Pindar's poetry, he refers only to epinician poetry: in chapters 4 and 5, discussing digressions in Pindar's praise poetry he distinguishes digressions closely related to the victor and those without any obvious connection to the victor. In chapter 38.1, when speaking about the metrical shape used by Pindar, he refers explicitly to the victory ode and its triadic structure; and at the end of the same chapter, he notes that his commentary consists of a selection from the victory odes.[10] These passages show that Eustathius worked mainly on Pindar's victory odes, and that, as the end of the *Introduction* indicates, he commented on these poems.[11]

This observation is supported by the quotations of Pindar's works adduced by Eustathius in this treatise. As the indices in the editions of Kambylis and Negri show, most of these quotations come from the victory odes known from the manuscript tradition.[12] A few others come from other works of Pindar lost today: six can be assigned to indirect transmission as they occur in other texts, namely in the works of Aristophanes (Comicus) (1), Athenaeus (1), and the *Vita Ambrosiana* (4).[13] Two other Pindaric quotations in this treatise can be assigned

---

8   Eust. *Prooem. ad Pind.* 34.1: ποιήματα δὲ πολλὰ γράψαι Πίνδαρος λέγεται, ὧν καὶ φέρονται οὐκ ὀλίγα, οὐ μὴν τὰ πάντα ὑπεμνηματισμένα (Kambylis; Negri inserts a comma after πάντα), with the discussion of Kambylis (1991b) 24–26 and Negri (1998) 227–231 and (2000) 89–94.
9   Negri (1998) and (2000) 265–273.
10 See below p. 537.
11 See also Kambylis (1991b) 22–23.
12 Kambylis (1991a) 78–79; Negri (2000) 211–212. Sometimes Eustathius provides readings different from the *paradosis*, often due to inaccurate quotation of Pindar's text: cf. Pind. *Ol.* 2.93 in Eust. *Prooem. ad Pind.* 11.2; Pind. *Ol.* 3.17 in Eust. *Prooem. ad Pind.* 21.2; Pind. *Ol.* 10.81 in Eust. *Prooem. ad Pind.* 16.1; Pind. *Pyth.* 4.47 in Eust. *Prooem. ad Pind.* 12.1; Pind. *Pyth.* 10.29 in Eust. *Prooem. ad Pind.* 12.1; Pind. *Nem.* 6.28 in Eust. *Prooem. ad Pind.* 21.5; Pind. *Isthm.* 7.44 in Eust. *Prooem. ad Pind.* 20.3; see Negri (2000) 211–212, and for Eust. *Prooem. ad Pind.* 20.3 and Pind. *Isthm.* 7.44 Negri (1994a). See also Kambylis (1991a) 136*–137*, with a general discussion of quotations of Pindar's works in Eustathius' *Introduction* to Pindar.
13 Aristophanes: Eust. *Prooem. ad Pind.* 28.1: Pind. fr. 76.1 = Ar. *Eq.* 1329. Athenaeus: Eust. *Prooem. ad Pind.* 16.1: Pind. fr. 123.6 = Ath. 13.601d. *Vita Ambrosiana*: Eust. *Prooem. ad Pind.* 27.12: Pind. fr. 37 = *Vit. Ambr.* p. 2.9 Drachmann; Eust. *Prooem. ad Pind.* 27.4: Pind. fr. 95.1–2

to an *Isthmian* ode lost today: Eustathius mentions the epithet ἐρισφάραγος in chapter 16.1 where he lists epithets invented by Pindar, and the adverb ἄκασκα is mentioned in chapter 21.3 as an example of the Doric dialect. Both epithets are recorded in a victory ode for a Megarian runner preserved on a papyrus containing a commentary on Pindar's *Isthmian* odes (P.Oxy. 26.2451 = Pind. fr. 6a[c] and [d]). In the course of manuscript transmission, the end of the book of the *Isthmian* odes was lost (today the book stops after the first verses of *Isthmian* 9), and so we may infer that Eustathius had access to the complete or at least a more complete copy. Other short quotations from Pindar's works are commonly listed under the fragments of the *Isthmian* odes, but in fact it is not possible to be certain which genre they were from.[14]

2.2 Features of Pindar's Poetry Indicated by Eustathius in His Introduction to Pindar

Eustathius gives an overview of the features of Pindar's poetry in the first part of his *Introduction*: he argues that he is one of the greatest lyric poets because of his rhetorical ability, and illustrates this observation by examining his use of digressions (chapters 3–7). In this context, he mentions several elements of the victory ode: praise of the victor and his family, historical references, descriptions of places, and myths and maxims. In chapter 8, he deals briefly with the dialects found in Pindar's poetry before focusing on its obscurity (chapters 9–24). As one element of Pindaric obscurity, Eustathius considers his diction at some length and mainly discusses inversion, negation, and periphrasis. He also gives a long list of epithets invented by Pindar that increase the obscurity of the poems. As another element of obscurity, Eustathius mentions historical digressions and myths that sometimes have no obvious connection with the rest of the poem. Finally, Pindar's use of the Doric dialect, illustrated by several examples, adds to the obscurity of his diction.[15]

All these features are mentioned occasionally in the ancient scholia on Pindar, but bringing them together in his *Introduction* to Pindar, Eustathius presented his own view on Pindar's poetry.[16] We will see below if we meet these features again when Eustathius refers to Pindar in his other works.

= *Vit. Ambr.* p. 2.5 Drachmann; Eust. *Prooem. ad Pind.* 27.3: Pind. fr. 193 = *Vit. Ambr.* p. 2.18 Drachmann; Eust. *Prooem. ad Pind.* 33.1: Pind. fr. 209 = *Vit. Ambr.* p. 4.6 Drachmann. On Eust. *Prooem. ad Pind.* 27.9 see Negri (1992), who rejects an attribution to Pindar (fr. 325).

14 Pind. fr. 10–27 and see Kambylis (1991b) 23–24; see also Negri (1999) 279–281; Negri (2000) 234n1; Adorjáni (2011) 78; D'Alessio (2012) 29.

15 For detailed studies of these features, see Kambylis (1991b) and Negri (2000) 178–206.

16 On the originality of Eustathius' *Introduction* to Pindar see Kambylis (1991b) 96–104; see also Adorjáni (2011) 82.

2.3 The Content of Eustathius' Commentary on Pindar

In the *Introduction*, Eustathius gives some indications about the content of his commentary. In chapter 10.1, he calls it a παρεκβολή and in chapter 36.1 he speaks of a παρεκβολικὴ πραγματεία. As Kambylis has demonstrated, Eustathius designates by these terms a treatise enriched by excerpts.[17] At the very end of his *Introduction*, in chapter 38.4, he specifies the content:

> But here, the proposal is a not unusual survey, to collect from Pindar's victory odes what is useful for all who wish to write or, in general, to understand. It is not an exegesis in the style of a commentary, but it selects from a large field all that those who love beautiful things and know the crowns of the Muses, would neither tread on nor disdain.[18]

By first pointing out that his study on Pindar's victory odes is a customary one, Eustathius seems to refer to his previous commentary on Aristophanes.[19] Eustathius then adds that his study of Pindar's victory odes is not an exegesis in the style of a commentary, but rather assembles what is useful for all who wish to write or, in general, to understand. It is thus a selection—he uses the verb ἀνθολογεῖν—for readers of Pindar's poetry. Taking these passages together, we may suppose that the commentary consisted of a study of excerpts from Pindar's victory odes.[20] However, it is interesting to note that Eustathius announces in chapter 11.2 that he will give many examples of Lycophron's imitation of Pindar. As there are no such examples in the *Introduction*, they must have been given in the commentary itself. We will return to the question of the content of the commentary on Pindar after having discussed references to it in Eustathius' other works.

---

17 Kambylis (1991b) 13–19.
18 Eust. *Prooem. ad Pind.* 38.4: ἐνταῦθα δὲ τὸ προκείμενον ἐπέλευσις οὐκ ἀσυνήθης τὰ ἐκ τῶν Πινδαρικῶν ἐπινικίων συλλέγουσα χρήσιμα εἰς εἴδησιν εὔχρηστον τοῖς καὶ γράφειν καὶ ἄλλως δέ πως νοεῖν ἐθέλουσι, καὶ τοῦτο οὐ κατὰ ὑπομνηματικὴν ἐξήγησιν, ἀλλ' εἰς ὅσον ἐκ πλατυτάτου λειμῶνος ἀνθολογῆσαι ὅσα οὐκ ἂν πατοῖτο ἢ ἄλλως ἐξαθερίζοιτο τοῖς γε φιλοκάλοις καὶ εἰδόσι τὰ τῶν Μουσῶν στεφανώματα. For different translations see Negri (2000) 63n2.
19 See Gallo (1977) 45–47 and Kambylis (1991b) 19.
20 For a detailed discussion, see Kambylis (1991b) 16–19.

3 Pindar in Eustathius' Commentaries on Homer and Dionysius Periegetes

In addition to his commentary on Pindar and other commentaries on ancient works, Eustathius wrote treatises on religious and clerical topics and many of his letters have also been preserved. However, most of his references to Pindar are to be found in his scholarly works.[21] In his *Introduction*, there is a reference to his previous commentary on Aristophanes, but none to any other commentary, while in his commentaries on Homer and Dionysius Periegetes there are some references to his commentary on Pindar so that we may assume that they were later works.[22] Cross-references in the commentaries on the *Iliad*, the *Odyssey*, and on Dionysius' *Periegesis* suggest that Eustathius worked on all three commentaries at the same time, completing that on Dionysius' *Periegesis* before those on the *Iliad* and the *Odyssey*.[23] Although it is obvious that Eustathius used the Homeric scholia for his own commentaries, it is disputed which scholia—there are different groups—he actually had access to.[24] The scholia on Dionysius' *Periegesis*, one of the most important geographical works in late antiquity, date to the fourth century CE and were used by Eustathius when he was writing his own commentary.[25]

Taking into account the scholia, Eustathius commented on Homer and Dionysius Periegetes verse by verse in an unusually detailed way. He gathered together all that he considered to be interesting for a reader of the poems, quoting a great number of ancient authors and works, and commenting on language and style as well as on historical and geographical topics. Later I will analyse some passages of Eustathius' commentaries where he refers to Pindar, but in order to give an idea of the organization of the entries in these commentaries, I quote here in full one passage in which Pindar is also mentioned. In Eustathius' commentary on *Iliad* 2.662, where the expression πατρὸς ἑοῖο φίλον μήτρωα designates Tlepolemus' great-uncle Licymnius, he explains the term μήτρως in the following way:

---

21 For references to Pindar in Eustathius' other works, cf. e.g. Eust. *Epist*. 3.68 and 45.92; see also Wirth (2000) 404. In what follows, the edition of van der Valk (1971–1987) is used for Eustathius' commentary on the *Iliad*, that of Stallbaum (1825–1826) for his commentary on the *Odyssey* and that of Müller (1861) for his commentary on Dionysius' *Periegesis*.
22 For these references to Pindar's commentary, see below p. 547.
23 See above, p. 534.
24 See van der Valk (1971–1987) vol. 1, pp. lx–lxiv (§ 71–71a) and vol. 2, pp. xli–xlii (§ 152).
25 On the use of these scholia, see Cohn (1907) 1455.68–1456.36.

They use μήτρως in the same way as πάτρως, because for Herodotus (2.133.2, etc.), πάτρως is the uncle from the paternal brother, so now the one from the maternal brother is the μήτρως. [The writers after Homer also call the ancestors generally from the father's line in this way, as Aristophanes of Byzantium shows in the work *On names of the same kind* (fr. 9 Nauck) by giving the following definition: τήθη is the mother of the father, for example Aerope is the paternal grandmother of Orestes, and the mother of the mother, as Leda is the maternal grandmother of Orestes. Some call them μάμμα and μαία. θεῖος is also the uncle, but according to some the father's brother, but also the mother's brother. And the same is true for τήθη. τηθίς, however, is equivalent to θεῖος; for it is the father's or mother's sister. Some call them πατράδελφος and μητράδελφος, whereas others use πάτρως and μήτρως: Pindar called the parents of the mother, not her brothers, μάτρωες; Stesichorus called the paternal ancestor πάτρως in the poem where Amphilochus said: 'my ancestor, godlike Melampus', because Melampus is the father of Antiphates, whose son is Oikles, whose son is Amphiaraos, whose son is Amphilochus. Thus you see how Melampus was a distant ancestor of Amphilochus.][26]

The square brackets indicate that most of Eustathius' explanation is a later addition in the margin of the autograph.[27] In his first comment on the term μήτρως, Eustathius referred only to Herodotus; later on, he mentioned the grammarian Aristophanes of Byzantium and quoted some poets who used the term differently, among them, Pindar.[28] Eustathius' comment shows that he considered it worth explaining the term in a detailed way (there is no explanation of it in the ancient scholia on the verse), providing a learned comment-

---

26 Eust. *Il.* 2.662 (1.491.12): μήτρως μὲν εἴρηται καθ' ὁμοιότητα τοῦ πάτρως· ὡς γὰρ παρ' Ἡροδότῳ (2.133.2, etc.) πάτρως ὁ ἀπὸ πατρικοῦ ἀδελφοῦ θεῖος, οὕτω νῦν ὁ ἀπὸ μητρικοῦ μήτρως. [οἱ δὲ μεθ' Ὅμηρον καὶ τοὺς ἁπλῶς κατὰ πατέρα προγόνους οὕτω καλοῦσιν, ὡς δηλοῖ καὶ ὁ ἐν τῷ Περὶ συγγενικῶν ὀνομάτων (Ar. Byz. fr. 9 Nauck) ὧδέ πως διαστείλας· τήθη ἐστὶν ἡ τοῦ πατρὸς μήτηρ, ὡς ἡ Ἀερόπη τῷ Ὀρέστῃ, καὶ ἡ τῆς μητρὸς δὲ μήτηρ, ὡς τῷ αὐτῷ ἡ Λήδα. ταύτας δὲ μάμμας τινές φασι καὶ μαίας. θεῖος δὲ ὁ καὶ νέννος κατά τινας πατρὸς ἀδελφός, ὁμοίως δὲ καὶ μητρὸς ἀδελφός. καὶ οὕτω μὲν ἡ τήθη. τηθὶς δὲ ἀνάλογόν τι τῷ θείῳ· πατρὸς γὰρ ἀδελφὴ ἢ μητρός. τούτους δὲ οἱ μὲν πατραδέλφους καὶ μητραδέλφους, οἱ δὲ πάτρωας καλοῦσι καὶ μήτρωας· Πίνδαρος δὲ οὐκ ἀδελφοὺς ἀλλὰ γονέας μητρὸς μάτρωας ἔφη, Στησίχορος (fr. 228 Page) δὲ πάτρωα τὸν κατὰ πατέρα πρόγονον εἶπεν, ἔνθα παρ' αὐτῷ Ἀμφίλοχος ἔφη τὸ 'πάτρωα ἐμὸν ἀντίθεον Μελάμποδα'. Μελάμπους γάρ, οὗ Ἀντιφάτης, οὗ Ὀϊκλῆς, οὗ Ἀμφιάραος, ὅθεν Ἀμφίλοχος. ὅρα οὖν, οἷος ὁ Μελάμπους ἦν πάτρως τῷ Ἀμφιλόχῳ οὕτω πόρρωθεν.]
27 van der Valk (1971–1987) vol. 1, pp. xii–xvi (§ 9–13) and p. cxl (§ 128).
28 See the discussion below, p. 546.

ary that would have been useful for a reader of his time who did not have access to a well-equipped library.

I shall now look at the following aspects of Eustathius' engagement with Pindar in his later commentaries: the corpus of Pindar's works used by him, the references themselves, Eustathius' understanding and handling of Pindar's poetry, and references to his commentary on Pindar.

3.1 The Corpus of Pindar's Works Used by Eustathius in His Later Commentaries

Eustathius worked mainly on Pindar's victory odes when he wrote his commentary on Pindar. In his commentaries on Homer and Dionysius Periegetes, most of the Pindaric quotations are also from the victory odes.[29] In a very few passages he refers to a specific epinician book or to a single ode.[30] In one case is there an explicit quotation from an *Isthmian* ode not otherwise known, which supports the hypothesis that he had a complete or at least a more complete copy of Pindar's *Isthmian* odes.[31] Furthermore, as in his *Introduction*, Eustathius mentions once in his commentary on the *Odyssey* the epithet ἐρισφάραγον which is known to come from an *Isthmian* ode.[32] He clearly made use of the scholia to the victory odes as well,[33] and twice refers to ancient commentators on the first line of *Olympian* 1.1.[34] As regards the texts quoted from the victory odes, they accord generally with the readings in the *recensio Vaticana* (codd. BD),[35] but in some instances, Eustathius quotes inaccurately, due to errors in his sources or by writing them down from memory,[36] as he used to do when

---

29 For Eustathius' commentary on the *Iliad* see Keizer (1995) 592–595. For his commentary on the *Odyssey* and on Dionysius' *Periegesis* see Maehler (1989) 212. For the use of ὁ Λυρικός instead of Πινδαρός cf. e.g. Eust. *Il.* 2.58 (1.265.22), *Il.* 4.281 (1.745.20), *Il.* 5.366 (2.93.8) and see van der Valk (1971–1987) vol. 2, p. l (§159); for the adjective Πινδαρικός, cf. e.g. Eust. *Il.* 1.213s. (1.140.27), *Il.* 2.667 (1.493.11), and *Il.* 2.755 (1.526.19); for the adverb Πινδαρικῶς, cf. e.g. Eust. *Il.* 1.6–7 (1.34.29), *Il.* 7.228 (2.451.24), and *Od.* 1.434 (1.74.22).

30 *Olympian* odes: Eust. *Il.* 3.54 (1.602.17), and *Il.* 8.306s. (2.586.15); Pind. *Ol.* 6: Eust. *Il.* 2.814 (1.551.19); Pind. *Ol.* 13: Eust. *Dionys. Per.* 1 (p. 216.39). *Pythian* odes: Eust. *Il.* 2.561 (1.442.24), and *Il.* 21.319 (4.507.18). *Isthmian* odes: Eust. *Il.* 1.129 (1.104.21), and *Od.* 12.99 (2.15.45).

31 Eust. *Od.* 12.99 (2.15.44): …, ὡς ἐμφαίνει Πίνδαρος ἐν Ἰσθμιονίκαις (fr. 8), εἰπών· 'τρία κράτα ἤτοι κράατα', with the discussion of Kambylis (1991b) 24; see also D'Alessio (2012) 29.

32 Eust. *Od.* 9.390 (1.351.43): Pind. fr. 6a(d), see above p. 536.

33 See below, pp. 545 and 549.

34 Eust. *Il.* 11.726 (3.314.17), and *Il.* 14.201 (3.615.11).

35 Cf. Eust. *Il.* 1.10 (1.39.7) quoting Pind. *Ol.* 9.44–46, and see van der Valk (1971–1987) vol. 1, p. xc (§94), n. 5.

36 E.g. Eust. *Il.* 14.267 (3.630.15) = Pind. *Isthm.* 7.16s.; Eust. *Il.* 15.60 (3.703.22) = Pind. *Ol.* 10.3; Eust. *Il.* 24.734 (4.980.5) = Pind. *Pyth.* 4.41.

quoting ancient works.[37] However, sometimes he provides readings not found in the manuscript tradition which are worth considering.[38] There are also quotations in which he indicates alternative readings by separating them with the particles ἤ or ἤτοι.[39]

Eustathius also refers to passages from Pindar's other works in his commentaries on Homer and Dionysius Periegetes. Most of them can be assigned to indirect transmission as they are also recorded in other texts, namely in the works of Aristophanes of Byzantium (1), Strabo (4), Pausanias (1) and Athenaeus (6),[40] writers frequently referred to in the commentaries. He found other Pindaric quotations in the scholia on Homer.[41] There are only three quotations where the source cannot be identified; they are likely to come either from some lost *Isthmian* odes or from indirect transmission.[42]

3.2   *References to Pindar in Eustathius' Later Commentaries*

In Eustathius' commentaries on Homer and Dionysius Periegetes, there are approximately 220 references to Pindar: in his extensive commentary on the *Iliad*, he refers to Pindar nearly 130 times; in the shorter commentary on the *Odyssey*, about 70 times; and in his commentary on Dionysius Periegetes, 20 times. Eustathius mentions Pindar in different contexts, but there are recurrent topics in his commentaries in which he frequently refers to Pindar's works.

---

37   See van der Valk (1971–1987) vol. 1, pp. lvi–lvii (§ 67).
38   E.g. Eust. *Od.* 8.190 (1.290.30) = Pind. *Isthm.* 1.25.
39   E.g. Eust. *Od.* 5.274 (1.216.39) = Pind. *Nem.* 2.11; Eust. *Od.* 12.99 (2.15.45) = Pind. fr. 8.
40   Aristophanes of Byzantium: Eust. *Il.* 11.679 (3.302.1): Pind. fr. 317 = Ar. Byz. fr. 42 Nauck.
    Strabo: Eust. *Il.* 16.233s. (3.844.10): Pind. fr. 59.3 = Strabo 7.7.10 (C 328.4); Eust. *Il.* 1.65 (1.79.18): Pind. fr. 170 = Strabo 3.3.7 (C 155.3); Eust. *Il.* 2.638 (1.483.25): Pind. fr. 183 = Strabo 9.5.5 (C 431.5); Eust. *Dionys. Per.* 64 (p. 228.25): Pind. fr. 256 = Strabo 3.5.5 (C 170.19).
    Pausanias: Eust. *Od.* 11.333 (1.422.30) and *Od.* 12.167 (2.5.32): Pind. fr. 52i.71 = Paus. 10.5.12.
    Athenaeus: Eust. *Od.* 17.315 (2.148.8): Pind. fr. 106.1–3 = Ath. 1.28a; Eust. *Od.* 1.138 (1.35.29): Pind. fr. 124c = Ath. 14.641b; Eust. *Od.* 8.383 (1.306.4): Pind. fr. 148 = Ath. 1.22b; Eust. *Od.* 4.179 (1.157.41): Pind. fr. 155 = Ath. 5.191f; Eust. *Il.* 13.6 (3.427.6): Pind. fr. 166 = Ath. 11.476b; Eust. *Od.* 10.515 (1.393.13): Pind. fr. 198b = Ath. 2.41e.
41   Eust. *Il.* 16.233s. (3.844.10): Pind. fr. 59 = schol. Hom. *Il.* 16.234c; Eust. *Il.* 11.242 (3.186.17): Pind. fr. 110 = schol. Hom. *Il.* 11.227c; Eust. *Il.* 1.1 (1.15.14): Pind. fr. 150 = schol. Hom. *Il.* 1.1; Eust. *Od.* 10.240 (1.379.31): Pind. fr. 236 = schol. Hom. *Od.* 10.240; Eust. *Il.* 10.435 (3.107.18): Pind. fr. 262 = schol. Hom. *Il.* 10.435a; Eust. *Il.* 21.22 (4.451.12): Pind. fr. 306 = schol. Hom. *Il.* 21.22b; and see above p. 535.
42   Eust. *Il.* 1.1 (1.16.5) and *Il.* 2.89 (1.275.3): Pind. fr. 151; Eust. *Il.* 1.423 (1.197.26) and *Od.* 1.156 (1.42.36): Pind. fr. 297; Eust. *Il.* 14.171 (3.606.24): Pind. fr. 305. Cf. also Eust. *Il.* 3.55 (1.604.23 = fr. 18 and 302 Turyn) with the study of Negri (1994b).

In his commentary on the *Iliad*, the reasons Eustathius cites Pindar are in line with what we would expect from the *Introduction*: for epithets;[43] as an example of the Doric dialect;[44] for stylistic similarities to Homer;[45] as evidence for places and people, especially in his commentary on the catalogue of ships in book 2 of the *Iliad*;[46] for myths;[47] and for maxims (only once).[48]

References to Pindar in Eustathius' commentary on the *Odyssey* relate to these same features, but particularly the Doric dialect,[49] places,[50] myths, and maxims (twice).[51]

In the commentary on Dionysius' *Periegesis*, Eustathius mentions Pindar mainly when commenting on places;[52] there are also some references to Pindar when he deals with people and myths.[53] Because the focus of his commentary is on geography, explanations of epithets, dialect, and diction with reference to Pindar are rare.[54]

Thus in his commentaries on Homer and Dionysius Periegetes, Eustathius referred to Pindar frequently when he dealt with the features of Pindar's poetry he had discussed in his *Introduction*. The frequent references to Pindar concerning geography also reveal his familiarity with Pindar's works, which had already been appreciated for their geographical information in antiquity.[55] His deep knowledge of Pindar's texts becomes even more striking if we compare the scholia on Homer and Dionysius Periegetes that Eustathius had at hand when he wrote his own commentaries: in the scholia on the *Iliad*, there are approximately fifty references to Pindar, mainly in comments on myths, one-third of which Eustathius included in his own commentary.[56] In the scholia on

---

43 Cf. Eust. *Il.* 1.75 (1.84.20), *Il.* 1.213s. (1.140.27), *Il.* 4.328 (1.757.7), etc.
44 Cf. Eust. *Il.* 1.15 (1.41.6), *Il.* 1.35 (1.52.11), *Il.* 1.279 (1.163.21), etc.
45 Cf. Eust. *Il.* 1.15 (1.41.14), *Il.* 1.312 (1.168.29), *Il.* 2.637 (1.480.10), etc.
46 Cf. Eust. *Il.* 2.506 (1.414.1), *Il.* 2.531 (1.425.25), *Il.* 2.570 (1.447.20), etc.
47 Cf. Eust. *Il.* 1.6s. (1.34.29), *Il.* 1.10 (1.39.7), *Il.* 1.250–252 (1.152.2), etc.
48 Cf. Eust. *Il.* 11.242 (3.186.17).
49 For epithets, cf. Eust. *Od.* 2.11 (1.78.8), *Od.* 4.131 (1.154.40), *Od.* 5.306 (1.227.1), etc. For diction, cf. Eust. *Od.* 2.190 (1.91.38), *Od.* 8.429 (1.309.13). For the Doric dialect, cf. Eust. *Od.* 1.51 (1.18.46), *Od.* 1.321ss. (1.61.22), *Od.* 1.415 (1.72.28), etc.
50 Cf. Eust. *Od.* 5.121 (1.205.20), *Od.* 10.515 (1.393.12), *Od.* 12.261 (2.23.38).
51 For myths, cf. Eust. *Od.* 9.65 (1.322.6), *Od.* 11.270 (1.414.2), *Od.* 11.316 (1.419.21), etc. For maxims, cf. Eust. *Od.* 8.148 (1.288.28), *Od.* 8.176 (1.290.8).
52 Cf. Eust. *Dionys. Per.* 64 (p. 228.25), 66 (p. 230.12), 213 (p. 254.25), etc.
53 For people, cf. Eust. *Dionys. Per.* 426 (p. 297.3), 820 (p. 361.31). For myths, cf. Eust. *Dionys. Per.* 144 (p. 243.21), 211 (p. 253.41), 213 (p. 254.25).
54 Cf. Eust. *Dionys. Per.* 820 (p. 361.31).
55 See Giannini (2006) 215–219.
56 Cf. e.g. schol. Hom. *Il.* 1.1d (= Eust. *Il.* 1.1 [1.15.14]), *Il.* 1.312 (= Eust. *Il.* 1.312 [1.168.29]). For references to Pindar in the scholia on the *Iliad*, see Erbse (1969–1988) vol. 6, pp. 103–104.

the *Odyssey*, there are very few references to Pindar.[57] In the voluminous scholia on Dionysius' *Periegesis*, there are no quotations from Pindar, although other poetry is quoted. Thus most of the references to Pindar in the commentaries on Homer and Dionysius Periegetes were by Eustathius himself.

3.3 *Eustathius' Understanding and Handling of Pindar's Poetry*

Most references to Pindar in Eustathius' commentaries on Homer and Dionysius Periegetes provide examples of something, for example the Doric dialect, or illustrate something mentioned in the verse commented on, without giving real insight into his understanding of a given passage in Pindar's works. I will now look at some passages where we can gain insight into how Eustathius understood Pindar and, at the same time, how he dealt with his poetry.

One of these passages is his commentary on *Iliad* 9.378: this verse is part of a long speech Achilles addresses to Odysseus, who presents to him Agamemnon's offer of reconciliation. Answering him that he detests Agamemnon's gifts and despises him, Achilles uses the otherwise unrecorded expression ἐν καρὸς αἴσῃ, which means something worthless. Eustathius comments on it at some length. Based on the ancient scholia, he lists different interpretations, among them the following:

> Others separate that expression into two parts and put an acute accent on the ending and still give it the same sense, saying that 'I honour him in a part of καρός', that is the head louse, that means 'I in no way honour him', that means 'not at all'. There are other ways to say in no way to esteem someone, for example as Sophocles (*Antig.* 1170–1171): 'I would purchase all the rest for a shadow of smoke', which seems to come from the Pindaric saying 'A dream of a shadow is man'.[58]

Eustathius states that some write the expression in one word as ἔγκαρος, whereas others say ἐν καρός denoting something worthless. In connection with this interpretation, Eustathius quotes verse 1170 of Sophocles' *Antigone*, where

---

57 Schol. Hom. *Od.* 1.327, *Od.* 10.3, *Od.* 10.240 (= Eust. *Od.* 10.240 [1.379.31]), *Od.* 11.309 (= Eust. *Od.* 11.316 [1.419.21]), *Od.* 19.457, *Od.* 21.303.

58 Eust. *Il.* 9.378 (2.734.13): ἕτεροι δὲ εἰς δύο τε μέρη διαιροῦσι τὴν λέξιν ταύτην καὶ ὀξύνουσι τὴν λήγουσαν καὶ τὴν αὐτὴν αὖθις ἀποδιδόασιν ἔννοιαν, λέγοντες, ὡς τιμῶ αὐτὸν ἐν μοίρᾳ καρός, ὅ ἐστι φθειρὸς τοῦ περὶ τὴν κεφαλήν, τουτέστι τοῦ μηδενὸς τιμῶμαι αὐτόν, μάλιστα δέ, τοῦ εὐτελεστάτου. τὸ γὰρ ἀξιοῦν τινα τοῦ μηδενὸς ἄλλως ἔστι φράζεσθαι, οἷον ὡς Σοφοκλῆς (*Antig.* 1170–1171) 'τἄλλα ἐγὼ καπνοῦ σκιᾶς οὐκ ἂν πριαίμην', ὃ δοκεῖ ἐκ Πινδαρικοῦ ῥητοῦ παρεξέσθαι τοῦ 'σκιᾶς ὄναρ ἄνθρωπος'.

the expression καπνοῦ σκιᾶς is used similarly. And he notes that the expression καπνοῦ σκιᾶς seems to come from Pindar's sentence σκιᾶς ὄναρ ἄνθρωπος ('a dream of a shadow is man'). In the tragedies, there are many parallels to the well-known sentence from *Pythian* 8.95-96: a closer one is verse 946-947 of Sophocles' *Philoctetes*, in which Philoctetes calls himself a νεκρόν, ἢ καπνοῦ σκιάν, εἴδωλον ἄλλως ('a corpse, a shadow of smoke, a mere phantom').[59] Nevertheless, we can state that Eustathius recognized here an example of intertextuality mentioned neither in the scholia on the *Iliad* nor in those on Pindar.

Sometimes, commenting on Homeric epithets, Eustathius provides explanations of epithets used by Pindar. There is one example in Eustathius' commentary on *Iliad* 1.75.[60] In this verse Apollo is called ἑκατηβελέτης ἄναξ. The meaning of the epithet had already been discussed in antiquity, as Eustathius' comment shows:

> For, the poets after the Poet [i.e. Homer] are not as dignified as him concerning the myths. For, where Homer called the holy Apollo ἑκατηβελέτης, Simonides (fr. 573 Page; fr. 117 Poltera) says that Apollo killed the dragon in Pytho with a hundred arrows, although he ought to have killed the beast with one stroke; for it is not an archer's virtue to harm by shooting many arrows. Thus such a person is ἑκατηβελέτης not for that reason, but because he shoots from afar. For that is the property of an archer. For that reason, ἑκάεργος is the same, as warding off from afar. Thus as ἑκάς and ἕκαθεν are two adverbs, ἑκηβόλος comes from ἑκάς and ἑκατηβελέτης from ἕκαθεν. But if someone likes to call Apollo ἑκατηβελέτης as deriving from a hundred arrows, it is better to call him that on the grounds that he has a hundred or many arrows. Thus Pindar also calls him εὐρυφαρέτρας.[61]

---

59   See Bagordo (2003) 6-7.
60   Other examples would be his explanation of ἐγχεικέραυνος in Eust. *Il.* 21.357 (4.517.15), that of εὐδείελος in Eust. *Od.* 9.21 (1.320.24) or that of ἐρισφάραγος in Eust. *Od.* 9.390 (1.351.43), which is also listed in Eust. *Prooem. ad Pind.* 16.1.
61   Eust. *Il.* 1.75 (1.84.11): ὅτι οὐχ᾽ ὁμοίως τῷ ποιητῇ σεμνοί εἰσιν ἐν τοῖς μύθοις οἱ μετ᾽ αὐτὸν ποιηταί. ποῦ γὰρ σεμνὸν Ὁμήρου ἑκατηβελέτην εἰπόντος τὸν Ἀπόλλωνα μυθεύεσθαι τὸν Σιμωνίδην (fr. 573 Page; fr. 117 Poltera), ὡς ἑκατὸν βέλεσιν ἀνεῖλεν ὁ Ἀπόλλων τὸν ἐν Πυθοῖ δράκοντα, δέον ὂν μιᾷ βολῇ νεκρῶσαι τὸ θηρίον· οὐ γὰρ ἀρετὴ τοξότου τὸ πολλὰ βαλόντα βλάψαι. οὔκουν ἑκατηβελέτης ὁ τοιοῦτος, ἀλλ᾽ ὁ ἕκαθεν βάλλων. τοῦτο γὰρ ἰδιότης τοξεύοντος. διὸ καὶ ἑκάεργος ὁ αὐτός, ὡς ἕκαθεν εἴργων. δύο οὖν ὄντων ἐπιρρημάτων τοῦ ἑκάς καὶ ἕκαθεν ἀπὸ μὲν τοῦ ἑκάς ἑκηβόλος λέγεται, ἀπὸ δὲ τοῦ ἕκαθεν ἑκατηβελέτης. εἰ δέ τις ἑκατηβελέτην Ἀπόλλωνα εἰπεῖν θέλει ὡς ἀπὸ ἑκατὸν βελῶν, κάλλιον οὕτως εἰπεῖν αὐτόν, ὡς ἑκατὸν ἤγουν πολλὰ ἔχοντα βέλη. διὸ καὶ Πίνδαρος εὐρυφαρέτραν αὐτὸν λέγει.

After rejecting Simonides' statement that Apollo killed the dragon Python with a hundred arrows, Eustathius explains that the epithet ἑκατηβελέτης derives from ἕκαθεν ('from afar') and means 'shooting from afar'.[62] He adds that it could also be considered as a compound with ἑκατόν, but in this case, it should be understood as 'having a hundred (or many) arrows'. And, as Eustathius notes, Pindar for that reason calls Apollo εὐρυφαρέτρας. This epithet, meaning 'with wide quiver', is recorded only in Pindar's works, once in a victory ode (*Pyth.* 9.26) and twice in the fragments (*Pae.* fr. 52 f.111; fr. 148). There is no explanation of it in the Pindaric scholia. Thus Eustathius understood the epithet εὐρυφαρέτρας against the background of the Homeric epithet ἑκατηβελέτης, interpreted as 'having a hundred arrows (in a wide quiver)'.

Another reference to Pindar in Eustathius' commentary on the *Iliad* reveals well how he handled Pindar's poetry. In his comment on *Iliad* 1.1, he lists different explanations of the term ῥαψῳδός, among them the following:

> Many of the ancients call the whole Homeric poem ῥαψῳδία and its singers ῥαψῳδοί; they also call the singers ῥαβδῳδοί because of the baton made of bay mentioned above; because of the same baton they also call them στιχῳδοί; for, as they say, some called the batons στίχοι. But they also call them ἀρνῳδοί, because they competed in Homeric song, and the winners received as a prize a lamb (ἀρήν). However, it does not please Pindar to call the rhapsodes from the baton, but from the verb ῥάπτειν ('stitch together'). To describe the rhapsodes, he calls them 'singers of verses stitched together'. ῥάπτειν means either simply, as has been written, to put together or to bring together separated parts in a sequence like a seam.[63]

In this passage, Eustathius states that the term ῥαψῳδός was understood as a compound of ῥάβδος ('rod, wand'), but that Pindar linked it to the verb ῥάπτειν ('stitch together') as is shown by the expression ῥαπτῶν ἐπέων ἀοιδούς, a quotation from *Nemean* 2.2. The scholia on Pindar's verse contain similar information,[64] which shows that Eustathius used the Pindaric scholia for his own

---

62 Cf. schol. Hom. *Il.* 1.75 (D) with a similar explanation.
63 Eust. *Il.* 1.1 (1.10.12): οἱ δὲ πλείους τῶν παλαιῶν τήν τε ὅλην Ὁμηρικὴν ποίησιν ῥαψῳδίαν λέγουσι καὶ ῥαψῳδοὺς τοὺς αὐτὴν ᾄδοντας· ἔτι δὲ καὶ ῥαβδῳδοὺς διὰ τὴν ἄνω ῥηθεῖσαν δαφνίνην ῥάβδον· διὰ δὲ τὴν αὐτὴν καὶ στιχῳδούς· στίχοι γάρ, φασίν, ὑπό τινων αἱ ῥάβδοι ἐλέγοντο. ἀλλὰ καὶ ἀρνῳδούς, ἐπειδὴ οἱ ἀγωνιζόμενοι ἐν ᾠδῇ Ὁμηρικῇ καὶ νικῶντες ἄρνα ἐλάμβανον ἔπαθλον. Πινδάρῳ δὲ ἀρέσκει οὐκ ἀπὸ ῥάβδου ἀλλ' ἐκ τοῦ ῥάπτειν τοὺς ῥαψῳδοὺς λέγεσθαι. περιφράζων γὰρ τοὺς ῥαψῳδοὺς 'ῥαπτῶν ἐπέων ἀοιδούς' αὐτοὺς λέγει. ῥάπτειν δὲ ἢ ἁπλῶς, ὡς εἴρηται, τὸ συντιθέναι ἢ τὸ κατὰ εἱρμόν τινα ῥαφῇ ὁμοίως εἰς ἓν ἄγειν τὰ διεστῶτα.
64 Cf. schol. Pind. *Nem.* 2.1d with van der Valk's critical apparatus at the passage quoted.

commentaries, without acknowledging them. There are many similar passages where he seems to take over material from the Pindaric scholia without revealing his source;[65] his use of Homeric scholia is similar.[66]

Although Eustathius consulted the scholia on Pindar, he sometimes misrepresents Pindaric usage. This can be observed, for instance, in his explanation of the word μήτρως cited in full above, where he states that Pindar uses this term for the mother's parents, not the mother's brothers. However, Pindar does use μάτρως to designate the mother's brother (*Nem.* 4.80, 5.43; *Isthm.* 6.62, 7.24) as well as the mother's ancestors (*Ol.* 6.77, 9.63; *Nem.* 10.37, 11.37), and a scholion to *Olympian* 9.63 states explicitly that μάτρως usually designates the mother's brother, but in this passage, the mother's father (schol. Pind. *Ol.* 9.96a).

Notice also Eustathius' comment on Dionysius Periegetes' description of the Peloponnese (403–408), where the outline of the region is compared to the leaf of a plane tree:

> For that place lies next to Hellas and resembles the leaf of the plane tree that tapers off at the end of its stalk or stem, narrowing and becoming as thin as the tail of a mouse. The isthmus of the Peloponnese is also, as he [i.e. Dionysius Periegetes] says, of forty stades, producing a strait, and it resembles the end of the stalk of a leaf, located in the north and heading toward Hellas, because Hellas lies directly after the isthmus, as has been said. The circumference of the Peloponnese resembles a leaf with many whorls because of its many valleys, curvatures, and bays similar to the leaf of a plane tree. Therefore, Pindar calls the Peloponnese a much-winding valley and the ancients call the Peloponnese the acropolis of Hellas.[67]

---

65 E.g. Eust. *Il.* 2.637 (1.480.10) and 5.339 (2.84.17) with schol. Pind. *Pyth.* 4.367a; Eust. *Od.* 3.6 (1.108.37) with schol. Pind. *Ol.* 13.99c; Eust. *Od.* 12.65 (2.11.2) with schol. Pind. *Nem.* 2.17c. For more passages, see Keizer (1995) 592–595.
66 See Cohn (1907) 1459.43–59.
67 Eust. *Dionys. Per.* 403 (p. 291.20): συνάπτει γὰρ ὁ τόπος ἐκεῖνος τῇ Ἑλλάδι, καὶ ἔοικε πλατάνου πετάλῳ μυουρίζοντι, τουτέστι κατὰ μυὸς οὐρὰν στενουμένῳ καὶ λεπτυνομένῳ, κατὰ τὸν ἄκρον μίσχον, ἤτοι κατὰ τὸν καυλόν, οὗ τὸ φύλλον ἐξήρτηται. καὶ ὁ μὲν ἰσθμός, φησί, τῆς Πελοποννήσου ὁ τεσσαρακονταστάδιος, εἰργόμενος στενός, ἔοικε τῷ ἄκρῳ μίσχῳ τοῦ φύλλου, βόρειος ὢν καὶ κοινὸν ἐφ' Ἑλλάδος ἴχνος ἐρείδων, ὡς τῆς Ἑλλάδος κατὰ συνέχειαν εὐθὺς κειμένης, ὡς εἴρηται, μετὰ τὸν ἰσθμόν. ἡ δὲ τῆς ἔσω ἠπείρου περίμετρος τῷ πολυδινήτῳ φύλλῳ παρέοικεν, ὡς πολλὰς ἐπικλάσεις ἔχουσα καὶ καμπὰς καὶ ἐγκολπώματα, καθ' ὁμοιότητα τοῦ τῆς πλατάνου φύλλου. διὸ καὶ ὁ Πίνδαρος πολύγναμπτον μυχὸν λέγει τὴν Πελοπόννησον· ἀκρόπολιν δὲ τῆς Ἑλλάδος οἱ παλαιοί φασι τὴν Πελοπόννησον.

Explaining the comparison, Eustathius points to the many valleys and bays of the Peloponnese and states that this is the reason that Pindar calls it a 'much-winding valley'. The reference must be to the second triad of *Olympian* 3, where he says that Heracles, setting off to search for olive trees for the Olympian grove, starts off 'from the mountains of Arcadia and its much-winding valleys' (Ἀρκαδίας ἀπὸ δειρᾶν καὶ πολυγνάμπτων μυχῶν: *Ol.* 3.27). Since Ἀρκαδίας is the genitive governing both δειρᾶν and πολυγνάμπτων μυχῶν, only the valleys of Arcadia are meant. Eustathius, however, recognized in πολύγναμπτον μυχόν a felicitous description of the whole Peloponnese. Thus his reference to Pindar shows both his deep familiarity with Pindar's odes and his tendency to handle the poet's words rather loosely.

3.4 *References in Eustathius' Later Commentaries to His Commentary on Pindar*

In the commentaries on Homer and Dionysius Periegetes, there are eight passages where Eustathius uses the expression ἐν τοῖς τοῦ Πινδάρου.[68] Because he uses the construction ἐν τοῖς τοῦ as a way of referring to authors (e.g. Athenaeus), it could in principle refer to Pindar's poetry itself.[69] However, the context in which it appears, points to another interpretation as is shown by the following four passages:

- Eust. *Il.* 3.209 (1.638.24): 'In the verse "Now when they mingled with the Trojans as they were gathered together", Menelaus and Odysseus are meant; the word ἀγρομένοισιν means the agora of the Trojans, and the verb ἔμιχθεν is not used in its literal sense, as for the meeting of the waters, but Pindar likes it as good diction, as it has been shown in the works of/on Pindar (ἐν τοῖς ἐκείνου).'[70]

---

68 For a discussion of these passages see also Gallo (1977) 49–50 and Kambylis (1991b) 19–22. On Eust. *Il.* 16.514 (3.893.14) δῆλον δὲ ὅτι Λυκηγενὴς Ἀπόλλων καὶ διὰ τὴν μικρὰν Λυκίαν ἐλέγετο, τὴν καὶ μικρὰν λεγομένην Τροίαν, ὡς ἐν τοῖς περὶ Πινδάρου προδεδήλωται, see van der Valk ad loc.: '*ne oblitus sis Eust. Comment. in Pindarum scripsisse (τὰ περὶ Πινδάρου), qua de causa error explicatur (debebat Πανδάρου)*'; cf. Eust. *Il.* 2.824–827 (1.554.5 and 1.555.11), *Il.* 4.101 (1.708.3).

69 For references to Athenaeus, cf. e.g. Eust. *Il.* 1.261 (1.157.12), *Il.* 2.219 (1.316.2), *Il.* 11.477 (3.237.9); cf. also Eust. *Il.* 2.353 (1.360.14) referring to Philostratus; Eust. *Il.* 2.571 (1.449.10) to Stephanus of Byzantium. See also van der Valk (1971–1987) vol. 1, p. lxxxvi (ἐν τοῖς τοῦ Ἀριστοφάνους).

70 ὅτι ἐν τῷ 'ἀλλ' ὅτε δὴ Τρώεσσιν ἐν ἀγρομένοισιν ἔμιχθεν', ὁ Μενέλαος δηλαδὴ καὶ ὁ Ὀδυσσεύς, τὸ μὲν ἀγρομένοισιν ἀγορὰν Τρώων ὑπολαλεῖ, τὸ δὲ ἔμιχθεν οὐ κυριολεκτεῖται μέν, καθὰ ἐπὶ μισγαγκείας ὑδάτων, ἐφιλήθη δὲ τῷ Πινδάρῳ τε ὡς ἀγαθὴ λέξις, καθὰ ἐν τοῖς ἐκείνου δεδήλωται.

Commenting on the Homeric use of the verb μίγνυμι, Eustathius mentions Pindar's preference for it, as it is found in *Nemean* 2.22 (στεφάνοις ἔμιχθεν). The perfect of the verb δηλόω in the reference points to an earlier, more detailed treatment of it, as his commentary on Pindar might have provided.[71]

- Eust. *Od.* 11.270 (1.414.1): 'The facts that the Sphinx, mentioned above, had an evil appearance and that Medusa was one of the Gorgons were also shown in the works of/on Pindar (ἐν τοῖς τοῦ Πινδάρου).'[72]

  Commenting on Oedipus' mother, Eustathius mentions the Sphinx, killed by Oedipus, and Medusa for their evil looks. No Pindaric mention of the Sphinx is preserved, but Medusa is mentioned in *Pythian* 12.16, so it is possible that Eustathius discussed the Sphinx in the context of Medusa in that poem.

- Eust. *Il.* 11.750 (3.320.20): 'The stories report that Heracles, too, had a long struggle in some places because of Ares. He was also scarcely unlucky in Thrace because of a robber, as it is shown in the works of/on Pindar (ἐν τοῖς τοῦ Πινδάρου).'[73]

  In order to explain the mention of the Moliones in the Homeric passage, Eustathius mentions Heracles, who killed the Moliones at Cleonae. Because Pindar tells this story in *Olympian* 10.26–38, Eustathius seems to have dealt with it in his commentary on Pindar where he would also have spoken about Thrace and the robber mentioned in his commentary on *Iliad* 11.750.[74]

- Eust. *Dionys. Per.* 211 (p. 253.37): 'Some say that the Zeus of that place is called Ammon from a shepherd of the same name who had founded the first sanctuary. There is also something said about Ammon in the works of/on Pindar (ἐν τοῖς τοῦ Πινδάρου).'[75]

  Zeus Ammon is mentioned in *Pythian* 4.16, and Eustathius seems to refer here to his previous commentary on that passage.

These four references to Pindar can all be connected to passages in Pindar's victory odes, and the formulation and context show that the expression ἐν τοῖς τοῦ Πινδάρου refers to Eustathius' commentary. In four other passages ἐν τοῖς τοῦ Πινδάρου no doubt refers to the commentary as well, but in these the ancient scholia provide similar information:

---

[71] See also Negri (1994b).

[72] ὅτι δὲ κατὰ τὴν εἰρημένην Σφίγγα κακὴ τὸ εἶδος ἦν καὶ ἡ Μέδουσα μία τῶν Γοργόνων, καὶ ἐν τοῖς τοῦ Πινδάρου δηλοῦται.

[73] ὅτι δὲ καὶ ὁ Ἡρακλῆς ἐνιαχοῦ ἀγῶνα πολὺν εἶχε διὰ τὸ τοῦ Ἐνυαλίου ξυνόν, αἱ ἱστορίαι δηλοῦσιν. ὃν καὶ ἡ Θρᾴκη παρὰ βραχὺ δυσπραγήσαντα εἶδεν ὑπὸ λῃστοῦ, ὡς ἐν τοῖς τοῦ Πινδάρου δηλοῦται.

[74] The story seems to be otherwise unknown. Kambylis (1991b) 20 considers relating the reference to Pind. *Nem.* 4.27ss. where, however, the Giant Alcyoneus is mentioned.

[75] οἱ δέ φασι τὸν ἐκεῖ Δία Ἄμμωνα κληθῆναι ἀπό τινος ὁμωνύμου ποιμένος, προκατάρξαντος τῆς τοῦ ἱεροῦ ἱδρύσεως. εἴρηται δέ τι περὶ Ἄμμωνος καὶ ἐν τοῖς τοῦ Πινδάρου.

- Eust. *Il.* 1.15 (1.40.30): 'The poet [i.e. Homer] attributes here the golden sceptre to Apollo, that is to Helius, because the metal of gold is attributed to Helius by the ancients, like silver to Selene and others to every planet, as it is mentioned in the works of/on Pindar (ἐν τοῖς τοῦ Πινδάρου).'[76]

  A similar comment on the attributes of deified celestial bodies is to be found in a scholion to *Isthmian* 5.1–3 where the association of Theia and gold is explained (schol. Pind. *Isthm.* 5.2b).

- Eust. *Il.* 2.783 (1.542.9): 'But if the same is called Typhaon as well, as it is also shown in the works of/on Pindar (ἐν τοῖς τοῦ Πινδάρου), the name of that divine being is therefore written in four different ways: Τυφωεύς and Τυφάων with the genitive Τυφάονος, whence the expression 'Typhaonian war-cry' (Oppian, *Halieutica* 3.25), and with crasis Τυφῶν, and with another ending Τυφῶς.'[77]

  Commenting on Typhon in *Pythian* 1.16, the scholion to this passage lists three different spellings of Typhon's name (schol. Pind. *Pyth.* 1.29a).

- Eust. *Il.* 2.756 (1.529.1): 'You must know that the Centaur was born of Nephele and was Magnesian, as it is shown in the works of/on Pindar (ἐν τοῖς τοῦ Πινδάρου), who also mentioned the Magnesian horses and showed that the Hippocentaurs were from such sperm and that they were called Magnesians by a famous man.'[78]

  The myth of the Centaur and his connection to Magnesia, mentioned in *Pythian* 2.44–48, are explained in the scholion to this passage (schol. Pind. *Pyth.* 2.78d).

- Eust. *Od.* 18.105 (2.170.39): 'It is a custom for the Dorians, as it is also shown in the works of/on Pindar (ἐν τοῖς τοῦ Πινδάρου), to sometimes combine the preposition ἐν with the accusative.'[79]

  Commenting on the Doric ἐνταυθοῖ, used in *Odyssey* 18.105, Eustathius refers to the Pindaric use of ἐν with the accusative. An example of this use is

---

76 τὸ δὲ σκῆπτρον χρυσοῦν ἐνταῦθα πλάττει ὁ ποιητὴς τῷ Ἀπόλλωνι, τουτέστι τῷ Ἡλίῳ, διὰ τὸ καὶ τὸ μέταλλον τοῦ χρυσοῦ Ἡλίῳ παρὰ τῶν παλαιῶν ἀνατίθεσθαι, ὡς τῇ Σελήνῃ τὸν ἄργυρον καὶ ἑτέρῳ τῶν πλανήτων ἄλλο τι, καθάπερ ἐν τοῖς τοῦ Πινδάρου φέρεται.

77 εἰ δὲ καὶ Τυφάων ὁ αὐτὸς ὀνομάζεται, καθὰ καὶ ἐν τοῖς τοῦ Πινδάρου δηλοῦται, τετραχῶς ἄρα σχηματίζεται τὸ δαιμόνιον. Τυφωεύς γὰρ καὶ Τυφάων Τυφάονος, ὅθεν τὸ 'Τυφαονίων ἀλαλητῶν' (Oppian, *Halieutica* 3.25), καὶ κατὰ κρᾶσιν Τυφῶν, καὶ ὡς ἐν δικαταληξίᾳ Τυφῶς.

78 ἰστέον δέ, ὅτι καὶ ὁ ἐκ Νεφέλης Κένταυρος Μάγνης ἦν, ὡς ἐν τοῖς τοῦ Πινδάρου δηλοῦται, ὃς καὶ Μαγνησίαις ἵπποις συναναχρωνύμενος ἐκ τοιούτου σπέρματος τοὺς Ἱπποκενταύρους ἔφηνε, καὶ ὅτι Μάγνητες ἐκλήθησαν ἀπὸ ἀνδρὸς ἐπιφανοῦς.

79 ἔθος Δωριεῦσιν, ὡς καὶ ἐν τοῖς τοῦ Πινδάρου φαίνεται, συντάσσειν ἔστιν ὅτε τὴν ἐν πρόθεσιν μετὰ αἰτιατικῆς.

provided by *Pythian* 2.11 where the scholion explains that ἐν is used instead of εἰς (schol. Pind. *Pyth.* 2.21).

In these four passages, the expression ἐν τοῖς τοῦ Πινδάρου refers again to Eustathius' commentary on Pindar, as the required information is not given in the Pindaric text itself nor provided by the scholia in exactly the same way.

The eight passages given above show that Eustathius refers to victory odes from all four books, namely *Olympian* 10, *Pythian* 1, 2, 4, 12, *Nemean* 2, and *Isthmian* 5. The passages reveal that he commented on diction and style and provided explanations concerning gods and myths. Thus we could imagine that his commentary on Pindar was similar to his later commentaries on Homer and Dionysius Periegetes, which were based on the ancient scholia, but enriched by a number of pieces of (secondary) information. These may have included the many references to Lycophron, announced in the *Introduction*, because this author is mentioned only once in the ancient scholia on Pindar.[80] However, since the *Introduction* seems to describe the commentary as covering excerpts of Pindar's works, it is difficult to evaluate how detailed his commentary on Pindar actually was.

4 Conclusion

Eustathius' *Introduction* makes it clear that his commentary on Pindar dealt with excerpts from the epinicia. The references to the commentary on Pindar in the other commentaries suggest that these included poems in all four books. The references to Pindar in the commentaries on Homer and Dionysius Periegetes may also provide other indirect evidence about Eustathius' commentary on Pindar. They are in general in line with what Eustathius tells us about his attitude to Pindar in the *Introduction*, but they give us the following additional pieces of information: first, they show that he used older Pindaric scholia; second, at the same time many of his references to Pindar in the commentaries on Homer and Dionysius Periegetes do not seem to come from older scholia, and these may be original insights of his own, showing a deep knowledge of the poet; third, although for the most part he uses Pindar's poems as evidence, for example to illustrate the Dorian dialect or to provide parallels to place names, his comments sometimes show signs of literary appreciation.

---

80 Cf. schol. Pind. *Nem.* 4.76. On the juxtaposition of Pindar to Lycophron in the first and second century CE, cf. Stat. *Silv.* 5.3.146–158 and Clem. Al. *Strom.* 5.8.50.2, and see Negri (1997) 107.

References

Adorjáni, Z. 2011. Eustathios und Pindar. *Acta Antiqua Academiae Scientiarum Hungaricae* 51: 77–85.

Bagordo, A. 2003. Sofocle e i lirici: tradizione e allusione. In *Il dramma sofocleo: testo, lingua, interpretazione*. Atti del seminario internazionale (Verona, 24–26 gennaio 2002), ed. G. Avezzù, 5–15. Stuttgart.

Braswell, B.K. 2013. *Didymos of Alexandria, Commentary on Pindar*. Basle.

Cohn, L. 1907. Eustathios. In *RE* VI 1.1452.50–89.3.

D'Alessio, G.B. 2012. The lost *Isthmian* odes of Pindar. In *Reading the Victory Ode*, ed. P. Agócs, C. Carey, and R. Rawles, 28–57. Cambridge.

Erbse, H. 1969–1988. *Scholia Graeca in Homeri Iliadem (Scholia vetera)*, 7 vols. Berlin.

Gallo, I. 1977. Eustazio commentatore di Pindaro. *QUCC* 25: 43–51.

Giannini, P. 2006. I riferimenti geografici negli epinici di Pindaro. In *I luoghi e la poesia nella Grecia antica*. Atti del Convegno, Università 'G. d'Annunzio' di Chieti-Pescara (20–22 aprile 2004), ed. M. Vetta and C. Catenacci, 213–226. Alessandria.

Irigoin, J. 1952. *Histoire du texte de Pindare*. Paris.

Kambylis, A. 1991a. *Eustathios von Thessalonike, Prooimion zum Pindarkommentar. Einleitung, kritischer Text, Indices*. Göttingen.

Kambylis, A. 1991b. *Eustathios über Pindars Epinikiendichtung: ein Kapitel der klassischen Philologie in Byzanz*. Göttingen.

Keizer, H.M. 1995. *Indices in Eustathii archiepiscopi Thessalonicensis Commentarios ad Homeri Iliadem pertinentes, ad fidem codicis Laurentiani editos a Marchino van der Valk*. Leiden.

Maehler, H. 1989. *Pindari carmina cum fragmentis. Pars II: Fragmenta, indices*. Leipzig.

Müller, C. 1861. *Eustathii commentarii in Dionysium Periegetem*. In *GGM* II 201–407. Paris.

Negri, M. 1992. Il frammento 325 di Pindaro: una nuova attribuzione? *Athenaeum* 80: 494–499.

Negri, M. 1994a. Una *varia lectio* per Pindaro, *Istmiche* 7, 44. *Maia* n.s. 46: 3–10.

Negri, M. 1994b. Due misconosciuti frammenti di Pindaro (Fr. 18 e 302 Turyn). *Athenaeum* 82: 221–223.

Negri, M. 1996. La Μοῖσα φιλοκερδής dei poeti lirici e il caso di Pindaro (Eustath. *Intr. Pind.* 7,2–5). *Athenaeum* 84: 598–604.

Negri, M. 1997. La sopravvivenza degli *Epinici* di Pindaro: le ragioni della scelta antica. In *Discentibus obvius: omaggio degli allievi a Domenico Magnino*, 87–108. Como.

Negri, M. 1998. Il catalogo delle opere di Pindaro in Eustazio (*Introd. Pind.* 34.1–2). *Aevum(ant)* 11: 217–231.

Negri, M. 1999. Per un'interpretazione di Pindaro, fr. 26 Mähler. *Athenaeum* 87: 279–290.

Negri, M. 2000. *Eustazio di Tessalonica, Introduzione al commentario a Pindaro*. Brescia.

Neumann-Hartmann, A. 2019. Belege griechischer Historiker in den Pindar-Scholien und ihre Bedeutung für die Pindar-Exegese. *Museum Helveticum* 76: 30–51.

Stallbaum, J.G. 1825–1826. *Eustathii archiepiscopi Thessalonicensis commentarii ad Homeri Odysseam ad fidem exempli Romani editi*, 2 vols. Leipzig.

van der Valk, M. 1971–1987. *Eustathii archiepiscopi Thessalonicensis commentarii ad Homeri Iliadem pertinentes*, 4 vols. Leiden.

Wirth, P. 2000. *Eustathii Thessalonicensis opera minora: magnam partem inedita*. Berlin.

Index of Passages

Aelius Aristides
Or.
2.129	417–418
24	417–435
24.3	421
24.4–40	426
24.14	426
24.22	419–420
24.50–51	426
24.52	427
24.53	428
24.53–54	430
24.54–56	431
24.59	422
25.17–33	421
27.42	418
32.24	433
43.40	12
45	424

Aelius Donatus
Vit. Verg.
44–45	530

Aelian
VH
10.13	182
12.50	423

Aeschines
1.16–20	376
1.6	373

Aeschylus
Cho.
50	230
Or.	230
Pers.	230, 234

Alcaeus
fr. 6	288–293, 432
fr. 15	485
fr. 38A	284
fr. 45	282–283
fr. 48	282–283
fr. 69	388
fr. 70	387–388
fr. 72	388
fr. 129	283, 286, 387–388
fr. 208	288–293
fr. 208a	432
fr. 249.6–9	4, 60–62
fr. 305b	433
fr. 306c	526
fr. 306i	433
fr. 307	282–283
fr. 308	526
fr. 325	282–283
fr. 326.1–2	329–331
fr. 338	528
fr. 342	528
fr. 345.1	282–283
fr. 350	282–283, 285
fr. 354	282–283
fr. 384	327
fr. 401B	268–269
fr. 428	283–285
fr. 432	282–283

Alcman
fr. 39	193
fr. 59a	191–194
See also Papyri	

Alexis
fr. 222 PCG	332–335

Anacreon
fr. 356	527
fr. 358	167–169
fr. 359	362
fr. 360	357
fr. 372	169–171
fr. 388	170–171
fr. 397	329–331
fr. 422	41
fr. 472	349

Anaxagoras
fr. 59 B22	349

Anonymus
Hymn to Asclepius   10

Antiphanes
Sappho   344

Apollodorus of Athens
   FGrH 244 F 112   358

Archilochus
   fr. 5   284–285
   fr. 9.10–11   401–402
   fr. 19   268–269
   fr. 108   401
   fr. 122   189
   fr. 129   188
   fr. 185   284
   fr. 253   198
   Telephus   143

Aristophanes
Ach.
   263–279   125
   637   212
   978–981   126
Av.   17
   217   135
   846–884   119–120
   895–921   119–120
   922–930   120–121
   931–945   121
   946–955   121
   1362–1363   141
   1373–1409   121–122
   1720–1742   122–123
   1748–1765   122–123
   1763   123–124
Eq.
   407–408   124
   1329   535
Lys.
   630–635   126
   1248–1272   124
   1291–1294   123–124
   1296–1320   124
Nub.   16
   330–339   122
   1314–1315   251
   1345–1362   117–119
   1363–1379   118
Pax   17, 242
   453–455   124
   694–700   118, 163
   734–740   138
   828–836   122
   1320–1359   123
Ran.
   363–367   122
   1491–1499   251
Thesm.   17, 105–106
   101–129   115
   130–170   115–117
   167   183
   159–163   177
   310–311   124
   947–1000   125
   1034–1037   123–124
Vesp.
   1222–1228   126
   1402–1413   118–119
Fragments
   fr. 235 PCG   95–96, 117
   fr. 696 PCG   162
   fr. 444 PCG   126

Aristophanes of Byzantium
   fr. 9   539
   fr. 42   541

Aristotle
Ath. Pol.   189, 385
   2.1   377
   5.2   138–139
   5.3   377, 385–387, 390
   5.10   138–139
   6.2–4   377
   12.1   51–55
Hist. an
   536b   194
Poet.   98–99, 116–117
   1149b24–31   117
   1447a1.3–15   98
   1447b14   130
   1448b24–27   192
   1448b34–1449a2   186–187
   1449a2–6   98
   1460a5–11   184–187

INDEX OF PASSAGES

Pol.
1273b35	377
1274a1–5	377
1296a19–20	377
1306b36	143
1327b40–1328a5	187–188
1339b10–42	157
1340a12–14	157

Rhet.
1356a4–13	117
1367a	103
1367a7–15	187
1375b34	52–55
1405a31	138–139
1418b23–32	188–189

Aristoxenus
fr. 89	157–158
frr. 92–93	153
fr. 98	349–350
fr. 117	164–166
frr. 122–127	154

Athenaeus
1.1b	345
1.21c	345
1.22b	541
1.28a	541
1.39.21d–f	162
2.39a–b	345–348
2.41e	541
2.54f	348–349
2.57d	348–349
4.182e	349
5.191f	541
8.338b	176
8.339c	350
9.389f–390a	193
9.391f	350–351
9.410d–e	351–352
10.424f–425a	352
10.425c–d	353
10.429b	182–183
10.450e–451b	353
10.456c	176
11.460d	347
11.462c–463e	331–339
11.463e	62, 347
11.475a	346–348
11.476b	541
12.533e	176
12.533e–534b	155–156, 169–171
12.554b	353–354
13	342, 349
13.563d	328–329
13.564c–e	357–358
13.566e	328–329
13.567a	328–329
13.567b	358
13.571c–d	328–329, 358–359
13.572c	359
13.573c	176
13.573c–574b	171–174
13.573e	452
13.596b–d	257–259, 262, 264–266, 269–272, 359–360
13.596b–605e	359
13.596e	361
13.597b–599b	361
13.598b–c	361–363
13.599c	176, 362
13.599c–d	167–169, 362–363
13.599d	363
13.600f	175–176, 191–194
13.601d	535
13.605e	363–364
13.611a	176
13.656c	176
14	349
14.619d–e	158
14.620c	176
14.635b	349–350
14.635e	425
14.639a	154, 349
14.653e	349–350
14.641b	541
14.656c–e	163
15.667c	483
15.668e	176
15.669c	330
15.674c–e	329–331, 354–355
15.687a–b	355–356
15.690e	354–355

Attic Scolia
891	60–62
893	126

Attic Scolia (cont.)
    894   126

Aulus Gellius
NA
    17.11.1   531
    17.21.8   531
    19.9   326
    19.9.4   531
    20.7.2   531

Bacchylides
    fr. 1B   478
    frr. 2–4   477
    fr. 6   477
    fr. 7   477
    fr. 9   477
    fr. 12   477
    fr. 13   224–425
    fr. 14   477
    Fr. 14B   477
    fr. 15   29, 477
    fr. 17   29, 210, 215–220, 222–224, 477, 483, 485
    fr. 18   478, 485
    fr. 19   216–217, 478
    frr. 20–20C   478
    fr. 23   478, 527–528
    See also Papyri

Callimachus
    fr. 64   11
    fr. 110.48   528
    fr. 215   528
    fr. 587   528

Catullus
    11   22, 279–286
    51   281

Chamaeleon
    fr. 6   196–198
    fr. 13   196
    fr. 25   175–176
    fr. 26   168, 176, 192–194
    fr. 27   191–194
    fr. 28   176, 190
    fr. 30   176
    fr. 31   171–174, 176, 452
    fr. 33   162–164, 176
    fr. 34   176
    fr. 35   176, 190
    fr. 36   169–171, 176
    fr. 37   190
    fr. 41   161–162
    frr. 43–44   161
    fr. 95   176

Cicero
Att.
    10.10.3 (fr. 105)   298
    12.5.1   298
    13.38.2 (fr. 213)   298
Fam.
    9.10.1   295–296
Fin.
    2.115   298
Nem.
    1.1   298
Or.
    4   298
Pis.
    73   296

Clearchus
    frr. 21–35   154
    fr. 22   195
    fr. 24   195
    fr. 25   155–156, 195
    fr. 32   194–195
    fr. 33   154–155, 195, 349–350
    fr. 34   131–132, 195

Critias
    B 44 DK   182
    fr. 4 W.   135–137

Demetrius of Phalerum
Eloc.
    106   281

Demosthenes
Or.
    19.252–254   373
    19.254–256   138
    29.102–104   376
    [59.97]   59

INDEX OF PASSAGES 557

Dicaearchus
  fr. 39   197–198
  frr. 73–89   153, 160
  fr. 88   156–157
  frr. 89–91   195
  frr. 105–109   195
  fr. 110   198

Dieuchidas of Megara
  FGH 485 F 6   101

Dio Chrysostom
Or.
  19.1–5   424
  31.18   419
  32.60–61   424
  48.7   427

Diodorus Siculus
Bibl. Hist.
  7.12.5–6   80–90
  7.12.6   57–58
  9.20   388
  12.10–11   85–86
  12.12–13   86
  18.18.5   373

Diogenes Laertius
  1.51   388
  1.57   101
  1.60   402
  1.61   396–397
  1.66–67   373

Dionysius Chalcus
  fr. 7   139

Dionysius of Halicarnassus
De imit.
  2.8   434

Dionysius Periegeta
  1   540
  64   541–542
  66   542
  144   542
  211   542, 547–550
  213   542
  403–408   546–547
  426   542
  820   542

Diphilus
Sappho
  fr. 71 PCG   363
Theseus
  fr. 49 PCG   353

Ephippus
Sappho
  fr. 20 PCG   359

Epicrates
Antilaïs
  fr. 4 PCG   363–364

Euenus
  fr. 8a W.   137–138

Eupolis
  fr. 148 PCG   124–125
  fr. 395 PCG   124–125

Euripides
Bacch.
  8   408
  274–285   233
El.
  434   215–217
Hel.
  185   135
IA
  1055–1057   215
IT
  146   135
  392–466   213, 215
  425–426   221
  427–429   215–217
Or.
  968   135
Tro.
  119   135
  137–138   230
  190–229   230

Eustathius of Thessalonica
Il.
                      538–539
  1.1   541–542, 545–546

Il. (cont.)

1.6 f.	542
1.10	540, 542
1.15	542, 547–550
1.35	542
1.65	541
1.75	542, 544–545
1.129	540
1.213 f.	542
1.250–252	542
1.279	542
1.312	542
1.423	541
2.89	541
2.506	542
2.531	542
2.561	540
2.570	542
2.637	542
2.638	541
2.662	538–540, 546
2.756	547–550
2.783	547–550
2.814	540
3.54	540
3.209	547–550
4.328	540
8.306 f.	540
9.378	543–544
11.242	541–542
11.679	541
11.726	540
11.750	547–550
13.6	541
14.171	541
14.201	540
14.267	540
15.60	540
16.233 f.	541
21.22	541
21.319	540
24.734	540

Od.

1.51	542
1.138	541
1.156	541
1.312 ff.	542
1.415	542
2.11	542
2.190	542
4.131	542
4.179	541
5.121	541
5.274	541
5.306	542
8.148	542
8.176	542
8.190	541
8.383	541
8.429	542
9.65	542
9.390	540
10.240	541, 543
10.435	541
10.515	541–542
11.270	542, 547–550
11.309	543
11.316	542–543
11.333	541
12.99	540–541
12.167	541
12.261	542
17.315	541
18.105	549–550

Prooem. ad Pind. 533–537

3–24	536
10.1	537
11.12	537
16.1	535–536
21.3	536
27.3	536
27.4	535
27.12	535
28.1	535
33.1	536
34.1	535
36.1	537
38.1	534
38.4	537

Gorgias

Hel.	20, 228, 230–234

Hecataeus

FGrH 1 F358	352

Heraclides Ponticus

frr. 157–163	153

538–539

INDEX OF PASSAGES 559

Heraclitus Grammaticus
Alleg.
  4   12
  5.5–9   433
Quaest. Hom.   23, 289

Hermesianax
  fr. 7   361–363

Hermogenes
Id.
  331   12
  334   12

Herodotus
Hist.   234
  1.5.4   376
  1.12   268–269
  1.29.1–33   376
  1.33   373
  2.133.2   539
  2.134–135   257–259, 269–272, 327, 359–360
  2.177.2   376
  3.121.1   101
  3.125.2–3   101
  5.95   268–269, 283–285
  5.102   268–269
  5.113   268–269

Hesiod
Op.
  311   405–406

Himerius
Or.
  9   12
  48   12

Hipponax
  fr. 153   134

Homer
Iliad
  1.1   545–546
  1.3–5   402–403
  1.75   544–545
  2.594–600   248–249
  9.378   543–544
  15.713–715   224
  21.21   224
  22.263   250
Odyssey   295, 387
  8.62–64   248
  11.362–372   117
  18.105   549
Hom. Hymn Ap.   246
Hom. Hymn 32   119

Horace
Ars P.
  73 ff.   530
  79   524
Carm.
  1.1   30
  1.1.32–34   517, 519, 525
  1.9   528
  1.10   30, 526
  1.12   30, 527
  1.14   22, 23, 30, 286–293, 433, 519
  1.15   30, 527–528
  1.18.1   528
  1.26.10 ff.   518–519
  1.27   527
  1.32   23, 30, 290–293
  1.32.3 ff.   519
  2.1.37–38   526
  2.13   23, 30
  2.13.21–28   291–292, 519–521
  2.13.31   30, 519, 523
  3.25   303
  3.30   298–306, 518, 520
  4.2   298
  4.2.5–8   12
  4.2.11–12   307
  4.3   522–523
  4.3.10 ff.   523
  4.6.35–36   523
  4.9   30, 523, 525–526
Epist.
  1.10   528
  1.19   30, 521, 524
  1.3.9–14   298
  2.2.99 ff.   523–524
Epod.
  6   524

Sat.
1.10.18	518
2.1.43	528
2.3	528
2.3.11–12	524
2.3.299	518

Ibycus
Fr. 282	228
fr. 287	177
fr. 310	177

Inscriptions
IG 11² 2311	96

Clara Rhodos
2.201.33	429
2.215.55	429

I.Lindos
2.197d	429
2.449	429

N. Suppl. Epigr. Rodio
175.29	429

Ion of Chios
fr. 27	332–335

Isocrates
Or.
2.42–43	138
15.232	373

Julian
Epist.
10	259

Licymnius of Chios
fr. 771 PMG	357–358

Livius Andronicus
Od. 295

Lycurgus
Leoc.
106	138

Lysias
30.28	376

Marius Victorinus
Gramm.
6.161	282

Menaechmus
De art.
FGrH 131 F4a	349–350
FGrH 131 F4b	349–350

Mimnermus
Smyrn.	143

Oppian
Hal.
3.25	549

Ovid
Her.
15	262–264
15.63–68	257–258, 263–264

Met.
15.871–879	304–306

Pont.
4.16.28	298
15.199–202	324

Papyri
P. Hercul. 1384 fr. 1	411
P. Oxy. 1790	464
P. Oxy. 1800 fr. 1.7f	257–258
P. Oxy. 2298 fr. 1	61, 326
P. Oxy. 2506 fr. 26	244, 252
P. Oxy. 2734	485
P. Oxy. 21.2306 col. 2	433
P. Oxy. 21.2307 fr. 14	433
P. Oxy. 21.2307 fr. 16	433

Alcman
P. Oxy. 2390	11

Bacchylides
P. Bacchylides A	465, 467–468
P. Bacchylides fr. 20C	463

Palladas
P. CtYBR inv. 4000	50

Pindar
P. Oxy. 5042	466
P. Pindar Π⁴	465, 467
P. Pindar Π¹⁰ *Partheneion*	466

INDEX OF PASSAGES 561

Sappho
  P. Berl. 9722 — 13
  P. Köln 429–430 — 326–327
  P. Köln 21351.1–8 — 520
  P. Oxy. 1787 — 322

Pausanias
  5.24.3 — 50
  10.5.12 — 541
  10.7.5–6 — 132–134, 143

Pherecrates
Chiron
  fr. 162.10 K.-A. — 137–138
  fr. 162.11–12 K.-A. — 135–136

Philodemus
De poem. 2
  fr. 117 Janko — 259

Photius
Lex — 269

Pindar
Ol.
  1 — 471
  1.1 — 540
  1.115b–116 — 3
  2 — 472
  2.1–2 — 527–528
  Σ 2.29d — 449
  3 — 28, 472
  3.1–2 — 28, 442
  Σ 3.1a–d — 442, 449
  3.27 — 547
  4 — 472
  5 — 472
  6 — 472, 540
  6.1–4 — 310–312
  Σ 6.55a — 447
  6.77 — 546
  Σ 6.158c — 447
  7 — 472
  7.54 — 450
  7.55–71 — 426
  Σ 7.100a — 450
  8 — 472
  9 — 472
  Σ 9.62b — 448
  9.63 — 546
  9.44–46 — 540
  10 — 472
  10.3 — 540
  11 — 472
  12 — 472
  13 — 171–174, 472, 540
  13.23 — 28, 451–452
  Σ 13.32b — 451–452, 458
  Σ 13.74d — 453
  Σ 13.74f — 453
  13.53–54 — 453
  14 — 472
Pyth.
  1 — 472
  1.16 — 549
  2 — 473
  2.11 — 550
  2.127 — 120
  3 — 473
  4 — 473
  4.41 — 540
  5 — 473
  6 — 473
  6.5–14 — 299–310
  6.7 — 23
  7 — 473
  8 — 473
  8.95–96 — 543–544
  9 — 473
  9.26 — 544–545
  10 — 466, 473
  11 — 466, 473
  11.38–40 — 445
  Σ 11.58a — 445
  12 — 473
Nem.
  1 — 28, 473
  Σ 1.3 — 449
  Σ 1.49c — 442–447
  2 — 473
  2.2 — 545–546
  2.11 — 541
  3 — 473
  3.13–14 — 28, 453
  Σ 3.16b — 448
  3.21 — 453–457
  Σ 3.21 — 453–458
  Σ 3.23 — 454–455

Nem. (cont.)		fr. 89b	477
3.28	457	fr. 94b	476
Σ 3.75	457	fr. 94c	476
3.43–52	457	fr. 95.1–2	535
Σ 4.53a	445–447	fr. 105	120–121, 476
4	473	fr. 106.1–3	541
4.33	445	fr. 109	476
4.80	546	fr. 110	476, 541
5	473	fr. 120–121	476
5.43	546	fr. 122	171–174
6	473	fr. 123.6	535
7	473	fr. 124c	541
8	465, 473, 479	fr. 128c	8, 125, 476, 480
10	465, 474	fr. 132.2–6	357
10.37	546	fr. 137	476
11.37	546	fr. 140b	477
Isthm.		fr. 148	541, 544–545
1	465, 474	fr. 150	541
1.25	541	fr. 151	541
2	474	fr. 155	541
3	465, 474	fr. 166	541
4	465, 474	fr. 170	541
4.48	400	fr. 183	541
5	465, 474, 479	fr. 193	536
Σ 5.63a	453	fr. 198b	541
6	474	fr. 209	536
6.62	546	fr. 236	541
7.16s	540	fr. 256	541
7.24	546	fr. 262	541
7.47	400	fr. 297	541
8	474	fr. 305	541
Fragments		fr. 306	541
frr. 2–3	474	fr. 317	541
fr. 4	474–475	*Vitae*	
fr. 6a	475	Drachmann 10–11	97
fr. 6a(c)	536	Vita Ambrosiana	535–536
fr. 6a(d)	536, 540	See also Papyri	
fr. 6a(i)	474		
fr. 6b	474	**Plato**	
fr. 6c	29, 474	*Criti.*	377
fr. 8	475, 527–528, 540–541	*Ion*	
		534d	3
fr. 36	475	*[Hipparch.]*	
fr. 37	475, 535	228b–c	100–102
fr. 52i.71	541	*Hp. mai.*	
fr. 52f.111	544–545	285e4	377
fr. 59	541	*Leg.*	
frr. 76–77	211–214, 232	700d–e	160
fr. 76	476, 479, 535	858c3	377

INDEX OF PASSAGES

700a–701a	228	156b–d	412–413
764d–e	96	403a	409–413
Meno		405	412
95d	141	*De Herod.*	398
Phdr.	239–254	871a	452
229b–c	250	[*De mus*]	12
229c	250	1132c	425
242c6–b1	177	1132d	135, 424
235c	327	1132e	425
237a	240	1133b–c	253
237a7–9	20	1134a	134
241d	240–244, 250–251	1134b	424
241e	241	1146b–c	422
243a–c	20, 239–240, 250–251	*Prae. ger. reip.*	
		813f	420
252b	243	*Quaest. conv.*	412–413
257a	241	622c	326
257b–c	247–249	*Quomodo adul.*	414
258c1	377	15a–e	398
277e5–b2	21	16a	398
277e–278b	245–246	16a–b	399–400
278d	246	17	399
Prm.		20c	399, 410
136e9–137a4	177	21a3–8	400–401
Prt.	177, 377	22a4–9	401
338e	243	23	399
338e–347a	119	23a–f	401
Resp.	21	25a–c	398
398d	160	26–27	396
487d–488e	430	27f	399, 401
596a	401	33d–e	402
3.394b–c	210	33d–34a	45
10.595c	98	33e	399
10.598d	98	35f	399, 410
10.605c	98	36d	399, 410
10.607a	98	*Vitae*	374–375, 378, 391
Symp.	366–367	*Vit. Alex.*	
176e	366	1.2	378
209a7	377	*Vit. Alex. et Caes.*	
212c–d	366	1.1–1.3	398
Tht.		*Vit. Luc.*	
152e	98	1.1	72
Ti.	377	6.6–10	75–80
		6.10	57–58
Plutarch		7	79
Amat.	27	*Vit. Per.*	
751e	409–413	1.3	398
Conv. sept. sap.	409	9–11	106–109
155f	381	13.9–11	108

Vit. Publ.	378
1.2	382
Vit. Sol.	25–27, 373–392, 395–414
1.1–2	379
1.3	398, 408
1.5–6	408
1.6.4–1.7.1	48
2	403–406
2.1–2.6	404–405
2.6	404–406
3.1	398
3.1–3.2	406–407
3.2	379, 385–387
3.3	398
3.3–4	407
3.3–5	379
4–7	379
12.1–3	380
13	380
14.1	380
15.6	380
16.1–2	380
16.5	380
17–25a	381
18.5	51–55
20.1	381
26–28	381
29–30	381
30.2–31.2	380
30.8	388
31.3	409–113
Vit. Sol.: Comp. Sol. & Public.	
1.1	383
1.5	401
[*X orat.*]	
841f	97

Pomponius Porphyrio
Ad Hor. Ars P.
97	528

Ad Hor. Carm.
1.1.34	517
1.10	526
1.12	527
1.15	527–528
1.15.1	527–528
1.16.22–24	518
1.26.11–12	519
1.27	527
2.13.23–25	520–521
2.13.26–27	521
4.6.35–36	523
4.9.8	523
4.9.11–12	523

Ad Hor. Epist.
1.1.45	528
1.19.23	521
1.19.25	522
1.19.28	520–522
1.19.29	522
1.19.30	522
1.19.34	522
2.2.99 ff.	523–524

Ad Hor. Epod.
5.41–42	520, 522

Ad Hor. Sat.
2.3.296	528

Commentum in Horatium Flaccum
	516–531
Vita ⟨H⟩oratii	517–518

Posidippus
Ep. 122 A.-B.   257–262, 264, 360

Praxiphanes
Commentary on Hesiod
fr. 22b	166–167

Proclus
Tim. 20e   52–55

Propertius
2.1.4	304
2.30	304
2.34	304
3.2	300–304
3.17	302–303
4.6	303

Quintilian
Inst.
1.8.6	531
8.6.44	287, 433
10.1.53–54	9
10.1.63	434

INDEX OF PASSAGES

Sappho
fr. 1 — 339
fr. 1.9–10 — 350–351
fr. 2 — 24, 62–63, 322, 325, 331–339, 344
fr. 2.13–16 — 333–335, 347–348
fr. 2.14 — 347
fr. 5 — 258, 263, 327
fr. 15 — 258, 272, 327
fr. 15.9–12 — 259
fr. 15.11 — 270
fr. 16.9 — 282
fr. 22 — 325, 339
fr. 24a — 324
fr. 27 — 323
fr. 35 — 282
fr. 44 — 104, 344
fr. 44.10 — 347
fr. 55 — 271–272
fr. 58 — 50, 322, 344. See also 'Tithonos song'
fr. 58.25–26 — 355–356
fr. 71 — 339
fr. 71.1–4 — 323–324
fr. 71.1/3 — 345–348
fr. 81 — 355
fr. 81.4–7 — 329–331
fr. 94 — 24, 325, 330–331, 339, 344
fr. 94.1 — 358
fr. 94.15–16 — 329–331, 354
fr. 94.19–20 — 354–355
fr. 96 — 282
fr. 98a — 282
fr. 101 — 351–352
fr. 105(c) — 281
fr. 106 — 432
fr. 122 — 155–156, 353–354
fr. 126 — 283, 325
fr. 137 — 103
fr. 138 — 357
fr. 141 — 345–348
fr. 141.1–3 — 345–348, 353
fr. 142 — 283, 325, 328–329, 358–359
fr. 143 — 348–349
fr. 160 — 283, 322, 325, 328–329, 339, 358–359
fr. 166 — 348–349
fr. 167 — 348–349
fr. 176 — 349
fr. 199 — 358
fr. 202 — 282
fr. 203a — 352
fr. 247 — 349–350
fr. 252 — 257–258
fr. 254c — 359–360
Brothers Song — 258, 266, 327
21–22 — 263
Tithonus Song — 7, 63–67. See also 'fr. 58'
Testimonia (Campbell)
8 — 167–169
39 — 350
Florentine ostrakon — 335–338
See also Papyri

Simonides
Elegies
fr. 7 — 163
fr. 11 — 104–105, 143, 211
Epigrams
11 — 59, 218
14 — 171–174
17 — 59–60
EG 14.1–2 — 451
Lyric Fragments
507 — 118, 470
511 — 470
514 — 470
519 — 471–480
530 — 471
531.7–8 — 211
532–538 — 471, 478
539 — 471, 478–479
550 — 471
562 — 471, 479
564 — 245
573 — 544–545

Solon
fr. 1.1–2 — 284
fr. 4 — 26, 138, 377, 384, 387–391
fr. 4a — 138
fr. 4b — 138
fr. 4c — 377, 385–388
fr. 5 — 51–55, 377, 384

Solon (cont.)

fr. 6	377, 387
fr. 10	377
fr. 11	26, 54, 377, 388–389
fr. 13	377, 404–405
fr. 15	26, 385–391, 406–407
fr. 18	409–413
fr. 19	268–269
fr. 20	401–402
fr. 22a	49, 52–55
fr. 24.1–6	404–405
fr. 25	27, 410–412, 414
fr. 26	27, 409–413
fr. 27	412
fr. 29	399–400
fr. 33	385, 387
fr. 34	387–388
fr. 37.1–3	377

Sophocles
Aj.

1185–1222	230

Ant.

1170–1171	543–544

Phil.

946–947	543–544

Trach.

441	408

Statius
Silv.

1 *praef.* 11–12	309
1.1.91–94	307–310
4.7.5	307
5.3.146–158	307
5.3.151–155	307
5.3.151–152	307
5.3.3	307

Stesichorus

fr. 240	241–242
fr. 277	157–158
fr. 278	241–242
Helen	239–254
Oresteia	
fr. 210.1	242
Palinode	5–6, 21, 239–240, 249, 251–254

Strabo

1.2.30	282–283
3.3.7	541
3.5.5	541
7.7.10	541
9.5.5	541
13.1.38	284
13.2.3	432
17.1.33	257–258, 269

Suda

αι 334	265–266
δ 1466	269
ρ 211	269
σ 107	259, 321

Theognis

19–38	3–4
27–28	141
33–36	141
39–42	56–57
53–68	389
175–176	528
183–192	389
213–218	392
237–254	142
261–269	140
457–460	141
667–682	430
993–1002	140
1081–1082b	56–57

Theophilus

fr. 6 PCG	141–142

Theophrastus
Hist. pl.

8.5.1	348

Thucydides

1.132	59

Timocles
Sappho

fr. 32 PCG	350

Timotheus
Pers.

	7, 20, 205–234
19	220

INDEX OF PASSAGES

31–39	220–223	fr. 5	78
31–33	224	fr. 12.31–34	58–59
37–39	218		
60–87	218	**Velleius Paterculus**	
86–87	218	2.18.3	434
121 ff.	230		
178	230	**Virgil**	
196–205	218–220	*G.*	
202–233	234	3.13	310–312
207	213	3.16	310–312
237–238	214–215	3.26–29	310–312
		3.34–36	310–312

Tragic Fragments
Adesp.

354	403	**Xenophanes**	
		fr. 1	331–335
		fr. 2	332–335
Tyrtaeus		fr. 21B 22	348
fr. 1.55	59		
fr. 2	78	**Xenophon**	
fr. 4	14–15, 57–58, 72–90	*Mem.*	
fr. 4.5	59	1.4.3	9
fr. 4.9	55		

Index of Subjects

Adonia   353
Adonis   358
Aeacus   508
Aelius Aristides   27, 417–438
Aeschylus   432
Aesop   381
Agathon   177
agathos/aristos   375, 386–390, 140–141
Alcaeus   5, 11–12, 16, 22–26, 30, 95, 115, 117, 160, 177, 187, 198, 282, 324, 326, 339, 343–344, 361–362, 390–391, 418, 433–434, 516–523, 525–526, 529–530
   and Sappho   103
   companions   322
   pederastic poetry   324
   stasiotica   279–294
Alcmaeonidae   384–385
Alcman   5, 8, 10, 95, 115, 120, 124, 175–176, 307, 343, 417, 427
   sphragis   199
Alexander of Cotiaeum   433
Alexandria   7, 97–99, 109–110
   Library   8, 97
Alexandrian scholarship   23, 45, 46, 295, 297, 462, 469, 505
   editions   29, 64, 281, 326, 351, 464, 496, 501
   exegesis   295, 297
allegory   12, 23, 287, 289, 292, 312, 430, 519
allusion   211, 216, 338, 435, 442, 452
Almeida, Joseph   378
Ammonius   446
Amphitrite   215, 218, 220–224, 233
Anacreon   4, 5, 10, 12, 16, 19, 95, 100–103, 105, 115, 117, 121, 154–155, 159, 177, 183, 190, 323, 327, 339, 343–344, 350, 354, 361, 525, 531
Andrews, Tara   46
anthologies   13, 17–18, 24, 45, 59, 139–140, 327, 395–396
Antimachus   125, 131, 186
Antiphanes   353
antiquarianism   19, 151, 154, 194–198
Aphrodite   157–158, 171–174, 334–336, 350–351, 358, 364, 453
Apollo   209, 218, 334, 481

Apollodorus of Athens   448
Archilochus   4, 5, 11, 30, 137, 159, 168, 182–183, 187, 190, 284–285, 322, 343–344, 363, 434, 516, 520, 524, 530
   and Lycambes   522
Archytas of Mytilene   175, 191
Archytas of Tarentum   175, 191–192
Arion of Methymna   432, 502–503
Aristarchus   8, 27, 28, 167, 296, 441–448, 462, 505–507, 533
Aristocyprus   268
Aristophanes, comic poet   5, 8–10, 16, 112–128, 161–165, 183, 210, 462, 507
Aristophanes of Byzantium   7–8, 462, 464, 507
Aristotle   7, 19, 97, 130, 151–152, 163, 166, 177, 185–189, 375, 379, 491–492, 497, 502, 504
   didaskalia   498
   on the lyric poets   184–189
Aristoxenus   18, 159–161, 192
Artemon   448, 457
Ascalon   282
Asclepiades of Myrlea   448
Asclepius   27
Assmann, Jan   1
Athenaeus   12, 22, 60, 63, 151, 269–271
   Sappho in Athenaeus   321–341, 342–372
Athens   5–7, 15–18, 43, 59, 139, 142, 176, 212–213, 214, 216–217, 220, 428, 469, 497, 499, 503
   and the lyric canon   95–111
Atlantis   392, 400, 409
Atthidographers   54, 376
auletes   96–98
aulodes   15, 96–98, 105, 109, 133–135
aulos   105, 133, 143
authenticity   14, 55–56, 72, 74, 113, 117
autobiography   182, 193, 199
author   46, 47, 113–119, 122, 182, 174
authority   85, 113–114, 220, 232, 343, 367, 401, 413, 450

Babylon   282
Bacchylides   5, 9, 12, 16, 19–20, 95, 124–125, 175, 177, 207–209, 230

INDEX OF SUBJECTS 569

lyric style   205, 217
titles of poems   461–515
Balot, Ryan   311–312
Barchiesi, Alessandro   297
barbitos   102–103, 349, 519
Barns, John   140
battle songs   523
Bein, Thomas   41–42
Behr, Charles   421
Bergk, Theodor   73
biography   7, 21–22, 25–26, 30, 152, 165, 251, 258, 518, 529–530
  biographical data   189, 153, 190, 529
  biographical anecdotes   177
  biographical fallacy   184
  biographical interpretation   19, 184, 191, 187, 353, 397
  Of Solon   373–416
Bion of Borysthenes   401
blame poetry   17, 136
  See also Invective
blindness   21, 246–248, 252–254
Blinkenberg, Christian   429
Blois, Lucas de   395
Blum, Rudolph   498, 500
Boedeker, Deborah   64
books   29, 166, 178, 217, 487, 504
Bowie, Ewen   55, 105, 109, 135, 137, 139–141, 399, 417, 427
Bowra, Cecile   265
Budelmann, Felix   205, 213
Burkert, Walter   246
Byzantine period   13, 31, 533–552

Callimachus   8, 10–11, 23, 303, 307, 482, 498, 507, 524, 529–530
Callinus   186
Callisthenes   491
Callistratus   126
canon   1, 4, 6, 9, 14–18, 21, 109, 124–126, 143, 247–249, 307, 466
  of nine lyric poets   15–16, 18, 95–111, 152, 165
capping   55
Carneia   501
Carruesco, Jesús   245
Cassandra   505
Catullus   11, 279–286, 518
Chaeris   28, 443–445, 448

Chamaeleon   7, 19, 97, 153, 160, 167–177, 184, 189, 199, 252, 362–363, 490
Charaxus   22, 257–276, 327, 359
chorus   133, 209, 230, 426–429, 418, 497, 503
'chunking'   12, 16, 18, 22
Cinesias   16, 121–122, 125, 498
Claranus   516
Clearchus of Soli   19, 175
Cleomenes of Rhegium   363
Colesanti, Giulio   131
Collins, Derek   57
comedy   5, 16, 112–128, 141, 153, 161–162, 165, 251, 327, 366
  Old Comedy   7, 16, 19, 161, 165
commentaries   2, 7, 27, 166, 170, 424, 441, 444–447, 533, 537, 459, 505, 516, 548, 550
  on Alcman   11
  commentary tradition   23, 297, 306, 313
competition   13, 153, 425, 497
conservatism   6, 54, 161
Corinna   9, 11, 110
Cormeau, Christoph   41–42
courtesan   *See Hetaira*
Critias   141, 183, 188
Csapo, Eric   205, 209, 215
Cydias   5
Cylon   380, 384
Cyprus   282

D'Alessio, Giambattista   483
Damon   6
Daniel, Robert   63
Delos   504
Delphi   282
democracy   54–56, 373, 377, 381–383, 392
Democritus   182–183
Demodocus   248
dialects   59, 61, 62, 536
  Aeolic   271, 423, 518, 523
  Attic   61, 63
  Doric   31, 59, 60, 536, 542
  Ionic   59, 61
  Lesbian   61
Dicaearchus   97, 160, 189
didactic poetry   17, 138, 141, 143, 263–264, 397–398, 407
didaskaliai   497–499, 500–502, 504
Didymus of Alexandria   11, 27, 444–450, 533

Diehl, Ernst 73
digressions 445, 535–536
Dio Chrysostom 423
Diodorus Siculus 14, 15, 72–91
Diogenes Laertius 151
Dionysia 5, 105, 120, 497, 500–501
Dionysus 209
Dionysodotus the Laconian 427
Dioscuri 28, 442
Diphilus 190, 363
dithyramb 5, 29, 30, 125, 119–121, 125, 153, 208–210, 212–217, 220, 226, 479, 482, 485, 535
  and choral projection 215
  choregic dedications 502
  choruses 122, 428
  contests 498
  didascalic lists 499–501, 504
  narrative structure 222
  performances 500
  titles 464, 488
  victories 498–499
dolphins 215
Doricha 22, 257–276, 327, 359, 360
  See also Rhodopis
Drachmann, Anders Bjørn 465
Draco 385
drinking 154, 409, 413, 346–347

editions 10, 18–19, 44–45, 55, 64, 177
  multiform 65
editors 505, 507
education 17, 102, 116, 119, 140–142, 307, 398, 411, 413, 516
Egypt 282
elegy 7, 8, 10, 16–18, 39–71, 84, 105, 126, 129–147, 152, 181, 186, 304, 382, 400, 524
Else, Gerald 130
emulation 297, 313
enargeia 223
encomium 117, 173, 214, 231, 233, 312, 417, 446, 483–484, 489, 535
Endymion 358
Ennius 306
Eos 358
epigram 260–262
epinician 12–13, 27, 31, 118, 120, 441–460, 480, 483–484, 489–496, 533, 535, 537, 540, 550

epithalamion See Wedding Songs
epithets 31, 217, 223, 225, 536, 542, 544–545
Eratosthenes 491
Ercoles, Marco 251
Eriphanis 195
Eros 356
erotic songs *See* Love songs
eroticism 12, 25, 169, 330–331, 351, 354, 361, 365, 408–409
ethos 117, 154, 190–191, 196–197, 375, 383, 389
Eudemus of Rhodes 159
Eupolis 16
Eustathius of Thessalonica 13, 31, 533–552
excerpts 11, 81, 140, 537, 550
exegesis 6, 449, 455

Faraone, Chris 58–59
Favorinus 59
Fearn, David 483
Ferrari, Franco 266
festivals 143, 153, 210, 442, 496–497
Finglass, Patrick 47
Firinu, Elena 213, 215, 220–221
first-person expressions 182, 199, 388, 397
Foucault, Michel 113

Gaisser, Julia 39
games 481, 492
garlands 354–355, 364
Genette, Gérard 461
genres 8, 17, 29, 112–147, 153, 190, 487–488
  lyric 16, 153, 160
Gentili, Bruno 40, 53, 59, 73, 83
Gkourogiannis, Theodoros 426
gnomai See maxims
Goldhill, Simon 227
Gronewald, Michael 63
gymnopaediae 427

habrosynē 356
Hardie, Alex 308–309
Harmodius song 16, 126
Hebrus 282
Hegemon 190
Helen 228, 231, 348
Hellenistic period 7–11, 45, 97–98, 153, 234, 445, 464
Hellenistic scholarship *See* Alexandrian scholarship

INDEX OF SUBJECTS 571

Heracles 28, 442–445
Hermesianax 168
Herodotus 5, 22, 234, 359, 502–503
Hesiod 28, 138
hetaira 24–26, 283, 324–327, 329, 338–339, 381–382, 388–389, 342–372
hetairos 24–26, 283, 322, 324, 329, 357, 388–390
Hieronymus of Rhodes 153
Hipparchus 5, 100–102
Hippias 491, 492
Hipponax 11, 13, 121, 159, 161, 168, 190, 343, 363
historiography 376, 441–460
Homer 20, 21, 153, 159, 221, 230, 245–247, 425, 433, 529
Horace 11, 20, 30, 286–294, 298–307, 309, 313, 516–532
hymenaion See wedding songs
hymns 10, 12, 27, 124–125, 253–254, 335, 337, 339, 397, 424, 482–483, 488, 535
    Cletic 12
Hyperboreans 282
hyporchema 120, 535

iambic poetry 10, 12, 16, 126, 136–137, 152, 259, 521, 524
Ibycus of Rhegium 11–12, 16, 19, 95, 115, 175, 177, 307, 343
imitation 130, 398, 404, 527, 528
    See also emulation
immortality 58, 261, 305–306, 526
Imperial Greek poetry 417–438
improvisation 43–45, 246
innovation 192, 210, 234
    Anchoring innovation 58
    See also invention
inspiration 195, 240, 242, 248, 253
interpolation 46, 167
    See also tragedy
intertextuality 206, 210–220, 224, 226, 229–230, 281, 285, 516, 528, 544
invective 136, 264, 266
    See also blame poetry
invention 193–195, 199, 349
    See also innovation
invocation 240, 242, 247, 336, 442
Ion of Chios 122, 335
Isthmian games 494–495

Jebb, Sir Richard 20, 207, 208, 229, 503
John Tzetzes 422
Julia Balbilla 11
Julian, Emperor 12

Kelly, Adrian 253, 254
kitharodia 15, 96–98, 103, 105, 109, 125, 210, 423–425, 432, 502

Labarbe, Jules 243
Lachmann, Karl 48
lament 17, 132–133, 135
Lamynthius of Miletus 132, 363
Larichus 263, 327, 352–353
Lasus of Hermione 6, 16, 119, 125, 159
Latin poetry See Romans
Lenaea 497
Lesbia 282
Lesbos 430–434
LeVen, Pauline 205, 211, 213, 221–222, 225–226
Lidov, Joel 265
Lindos 429
literacy 140, 246
    See also reading and writing
literary criticism 19, 152, 184, 190, 206–210, 296, 447
literary history 161, 190, 208, 216, 456
Lobel, Edgar 63, 336
Locrian songs 154–155, 350
love songs 27, 116, 154, 155, 175–176, 192, 194, 304, 364, 366, 408, 411, 414, 521
    erotic catalogue 359
    erotic themes 140, 250
Lycambes 30, 522, 524
Lyceum 159, 160, 166
Lycophron 307, 537, 550
Lycurgus, Athenian statesman 4, 48–49, 138
Lycurgus, Spartan lawgiver 14–15, 58, 74–75, 79–80, 82–89, 395
Lydia (region) 282

Maehler, Herwig 527
marriage song See wedding song
Martin, Richard 269
maxims 13, 17, 140–141, 390, 432, 542
Medea 452–453
Megacles 385
Meier, Mischa 73, 79

Meleager   45
Melanippus   284–285
Melanippides of Melos   7, 9, 499
Meletus   363
melody   133, 135, 143
melos   119, 126, 131–132
memory   45, 141, 540
Menander Rhetor   12, 417
metaphor   232, 300, 306, 309, 313, 427–428, 444
   architectural   23, 211, 295–317
   avian   121
   nautical   22–23, 286–294, 430–435, 519
   political   430, 433
metapoetics   131, 212, 298, 309
metatexts   216, 218, 457
metonymy   442, 521
metre   60, 64, 136, 140, 143, 244, 250, 281, 464, 485, 518, 535
   dactylic hexameter   131–136
   melic   133
   metrical cola   8–9
   Sapphic stanzas   518, 523
   'three of Stesichorus'   249, 251
Miller, John   300
mimesis   115–116, 130, 184–185, 194, 199, 218, 399–401
Mimnermus   4, 57, 133, 181, 343, 401–402
Minos   220
moderation   378–380, 382, 386–387, 390
money   403–406
mousike   6, 19, 154, 157, 409
Muse   241
music   8–9, 21, 131–132, 134, 154, 159–160, 196, 198, 246, 339, 349, 417–438, 519
   See also New Music
Myrmidons   453, 455
myth   209–210, 215, 400, 450, 445–446, 536, 542
Mytilene   432, 434

Nagy, Gregory   3, 56
Nafissi, Massimo   83, 89
narrative   18, 143, 210, 218, 229, 488
nature   226–227, 336–337
Naucratis   282
Negri, Monica   533–535
Nemean games   494–495
Neoboule   30, 522

Nereids   215–216, 224, 258, 263
Nereus   527
New Music   5, 7, 18–20, 160–161, 164–165, 195, 205–238
New Philology   14, 39–71, 74
Newlands, Carole   310
Nonnus   12
Noussia-Fantuzzi, Maria   54–55

Obbink, Dirk   266
Odeum of Pericles   106–109
old age   163, 409, 411
oligarchy   6, 56, 373
Olympia   442
Olympic games   491–493
oracles   57, 58, 73, 75, 78, 80, 83–85, 87–89
orality   3, 40, 41, 44, 54, 129, 246, 306, 337
orators, Attic   375–376
originality   14–15, 22, 50, 54, 73–74, 521
Orpheus   432, 520
Ovid   22, 23, 259, 304–307, 309, 313

paean   123, 125, 164–165, 218, 428, 481, 488, 504, 507, 535
Page, Denis   265, 289–290, 336
paideia   17, 138, 141–143, 251, 375, 381, 388, 389
palinode   249, 251–254
Palladas   50
Panathenaea   6, 15–16, 18, 21, 96, 246
Panhellenism   3–4, 43, 142, 219, 533
paratext   20, 23, 249–251, 295–317, 465
Parker, Holt   321–324, 328, 338
Parmenides   231
parody   190, 210, 212
partheneion   115, 120–121, 124, 192, 482, 535
patrons   164
Pausanias   12, 59, 60, 89
pederasty   250, 324, 408, 410–411
pektis   349–350
Peloponnese   546–547
performance   3–6, 16–17, 24, 29, 43, 96, 98–99, 245–246, 425
   culture   129–130
   context   157, 213, 228, 234, 496
   sympotic   44, 64, 325
   of archaic Greek elegy   105

INDEX OF SUBJECTS

perfumes 354, 364
Periander 525
Pericles 106–109
Peripatetics 7, 18–20, 97, 131, 151–202
Pernot, Laurent 425
Persian wars 28, 214, 220, 451–453
persona 3, 19, 22, 183, 245–246, 253–254, 457
Phaon 30, 361, 520–521
Philitas 303
phenomenology 151, 166
Philocyprus 268
Philodemus 196–197
philosophy 377, 379, 392, 398, 404, 406, 409
  See also sophists
Philoxenus 16, 122, 125, 161, 502
Phlegon of Tralles 491
Phocylides 138
Pindar 4, 5, 12, 19–20, 23, 95, 117, 153, 159, 177, 190, 215, 220, 343, 525, 527, 533–552
  commentaries on 31, 313, 450
  epinicians 13, 27, 441–460
  reception in Roman poetry 295–317
  titles of poems 461–516
Pindar's *Epinicia* 13, 27
'Pisistratean recension' 15
Pisistratus 385, 388, 408
Pittacus 388, 391, 432
Plato 5, 8, 19, 160–161, 165, 206–208, 210, 239–256, 377, 406
Plutarch 14, 15, 54–55, 72–91, 326, 373–394, 395–416, 452
politics 22, 52, 54, 142, 177, 377, 387, 391, 397, 417–438
Polycrates 101, 228, 323
Polydorus 78, 79
Polyidus of Selymbria 499
Polyxenus of Cyrene 122
Porphyrio 516–532
Porro, Antonietta 433
Posidippus 22, 259
poststructuralism 40
Power, Timothy 103, 104, 109, 205, 211, 424
praise 16, 136, 212, 214, 232–233, 303, 312, 484, 520
praise poetry 17, 490
Prato, Carlo 53, 73, 83
Praxiphanes 159
Proclus 53–54

Prodicus 233
prooimion 425–426
Propertius 23, 306, 310, 313, 524
prosodia 119, 482, 488, 535
Proteus 527
prôtos heuretês 518
Publius Valerius Publicola 382–383
Pythian games 425, 491–493
Pythii 78

quotations 171, 177, 249–251, 326, 343–344, 367, 395–416, 535, 540

reading 6, 9, 441, 456
  See also Literacy
reception 14, 29–30, 74, 129, 205–256, 373–394
reperformance 4, 16, 40, 41, 47, 50, 96, 158
rhapsodes 15, 21, 96, 98, 246, 545
rhetoric 226–228, 230, 234, 376, 391, 418, 424, 434, 447, 536, 455
  See also orators, Attic
rhetra 57–58, 74–80
Rhodes 418–420, 423–424, 426–429, 434–435
Rhodopis 22, 257–276, 359
  See also Doricha
riddles 353
ritual 122, 157, 158, 171
Romans 9, 11–12, 30, 365, 429, 516, 531
  Roman poets 22–23, 295–317
Rosenmeyer, Patricia 11
Rossi, Luigi Enrico 130–131, 144
Rufus 298
Rutherford, Ian 527

Sacadas of Argos 4
sadness 521
sage 376, 379–381, 395, 399, 404, 406
  See also Seven Sages
Sappho 4, 5, 11–12, 22, 24–25, 30, 95, 114, 123–124, 154–156, 159, 187, 190, 307, 516–518, 520, 522–523, 525, 529–531
  and Alcaeus 103
  kertomia 257–276
  lovers 167–168
  schoolmistress 322–323
  See also Athenaeus, metre

scholia 11, 27–29, 297
  on Homer 541
  on Pindar 31, 300, 302, 312, 441–459, 465, 533, 540, 545–546
schools 11, 161, 433, 447, 529, 533
Schröder, Bianca-Jeanette 462, 486
scribes 46
  scribal errors 41, 51–52, 57, 65
Second Sophistic 12, 24–27, 417–438
Segal, Charles 225
Selene 358
Semonides 343, 349
Seven Sages 376, 379
  See also sage
sexuality 266, 351
  heterosexuality 363, 366, 410
  homosexuality 116, 365, 408, 410, 520, 522
  See also eroticism, pederasty
Shear, Julia 428
'ship of state' See metaphor
Sicily 8
Sider, David 252
Simonides 4–7, 11, 12, 28–29, 95, 100–102, 117–120, 124, 138, 153, 159, 162–164, 173–174, 177, 190, 220, 223, 230, 232, 243, 268, 343, 525–526
  intertextuality 214
  titles of poems 461–515
skolia 4, 16, 55, 60–61, 117, 120, 126, 156–157, 173, 195, 483–484
Smyth, Herbert Weir 265
Snell, Bruno 468
Society for Classical Studies 39
Socrates 20, 21, 141, 177, 247
Solon 25–27, 53–55, 57, 84, 138, 141, 189, 268, 326, 343, 426
  in Plutarch 373–394, 395–416
song culture 114, 119, 126, 157
sophists 7, 140, 206, 226–234, 373, 417–438
Sophocles 153, 428
Sparta 5, 8, 87, 88, 176, 213–214, 234, 422, 424–425, 427, 501
  See also Rhetra
sphragis 114, 192, 199, 213, 218, 230, 304, 306, 518, 520
Stackmann, Karl 40
stasis 26, 374, 379–380, 382, 418, 420–423, 425–426, 430–435

Statius 23, 307–310, 313
Stehle, Eva 321–323, 328
Stesichorus 4, 8, 11, 95, 124–125, 223, 307, 343, 525, 539
  and Homer 20–21
  in Plato's *Phaedrus* 239–256
Stobaeus 13, 59, 151
Suetonius 517
symposium 12, 16, 24–25, 43, 54, 59, 99, 101, 103, 115, 117–118, 126, 154, 156–157, 195, 249, 251, 324–327, 329–331, 334–339, 365–366, 389, 409, 411, 413
  in Athenaeus 342–372
  sympotic poetry 4, 116, 140, 142–143, 326–327, 338, 411

Tarrant, Richard 40, 48
Terpander 10, 27, 234, 417–438
texts 15, 29, 41, 44, 96, 98–99, 129, 166–167, 176–178, 357, 486
  emendation of 167, 399, 402
  fixed texts 21, 45, 246
  See also variations in texts
Thales 406
Thaletas 10, 422–423, 427
Thamyris 248–249
Thargelia 120
Theagenes of Rhegium 6
Theogenes 28
Theognis 6, 10, 13, 55–57, 138, 324, 343, 401, 528–530
  Theognidea 3–4, 44, 55, 57, 61, 116–117, 139, 141–142, 326, 331, 338
Theon 11, 447, 450
Theophrastus 159
Theopompus 78, 79
Theoxenia 28, 442
Theseus 485, 503
Thomas, Richard 311–312
Thrace 282
threnos 125, 132, 482, 526, 535
Thucydides 136
Timotheus of Miletus 205–238
Tiresias 28, 444
Tithonus 358
titles of poems 29, 30, 461–515
tragedy 5, 16, 47, 48–49, 160
  actors' interpolations in 50

INDEX OF SUBJECTS

transmission   1, 3–6, 14–15, 17–18, 29–30, 39–71, 151–181, 245–249, 418, 463–470
Troy   282, 527
Tryphon of Alexandria   11
Tynnichus   3, 5
tyranny   30, 56, 163, 382, 391, 432–434, 519, 523, 530
Tyrtaeus   11, 14, 15, 72–91, 138

van Wees, Hans   73, 89
variations in texts   39–71
   as result of deliberate changes   49, 50, 54, 57, 63, 65
   significant variation   49
Varro of Atax   304
Vassilaki, Ekaterina   441–442
victory odes   *See* epinician
Virgil   23, 310–313
Von der Vogelweide, Walter   41–43

Wade-Gery   83
Wardy, Robert   31, 232

wedding songs   122–125, 281, 322–323
   See also epithalamion
Welcker, Friedrich   321–323, 327
West, Martin Lichfield   50–53, 72–73
Wilamowitz-Moellendorff, Ulrich von   9, 15, 48, 95–96, 321
Wilson, Peter   428, 429
wisdom poetry   *See* Didactic poetry
wise advisor   373, 376, 391
writing   3–4, 44, 129, 166, 306

xenia   324, 442
Xenocritus of Locri   4
Xenophanes   338
Xenophon   6

Yatromanolakis, Dimitrios   327
Yunis, Harvey   242

Zenodotus   8